James D. McCawley

Everything that Linguists have Always Wanted to Know about Logic*

*but were ashamed to ask

Second Edition

The University of Chicago Press

Chicago and London

The University of Chicago Press, Chicago 60637
The University of Chicago Press, Ltd., London
© 1981, 1993 by The University of Chicago
All rights reserved. Published 1993
Printed in the United States of America
09 08 07 06 05 04 03 02 01 00 99 2 3 4 5 6 7

ISBN (cloth): 0-226-55610-7
ISBN (paper): 0-226-55611-5

Library of Congress Cataloging-in-Publication Data

McCawley, James D.
    Everything that linguists have always wanted to know about logic
but were ashamed to ask / James D. McCawley, — 2nd ed.
        p.   cm.
    Includes bibliographical references and index.
    1. Language and logic. I. Title.
P39.M3   1993
401—dc20   92-30744

Everything that Linguists
have Always Wanted to Know
about Logic*

*but were ashamed to ask

Contents

Contents

Preface to the Second Edition

Inevitably, this volume will be referred to as *Everything That Linguists Have Always Wanted to Know about Logic—But Were Ashamed to Ask,* second edition. Nonetheless, it may help readers if they take the trouble to notice the change in the title, which they might otherwise overlook: this book is entitled *Everything That Linguists Have Always Wanted to Know about Logic—But Were Ashamed to Ask,* whereas the book that appeared in 1981 was entitled *Everything That Linguists Have Always Wanted to Know about Logic—But Were Ashamed to Ask.* Had I retained the original title, the words printed on the cover would have to be *Everything That Linguists in 1981 Had Always Wanted to Know About Logic—But Were Ashamed to Ask,* and what would really have been just a second edition of the 1981 book would have taken on the misleading appearance of a new book with a new title.[1] However, I will bow to the inevitable and refer to the present book henceforth as the second edition, a policy that can be defended at least on the grounds that many of its sections are lineal descendants of corresponding sections in the original book, and thus its content is such as would easily merit a designation as "second edition" if the title did not involve a present tense whose deictic anchorage had changed between the two editions.

Some of the differences between this book and its predecessor reflect the difference between the two titles: the range of things in logic that linguists in 1993 have always wanted to know is considerably larger than the range of things that linguists in 1981 had always wanted to know. Indeed, there is now a sufficiently broad range of areas of logic in which at least some linguists have a serious interest that reviewers of this book may well castigate me for failing to give my readers the full universal-quantifier's-worth of content that my title (with its present perfect deictically anchored in the early 1990s) promises, a fault that was not among those that any of the reviewers of the first edition found in it. If I encounter that objection this time around, I may be able to defend myself by arguing that the omissions are topics that linguists are no longer ashamed to ask about. In any event, I have added to the book a fair amount of material on a number of topics on which important work has appeared since I finished the first edition, most notably the logic of conditional sentences (on which a vast literature now exists), the application of type theory to various questions of natural language semantics, Anil Gupta's work on "principles of identity" and the way they distinguish the semantic roles of common nouns from those of other syntactic/semantic elements, and the "generalized quantifier" approach to the logical properties of "determiners."

However, my reason for writing this second edition is not so much a desire to make it timely and topical as the fact that I have become dissatisfied in many ways with the first edition and want to replace it with something that will let me once again have the pleasure of teaching my linguistically oriented logic courses using a textbook that I find congenial. The reasons that I no longer find the first edition as pleasurable an adjunct to my teaching as I previously had are:

1. My ideas about syntax have changed considerably since the late seventies, and the syntactic analyses to which I relate the logical analyses in the first edition reflect my ideas then rather than the much better worked out conception of syntax given in *The Syntactic Phenomena of English* (McCawley 1988a). One of the most important areas in which my thinking about syntax has changed is my conception of syntactic category, and in view of the major role that questions of syntactic category assignment play throughout this book, I have added a section about syntactic categories and other relevant notions of syntax to chapter 1.

2. I made some bad decisions about the order in which to present things (some of which were the result mainly of inertia, e.g., the various sections of the last chapter of the first edition really belong in earlier chapters but were grouped together as a final chapter mainly because I didn't get my act together and write sections on those topics until I had already written the other thirteen chapters). One of the bad decisions was to follow the usual practice of modern logic textbooks and present propositional logic before predicate logic. In the present volume, following the lead of Geach 1976, I have put the chapter on the "syntax" (formation rules and rules of inference) for predicate logic before the chapter on the syntax of propositional logic, thereby not only partially recapitulating the history of logic (Aristotle had a highly developed predicate logic two centuries before the Stoic logicians developed a full-fledged propositional logic) but also increasing the likelihood that my readers will come to share my view of the ubiquitous "unrestricted quantification" of modern formal logic as a pernicious aberration. I still have the chapter about the seman-

tics of propositional logic before the section on the semantics of predicate logic (a decision that I may regret before the ink is dry on this new edition), but at least the possibly undesirable effects of that feature of organization will be mitigated by my beginning the book with the chapters on the syntax of predicate logic and propositional logic in what I regard as the right order.

3. In the process of writing *The Syntactic Phenomena of English,* I achieved considerably greater mastery of the art of textbook writing than I possessed in the latter seventies, and my standards with regard to style appropriate for textbooks, quantity and utility of exercises, and the like, have accordingly become much higher than they were then. In particular, I now think that in many of the chapters of the first edition, the exercises were insufficient in number and didn't adequately cover the important points that were dealt with in the chapter.

4. There are quite a few matters that I understand considerably better now than I did twelve or thirteen years ago which I can accordingly present more lucidly, smoothly, and compactly than I did then (this includes the one thing that I would say I did a shoddy job of the first time around, namely, model theory for predicate logic, to which section 6.1 of the first edition was devoted).

5. There are several topics to which I gave scanty treatment the first time around (e.g., λ-calculus and conventional implicature) but which clearly deserve to be presented in more detail and exploited more fully than they were in the first edition.

6. In some of the later chapters of the first edition, I made an inexcusable and cowardly retreat from some of the policies that I had followed in the earlier chapters, as in the chapter on modal logic, where I strayed from the "natural deduction" framework of most of the book by reverting to an "axiomatic" style.

In the present edition, I have corrected these faults, at least to the point that the drafts I have used in the recent incarnations of my logic courses have helped make the courses enjoyable to me and at least a fair proportion of the students. I have also added material to most of the sections of the first edition to add coherence and detail to what in many cases were somewhat capricious selections of material from such vast areas as relevance logic. However, notwithstanding these numerous additions and the substantially enlarged exercise sections, the total bulk of the book has increased by only a small amount, since I have been able to shorten many other parts of the book by finding more straightforward ways of treating the matters alluded to in paragraph 4 above.

For calling to my attention errors that I had missed in the first edition or in drafts of this edition and/or making helpful suggestions for revisions, I am grateful to Barbara Abbott, Tista Bagchi, Peter Daniels, Geoffrey Huck, Sotaro Kita, Mitchell Marks, Younghee Na, Greg Oden, Barbara Partee, Kent Wilson, and an anonymous referee.

Preface to the First Edition

I didn't really want to write this book, but I decided in 1974 that it would be easier for me to write it than to not write it, assuming, that is, that I was going to continue teaching courses on logic for linguists regularly. While there are many admirable logic textbooks, several of which I had used to considerable advantage in my courses (those of Reichenbach, Strawson, Thomason, and Massey), none matched very well my conception of what a course of logic for linguists should provide: a survey of those areas of logic that are of real or potential use in the analysis of natural language (not just "basic" areas of logic, but areas such as presuppositional logic and fuzzy logic that are usually ignored in elementary logic courses), rich in analyses of linguistically interesting natural language examples, doing justice both to the logician's concerns and to the linguist's in the analysis of those examples, and making clear to the linguist what the logician's concerns are, in particular, what reasons logicians have for doing many things that may strike a linguist as perverse. I was able to offer a course along these lines only by supplementing an assigned textbook with numerous extra readings and lectures aimed at filling in what from my point of view were major gaps in the textbook and correcting naive and superficial treatments of linguistic matters. I soon concluded that the only way I was likely to be able to offer a relatively exasperation-free course on logic for linguists would be to write a textbook that conformed to my list of desiderata.

I intend this book to be useful as a textbook in courses of logic that give heavy emphasis to considerations of the analysis of natural language, especially courses aimed at students in linguistics. I have used preliminary versions of it in a two-quarter sequence on linguistic logic at the University of Chicago in which I have generally covered chapters 1–6 and selected sections of chapters 7–10 in the first quarter and the bulk of the remainder in the second quarter.[2] The students in these courses have typically been advanced undergraduate and first-year graduate linguistics majors, with a sprinkling of students from philosophy and psychology. The prerequisite for this sequence has been an introductory syntax course, and this book correspondingly presumes some familiarity on the reader's part with the kind of analysis and use of linguistic data that is familiar in transformational grammar, though not with arcane points of transformational syntactic theory. Where linguistic questions have raised their heads, I have cited literature that the reader can consult for further exposition. I anticipate that this book will also prove useful for individual study and reference, though its fetal forms have not been tested in that capacity.

What the student can hope to get out of this book, besides familiarity with a number of areas of logic and their relation to linguistic questions, includes: (i) training of his semantic perceptions through exposure to linguistic examples in which considerations of logic help bring out certain subtle details of meaning; (ii) awareness of the intimate relationship between many linguistic problems (such as that of accounting for the distribution of reflexive pronouns) and many philosophical problems, particularly those relating to reference; (iii) development of an awareness of the distinction between those details of standard formal logic that represent serious conclusions worth defending and those details that merely reflect arbitrary decisions on the part of earlier logicians, and concomitant realization that standard versions of logic need not be accepted as package deals (this sort of perspective is of course something that linguistics students should hope to get not only from logic courses but also from their linguistics courses: a course in transformational syntax does a great disservice to students if it merely teaches them to do transformational analyses like a native but gives them no appreciation that those analyses embody both serious claims for which there is substantial backing and uncritical repetitions of features of earlier analyses that no one has seen fit to either provide support for or challenge); (iv) a conception of logic as a resource to be exploited according to one's own aims rather than as a legal code to be obeyed, and of logicians as merchants and manufacturers of potentially useful products that one is free to buy or not, according to one's needs and resources, with no obligation to buy all the standard accessories. In one's consultations with logicians, as with any other experts, one should keep in mind the advice of Bakunin (1871; p. 32 of 1970 reprint of 1916 translation):

> Does it follow that I reject all authority? Far from me such a thought. In the matter of boots, I refer to the authority of the bootmaker; concerning houses, canals, or railroads, I consult that of the architect or engineer. For such or such special knowledge I apply to such or such a *savant*. But I allow neither the bootmaker nor the architect nor the *savant* to impose his

authority upon me. I listen to them freely and with all the respect merited by their intelligence, their character, their knowledge, reserving always my incontestable right of criticism and censure. I do not content myself with consulting a single authority in any special branch; I consult several; I compare their opinions, and choose that which seems to me the soundest. But I recognize no infallible authority, even in special questions; consequently, whatever respect I may have for the honesty and sincerity of such or such an individual, I have no absolute faith in any person. Such a faith would be fatal to my reason, to my liberty, and even to the success of my undertakings; it would immediately transform me into a stupid slave, an instrument of the will and interests of others.

Finally I hope that the student will develop an appreciation of the way that considerations of logic, especially of the supposedly more esoteric areas that this book deals with, can help one to gain insight into important problems outside of logic and mathematics. Besides the various problems in linguistics and in philosophy of language that are dealt with in this book, I can mention a number of other areas to which certain points taken up below are relevant. Anderson and Belnap's relevant entailment logic (11.4) allows one to reevaluate the role of contradiction in the philosophy of science developed by Sir Karl Popper and his students. Popper lays great emphasis on the fact that in standard logic a contradiction causes all hell to break loose: "For it can easily be shown that if one were to accept contradictions then one would have to give up any kind of scientific activity: it would mean a complete breakdown of science. This can be shown by proving that *if two contradictory statements are admitted, any statement whatever must be admitted;* for from a couple of contradictory statements any statement whatever can be validly inferred" (Popper 1962:317, original emphasis). But for Anderson and Belnap, a contradiction causes only **some** hell to break loose: a contradiction implies only propositions to which it is relevant, and not even all of those. Thus adoption of Anderson and Belnap's version of logic allows the philosopher of science to demote contradictions in science from the status of crises to that of problems, not necessarily greater in importance than other types of "problem" with which a scientific community may be faced. (See Laudan 1976 for insightful discussion of the notion of "problem" in the history and philosophy of science). The arguments given by such economists as Frederic Bastiat (1850) for a free market economy implicitly involve a possible worlds semantics in which individuals can be identified across worlds but individuals existing in one world need not exist in all other worlds. In saying "Let us accustom ourselves, then, not to judge things solely by *what is seen,* but rather by *what is* *not seen"* (Bastiat 1850:9), Bastiat was contrasting the events and objects in the real world (what is seen) with those that exist in alternative worlds in which different laws were enforced (what is not seen). For example, the prosperity of existing weavers in a state that imposes a high import tariff on textiles does not in itself justify the tariff: their actual prosperity must be weighed against the interests of other workers who would have access to currently nonexistent jobs that would exist if textiles could be imported without tariff, of the consumers who would have access to cheaper clothing, and of those dealing in goods that consumers might buy more of if clothing were cheaper. Finally, fuzzy logic (chapter 13) has a bearing on the status of legal distinctions such as adult/minor, sane/insane, and human/nonhuman. Legal codes are normally drawn up in such a way that they provide a simple two-way distinction, with fine details of the drawing of the distinction having profound effects on who will go to prison and who will go free, what rights different persons have, and even who will live and who will die. However each distinction is drawn, legal decisions relating to persons on one side of the dividing line have no bearing on persons on the other side; for example, rights that adults accused of crimes have been held to possess are not automatically extended to minors, with the result that minors are often at a serious legal disadvantage in comparison with adults, even though special provisions for minors have in most cases been legislated for the purpose of protecting minors. The anomaly could be alleviated if laws recognized fuzzy rather than sharp distinctions, for example, if laws providing for a different status for adults and minors admitted a broad range of "borderline cases," within which the person in question could choose the status which he was to be treated as having.[3]

This book is unconventional not only in its goals and the choice of topics but also in the attitudes that I take in it and some of the conclusions that I arrive at. For example:

1. In keeping with Lakoff's (1972a) program of "natural logic," I take the subject matter of logic to be open-ended: I hold that all elements of meaning can play a role in inference and in truth conditions and that it is only by historical accident that logicians have largely confined themselves to the study of the logical properties of comparatively few elements of meaning (those expressed by *and, or, not, if, all, some, may,* and *must*). I thus reject the distinction that is usually drawn between "logical" and "nonlogical" vocabulary. In the process of writing this book I have realized that my rejection of that distinction forces me to reject another standard distinction, namely, that between axioms and rules of inference on the one hand and meaning postulates on the other: meaning postulates, in the sense of Carnap (1947), are axioms and rules

of inference for "nonlogical vocabulary," and there is no more grounds for singling them out for special status than there is for distinguishing "logical" from "nonlogical" vocabulary.

2. I take the units that one does "the logic of" to be the elements of meaning and thus to be in the province of linguistics as much as of logic. Logic is an empirical enterprise at least to the extent that investigation of natural language provides evidence about what elements of meaning there are and what their combinatoric possibilities are (see, e.g., section 3.5 for arguments from natural language facts to the conclusion that the logical counterparts of *and* and *or* combine not with just two propositions at a time, as is standardly assumed in logic, but with any number at a time).

3. I take as mentalistic a position with regard to logical units as I do with regard to linguistic units. In particular, I feel free to distinguish in logic between conceptually distinct entities regardless of whether they ever have distinct denotations. This policy is responsible for the terminological detail in this book that is likely to offend the greatest number of logicians: my use of "proposition" to refer to a conceptual unit rather than to a function giving truth conditions. To most modern logicians, a proposition is simply a function associating a truth value to each state of affairs. Under that conception of "proposition," any two self-contradictory sentences correspond to the same proposition: the function that associates the value "false" to every state of affairs. As "proposition" is used here, there are infinitely many different self-contradictory propositions, and any self-contradictory sentence can be said to express some particular self-contradictory proposition. (Note also that I use the term "proposition" in such a way that it makes perfect sense to speak of a sentence as expressing a proposition, whereas the way that modern logicians usually use "proposition," a sentence does not strictly speaking **express** but only **denotes** a proposition, the way that a proper name denotes the individual that it is used as a name of).

4. I disown the prescriptive attitude toward natural language that logicians commonly adopt (with notable exceptions, such as the authors alluded to at the beginning of this preface): the attitude that formal logic must remedy deficiencies in natural language that render at best a clumsy and limited tool for reasoning. I hold rather that in instances where formal logic has allegedly improved on natural language, it has merely given prominence to features that natural language has had all along though they have been overlooked in superficial analyses of natural language; for example, I have argued (McCawley 1970, 1972) that the "referential indices" of formal logic are linguistically real and play a role in such syntactic phenomena as the occurrence of reflexive pronouns and of understood subjects of infinitives. Apparent discrepancies

between natural language and formal logic provide no evidence of any defect in natural language: they are rather evidence that our analysis of natural language is deficient, or our formalization of logic is deficient, or our understanding of the relationship between language and logic is deficient, or our data reflect the interaction of language and logic with some third factor that we have not yet properly accounted for. See 9.2 for discussion of one factor that is responsible for many of the apparent discrepancies between standard formal logic and natural language, namely, Grice's (1967) principles of cooperativity in language use. While Grice's approach allows one to explain away many of the better-known putative examples where formal logic conflicts with natural language, it does not serve to explain them all away: certain properties of conditional sentences and of sentences containing *all* or *every* diverge from those of their counterparts in standard formal logic in ways that are not attributable to Grice's cooperative principles. In those particular cases, I have accordingly concluded that standard formal logic misrepresents the elements of meaning that it purports to deal with, and I have indicated how the logic might be done differently so as to avoid those discrepancies.

5. I have rejected (on the basis of several arguments given in chapter 6) one of the most universally accepted policies of modern formal logic, namely, that of "unrestricted quantification." I regard that policy as the most pernicious and perverted idea in the history of logic and hold it responsible for an immense volume of pseudo-problems (particularly the alleged difficulties raised by the recognition of "nonexistent objects") that have consumed the energies of many otherwise productive philosophers.

6. I have adopted a highly idiosyncratic notational system from the outset, rather than indoctrinating the student first in more widely used notational systems. Since students in a course of logic for linguists can reasonably expect to derive from the course some facility in reading the logical formulas that appear in existing works by linguists and philosophers, I have provided exercises in which the student is required to translate from standard notations into the notation of this book. The student who faithfully does all the exercises in this book can thus expect to acquire a useful reading knowledge of standard notations but will probably never be able to pass for a native speaker of them. When he is laughed at for his foreign accent, he can take consolation in the fact that his vocabulary is probably much larger than that of his derogators.

I have learned more in the process of writing this book than in any other project that I have ever undertaken. In attempting to produce a book that I, at least, find satisfactory both as logic and as linguistics, I have had to grapple with countless important questions in both fields that I had never thought about before, not only questions relating to fairly esoteric areas, but quite fundamental questions, such as what a proposition is and what it is to call a proposition true or false. I do not mean to suggest that this educational experience is complete, and I will not be surprised if comments of readers cause me to change my thinking substantially on many of the points covered here.

In preparing this book, I have derived much benefit from the comments, questions, and suggestions of many persons, including Gilbert Harman, S.-Y. Kuroda, Larry Martin, Uwe Mönnich, Alan Reeves, Valerie Reyna, Ivan Sag, Takashi Sugimoto, Richmond Thomason, Bas van Fraassen, and the many students who have used preliminary versions of parts of this book in my courses at the University of Chicago and at the 1977 Linguistic Institute at the University of Hawaii. I am particularly grateful to Richmond Thomason for detailed criticisms of the final draft of this book, criticisms which have left me with a significantly sharpened understanding of many of the matters with which I deal; while I have not accepted all of his advice, I may eventually wish that I had. Finally, I wish to acknowledge the stimulation that I have received from several scholars whose influence on my thinking is in part responsible for the fact that this book takes the form that it does: Noam Chomsky, from whom I learned to turn my questions about language into questions about human beings and their minds; George Lakoff, who has nearly convinced me that I should do the same with my questions about logic; Peter Geach, who has provided logic with an ample supply of that most basic necessity for scientific endeavor, namely, problems; Paul Grice, from whom I have learned to look for the effects of context on linguistic examples, especially of that particularly potent context, the null context; and Paul Feyerabend, from whom I have learned that diversity is as essential to the quality of life in science as in any other human endeavor.

1. The Subject Matter of Logic

1.1 Logic and "Logical Form"

Logic is concerned with **truth** and **inference;** that is, with determining the conditions under which a proposition is true and the conditions under which one proposition may be inferred or deduced from other propositions. For example, an adequate system of logic must provide an account of the fact that the proposition expressed by example 1.1.1a is always true, that expressed by 1.1.1b can be true on some occasions and false on others, and that expressed by 1.1.1c is always false:

1.1.1   a. Either there are unicorns or there aren't any unicorns.
         b. The number of books in the Library of Congress is a multiple of 7.
         c. All linguists are insane, and some linguists are not insane.

It must provide an account of the fact that the conclusion in 1.1.2a follows from the premises but the conclusion in 1.1.2b does not:

1.1.2   a. All linguists are insane.
          Some linguists are musicians.
          Therefore, some musicians are insane.
        b. All linguists are insane.
          Most linguists are musicians.
          Therefore, most musicians are insane.

These two tasks are intimately related in that principles of inference can be regarded as acceptable only if they always yield true conclusions when applied to true premises; that is, if given principles of inference allow one to deduce a certain conclusion from given premises, then the conditions for truth of propositions must insure that that conclusion is true in all cases in which the premises are all true.

Logic is of necessity also concerned with **semantic analysis,** that is, with

1

determining what propositions are expressed by or involved in the sentences of natural languages such as English or Japanese or Wolof: since inferences framed in ordinary language form a major part of the "data" that logicians must provide an account of, semantic analysis will be a major part of the practising logician's activity and of what must be learned in order to understand logic, regardless of whether one regards semantic analysis as a part of logic or as something outside of logic that is a prerequisite for the application of logic.

In this book I will give the analysis of natural language a much more central role than is generally assigned to it in logic textbooks. Specifically, I will adopt the following policies:

i. I will assume that the linguist's semantic analysis and the logician's have the same subject matter and that the linguist's goals do not conflict with the logician's. Thus I will assume that it is possible to provide an analysis of "content" that is appropriate both for the linguist's goal of specifying what sentences are possible in a given natural language and how they are related to their meanings and for the logician's goal of formulating truth conditions and rules of inference.

ii. Accordingly, I will assume that linguistic facts are relevant to choosing among otherwise equivalent proposals for the "logical form" of various propositions. For example, I will reject the traditional policy of logicians of taking *and* as basically conjoining propositions two at a time (and thus of analyzing all apparent conjunctions of three or more propositions as iterated two-term conjoining) and will treat it instead as conjoining arbitrarily many propositions at a time. Among my reasons for this is the fact (see section 3.5 for details) that the syntactic rules of English and other languages respect the distinction among "(p and q) and r," "p and (q and r)" and "p and q and r." A less trivial example of this policy in action is given by my treatment of the expression *only if*. Logicians (e.g., Quine 1962:41) have generally treated "p only if q" as merely an alternative expression (an "idiomatic variant," in Quine's words) of "If p, then q" or "q if p," and thus make *only if* appear to be merely an idiosyncratic way of expressing the converse of *if*. *Only* does not otherwise express the notion of "converse," for example, *John only likes Mary* does not express the proposition that Mary likes John. However, the expression *only if* clearly is not just an idiom (like *kick the bucket* or *go for broke*), whose meaning is not predictable from the meanings of its constituents: an English speaker who knows the use of the words *only* and *if* can understand and use *only if* without having to learn anything extra about that combination of words. I thus will not be satisfied with an analysis of *only if* unless it treats *only if* as put together from *only* and *if* by ordinary syntactic rules and as having a meaning derived from the meanings of *only* and *if* in the same way that the meanings of syntactically similar expressions such as *even when* are derived from the meanings of their parts. Since the traditional renderings of *only* and *if* by logicians cannot be combined with each other in any coherent way, either *only* or *if* will have to be given a treatment different from the one logicians generally give it; see 3.4 and chapter 15 for considerations suggesting that *if* is the one requiring a nonstandard analysis and for an analysis of *if* that makes it syntactically and semantically compatible with *only, even,* and the other things that it combines with.

    iii. I will take the domain of logic as encompassing all elements of meaning; that is, I will not draw any distinction between "logical" and "nonlogical" elements of meaning. I thus take the logical properties of *and, or, not, if, all,* and *some* as forming neither the whole of logic nor even the core of logic but as simply the part of logic which happens, in part through historical accident, to be the most thoroughly investigated and best understood.

1.2. On the Nature of Propositions

    In the last section, I used the term "proposition" repeatedly but did not define or explain it. Since propositions are whatever logic is done on if logic is to provide an account of truth and inference, propositions must be things that can be said to be true or false and must also be things that can serve as premises or conclusions of inferences.

    A proposition cannot be simply a sentence of English (or Japanese or Wolof or . . .). For example, it makes no sense to speak of the English sentence 1.2.1 as being in itself true or false:

1.2.1   It was raining.

This is because different occurrences of 1.2.1 express different propositions, sometimes a true proposition (if it was in fact raining at the place the speaker was referring to at the time he was referring to) and sometimes a false one (if it was not raining at that time and place). Thus, 1.2.1 can express any of an infinite number of propositions (one for each combination of time and place that might be the ones in question), but it is still the same sentence in each case. Accordingly, the closest thing to a sentence that one might be able to take as fulfilling the role of a proposition is a sentence supplemented by information about **reference,** in particular, the time and place that that particular occurrence of the sentence purports to refer to. The same conclusion follows from a consideration of 1.2.2:

1.2.2   John told Fred's father that he was expected to help him.

There are a great many possibilities for the reference of the *he* and the *him* of 1.2.2: either could refer to John or to Fred or to Fred's father or to some fourth person (and if *he* refers to some fourth person, *him* might refer to some fifth person).

The reference of the various elements of the sentence (and of elements that are only understood, such as the place in 1.2.1) is also relevant to the question of whether inferences in which they appear are valid. Consider the inferences:

1.2.3   a. Bill knew that it was raining.
              Sam told Bill that it was raining.
              Therefore, Sam told Bill something that Bill knew.
          b. Bill knew that John had told Fred's father that he was expected
              to help him.
              Sam told Bill that John had told Fred's father that he was
              expected to help him.
              Therefore, Sam told Bill something that Bill knew.

Whether 1.2.3a is **valid** will depend on whether the two premises purport to refer to the meteorological conditions of the same place and the same time. If the first premise refers to Bill's knowledge about the weather at some time and place referred to earlier in the discourse (say, 1.2.3a comes in the middle of a report of a conversation about one of the Boston Strangler's crimes and the first premise refers to Bill's knowledge about what the weather was doing when that crime was committed) but the second premise refers to the weather at the time Sam uttered his statement to Bill, then the conclusion does not follow from the premises: in that case what Sam told Bill was not necessarily something that Bill knew. Similarly, 1.2.3b is not valid unless the two *he*'s have the same reference and the two *him*'s do: if the first premise relates to Fred's being expected to help John and the second premise to Bill's being expected to help Fred's father, then what Sam told Bill need not be something that Bill knew, and thus 1.2.3b is invalid. Thus, whatever rule of inference gets one from the premises to the conclusion in 1.2.3a and b must be sensitive to the purported reference of the various parts of the premises: if the references do not match, the rule of inference must not apply.

However, it will not do just to take a sentence supplemented with referential information as filling the role of a "proposition." Consider the inference:

1.2.4   All experts think that Bush likes Gorbachev better than Saddam.
          Mike Royko is an expert.
          Therefore, Mike Royko thinks that Bush likes Gorbachev better
          than Saddam.

The first premise and the conclusion of 1.2.4 are ambiguous. *Bush likes Gorbachev better than Saddam* may mean either "Bush likes Gorbachev better than he likes Saddam" or "Bush likes Gorbachev better than Saddam likes Gorbachev." It only makes sense to speak of 1.2.4 as valid or invalid if one assigns a specific interpretation to each of the sentences in it. Thus, 1.2.4 strictly speaking is not **an** inference but something ambiguous among four different inferences.[1] Two of those inferences are valid (namely, the two in which the premise and conclusion are given like interpretations), and the other two are invalid.

If the different meanings of a sentence must be kept separate in determining the validity or invalidity of an inference apparently involving that sentence, one must ask whether it is not in fact simply the meanings that function as the premises and conclusions of arguments. Since the validity of an argument clearly depends on the meanings of the sentences that are used to frame the argument but does not obviously depend in any way on the sentences themselves (that is, it does not obviously depend in any way on the choice of words used to express those meanings), I will assume provisionally that the things that constitute the premises and conclusions of inferences are simply meanings such as can be expressed by sentences, with the qualification that "meaning" here must be taken as including reference, in accordance with the discussion of 1.2.1 above.

This provisional conclusion raises a huge number of questions, of which the most important are: (i) What is the structure of a meaning? That is, what are the bits and pieces of which a meaning consists, and how do they fit together? (ii) How does one identify the bits and pieces of the meaning (or rather, of each of the meanings) expressible by a given sentence? (iii) How does one individuate meanings? That is, how does one tell whether a particular sentence is really ambiguous, as opposed to just having a single meaning that happens to be applicable to a broad range of cases? These are not easy questions to answer, and it is easy to find disagreement as to their answers, even disagreement as to whether they have answers. In the course of this book, I will offer partial answers to each of these questions. However, the reader would do well to think critically about the answers offered, since he can rest assured that any position whatever regarding these questions will be controversial.

1.3. Ambiguity

In the chapters that follow, we will often have reason to ask whether some class of sentence is ambiguous.[2] For example, consider the question of whether the logicians' standard account of *and* really accords with the use of *and* in ordinary English. This logicians' rendition of *and*, which I will henceforth symbolize with ∧, is completely symmetric: A ∧ B is true under the same circumstances as is B ∧ A, and anything that can be inferred from A ∧ B can be inferred from B ∧ A. But there are instances in which ordinary English *and* appears to be asymmetric; for example, under the most obvious interpretation, 1.3.1a would be true under different circumstances from those under which 1.3.1b is true:

1.3.1   a. John got up and fell down.
         b. John fell down and got up.

These sentences are normally taken as referring to an order of events that matches the order of the conjuncts: in 1.3.1a the rising precedes the falling, and in 1.3.1b the falling precedes the rising.

Logicians who have confronted sentences such as 1.3.1 have generally adopted the position that English *and* is ambiguous between (at least) two senses: a "symmetric" sense which conforms to the logicians' ∧, and a "consecutive" sense in which the order of the conjuncts agrees with the purported temporal order of the events reported in the conjuncts (Massey 1970:5). This conclusion may very well be correct. However, logicians have been remiss in simply accepting it without even attempting to provide arguments that English *and* really is ambiguous. There are a number of possible alternatives to the position that *and* is ambiguous: (i) Perhaps there is only one *and*, it is basically asymmetric, and the logicians who have concerned themselves with a symmetric *and* have deluded themselves by restricting their attention to instances where the order of the conjuncts happened not to be of any particular significance. (ii) Perhaps there is only one *and*, it is basically symmetric, and the supposed asymmetry of *and* in 1.3.1 is really something else, namely, either (iia) an ambiguity in some other element of the sentence (for example, in the past tense marker) or (iib) the result of something outside of logic and grammar, for example, principles of sportsmanlike behavior that would dictate that one avoid misleading one's hearers; these principles might dictate that one provide an overt signal whenever one relates events in an order that is not (or is not known to be) the order in which they happened.

In order to choose among these alternatives, it will be necessary to invoke an account of the notion of ambiguity which provides a basis for determining whether a sentence has some putative ambiguity or does not, and for identifying the exact nature of the ambiguity. To develop such an account, it will be worthwhile to start with some clear cases of ambiguity and clear cases of nonambiguity and determine what characteristics of the two classes of cases might be used as tests to settle the unclear cases. Let us start by seeing if we can come up with a principled basis for accepting the proposition that *bastard* is ambiguous between the senses "person whose parents were not married" and "nasty person," and for rejecting the proposition that *carp* is ambiguous between the senses "male member of the species *Cyprinus carpio*" and "female member of the species *Cyprinus carpio*." There is, of course, an obvious definition, namely, "member of the species *Cyprinus carpio*," that would cover the domains of applicability of both of the supposed senses of *carp,* whereas there does not appear to be any way of defining *bastard* so as to take in both illegitimate persons and nasty persons without at least in effect enumerating the two cases ("person who either is nasty or is the offspring of persons who were not married to each other").

While these observations lend plausibility to the claim that *bastard* has two separate senses but *carp* has a single general sense that covers the cases taken in by each of the putative senses, they do not settle the issue. For one thing, we have no basis for assuming that a single sense cannot involve a list of separate cases; thus, dictionaries might be correct when they give "female ruler or wife of male ruler" as a definition of a supposed single sense of *queen.* For another, our failure to come up with a single definition that covers both "illegitimate person" and "nasty person" may be merely the result of insufficient ingenuity on our parts, and we have no justification for calling *bastard* ambiguous just on the basis of an argument from ignorance. In fact, the problematic sense of *queen* just noted can be defined, as Michael LaGaly has observed, as "enthroned female." Perhaps our perplexity about *bastard* may vanish when someone with LaGaly's ingenuity hits upon a nonenumerative definition that covers both "nasty person" and "illegitimate person." Finally, the existence of a sense that covers the whole domain of applicability of a word does not imply that it does not have additional more restricted senses; for example, I will argue that *Yankee* is ambiguous among the three senses "native of the U.S.A.," "native of the north of the U.S.A.," and "native of New England."

A question of ambiguity can often be resolved by a consideration of grammatical phenomena that depend on whether the two items are identical. Consider, for example, deletion of repeated verb phrases.[3]

1.3.2   a. Marcella has won a prize in the lottery, and Ben has too.
         b. I'm sure that Bert can play the tuba, but I doubt that Harry can.
         c. Martha bought a computer before George did.

I will assume that these sentences are derived from a more complete underlying structure by a grammatical transformation that deletes one of two identical verb phrases; I will refer to this transformation as **V'-deletion,** anticipating the terminology for categories that will be introduced in section 1.5, in which V′ will be the symbol for "verb phrase." Let us see whether this transformation respects the putative differences between *bastard* 'illegitimate person' and *bastard* 'nasty person' and between *carp* 'male *Cyprinus carpio*' and *carp* 'female *Cyprinus carpio.*' If there are two distinct items *bastard*$_1$ 'illegitimate person' and *bastard*$_2$ 'nasty person', then 1.3.3a–b involve two identical nouns and 1.3.3c–d involve two distinct nouns, and thus only 1.3.3a–b ought to give rise to 1.3.3e by deletion of a repeated verb phrase:

1.3.3   a. Maxine married a bastard$_1$, and then Frieda married a bastard$_1$.
          b. Maxine married a bastard$_2$, and then Frieda married a bastard$_2$.
          c. Maxine married a bastard$_1$, and then Frieda married a bastard$_2$.
          d. Maxine married a bastard$_2$, and then Frieda married a bastard$_1$.
          e. Maxine married a bastard, and then Frieda did.

This is in fact the case: 1.3.3e can be used with reference to Maxine and Frieda both marrying illegitimate sons or to their both marrying nasty persons but not with reference to one of them marrying an illegitimate but nice man and the other marrying a nasty man whose parents were married. By contrast, a putative difference between *carp* 'male *Cyprinus*' and *carp* 'female *Cyprinus*' is ignored when verb phrase deletion (henceforth, V′-deletion) applies—1.3.4 can be used just as well when Susan has caught a male carp and George a female one as when both have caught female carps:

1.3.4   Susan caught a carp, and then George did.

The same conclusion can be arrived at by a consideration of the transformation that deletes a repeated noun:[4]

1.3.5   a. Sam owns four *sweaters* and Bill owns five.
          b. John owns four *portraits of Napoleon* and Mary owns five.

Sentences such as could be obtained by deleting a repetition of *bastard* cannot be interpreted as mixing the two putative senses of *bastard* (thus 1.3.6a cannot refer to Maxine marrying an amiable man who was sired by his mother's chauffeur and Frieda marrying a disagreeable man of impeccable parentage), but sentences such as could be derived by deleting a repetition of *carp* are noncommittal with regard to whether the two carps referred to are of the same sex:[5]

1.3.6   a. Maxine married a bastard, and then Frieda married one.
          b. Susan caught a carp, and then George caught one.

Let us apply this test to a case where it is not so obvious whether the word is ambiguous. The word *uncle* is occasionally claimed to be ambiguous among the four senses 'brother of father', 'brother of mother', 'husband of sister of father', and 'husband of sister of mother'. To see whether it has these four senses or instead has a single sense that covers all four cases (or has two senses, each of which covers two of the cases, or . . .), let us consider:

1.3.7   Bill is Marty's uncle, and Tom is too.

One can use 1.3.7 not only in the four cases in which Bill and Tom have the same genealogical relation to Marty (they are both brothers of Marty's father; they are both husbands of sisters of Marty's father; . . . .) but also in the 12 cases in which they have different genealogical relations to Marty (e.g., Bill is Marty's father's brother, and Tom is the husband of Marty's mother's sister). Thus the difference between the putative four senses of *uncle* is not respected by V'-deletion, and there is thus a single sense of *uncle* that covers all four genealogical relationships. (Giving a nonenumerative definition that covers all four cases is another matter; it turns out not to be at all easy to do).

One can also test whether an expression has a putative ambiguity by determining whether a single occurrence of it can simultaneously cover things corresponding to each of the putative senses. Thus, 1.3.8a can be an accurate description of your having caught a male Cyprinus at 2:00 yesterday and a female Cyprinus at 3:00 yesterday and 1.3.8b is a normal description of a situation in which Marty's mother has a brother and a married sister, but 1.3.8c does not accurately describe your meeting a pleasant man whose parents weren't married and an unpleasant man whose parents were married:[6]

1.3.8   a. I caught two carp yesterday.
         b. Marty has two uncles.
         c. I met two bastards yesterday.

Likewise, the following sign is normal on a shop that sells material for making fences (in which case *all kinds* is to be interpreted as "picket, chain link, barbed wire, . . .") or on a school that teaches sword-fighting (in which case *all kinds* is to be interpreted as "foil, epée, sabre, . . ."), but, except as a joke, could not be used to mean that picket fencing, foil, chain link, epée, etc., were all available:

1.3.9   FENCING
             ALL KINDS

The test embodied in 1.3.3–7 gives fairly clear results when the putative senses are nonoverlapping (or where their overlap is only fortuitous, as in the case of *bastard:* some people are both illegitimate *and* nasty). It is important that we find a test that will be applicable even in the case where one of the putative senses is contained in another, since many plausible cases of ambiguity are of this type (for example, *Yankee*). Consider questions such as

1.3.10   a. Is Bill Marty's uncle?
         b. Is John a bastard?
         c. Is Barney a Yankee?

If you know the exact genealogical relationship between Bill and Marty, you know the answer to 1.3.10a: if Bill is related to Marty in any of the four ways listed above, the answer is "Yes," and otherwise the answer is "No." Suppose now that you have full information about whether John's parents were married and whether he is a nasty person. Are you in a position then to answer 1.3.10b? If John is nasty and illegitimate, the answer to 1.3.10b will be "Yes," and if he is pleasant and legitimate, the answer will be "No." But what about the case where he is pleasant and illegitimate or where he is nasty and legitimate? If there were just a single sense "illegitimate or nasty," then the answer ought to be "Yes," since John in these cases does meet the condition "illegitimate or nasty." But in these cases, the answer sometimes is "Yes" and sometimes is "No," depending on the intentions of the person who asked the question: either he was asking whether John is illegitimate or he was asking whether John is nasty, and to answer the question you have to know which question he was asking.[7] Things are similar with 1.3.10c: if Barney comes from Birmingham, Alabama, then the right answer to 1.3.10c may be either "Yes" (if it was a question about Barney's nationality) or "No" (if it was a question about what part of the country Barney is from).[8]

The negative sentences 1.3.11 are exactly parallel to the questions 1.3.10:

1.3.11   a. Bill isn't Mary's uncle.
         b. John isn't a bastard.
         c. Barney isn't a Yankee.

While 1.3.11a is true if Bill holds none of the four relationships to Marty and false if he holds one of them, it does not make sense to speak of 1.3.11b as being true or as being false in the case where John is a nasty person whose parents were married. Example 1.3.11b has to be assigned two distinct senses. The one sense of 1.3.11b is true and the other one false in the case just mentioned, and it makes no more sense to ask whether 1.3.11b itself is true or false in this case than to ask whether Springfield (not specifically Springfield, Missouri, or Springfield, Illinois, or Springfield, Massachusetts, but just plain Springfield) is west of the Mississippi.

We are now in a position to obtain a partial answer to our questions about whether *and* is ambiguous between a symmetric sense and a consecutive sense. Consider the question

1.3.12   Did John get up and fall down?

If John got up and fell down, in that order, then the answer to 1.3.12 is clearly "Yes." What if he fell down and then got up without then falling down again? Are we then in a quandary about how to answer 1.3.12; that is, can 1.3.12 be taken either as asking whether he got up and then fell down (in which case the answer would be "No") or as asking whether he both got up and fell down, irrespective of order (in which case the answer should be "Yes")? The judgment is fairly subtle, but I believe that there in fact is such a quandary here (i.e., that either answer might be correct, depending on how the speaker intended the question, and that one cannot answer the question without deciding which way the speaker meant it). This supports, albeit weakly, the conclusion that there is both such a thing as a symmetric *and* and a temporally consecutive *and*[9] and shows that logicians have not been engaging in a total flight of fancy when they speak of such a thing as a symmetric **sense** of *and* (as opposed to merely cases where, perhaps fortuitously, the order of the conjuncts does not matter).

1.4. Logic and the Division of Labor

To a far greater extent than is generally recognized, logic is an empirical science. Putative rules of inference and truth conditions are not self-evident propositions that one is obliged to accept at all costs: they might turn out to be wrong, and facts about the use and interpretation of sentences of ordinary language are relevant to the confirmation or refutation of hypothesized principles of logic. However, logic is only one of several factors that may play a role in any fact about language. For example, several things interact in a person's judgment that there is something wrong with each of the following arguments:

1.4.1   If the door is unlocked, someone has entered the house. Someone has entered the house. Therefore, the door is unlocked.

1.4.2   Nothing is a square circle. Otto bought nothing. Therefore, Otto bought a square circle.

1.4.3   Chicago is in Illinois. Therefore, Chicago is in either Illinois or Uruguay.

In judging that these arguments are "unacceptable," one makes use not only of one's knowledge of and abilities in logic but also of one's knowledge of the syntax and vocabulary of the English language, of the uses that such arguments play in exposition and discussion, and of how behavior (such as the uttering of the above sentences) relates to the context in which it takes place and to one's goals.

The source of the unacceptability might be purely a matter of logic: that there are no general principles guaranteeing that the conclusion is true whenever the premises are true. But the unacceptability might rest in part or in total on a faulty linguistic analysis, in which two expressions that make different contributions to the meanings of the sentences in which they occur are mistakenly treated alike. For example, one could reasonably maintain that 1.4.2 is faulty because it wrongly treats *nothing* and *is* as if they figured in 1.4.2 the same way that *a pen* and *is* figure in 1.4.2':

1.4.2'   A pen is a writing instrument. Otto bought a pen. Therefore, Otto bought a writing instrument.

Or the unacceptability of an argument might simply rest on its pointlessness. For example, one could reasonably hold that 1.4.3 sounds as odd as it does simply because no reasonable purpose would be served by drawing its conclusion from its premise, since its conclusion contains less information than does its premise, and one is normally expected to be informative. On this account, the unacceptability of 1.4.3 is like the unacceptability of opening a chess game by moving P-KB3: it is a legal move but a stupid one, since other moves (such as P-K4) put one in a better position to accomplish the presumed goal of winning the game (though it might be a clever move if the goal were different, say, if one were in a contest to see who could play the longest chess game). In 3.2 this account of 1.4.3 will be defended and it will be pointed out that arguments of the form of 1.4.3 are perfectly acceptable provided that they are used as parts of larger arguments rather than by themselves.

Similarly, a sentence may in some sense conflict with the facts without necessarily expressing a false proposition: it might just be a pointless or stupid or misleading thing to say, given what the facts are. For example, Grice (1967) has argued that sentences such as the conclusion of 1.4.3 will convey that the speaker does not know which alternative is correct (in this case, that he does not know whether Chicago is in Illinois or in Uruguay) and will thus be misleading if he does know, since if he does know, he is in a position to utter the shorter and more informative sentence *Chicago is in Illinois* and is thus going out of his way to be uninformative if he utters instead the sentence *Chicago is in either Illinois or Uruguay*. Here what is in conflict with the facts is not the proposition expressed by the sentence but the speaker's behavior in choosing to utter that sentence rather than one of the alternatives available to him.

The fact that a given ordinary language argument is in some way unacceptable is generally of some relevance to logic, but what exactly its relevance is cannot be determined without exploration of the linguistic, psychological, and sociological factors that might be involved in its unacceptability. The more thorough knowledge one has of those factors, the better prepared one is to identify whether the argument is wrong in any strictly logical way (i.e., is not merely "unacceptable" but "invalid"). Thus, to place claims about logic on a really firm footing, one must have a firm understanding of the linguistic structures, the meanings of the words, the principles of language use, and perhaps many other things that interact with logical principles in the construction and evaluation of arguments in natural language. A serious but not fully systematic attempt has been made in the following chapters to give due consideration to these factors.

1.5. Some Syntactic Prerequisites

A number of notions that derive from linguistic syntax (as opposed to what logicians call "syntax"; see 2.1) will play a role below, not only in discussing the relationship between linguistic form and logical form but also in describing logical form itself. In this section, I will sketch some of these notions.

While no one conception of syntactic structure enjoys universal acceptance among linguists, there is at least widespread agreement that the information represented in diagrams such as 1.5.1 comprises (or at least makes up a major part of) a syntactic structure:[10]

1.5.1

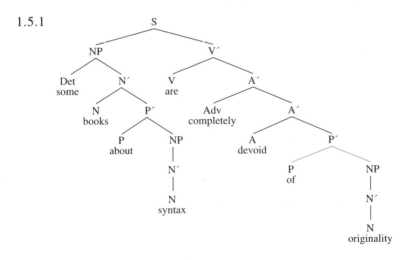

The lines in a diagram represent the relation of **constituency:** they indicate what smaller units the whole sentence and its various parts consist of; the **labels** indicate the category to which each of these units belongs; and the left-to-right orientation of the various units indicates what unit precedes what unit. For example, in 1.5.1 the two lines leading down from the unit labeled S indicate that that unit consists of a unit *some books about syntax* and another unit *are completely devoid of originality,* the labels indicate that the one unit belongs to the category NP and the other to the category V', and the fact that the words making up the one unit are to the left of those making up the other unit indicates that the one unit precedes the other unit. These units are called **constituents;** each line in a diagram like 1.5.1 indicates that the lower unit is an **immediate constituent** of the upper unit (thus, here the immediate constituents of the NP *some books about syntax* are the Det *some* and the N' *books about syntax*). It is usual to refer to the units (or **nodes**) of such a structure in terms derived from those of kinship relations: a node is the **mother** of those nodes that are its immediate constituents (its **daughters**); nodes having the same mother are **sisters** of one another.

An entity having the sort of structure that is represented in such a diagram is an **ordered labeled tree,** provided the relations of constituency, labeling, and precedence satisfy certain conditions that are held in such works as Wall (1972:149) and McCawley (1988a:39–40) to characterize the relevant linguistic notions. Thus, approaches that hold that the sentences of natural languages have that sort of structure make the claim that a sentence **is** an ordered labeled tree. (To avoid confusion, it is important to keep in mind that a diagram such as 1.5.1, known as a **tree diagram,** is not an [ordered labeled] tree but merely **represents** a tree; the question at issue here is not the absurd question of whether a sentence is a diagram of a certain kind but the quite sensible question of whether a sentence has the kind of structure that is represented by such a diagram). In saying that sentences have such a structure, linguists are saying that linguistic phenomena operate in terms of such a structure: that the phonological, morphological, syntactic, and semantic characteristics of individual sentences depend on the sort of organization that is represented in a diagram such as 1.5.1.

I will not attempt to justify the gigantic claim that is made in the last sentence (interested readers are directed to McCawley 1988a for a detailed demonstration that all of the major syntactic constructions of English lend themselves in a reasonably straightforward way to analysis in terms of this sort of syntactic structure). Rather I will content myself with giving one example that shows that sentences are more than simply sequences of words. The syntactic possibilities of the comparative construction with *more/-er . . . than* and of the comparative construction with *as . . . as* are virtually identical:

1.5.2   a.   John is taller than Mary thinks Roger is.
         a′. John is as tall as Mary thinks Roger is.
         b.   John owns a bigger car than Mary does.
         b′. John owns as big a car as Mary does.[11]
         c.   John owns more books about than portraits of Benjamin
              Franklin.
         c′. John owns as many books about as portraits of Benjamin
              Franklin.

However, there is a small class of cases in which normal *more/-er . . . than*
comparatives correspond to decidedly abnormal-sounding *as . . . as* comparatives:[12]

1.5.3   a.   You can earn more money as a lawyer than you can earn as a
              linguist.
         a′. You can earn as much money as a lawyer as you can earn as a
              linguist.
         b.   You can earn more money as a lawyer than as a linguist.
         b′. ??You can earn as much money as a lawyer as as a linguist.

The normal rules for "reducing" *than* and *as* expressions, as in the reduction
of 1.5.3a to 1.5.3b, yield the deviant result 1.5.3b′ when applied to 1.5.3a′.
The reason for the deviance of 1.5.3b′ is presumably the double *as,* and it
might seem at this point that one needs only to add a rule excluding the sequence of words *as as* (i.e., a rule that would depend only on the sequence in
which words occur and not on constituency relations) to account for the deviance of 1.5.3b′. But such a rule would in fact incorrectly exclude such perfectly normal sentences as *I'm as polite to people that I'm as big as as to
people that I'm smaller than* or *John gives people that he's as smart as as
much of his time as they want,* in which a phrase that happens to end in *as* is
immediately followed by an extraneous phrase that begins with *as.* What is
excluded is not the sequence of words *as as* but rather a combination in which
as is combined with an expression that is itself an *as*-phrase, i.e., a combination having the following structure.[13]

1.5.4
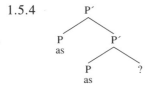

I make this point largely because in this book I reject the common view that a logical form **does** have the structure simply of a string of symbols. I wish to claim that logical structures are themselves syntactic structures of the sorts considered here, and that the "formation rules," "rules of inference," and "truth conditions" that logicians have given are most plausibly interpreted in terms of trees rather than in terms of strings of symbols. Logicians commonly discuss their formulas as if they were simply strings of symbols (and treat parentheses as if they were on a par with any other kind of symbol, rather than as simply being a typographical device to indicate constituency relations); however, when they give the rule of inference 1.5.5 (the rule by which, say, from *John is angry and Mary is disgusted* one is entitled to infer *Mary is disgusted;* ∧ is the symbol for 'and') they do not mean it to apply to just any formula that has an 'and' in the middle:

1.5.5   A ∧ B
         B

For example, they do not mean for it to be applicable when the ∧ is in the middle of an 'if' construction (as in *If Lucy has read your letter, then John is angry and Mary is disgusted,* from which one is not entitled to infer that Mary is disgusted). The interpretation that is put on 1.5.5 is that it is applicable to structures such as 1.5.6a, in which the 'and' and two sentences are combined directly into the given sentence, but not to structures such as 1.5.6b that merely have an 'and' **somewhere** within them:

1.5.6   a.   b.

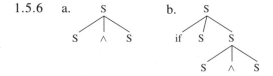

The labels that appear in 1.5.1 will be unfamiliar to many readers and will be used here in ways that will be unfamiliar to some readers who are familiar with the symbols themselves. Specifically, I will adopt here a conception of syntactic categories as defined by a set of factors that affect the syntactic behavior of linguistic units (McCawley 1988a: chap. 7). Three of these factors are represented directly or indirectly in the symbols that are used here as labels: (i) the **part of speech** of the **head** of the unit; (ii) the difference between a **word-level** unit and a **phrasal** unit; and (iii) the **logical category** of the unit. The symbols N (noun), V (verb), A (adjective), P (preposition), and Adv (adverb) will be used here both by themselves, indicating a word-level unit belonging to the given part of speech, and in such symbols as V′ (verb phrase)

and A′ (adjective phrase), indicating a phrasal unit consisting of an item belonging to the given part of speech, along with whatever "objects" it has, taking "object" in the broad sense that includes not only objects of verbs and prepositions (*drink the beer, at the office*) but also "objects" of nouns and adjectives (*inventor of the lightbulb, afraid of snakes*). "Phrasal unit" is taken as covering a one-word unit if the word has no "object," as with an intransitive verb or the "intransitive nouns" *syntax* and *originality* in 1.5.1. Note that the notion of constituency that is assumed here thus does not require that all units "branch": some N′s consist of N + P′ and other N′s consist of just N.

In consequence of an unfortunate historical accident, the term "noun phrase" (NP) has become firmly established with a different meaning from what one might expect. The term suggests something that is to "noun" as "verb phrase" and "adjective phrase" are to "verb" and "adjective" (i.e., it suggests what we are calling N′ here), but it is used instead with a meaning that relates to factor (iii) rather than to factors (i)–(ii). "NP" is most often used by linguists to take in all of the diverse things that are used as the subjects and objects of verbs, adjectives, etc., not only expressions in which an N′ is combined with an article or quantifier, but also subordinate clauses and reduced forms of subordinate clauses when they fill a subject or object position:

1.5.7   a. Some books about syntax are completely devoid of originality.
         b. That the butler had blood on his hands proves nothing.
         c. Being tired is no excuse for neglecting your duties.

What unites these diverse expressions into a category is their role in logical structure: they denote things of which properties are "predicated." The notion of "sentence" is likewise one of logical category: the linguistic category S corresponds to the logical category "proposition";[14] similarly, the linguistic category "determiner" (Det) corresponds to the logical notion of "quantifier," understood somewhat more broadly than is usual among logicians.

I will also assume here that "modifiers" combine with units of some category to form larger units of the same category, as in 1.5.1, where *completely* combines with the A′ *devoid of content* to yield the A′ *completely devoid of content*.[15] Contrary to the policy of many linguists, I do not classify articles and quantifiers as modifiers and thus do not take my policy on modifiers as implying that *some books about syntax* is an N′.

If syntactic structures are conceived of as ordered labeled trees, there is a simple way in which one can give a set of rules (a **grammar**) that will define a set of trees. Specifically, suppose that one gives a list of admissible syntactic configurations (e.g., a S can have as its immediate constituents a NP and a V′, in that order) and a list of the words that make up each part of speech. The syntactic configurations can be listed in diagrammatic form, as in 1.5.8a, or more compactly, by formulas, as in 1.5.8b, in which the colon can be read "can consist of":

1.5.8   a.

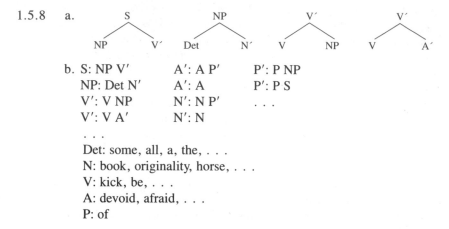

   b. S: NP V'   A': A P'   P': P NP
      NP: Det N'   A': A   P': P S
      V': V NP   N': N P'   . . .
      V': V A'   N': N

      . . .

      Det: some, all, a, the, . . .
      N: book, originality, horse, . . .
      V: kick, be, . . .
      A: devoid, afraid, . . .
      P: of

A tree will **conform to** a grammar of this form if: (i) for each of its **nonterminal nodes** (i.e., nodes below which other nodes stand) the label occurs to the left of the colon in one of the rules and the nodes directly below that node have the labels that appear after the colon, and (ii) each of its **terminal nodes** is labeled with one of the part of speech labels and with a word that appears in the list of words of that part of speech.

    While grammars of the form just described are not up to the task of specifying the possible syntactic structures in a natural language (though extended versions of such grammars, supplemented by machinery that goes considerably beyond what is given above, may be up to that task; see Gazdar et al. 1985), such grammars will play a major role in the **formation rules** of the logical systems taken up below, i.e., the rules that specify what is a possible logical structure.

Exercises

    1. Give facts that are relevant to deciding which of the following is a real ambiguity:

   a. Two putative senses of *apple,* one referring to a fruit with red skin and one referring to a fruit with green or yellow skin.
   b. Two putative senses of *coffee,* one referring to the beans from which a certain beverage is made and the other referring to that beverage.

c. Two putative interpretations of the sentence *Someone has rented a house*, one in which *someone* refers to the landlord (cf. *Someone rented me a house for $400 a month*) and one in which *someone* refers to the tenant (cf. *I rented a house from Schwartz for $400 a month*). NB: these two putative senses have exactly the same truth conditions.

d. Two putative senses of *may:* "permitted" and "possible," as in the interpretation of *Shirley may dance* as "Shirley is permitted to dance" or as "It is possible that Shirley dances."

e. Two putative interpretations of the sentence *I enjoy tennis*, one referring to enjoyment of playing tennis and one referring to enjoyment of watching tennis as a spectator.

2. Determine whether the structures represented in the following diagrams conform to the grammar in 1.5.8b:

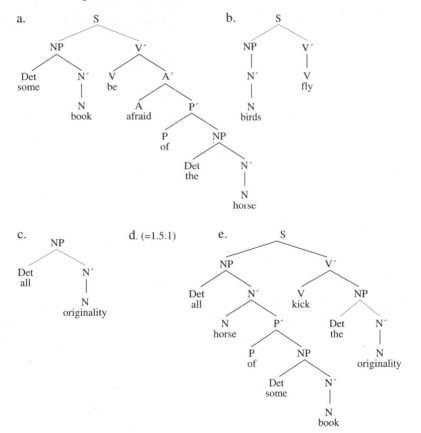

Where you give a negative answer, indicate where exactly the structure fails to conform to the grammar. Consider only the rules that are actually given in 1.5.8b, i.e., ignore the " . . . " that indicates additional rules beyond those given.

3. a. Construct a valid argument with false premises and a false conclusion.
   b. Construct a valid argument with false premises and a true conclusion.
   c. Construct an invalid argument with true premises and a true conclusion.
   d. Construct an invalid argument with true premises and a false conclusion.
   e. Construct an invalid argument with false premises and a true conclusion.
   f. Construct an invalid argument with false premises and a false conclusion.

4. Suppose that a Navaho linguist interested in the question of whether different languages can reflect different logical systems carries out fieldwork on the language of an exotic tribe, the Anglos. After several years of investigation he publishes an article in which he makes the following claims: (i) in the language of the Anglos, the negation of a declarative clause is formed by putting *not* or *n't* after the first auxiliary verb (and creating an auxiliary verb out of *do* and the tense marker if there was no auxiliary verb there to begin with); (ii) Anglos readily assent to many sentences of the form "*p* and negation-*p*," for example, *Some men are bald and some men aren't bald;* and (iii) therefore in the logic of the Anglos the familiar (to the Navahos) "law of non-contradiction" (according to which a proposition "*p* and negation-*p*" can never be true) is invalid. How could one argue against the Navaho linguist's claim that Anglo logic is different from Navaho logic? (Note: a large part of this problem revolves about the question of how one can tell whether one sentence "is the negation of" another sentence). Don't expect to solve this problem, only to gain appreciation of the fact that it poses a serious problem.

2.   Predicate Logic I: Syntax

2.1. The Notion of "System of Formal Logic"

Logicians have widely adopted the terms "syntax" and "semantics" to refer to certain portions of their endeavors. A logician is doing "syntax" when he is constructing **rules of inference,** that is, general principles that specify what conclusions may be inferred from what premises, or is investigating the implications of particular rules of inference. He is also doing "syntax" when he is constructing **formation rules,** that is, rules that specify the class of propositions he is dealing with. A logician is doing "semantics" when he is setting up conditions on what the **truth values** of the various propositions under consideration can be.[1] For example, a logician dealing with an extremely restricted portion of logic might state the following "logical principles":

2.1.1   Formation rules:

God is good is a proposition.

Cincinnati is in Mongolia is a proposition.

Bamboo shoot goes good with mushrooms is a proposition.

If *A* and *B* are propositions, then *A and B* is a proposition.

Rules of inference:

From *A and B* you may infer *A*.

From *A and B* you may infer *B*.

From *A and B* you may infer *A and B*.

Truth conditions:

Every proposition is either true or false (but not both).

If *A* and *B* are both true, then *A and B* is true.

Otherwise, *A and B* is false.

The formation rules, though only four in number, commit one to recognizing an infinite number of propositions: anything that one can get from the three given **atomic** propositions by conjoining them to one's heart's content will be a proposition of this system. For example, the formation rules of 2.1.1 imply that ((*God is good and Cincinnati is in Mongolia*) *and* (((*God is good and bamboo shoot goes good with mushrooms*) *and* (*God is good and God is good*)) *and* (*Cincinnati is in Mongolia and bamboo shoot goes good with mushrooms*))) is a proposition.[2] The rules of inference sanction such reasonable (albeit trivial) inferences as 2.1.2:

2.1.2   God is good and bamboo shoot goes good with mushrooms.
            Therefore, God is good.

The truth conditions restrict the class of "states of affairs" that can come into consideration. In a state of affairs in which *God is good* is true, *Cincinnati is in Mongolia* false, and *Bamboo shoot goes good with mushrooms* true, it will have to be the case that *God is good and bamboo shoot goes good with mushrooms* is true and *God is good and Cincinnati is in Mongolia* false if the "truth conditions" given in 2.1.1 are to be satisfied. While these truth conditions have been given just by fiat in 2.1.1, they are eminently reasonable: one could not assign truth values in violation of 2.1.1 without being blatantly inconsistent. Note, though that 2.1.1 places no constraint on what truth values the atomic propositions have; 2.1.1 thus allows for states of affairs in which *Cincinnati is in Mongolia* is true and *God is good* false.

While "rules of inference" and "truth conditions" are separate parts of a "logical system" such as the fragment of logic given in 2.1.1, they must fit together properly if the "system" is to make any sense. When rules of inference are applied to true premises, true conclusions must result: a rule of inference is supposed to be a guarantee that the conclusion resulting from applying it to true premises will be true. The rules in 2.1.1 meet this criterion of "fit": the truth conditions have been set up in such a way that anything that the rules of inference of 2.1.1 allow you to infer from any given true premises will also be true. The rules 2.1.1 in fact satisfy an even tighter criterion of "fit": if the truth conditions in 2.1.1 guarantee that some proposition B will be true whenever some proposition A is true, then B is inferrable from A by the rules of inference of 2.1.1 (possibly in several steps, but inferrable all the same). This means that what is inferrable from a particular proposition A is **precisely** the propositions that have to be true when A is true. The first criterion of "fit" says that the rules of inference work; the second criterion says that they work as well as anyone could demand of them: that there is nothing that you ought to be able to infer (within the set of propositions under consideration) but can't.

In this text, I will often treat "syntax" and "semantics" separately, simply to impress on the reader the fact that they are separate and that making them "fit together" is a nontrivial task. The remainder of this chapter will be concerned with the "syntax" of **quantifiers:** elements of logical structure that correspond to words like *all, some,* and *most,* which say which or how many of some set of things have a given property.

2.2. Quantifiers, Predicates, and Variables

It is easy to convince oneself that 2.2.1a is a valid argument, while 2.2.1b is invalid:

2.2.1   a. Many politicians are crooks.
             All crooks tell lies.
             Therefore, many politicians tell lies.
         b. Many politicians are crooks.
             Most crooks tell lies.
             Therefore, many politicians tell lies.

The enterprise of constructing rules of inference will involve us in such tasks as identifying why the one argument is valid and the other invalid. Since the only apparent difference between 2.2.1a and 2.2.1b is in the **quantifier** of the second premise, i.e., *all* versus *most,* that item is the most promising candidate for a factor on which the validity of these arguments hinges.

A quantifier is a word or expression that specifies which or how many of some kind of things have some property, as here, where *All/Most crooks tell lies* says which crooks or how many crooks have the property of telling lies. This informal description divides the meaning of such a sentence into three parts: a **domain expression** (here, *crook*), which specifies some kind of thing that is under consideration, a **matrix** (here, *x tells lies*), which specifies a property that a thing of that kind might or might not have, and a **quantifier,** specifying which or how many things of that kind have that property. The matrix involves a **variable** such as the *x* of *x tells lies.* A variable marks a position into which things of some kind can be inserted, and the domain expression specifies the kind of things that are under consideration for insertion into that position. A formula such as is posited here as the matrix defines a **propositional function:** to each value of the variable it associates a proposition, e.g., substituting Reagan for the variable yields the proposition that Reagan tells lies, substituting Dukakis for the variable yields the proposition that Dukakis tells lies, etc.

Since the quantifier and the domain expression are normally expressed as parts of a single syntactic unit (here, the noun phrase *all crooks* or *most crooks*), I will provisionally adopt a policy of grouping the quantifier together with the domain expression in the logical structures that will be given here, and will thus give the logical structure of *All crooks tell lies* in either of the forms given in 2.2.2, which are equivalent except for the information about categories that is indicated as labels on the nodes in 2.2.2b:[3]

2.2.2   a. (all: crook)$_x$ (x tells lies)
          b.

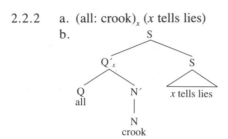

The prime means, as usual, "phrasal unit," the quantified NP here being treated as having the quantifier as its head and the domain expression as dependent on the quantifier;[4] the symbol Q′ will be used here not only for quantified NPs such as *all crooks* but also for quantified expressions of other categories such as *never before* and *ever since the earthquake*. The subscript on the label Q′ indicates what **bound variable** corresponds to the given quantified NP, i.e., what variable it defines a domain of values for. In the simple example that is given here, the subscript is superfluous, since only one variable, namely x, could possibly play the role of the bound variable; however, when we get to examples in which there is more than one variable, cases will arise where there could be indeterminacy as to which variable goes with which quantifier if that were not indicated explicitly. The domain expression is given the label N′ here because the domain expression of a quantifier is not limited to simply a noun but covers the whole gamut of phrasal expressions whose heads are nouns: *all admirers of Elvis Presley, most former owners of Edsels, many occasions on which tax repeal has been discussed.*

Let us for at least the present treat quantifiers as combining with sentences in the fashion illustrated in 2.2.2a. We can then easily construct a logical structure for a sentence that contains two quantifiers, such as *Many politicians admire most crooks*. We will need a structure that contains a sentence *x admires y* in which there are two variables, one for each of the two quantifiers. That sentence can be combined with the two quantifiers and domain expressions by simply iterating the structure of 2.2.2. Combining *most* with *crook* and combining the result with *x admires y*, we obtain a structure corresponding to *x admires most crooks:*

2.2.3

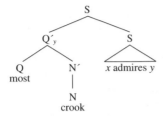

This structure can now play the role of the embedded S in a structure of the same form, and combining that with *many politicians,* we obtain:

2.2.4

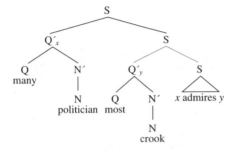

The sentence *Many politicians admire most crooks* is in fact ambiguous: it can mean either (i) that the number of politicians who admire most crooks is large or (ii) that the crooks whom many politicians admire are a majority of all crooks. The style of logical forms introduced in this section readily accommodates both of these interpretations. The structure in 2.2.4 corresponds to (i): it combines *many politicians* with a S that says "*x* admires most crooks," and (i) says that many politicians have the property "*x* admires most crooks." One can obtain a logical form corresponding to (ii) by simply interchanging the two Q's:

2.2.5

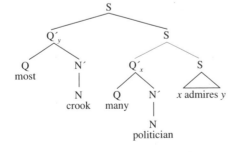

In 2.2.5, *most crooks* is combined with a sentence that corresponds to "many politicians admire *y*," and (ii) says that most crooks have the property that is expressed by the latter sentence.

At this point, it will be useful to introduce some terminology. In 2.2.5, the symbol S appears as a label on three different constituents: the whole structure, which corresponds to a **proposition;** the expression with which *most crooks* is combined, which corresponds to a **one-place propositional function** (paraphrasable as *Many politicians admire x*); and the **two-place propositional function** *x admires y.* The number of "places" is the number of **free** variables, i.e., variables that are not **bound** by a quantifier or other **binder** within the propositional function itself. I will allow in principle the possibility of three-place, four-place, etc., propositional functions, e.g., *x is between y and z* and *x resents y for z* would correspond to three-place propositional functions: there are three distinct variables, each of which is available for replacement by a particular value for the variable or for combination with a Q′, as when one derives the two-place propositional function *Pittsburgh is between y and z* by substitution of a particular value for *x* in the three-place function *x is between y and z* or when one derives the two-place propositional function *x resents many football players for z* by combining the three-place function *x resents y for z* with *many football players* as a binder of the variable *y.* Since combining a propositional function of any number of places with a binder of one of its variables yields a propositional function having one fewer place (binding one of the variables of a three-place predicate yields a two-place predicate, binding one of the variables of a two-place predicate yields a one-place predicate), we are entitled to regard a proposition (i.e., the sort of thing that one can obtain by binding the one free variable of a one-place predicate) as a zero-place predicate, which would provide a rationale for our using the same symbol (S) as a label for both propositions and propositional functions. This choice of a symbol reflects the usage of many logicians, who use the term **open sentence** for a sentence-like object that contains a free variable and the term **closed sentence** for a sentence-like object that does not contain any free variables.

Simple propositions such as *Bert admires Lincoln* and simple propositional functions such as *x admires y* consist of a **predicate** (here, *admire*) combined with what are called **arguments** of the predicate. It is important to distinguish between names such as *Bert* and *Lincoln* and the entities that those names purport to refer to, since predicates differ with regard to whether they say something about the entity that the name refers to or about the name itself. For example, in 2.2.6a, *Jonathan* refers to a person (to whom they introduced their son) and in 2.2.6b, it refers to a name (which they gave to their son):

2.2.6   a. They introduced their son to Jonathan.
           b. They named their son Jonathan.

Different kinds of pronouns that have a proper noun such as *Jonathan* as antecedent differ with regard to whether the pronoun refers to the person bearing
that name or to the name itself, as in the well-known example 2.2.7 (Quine
1953:139–41):

2.2.7   Giorgione is <u>so</u>-called because of <u>his</u> size.

Here *his* refers to the person Giorgione and *so* refers to the name "Giorgione"
(the Italian augmentative suffix *-one* is usually reserved for big things); since
the person in question bore the family name Barbarelli, 2.2.7 could be paraphrased *Barbarelli is called Giorgione because of his size*. While drawing the
appropriate distinctions will sometimes be cumbersome, it will ultimately
avoid much confusion if we adopt a firm policy of distinguishing between
individual constants that correspond directly to entities that are referred to,
and names such as *Jonathan* or *Napoleon* by which one often refers to various
entities. I will adopt the policy of using letters from the beginning of the alphabet (a, b, c, d) for constants and letters from the end of the alphabet (w, x,
y, z) for variables, supplemented by ad hoc devices such as primes or subscripts (a', a'', x_1, x_2) when that is a more convenient way of distinguishing
between different constants and different variables. I will accordingly speak of
Bert admires Lincoln as having a logical form *b admires c*, with two constants
rather than two names occupying the two argument positions of the predicate
admire. (When spelled out in full, the logical structure of *Bert admires Lincoln* should involve the names *Bert* and *Lincoln* **in addition to** corresponding
constants, in clauses "*b* is called Bert" and "*c* is called Lincoln," but in the
remainder of this book I will ignore the role that names play in references to
persons and places.)
      Let us now attempt to give formation rules for the formulas of predicate
logic with which we are dealing in this chapter. As a first approximation to
appropriate formation rules, let us simply list the structural configurations that
have figured in our analyses so far, using the notation introduced in 1.5. The
list will have to include at least the following:

2.2.8   S: Q' S
           Q': Q N'

What else the list will contain will depend on what internal structure we assume for "simple" Ss. These consist of a predicate and one or more arguments. Logicians commonly treat the various arguments of a predicate as all

on a par with one another and accordingly write formulas such as 2.2.9a or
2.2.9a', which are equivalent to structures such as 2.2.9b:[5]

2.2.9   a.   Admire *b c*
         a'. Admire(*b, c*)
         b.

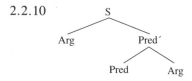

Alternatively, one might treat the simple Ss of logical structure as having the
same sort of internal structure as do corresponding sentences of most natural
languages, in which one argument (the **subject**) has a special role and is separate from a phrasal unit consisting of the predicate and the remaining arguments, as in 2.2.10, in which ' continues to be used to indicate "phrasal unit"
(as in N', V'):

2.2.10

Let us provisionally adopt structures as in 2.2.10 and accordingly add 2.2.11
to the list of configurations that was begun in 2.2.8:

2.2.11   S: Arg Pred'
           Pred': Pred (Arg) ... (Arg)

In the second entry in 2.2.11, I have utilized two common notational devices
in an informal way: parentheses to indicate optionality, and ... to indicate
arbitrary terms in a sequence; the meaning is that a Pred' can consist of a Pred
and zero or more arguments.

It will in fact be convenient to use the notation of 2.2.9 side by side with
that of 2.2.10, with the choice between the two determined by whether the
"Pred" is represented by something looking like a word (such as "Admire"
here) or by an "abstract" symbol such as the F, G, H that are commonly used
in predicate logic. While I wish to assume the constituent structure of 2.2.10
throughout this book, the order in which I will put the elements of linear
formula will have the Pred second in formulas such as "*b* Admire *c*" but the
Pred first in formulas such as "F*bc*." The rationale for this policy is that the
order of elements will be like English in formulas containing elements that
look roughly like English, but will be like that commonly used in formal logic

in formulas whose elements are symbolized as in standard versions of formal logic.

To complete this system of rules, we need to give rules specifying what an N' can consist of and to give lists of the "atomic" members of the various categories. Let us begin with the second of these tasks. For the category Q, all we need to do is make a list of the quantifiers: *all, each, every, any, most, few,* . . . . (This task is in fact not completely trivial, since there are some tricky problems involved in determining what elements are in fact quantifiers, a question that will be taken up seriously in 7.4.) Our lists of predicates will have to distinguish among one-place, two-place, three-place, . . . predicates, so that our rules can distinguish between logical structures in which each predicate is combined with the right number of arguments and (ill-formed) structures in which a predicate is combined with too many arguments (as in *John slept a grand piano*) or too few (*This number exceeds*). Since, aside from its subject, the arguments of a predicate are its sisters, we can draw the necessary distinctions by listing what each predicate allows as its sisters. Specifically, let us supplement the notation of 1.5 with the symbol (/) (read "in the environment") for restrictions on where the items in question can be used:

2.2.12   Q: All, Each, Every, Any, Some, Most, ...
           Arg: $x, x_1, x_2, ..., y, y_1, y_2, ..., a, a_1, a_2, ..., b, b_1, b_2, ...$
           Pred: Sleep, Breathe, Tall, Hungry, ... /_____
           Pred: Admire, Love, Similar, At, ... /_____ Arg
           Pred: Between /_____ Arg Arg

What follows the / is a specification of what can appear as sisters of the given item, whose position relative to its sisters is indicated by _____; the _____ by itself in the third line of 2.2.12 indicates that "sleep," etc., are not allowed to have sisters.

The lists in 2.2.12 call for some comment. Strictly speaking, what belongs in these lists is not English words but rather units of meaning that may well correspond to English words but need not correspond to any particular word of English or whatever language is under consideration. In cases where I wish to posit a semantic unit that corresponds to (one sense of) some particular English word, I will designate that unit informally by capitalizing the word in question, as I have here. In the lists in 2.2.12, items of different parts of speech occur: verbs, adjectives, prepositions. The notion of predicate, as it figures in modern logic, is largely independent of that of part of speech: a two-place predicate corresponds to a relationship between one entity and another, irrespective of whether that relationship is expressed by a verb (*The stadium borders on the park*), an adjective (*The stadium is close to the park*), or a preposition *(The stadium is by the park)*. This policy is plausible, in that the categorical notions most relevant to logic are categories of meaning, and there is only a loose connection between the meanings of words and the parts of speech to which they belong. For example, there are a fair number of cases in which the same meaning can be expressed both by a verb and by an adjective *Mary likes John, Mary is fond of John.*

What then about (common) nouns? Should the notion of predicate that is being elaborated here be taken as including semantic units that correspond to nouns, e.g., should the list of two-place predicates in 2.2.12 include an element Brother that corresponds to the relationship of being a brother of? In 11.3, I will argue for an analysis (due to Gupta 1980) according to which the meaning of a common noun is in fact more than a predicate: it provides something (a "principle of identity") that is not part of the meanings of verbs, adjectives, and prepositions. In the earlier chapters of this book, however, I will follow the more usual policy of treating nouns, along with verbs, adjectives, and prepositions, as having meanings that correspond to predicates.

If nouns are to be assimilated to the logical category of predicate, then should the rule Q': Q N' perhaps be changed so as to avoid its reference to the category "noun"? This is not an easy question to answer. The expression with which a quantifier combines must in fact be an N' and not a V', an A', or (with the possible exception of such expressions as *many of your friends*) a P':

2.2.13   *every composed by Beethoven
              *most ashamed of their pasts
              *all under the sofa

It is not obvious, though, whether the deviance of expressions such as those in 2.2.13 is of a semantic or of a syntactic nature: perhaps the various elements of meaning are not combined in a semantically coherent way in 2.2.13, but then again, perhaps the expressions in 2.2.13 correspond to semantically impeccable combinations that violate a syntactic constraint requiring that what a quantifier combines with have a noun as its head. In line with my intention to pursue relatively traditional analyses in the earlier chapters of this book and reserve for later chapters alternative analyses in which traditional assumptions are challenged, I will provisionally adopt the latter of these two alternatives and indeed take it a step further in the direction of traditional analyses by proposing that in logical structures a quantifier combines not with a N' or Pred' such as Politician but rather with a S such as *x (is a) Politician* in which the noun does not just belong to the category Pred but indeed appears in a **predicate position,** so that instead of 2.2.4 we will have logical structures such as 2.2.14:

2.2.14

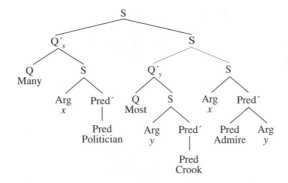

I will accordingly revise my use of the term "domain expression" and speak of a S such as *"x (is a) Politician"* rather than the Pred' "Politician" as the domain expression for the quantifier in question; note that under this revised conception of "domain expression," a domain expression is a condition that an entity must meet in order to belong to the domain of the given variable, e.g., a value of x must meet the condition "x is a Politician" in order to play a role in the interpretation of 2.2.14. Treating the N's of quantified NPs as reduced sentences will turn out (see 2.5) to provide a simple way of accommodating combinations of quantifier and relative clause, as in *every person who voted for Nixon* or *most problems that have been studied by linguists:* it will be possible to treat the relative clause as conjoined with the S that provides the head noun *(x is a person and x voted for Nixon),* and so treating them accounts in a straightforward way for the relationship between their contribution to semantic interpretation and the way in which they fit into syntactic structure.

2.3. Coherence Conditions on Variables

There is one important detail of the structures that are proposed here that is not accounted for in the rules 2.2.8, 11, and 12, namely, the subscript variable on the Q'. Before attempting to rectify that omission, it will be necessary to first take up a question that we have pushed aside so far, namely that of how variables affect the semantic coherence of logical structures. Note first that there are many cases in which it is appropriate to have the same variable appear several times in a single structure. For example, in representing the meanings of sentences such as 2.3.1a,b, it is natural to propose formulas such as 2.3.1a',b', in which repetition of a variable corresponds to there being "places" into which the same value must be substituted:

2.3.1　a.　Every philosopher admires himself.
　　　　a'.　(Every: x Philosopher)$_x$ (x Admire x)
　　　　b.　Most linguists respect all of their teachers.
　　　　b'.　(Most: x Linguist)$_x$ (All: y Teacher x)$_y$ (x Respect y)

That is, in determining whether 2.3.1a is true, it is relevant whether Quine admires Quine, but it doesn't matter whether Quine admires Putnam or Kripke; in determining whether 2.3.1b is true, it matters whether Chomsky respects all of his (Chomsky's) teachers, but not whether he respects all of Labov's teachers or all of Hockett's teachers. Thus, I do not wish to impose any restriction that would prevent distinct occurrences of the same variable from occurring in a single formula.

However, the choice of variables as subscripts on Q's is not as unrestricted as the choice of variables that serve as arguments of predicates. For example, if both Q's in 2.2.14 had the subscript x, the resulting formula would be unintelligible:

2.3.2　　　(Many: x Politician)$_x$ (Most: y Crook)$_x$ (x Admire y)

There are two respects in which 2.3.2 is bizarre. First, the subscript on the second Q' indicates that its domain expression is supposed to define a domain for the variable x, but that variable does not appear in the domain expression; a condition involving only the variable y does not define a domain for the variable x. Second, two different Q's purport to lay claim to the same variable in the matrix "x Admire y." The second kind of bizarreness becomes more pronounced if the first kind is removed, by changing the variable in the second domain expression to x:

2.3.3　　　(Many: x Politician)$_x$ (Most: x Crook)$_x$ (x Admire y)

According to the first Q', the values of x that are relevant to the truth or falsehood of 2.3.3 are those which are politicians, and according to the second Q', the relevant values of x are those that meet the quite distinct condition of being crooks.

There are two principal ways of dealing with formulas such as 2.3.3: either set up one's formation rules so as to exclude them, or admit them and, by hook or crook, impose an interpretation on them. Logicians have generally opted for the second of these alternatives: they have adopted highly permissive formation rules that allow for many formulas (such as 2.3.3) that one might strongly prefer to do without, and they adopt a policy whereby the outermost of two quantifiers that bind the same variable is ignored in interpreting a formula (so that 2.3.3 is interpreted as saying that most crooks admire y, just as if the first Q' were not there). In this case I will part company with the logicians, on the grounds that admitting formulas such as 2.3.3 requires that one complicate one's rules of inference for quantifiers so as to avoid inadvertently deriving formulas like 2.3.3. If there is no general constraint against formulas like 2.3.3 and they are interpreted as in the policy just described, then restrictions to prevent one from inadvertently drawing a conclusion that is irrelevant to the premises will have to be built into those rules of inference that introduce variables; for example, if one's choice of the variable were not prevented from coinciding with another bound variable, the rule of "Universal quantifier introduction," which entitles one under certain circumstances to draw a conclusion 2.3.4a, corresponding to *Every man loves some woman,* could yield a conclusion 2.3.4b that was given the same interpretation as *Some woman loves herself,* a conclusion that one generally is not entitled to draw in cases which one is entitled to draw the conclusion that every man loves some woman:

2.3.4   a. (Every: x Man)$_x$ (Some: y Woman)$_y$ (x Love y)
    b. (Every: y Man)$_y$ (Some: y Woman)$_y$ (y Love y)

By excluding formulas like 2.3.3 and 2.3.4b tout court, one allows rules like "Universal quantifier introduction" to be formulated in their pristine purity without letting oneself in thereby for unwanted inferences. I thus choose to supplement the rules in 2.2.12–13 by conditions on the occurrence of variables that will serve to exclude formulas such as 2.3.3 from the class of admissible logical structures.

Before giving these conditions, let me point out some other kinds of formulas that one may wish to exclude on the grounds that the variables are employed incoherently:

2.3.5   a. (All: x Linguist)$_x$ (a Admire b)
    b. (All: a Admire b)$_x$ (x Hate x)
    c. (All: x Teacher y)$_y$ (All: x Linguist)$_x$ (x Respect y)

In 2.3.5a, the matrix corresponds to something such as *Thatcher admires Reagan,* that does not contain anything for the quantifier to bind; it is at best an egregiously roundabout way of saying something in which the quantifier does not even appear. In 2.3.5b, the domain expression does not give any condition on the bound variable, i.e., it gives a condition that will be met or not depending just on whether (say) Thatcher admires Reagan, irrespective of what value one assigns to the variable x. In 2.3.5c, the first Q' contains an occurrence of x that is outside of the scope of the Q' that binds x: the second Q' tells what values of x are relevant to the interpretation of "x Respect y," but plays no role in the interpretation of material outside of that S.

The following conditions will suffice to exclude the classes of formulas that I have suggested excluding:

2.3.6   For any variable x and any expression of the form

   i. S_1 must contain x.
  ii. S_2 must contain x.
 iii. S_1 and S_2 must not contain Q'_x.

These conditions respectively exclude formulas like 2.3.5b, 2.3.5a, and 2.3.3. Strictly speaking, they do not exclude 2.3.5c entirely; however, they prevent such formulas from being constituents of propositions (= closed sentences): to combine 2.3.5c with other material into a proposition, one would have to combine it (or something containing it) with a quantifier that binds the occurrence of x that is not bound in 2.3.5c, and the resulting formula would then violate 2.3.6iii, since the latter quantifier would then bind x and be combined with an S_1 that also contains Q'_x.

The coherence conditions in 2.3.6 are not expressible in the form of "constituent structure rules" such as have figured in the "grammars" given above: a constituent structure rule gives only a "local" condition on what a structure may contain (i.e., it tells what may be directly under a given node, possibly subject to a restriction on what is adjacent to that node), whereas the coherence conditions are "overall" conditions. To determine whether a particular Q is used coherently, it is necessary to examine not only the nodes that are immediately below or adjacent to the Q-node, but also nodes that are an arbitrary distance down the tree from it. For example, in the structure in 2.3.7, the logical structure of a sentence such as *Every admirer of all the brothers of most philosophers is out of his mind*, the only occurrence of x under the Q' that binds it is 4 steps down the tree from it, and by appropriate combination of the available logical elements, one could easily construct structures in which a Q'_x was 10 or 100 steps above the closest occurrence of x:

2.3.7

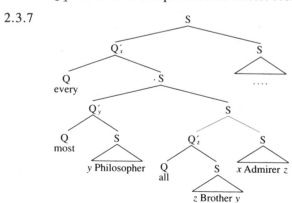

Thus, the grammars of systems of logic must be allowed to contain at least two kinds of rules: constituent structure rules and rules for "overall conditions." In this respect, logical structure is like ordinary syntactic structure, in which there are not only rules specifying what a NP or the like may consist of but also overall structural conditions on the location of a pronoun relative to its antecedent, or of a negative polarity item such as *a red cent* (as in *Phil hasn't given Lucy a red cent;* see 3.4 for some discussion of negative polarity items) in relation to a negative element that licenses it.

In many cases, the subscripts on the Q's are predictable from the rest of the structure plus the coherence conditions in 2.3.6, in the sense that only one way of subscripting them would conform to the conditions, e.g., in 2.3.7, the lower Q' has to have the subscript y, since otherwise 2.3.7 would violate 2.3.6i (y is the only variable within the domain expression), and for the same reason the upper Q' has to have the subscript x. It is indeed rather hard to devise structures that conform to 2.3.6 but in which the subscripts on the Q's are not predictable from the rest of the structure, and indeed only in structures containing at least four Q's does it ever happen that there are two distinct ways of subscripting the Q's without violating 2.3.6, as in 2.3.8a, which is ambiguous between interpretations of the forms 2.3.8b and 2.3.8b':

2.3.8   a.

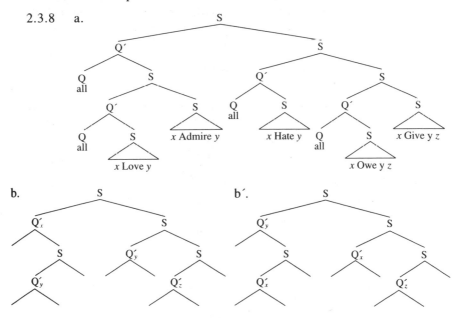

Using numerical subscripts to indicate the antecedents of the pronouns, one can paraphrase interpretation 2.3.8b roughly as "All people$_1$ who admire all people that they$_1$ love give all people$_2$ that they$_1$ hate all things that they$_1$ owe them$_2$." Interpretation 2.3.8b′ can be paraphrased roughly as "All people$_1$ who are admired by all people that love them$_1$ are given by all people$_2$ that hate them$_1$ all things that they$_2$ owe them$_1$." These two interpretations are thus quite different meanings (though you should think for a minute about the paraphrases that I have just given before taking my word that they are different) and they could very well differ in truth value. The paraphrases are rough in that 2.3.8a contains nothing corresponding to the nouns *people* and *things* that appear in the paraphrases. If predicates corresponding to those nouns were incorporated into 2.3.8a in the obvious way (e.g., instead of "*x* Love *y*" we would have "*y* Person and *x* Love *y*," the structures would then be unambiguous about which Q binds which variable: depending on whether you have "*x* Person" or "*y* Person" combined with the first *all*, the first Q would have to bind *x* or *y* respectively. Thus, while 2.3.6 does not enable one to predict the subscripts in 2.3.8a from the rest of the structure, it is conceivable that the structures in which the subscripts are not predictable might all violate some defensible requirement that there be "sufficiently many nouns" in logical structures. Since for the time being, however, I am not in a position to formulate such a condition, I will thus henceforth assume that the Q′s are subscripted with the variables that they bind, though I will often omit the subscripts in cases where they are predictable through the coherency conditions.

2.4. The Logicians' Favorite Quantifiers

Most modern works on logic operate in terms of just two quantifiers: a **universal quantifier** and an **existential quantifier.** The so-called universal quantifier corresponds to several different English words: *all, every, any, each;* the existential quantifier corresponds to certain uses of the words *some* and *a/an.* Thus, most logicians would assign (or at least, would expect their pupils to assign) the same logical formula to the sentences

2.4.1   a. All doctors will tell you that Stopsneeze helps.
         b. Every doctor will tell you that Stopsneeze helps.
         c. Any doctor will tell you that Stopsneeze helps.
         d. Each doctor will tell you that Stopsneeze helps.

These sentences in fact are not interchangeable, as was noted in an insightful discussion of the differences in the conditions of use of the four "universal quantifier words" by Vendler (1967b). For example, 2.4.1c refers to a hypothetical situation (if you solicit any doctor's opinion about Stopsneeze, he will tell you that it helps) and can be true even if many doctors never express an opinion about Stopsneeze; however, the other sentences will not be true unless every doctor expresses a favorable opinion about Stopsneeze.

Example 2.4.1d refers to a sequence of events (i.e., it suggests that you will consult the doctors one by one), whereas the other sentences leave open the possibility that you will get all the opinions simultaneously. More generally, *each* requires a "matching" between the domain of the quantifier and the objects or events referred to in a way that *every*, *any*, and *all* do not. For example, the difference in normalness between 2.4.2a and 2.4.2b correlates with the fact that in our society a woman has her husbands in succession but has her uncles at the same time:

2.4.2   a.   Marge admired each of her husbands.
          b.   ?Marge admired each of her uncles.
          b′. Marge admired each of her uncles in a different way.

In 2.4.2a the *each* matches the various periods when Marge was married with the proposition that at the time she loved her current husband. The addition of *in a different way* to 2.4.2b yields the requisite matching: each uncle is matched with a way of admiring someone.

All differs from *each, any,* and *every* in allowing not only a **distributive** interpretation, in which it says something about each of the entities taken in by the expression that it combines with, but also a **collective** interpretation, in which it says something about the whole body made up by those entities, as in 2.4.3a and in one interpretation of 2.4.3b:

2.4.3   a.   Köchel compiled a catalog of all of Mozart's works.
          b.   All of the boys carried the piano upstairs.

Since a catalog must be of a set of things and not of a single thing (e.g., one could not speak of "a catalog of the C minor mass," except perhaps in the extended sense of a catalog of the editions, performances, and/or recordings of that composition), 2.4.3a has only a collective interpretation. The distributive interpretation of 2.4.3b refers to several events of carrying the piano, one involving each boy (in that interpretation, it can be paraphrased *Each of the boys carried the piano upstairs*); the collective interpretation refers to an event (or perhaps several events) in which all the boys participated.

A second respect in which *all* behaves differently from *each* and *every* emerges from a consideration of sentences such as these in 2.4.4, in which these quantifiers are combined directly with an N′ (rather than with *of NP*):

2.4.4   a.   He served each/every dish on a silver platter.
          a′. He served all dishes on a silver platter.

      b. Every student passed the exam in my syntax course.

      b'. ??All students passed the exam in my syntax course. (Cf. All
          (of) the students . . .)

In 2.4.4a, *each dish* or *every dish* can be interpreted as taking only a particular set of dishes into account, say, the various dishes that were served at one particular dinner. By contrast, 2.4.4a' allows only a "habitual" reading, in which it does not refer to a particular set of dishes but rather says that (during whatever past time period is referred to) the chef in question used only silver platters as serving vessels. The lexical material in 2.4.4b–b' is chosen so as to make plausible only an interpretation in which a particular set of students are referred to (namely, those taking the course in question), and while *every* sounds normal, *all* sounds quite strange.

    The possibility of a collective interpretation of *all* brings out an important respect in which *all* differs from the universal quantifier of standard logic, namely, that from universal propositions one is allowed to infer particular cases, as in 2.4.5a–d, but the collective use of *all* does not allow that inference:

2.4.5   a. Every one of Mozart's works is a masterpiece.
         The quintet for horn and strings is one of Mozart's works.
         Therefore, the quintet for horn and strings is a masterpiece.

      b. Each speaker answered questions.
         Schwartz was a speaker.
         Therefore, Schwartz answered questions.

      c. Any doctor will tell you that Stopsneeze helps.
         Dr. Krankheit is a doctor.
         Therefore, Dr. Krankheit will tell you that Stopsneeze helps (if
          you ask him).

      d. All men are mortal.
         Socrates is a man.
         Therefore, Socrates is mortal.

      e. Köchel compiled a catalog of all of Mozart's works.
         The C minor mass is one of Mozart's works.
         *Therefore, Köchel compiled a catalog of the C minor mass.

Actually, even the collective use of *all* can be regarded as allowing the inference to special cases, provided we take an appropriate view of what a "special case" of a proposition with collective *all* is. Note that collective *all* is not equivalent to a simple plural NP denoting the group, since it implies that every member was involved in the event or state in question (thus, 2.4.6a is valid), whereas the simple plural does not (2.4.6b is invalid):

2.4.6   a. All of the boys carried the piano upstairs. (collective
              interpretation)
          Billy is one of the boys.
          Therefore, Billy was involved in carrying the piano upstairs.
        b. The boys carried the piano upstairs.
          Billy is one of the boys.
          *Therefore, Billy was involved in carrying the piano upstairs.

The fact that even collective *all* can be interpreted as allowing this rule of inference suggests that logicians have not been unreasonable in factoring out a single "universal quantifier" from *each, every, any,* and *all* and giving rules of inference for that single quantifier rather than separate rules for *each, any, every,* and *all.* The sketch given above of the differences among those four words suggests that it may in fact be possible to analyze them all as involving the same quantifier (henceforth symbolized as ∀), with the four words differing from one another with regard to either the class of contexts to which they are restricted or what additional material besides ∀ goes into their meaning. If that is in fact the case, then what is wrong with logical forms as in 2.4.7 for the first premise of each of 2.4.5 is that some or all of them are incomplete—while the ∀ is correct, there is more than that to the logical forms of at least some of the sentences:

2.4.7   a. (∀: x is one of Mozart's works)(x is a masterpiece)
        b. (∀: x is a speaker)(x answered questions).
        c. (∀: x is a doctor)(x will tell you that Stopsneeze helps)
        d. (∀: x is a man)(x is mortal)

One particularly influential proposal in which a universal quantifier word is analyzed as a contextual variant of ∀ is Quine's (1960:138–41) proposal that *any* is a universal quantifier with "wide scope," while *every* and *all* have "narrow scope." According to Quine's proposal (adapted to the general style of logical forms adopted in this section), 2.4.8a–d have logical forms as indicated below:

2.4.8   a. If you ask any doctor, you'll be arrested.
          (∀: x is a doctor)$_x$ (if you ask x, you'll be arrested)
        b. If you ask every doctor, you'll be arrested.
          if [(∀: x is a doctor)$_x$ (you ask x)], you'll be arrested.

    c. John didn't criticize any candidate.

      ($\forall$: x is a candidate)$_x$ not(John criticized x)

    d. John didn't criticize every candidate.

      not($\forall$: x is a candidate)$_x$ (John criticized x)

That is, he took *any* to be the form that a universal quantifier assumes when certain logical elements (such as the *if* in 2.4.8a and the *not* in 2.4.8c) inter-vene between it and the clause containing the variable that it binds. For Quine, thus, the difference in meaning between 2.4.8a and 2.4.8b or between 2.4.8c and 2.4.8d corresponded not to a difference in meaning between *any* and *every* but to a difference in scope that is signaled by the superficial difference be-tween *any* and *every*. Certain other instances where *any* and *every* appear to contrast in meaning can be analyzed in accordance with Quine's proposal, provided the language in which the analysis is carried out is richer than that of ordinary predicate logic. For example, 2.4.9a,b (taken from Geach 1972:7) can be analyzed as 2.4.9a′, b′ provided one admits *may* as combining with sentences:

2.4.9   a. You may marry anyone you want to.

        a′. ($\forall$: you want (you marry x))$_x$ may (you marry x)

        b. You may marry everyone you want to.

        b′. may ($\forall$: you want (you marry x))$_x$ (you marry x)

It is far from clear, however, that all instances of *any* can be analyzed as $\forall$ with wide scope. For example, if *any* were just a universal quantifier with wide scope, there would be no reason why it should not combine with *almost* the way that *all* and *every* do (*Almost all of the glasses are cracked; Almost every student found problem 3 difficult*); but the *any* of 2.4.8c does not allow *almost*: **John didn't talk to almost anyone.*[6] Moreover, there is no obvious way of providing a "wide scope" analysis for such sentences as *Hardly any Americans enjoy opera*. It is also not clear that a distinction between "wide scope" and "narrow scope" can be drawn in such a way as to accord with the use of *any* versus *every*. The instances of "wide scope" discussed above all involve a universal quantifier commanding a *not* or *if* or *may* that commands the variable which the quantifier binds. But what happens when the interven-ing "operator" is a conjunction or a quantifier, or if more than one operator intervenes—can the universal quantifier then be realized as *any?* Or as *every?* Or can it be rendered into normal English at all? Exploration of this series of questions is left to the reader as an exercise.[7]

    For the purposes of this book, I will adopt the position that $\forall$ should be part of the vocabulary available for representing meanings, that it is all or part of the meanings of *all, every, each,* and *any* (or at least, the use of *any* found in 2.4.1c), and that the differences in meaning among those four words correspond to extra material that in some cases may legitimately be ignored.

Before leaving the topic of universal quantifiers, I wish to mention briefly an important class of words in which the usual four-way contrast of *each/ every/any/all* is reduced to a two-way contrast, namely, the universal "indefinite pronouns" *everyone, anyone, everything, anything, everywhere, anywhere,* etc. In each of these words (as in their existentially quantified counterparts *someone, something, somewhere,* etc.), a quantifier is combined with an element that indicates the domain of its bound variable, e.g., the bound variable in *everyone* or *everybody* ranges over persons and the bound variable in *everywhere* ranges over places. (There are both morphological irregularities and morphological gaps in these paradigms: *always* is used where one might expect **everytimes,* and there is no universally quantified counterpart of *somehow,* not even such a word as **everyhow.*) When dealing with sentences containing words of the *every-* series, it is important to keep in mind that the *every-* does not always mean "every" but sometimes means "all," as can be seen from the fact that words of the *every-* series can be used not only like NPs of the form *every N'* but also like NPs of the form *all N's:*

2.4.10   a.   He took a photograph of everyone in the room.
        a'.   He took a photograph of every person in the room.
        a.   He took a photograph of all the people in the room.
        b.   Köchel compiled a catalog of everything that Mozart ever wrote.
        b'.   ??Köchel compiled a catalog of every work that Mozart ever wrote.
        b''.   Köchel compiled a catalog of all the works that Mozart ever wrote.
        c.   Everyone assembled in the auditorium.
        c'.   *Every one of them assembled in the auditorium.
        c''.   All of them assembled in the auditorium.

For example, like 2.4.10a'' and unlike 2.4.10a', 2.4.10a allows a collective interpretation, i.e., an interpretation that refers to a single group photograph rather than several individual photographs. When the *every-* word appears in a context that requires a NP to be interpreted collectively, as in 2.4.10b,c, corresponding sentences with *all* are fully acceptable while corresponding sentences with *every N'* are not fully acceptable.[8]

Logicians also usually recognize a single **existential quantifier,** henceforth represented by the symbol ∃, that is supposed to correspond indiscriminately to a number of things that natural languages often distinguish, for example, *a/an* in such sentences as 2.4.11a, the zero article in 2.4.11b, and *some* in such sentences as 2.4.11c–c′:[9]

2.4.11   a.   A friend of mine phoned me this morning.
          b.   Birds were singing.
          c.   Some politician was saying stupid things.
          c′.   Some politicians were saying stupid things.

Formulas such as $(\exists: x \text{ Politician})_x$ (x was saying stupid things), which would correspond indiscriminately to both 2.4.11c and 2.4.11c′, are supposed to be noncommittal as to whether one or more than one individual that satisfies the domain expression satisfies the matrix expression, and in fact the most accurate natural language paraphrase of $\exists$ may be "at least one." The formulas of standard logic thus usually ignore a pervasive feature of all European languages (though not all languages by any means), namely, the singular/plural distinction in nouns: when one uses a noun in an English sentence, one usually is required by the language to commit oneself as to whether one is referring to one or more than one object, regardless of whether one has any interest in conveying that information. For example, if you have one nephew and three nieces, you have to use the singular form *nephew* and the plural form *nieces* in the sentence *I'm shopping for Christmas presents for my nephew and nieces* even if all that you want to convey is that the presents are for the children of whom you are an uncle or aunt, and you have no particular reason to inform your hearers about how many of the children are of each sex.

The information conveyed by the singular/plural distinction sometimes is part of the information that one wishes to convey in what one says, and sometimes it is not, and if a system of logic is to deal with the propositions that are intended in the various sentences that are used in stating arguments, rather than the propositions that happen to be conveyed as a result of quirks of a particular language, it will be necessary to allow logical formulas to contain elements that are unspecified with regard to the singular/plural distinction but which may be combined, when appropriate, with elements that specify whether one object or more than one is being referred to.

All natural languages contain words that appear in the same positions as do *all* and *some* (or their equivalents in the language in question) but which are not identifiable with $\forall$ or $\exists$. For example, there are such words as *most, many, few, no, several,* and the numerals (*one, two, three, . . .*), as well as such compound expressions as *almost all, all but one, hardly any, at least five.* In some cases an analysis of the word as a combination of $\forall$ or $\exists$ with other material is possible. For example, it is reasonable to propose that *no* means "*not* $\exists$," for example,

2.4.12   No Republican admires Truman.

        not ($\exists$: x Republican)(x Admire Truman)

However, the "other material" may have to be something other than just propositional connectives. For example, in section 7.4 I will propose and defend an analysis of *Many Americans enjoy sports* as involving an existential quantifier ("There is a set of Americans such that . . ."), a universal quantifier ("All the individuals in that set enjoy sports"), and a size specification ("That set is large"). That analysis involves the conceptual apparatus of set theory (the notion of a set, the notion of being a member of a set), as well as the conceptual apparatus involved in notions of size; and an adequate treatment of notions of size may be fairly involved, since it is necessary to refer to relative sizes rather than just to absolute sizes and since such notions as "normal" or "expected" may be involved in determining how many shall count as "many" or as "few" (for example, one might say *Very few people went to the football game* when there were 5000 in attendance, yet *Lots of people came to Fred's party* when 50 people came). For the present, I will leave open the question of whether it is reasonable to analyze all other quantifiers into combinations of $\forall$ and/or $\exists$ with other material. The discussion in the rest of this chapter and in chapter 6 will in fact concentrate on $\forall$ and $\exists$, though occasional references will be made to other quantifiers. I will make a point, however, of avoiding an error that is easy to fall into: the error of taking properties that $\forall$ and $\exists$ share to be properties of quantifiers in general. For example, by interchanging consecutive Q's that both have $\forall$ or both have $\exists$ as the quantifier, one obtains a result that has the same truth conditions as does the original formula:[10]

2.4.13   a. ($\forall$: Fx)$_x$ [($\forall$: Gy)$_y$ Hxy]   a'. ($\forall$: Gy)$_y$ [($\forall$: Fx)$_x$ Hxy]
           b. ($\exists$: Fx)$_x$ [($\exists$: Gy)$_y$ Hxy]   b'. ($\exists$: Gy)$_y$ [($\exists$: Fx)$_x$ Hxy]

However, this fact must not lead one to conclude that the result of interchanging consecutive occurrences of the same quantifier always preserves truth conditions. For example, interchanging consecutive occurrences of *most* can turn a true proposition into a false one. Suppose that (Most: Fx)$_x$ Gx is true if more than half of the things that have the property F also have the property G and is false otherwise.[11] Example 2.4.14a is three-ways ambiguous, having the interpretations 2.4.14b–d, where B stands for "is one of the boys," G for "is one of the girls," and D for "danced with":

2.4.14   a. Most of the boys danced with most of the girls.
         b. (Most: Bx)[(Most: Gy) Dxy]
         c. (Most: Gy)[(Most: Bx) Dxy]
         d. The dancing involved most of the boys and most of the girls.

I will ignore 2.4.14d, which is listed here only for the sake of completeness; in fact it does not fit neatly into the notational scheme being developed here. It is easy to set up a possible state of affairs in which 2.4.14b and 2.4.14c differ in truth value. Let lines indicate who danced with whom:

2.4.15

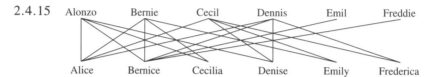

Alonzo danced with most of the girls (namely, with four of them); so also did Bernie, Cecil, and Dennis. Thus there are four boys who danced with most of the girls, and since four is most of the boys, 2.4.14b is true. But there are only two of the girls that most of the boys danced with: four boys danced with Alice and five with Bernice, but at most three boys danced with any of the other girls. Thus "(Most: Bx)Dxy" is true of only two of the girls and is thus not true of most of the girls, which means that 2.4.14c is false. Thus, interchanging (Most: Bx) with (Most: Gy) may change the truth value. The same is true of interchanging occurrences of *many* or of *almost all* or of *all but one,* as can be seen by constructing an appropriate state of affairs. The property of $\forall$ and $\exists$ noted for 2.4.13, far from being a general property of quantifiers, appears to be shared by no other quantifiers.

2.5. Rules of Inference

In this section we will take up rules of inference for the two favorite quantifiers of logicians, $\forall$ and $\exists$. Here, as with the elements of meaning that will be taken up in subsequent chapters, it will be necessary to have two rules for each quantifier: a rule of **introduction,** which gives conditions under which one is justified in drawing a conclusion involving the given quantifier (e.g., $\forall$-introduction will be a rule that licenses a class of inferences whose conclusion is a universal proposition), and a rule of **exploitation,** which specifies how premises that involve the given quantifier can be used in drawing conclusions.[12]

The rule of $\forall$-exploitation is the rule that allows one to go from a universal proposition to a special case of that proposition, for example,

2.5.1   All human beings are mortal.
           Socrates is a human being.
           Therefore, Socrates is mortal.

Expressed in the notation used in this chapter, the general pattern of inference
is the following:

2.5.2 $(\forall: Fx)_x\ Gx$
           Fa
           Ga

The rule of $\forall$-introduction is best introduced through an example of how
one can argue for a universal proposition. Suppose that you want to show that
the square of every odd number is odd. To do that, take an arbitrary odd number n. An odd number is one more than an even number, so n will be equal to
$2m + 1$ for some whole number m (an even number is twice a whole number). Since $n^2 = (2m + 1)^2 = 4m^2 + 4m + 1 = 2(2m^2 + 2m) + 1$, n^2
is one more than twice a whole number and is thus odd. This will be the case
no matter what odd number we pick, and so every odd number will have an
odd number for its square.

The important feature of this argument is the subproof in which one "picks
an arbitrary element" and shows, on the basis of what has already been established, that that element, no matter what it is, will have the characteristic in
question. The words "pick an arbitrary element" are misleading, since there
isn't any "picking" involved (you don't, for example, say "Let's pick 37,
since that's as arbitrary an odd number as you're likely to find"). What is
going on, rather, is that a subproof is set up in which a supposition is made
involving something that has not hitherto appeared in the proof. The only
"information" in which that thing appears is the supposition (e.g., all that you
know about n is that it is an odd number). The scheme of inference can be
displayed as follows:

2.5.3
$$
\begin{array}{|l}
\hline
Fu \\
\hline
\cdots \\
Gu \\
\end{array}
$$
$(\forall: Fx)_xGx$

In the given case, "Fu" is "u is an odd number" and "Gu" is "u^2 is an odd
number." The vertical line here marks off a **subproof** from a larger inference
of which it is a part; the horizontal line separates the **supposition** from the
remainder of the subproof, in which consequences of that supposition are
drawn: you suppose you have an odd number and see what follows from that.

Here u is strictly speaking neither a constant nor a variable but rather an **indeterminate**: a symbol that does not have a determinate value but rather represents an "arbitrarily selected member" of some domain; indeterminates figure in proofs like the one here, where one can prove something by showing that irrespective of what element one selects that meets some condition, such-and-such conclusion about it follows.

The rules of ∀-exploitation and ∀-introduction are both involved in the following inference, in which from "All politicians are crooks" and "All crooks are obnoxious" one deduces "All politicians are obnoxious":

2.5.4
1	$(\forall : x\ \text{Pol})_x(x\ \text{Crook})$	supp
2	$(\forall : x\ \text{Crook})_x(x\ \text{Obn})$	supp
3	$u\ \text{Pol}$	supp
4	$u\ \text{Crook}$	1, 3, ∀ -expl
5	$u\ \text{Obn}$	2, 4, ∀ -expl
6	$(\forall : x\ \text{Pol})_x(x\ \text{Obn})$	3–5, ∀ -intro

In this example, I have introduced a format that will figure in all proofs to be given subsequently in this book: the lines are numbered, and each line is provided with a **justification.** The justification will be simply "supp(osition)" for those lines which either are premises of the whole proof, here lines 1–2, or suppositions whose implications are explored in a subordinate proof, here line 3, from which inferences are drawn in the subproof that runs from line 3 to line 5 (subproof 3–5, for short). The justification for a line that is inferred from earlier lines will consist of the numbers of those lines and the name of the rule of inference that licenses the inference. In 2.5.4 we have proved that all politicians are obnoxious by setting up a subordinate proof in which we pick any politician, infer that he is a crook (which we can do because we are given that all politicians are crooks), then infer that he is obnoxious (which we can do because we are given that all crooks are obnoxious), which enables us to emerge from the subordinate proof with the conclusion that all politicians are obnoxious (the subordinate proof establishes that no matter what politician we pick, he will be obnoxious).

Let us turn to the rules of inference for ∃, of which there will again be two: a rule of ∃-introduction, giving circumstances in which we are entitled to draw an existential proposition as a conclusion, and one of ∃-exploitation, saying how we can use existential propositions in drawing inferences. The rule of ∃-introduction allows one to go from propositions about a particular individual to the conclusion that there is an individual having the properties that figure in those propositions, as when one shows that some man is bald by giving Aristotle as an example of a man who is bald. Here one goes from the premises "Aristotle is a man" and "Aristotle is bald" to the conclusion "Some man is bald" by a scheme of inference that can be represented as:

2.5.5 Fa
        Ga
        $(\exists{:}\ Fx)Gx$

The rule of $\exists$-exploitation is somewhat more complicated and is best introduced through an example. From the premise "Every person has a father" you can deduce the conclusion "Every person has a grandfather." Take an arbitrary person. Then there will be a second person who is the father of the first person. But the second person also has a father (since every person has a father), and so there is a third person who is the father of the second person. The father of the father of a person is that person's grandfather; thus, the third person is the first person's grandfather. Thus, the first person has a grandfather, and since the first person could be anyone at all, that means that every person has a grandfather. This argument can be given a formalization that begins as follows:[13]

2.5.6

1	$(\forall{:}\ x\ \text{person})(\exists{:}\ y\ \text{person})(y\ \text{father}\ x)$		supp
2	u person		supp
3	$(\exists{:}\ y\ \text{person})(y\ \text{father}\ u)$		1, 2, $\forall$-expl
4		v person	supp
5		v father u	supp
6		$(\exists{:}\ y\ \text{person})(y\ \text{father}\ v)$	1, 4, $\forall$-expl
7			w person	supp
8			w father v	supp
9			w grandfather u	5, 8, definition of *grandfather*
10		$(\exists{:}\ y\ \text{person})_y(y\ \text{grandfather}\ u)$	7, 9, $\exists$-intro

The line at which 2.5.6 breaks off says that u has a grandfather, which is what we need in order to establish that every person has a grandfather, but it is the conclusion of the wrong subproof: we need it as the conclusion of the subproof that starts at line 2, but it is actually the conclusion of the subproof that begins at line 7. However, we ought to be able to "export" it from the latter subproof, since it is independent of the indeterminate w that was introduced in the suppositions of subproof 7–10: we have shown that no matter who v's father is (i.e., no matter who w is), u has a grandfather. Suppose that we identify as the rule of $\exists$-exploitation a rule that says one may export such a conclusion to the higher proof: a conclusion that is drawn from the supposition that one has an entity such as the given existential proposition says exists, but is independent of the identity of that entity. That amounts to a pattern of inference with a subproof whose suppositions introduce an indeterminate but whose conclusion does not involve that indeterminate, which can be represented schematically as in 2.5.7:

2.5.7 $(\exists: Fx)Gx$

> Fu
> Gu
> ———
>
> . . .
>
> A (u does not occur in A)

A

We can then complete 2.5.6 as follows, exporting the conclusion of subproof 7–10 to successively higher subproofs until we have it in the subproof that we have set up in order to apply $\forall$-exploitation:

2.5.8

1	$(\forall: x\ \text{person})(\exists: y\ \text{person})(y\ \text{father}\ x)$	supp
2	u person	supp
3	$(\exists: y\ \text{person})(y\ \text{father}\ u)$	1, 2, $\forall$-expl
4	v person	supp
5	v father u	supp
6	$(\exists: y\ \text{person})(y\ \text{father}\ v)$	1, 4, $\forall$-expl
7	w person	supp
8	w father v	supp
9	w grandfather u	5, 8, definition of grandfather
10	$(\exists: y\ \text{person})_y(y\ \text{grandfather}\ u)$	7, 9, $\exists$-intro
11	$(\exists: y\ \text{person})_y(y\ \text{grandfather}\ u)$	6, 7–10, $\exists$-expl
12	$(\exists: y\ \text{person})_y(y\ \text{grandfather}\ u)$	3, 4–11, $\exists$-expl
13	$(\forall: \text{person}\ x)_x(\exists: y\ \text{person})_y(y\ \text{grandfather}\ x)$	2–12, $\forall$-intro

Note that lines 10, 11, and 12 are identical, but they nonetheless play different roles in the whole proof: each enables one to emerge from a particular subproof, and it is only by emerging from subproofs 7–10 and 4–11 that one gets to the position of being able to apply $\forall$-exploitation.

   One caveat must be added to the statement of $\forall$-introduction and $\exists$-introduction given above. In both of these rules a bound variable is introduced, together with a quantifier that binds it. The absolute identities of the bound variables are of no significance; that is, the following all represent exactly the same proposition:

2.5.9   a. (∀: x man)$_x$ (x mortal)
        b. (∀: y man)$_y$ (y mortal)
        c. (∀: z man)$_z$ (z mortal)

However, it does matter whether the variables occurring in two positions are the same or different. Thus, while 2.5.10a and 2.5.10b represent the same proposition, 2.5.10c is incoherent (it violates 2.3.6iii) and represents no proposition at all:

2.5.10   a. (∀: x man)$_x$ (∃: y woman)$_y$ (x love y)
        b. (∀: y man)$_y$ (∃: x woman)$_x$ (y love x)
        c. (∀: x man)$_x$ (∃: x woman)$_x$ (x love x)

In applying ∀-introduction and ∃-introduction, the new bound variable must be chosen in such a way that the resulting combination is coherent. For all practical purposes, what this will mean is that the new bound variable must not appear in the lines of the proof from which the conclusion is inferred by ∀-introduction or ∃-introduction. I will assume henceforth that statements of rules of inference apply only to "coherent" formulas; that is, the incoherence of a line of a proof is sufficient to exclude the proof, regardless of whether the proof conforms in all other details to the rules of inference. Thus, a proof containing the following would be excluded, though conforming to the rules of inference, since it contains an incoherent line:

2.5.11

w man
. . .
(∃: x woman)$_x$(w love x)
(∀: x man)$_x$(∃: x woman)$_x$(x love x)

Largely in order to broaden the range of exercises that can be given in this chapter, I will introduce here something that involves notions of propositional logic that will not be taken up in detail until chapter 3: an analysis of restrictive relative clauses in terms of conjoining. The interpretation of such sentences is parallel to that of the examples considered so far, provided that the relative clause is interpreted as part of the domain expression:

2.5.12   a. Every linguist who has read Bloomfield knows what a
           phoneme is.
        b. Most philosophers who write about language are ignorant of
           linguistics.

That is, in 2.5.12a, the individuals who are said to all know what a phoneme is are those who meet the condition "x is a linguist who has read Bloomfield," and in 2.5.12b, it is a majority of the individuals who meet the condition "*x* is a philosopher who writes about language" that are said to be ignorant of linguistics. These conditions can be treated as conjunctions of two propositional functions, one providing the noun and one corresponding to the relative clause, e.g., "*x* is a linguist who has read Bloomfield" can be analysed as "*x* is a linguist and *x* has read Bloomfield," and "*x* is a philosopher who writes about language" as "*x* is a philosopher and *x* writes about language." Anticipating the notation and the conclusions of chapter 3, let us write ∧ before two or more propositions to indicate their *and*-conjunction, i.e., ∧(*x* is a linguist, *x* has read Bloomfield) will represent "*x* is a linguist who has read Bloomfield." [14] The relevant formation rule for ∧ is 2.5.13, which says that a S may consist of ∧ and two Ss:

2.5.13

(This is a simplified version of the formation rule that will be given in 3.1, which will allow ∧ to conjoin any number of Ss at a time; for the purposes of this chapter only conjoining of Ss two at a time will play any role). Then, fudging details such as the present perfect *have,* we can give 2.5.14 as the logical structure of (one interpretation of) *Every linguist who has read Bloomfield resents most philosophers who write about language:*

2.5.14

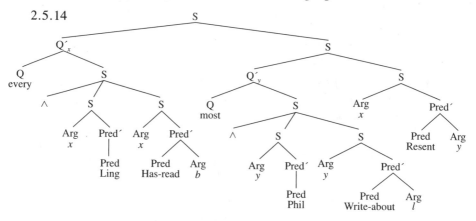

If we combine the rules of inference of this section with the rule of inference for ∧ that will be given in section 3.2, we are in a position to account for the validity of certain inferences that involve relative clauses in addition to universal and existential quantifiers. The rules of inference for ∧ are

∧-introduction, which entitles one to infer a conjoined proposition once the individual conjuncts have been established, and ∧-exploitation, which entitles one to infer any of the conjuncts once a conjoined proposition has been established:

2.5.15   a. ∧-introduction   b. ∧-exploitation

A	∧AB ∧AB
B	A B
∧AB	

Thus, 2.5.16b serves as a formalization of the inference given in English in 2.5.16a:

2.5.16   a. Every philosopher who admires Quine despises Derrida.
Jones is a philosopher.
Jones admires Quine.
Therefore, Jones despises Derrida.

b. 1 ($\forall$: $\wedge$(x Phil, x Adm q))$_x$ (x Desp d)   supp
   2 j Phil   supp
   3 j Adm q supp
   _____
   4 $\wedge$(j Phil, j Adm q)   2, 3, ∧-intro
   5 j Desp d 1, 4, $\forall$-expl

We are able to invoke $\forall$-expl in line 5 because in line 4 we have shown that j meets the condition that the universal quantifier in line 1 imposes on its variable.

We now have at our disposal two resources that allow us to set up logical structures for sentences that involve complex quantified noun phrases. Besides being able to use the above analysis of restrictive relative clauses, we also are able to represent certain nouns as two-place predicates, e.g., sentences that involve the noun *brother* will have logical forms that involve a two-place predicate "*x* is a brother of *y*," and the analysis of a sentence that contains *every philosopher who admires all of his teachers* will be in terms of a two-place predicate "*x* is a teacher of *y*" (not to be confused with the one-place predicate "*x* is a teacher"). For example, we can assign to 2.5.17a the logical form that is represented equivalently as in 2.5.17b or 2.5.17b':

2.5.17   a. Every philosopher who admires all of his teachers despises most of his students.
b. (Every: $\wedge$(x Phil, (All: y Teacher x)$_y$ (x Adm y)))$_x$ (Most: z Student x)$_z$ (x Despise z)

b′.

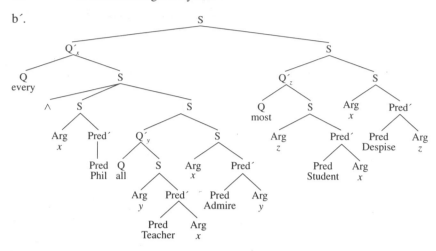

Let us illustrate the formalization of an ordinary language argument involving expressions that require the use of these devices.

2.5.18   Some philosophers who admire Aristotle are saintly.
Aristotle is a Greek.
All linguists respect every philosopher who admires a Greek.
Therefore, all linguists respect some philosophers who are saintly.

1	(∃: ∧(x Phil, x Adm a))ₓ (x Saintly)	supp
2	a Greek	supp
3	(∀: x Ling)ₓ(∀: ∧(y Phil, (∃: z Greek)₂(y Adm z)))ᵧ(x Resp y)	supp
4	u Ling	supp
5	(∀: ∧(y Phil,(∃: z Greek)(y Adm z)))(u Resp y)	3, 4, ∀-expl
6	∧(v Phil, v Adm a)	supp
7	v Saintly	supp
8	v Adm a	6, ∧-expl
9	(∃: z Greek)(v Adm z)	2, 8, ∃-intro
10	v Phil	6, ∧-expl
11	∧(v Phil,(∃: z Greek)(v Adm z))	10, 9, ∧-intro
12	u Resp v	5, 11, ∀-expl
13	∧(v Phil, v Saintly)	10, 7, ∧-intro
14	(∃: ∧(y Phil, y Saintly))ᵧ(u Resp y)	13, 12, ∃-intro
15	(∃: ∧(y Phil, y Saintly))ᵧ(u Resp y)	1, 6–14, ∃-expl
16	(∀: x Ling)ₓ(∃: ∧(y Phil, y Saintly))ᵧ(x Resp y)	4–15, ∀-intro

Note the supposition $\wedge(v$ Phil, v Adm $a)$ in line 6. Not only is it proper to use a syntactically complex expression such as this as a supposition, but it is indeed essential that that supposition appear at the beginning of a subproof that is to terminate with an application of ∃-expl that invokes line 1: $\wedge(x$ Phil, x Adm $a)$ is the domain expression of the existential proposition in line 1, and only a supposition that corresponds to that domain expression can yield a subproof that will fit the template of ∃-expl. It would indeed be a serious error to set up a subproof with suppositions from which one could derive $\wedge(v$ Phil, v Adm $a)$ by $\wedge$-intro:

2.5.18′	· · ·		
	6	v Phil	supp
	7	v Adm a	supp
	8	v Saintly	supp
	9	$\wedge(v$ Phil, v Adm $a)$	6, 7, $\wedge$-intro

An occurrence of $\wedge(v$ Phil, v Adm $a)$ that is derived by $\wedge$-intro is not a supposition and thus cannot fulfill the role that it must fulfill if ∃-expl is to be invoked in line 15. Thus, if one had deviated from 2.5.18 in the manner indicated in 2.5.18′, one would have made it impossible to apply ∃-expl and thereby exit from the subproof.

To conclude this section, I will illustrate some important results that the rules of inference given in this section enable us to prove. In stating these results, it will be convenient to use two special symbols that will recur throughout the book. The symbol ⊢ (read "turnstile") indicates that from the propositions listed before it one can infer the conclusion that is written after it. For example, the inference that was given at the very beginning of this section might be represented, using "Hx" to stand for "x is a human being," "Mx" for "x is mortal," and "a" for Socrates, as:

2.5.19 $(\forall: Hx)Mx, Ha \vdash Ma$

It often turns out that two propositions are **deductively equivalent,** in the sense that each can be inferred from the other. We will represent deductive equivalence by back-to-back turnstiles, so that 2.5.20a will serve as an abbreviation for 2.5.20b:

2.5.20   a. $p \dashv\vdash q$
         b. $p \vdash q$ and $q \vdash p$

The following results illustrate some ways in which the rules of inference given here can be combined into proofs of some complexity:

2.5.21 $(\forall: fx)(\forall: gy)hxy \dashv\vdash (\forall: gy)(\forall: fx)hxy$
          Proof that the first formula $\vdash$ the second formula:

1	$(\forall: fx)(\forall: gy)hxy$	supp
2	gu	supp
3	fv	supp
4	$(\forall: gy)hvy$	1, 3, $\forall$-expl
5	hvu	2, 4, $\forall$-expl
6	$(\forall: fx)hxu$	3–5, $\forall$-intro
7	$(\forall: gy)(\forall: fx)hxy$	2–6, $\forall$-intro

Proof that the second formula $\vdash$ the first formula: essentially identical to the proof just given.

2.5.22 $(\exists: fx)(\exists: gy)hxy \dashv\vdash (\exists: gy)(\exists: fx)hxy$
          Proof that the first formula $\vdash$ the second:

1	$(\exists: fx)(\exists: gy)hxy$	supp
2	fu	supp
3	$(\exists: gy)huy$	supp
4	gv	supp
5	huv	supp
6	$(\exists: fx)hxv$	2, 5, $\exists$-intro
7	$(\exists: gy)(\exists: fx)hxy$	4, 6, $\exists$-intro
8	$(\exists: gy)(\exists: fx)hxy$	3, 4–7, $\exists$-expl
9	$(\exists: gy)(\exists: fx)hxy$	1, 2–8, $\exists$-expl

Proof that the second formula $\vdash$ the first: essentially identical to the above proof.

2.5.23 $(\exists: fx)(\forall: gy)hxy \vdash (\forall: gy)(\exists: fx)hxy$
          Proof:

1	$(\exists: fx)(\forall: gy)hxy$	supp
2	fv	supp
3	$(\forall: gy)hvy$	supp
4	gu	supp
5	hvu	3, 4, $\forall$-expl
6	$(\exists: fx)hxu$	2, 5, $\exists$-intro
7	$(\forall: gy)(\exists: fx)hxy$	4–6, $\forall$-intro
8	$(\forall: gy)(\exists: fx)hxy$	1, 2–7, $\forall$-intro

You should be able to identify why the converse of 2.5.23 is **not** provable.

Exercises

1. For each of the following sentences, give a logical structure for it that conforms to the formation rules given in this chapter:

    a. Some students admire most teachers.
    b. Many persons admire all of their relatives.
    c. Many persons$_i$ who respect all of their$_i$ relatives admire all philosophers.
    d. Few students who admire all authors love most teachers who hate many authors.
    e. Every person$_i$ who respects himself$_i$ admires all of his$_i$ teachers.
    f. Every linguist$_i$ loves all students of his$_i$ who own all books of which he$_i$ is the author.
    g. Most philosophers$_i$ who love many persons who admire them$_i$ respect few of their$_i$ relatives.
    h. Many philosophers$_i$ who are admired by all students of all of their$_i$ colleagues mistreat most of their$_i$ own students.

Treat the various quantifiers (*some, many, most, few, all, . . .*) as unanalyzable (i.e., don't try to analyze any of them into more primitive notions), treat pronouns as having as antecedent the NP with the matching subscript, and analyze all restrictive relative clauses in terms of coordination (e.g., "x is a student who admires Freud" $= \wedge(x$ Stud, x Adm Freud). Use the following predicates:

x Stud $=$ "x is a student"	x Adm y $=$ "x admires y"
x Tea $=$ "x is a teacher"	x Resp y $=$ "x respects y"
x Per $=$ "x is a person"	x Rel y $=$ "x is a relative of y"
x Book $=$ "x is a book"	x Love y $=$ "x loves y"
x Ling $=$ "x is a linguist"	x Col y $=$ "x is a colleague of y"
x Phil $=$ "x is a philosopher"	x Mistr y $=$ "x mistreats y"
x Tch y $=$ "x is a teacher of y"	x Hate y $=$ "x hates y"

2. Give two versions of the logical form of *Many students$_i$ respect few persons who are relatives of any of their$_i$ friends,*

    a. if *any* is regarded as a universal quantifier.
    b. if *any* is regarded as the alternate form that *some* takes when it is in the scope of a negative word (such as *few*).

Be especially careful to assign the correct scope to the quantifier that corresponds to *any* and to come up with formulas that are plausible representations of the presumed meaning of the sentence.

3. Test the generality of Quine's proposed analysis of *any* by

a. picking any two sentences in which *any* appears in combinations other than those discussed in this chapter and determining whether an analysis of *any* as a wide-scope universal quantifier is plausible.

b. constructing two logical forms in which a universal quantifier has wide scope in relation to its host sentence and determining whether a corresponding sentence with *any* can express the meaning in question.

4. Give formal proofs that lead from the premises to the given conclusion, following the format adopted in this chapter and filling in whatever intermediate steps are needed. If you need to supply extra premises that are in some sense trivial (e.g., a premise like "Every philosopher is a person"), do so and say explicitly that you are doing so.

a. Every linguist hates some philosopher who has criticized Chomsky.
Chomsky is a linguist.
Every philosopher who has criticized a linguist is a positivist.
Therefore, every linguist hates some positivist.

b. Every person$_i$ who respects himself$_i$ admires all of his$_i$ teachers.
Some philosophers respect themselves.
Therefore, some philosophers admire all of their teachers.

3. Propositional Logic 1: Syntax

3.1. Propositional Connectives and Their Formation Rules

This chapter will be concerned with the logical "syntax" of garden-variety uses of the words *and, or, if,* and *not;* that is, we will be concerned with giving for corresponding elements of logical structure both formation rules (rules specifying what are possible well-formed logical structures containing those elements) and rules of inference. We will postpone until chapter 4 any systematic treatment of the semantics of those elements, that is, of rules giving the conditions under which propositions involving those elements are true or false.

For the purposes of most of this chapter, we will be concerned with **pure** propositional logic, that is, with logical properties that depend only on how our four **propositional connectives** fit into the logical form of a proposition and not on the roles played by any other elements of meaning. This means that we will treat as **atomic** (that is, ignore the internal structure of) any propositions that are not decomposable into simpler propositions combined with *and, or, if,* and *not.* We will use lower-case letters such as *p, q, r, s* to stand for atomic propositions; capital letters such as A, B, C will be reserved for (not necessarily atomic) propositions. We will use the following symbols, all of which are in common use, for the propositional connectives:

3.1.1   and $\wedge$
        or $\vee$
        not $\sim$
        if(. . . then) $\supset$

Let A be any proposition. Then $\sim$A is the negation of A; for example, if A is the proposition that Cincinnati is in Mongolia, then $\sim$A is the proposition that Cincinnati isn't in Mongolia. *Not* (or its contracted form *n't*) expresses negation; for example, *Cincinnati isn't in Mongolia* expresses the negation of the proposition expressed by *Cincinnati is in Mongolia.* However, striking out *n't* doesn't always take you from one proposition to another of which it is the negation. For example, if you strike out the *n't* of 3.1.2a, you get something (3.1.2b) that isn't quite what 3.1.2a is the negation of, and if you strike out the *n't* of 3.1.3a, you get something (3.1.3b) of which 3.1.3a is clearly not the negation:

3.1.2   a. John doesn't love his wife.
          b. John does love his wife.

3.1.3   a. Some people aren't afraid of dying.
          b. Some people are afraid of dying.

The fact that the proposition whose negation 3.1.2a expresses is normally expressed not by the somewhat odd-sounding 3.1.2b[2] but by *John loves his wife* reflects a peculiarity of English: *n't* and the tense marker (here, the *-s* of *loves*) must be suffixed to an auxiliary verb, and if there isn't any auxiliary verb there, a *do* is supplied to meet that demand. The propositions expressed by 3.1.3a and 3.1.3b are not mutually contradictory; indeed, they clearly are both true. That doesn't mean that the *n't* of 3.1.3a doesn't express negation. It does express negation, but not negation of the whole proposition expressed by 3.1.3b: in the most obvious interpretation of 3.1.3b, the scope of the negation is "x is afraid of dying" and the matrix that the quantified NP is combined with is $\sim(x$ is afraid of dying). For the purposes of (pure) propositional logic, 3.1.3b is thus not of the form $\sim A$: it **contains** a negation but is not itself the negation of anything. Thus a proposition expressed by a sentence containing *not* or *n't* need not fit the formula $\sim A$: it can contain a proposition (or propositional function) of that form without itself being of that form.

   Logic texts generally adopt the practice of writing formulas as in 3.1.4 for propositions in which *and* or *or* conjoins two propositions:

3.1.4   a. A∧B
          b. A∨B

For example, if *p* is the proposition expressed by *John loves his wife* and *q* the proposition expressed by *Bert loves his parakeet,* then the proposition expressed by *John loves his wife and Bert loves his parakeet* is *p∧q*. I will deviate from this practise by writing the ∧ or ∨ before the propositions that it conjoins,[3] for example:

3.1.5   a. ∧AB [alternatively: ∧(A, B)]
          b. ∨AB [alternatively: ∨(A, B)]

I adopt this policy because (i) *and* and *or* can conjoin any number of propositions at a time, not just two (see section 3.5 for justification of this claim); (ii) to write A∧B∧C∧D for the *and*-conjunction of A, B, C, and D, as is often done, is misleading, since three ∧'s appear in the formula, whereas the meaning involves only a single conjunction, and (iii) if there is to be a uniform notation for conjunctions of arbitrarily many propositions, the extreme beginning and the extreme end are the most innocuous places to write the ∧ or ∨ (there are other possibilities, such as writing the ∧ or ∨ after the first of the conjunct propositions, regardless of how many of them there are; however, such a notation is baroque to no apparent purpose).

"Coordinating conjunctions" such as *and* and *or* have an important characteristic which it is worth devoting some attention to at this point, since it will recur throughout the examples to be given in this book. When sentences that are the same except for one item are conjoined by *and* or *or*, they can optionally be replaced by a simple sentence with a conjoined part. For example, the meaning of the first member of each of the following pairs of examples can be expressed by the second member of the pair:

3.1.6   a.   Fred is an athlete, and Myron is an athlete (too).
      a′.   Fred and Myron are athletes.
      b.   Brazil is larger than Baffin Island, and it is more densely populated than Baffin Island.
      b′.   Brazil is (both) larger and more densely populated than Baffin Island.
      c.   Either the poem was written by Whitman or it was written by Tennyson or it was written by e.e. cummings.
      c′.   The poem was written by either Whitman or Tennyson or e.e. cummings.
      d.   Jack admires Ribbentrop and he respects Ribbentrop.
      d′.   Jack (both) admires and respects Ribbentrop.

In the syntactic derivation of the second member of each of these pairs, there is an application of the grammatical transformation of **Conjunction Reduction,**[4] which replaces conjoined structure whose "conjuncts" are identical except for one part where they contrast by a simple structure in which the contrasting parts are conjoined in the place where the conjuncts contrast with each other.

This is not to say that all sentences having conjoined parts are derived from conjoined sentences; indeed there are clear cases of conjoined elements that do not admit such a derivation:

3.1.7   a. John and Mary are an amiable couple.
      b. Bush or Dukakis was a disconcerting choice.

The meaning of 3.1.7a could not be expressed by *John is an amiable couple and Mary is an amiable couple,* whose meaning is a blatant falsehood (neither John nor Mary can be a couple, let alone an amiable couple); it could not even be expressed by *John is amiable and Mary is amiable,* since that sentence does not even imply that John and Mary are a couple, let alone that they are an amiable one, and even if one assumes that they are indeed a couple, they can be amiable individually without being an amiable couple—they might be two very amiable persons who become nasty when they are together. Likewise, 3.1.7b cannot be paraphrased by *(Either) Bush was a disconcerting choice or Dukakis was a disconcerting choice,* since that sentence is not intelligible unless *choice* is interpreted differently than in 3.1.7b: as "thing chosen" rather than as "list of alternatives from which one must choose."[5]

There are also sentences with conjoined pieces that can in fact be treated as having Conjunction Reduction in their derivations, but only if Conjunction Reduction is taken as applying not to the whole sentence but to a subordinate sentence in its underlying structure. Thus, the most simple-minded way of undoing Conjunction Reduction in 3.1.8a and 3.1.8b yields sentences that are not accurate paraphrases of the originals; 3.1.8a says that John is neither athlete nor musician, whereas 3.1.8a′ says only that he isn't both, and 3.1.8b says that Bill is obliged to take one of the two actions (with the choice perhaps being left up to him), while 3.1.8b′ says that Bill is under one or other of two obligations (though you don't remember which of the two):

3.1.8   a.   John isn't an athlete or a musician.
         a′. Either John isn't an athlete or he isn't a musician.
         b.   Bill must either buy you a new car or give you his car.
         b′. Either Bill must buy you a new car or he must give you his car.

To treat 3.1.8a and 3.1.8b in terms of Conjunction Reduction, one must analyze them not as in 3.1.8a′ or 3.1.8b′ but as containing a conjoined sentence that is either negated (3.1.8a $= \sim \vee pq,$ where p is "John is an athlete" and q is "John is a musician") or combined with *must* (3.1.8b $=$ Must $(\vee pq)$, where p is "Bill will buy you a new car" and q is "Bill will give you his car"). Their deep structures are then roughly as in 3.1.9:

3.1.9   a.   b.

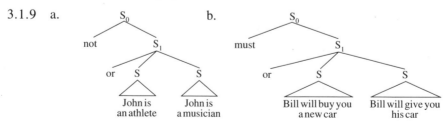

In the derivation of these sentences, Conjunction Reduction will apply to S_1 (which, as the only conjoined S in the structure, is the only S that could be the domain to which it applies), and thus the invocation of Conjunction Reduction does not require an underlying structure corresponding to 3.1.8a′ or 3.1.8b′.

The same point can be made about 3.1.10a,b:

3.1.10   a.   Richie wants to buy either a Mustang or a Chevy.
         a′. Either Richie wants to buy a Mustang or he wants to buy a Chevy.
         b.   Richie wants either a Mustang or a Chevy.
         b′. Either Richie wants a Mustang or he wants a Chevy.

Both 3.1.10a and 3.1.10b are ambiguous. One interpretation of 3.1.10a corresponds to 3.1.10a′. Its other interpretation can most easily be described in terms of the analysis that posits an embedded S as underlying the infinitive phrase (thus, *Richie wants to buy a Mustang* would have an underlying structure *Richie wants [he buy a Mustang]*, with *he* referring to Richie); the second interpretation is one in which *either . . . or* conjoins not main Ss but subordinate Ss, i.e., one with an underlying structure *Richie wants [[he buy a Mustang] or [he buy a Chevy]]*. The first interpretation of 3.1.10a suggests that the speaker doesn't know which of two desires Richie has, while the second interpretation suggests no uncertainty on the speaker's part but rather a desire on Richie's part that could be fulfilled in either of two ways. The sentence can be interpreted as reflecting Conjunction Reduction even in its second interpretation, just as long as the underlying structure is as just indicated and Conjunction Reduction applies to the embedded S rather than to the main S. There is the same ambiguity in 3.1.10b: in one interpretation, it says that Richie has one of two desires (and the speaker presumably does not know which one), and in the other interpretation it says that Richie has a certain desire that can be fulfilled in two ways (by his having a Mustang or by his having a Chevy). It is possible to analyse these two interpretations as differing the same way that the two interpretations of 3.1.10a do, provided one analyses sentences like *Richie wants a Mustang* as having an embedded S, e.g., as being a reduced form of *Richie wants to have a Mustang,* thus as being subject not only to Equi-NP-deletion, which deletes the subject of a nonfinite S if it is coreferential to a certain NP in the S to which it is subordinate, but also to a rule that (when the verb belongs to a limited class that includes *want*) deletes *have* if that is the main verb of the embedded S.[6]

While the examples in 3.1.8–10 thus **can** be analyzed as involving Conjunction Reduction, they should put one on one's guard against a mistake that is easily made: the fact that a sentence contains *and* or *or* does not imply that its meaning **is** a conjoined proposition—its meaning may merely **contain** a conjoined proposition.

In conformity with my notation for the "operators" taken up so far, which I write to the left of the propositions that they are combined with, I will also write the symbol for "if (. . . then)" before the propositions in question:

3.1.11 $\supset pq$ [alternatively: $\supset(p, q)$]

The standard notation is $p\supset q$. It must be kept in mind that while $\wedge$ and $\vee$ can combine with any number of propositions at a time, $\supset$ can only combine with two at a time; thus 3.1.12a makes sense but 3.1.12b does not:

3.1.12   a. $\wedge(p, q, r)$
　　　　 b. $\supset(p, q, r)$

The function of the parentheses in 3.1.5, 3.1.11, and 3.1.12 is to indicate how the elements of meaning are grouped together. That the grouping is significant can be seen by comparing the expressions

3.1.13   a. $\wedge(\vee(p, q, r),s)$
　　　　 b. $\wedge(\vee(p, q), r, s)$

These formulas correspond to clearly distinct meanings, for example,

3.1.14   a. Either Tom or Dick or Harry is sick, and George is sick (too).
　　　　 b. Either Tom or Dick is sick, and Harry is sick, and George is sick (too).

From 3.1.13b one can infer r, but from 3.1.13a one cannot.

Following the policy that I stated in 1.5 of regarding logical structures not as simply strings of symbols but as entities having a constituent structure (i.e., as trees), I maintain that it is not the parentheses themselves in formulas such as 3.1.13 that are significant but rather the grouping of elements that is represented by the parentheses. I thus relegate the differences among $\sim p$, $\sim(p)$, and $(\sim p)$ to the realm of typography: the differences can be ignored in the same way that we ignore the difference between 8-point and 10-point type or ignore spaces (i.e., "$p\wedge q$" and "$p \wedge q$" count as the same expression). The grouping can be indicated more perspicuously in the form of tree diagrams:

3.1.15   a. 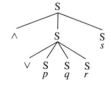   b.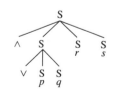

We are now in a position to give formation rules for propositional logic. As in section 2.2, the formation rules will be simply a list of the admissible ways in which the various elements (here, connectives and atomic propositions) can fit into logical structures:

3.1.16 $S: \vee S^n$ $(n \geq 2)$ $S: p$
          $S: \wedge S^n$ $(n \geq 2)$ $S: q$
          $S: \sim S$ $S: r$
          $S: \supset S\ S$ $S: s$

                                           ...

As before, the interpretation of a "grammar" such as 3.1.16 is that a tree conforms to it if and only if its topmost node is labeled S, its nonterminal nodes all have immediately under them nodes with labels fitting the expression that follows the colon in one or other of the rules, and its terminal symbols are all labeled by terminal symbols (here, $\wedge$, $\vee$, $\sim$, $\supset$, p, q, r, ...). For example, in 3.1.15a the terminal nodes have the labels $\wedge$, $\vee$, p, q, r, s, all of which are terminal symbols; the topmost node is labeled S and has under it nodes labeled $\wedge$SS, in that order, and thus conforms to the second rule of 3.1.16, which allows a node labeled S to have directly under it a node labeled $\wedge$, followed by two or more nodes labeled S; the four remaining nonterminal nodes conform to other rules of 3.1.16; for example the first of them conforms to the fifth rule of 3.1.16, since it bears the category label S and the terminal symbol p and does not have under it any other nodes.

By contrast, the following trees are not well formed relative to the rules of 3.1.16:

3.1.17   a. ... b. ... c. ...

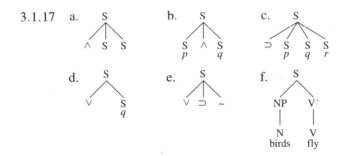

Example 3.1.17a is ill formed, since it has terminal nodes which are not labeled with terminal symbols; of course, addition of, say, the symbol p to one of the lower S-nodes and r to the other one would convert it into a well-formed

tree. Example 3.1.17b is ill formed since it has an ∧ between the two Ss that the ∧ is combined with, whereas 3.1.16 only allows a ∧ to precede the Ss that it is combined with; of course, had we chosen to write conjunctions between rather than before the conjuncts, we would have set up a different system of formation rules and, relative to **those** rules, 3.1.17b would have been well formed. Example 3.1.17c is ill formed because the ⊃ is combined with three Ss, whereas 3.1.16 only allows it to be combined with two, and 3.1.17d is ill formed because the ∨ is combined with only one S, whereas 3.1.16 only allows ∨ to be combined with two or more Ss. Example 3.1.17e is ill formed because none of the three "connectives" is combined with Ss, as they are required to be by 3.1.16. Finally, 3.1.17f is ill formed relative to 3.1.16 since it involves node labels that do not appear in 3.1.16 (NP, V, *birds, fly*). Of course, if we were to modify 3.1.16 so as to allow English (or Englishlike) expressions rather than *p*s and *q*s as the atomic propositions, 3.1.17f might very well be well formed relative to **those** rules.

Throughout most of the book I will use parenthesized formulas rather than tree diagrams to represent propositions. However, I will regard the parenthesized formulas as only an informal makeshift for representing information that appears more directly in tree diagrams. Actually, to a large extent, parentheses will be unnecessary; for example, the formulas in 3.1.18 can be given a coherent interpretation only if they are assigned the structures in 3.1.19:

3.1.18   a. ⊃∧~∨*pqpr*
           b. ~∧⊃*p*~∨*qrq*

3.1.19   a. 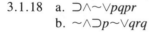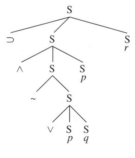   b.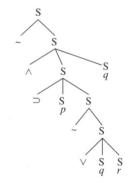

In fact, if conjoining (both *and*-conjoining and *or*-conjoining) were restricted to two conjuncts at a time, parentheses would be unnecessary when the connectives are written before the propositions that they combine with, as they are here; a proof of this claim will be given in section 5.7. However, if conjunctions of arbitrarily many conjuncts at a time are allowed, a formula without parentheses could be ambiguous with regard to constituent structure; for example, the formula $\wedge\vee pqrs$ would be ambiguous between interpretations corresponding to 3.1.13a and 3.1.13b, and that ambiguity would be pernicious, because those two interpretations have different truth conditions; for example, falsehood of r does not preclude the truth of the first interpretation $(\wedge(\vee pqr, s)$, which would be true if p and s are true) but is sufficient to guarantee the falsehood of the second interpretation $(\wedge(\vee pq, r, s))$. While the possibility of a parenthesis-free notation is of some inherent interest (and such a notation has even been given a name: "Polish notation" or "Polish parenthesis-free notation"), the possibility of omitting parentheses is of no particular relevance to the issues treated in this book. Thus, having advised the reader that if conjunctions are restricted to two conjuncts at a time, the notational scheme adopted here is for all practical purposes identical to "Polish parenthesis-free notation,"[7] I will proceed to write parentheses anywhere that they lend clarity to the formulas in question, even when, strictly speaking, they are superfluous.

3.2. Rules of Inference

In accordance with the approach to rules of inference that was introduced in 2.5, we now have the task of giving two rules of inference for each connective: a rule of **exploitation,** stating how premises containing that connective may be used in inferring conclusions, and a rule of **introduction,** stating how conclusions containing that connective may be inferred.

A simplified version of the two rules for $\wedge$ was given in 2.5.20; the simplification consisted in the fact that the rules given there applied only to conjunctions having two conjuncts. The more general rules of inference that those rules are special cases of are:

3.2.1   a. $\wedge$-exploitation. From a proposition $\wedge A_1 A_2...A_n$, any of the conjuncts A_i may be inferred.

b. $\wedge$-introduction. From the propositions A_1, A_2, ..., A_n, the conjunction $\wedge A_1 A_2...A_n$ may be inferred.

For example, from "Trivandrum is in India, Bhadgaon is in Nepal, and Luang Prabang is in Laos," $\wedge$-exploitation allows one to infer "Bhadgaon is in Nepal." From the three propositions "Mantle was a center-fielder," "Rizzuto was a shortstop," and "Mize was a first-baseman," $\wedge$-introduction allows one to infer the conclusion "Mantle was a center-fielder, Rizzuto was a shortstop, and Mize was a first-baseman." When used alone, as in these examples, the rules of inference for $\wedge$ seem to be totally trivial, but they often play an important role as steps in more complicated inferences, as may become clear from examples later in this chapter.

The rule of ⊃-**exploitation** says that from ⊃AB and A you may infer B. For example, from "If Socrates is a man, then he is mortal" and "Socrates is a man," you may infer "Socrates is mortal." The rule of ⊃-exploitation is better known by the name of **modus ponens**; however, I will use the name ⊃-exploitation in this book in order to make clearer the role that this rule of inference plays in the entire system of rules of inference. The rule of ⊃-**introduction** is best introduced via an example:

3.2.2   Whoever committed the murder left by the window.
               Anyone who left by the window would have mud on his shoes.
               Suppose that the butler committed the murder. Then he left by
                    the window. In that case, he has mud on his shoes.
               So if the butler committed the murder, he has mud on his shoes.

The conclusion of 3.2.2 is of the form ⊃pq (p is "The butler committed the murder," q is "The butler has mud on his shoes"). The way that the conclusion is proved is by setting up a subproof in which you suppose p and infer q from that supposition plus whatever propositions have been established up to that point. The structure of the argument 3.2.2 can be displayed in the diagram:

3.2.3   ...

               ...

               ┌─── p
               │   ...
               │ q
               ⊃pq

The following are some simple illustrations of proofs in which the above rules of inference figure. As in the notation introduced in section 2.5, each line is supplied with a "justification" (either the specification that it is a supposition, which is also indicated by its appearing above the horizontal line that separates the suppositions of each proof from the inferences that are drawn within the proof, or a specification of the earlier lines of the proof from which it is inferred and the rule of inference that allows it to be inferred from those lines):

3.2.4

1	⊃(p, ⊃qr)	supp
2	∧pq	supp
3	p	2, ∧-expl
4	⊃qr	1, 3, ⊃-expl
5	q	2, ∧-expl
6	r	4, 5, ⊃-expl
7	⊃(∧pq, r)	2–6, ⊃-intro

3.2.5   1 $\supset(\wedge\, pq, r)$ supp
             2 p supp
             3   q supp
             4        $\wedge pq$ 2, 3, $\wedge$-intro
             5   r 1, 4, $\supset$-expl
             6 $\supset qr$ 3–5, $\supset$-intro
             7 $\supset(p, \supset qr)$ 2–6, $\supset$-intro

Note that, as in 2.5.8, in 3.2.5 there is a subproof embedded within a sub-proof; the rules of inference that involve subproofs apply without regard to whether the subproofs are themselves embedded in subproofs and thus license proofs in which subproofs are embedded within one another to any finite depth.

Before going on, it will be worthwhile to repeat the points that were made with regard to 2.5.18 about the suppositions that figure in subordinate proofs. There is no restriction on what proposition or propositions can appear as sup-position(s) of any subordinate proof. In particular, there is no requirement that a supposition be syntactically simple (note the conjoined proposition $\wedge pq$ that figures as the supposition of 3.2.4). Not only is it legitimate to have a suppos-ition of any degree of internal complexity, but it is a serious error to suppose that complex propositions such as the $\wedge pq$ of 3.2.4 have to be derived from something: if one is to use $\supset$-intro to draw a conclusion of the form $\supset AB$, in which A is syntactically complex, the subproof in question **must** have that complex proposition as its supposition: otherwise there would be no way for $\supset$-intro to license the drawing of $\supset AB$ as a conclusion. In particular, if one were to set up a subordinate proof that had as suppositions the two simple propositions from which one can infer $\wedge pq$ (by $\wedge$-intro), none of the rules of inference that will be given in this chapter would provide any way for one to exit from the subordinate proof, because each of those rules of inference re-quires a subordinate proof having **one** supposition and does not license one's exit from a subordinate proof having two or more suppositions. The various rules of inference that involve subordinate proofs ($\supset$-intro, as well as $\sim$-intro and $\vee$-expl, which will be presented shortly, $\forall$-intro and $\exists$-expl from 2.5, and some other rules to be given in later chapters) do not merely entitle one to enter a subordinate proof but also provide very specific ways in which one is entitled to emerge from the subordinate proof. While there is no constraint on what propositions (or on how many of them) can serve as suppositions of a subordinate proof, one will accomplish nothing with a subordinate proof un-less one chooses the supposition(s) in such a way as to enable one to exit from the subordinate proof and emerge with a conclusion that either is or brings one closer to the result that one is endeavoring to prove. Thus, if one wishes to prove that from certain premises it follows that $\supset(\vee pq, \sim r)$, it may well be to one's advantage to set up a subordinate proof with the supposition $\vee pq$, but it is unlikely that a subordinate proof with any other supposition would lead one anywhere other than around in circles.

Similarly, the freedom to make suppositions in the main proof is quite innocuous: while there is inherent interest in what can be inferred from Euclid's axioms for geometry, there is no particular interest in what can be inferred from the premises "Bertrand Russell's native language was Kikuyu" and "All cities of population over 2 million are located in Tierra del Fuego." A pearl of wisdom from the domain of computer programming is worth quoting here: "Garbage in, garbage out."

The rule of **$\sim$-exploitation** is simply a rule of cancelling out double negations: from "it is not the case that not p," one can infer p. It should be emphasized that this rule refers to **double** negation, that is, to a negation of a negation, rather than to just anything that contains two negations. Thus, it doesn't justify your going from $\sim\supset(\sim p, q)$ to $\supset pq$, since $\supset(\sim p, q)$ is not the negation of $\supset pq$, and thus $\sim\supset(\sim p, q)$ is not a double negation.

The rule of **$\sim$-introduction** involves a subproof: you prove $\sim A$ by supposing A and showing that a contradiction follows. For example:

3.2.6   The butler doesn't have mud on his shoes.
           If the butler is the murderer, he left by the window.
           If he left by the window, he has mud on his shoes.
           Suppose the butler is the murderer. Then he left by the window
               and thus he had mud on his shoes. But he doesn't have mud
               on his shoes.
           Therefore, the butler isn't the murderer.

The argument which 3.2.6 spells out in such laborious detail can be spelled out equally laboriously in the following graphic form:

3.2.7   1 $\sim r$ supp
           2 $\supset pq$ supp
           3 $\supset qr$ supp
           4 | p supp
           5 | q 2, 4, $\supset$-expl
           6 | r 3, 5, $\supset$-expl
           7 | $\sim r$ $(=1)$
           8 $\sim p$ 4–7, $\sim$-intro

Arguments in which the conclusion is established by $\sim$-introduction are generally referred to as arguments by **reductio ad absurdum.**

Step 7 in 3.2.7, in which one of the suppositions of the main proof is repeated, deserves special comment. This step fits exactly one of the steps in 3.2.6 and seems reasonable here, since a contradiction involving suppositions of the main proof is just as much a ground for rejecting a proposition as a contradiction involving only matter in the subordinate proof. I will thus assume that there is a rule of inference, called **reiteration,** which allows one to repeat any line of a proof as a line of a subproof that occurs later and "subordinate to" the line in question.

The following are some examples of proofs that conform to the rules of inference given so far:

3.2.8   a. 1 $\supset pq$ supp
        2    $\sim q$ supp
        3   p supp
        4   q 1, 3, $\supset$-expl
        5    $\sim q$ 2, reit
        6    $\sim p$ 3–5, $\sim$-intro
        7 $\supset (\sim q, \sim p)$ 2–6, $\supset$-intro

      b. 1 $\sim\sim p$ supp
        2    $\wedge pq$ supp
        3   p 2, $\wedge$-expl
        4    $\sim p$ 1, reit
        5 $\sim\wedge pq$ 2–4, $\sim$-intro

      c. 1 $\wedge(p, \sim q)$ supp
        2    $\supset pq$ supp
        3   p 1, $\wedge$-expl
        4   q 2, 3, $\supset$-expl
        5    $\sim q$ 1, $\wedge$-expl
        6 $\sim\supset pq$ 2–5, $\sim$-intro

      d. 1 $\sim\supset pq$ supp
        2    $\sim p$ supp
        3   p supp
        4        $\sim q$ supp
        5   p 3, reit
        6      $\sim p$ 2, reit
        7      $\sim\sim q$ 4–6, $\sim$-intro
        8   q 7, $\sim$-expl
        9    $\supset pq$ 3–8, $\supset$-intro
        10 $\sim\supset pq$ 1, reit

11	$\sim\sim p$	2–10, $\sim$-intro
12	p	11, $\sim$-expl
13	q	supp
14	p	supp
15	q	13, reit
16	$\supset pq$	14–15, $\supset$-intro
17	$\sim\supset pq$	1, reit
18	$\sim q$	13–17, $\sim$-intro
19	$\wedge(p, \sim q)$	12, 18, $\wedge$-intro
e. 1	p	supp
2	$\sim p$	supp
3	$\sim q$	supp
4	p	1, reit
5	$\sim p$	2, reit
6	$\sim\sim q$	3–5, $\sim$-intro
7	q	6, $\sim$-expl

The results proved in 3.2.8a–c are quite reasonable (although I will shortly (in section 3.4) give some grounds for being suspicious of 3.2.8a): from "If p, then q" you can infer "If not q, then not p"; from "Not p" you can infer "Not both p and q"; from "p and not q" you can infer "It is not the case that if p then q." The other two results are much less obviously reasonable. While they conform in all details to the rules of inference given so far, they contain steps that may feel somewhat fishy, and both results are matters of serious controversy in logic and philosophy. If the result in 3.2.8d is correct, then not only is the truth of p and falsehood of q sufficient to make $\supset pq$ false (which is what 3.2.8c shows), but it is indeed the **only** way that $\supset pq$ can be false, which seems to make it disconcertingly easy for conditional propositions to be true. The result in 3.2.8e is particularly controversial: from contradictory premises you can infer any conclusion whatever. That result can be rationalized in a number of ways; for example, one might say that all a proof is supposed to do is show that in any state of affairs in which the premises are all true, the conclusion is also true, and since there is no state of affairs in which contradictory premises are all true, it is really not saying anything to say that q (or anything else you might pick) is true in any state of affairs in which p and $\sim p$ are both true. However, one should not be too hasty in accepting such rationalizations. There remains something quite odd about the conclusion that any contradiction causes **all** hell to break loose; can we not perhaps set things up differently, so that minor contradictions cause only a little bit of hell to break loose? Many attempts have been made in such a direction; the one that has been developed the most thoroughly is the "relevant entailment logic" of Anderson and Belnap 1975, sketched below in section 11.4. Anderson and Belnap's approach consists in imposing on the rules of inference a restriction requiring the suppositions of subproofs to actually be used in establishing the conclusion of the subproof, a condition that clearly is not met in 3.2.8e, as one can see by noting that line 3 (the supposition of the subproof) does not figure in the justification of any conclusion of that subproof; it can indeed be shown that no proof with p and $\sim p$ as premises and q as conclusion can satisfy Anderson and Belnap's restriction, and thus in their version of propositional logic neither 3.2.8e nor many other results that they disparage as "fallacies of relevance" can be proven.

Let us drop this matter for the present and return to the survey of rules of inference, though at least keeping in mind the possibility that the "classical" rules of inference which we will assume may have to be revised in the direction of "relevant entailment logic" in view of certain relatively bizarre conclusions that they lead to.

The rule of ∨-**exploitation** allows one to infer from an *or*-conjunction any proposition that can be inferred from all of the conjuncts. It is illustrated by inferences like the following:

3.2.9   Creepy Calabresi got off the plane in either Chicago, Kansas City, or Las Vegas.
             Suppose he got off in Chicago; then he would have called his brother; but his brother doesn't like Creepy and would have tipped off the Feds.
             Suppose Creepy got off the plane in Kansas City; then he would have called his girlfriend; but his girlfriend is working for the IRS, and she would have tipped off the Feds.
             Suppose Creepy got off the plane at Las Vegas; then he would have called the Fettucini Kid; but the Fettucini Kid has been arrested and the fuzz would have a stoolie taking the phone calls, and he would have tipped off the Feds.
             So someone has tipped off the Feds.

The first premise of this argument is of the form $\vee(p, q, r)$. There then follow subproofs, one with the supposition p, one with the supposition q, and one with the supposition r. In each case the subproof establishes: "Someone has tipped off the Feds." (Actually, the statement of each of the above subproofs stops just short of saying "Someone has tipped off the Feds"; however, the purpose of each of the subproofs is in fact to establish that). The conclusion is the proposition that is the common conclusion of those subproofs: "Someone has tipped off the Feds."

The rule of ∨-**introduction** allows one to infer from any proposition a conclusion which is an *or*-conjunction which has that proposition as one of its conjuncts. Any simple instance of ∨-introduction will sound quite fishy because the conclusion would be a misleading thing to assert if you already knew the premise:

3.2.10   Kathmandu is the capital of Nepal.
              Therefore, either Jersey City or Kathmandu or Istanbul is the
              capital of Nepal.

If you know what the capital of Nepal is, it is misleading to say something that suggests you have narrowed it down to three possibilities but (presumably) don't know which one of them is the capital. However, this fishiness vanishes when ∨-introduction is embedded in a larger proof and the proposition to which it applies is not **being asserted.** For example:

3.2.11   1 $\wedge(\vee pq, r)$ supp
           2 $\vee pq$ 1, ∧-expl
           3 │ p supp
           4 │ r 1, ∧-expl
           5 │ $\wedge pr$ 3, 4, ∧-intro
           6 │ $\vee(\wedge pr, \wedge qr)$ 5, ∨-intro
           7 │ q supp
           8 │ r 1, ∧-expl
           9 │ $\wedge qr$ 7, 8, ∧-intro
          10 │ $\vee(\wedge pr, \wedge qr)$ 9, ∨-intro
          11 $\vee(\wedge pr, \wedge qr)$ 2, 3–6, 7–10, ∨-expl

Here ∨-introduction is used in a quite reasonable inference; for example, the inference would take you from the premise "He's in either Kansas City or Las Vegas, and he's been arrested" to the conclusion "Either he's in Kansas City and he's been arrested, or he's in Las Vegas and he's been arrested." The difference between the fishiness of 3.2.10 and the innocuousness of 3.2.11 can be attributed to the fact that in 3.2.10 ∨-introduction was applied to something that had been asserted, whereas in 2.2.11 it was applied (steps 6 and 10) to "hypothetical" propositions: propositions that are only parts of subproofs and do not serve as lines of the main proof. It thus appears as if ∨-introduction is a valid rule of inference (i.e., it does in fact lead to true conclusions when applied to true premises), and the apparent fishiness of certain arguments in which it is used merely reflects the fact that the conclusions that it leads to, while true, are less informative than the premises to which it was applied, and it is misleading to assert something which takes more words to say but is less informative than another thing that you were in a position to assert.

One qualification must be made, relating to a possible ambiguity in the word *or*. The English word *or* can be used both "inclusively," as in *Shirley visited either Ayuddha or Lopburi last year,* which does not rule out the possibility that she visited both Ayuddha and Lopburi, and "exclusively," as in *On the $2.95 lunch you can have either a soup or a dessert,* which grants you permission to take one or the other but does not grant you permission to take both a soup and a dessert for your $2.95. Assuming for the moment that it makes sense to distinguish between two connectives, an **inclusive or,** which is true when at least one of the conjuncts is true and false otherwise, and an **exclusive or,** which is true when exactly one of the conjuncts is true and false otherwise, the rule of ∨-introduction given above clearly relates only to inclusive *or:* the truth of one conjunct is enough to insure that an inclusive *or* is true, but all the conjuncts would have to be examined to determine whether an exclusive *or* was true. There is actually some doubt about whether an exclusive *or* has to be recognized; in section 9.2, I will present considerations that suggest that English has only an inclusive *or,* and that supposed instances of exclusive *or* are really instances of inclusive *or* whose nature is masked by interactions with other factors. For the moment, though, I leave open the question of whether an exclusive *or* must be recognized. In any case, the rule of ∨-introduction given above has to do only with inclusive *or,* not with exclusive *or,* if there is such a thing.[8]

We have now gone through the complete system of rules of inference for propositional logic. The rules can be summarized in graphic form as in 3.2.12 (see next page). In each of these diagrams, the bottom line indicates what may be inferred from the lines above. The lines prior to the last line need not be consecutive (i.e., other lines can intervene in any proof in which these rules are applied) and need not be in the order given here, though the arrangement into "main" and "subordinate" proofs must be as given here. Strictly speaking, the rule of reiteration displayed in 3.2.12 allows one to reiterate a line only into an **immediately** subordinate proof; however, by repeated application of the rule given in 3.2.12 one can duplicate the effect of the reiteration rule in its full glory and reiterate lines down into an arbitrary depth of subordination.

3.2.12 ∧-introduction   ∧-exploitation

A_1

A_2 ∧$(A_1, A_2, ..., A_n)$

... A_i $[1 \leq i \leq n]$

A_n

∧$(A_1, A_2, ..., A_n)$

∨-introduction   ∨-exploitation

A_i ∨$(A_1, A_2, ..., A_n)$

∨$(A_1, ..., A_n)$ $[1 \leq i \leq n]$ | A_1

             | ...

             | B

             ...

             | A_n

             | ...

             | B

           B

~-introduction   ~-exploitation

| A   ~~A

| ...   A

| B

| ~B

~A

⊃-introduction   ⊃-exploitation

| A   ⊃ AB

| ...   A

| B   B

⊃ AB

---

reiteration

A

| ...

| ...

| A

Let us now go through some proofs illustrating the whole system of rules of inference and what can be done with them.

3.2.13   a. 1   ~ ∨ AB   supp
            2 | A   supp
            3 | ∨ AB   2, ∨-intro
            4 | ~∨ AB   1, reit
            5   ~ A   2–4, ~-intro
            6 | B   supp
            7 | ∨ AB   6, ∨-intro
            8 | ~∨ AB   1, reit
            9   ~ B   6–8, ~-intro
           10   ∧(~A, ~B)   5, 9, ∧-intro
         b. 1   ∧(~A, ~B)   supp
            2 | ∨ AB   supp
            3 | | A   supp
            4 | | ~ A   1, ∧-expl
            5 | | B   3, 4, 3.2.8e
            6 | | B   supp
            7 | | B   6, reit
            8 | B   2, 3–5, 6-7, ∨-expl
            9 | ~ B   1, ∧-expl
           10   ~ ∨ AB   2–9, ~-intro
         c. 1   ∨ AB   supp
            2   ~A   supp
            3 | A   supp
            4 | ~ A   2, reit
            5 | B   3, 4, 3.2.8e
            6 | B   supp
            7 | B   6, reit
            8 B   1, 3–5, 6–7, ∨-expl

The result proved in 3.2.13c is widely known as the **disjunctive syllogism** and is often given as a rule of inference; while it is not, strictly speaking, a rule of inference of the system of logic adopted here, it is a **derived rule of inference,** in the sense that it can be simulated by a combination of applications of rules of this system. The proofs given in 3.2.13b and 3.2.13c conform to our rules of inference only in an extended sense, since the justification given for step 5 is not one of the rules of inference; however, since the steps that were carried out in establishing 3.2.8e could have been repeated at the places where 3.2.8e is invoked in these proofs, 3.2.13b and 3.2.13c establish that there are proofs leading from the given premises to the conclusions, with every step conforming to one of the rules in 3.3.12. From here on I will feel free to give justifications such as 3.2.8e and not distinguish between proofs in which all the steps are spelled out in laborious detail and proofs in which the reader is referred to other proofs in the justification of some step.

3.2.14 a. 1   A   supp
          2   B   supp
          3   A   1, reit
          4   ⊃BA   2–3, ⊃-intro
          5 ⊃(A, ⊃BA)   1–4, ⊃-intro
    b.   1   ∧(A, ~A)   supp
          2   A   1, ∧-expl
          3   ~A   1, ∧-expl
          4 ~∧(A, ~A)   1–3, ~-intro
    c.   1   ~∨(A, ~A)   supp
          2   ∧(~A, ~ ~A)   1, 3.2.13*a*
          3   ~A   2, ∧-expl
          4   ~ ~A   2, ∧-expl
          5 ~ ~∨(A, A)   1–4, ~-intro
          6 ∨(A, ~A)   5, ~-expl

In 3.2.14 the main proofs have no premises (i.e., the only "suppositions" are suppositions of subordinate proofs). Thus, the three conclusions have been established "categorically," in contrast with the proofs in 3.2.13, where the conclusions were proven from the given premises. A conclusion that can be proven categorically in a given system is called a **theorem** of that system. The theorems proven in 3.2.14b–c are well known under the names of the **law of noncontradiction** and the **law of the excluded middle,** respectively.[9]

Note the appropriateness of invoking 3.2.13a in step 2 of 3.2.13c; while 3.2.13a was presented in the form of a derivation of ∧(~A, ~B) from ~∨AB, the exact same steps would be carried out even if something else were substituted for A and for B throughout 3.2.13a, in particular, if A were substituted for B, in which case the proof 3.2.13a would become a proof of line 2 of 3.2.14c from line 1.

3.2.15 a. 1   ∧(⊃AC, ⊃BC)   supp
          2   ∨AB   supp
          3   A   supp
          4   ⊃AC   1, ∧-expl
          5   C   4, 3, ⊃-expl

6	B	supp
7	⊃BC	1, ∧-expl
8	C	7, 6, ⊃-expl
9	C	2, 3–5, 6–8, ∨-expl
10	⊃(∨AB, C)	2–9, ⊃-intro

b.
1	∧(A, ∨ BC)	supp
2	A	1, ∧-expl
3	∨ BC	1, ∧-expl
4	B	supp
5	∧AB	2, 4, ∧-intro
6	∨(∧AB, ∧AC)	5, ∨-intro
7	C	supp
8	∧AC	2, 7, ∧-intro
9	∨(∧AB, ∧AC)	8, ∨-intro
10	∨(∧AB, ∧AC)	3, 4–6, 7–9, ∨-expl

Both of the results in 3.2.15 can be turned around: not only can you infer ⊃(∨AB, C) from ∧(⊃AC, ⊃BC), but you can also infer ∧ (⊃AC, ⊃BC) from ⊃(∨ AB, C); not only can you infer ∨(∧AB, ∧AC) from ∧(A, ∨BC), but you can also infer ∧(A, ∨ BC) from ∨(∧AB, ∧AC); proof of these claims is left to the reader as an exercise. The proofs thus establish that the formulas in each pair are deductively equivalent:

3.2.16   a. ∧(⊃AC, ⊃BC) ⊣⊢ ⊃(∨AB, C)
         b. ∧(A, ∨BC) ⊣⊢ ∨(∧AB, ∧AC)

The following proofs establish another well-known deductive equivalence:

3.2.17   a.
1	~∧AB	supp
2	~∨(~A, ~B)	supp
3	∧(~ ~A, ~ ~B)	2, 3.2.13a
4	~ ~ A	3, ∧-expl
5	~ ~ B	3, ∧-expl
6	A	4, ~-expl
7	B	5, ~-expl
8	∧AB	6, 7, ∧-intro
9	~∧AB	1, reit
10	~ ~∨(~A, ~B)	2–9, ~-intro
11	∨(~A, ~B)	10, ~-expl

b.
1	∨(~A, ~B)	supp
2	~A	supp
3	∧AB	supp
4	A	3, ∧-expl
5	~A	2, reit
6	~∧AB	3–5, ~-intro
7	~B	supp
8	∧AB	supp
9	B	8, ∧-expl
10	~B	7, reit
11	~∧AB	8–10, ~-intro
12	~∧AB	1, 2–6, 7–11, ∨-expl

This result and the result established in 3.2.13 are known collectively as the de Morgan laws:

3.2.18   a. ~∨AB ⊣⊢ ∧(~A, ~B)
       b. ~∧AB ⊣⊢ ∨(~A, ~B)

The de Morgan laws show that ∧ and ∨ are **duals** with regard to negation, that is, that negating a conjoined proposition is equivalent to conjoining with the other conjunction the negations of the conjuncts.

    I will conclude this section with the proof of one more deductive equivalence:

3.2.19   ⊃AB ⊣⊢ ∨(~A, B)

a.
1	⊃AB	supp
2	~∨(~A, B)	supp
3	∧(~ ~A, ~B)	2, 3.2.18a
4	~ ~A	3, ∧-expl
5	A	4, ~-expl
6	B	1, 5, ⊃-expl
7	~ B	3, ∧-expl
8	~ ~∨(~A, B)	2–7, ~-intro
9	∨(~A, B)	8, ~-expl

b.
1	∨(~A, B)	supp
2	A	supp
3	~A	supp
4	B	2, 3, 3.2.8e

```
5     |  | B  _____      supp
6     |  |‾ B                  5, reit
7     | B                      1, 3–4, 5–6, ∨-expl
8   ⊃AB                        2–7, ⊃-intro
```

3.3 Axiom versus Rule of Inference versus Meaning Postulate

In addition to formation rules, rules of inference, and truth conditions, formal treatments of logic often involve what appears to be yet another type of formal apparatus, namely, **axioms.** For example, the system presented in chapter 5 of Thomason 1970 does without the rules of ⊃-introduction, ∼-introduction, and ∼-exploitation but has instead the axioms:[10]

3.3.1   a. ⊃(A, ⊃BA)
        b. ⊃(⊃(A, ⊃BC), ⊃(⊃AB, ⊃AC))
        c. ⊃(⊃(∼B, ∼A), ⊃AB)

The role of the axioms in proofs is that any **substitution instance** of an axiom (that is, any formula obtainable from an axiom by substituting some formula for all occurrences of A, some formula for all occurrences of B, and some formula for all occurrences of C) may appear at any point in a proof.

There is a large amount of trade-off between axioms and rules of inference. For example, the three formulas 3.3.1a–c are all theorems relative to the rules of inference given earlier in this chapter (we have already given proofs of two of them), which means that if those rules of inference are accepted, there is no need to assume any of the axioms 3.3.1a–c. Conversely, any theorem that can be proven by means of ⊃-exploitation, ⊃-introduction, ∼-exploitation, and ∼-introduction can also be proven by means of ⊃-exploitation and the axioms 3.3.1a–c (this is in effect proven in Thomason 1970, chapter 5), and thus one could do without three of the rules of inference if one accepts instead the axioms 3.3.1a–c.

The difference between "axiom" and "rule of inference" is one of detail rather than one of general nature: axioms are merely rules of inference that involve no premises. Note that we have seen above both rules of inference that involve one premise (∨-introduction, ∧-exploitation, ∼-exploitation) and rules of inference that involve two premises (⊃-exploitation, ∧-introduction). The difference between axioms and one-premise rules of inference is comparable to that between one-premise rules of inference and two-premise rules of inference: they differ in regard to how much of the earlier part of the proof plays a role in justifying the line of the proof that is at issue. For a system of rules of inference (including axioms, if any) to be of interest, it will have to include rules that have premises, since otherwise all that could be derived would be substitution instances of axioms, which would not be a very interesting system of inference; indeed, it will have to include at least one rule of inference that has more than one premise, since if there were only zero-premise and one-premise rules of inference, the kinds of interactions between premises that provide both the fun and the glory of logic would not be possible. However, provided that there are rules of inference with more than one premise, there is a great deal of freedom in how much of the inferential apparatus of the system one chooses to embody in the form of zero-premise rules (= axioms) and how much in the form of rules that refer to premises. For example, it will not particularly matter whether we have the rule of ~-exploitation or the axiom ⊃(~~A, A), provided that we have the rules of ⊃-introduction and ⊃-exploitation available.

Different sets of rules of inference (including axioms, if any) thus may perfectly well sanction exactly the same inferences. In that event the rules of either system will be **derived** rules of the other system; that is, the effect of any rule of the one system can be replicated by a series of applications of the rules of the other system, and any proof in the one system can be converted into a proof of the other system by replacing each step by the corresponding sequence of applications of the rules of the other system. The difference between "basic" and "derived" rules of inference is thus somewhat arbitrary. The only real advantage of the choice I have made about what rules of inference to take as basic is the relatively systematic structure of the set of rules presented here: aside from the rule of reiteration what we have is for each connective a rule saying how to use premises that contain it and a rule saying how to derive conclusions that contain it. By contrast, the three axioms 3.3.1a–c simply appear to give fairly esoteric properties of ⊃ and ~ which are not correlated with obvious functions in constructing inferences, although in reality 3.3.1 plus ⊃-exploitation justifies exactly the same inferences as do the rules for introduction and exploitation of ⊃ and ~ given in section 3.2.

The term **meaning postulate** also occasionally occurs in expositions of the details of a logical system (e.g., Carnap 1956:222–29). The term has generally been used in connection with "nonlogical elements" that might play a role in a formal analysis. For example, one might encounter the meaning postulate 3.3.2 in an analysis in which propositions of the form "x knows A" play a role:

3.3.2   ⊃(x Know A, A).

Meaning postulates are supposed to supply steps in inferences that follow from the meaning of the "nonlogical element" in question (here, the fact that you can only know a proposition which is true, as contrasted with the fact that you can believe false propositions as well as true ones). The distinction between meaning postulate and rule of inference is only as good as the difference between "nonlogical element" and "logical element," which is to say that it is far from clear that the difference has any substance. Rules of inference can be thought of as meaning postulates for the "logical elements," that is, they distinguish among the various "logical elements" on the basis of characteristics of their roles in inference that are associated with their meanings. I will avoid the term "meaning postulate" on the grounds that it is superfluous and creates pseudoproblems regarding the application of the term "meaning." Meaning postulates are not strictly speaking parts of the meanings of the elements involved. Any logical system will provide a set of "primitive" elements which figure in its logical structures, and those elements are the "elements of meaning." The meaning postulates can distinguish among those elements of meaning, much as facts about about the location and population of cities can distinguish among the meanings of the words *Vienna, Brussels,* and *Istanbul,* although the fact that Vienna is on the Danube is not part of the meaning of the word *Vienna.*

3.4 More on *If*

Elementary logic texts commonly contain statements to the effect that "If A, then B" can be paraphrased by "A only if B," as when Quine (1962:41) says, "But whereas 'if' is thus ordinarily a sign of the antecedent, the attachment of 'only' reverses it; 'only if' is a sign of the consequent." Thus the student is generally directed to assign the same logical form to pairs of sentences such as:

3.4.1   a.   If all men are mortal, then Aristotle is mortal.
         a′. All men are mortal only if Aristotle is mortal.
         b.   If a set has only finitely many subsets, it is finite.
         b′. A set has only finitely many subsets only if it is finite.

While it is reasonable to regard 3.4.1a and 3.4.1a′, or 3.4.1b and 3.4.1b′, as merely variant ways of expressing the same idea, it is in fact not at all easy to find pairs of sentences like 3.4.1a and b, where a sentence "If A, (then) B" and a sentence "A only if B" sound equally normal and appear to express the same thing. Consider the following sample pairs of sentences in which "If A, (then) B," and "A only if B" are not interchangeable:"[11]

3.4.2   a.   If you're boiled in oil, you'll die.
         a′. You'll be boiled in oil only if you die.[12]

    b. If Mike straightens his tie once more, I'll kill him.

    b'. Mike will straighten his tie once more only if I kill him.

    c. If butter is heated, it melts.

    c'. Butter is heated only if it melts.

    d. If Pittsburgh won the 1971 World Series, I've lost my bet.

    d'. ?Pittsburgh won the 1971 World Series only if I've lost my bet.

    e. If we're having fish, we should order white wine.

    e'. ?We're having fish only if we should order white wine.

    f. If you're insured, you have nothing to worry about.

    f'. You're insured only if you have nothing to worry about.

In 3.4.2, a perfectly banal sentence *If A, (then) B* is paralleled by a sentence *A only if B* that suggests something either bizarre (e.g., 3.4.2b' suggests that Mike will not straighten his tie until you have first killed him) or quite different from what the original sentence suggests (e.g., 3.4.2f suggests that insurance companies are generous in paying benefits, 3.4.2f' that insurance companies deviously exclude any clients who would receive any benefits). In many cases the sentence with *only if* reverses the temporal or causal relations expressed by the sentence with *if*, as where 3.4.2a' refers to boiling in oil following one's death, while 3.4.2a refers to death resulting from one's being boiled in oil. In 3.4.3, the same reversal takes place, but with the *only if* sentence expressing something normal and the *if* sentence something bizarre:

3.4.3   a. I'll leave only if you have somebody to take my place.

           a'. If I leave, you('ll) have somebody to take my place.

           b. My pulse goes above 100 only if I do heavy exercise.

           b'. If my pulse goes above 100, I do heavy exercise.

           c. You're in danger only if the police start tapping your phone.

           c'. If you're in danger, the police start tapping your phone.

While *If A, then B* is thus often a poor paraphrase of *A only if B*, often *If not B, then not A* is a rather good paraphrase of it; compare 3.4.3a, b, and c with:

3.4.4   a. If you don't have somebody to take my place, I won't leave.

           b. If I don't do heavy exercise, my pulse doesn't go above 100.

           c. If the police don't start tapping your phone, you're not in danger.

The fact that *If not B, then not A* is so much better a paraphrase than is *If A, then B* is a bit surprising since the logical formulas that those two sentence forms correspond most directly to are deductively equivalent according to the rules of inference of this chapter:

3.4.5 $\supset AB \dashv\vdash \supset(\sim B, \sim A)$

However, in the cases given in 3.4.3, the law of "contraposition" 3.4.5 appears to fail (e.g., 3.4.4a $\neq$ 3.4.3a′), and this fact suggests that either the logical system should be revised so that 3.4.5 does not hold (or holds only in a restricted class of cases) or ordinary *if* should not be identified with $\supset$.

Only behaves syntactically like a negative (3.4.6a, b) in virtue of supporting **negative polarity items** such as *any* and *give a hoot,* and it allows a paraphrase with a negative, such as *No X other than Y* or *No X except Y:*

3.4.6   a.   Only John said anything.
         a′. *John said anything.
         a″. No one said anything.
         b.   Only your wife gives a hoot about what happens to you.
         b′. *Your wife gives a hoot about what happens to you.
         b″. No one gives a hoot about what happens to you.

3.4.7   a.   John read only the first chapter.
         a′. John read nothing other than the first chapter.
         b.   Only Susan has a key to this room.
         b′. No one except Susan has a key to this room.

In combination with these observations, the fact that *Not A if not B* is so much better a paraphrase of *A only if B* than is *If A, then B* (or *B if A*) suggests that one should search for an analysis of *A only if B* in which the *only* is identified with the ordinary *only* of sentences such as 3.4.7a–b, with the *only* in turn being analyzed in terms of negation (e.g., *only John* = "no one except for John") in a way that allows it to be combined with *if B* as well as with NPs. Such an analysis (due to Geis 1973) will be sketched in section 15.2: *if B* will be analyzed as "in cases in which B," and *A only if B* will then be "Not A, except in cases in which B." Under this approach, *A only if B* implies *Not A if not B,* though the latter implies the former only under certain conditions.

Braine (1978) has presented experimental data that argue that *A only if B* is closer to *Not A if not B* than to *If A, then B.* Specifically, Braine replicated experiments in which Wason and Johnson-Laird (1972) had demonstrated sharp differences between subjects' abilities to evaluate "modus ponens" arguments (3.4.8a) and "modus tollens" arguments (3.4.8b):

3.4.8   a. If A, (then) B   b. If A, (then) B
         A   Not B
         Therefore, B.   Therefore, not A

When asked to judge arguments of these forms for validity, subjects usually make few errors and give rapid responses for modus ponens arguments but make many errors and give slower responses for modus tollens arguments. In his replication of Wason and Johnson-Laird's experiments, Braine included additional stimuli in which the first premise had the form *A only if B* and found that with such stimuli the difference between modus ponens and modus tollens disappeared or even was reversed. But note that what Braine here calls modus ponens (3.4.9a) is an instance of modus tollens and what he calls modus tollens is an instance of modus ponens (3.4.9b) if one relates *A only if B* not to *If A, then B* but to *Not A except if B* and thus indirectly to *Not A if not B:*

3.4.9   a. A only if B   b. A only if B
            (Not A if not B.)   (Not A if not B.)
            A   Not B
            B   Not A

Thus, if one of the two should yield faster and more accurate responses, it should be 3.4.9b, whose conclusion is inferred from the preceding two lines by modus ponens, though the difference should be less sharp because of the less transparent relationship between the sentences and their logical forms.

Since expressions such as *only if, even if, except if,* and *especially if* appear to be immediately intelligible to anyone who knows the words of which they are composed (i.e., they are in no sense idioms), an analysis in which *only if* is treated as ordinary *only* plus ordinary *if* seems to be inescapable. Note that the logicians' standard analysis, in which *only if* is regarded as simply the converse of *if,* treat *only if* as an idiom, since *only* does not otherwise mean "converse"; for example 3.4.10a cannot be paraphrased as 3.4.10b:

3.4.10   a. Bill only kissed Betty.
         b. Betty kissed Bill.

Suppose that we grant that the *only* of *only if* is the same *only* that appears in 3.4.10a. Before we can combine an analysis of *if* with an analysis of *only,* we have to decide what the **focus** of *only* is in sentences containing *only if,* that is, the expression that is implicitly contrasted with alternatives, as in 3.4.11a (pronounced with stress as indicated), which conveys 3.4.11a′, and 3.4.11b, which conveys 3.4.11b′:

3.4.11   a.   Bill only kíssed Betty. (focus = *kiss*)
         a'. Bill didn't hug Betty, he didn't caress her, . . .
         b.   Bill only kissed Bétty. (focus = *Betty*)
         b'. Bill didn't kiss Ann, he didn't kiss Clara, he didn't kiss Dora,

         . . .

The focus of *only* in 3.4.12a can't be *if,* since it doesn't convey propositions such as 3.4.12b–b', in which *if* is contrasted with the "propositional connectives" that it is usually classed with in propositional logic, nor propositions such as 3.4.12c–c', in which it is contrasted with other "subordinating conjunctions":

3.4.12   a.   I'll leave only if you ask me to.
         b.   It's not the case that I'll leave and you'll ask me to.
         b'. It's not the case that I'll leave or you'll ask me to.
         c.   It's not the case that I'll leave after you ask me to.
         c'. It's not the case that I'll leave although you'll ask me to.

For example, 3.4.12a does not convey 3.4.12b–b', since it clearly allows for the possibility that you will ask me to leave and I will leave, whereas 3.4.12b–b' do not. The only expressions that could conceivably be the focus of *only* in 3.4.12a are *if you ask me to* and *you ask me to,* e.g., 3.4.12a does convey 3.4.13.

3.4.13   I won't leave if you say you want me to stay; I won't leave if
              you express no opinion about whether I leave or stay; . . .

To treat either of those expressions as the focus of *only,* though, it will be necessary to replace the constituent structure 3.4.14a, in which, as logicians have virtually always assumed, the counterpart to *if* is combined simultaneously with the two Ss that it appears in combination with, by a structure 3.4.14b, in which, as linguists have generally assumed, *if* combines with the **antecedent** (or **protasis**) of the conditional construction, yielding an expression that combines with **consequent** (or **apodosis**) of the construction:

3.4.14   a.   b.

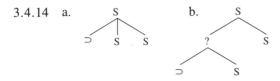

The reason for this is that *only* must immediately precede a syntactic unit that contains the focus, and unless *if you ask me to* is a syntactic unit, that condition would not be met. In Geis's treatment of *if* as "in cases in which", which will be taken up in section 15.2, *if* fits into a structure like 3.4.14b that provides an appropriate focus for *only*. Under Geis's analysis, *If Bill comes tomorrow, I'll give him the books* is analyzed as "In (all) cases in which Bill comes tomorrow, I'll give him the books", which allows *I'll give Bill the books only if he comes tomorrow* to be analyzed as "I'll give Bill the books only in cases in which he comes tomorrow", which amounts to "I won't give Bill the books, except in cases in which he comes tomorrow". The notion of "case" that figures in these paraphrases is heavily context-dependent: the "cases" over which the implicit bound variable ranges are those states of affairs that are relevant in appropriate respects to the given utterance. The logician's ⊃ can be interpreted as corresponding to the degenerate notion of "case" in which only the actual state of affairs counts as a "case". For the purposes of the earlier chapters of this book, however, I will operate in terms of the ⊃ of standard logic, with the constituent structure 3.4.14a that is usually assumed.

The differences noted above between *If A, then B* and *If not B, then not A* also manifest themselves when one considers sentences involving the expression *if and only if*. I maintain that *A if and only if B* is exactly what the words suggest it is: the conjunction of *A if B* and *A only if B*. In view of what I argued above, 3.4.15a ought to be better paraphrased by 3.4.15c–c' than by 3.4.15b:

3.4.15   a.   A if and only if B.
            b.   If A, then B, and if B, then A.
            c.   If not B, then not A, and if B, then A.
            c'. If B, then A, and if not B, then not A.

This prediction is borne out by examples formed on the analogy of 3.4.2 and 3.4.13:

3.4.16   a.   I'll leave if and only if you have someone to take my place.
            a'. If I leave, you'll have someone to take my place, and if you have someone to take my place, I'll leave.
            a''. If you have someone to take my place, I'll leave, and if you don't have anyone to take my place, I won't leave.
            b.   My pulse goes above 100 if and only if I do heavy exercise.
            b'. If my pulse goes above 100, I do heavy exercise, and if I do heavy exercise, my pulse goes above 100.
            b''. If I do heavy exercise, my pulse goes above 100, and if I don't do heavy exercise, my pulse doesn't go above 100.

    c. Butter melts if and only if it is heated.
    c'. If butter melts, it is heated, and if butter is heated, it melts.
    c". If butter is heated, it melts, and if butter is not heated, it
          doesn't melt.

The third sentence of each group is in each instance an excellent paraphrase of the first sentence. The second sentence of each group is at best a paraphrase of an extra interpretation that the first sentence allows, over and above its most obvious interpretation.

It follows from these observations that the expression *if and only if* is **asymmetric,** that is, that *A if and only if B* is not interchangeable with *B if and only if A:* while 3.4.15b is symmetric with respect to A and B (i.e., if you interchange A and B, the result is essentially the same as what you started with), 3.4.15c is not. This conclusion is likewise borne out by the facts. Note the result of interchanging A and B in 3.4.16a, b, and c:

3.4.17   a. You'll have someone to take my place if and only if I leave.
          b. I do heavy exercise if and only if my pulse goes above 100.
          c. Butter is heated if and only if it melts.

In each case the temporal and/or causal relations between the two clauses are the reverse of what they were in 3.4.16a, b, and c. For example 3.4.16b treats the exercise as the cause of the rise in your pulse, whereas 3.4.17b makes it sound as if a prior change in your pulse is the reason for which you do heavy exercise (perhaps because of the mistaken belief that doing heavy exercise will lower your pulse).

I thus take it as unfortunate that logicians have generally identified the expression *if and only if* with a putative logical connective (most frequently written with the symbol $\equiv$) which is symmetric both syntactically (i.e., $\equiv AB \dashv\vdash \equiv BA$) and semantically (i.e., the truth conditions are symmetric: $\equiv AB$ is true if A and B have the same truth value and is false if they have different truth values). While these properties are in fact possessed by the formula that is most often offered as a "definition" of $\equiv AB$, namely, $\wedge(\supset AB, \supset BA)$, those properties do not carry over to the English expression *if and only if* (or its counterparts in other languages, e.g., German *wenn und nur wenn*), with which it is generally equated.

3.5. More on Conjunction

I now turn to justification for my repeated statement that *and* and *or* (and their counterparts in logical structure) are not restricted to conjoining things two at a time but can conjoin arbitrarily many things at a time. The clearest syntactic arguments for this conclusion come from the various syntactic phenomena that affect all conjuncts (or all but the first of them) of a coordinate structure, which become barely tractable problems if conjoining is restricted to two conjuncts at a time but whose description is almost trivial if coordination of arbitrarily many conjuncts is admitted.

Under the popular (but, I maintain, incorrect) assumption that a sentence like 3.5.1 involves iterated two-term conjoining, one must allow optional deletion of a repeated conjunction in structures such as *A and (B and C)*.

3.5.1   Alice ordered pork chops, Ben ordered liver, and Sylvia ordered lasagna.

Let us see how that supposedly optional deletion interacts with such phenomena as **Gapping,** in which repeated material is deleted from all conjuncts after the first if the conjuncts are identical except for one item outside the V' and one item inside the V' in each conjunct:

3.5.2   a.   Alice ordered pork chops, Ben liver, and Sylvia lasagna.
        b.   ?Alice ordered pork chops, Ben liver, and Sylvia ordered lasagna.
        b'.   ??Alice ordered pork chops, Ben ordered liver, and Sylvia lasagna.

There is no viable alternative to describing this 'across-the-boards' deletion in terms of a single coordinate structure with multiple conjuncts of the same shape. If Gapping had to apply to nested two-term conjoined structures, it would have to be divided into two separate transformations, one applying to structures of the form [S Conj S] in which the two Ss had the requisite parallelism for Gapping, and one applying to structures of the form [S_1 Conj [S_2 Conj S_3]] (or its mirror image) in which Gapping had already applied to the inner conjoined structure and S_1 had the requisite parallelism to either S_2 or S_3, and the latter transformation would have to apply not only to structures in which, as here, there are only three ultimate conjuncts, but to iterated coordinate structures of arbitrary complexity, in which the material to be deleted is arbitrarily far from the "full" conjunct to which it must be matched. Moreover, the normally optional deletion of the repeated conjunction that the proponent of the "two conjuncts at a time" approach is committed to must be prevented from applying in cases like 3.5.2b–b' in which only the "inner" Gapping is carried out; cf. the normal-sounding 3.5.3b–b':

3.5.3   b.   Alice ordered pork chops and Ben liver, and Sylvia ordered lasagna.

   b′. Alice ordered porkchops, and Ben ordered liver and Sylvia
        lasagna.

A second serious difficulty that Gapping poses for a conception of conjoining as always two conjuncts at a time is that it should then be possible to apply
Gapping when two consecutive conjuncts in *A, B, and C* have the requisite
parallelism but that parallelism does not extend to the remaining conjunct;
however, Gapping is in fact not possible in such cases:

3.5.4   a. *Alice ate a hamburger, Ben drank some beer, and Sylvia a
             Coke.
         b. ??Alice ate a hamburger, Ben a hot dog, and Sylvia drank a
             Coke.

A third is that conjuncts can sometimes be factored into shared and contrasting parts in more than one way. For example, 3.5.5a can be taken either as
involving three instances of the frame "＿＿＿＿ *wrote* ＿＿＿＿," with *about
quasars* contrasting with *about black holes* and *about supernovas,* or three
instances of the frame "＿＿＿＿ *wrote about* ＿＿＿＿," with *quasars* contrasting with *black holes* and *supernovas.* Gapping requires that a uniform factoring of all the conjuncts be used:

3.5.5   a. Alice wrote about quasars, Ted wrote about black holes, and
             Oscar wrote about supernovas.
         b. Alice wrote about quasars, Tom black holes, and Oscar
             supernovas.
         b′. Alice wrote about quasars, Tom about black holes, and Oscar
             about supernovas.
         c. *Alice wrote about quasars, Tom black holes, and Oscar about
             supernovas.
         c′. *Alice wrote about quasars, Tom about black holes, and Oscar
             supernovas.

If Gapping applied separately to the third conjunct and to the second conjunct,
there would be nothing to prevent the first and second conjunct from being
factored differently than the second and third were, and thus nothing to exclude a derivation of 3.5.5c–c′.
    Conjoining is normal only when the conjuncts are related in one of the
ways that motivate the use of a conjoined structure. Coordinate structures are
commonly used, for example, to describe complex events, with each conjunct
describing one of the simpler events that the larger event is composed of, as
in 3.5.6a:

3.5.6   a.   The sheriff drew his gun, aimed at the fleeing bandits, and
              fired.
         b.   *The sheriff had a disgusted expression on his face, drew his
              gun, and fired.
         b′. With a disgusted expression on his face, the sheriff drew his
              gun and fired.
         b″. The sheriff grimaced in disgust, drew his gun, and fired.

While the three conjuncts in 3.5.6a describe salient subevents in the structure
of a complex event, two of the three conjuncts in the bizarre 3.5.6b describe
parts of a complex event and the other conjunct describes a condition that
accompanies that event; the unacceptability of 3.5.6b should be contrasted
with the acceptability of 3.5.6b′, in which the material that figures in 3.5.6b
is recast in the form of a conjoined structure that describes a complex event in
terms of its parts, combined with a modifier that describes the accompanying
condition, or 3.5.6b″, in which the event that brings about that condition is
conceived of as part of a more complex event.

A second case in which conjoining is normal is that in which the conjuncts
instantiate some more general proposition. In that case, the applicability of
Conjunction Reduction (including the generalized version of it that applies in
the derivation of such sentences as *John and Mary ordered pizza and lasagna,
respectively*) is contingent on the contrasting parts of the conjuncts corresponding to the same part of that general proposition (here, "they each ordered some food," with *John* and *Mary* both instantiating "they," and *pizza*
and *lasagna* both instantiating "some food"). Thus, 3.5.7a′ is quite odd in
comparison with 3.5.7a, since *is in Seattle* and *is in jail* can be thought of as
two current bits of news about John, but *Seattle* and *jail* do not count as, e.g.,
two things that John is in, and while 3.5.7b is odd to the extent that it is
difficult to find a general proposition that the two conjuncts instantiate (perhaps "Two conditions characterized Western European intellectual life in the
early 1600s" would fill that bill),[13] Conjunction Reduction renders it thoroughly bizarre (3.5.7b′), since *Galileo* and *adolescents* (likewise, *scanned
the skies* and *scorned the schools*) are very difficult to match to any part of
such a general proposition:

3.5.7   a.   John is in Seattle and is in jail.
         a′. ??John is in Seattle and jail.
         b.   ?Galileo scanned the skies and adolescents scorned the
              schools.
         b′. *Galileo and adolescents scanned the skies and scorned the
              schools, respectively.

The oddity of examples in which Conjunction Reduction is not normal cannot in general be attributed to any inherent inability of the conjuncts to conjoin with each other, since the conjuncts that figure in an example of unacceptable Conjunction Reduction (e.g., 3.5.8a′) may recur in a perfectly acceptable instance of Conjunction Reduction (e.g., 3.5.8b) as long as they can be conceived of as filling the same role in an appropriate general proposition:

3.5.8   a.   The score was tied and Yastrzemski was at bat.
         a′.   *The score and Yastrzemski were tied and at bat, respectively.
         b.   The score and Yastrzemski worried the manager and the
               pitcher, respectively.

Different ways of conjoining the same ultimate conjuncts often correspond to different ways of conceiving of a general proposition that the conjuncts instantiate, as in the contrast among 3.5.9a–c:

3.5.9   a.   John is overweight, and Myra is overweight and nearsighted.
         b.   John and Myra are overweight, and Myra is nearsighted.
         c.   John is overweight, Myra is overweight, and Myra is
               nearsighted.

The first sentence would be appropriate in situations where Myra's being overweight and her being nearsighted are conceived of as instances of the same thing, as when one uses it to convey that each of his friends suffers from minor physical problems (the first part specifies John's problems, the second part Myra's problems), while the second would be appropriate in situations in which Myra's being overweight and John's being overweight are conceived of as instances of the same thing, as when, say, one is helping an experimenter who seeks experimental subjects who suffer from various conditions that he is investigating. The third sentence is appropriate in situations in which each of the ultimate conjuncts is conceived of as conveying the same sort of information as the others, as when one uses it to list independent reasons why John and Myra should not be named "Mr. and Mrs. Physical Fitness." Distinguishing among the three sentences requires that one distinguish different underlying constituent structures (3.5.10a–c, respectively), with the applicability of Conjunction Reduction contingent on the underlying structure containing a constituent to which it is applicable, and the three groupings of the conjuncts correspond to different possibilities for one's understanding of the three sentences:

3.5.10 a.

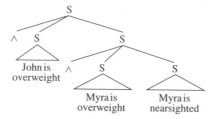

b.

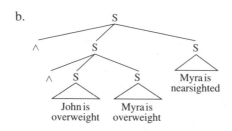

c.

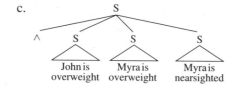

The standard policy in logic of "defining away" many-termed conjunction obliterates this distinction, since it forces 3.5.9c to be identified with 3.5.9a or 3.5.9b. Wundt (1900:310) made the same point with regard to the German equivalents of 3.5.11a–b:

3.5.11 a. Caesar and Alexander were both great generals and excellent statesmen.
        b. Caesar was a great general, Caesar was an excellent statesman, Alexander was a great general, and Alexander was an excellent statesman.

Example 3.5.11a conveys something that is not conveyed by 3.5.11b, namely, that Caesar and Alexander had something in common: the property of being both a great general and an excellent statesman. By contrast, 3.5.11b would be a more appropriate answer than 3.5.11a to a request "Tell me something about some famous figures of antiquity."

3.6. On the Structure of Proofs

Consider the following illegitimate variant of the proof given in 3.2.11:

3.6.1

1	$\wedge(\vee pq, r)$	supp
2	$\vee pq$	1, $\wedge$-expl
3	p	supp
4	r	1, $\wedge$-expl
5	$\wedge pr$	3, 4, $\wedge$-intro
6	$\vee(\wedge pr, \wedge qr)$	5, $\vee$-intro
7	q	supp
8	p	5, $\wedge$-expl
9	...	

Where the proof goes from that point on doesn't particularly matter. What I wish to call attention to is the illegitimacy of step 8: it makes reference to a part of the proof that has nothing to do with the subproof to which step 8 belongs. Line 8 belongs to a subproof with the supposition q; line 5 belongs to a subproof with the supposition p and that subproof does not contain the one in which line 8 occurs. The same illegitimacy is found in the following argument:

3.6.2   Creepy Calabresi got off the plane either in Las Vegas or in LA.
             Suppose he got off in Las Vegas; then he called the Fettucini Kid
                and the Fettucini Kid tipped off the feds.
             Suppose he got off in LA; since the Fettucini Kid tipped off the
                Feds, they must have been waiting for him at the airport.

In a legitimate proof based on $\vee$-exploitation, you are considering two or more alternatives separately, and what happens in one of those alternative states of affairs need not be the case in other alternatives; for example, what happens if Creepy Calabresi gets off the plane in Las Vegas need not be the same as what happens if he gets off in LA.

To see more clearly the source of the illegitimacy of 3.6.1–2, it may help to display the structure of a proof as a tree diagram, with the various subordinate proofs that are marked off by vertical lines corresponding to nodes that are labeled "Proof." For example, 3.6.3 has the structure that is represented in 3.6.4, in which a superscript $^+$ is used to mark the suppositions of each proof:

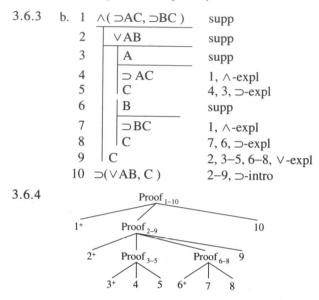

3.6.3   b.   1   ∧(⊃AC, ⊃BC)   supp
              2   │ ∨AB   supp
              3   │ │ A   supp
              4   │ │ ⊃ AC   1, ∧-expl
              5   │ │ C   4, 3, ⊃-expl
              6   │ │ B   supp
              7   │ │ ⊃BC   1, ∧-expl
              8   │ │ C   7, 6, ⊃-expl
              9   │ C   2, 3–5, 6–8, ∨-expl
             10   ⊃(∨AB, C)   2–9, ⊃-intro

3.6.4

The supposition 1 is "operative" in the whole proof, in the sense that a line anywhere in the proof could in principle include 1 in its justifications, whereas the supposition 3 is operative only in the subproof 3–5 and the supposition 6 is operative only in the subproof 6–8. More generally, it is legitimate to justify a line in terms of a line that is either in the same (sub-) proof or a superordinate proof (e.g., 1, 2, 6, or 7 could in principle figure in the justification of 8), but it is not legitimate to justify it in terms of a line that is in a separate proof or in a lower proof (3 could not figure in the justification of 8 or of 9; the whole subproof 3–5 can and does figure in the justification of 9, but individual lines of that subproof, such as 3, cannot).

   In the last paragraph, I have been hinting at a generalization about what parts of a proof can "influence" any given line of a proof. It will be convenient to give that generalization in terms of a notion that has figured prominently in linguistic studies of restrictions on what parts of a syntactic structure can influence other parts. Langacker (1969) described situations in which an element can influence elements contained in some unit that it is a part of but not elements that are outside of that unit in terms of a relationship that he called **command.** For example, "negative polarity items" such as *a red cent*, which normally can be used only in combination with a negation, are acceptable when the negation is in the same clause[14] or when it is in a clause superordinate to the item, but not when the negation is in a clause that is subordinate to or simply separate from the item:

3.6.5   a. No one gave him a red cent.
         b. I didn't expect that they would give him a red cent.
         c. *Someone who doesn't know John gave him a red cent.
         d. *That you don't have high standards suggests that you would
             give John a red cent.

In Langacker's terminology, the negative word commands *a red cent* in the
two acceptable examples but does not command it in the two unacceptable
examples.

   A simple procedure can be given for determining whether one node *a* commands another node *b:* trace up the branches of the tree from *a* until one hits a
node that is labeled S; if one can reach *b* by tracing down the branches of the
tree from that node, then *a* commands *b*, and otherwise it does not command
b. For example, in 3.6.6, the V/*didn't* node commands all the nodes in the
tree (because the lowest S node that dominates it is the "root" of the tree,
which dominates all of the other nodes), whereas the V/*give* and NP/*they*
nodes command only those nodes that are dominated by the bottom S node:

3.6.6

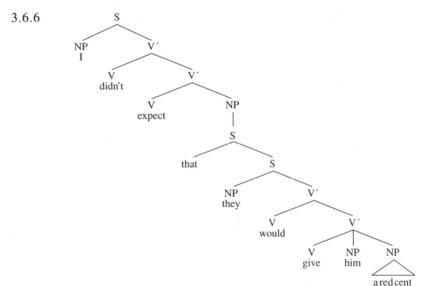

   In discussing various kinds of "influence" that one syntactic unit can have
on others, various linguists have proposed several different "command relations" that differ from one another with regard to the condition that defines the
"bounding node" from which one traces down to the commanded nodes: for
Langacker's notion of command, the condition is that the node be labeled S;

for a notion introduced in Lasnik (1976), the condition is that it be labeled S or NP; for a notion introduced in Reinhart (1976) it is that the node "branch" (i.e., that it have at least two daughters); and for a notion introduced in Mc-Cawley (1984) it is that the node be labeled with a "major category." More generally, Barker and Pullum (1990) have defined a family of notions of command that includes all these notions as special cases:

3.6.7   For any condition X on nodes of a tree, a node *a* X-commands a node *b* if the lowest node that dominates *a* and meets the condition X also dominates *b*.

Suppose we introduce the term "Proof-command" for the relation that is defined by the condition "belongs to the category Proof." Then the restrictions that we discussed above amount to the condition that:

3.6.8   The justification of any line in a proof can make reference only to lines and subproofs that both precede and Proof-command that line.

3.7. Predicate Logic Supplemented by Propositional Logic

The logical machinery developed in this chapter and the last can of course be combined into a single system of logic whose rules of inference are those of 2.5 and 3.2 and whose formation rules are those of 2.2. and 3.1, with the omission of the rules that allow for atomic propositions: in that system, which is the subject of this section, all propositions have some internal structure, the simplest being those that consist of a predicate and an appropriate number of arguments.

We will devote this short section to giving a number of proofs in which the rules of both predicate logic and propositional logic play a role. The first pair of results are the quantificational analog to the de Morgan laws (3.2.18):

3.7.1   a. $\sim(\forall: Fx)\,Gx \dashv\vdash (\exists: Fx)\,\sim Gx$
             Proof that $\sim(\forall: Fx)Gx \vdash (\exists: Fx)\,\sim Gx$:

1	$\sim(\forall: Fx)Gx$			supp
2		$\sim(\exists: Fx)\sim Gx$		supp
3			Fu	supp
4				$\sim Gu$	supp
5				$(\exists: Fx)\sim Gx$	3, 4, $\exists$-intro
6				$\sim(\exists: Fx)\sim Gx$	2, reit

7	$\sim\sim Gu$	4–6, $\sim$-intro
8	Gu	7, $\sim$-expl
9	$(\forall : Fx)Gx$	3–8, $\forall$-intro
10	$\sim(\forall : Fx)Gx$	1, reit
11	$\sim\sim(\exists : Fx)\sim Gx$	2–10, $\sim$-intro
12	$(\exists : Fx)\sim Gx$	11, $\sim$-expl

Proof that $(\exists : Fx)\sim Gx \vdash \sim(\forall : Fx)Gx$:

1	$(\exists : Fx)\sim Gx$	supp
2	Fu	supp
3	$\sim Gu$	supp
4	$(\forall : Fx)Gx$	supp
5	Gu	4, 2, $\forall$-expl
6	$\sim Gu$	3, reit
7	$\sim(\forall : Fx)Gx$	4–6, $\sim$-intro
8	$\sim(\forall : Fx)Gx$	1, 2–7, $\exists$-expl

b. $\sim(\exists : Fx)Gx \dashv\vdash (\forall : Fx)\sim Gx$

Proof that $\sim(\exists : Fx)Gx \vdash (\forall : Fx)\sim Gx$:

1	$\sim(\exists : Fx)Gx$	supp
2	Fu	supp
3	Gu	supp
4	$(\exists : Fx)Gx$	2, 3, $\exists$-intro
5	$\sim(\exists : Fx)Gx$	1, reit
6	$\sim Gu$	3–5, $\sim$-intro
7	$(\forall : Fx)\sim Gx$	2–6, $\forall$-intro

Proof that $(\forall : Fx)\sim Gx \vdash \sim(\exists : Fx)Gx$:

1	$(\forall : Fx)\sim Gx$	supp
2	$(\exists : Fx)Gx$	supp
3	Fu	supp
4	Gu	supp
5	$\sim Gu$	1, 3, $\forall$-expl
6	$\wedge(A,\sim A)$	4, 5, 3.2.8e [A can be any sentence not involving u]
7	$\wedge(A,\sim A)$	2, 3–6, $\exists$-expl
8	A	7, $\wedge$-expl
9	$\sim A$	7, $\wedge$-expl
10	$\sim(\exists : Fx)Gx$	2–9, $\sim$-intro

3.7.2 $(\forall: Fx) \supset (Gx, A) \dashv\vdash \supset((\exists: Fx)Gx, A)$,
               where A is any sentence not involving x
               Proof that $(\forall: Fx) \supset (Gx, A) \vdash \supset((\exists: Fx)Gx, A)$:

1	$(\forall: Fx) \supset (Gx, A)$	supp
2	$(\exists: Fx) Gx$	supp
3	Fu	supp
4	Gu	supp
5	$\supset(Gu, A)$	1, 3, $\forall$-expl
6	A	5, 4, $\supset$-expl
7	A	2, 3–6, $\exists$-expl
8	$\supset((\exists: Fx) Gx, A)$	2–7, $\supset$-intro

               Proof of the converse left to the reader as an exercise.

3.7.3 $\vee((\forall: Fx) Gx, (\forall: Fx) Hx) \vdash (\forall: Fx) \vee(Gx, Hx)$
               Proof:

1	$\vee((\forall: Fx) Gx, (\forall: Fx) Hx)$	supp
2	$(\forall: Fx) Gx$	supp
3	Fu	supp
4	Gu	2, 3, $\forall$-expl
5	$\vee(Gu, Hu)$	4, $\vee$-intro
6	$(\forall: Fx) \vee(Gx, Hx)$	3–5, $\forall$-intro
7	$(\forall: Fx) Hx$	supp
8	Fu	supp
9	Hu	7, 8, $\forall$-expl
10	$\vee(Gu, Hu)$	9, $\vee$-intro
11	$(\forall: Fx) \vee(Gx, Hx)$	8–10, $\forall$-intro
12	$(\forall: Fx) \vee(Gx, Hx)$	1, 2–6, 7–11, $\vee$-expl

You should be able to identify why the converse of 3.7.3 ought not to be provable.

I will conclude this section by commenting on some steps in the above proofs that some readers will undoubtedly find suspicious. (i) Line 6 of the second half of 3.7.1b is clearly a trick: the already suspicious theorem that "anything whatever follows from a contradiction" is used to create a line that can be exported from the innermost subproof in such a way as to allow the contradiction that arose in that subproof to make itself felt in a superordinate proof. What this trickery establishes is something eminently reasonable: that an existential proposition should be treated as "leading to a contradiction" if a contradiction arises no matter what instantiates the existential proposition; it would just be nice if that could be established without resorting to such sneaky dodges. (ii) In line 5 of the first half of 3.7.1a and line 4 of the first half of 3.7.1b, ∃-intro is invoked even though the lines from which the existential proposition is inferred involve not a constant but rather an "indeterminate." Given the way that ∀ is interpreted, the use of ∃-intro to establish the universal proposition that is the conclusion of the latter proof is innocuous: the conclusion is not supposed to imply that there are any Fs, only that whatever Fs there are, if any, are not Gs, and the proof establishes that by supposing that there is an F and showing that a contradiction arises unless it is not a G. If the result to be proved involved not ∀ but a universal quantifier such as *every* that implies that the domain of its variable is nonempty, ∀-intro would not suffice to draw the conclusion: to draw a conclusion with *every,* it would be necessary to have established that there were Fs; note, though, that it is then not the step where ∃-intro is invoked but the step where the universal quantifier is introduced whose legitimacy would depend on establishing that there are Fs.

The other proof in which ∃-intro is invoked to replace an indeterminate by an existentially quantified variable is not so innocuous, however, and indeed there is a major school of logic and of the philosophy of mathematics, namely **intuitionism** (covered insightfully in Dummett 1977), that rejects proofs in which, as in the first half of 3.7.1a, an existential proposition is established by showing that its negation leads to a contradiction rather than by exhibiting an object such as it says exists. Intuitionists in fact reject that particular part of the quantificational de Morgan laws (they accept the other half of 3.7.1a and both parts of 3.7.1b), as well as the corresponding part of the propositional de Morgan laws (for intuitionists, ∼∧AB does not imply ∨(∼A, ∼B)). Here, though, what intuitionists reject is not the step in which ∃-intro was invoked but rather the use that was made of ∼-intro in the first half of 3.7.1a.

In the remainder of this book, I will treat the uses of ∃-intro that are made in 3.7.1–2 as legitimate.

Exercises

1. Represent the meanings of the following sentences in the notational scheme used in this chapter, indicating what you take $p,q,$ ... to stand for in each case.

   a. They won't catch me if I keep quiet.
   b. If you quit, then I'll quit if they don't hire someone else.
   c. Tom will quit if they don't promote him, and if Tom doesn't quit, Bert will ask for a transfer.

2. For each of the following arguments, (i) translate the premises and conclusion into the notational system used in this chapter, to the extent that that is possible, (ii) state whether the conclusion follows from the premises or not, according to the rules of inference given here, and (iii) if the conclusion does in fact follow from the premises, spell out in detail how it can be derived from the premises by means of the rules of inference of this chapter.

   a. If Sam lives in Manhattan, he doesn't have a car. Sam has a car. Therefore, Sam doesn't live in Manhattan.
   b. Today is either Saturday or Sunday. If today is Sunday, there isn't any mail delivery today. So if there's a mail delivery today, it's Saturday.
   c. If the attorney general is a burglar, then if the postmaster general is an embezzler, the president is a dolt. Therefore, if the postmaster general is an embezzler and the president isn't a dolt, the attorney general isn't a burglar.
   d. All men are mortal. Socrates is a man. Therefore, Socrates is mortal.
   e. If federal spending increases and taxes don't go up, there will be inflation. If there is inflation, a lot of congressmen will be defeated in the next election. Therefore, if taxes go up, not many congressmen will be defeated in the next election.

3. In the notational schemes used in most publications on logic, ∨, ∧, and ⊃ are written between rather than before the items that they combine with. Convert the following formulas in the most direct way possible from that notational scheme into the one used in this book.

   a. A⊃~(B∧C)
   b. (A∧B)⊃(~C ∨~D)

   c. ~(A⊃B) ∨ ~(C⊃D)
   d. A ∨ (B ∨ (C∨D))
   e. (A ∧ (C⊃~B)) ⊃ (~B⊃(~A∨C))

4. Supply details of proofs showing that:

   a. ∨AA ⊢ A
   b. ⊃(~B, ~A) ⊢ ⊃ AB
   c. ∨(A, ∧(~A, B))⊢ ∨AB
   d. ~A ⊢ ⊃AB
   e. ⊃(A, ⊃BC) ⊢ ⊃(⊃AB, ⊃AC)
   f. ∨AB ⊢ ∨BA
   g. ⊃AB ⊢⊃(∧ AC, ∧ BC)
   h. A ⊣⊢~~A
   i. ⊃(∨AB, C) ⊣⊢ ∨(⊃ AC, ⊃BC)
   j. ∨(∧AB, ∧AC) ⊣⊢ ∧(A, ∨BC)

5. For each of the following sentences, either sketch how the conjoined constituents might plausibly be derived from conjoined clauses by conjunction reduction, or provide reasons for maintaining that they cannot plausibly be derived from conjoined clauses.

   a. He wept and wept.
   b. John invited Bill and either Maureen or Sheila.
   c. All work and no play makes Jack a dull boy.
   d. Tom promised Cheryl a fur coat and a diamond ring.
   e. How much is five and three?

6. Suppose that the rule of ~-introduction given in this chapter were replaced by the following rule of inference:

$$~\text{-intro}' \quad B$$

$$\begin{array}{|l} A \\ \hline \cdots \\ ~B \end{array}$$

$$~A$$

(i.e., you may infer ~A if the supposition A leads to a conclusion that contradicts something you have already established).

   a. Find a proof in chapter 3 that involves ~-intro that, with minor revisions, would remain valid under this alternative version of ~-intro.

   b. Find one which no minor alteration could make conform to this alternative version of ~-intro.

7. For each part of exercise 4, construct English sentences that have the logical forms corresponding to the premise and conclusion, and comment on whether the inference from the premise to the conclusion sounds plausible.

8. a. Identify where the assumption "A does not involve x" is used in the proof 3.7.2.

    b. Prove the other half of 3.7.2

    c. Prove: $(\forall{:}Fx)Hx \vdash (\forall{:}\wedge(Fx, Gx))Hx$

4   Propositional Logic II: Semantics

4.1. Truth Tables

Logicians have generally taken ∧, ∨, ~, and ⊃ to be **truth-functional;** that is, they have held that to tell whether ∧AB (likewise, ∨AB, ~A, ⊃AB) is true, all one needs to know is whether A is true and whether B is true. Specifically, they have held that the relationship between the truth-value of a complex proposition and the truth-values of its constituents is given by the following **truth tables:**

4.1.1

A	~A
T	F
F	T

A	B	∧ AB	∨ AB	⊃ AB
T	T	T	T	T
T	F	F	T	F
F	T	F	T	T
F	F	F	F	T

We assume here that every proposition is either true or false (in chapter 10 we will consider a way in which this assumption might be relaxed and propositions allowed to sometimes be neither true nor false). Each line of the truth table corresponds to a possible combination of truth values for the constituent propositions. Except for the column corresponding to ⊃, these truth tables are not particularly controversial. They say that (i) a proposition and its negation have opposite truth-values, (ii) an *and*-conjunction is true when both (more generally, all) of its conjuncts are true, and false when at least one of its conjuncts is false, (iii) and *or*-conjunction is true when at least one of its conjuncts is true, and false when both (more generally, all) of them are false, and (iv) an *if-then* proposition is false when the protasis is true and the apodosis false, and is true otherwise.

Claim iv is a bit hard to swallow: it means that not only do the sentences in 4.1.2 count as true, which is reasonable, but so do those of 4.1.3, which isn't so reasonable:

4.1.2   a. If 6 is an even number, then 7 is an odd number.
         b. If 3 is an even number, then 6 is an even number.
         c. If 3 is an even number, then 4 is an odd number.

4.1.3   a. If 6 is an even number, then Kathmandu is in Nepal.
         b. If 6 is an odd number, then Kathmandu is in Nepal.
         c. If Kathmandu is in Denmark, then Lima, Peru, is farther west
            than Miami.[1]

The following alternatives are open to one: either deny that ⊃ is truth-functional and allow some instances of ⊃AB to be true and others false in the cases where the truth table has T (e.g., treat 4.1.2a as true and 4.1.3a as false, even though in both cases the protasis is true and the apodosis true), or accept the standard truth table and attribute the oddity of such sentences 4.1.3 to something other than falsehood. For example, Grice (1967) has argued that sentences like those in 4.1.3 are really true, but that it would not be normal behavior for a person to assert them, since if one had the knowledge necessary to know that they were true, one could say something more informative without exerting oneself to any greater extent (e.g., if you know that 6 is an even number and that Kathmandu is in Nepal, you could be more informative to your hearers by asserting either of those propositions separately than by asserting 4.1.3a).

A third alternative, namely, that ⊃ is truth-functional but has a different truth table from the standard one, can be rejected outright. The second line has to be F, since if ⊃AB were true in that case, it would be possible to infer a false conclusion (B) from true premises (⊃AB and A) by ⊃-exploitation, and if there is any rule of inference that we must retain at all costs, it is ⊃-exploitation. If ⊃ is to be truth-functional and to be in reasonable accord with ordinary language, the first and last lines had better well both be T, since ordinary language abounds in cases in which A and B are both true and in cases in which A and B are both false (e.g., "If the butler is the murderer, he left before 10:00. But he didn't leave until 10:45, so . . ."), where "If A, then B" is accepted as true. Thus, if ⊃ is to be truth-functional, the only place where it could conceivably diverge from the standard table is the case where A is false and B true. However, if ⊃AB were uniformly false in that case, then ⊃AB and ⊃BA would be true under exactly the same circumstances, namely, when A and B agreed in truth value. There would then be a serious mismatch between rules of inference and truth conditions: with regard to truth conditions, ⊃ would be symmetric (i.e., you could always interchange protasis and apodosis without changing the truth value of the whole proposition), whereas with regard to inference, ⊃ is asymmetric, that is, you can infer different things from ⊃AB than you can infer from ⊃BA.[2] (For example, from "If Joe is married, he's over 21" and "Joe is married," you can infer "Joe is over 21," however, from "If Joe is over 21, then he's married" and "Joe is married," you can't infer "Joe is over 21").

The following argument provides further reason for saying that if ⊃ is truth-functional, its truth conditions must conform to the standard truth table. The following three assumptions are reasonably noncontroversial: (i) from a "universal" proposition one can infer all of the "special cases" of that proposition (e.g., from "All men are mortal" one can infer "Frank Sinatra is mortal," "Luciano Pavarotti is mortal," "Dan Quayle is mortal," etc.); (ii) 4.1.4 expresses a universal proposition in which "If x is over 6'8" tall, then x has trouble buying clothes" is applied to all persons; and (iii) 4.1.4 is true:

4.1.4   If a person is over 6'8" tall, he has trouble buying clothes.

Under these assumptions, the following conclusions can be inferred from 4.1.4 and thus are true:

4.1.5   a. If Wilt Chamberlain is over 6'8" tall, he has trouble buying clothes.
          b. If Max Abramowitz is over 6'8" tall, he has trouble buying clothes.
          c. If Angel Gonzales is over 6'8" tall, he has trouble buying clothes.

Wilt Chamberlain is about 7 feet tall and has trouble buying clothes; thus 4.1.5a is a true conditional in which both protasis and apodosis are true. Max Abramowitz is 5'3" tall, weighs 380 pounds, and has arms that reach down to his knees, and accordingly he has trouble buying clothes; thus 4.1.5b is a true conditional in which the protasis is false and the apodosis true. Finally, Angel Gonzales is 5'6" tall, weighs 130 pounds, and has no trouble whatever in buying clothes; thus 4.1.5c is a true conditional in which both protasis and apodosis are false. Moreover, the facts given here about Wilt Chamberlain, Max Abramowitz, and Angel Gonzales are clearly consistent with 4.1.4. But then for every line where the standard truth table for ⊃ has T, there are conditionals that conform to that line of the table (and must conform to it if assumptions i–iii are to be maintained), and consequently, if ⊃ is truth-functional, its truth table must be the standard one.

In sections 4.2, 10.3, 11.4, and 15.2, I will discuss in some detail the possibility that ⊃ is not truth-functional. For the time being, however, let's assume that it is truth-functional and, since any other truth table would entail even stranger conclusions than does the standard one, that its truth table is the

standard one. We have already accepted the idea that the other three connectives of propositional logic are truth-functional. There is then a mechanical
procedure whereby one can determine the truth value of any complex proposition of propositional logic, given the truth values of the atomic propositions.
For example, suppose that p is true, q false, r true, and s false. Consider the
proposition

4.1.6

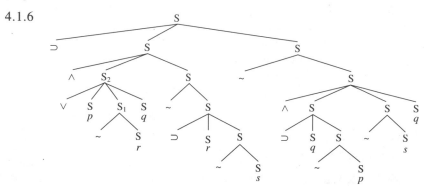

The truth value of 4.1.6 can be determined by starting from the bottom of the
tree and working one's way up, attaching a truth value to each S-node on the
basis of the truth values associated with the nodes that it directly dominates.
For example, since r is T, the truth value associated with S_1 in 4.1.6 would be
F, and since S_2 is then an *or*-conjunction of propositions that are T, F, and F,
respectively, S_2 would be T.

The computation may be facilitated by writing the Ts and Fs on the diagram
as one does the computation:

4.1.7

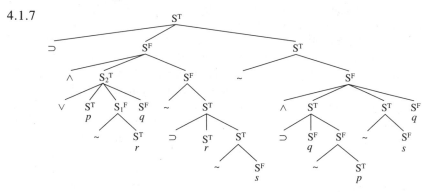

The same steps can be carried out using a linear representation instead of a
tree diagram, by writing a truth value under each connective to indicate the

truth value of the constituent composed of that connective and whatever it is combined with:

4.1.8 $\supset(\sim p, \wedge(q, \sim\supset pq))$
             T FT F F T FTF

The order of the steps in this computation is as indicated in 4.1.9:

4.1.9 $\supset(\sim p, \wedge(q, \sim\supset pq))$

```
0  |   |T |  F  | |TF
1  |   | F |     | F
2  |         |       T
3  |       F
4  T
```

4.2. How Do the Rules of Inference Constrain Truth Values?

Rules of inference are supposed to lead to true conclusions when applied to true premises. Let us assume that the rules of inference that were presented in section 3.2 do what they are supposed to do. Then some sharp constraints are imposed on the relationship between the truth value of a complex proposition and the truth values of its constituents. For example, $\wedge$ must conform to the standard truth table if $\wedge$-introduction and $\wedge$-exploitation are to lead from true premises to true conclusions. When A and B are both true, $\wedge$AB must also be true, since it is inferrable from them (by $\wedge$-introduction) and since, by assumption, the given rules of inference yield true conclusions when applied to true premises. If either or both of A and B is false, then $\wedge$AB must be false, since if it were true one could infer a false conclusion (A or B, as the case may be) from a true premise ($\wedge$AB) by $\wedge$-exploitation. Thus, if the given rules of inference lead to true conclusions when applied to true premises, $\wedge$ must be truth-functional and indeed conform to the standard truth table. (It is easy to generalize this argument so that it covers $\wedge$-conjunctions of arbitrarily many conjuncts: if the given rules of inference always yield true conclusions when applied to true premises, then an *and*-conjunction must be true when all of the conjuncts are true and must be false when one or more of the conjuncts are false.)

The fact that the rules of inference force $\wedge$ to be truth-functional is of considerable interest, since there is no reason to assume that an understanding of how a particular connective functions in inferences will carry with it a means for assigning truth values in all cases, nor that the truth values will depend only on the truth values (rather than on the content) of the constituent propositions. It is quite easy to come up with connectives that are non–truth-functional. For example, the connective "logically implies" is not truth-functional, where one proposition is said to logically imply another if the second proposition can be deduced from the first by the rules of inference of the logical system under discussion. "Aristotle taught Alexander, and Haydn taught Beethoven" logically implies "Aristotle taught Alexander," but "Aristotle taught Alexander" does not logically imply "Ankara is the capital of Turkey." In both cases the various propositions are true, but only in the first case does the first proposition logically imply the second. Thus, the fact that A is true and the fact that B is true do not provide enough information to determine whether "A logically implies B" is true, and thus "logically implies" is not truth-functional.

What about the other three connectives? Do they have to be truth-functional if the given rules of inference are to lead to true conclusions when applied to true premises? Negation looks like a prime candidate for truth-functionality, and surely ought to conform to the standard table:

4.2.1

A	~A
T	F
F	T

Let us see whether the given rules of inference force 4.2.1 on us, under the assumption that they lead to true conclusions when applied to true premises. Given just that one assumption, they in fact do not force 4.2.1 on us. For example, nothing in the rules of inference conflicts with the absurd possibility that all propositions might be true, since if all propositions are true, then no matter what the rules of inference are, they yield true conclusions when applied to true premises. And obviously, if there is a state of affairs in which all propositions are true, then negation does not conform to 4.2.1, since in that state of affairs there would be true propositions whose negations were true, contrary to the demand of 4.2.1 that their negations be false.

Clearly we ought to impose some restriction which would exclude something as outlandish as a "state of affairs" in which all propositions are true. However, before making any specific proposals for such a restriction, let's get clear what we're talking about. Propositional logic is generally discussed at an extremely high level of generality and abstraction. When a logician is doing propositional logic, he cares whether a proposition is the *and*-conjunction of two other propositions, but he doesn't care whether the first of the conjuncts is "The moon is made of styrofoam" or "Sea cucumbers expel their intestines when frightened." In propositional logic, the ultimate units into which complex propositions are analyzed are connectives and atomic propositions, and all that matters about the individual atomic propositions is (i) that one can tell whether two atomic propositions are the same or different, and (ii) what the truth value of each proposition (atomic or not) is in each state of affairs that comes into consideration. For the purposes of propositional logic, a state of affairs can thus be identified with an assignment of truth values: the only difference between states of affairs that ever plays a role in propositional logic is a difference with regard to which propositions are true and which ones false.

The kind of restriction on the use of the term "true" called for in propositional logic is not a condition on how one ought to apply the term "true" to concrete propositions (e.g., a condition that would force one to say that "The moon is made of styrofoam" is false and that "Sea cucumbers expel their intestines when frightened" is true) but rather a **formal** condition (i.e., a condition that does not make reference to the content of individual propositions) on the assignment of truth values to propositions that will rule out assignments of truth values are not internally coherent. One possible condition of this type would be the condition that a proposition and its negation must have opposite truth values in any state of affairs. That condition is of course equivalent to the truth table 4.2.1.

Let's see, however, if 4.2.1 follows from some less stringent condition. Suppose, as a first try, that we impose the minimum condition that would exclude the absurd state of affairs in which all propositions are true, namely, the condition that we will only admit states of affairs in which at least one proposition (N.B.: not necessarily an atomic proposition) is false. That condition in fact forces on us the first line of 4.2.1; that is, it implies that if our rules of inference yield true conclusions when applied to true premises, then in any admissible state of affairs, the negation of every true proposition must be false. Recall that we have shown (3.2.8e) that from a contradiction anything whatever can be inferred. Suppose that in some state of affairs there were a proposition A such that both A and $\sim$A were true. Since we are assuming that in every state of affairs there are false propositions, there is some proposition B which is false in this state of affairs. But then we can derive a false conclusion (B) from true premises (A and $\sim$A) by our rules of inference. Thus, if our rules of inference are to lead from true premises to true conclusions and if we only allow states of affairs in which there are at least some false propositions, then we can only admit states of affairs in which the negation of any true proposition is false.

Okay—from a nice innocuous assumption we've been able to get the first line of 4.2.1; can we get the second line too? I will argue shortly that we can't, that nothing said so far rules out states of affairs in which there are false propositions whose negations are also false. For the time being, let's just observe that the rules of inference for negation don't appear to rule out the possibility of a proposition and its negation both being false. For example, ∼-exploitation only shows that if A and ∼A are both false, then ∼∼A must also be false (since if it were true, you could derive the false conclusion A from the true premise ∼∼A). The rule of ∼-introduction won't help either. If A and ∼A were both false, then deriving something false from them by ∼-introduction would not show any breakdown of the system (since only inferences from **true** premises provide a test for the system), and deriving the contradictory false propositions A and ∼A in the course of an argument that used ∼-introduction would indicate no more of a breakdown than would deriving either of them alone.

Let's then turn to (inclusive) ∨ and see how much of its truth table is forced on us by our assumptions. The standard truth table for ∨ is

4.2.2

A	B	∨ AB
T	T	T
T	F	T
F	T	T
F	F	F

The first three lines of 4.2.2 are forced on us by ∨-introduction. From A you can infer ∨AB, so when A is true (the first two lines), ∨AB must also be true, since otherwise you could infer a false conclusion (∨AB) from a true premise (A). Similarly, the third line must also have T as the value for ∨AB: if it were F, then you could derive a false conclusion (∨AB) from a true premise (B). This leaves the last line, which ought to be a snap—surely we can show that when A and B are both false, ∨AB must also be false. So let's see if we can figure out how to show that. The obvious rule of inference to try to put to work is ∨-exploitation, which says that if you can infer something from each conjunct of an ∨-conjunction, you can infer it from the whole ∨-conjunction. Our job will be over if, given false A and false B, we can always come up with a proposition C such that (i) we can show that C has to be false, (ii) C can be inferred from A, (iii) C can be inferred from B. If we have such a proposition, then ∨AB would have to be false: if ∨AB were true, then we would be able to infer a false conclusion (C) from a true premise (∨AB). As an exercise, you should spend a few minutes trying to construct such a C; I guarantee that you won't find one.

If that doesn't work, maybe we can employ some of the many theorems about ∨ to justify the fourth line of 4.2.2. For example, we have the de Morgan laws. So let's assume that A and B are both false and see what we can conclude from the deductive equivalence of ∼∨AB and ∧(∼A, ∼B). Suppose that ∨AB were true. Then ∼∨AB would be false (since the assumptions in force here allow only states of affairs in which the negation of every true proposition is false). Thus ∧(∼A, ∼B) is also false: deductive equivalents must have the same truth value, since if they didn't you would be able to deduce the false one from the true one and the system would break down. Since we have established that ∧ must conform to the standard table, that means that either ∼A or ∼B must be false. If we knew that negation was truth-functional, we would be home: saying that either ∼A or ∼B is false would be equivalent to saying that either A or B is true, which would conflict with the assumption that A and B were both false. But for the moment the truth-functionality of negation is up in the air: we haven't conclusively ruled out the possibility of a proposition and its negation both being false, and if A and B were such that they and their negations were all false, we might for all we know be in a situation in which A and B were both false but ∨AB was true.

It's beginning to look as if whether ∨ is truth-functional hinges on whether ∼ is truth-functional. In fact it does, as does the truth-functionality of ⊃. I will prove shortly that negation is truth-functional if and only if *or*-conjunction is truth-functional and that negation is truth-functional if and only if ⊃ is truth functional. First, though, let us briefly take up the question of the extent to which the rules of inference of chapter 3 force ⊃ to be truth functional. The first and third lines of the standard truth table for ⊃ are in fact forced on us by ⊃-introduction, since we can infer ⊃AB from B:

4.2.3   1 B   supp
          2   A   supp
          3   B   1, reit
          4 ⊃AB   2, 3, ⊃-intro

Thus, if ⊃-introduction is to draw only true conclusions when it applies to true premises, ⊃AB must be true in all states of affairs in which B is true. The second line is likewise forced on us, in that if there were any state of affairs in which there was a true proposition A and a false proposition B for which ⊃AB was true, a false conclusion (B) could be inferred from true premises (A and ⊃AB); to exclude such states of affairs is to require that ⊃AB be false when A is true and B false. One case remains: that in which A and B are both false. It was shown in 3.2.19 that ⊃AB is deductively equivalent to ∨(∼A, B). Deductive equivalents must always have the same truth value, since otherwise there would be a state of affairs in which one of them was false and the other true, and so a false proposition could be inferred from a true one. The question of whether $\supset$AB must be true whenever A and B are both false thus reduces to the question of whether $\vee(\sim A, B)$ must be true. If the negation of the (by assumption, false) proposition A is true, then of course $\vee(\sim A, B)$ and thus $\supset$AB will be true. But if A and its negation are simultaneously false, a possibility that we have not yet excluded, then we are in the as yet unresolved situation of the last paragraph, with an $\vee$-conjunction of false propositions.

Since the possibility of a proposition and its negation being simultaneously false keeps arising at every turn, it will be worthwhile to digress briefly and show that that idea isn't as outlandish as it at first might seem. Consider the sentence:

4.2.4   Queen Elizabeth regrets that she had an affair with George
          Burns.

Given the factual assumption that Queen Elizabeth has never had an affair with George Burns, no one would want to call the proposition expressed by 4.2.4 true. However, few would want to call the proposition expressed by its negation true either:

4.2.5   Queen Elizabeth doesn't regret that she had an affair with
          George Burns.

The following choices are available: (i) say that the falsehood of the "presupposition" embodied in 4.2.4 and 4.2.5 (namely, the presupposition that Queen Elizabeth had an affair with George Burns) causes them to have no truth value at all, that is, to be neither true nor false; (ii) say that 4.2.4 is false and 4.2.5 true and forget about the uneasiness that one might feel at calling 4.2.5 true; or (iii) say that 4.2.4 and 4.2.5 are both false.[3] Choices i and iii are actually not all that different from each other. Indeed, they differ only in how broadly one interprets the word "false": it is given a narrow interpretation in (i) but a broad interpretation in (iii). Both in (i) and in (iii) one allows for the possibility of a proposition such that neither it nor its negation is true, and the only apparent difference between (i) and (iii) is whether one takes such a proposition to count as "false." I will not attempt to choose among (i), (ii), and (iii) here; it will suffice to point out that (iii) is not any less plausible than the available alternatives, and thus the possibility of a proposition and its negation being simultaneously false cannot be dismissed out of hand. While "classical" logic in fact rules out that possibility, and while a large part of this book is concerned with classical logic, it is worth giving serious consideration here to what classical logic rules out in this case.

Given the rules of inference of chapter 3 plus the assumptions that those rules lead to true conclusions when applied to true premises and that only states of affairs in which at least one proposition is false come into consideration, two alternatives are open to us: either negation is truth-functional, in which case all of the other connectives are truth-functional and have their standard truth tables, or negation is not truth-functional, in which case ∨ and ⊃ are not truth-functional either, though their deviation from truth-functionality is limited to the cells marked T/F in 4.2.6:

4.2.6   a. If negation is truth-functional:

A	~A
T	F
F	T

A	B	∧ AB	∨ AB	⊃AB
T	T	T	T	T
T	F	F	T	F
F	T	F	T	T
F	F	F	F	T

b. If negation is not truth-functional:

A	~A
T	F
F	T/F

A	B	∧ AB	∨ AB	⊃AB
T	T	T	T	T
T	F	F	T	F
F	T	F	T	T
F	F	F	T/F	T/F

To show that these are the alternatives, what I still have to show is the following: (i) if negation is truth-functional, then ⊃ is truth-functional and conforms to the standard table; (ii) it is possible to assign truth values consistently in such a way that negation is not truth-functional; and (iii) under such an assignment of truth values, there are choices of false A and false B which make ∨AB true and other choices which make ∨AB false, and there are choices of false A and false B which make ⊃AB true and others which make it false. Let's take up (i)–(iii) in turn:

i. Suppose that negation is truth-functional in some state of affairs. Since ⊃AB and ∨(~A, B) are deductively equivalent, they always have the same truth value. It was proved earlier in this section that if ~ is truth-functional, then ∨ conforms to the standard truth table. Thus, if ~ is truth-functional, then the truth value of ⊃AB is what results by computing the truth value of ∨(~A, B) according to the standard tables, which in fact is the truth value of ⊃AB according to the standard tables.

ii. Suppose you were to demand the most stringent possible standard of truth: you accept as true only what can be proven true (on the basis of the rules of inference adopted here) and call everything else false.[4] This assignment of truth values is consistent with the rules of inference assumed here; when you apply the rules of inference to true premises, you get a true conclusion: since the premises are provable (that's the only way they can be true, according to this standard of truth), you can put together the proofs of the premises and the step that leads you from the premises to the conclusion, which will add up to a proof of the conclusion, and thus the conclusion will be true. Under this assignment of truth values, negation is not truth-functional. For example, any atomic proposition will be a false proposition whose negation is false: under this assignment of truth values, any atomic proposition has to be false, since you cannot prove an atomic proposition (think what hell would break loose if you could!), and the same is true of the negation of any atomic proposition. There would also be false propositions whose negations were true. For example, $\wedge(p, \sim p)$ would be a false proposition whose negation was true, since its negation is a theorem.

This is not the only way that you could assign truth values to allow cases where a proposition and its negation were both false. For example, if you were to admit as true not just propositions that can be proved categorically but also those which are provable from some given consistent set $\{A_1, A_2, ..., A_n\}$ of premises, with all other propositions assigned the value F, the assignment of truth values would still allow for a proposition and its negation being simultaneously false unless the set of premises were so big as to allow you to prove or disprove all propositions expressible in the language of the given system.

iii. Suppose that we have assigned truth values in a way that conforms to the rules of inference but leaves negation not truth-functional. We can then find both false propositions whose $\vee$-conjunction is false and false propositions whose $\vee$-conjunction is true. Since negation is not truth-functional in the given assignment of truth values, there is some proposition A such that both A and $\sim$A are false. The proposition $\vee(A, \sim A)$ is provable categorically and is thus provable from any set of premises; thus if there are any true propositions in the given assignment of truth values, $\vee(A, \sim A)$ will have to be true. Strictly speaking, nothing we have said so far rules out the absurd state of affairs in which all propositions are false, and in that state of affairs it would be "vacuously true" that any rules of inference lead to true conclusions when applied to true premises. Let us supplement our earlier stipulation to admit only states of affairs in which at least some propositions are false with the further stipulation that we will consider only states of affairs in which at least some propositions are true. Then, in any state of affairs remaining in consideration, if A and $\sim$A are both false, then $\vee (A, \sim A)$ is a true $\vee$-conjunction of false conjuncts. To find an example of a false $\vee$-conjunction of false conjuncts, take any contradictory proposition, say $\wedge(p, {\sim}p)$, and or-conjoin it with a copy of itself:

4.2.7 $\vee(\wedge(p,{\sim}p), \wedge(p, {\sim}p))$.

Since $\vee$AA is deductively equivalent to A, 4.2.7 will have to have the same truth value as $\wedge(p, {\sim}p)$, and is thus false, since the negation of $\wedge(p, {\sim}p)$ is a theorem and is thus true under any admissible assignment of truth values. This establishes that if negation is not truth-functional, then just from the fact that C and D are both false you can't tell whether $\vee$CD is true or false.

The same is true of $\supset$. Suppose that $\sim$ is not truth-functional. Then there is a proposition A such that A and $\sim$A are both false. Then $\supset$(A, $\sim$A) will be false, since it is deductively equivalent to $\vee({\sim}A, {\sim}A)$, which is in turn deductively equivalent to $\sim$A, which is by assumption false. But there are also cases where two propositions are false but the result of combining them with $\supset$ is true. A trivial example of that is $\supset$BB, where B is any false proposition: $\supset$BB is provable and hence true. Thus, if negation is not truth-functional, then just from the fact that C and D are both false, you can't tell whether $\supset$CD is false or true.

The truth table 4.2.6b, corresponding to states of affairs in which negation is not truth-functional, can be sharpened if one notes that in the cells where T/F appears, one of the two values will be attested in every state of affairs (e.g., in any admissible assignment of truth values, there will be false propositions whose negations are true) but the other one will not occur in every state of affairs (e.g., there are admissible assignments of truth values in which the negation of every false proposition is true). Using parentheses to indicate those truth values which do not figure in every state of affairs, 4.2.6b can be revised to

4.2.8

A	$\sim$A
T	F
F	T/(F)

A	B	$\wedge$AB	$\vee$AB	$\supset$AB
T	T	T	T	T
T	F	F	T	F
F	T	F	T	T
F	F	F	F/(T)	T/(F)

In every state of affairs there are false propositions whose negations are true: $\supset$AA is a theorem and thus true in every state of affairs, and $\sim\supset$AA is thus false; thus $\sim\supset$AA is a false proposition whose negation (${\sim}{\sim}\supset$AA, which is of course deductively equivalent to $\supset$AA) is true, since it is a theorem. In every state of affairs, there will be false propositions whose or-conjunction is false: $\vee({\sim}\supset$AA, $\sim\supset$AA) will be an or-conjunction of false propositions which is false, since its negation, being deductively equivalent to the theorem ⊃AA, will be true. And in every state of affairs, there will be true conditional propositions with false protasis and false apodosis, since ⊃(~⊃AA, ~⊃AA) is a theorem and hence true but has as protasis and apodosis propositions which are the negations of theorems and are thus false. If a state of affairs includes an instance of any of the three parenthesized values in 4.2.8, it will include instances of the other two; this has in effect already been proved.[5]

4.3. Language and Metalanguage

Almost all of the symbols introduced so far have belonged to the vocabulary of a system of formal logic; that is, the symbols represent various elements of meaning that are parts of the propositions that figure as premises and conclusions of inferences in that system of logic. However, two symbols, namely the turnstile, ⊢, and its derivative, ⊣⊢ (back-to-back turnstiles), are not part of the system of logic itself but rather part of a **metalanguage** in which one talks about that system of logic. These symbols do not figure in the proofs of the given system of logic but only in our statements about what can be proven in that system. I will devote this brief section to enlarging somewhat the limited vocabularies of both our formal metalanguage (in which such symbols as ⊢ appear) and our informal metalanguage (in which words such as "provable" and "consistent" appear).

In most of the proofs given so far, a conclusion was inferred from one or more premises. However, in the three proofs in 3.2.14, a conclusion was inferred without reference to premises. It will be useful to extend the ⊢ notation to these cases by writing the result in question to the right of a turnstile that has nothing to its left:

4.3.1   a. ⊢ ⊃(A, ⊃BA))   (= 3.2.14a)
         b. ⊢ ~∧(A, ~A)   (law of noncontradiction, = 3.2.14b)
         c. ⊢ ∨(A, ~A)   (law of excluded middle, = 3.2.14c)

This notation is fairly natural, in that the turnstile can be regarded as connecting a set of premises to a conclusion that can be inferred from that set of premises, and saying that a proposition can be proven "categorically," as in 4.3.1, amounts to saying that it can be inferred from an **empty** set of premises. The notation in 4.3.1 can then be regarded as an abbreviation for such metalinguistic statements as "∅ ⊢ ∨(A, ~A)," where ∅ is the symbol that will be introduced in 5.2 to represent the empty set. A proposition that can be proven categorically in a given system of logic is called a **theorem** of that system.

In view of the rules of ⊃-introduction, ⊃-exploitation, ∧-introduction, and ∧-exploitation, it is largely a matter of convenience whether one states a result as a theorem or as the inferrability of a conclusion from a certain set of premises. For example, the proof (3.2.8e) by which we established 4.3.2a could be altered in a trivial way to yield a proof of the theorem 4.3.2b, and likewise, any proof of 4.3.2b by means of the given rules of inference (not necessarily the proof obtained by trivial alteration of 3.2.8e) could be altered equally trivially to yield a proof of 4.3.2a:

4.3.2   a. A, ~A ⊢ B
         b. ⊢ ⊃(∧ (A, ~A), B)

Specifically, it is fairly easy to prove the following metalinguistic results about the system of chapter 3:

4.3.3   a. $A_1, A_2, \ldots A_n$ ⊢ B if and only if $\wedge(A_1, A_2, \ldots A_n)$ ⊢ B
         b. A ⊢ B if and only if ⊢ ⊃AB

For example, we can verify the left-to-right half of 4.3.3b by noting that if we have a proof that derives B from the premise A, we can convert it into the following demonstration that ⊢ ⊃AB:

4.3.4   1   │ A   supp
                   │ ...
               n │ B   (lines 2 to n as in the given proof of B
                                from A)
             $n+1$ ⊃AB   1-n, ⊃-intro

Similarly, we can verify the right-to-left half of 4.3.3b by noting that if we have a categorical proof of ⊃AB, we can convert it into the following proof of B from A:

4.3.5   1   A
                    ...
                    ...   ⎫ the given proof of ⊃AB
               n ⊃AB   ⎬
             $n+1$ B   ⎭ n, 1, ⊃-expl

However, one should be careful not to let the limited trade-off between ⊃ and ⊢ stated in 4.3.3b lead one to confuse ⊢ with ⊃. The turnstile ⊢ is a symbol of our metalanguage; it does not figure in the formation rules and rules of inference of chapter 3 nor the truth conditions of this chapter, and it may not be embedded in complex formulas the way that ⊃ can be. (It is for these reasons that I have not included metalinguistic symbols such as ⊢ in my policy of using "Polish" notation for connectives: I write $\supset AB$, but $A \vdash B$). It makes sense to speak of a formula $\supset AB$ as being true or as being false in a particular state of affairs, However, it makes no sense to speak of $A \vdash B$ as being true or false in such-and-such state of affairs: the truth of $A \vdash B$ has nothing to do with any state of affairs but with whether the rules of inference of the system of logic in which one is operating allow one to infer B from A.

It should be emphasized that $\vdash$ refers to provability in the particular logical system under discussion, and a formula can be a theorem relative to one particular system of logic without being a theorem relative to some other system. For example, while $\supset(\wedge (A, \sim A), B)$ is a theorem in the classical logic under discussion here, it is not a theorem of the relevant entailment logic that was alluded to briefly in the last section. When there is need to make explicit the system of logic being referred to, this can be done with a subscript on the turnstile. Thus, if C denotes classical propositional logic and E denotes relevant entailment propositional logic, 4.3.6a is correct but 4.3.6b is incorrect:

4.3.6   a. $\vdash_C \supset(\wedge(A, \sim A), B)$
         b. $\vdash_E \supset(\wedge(A, \sim A), B)$

Two important metatheoretic notions based on the notion of a proposition being proven from a given set of premises are the notions of **consistency** and of **inconsistency**. A set of propositions is inconsistent if contradictory propositions can be inferred from it, that is, $\{A_1, A_2, ..., A_n\}$ is inconsistent if and only if there is a proposition B such that $A_1, A_2, ..., A_n \vdash B$ and $A_1, A_2, ..., A_n \vdash \sim B$. A set of propositions is consistent if and only if it is not inconsistent, that is, to say that $\{A_1, A_2, ..., A_n\}$ is consistent is to say that for any B for which $A_1, A_2, ..., A_n \vdash B$, it is not the case that $A_1, A_2, ..., A_n \vdash \sim B$. It should be emphasized that the notion of consistency is relative to a given system of rules of inference. Thus, a set of propositions that is inconsistent with respect to one system of rules of inference could very well be consistent with respect to a weaker system. Since the rules of inference with which we are operating here allow any conclusion whatever to be inferred from contradictory premises (this was proved in 3.2.8e), a set of propositions is inconsistent relative to these rules of inference only if **all** propositions can be inferred from it, that is, a set of propositions is consistent if and only if some propositions cannot be inferred from it.

Let us turn now to the metalinguistic notion of **deductive equivalence** that was introduced in section 2.5. This notion figures in a principle that often allows one to simplify proofs that otherwise would be quite long. The principle of **substitution of deductive equivalents (SDE),** which is valid for the system of propositional logic of chapter 3 (and for many other systems of logic, though not all systems) says that any formula is deductively equivalent to a formula obtained from it by replacing a subformula by anything deductively equivalent to that subformula. In view of the deductive equivalence of ~~B to B, if one has reached line 38 in a proof 4.3.7a, SDE allows one to obtain the next line directly by substituting ~~B for B, rather than going through the steps in 4.3.7b that one would otherwise need to go through:

4.3.7   a. 38 ⊃(∧(A, ~ ~B), C)
             39 ⊃(∧AB, C)   38, SDE

         b. 38 ⊃(∧(A, ~ ~B), C)
             39 │ ∧AB   supp
             40 │ A   39, ∧-expl
             41 │ B   39, ∧-expl
             42 │   │─ ~ B   supp
             43 │   │ B   41, reit
             44 │   │ ~ B   42, reit
             45 │ ~ ~B   42–44, ~-intro
             46 │ ∧(A, ~ ~B)   40, 45, ∧-intro
             47 │ C   38, 46, ⊃-expl
             48 ⊃(∧AB, C)   39–44, ⊃-intro

Since there is another quite distinct substitution principle that has raised its head already, it would be worthwhile to contrast the two principles here lest they be confused in any proofs in which a substitution plays a role. In line 3 of 3.2.17a, we invoked the result repeated in 4.3.8a to justify the step that is repeated here in 4.3.8b:

4.3.8   a. ~∨AB ⊢ ∧(~A, ~B)   (= 3.1.13a)
         b. 2 ~∨(~A, ~B)
            3 ∧(~~A, ~~B)

Line 2 is what you would get from the left half of 4.3.8a by substituting ~A for A and ~B for B; line 3 is what you would get by making the same substitution in the right half of 4.3.8a. Theorem 4.3.8a provides justification for the step from line 2 to line 3, since the steps involved in the proof of 4.3.8a are equally valid if some complex proposition stands in place of A (or of B), just as long as the same expression stands in place of A (or of B) in the conclusion. This follows from the fact that the rules of inference are sensitive to what the **immediate** constituents of a formula are (e.g., to whether the formula is of the form ⊃ AB) but not to what its **ultimate** constituents are. This principle is not restricted to the replacement of (all occurrences of) **one** symbol by a given formula: two or more substitutions can be performed simultaneously (as in the proof under discussion), just as long as each occurrence of any proposition letter is replaced by the same formula (e.g., each occurrence of A is replaced by ~A and each occurrence of B is replaced by ~B). Note that it is a mistake to speak of "setting A equal to ~A" here. Of course, A could not possibly be "equal to ~A." Rather than taking the original letter to be "equal to" the substituted formula in any sense, one is merely recognizing that if the substituted formula had stood in place of that letter in the original proof, the proof would still have gone through. Let us refer to this substitution principle as **substitution for propositional variables (SPV)**.

SPV works quite differently from SDE, which, unlike SPV, does involve a kind of equality, namely deductive equivalence. According to SDE, for any two formulas ϕ and ψ of arbitrary complexity, if $\phi \dashv\vdash \psi$, then from any formula one may infer the result obtained by substituting ψ for any occurrence of ϕ in the formula, e.g., on the basis of the deductive equivalence 4.3.9a, one is entitled to carry out the step indicated in 4.3.9b, in which one has replaced an occurrence of $\supset(\sim B, \sim A)$ by something that is deductively equivalent to it:

4.3.9   a. $\supset AB \dashv\vdash \supset(\sim B, \sim A)$
         b. ...
             17 $\supset(\supset(\sim B, \sim A), C)$
             18 $\supset(\supset AB, C)$ 17, 4.3.9a, SDE

Let us list the differences between SPV and SDE. (i) In SPV, an atomic proposition symbol is replaced, whereas in SDE, what is replaced can be as complex as one pleases. (ii) In SPV, all occurrences of the given symbol must be replaced, whereas in SDE, different occurrences of the expression in question can be replaced or left alone, as one pleases; for example, 4.3.10b–b″ can all be obtained from 4.3.10a by SDE:

4.3.10   a. $\supset(\supset AB, \supset(\sim B, \sim A))$
         b. $\supset(\supset(\sim\sim A, B), \supset(\sim B, \sim A))$
         b′. $\supset(\supset AB, \supset(\sim B, \sim\sim\sim A))$
         b″. $\supset(\supset(\sim\sim A, B), \supset(\sim B, \sim\sim\sim A))$

(iii) In SPV, any formula at all can replace the atomic proposition symbol, whereas in SDE, only a formula deductively equivalent to the given formula may replace it. (iv) SPV is applicable only to the proposition symbols appearing in a theorem $\vdash A$ or in a proven inference $\{B_1, \ldots, B_n\} \vdash A$, whereas SDE is applicable to constituents of any line of a proof.

These four remarks have had to do with the applicability of the two principles. To this, let us add a couple of remarks about what it takes to establish their validity. First, it is quite easy to show that SPV follows from the given rules of inference, but relatively difficult to show that SDE does. Second, the validity of both principles depends on details of the logical system to which they refer, and thus one cannot blithely assume that they will be valid in all other logical systems. One could not expect, for example, that SDE would be valid in a system of logic that covered not only negation, *if*, etc., but also such notions as belief. Note that, given that S_1 is deductively equivalent to S_2 and that Larry believes that S_1, one cannot conclude that Larry believes that S_2: one can hold a belief without recognizing what all its logical consequences are.

I turn now to some metalinguistic notions having to do with truth conditions. For the remainder of this section, let us assume that all the connectives have their standard truth tables. Certain complex propositions are true in all states of affairs; others are false in all states of affairs; others are true in some states of affairs but false in others. For example, $\supset(\supset AB, \supset(\sim B, \sim A))$ is true in all states of affairs (or at least, in all states of affairs such as we are admitting into consideration), as can be shown simply by computing its truth value for each combination of truth values for A and B:

4.3.11

A	B	$\supset(\supset AB, \supset(\sim A, \sim B))$				
T	T	T	T	T	F	F
T	F	T	F	F	T	F
F	T	T	T	T	F	T
F	F	T	T	T	T	T

The proposition $\supset(\supset AB, \supset(\sim A, \sim B))$ is true in some states of affairs and false in others; specifically, it is false when A is false and B true, and it is true otherwise:

4.3.12

A	B	$\supset(\supset AB, \supset(\sim B, \sim A))$				
T	T	T	T	T	F	F
T	F	T	F	T	F	T
F	T	F	T	F	T	F
F	F	T	T	T	T	T

The proposition $\wedge(A, \supset(A, \sim A))$ is false in all states of affairs:

4.3.13

A	$\wedge(A, \supset(A, \sim A))$				
T	F	T	F	T	F
F	F	F	T	F	T

A proposition which is true in at least one state of affairs is said to be **satisfiable.** A proposition which is true in all states of affairs is said to be **valid.** This terminology is unfortunate, since "valid" is used in a different sense with regard to inferences: an inference is said to be valid if its conclusion follows from its premises. However, the use of valid in the sense of "true in all states of affairs" is sufficiently standard in logic that there is little point in avoiding the term. Valid propositions are also called **tautologies.**

Note that proving a proposition isn't the same thing as proving that it is valid: proving the proposition means showing that it follows from the rules of inference, whereas proving that it is valid means showing that its truth value is T regardless of what the truth values of the atomic propositions in it are. Nonetheless, if everything works right, the propositions that you can prove ought to be precisely the ones that are valid, that is, the logical system ought to be **semantically complete.**

The logical system that we are talking about, that is, the logical system whose rules of inference are the nine that were given in the last chapter and whose truth conditions are given by the standard truth tables, can in fact be proved to be semantically complete. Half of this result is fairly easy to prove, namely, the half that says that if a proposition is provable, then it is valid, though making the proof explicit is a little tricky, as a result of the complete freedom that we have to make suppositions in subordinate proofs and the freedom we have to reiterate any line of a superordinate proof. Note in particular that the suppositions of the subordinate proofs are not required to be true; indeed, it is essential that they not be required to be true, since the results proved have to be true regardless of whether the suppositions are true; for example, if you prove $\supset$AB by $\supset$-introduction, you make the supposition A in a subordinate proof, but your result has to be true regardless of whether A is true. Note also that suppositions are the only way that the various proposition symbols get into the proof; that is, without suppositions you can't prove anything categorically.[6]

For those rules of inference that do not involve subordinate proofs, one can verify that they lead from true premises to true conclusions simply by checking the truth tables, e.g., to check that $\supset$-expl always yields a true conclusion when applied to true premises, one need only note that the truth tables allow $\supset$AB and A to be true only in cases in which B is also true. It is a considerably more complicated enterprise to show that the rules that do involve subordinate proofs likewise lead only to true conclusions when applied to true premises. To illustrate how this might be done, let us consider a proof in which a conclusion is derived by $\vee$-exploitation:

4.3.14

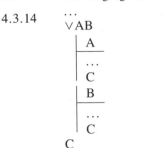

Suppose that ∨-expl did not always yield a true conclusion when applied to a true premise. Then there would be a proof of the form 4.3.14 in which ∨AB is true, C is false, and the two subordinate proofs conform to the assumed rules of inference. Since ∨AB is true and (by our previous assumption) the standard truth tables hold, one or the other of A and B must be true. But that means that one or the other of the two subordinate proofs leads from a true premise to a false conclusion, and thus that the step in which that conclusion was drawn is the one responsible for 4.3.14 having a true premise and a false conclusion. Thus, something other than the given application of ∨-expl must be to blame if a proof conforming to the assumed rules of inference leads from true premises to a false conclusion. The same sort of argument can be given for ⊃-intro and ∼-intro: in any proof in which the rule derives a false conclusion from true premises, some step in one of the subordinate proofs will also derive a false conclusion from true premises, and the blame for the false conclusion can then be shifted onto that step.

This means that the "goodness" of the whole proof hinges on the goodness of the subordinate proofs, which will in turn hinge on the goodness of any proofs that are subordinate to them, etc. However, as you burrow into the depths of a proof, you will eventually hit bedrock, which in this case means proofs to which nothing is subordinate. But the goodness of the bedrock proofs has been established (or at least, it has if you've checked the truth tables to verify the claim that I made at the beginning of this paragraph: that the rules of inference that do not involve subordinate proofs all lead to true conclusions when applied to true premises). Putting these results together, we obtain the conclusion that for any argument that conforms to the given rules of inference, its conclusion is true in any state of affairs in which the suppositions of the whole argument (i.e., the premises) are true. But note that this is the case even if there aren't any premises (i.e., if the only suppositions are those of subordinate proofs, not of the main proof). With a bit of meditation, you should be able to convince yourself that that means that if the argument has no premises, its conclusion is true in any state of affairs whatever. But that is precisely what we are trying to prove.

Or at least, it's the easier half of what we want to prove. We have sketched a proof that every provable formula is valid; that is, if a formula can be proved by means of the given rules of inference, it is true in all states of affairs. We have yet to prove the converse: that every valid formula is provable. Proving that result is quite involved; accordingly, I have banished a sketch of the proof to an appendix (4.6), so that anyone who does not feel up to going through it can skip it easily. However, you should at least think about the result long enough to appreciate why it would be difficult to prove it: one is required not just to come up with a proof of some formula but to show that for any formula, no matter how complicated, if it is true in all states of affairs, then there is a way of proving it by means of the given rules of inference. The task of establishing this theorem is made easier if we concentrate our energies on establishing an equivalent result: any formula that is not provable is not valid, that is, if a formula is not provable from the given rules of inference, then there is a state of affairs in which it is false. Note that to establish this result one must make use of fine details of the rules of inference: the result shows that the rules of inference allow you to prove the maximum that you could hope to prove, and you can thus expect that if you were to drop or weaken one of the rules the result need not remain true.[7]

The semantic completeness theorem provides us with a **decision procedure** for the deductive system of chapter 3: given any formula of propositional logic, one can determine whether it is provable by the given rules of inference by determining whether it is valid according to the classical truth tables, which one can do simply by computing its truth value for each possible combination of truth values of the atomic propositions contained in it. If there are n different atomic propositions in a given complex proposition A, one can determine its truth value for each of the 2^n combinations of truth values for those atomic propositions; if the value in each case is T, then A can be proved by the rules of inference of section 3.2, and if the value in any of the 2^n cases is F, it cannot be proved. The classical truth tables are thus valuable tools even if one does not think they give an accurate account of truth values; one can accept the less constrained account of truth values given in 4.2 but still use the classical truth tables as a device for determining whether a given proposition is provable by the rules of inference of chapter 3.

The symbol $\vDash$ is commonly used to indicate "true in all states of affairs," that is, $\vDash$ A means "A is true in all states of affairs," that is, "A is valid." Just as $\vdash$ is used not only to indicate that a proposition is provable categorically but also to indicate that it is provable from given premises, $\models$ is used not only to indicate that a proposition is valid but also to indicate that it is true whenever given propositions are true, that is, "B_1, B_2, ..., B_n $\models$ A" means "in all states of affairs in which B_1, B_2, ..., B_n are true, A is also true." The term **entailment** (or **semantic entailment**) is commonly used for this relationship, that is, we say that the set of propositions $\{B_1, B_2, ..., B_n\}$ (semantically) entails A if B_1, B_2, ..., B_n $\models$ A. As in the case of $\vdash$, $\models$ is used relative to a particular system of logic. The intended system of logic can be made explicit by a subscript whenever the occasion arises (say, whenever one is comparing two or more different systems), for example, if c is the system of classical propositional logic having the formation rules and rules of inference of chapter 3 and the truth conditions embodied in the truth tables of 4.1, one can write $\models_c$ A to mean that A is true in all states of affairs that conform to the classical truth tables, just as one writes $\vdash_c$ A to indicate that A is provable according to the classical rules of inference. The semantic completeness theorem referred to in this section can be restated as: For any proposition A of propositional logic, $\vdash_c$ A if and only if $\models_c$ A.

4.4. Different Kinds of Completeness

The term "completeness" is used to cover a number of quite distinct properties of logical systems; the only thing that these properties have in common is that each is some kind of maximum demand that one could reasonably impose on a system. This section, which is a brief summary of three notions referred to by the word "completeness," is inserted solely for the sake of clarity—for example, so as to decrease the likelihood that the reader will assume that "Gödel's incompleteness theorem" has something to do with semantic completeness.

A logical system is said to be **semantically complete** if its rules of inference allow you to prove all the propositions that could stand a chance of being proved, that is, all propositions that are true in all states of affairs. (If the system is consistent, then the fact that a given proposition is false in some state of affairs guarantees that that proposition cannot be proved in the system).

A second kind of completeness is **syntactic completeness**: a system is said to be syntactically complete if for every proposition A of the system, either A or ~A is a theorem of the system. A system is syntactically complete if it imposes the most stringent possible restriction on states of affairs: that there is only one state of affairs in which the rules of the system lead only to true conclusions when applied to true premises. The question of syntactic completeness arises not in connection with systems that would normally be spoken of as systems **of** logic, but rather in connection with systems that include axioms for a particular subject matter, for example, a formal system that is intended as an axiomatization of the arithmetic of positive whole numbers or as an axiomatization of atomic physics. The most celebrated result about syntactic completeness is Gödel's incompleteness theorem, which says that an axiomatization of the arithmetic of positive integers cannot be syntactically complete if it is consistent (that is, if it doesn't allow you to deduce contradictions); this shows that if a supposed system of axioms for arithmetic is consistent, then there are "undecidable" propositions of arithmetic relative to those axioms, that is, propositions A such that the axioms provide neither a proof of A nor a proof of $\sim$A.

A third kind of completeness that is often mentioned in logic texts is **expressive completeness.** A system is "expressively complete" if the formulas that it provides are sufficient to draw all possible distinctions among states of affairs. A state of affairs in this case is taken to be a set of truth values for the atomic propositions of the system, that is, a state of affairs amounts to a line of a truth table.[8] To say that the system is expressively complete is to say that for any set of states of affairs, there is a formula of the system which is true in those states of affairs and false in all other states of affairs. It is obvious that the system of propositional logic that we have been discussing here is expressively complete. For any one state of affairs there is a formula that is true only in that state of affairs (e.g., suppose the given state of affairs is "p true, q true, and r false"; then $\wedge(p, q, \sim r)$ is true precisely in that state of affairs). So for any finite set of states of affairs, we can get a formula which is true in those states of affairs and false otherwise: for each state of affairs, construct a proposition that is true in that state of affairs and false in any other state of affairs, and form the $\vee$-conjunction of those propositions. For example, given the three states of affairs "p true, q true, r false," "p true, q false, r false," and "p false, q false, r true," the following formula would be true in those states of affairs and false otherwise:

4.4.1 $\vee(\wedge(p, q, \sim r), \wedge(p, \sim q, \sim r), \wedge(\sim p, \sim q, r)).$

It is interesting to note that expressive completeness can be attained without some of the connectives of the given system. For example, observe that the procedure just given for finding a formula true only in given states of affairs utilizes only three of the four connectives: no use is made of $\supset$. In fact, you could get along with two, since $\vee(p_1, ..., p_n)$ has the same truth value as $\sim\wedge(\sim p_1, ..., \sim p_n)$ and thus you could eliminate the $\vee$'s in favor of combinations of $\sim$'s and $\wedge$'s without changing the set of states of affairs in which the formula is true. Likewise, since $\wedge(p_1, \ldots, p_n)$ has the same truth value as $\sim\vee(\sim p_1, \ldots, \sim p_n)$, you could replace all the $\wedge$'s by combinations of $\sim$'s and $\vee$'s without changing the set of states of affairs in which the formula is true. Thus, just $\sim$ and $\vee$ (or just $\sim$ and $\wedge$ or just $\sim$ and $\supset$) would be sufficient in order for the system to be expressively complete. What this means is that if all you care about is the conditions under which formulas are true, you can define two of the connectives away: for any formula of the given system, you can find another that involves only $\sim$ and $\vee$ and which is true under exactly the same conditions as is the given formula.

You can't get expressive completeness with just one of the given connectives, as you should be able to convince yourself by thinking about the truth tables (for example, why can't you get a formula containing only $\wedge$'s which is true when p is false and is false otherwise?). However, it is possible to have expressive completeness in a system with just one connective, provided you allow that connective to be something nonstandard. Specifically, suppose that there is a two-place connective | (read "stroke") which has the following truth table (and thus corresponds to English *neither . . . nor*):

4.4.2

A	B	A|B
T	T	F
T	F	F
F	T	F
F	F	T

It is then possible to construct formulas involving no connective other than | which have the same truth conditions as $\sim p$, $\vee pq$, $\wedge pq$, and $\supset pq$:

4.4.3
$\sim p$ $p|p$
$\wedge pq$ $(p|p)|(q|q)$
$\vee pq$ $(p|q)|(p|q)$
$\supset pq$ $((p|p)|q)|((p|p)|q)$

There is no loss of expressive completeness if $\vee$ and $\wedge$ are restricted to two conjuncts at a time. This follows from the fact that an n-term $\vee$-conjunction or $\wedge$-conjunction has the same truth conditions as a repeated two-term conjunction. For example, each of the formulas in 4.4.4 is true if at least one out of A, B, C, D, E is true, and is false otherwise, and each of the formulas in 4.4.5 is true if all of A, B, C, D are true and is false otherwise:

4.4.4   a. $\vee$(A, B, C, D, E)
         b. $\vee$(A, $\vee$(B, $\vee$(C, $\vee$DE)))

    c. $\vee(\vee(\vee(\vee AB, C), D), E)$

    d. $\vee(\vee(\vee AB, C), \vee DE)$

4.4.5   a. $\wedge(A, B, C, D)$

      b. $\wedge(A, \wedge(B, \wedge CD))$

      c. $\wedge(\wedge AB, \wedge CD)$

It is this fact which has led logicians generally to operate only in terms of two-term conjoining: if all you are interested in is truth conditions, you can define away conjunctions of 3 or more conjuncts (e.g., "define" 4.4.4a as "meaning" 4.4.4b or 4.4.c; it is of course arbitrary which of the nested two-term conjunctions one would take as the definiens). In section 3.5, I rejected this common policy of logicians in virtue of arguments that the natural language counterparts of $\wedge$ and $\vee$ as conjoin things arbitrarily many at a time, along with the lack of any obstacle to treating $\wedge$ and $\vee$ as parallel to their natural language counterparts in this respect.

This discussion of expressive completeness is perhaps the best place at which to take up "exclusive *or,*" which I have so far neglected in this book.[9] If exclusive *or* is to be truth-functional and is to be distinct from inclusive *or,* the only conceivable truth table it might have is 4.4.6, since only in a state of affairs in which both conjuncts are true might a two-term exclusive *or* and an inclusive *or* yield different truth values:

4.4.6

A	B	$\vee_e AB$
T	T	F
T	F	T
F	T	T
F	F	F

If we embed an $\vee_e$-conjunction in an $\vee_e$-conjunction and compute the truth conditions according to 4.4.6, it becomes clear that multiterm $\vee_e$-conjunction cannot be defined away in terms of iterated two-term conjunction, the way logicians have "defined away" multiterm $\vee$- and $\wedge$-conjunctions.

4.4.7

A	B	C	$\vee_e(A, \vee_e BC)$		
T	T	T	T	T	F
T	T	F	F	T	T
T	F	T	F	T	T
T	F	F	T	T	F
F	T	T	F	F	F
F	T	F	T	F	T
F	F	T	T	F	T
F	F	F	F	F	F

The iterated two-term conjunction is true when one of the three ultimate conjuncts is true or when all three of them are true, and is false when none of them is true or when two of them are. More generally, any iterated two-term $\vee_e$-conjunction of any number of items will be true if an odd number of those items are true and false if an even number of them are true. For example, the following expression will be true if one, three, or five of A, B, C, D, E, F are true and will be false if none, two, four, or six of them are true:

4.4.8

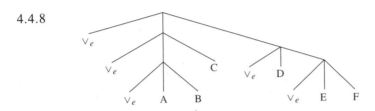

However, the truth conditions of English sentences in which *or* could be held to be used in an exclusive sense with more than two conjuncts do not conform to this pattern. For example, *On the $2.95 lunch you can have french fries, boiled potato, or mashed potato* does not invite you to take one or three but not two of the alternatives: it simply invites you to take one. Likewise, the question *Did Larry study physics, chemistry, or `geology?* (` indicates falling intonation on the word to which it is attached) presupposes that Larry studied one of the three subjects, not that he studied an odd number of them. Thus, the natural generalization of the truth table 4.4.6 to an $\vee_e$-conjunction of arbitrarily many conjuncts is that $\vee_e(A_1, \ldots, A_n)$ is true when exactly one of the conjuncts is true and is false otherwise, i.e., when either none of them or more than one of them is true. The most natural truth table for n-term $\vee_e$-conjunctions is thus distinct from that for an iterated two-term $\vee_e$-conjunction: when the number of true conjuncts is odd and greater than one, the former is false but the latter true.[10]

Thus, if $\vee_e$ is to be one of the connectives of a logical system and if its logical properties are to match those of apparent exclusive uses of *or* in English, it cannot be a two-term conjunction: it will have to be allowed to conjoin any number of propositions at a time, from two on up. This conclusion then yields an additional argument (albeit a weak one, in view of the controversial status of $\vee_e$ as an element of logical structure) that (inclusive) $\vee$ and $\wedge$ must also be allowed to conjoin any number of propositions at a time: there is no syntactic difference between, on the one hand, $\vee_e$, and on the other hand, $\vee$

and $\wedge$; any number of conjuncts have to be allowed with $\vee_e$, since otherwise the truth conditions come out wrong; but then $\vee$ and $\wedge$ must also be allowed to take any number of conjuncts, since otherwise a spurious syntactic difference among the three conjunctions would be created.

4.5. Appendix A: More on Metalanguage

It is important to distinguish between proving results **about** a logical system and proving results **in** that system. In the course of this chapter, we have proved many things about the system of propositional logic that was given in chapter 3 and about the notion of truth for that system. These proofs have often involved elements of meaning and principles of logic that are not part of propositional logic, for example, logical principles governing the notion of "all," and the so-called principle of induction (section 5.7), which allows one to prove a result about complex propositions by showing that the result holds for simple propositions and that it is preserved as one builds up complex propositions from simple pieces. Indeed to prove results **about** propositional logic that are of any interest, it will be necessary to use much richer logical principles and a much richer analysis of logical structure than is available in propositional logic.

We have accordingly been making informal use of powerful logical tools in proving results about the formal proofs of a very rudimentary system. One may find this situation disturbing; isn't it rather like using a filthy scalpel and rusty clamps in applying a well-sterilized bandaid to someone's aorta? It can be made a little less disturbing if one takes the attitude that in making informal use of powerful logic in proving results about a rigorously formalized but elementary logical system, one is offering a promissory note that is payable by eventual formalization of the powerful system that is at present being used informally. However, this attempt to allay one's worries raises a separate worry: has the logician thereby committed himself to a policy of perpetual deficit financing, in which he is at every step proving results about one logical system by the informal use of a more powerful logical system whose formalization he must put on the agenda for subsequent years? Or will one eventually reach an all-encompassing logical system which will contain all the logical apparatus that one needs to prove all conceivable results about that very system?

Whatever the answer to these mind-boggling questions, you will have to resign yourself at least temporarily to some deficit financing. In particular, you should recognize that until we have arrived at the promised land of the all-encompassing logical system, it will not be possible to force proofs **about** a system into the format adopted for proofs **in** the system. Indeed, it would be quite misguided to try to force into the format for proofs in propositional logic such "metaproofs" as the proof that every formula that is provable in propositional logic is true in all states of affairs. When you prove something about proofs in propositional logic, you have to keep the proofs that you're talking about separate from the proof that you're doing (the metaproof). You in fact would still have to keep them separate in the promised land of the all-encompassing logic, since what you're doing and what you're talking about are in any event distinct; but it is even more essential to keep them apart when (as is the case here) the metaproofs involve the logical apparatus of a much richer system than the one about which something is being proved in the metaproof.

The distinction between language and metalanguage must also be maintained. The "language" of propositional logic is quite rudimentary: propositions are built up from atomic propositions by means of just four connectives, and propositions are arranged into proofs having the structures given by the nine rules of inference. Distinguishing between a metalanguage[11] and the **object language** that you discuss in it is essential if you are to avoid getting tangled up in your own feet. For example, it is essential to be clear than when one speaks of a formula having the form $\vee AB$, the symbols A and B belong to the metalanguage rather than to the object language: the ultimate constituents of the formulas of propositional logic are atomic propositions (for which p, q, r, ... have been used here as symbols), and the As and Bs that have appeared in the statements of the rules of inference and the various metaproofs have been symbols of the metalanguage and have stood for formulas of arbitrary complexity (i.e., not necessarily atomic formulas) of the object language. This distinction is essential, for example, to an understanding of the proof that negation need not be truth-functional for the rules of inference to work; thus, I was able to speak of assigning truth values so that "A is true only if A is provable" but was still able to say that no atomic proposition is provable and thus that all atomic propositions are false under that assignment of truth values.

4.6. Appendix B: Sketch of a Proof of Semantic Completeness

I will sketch here how semantic completeness can be proved for the system of propositional logic developed here and in chapter 3. This is but a rough sketch, given only to show the reader how such a proof can be constructed (for a more detailed treatment relating to a different version of propositional logic, but easily modified to fit the present system, see chap. 7 of Thomason 1970).

I have already sketched a proof of the easy half of the completeness theorem: if a formula is provable by the rules of inference of chapter 3, then it is true according to every assignment of truth values that conforms to the truth tables of 4.1.1. What we must now prove is that if a formula is true according to every such assignment of truth values, then it is provable by the given rules of inference, or equivalently, if a formula is not provable by the given rules of inference, then it is false in at least one such assignment of truth values.

The proof, which was originally worked out by Leon Henkin (1950), will make use of the notion of a **saturated** set of formulas. A set of formulas is saturated (with respect to a given inventory of atomic propositions) if (i) it is consistent and (ii) for every formula built up from the given atomic propositions and the propositional connectives, either it or its negation belongs to the set. A saturated set of formulas is thus a maximal consistent set of formulas: it is consistent, and it could not be made any larger without becoming inconsistent. It can be proved that every consistent set of formulas can be expanded into a saturated set. Specifically, let M be a consistent set of formulas, and let $A_1, A_2, A_3, \ldots$ be a complete enumeration of the (infinitely many) formulas of propositional logic that can be built up from the given inventory of atomic propositions.[12] Define a sequence of increasingly large consistent sets as follows: $M_0 = M$, and for each $i \geq 1$, let $M_i = M_{i-1} \cup \{A_i\}$ if $M_{i-1} \cup \{A_i\}$ is consistent, and let $M_i = M_{i-1} \cup \{\sim A_i\}$ otherwise. It can be shown that the union of all the M_i is a saturated set, and since it contains M, that shows that M is contained in a saturated set. It can also be proved that every saturated set of formulas is closed under the given rules of inference, that is, if M is a saturated set of formulas and M ⊢ A, then A ∈ M.

For any saturated set M of formulas, we can define an assignment of truth values V_M as follows: if p is an atomic formula, then $V_M(p) = T$ if $p \in M$, and $V_M(p) = F$ if $p \notin M$; if A is not atomic, then $V_M(A)$ is what is computed from the values under V_M of the atomic constituents of A according to the truth tables of 4.1.1. It can be proved that $V_M(A) = T$ if and only if $A \in M$. The proof of this latter result relies heavily on the details of the rules of inference. It is an inductive proof, constructed by supposing that the result holds for all formulas whose "degree of complexity" (measured, say, by the depth to which the most deeply embedded atomic constituent is embedded in the formula) is less than an amount n and showing that it must then also hold for formulas of complexity n. Let A be any formula of complexity n. To show that $V_M(A) = T$ if and only if $A \in M$, it is necessary to go one by one through all the possibilities for the gross form of A. For example, suppose that for all formulas C of complexity less than n, $V_M(C) = T$ if and only if $C \in M$, and suppose that A is an *or*-conjunction, that is, $A = \vee(B_1, \ldots, B_m)$. Suppose $V_M(A) = T$; then for some i, $V(B_i) = T$ (since V_M satisfies the truth table for $\vee$); then (by the inductive hypothesis) $B_i \in M$ and thus (since A can be deduced from B_i by $\vee$-introduction and saturated sets are closed under the rules of inference) $A \in M$. Suppose that $V_M(A) = F$; then $V_M(B_1) = \ldots = V_M(B_m)$ $= F$ (since V_M conforms to the truth table for $\vee$); according to the inductive hypothesis, this means that each $B_i \notin M$ and thus each $\sim B_i \in M$ (since M is saturated), whence $\wedge(\sim B_i, \sim B_2, \ldots, \sim B_m) \in M$ (since M is closed under a set of rules of inference that includes $\wedge$-introduction), thus $\sim\vee(B_1, B_2, \ldots, B_m) \in M$, that is, $\sim A \in M$, and thus $A \notin M$, since M is saturated. Similar proofs can be given for all the other possibilities for the form of A. Thus, $A \in M$ if and only if $V_M(A) = T$, and the principle of induction allows us to conclude that that is the case for all formulas A.

We are now in a position to prove the theorem. Suppose we have a formula A that cannot be proved by the given rules of inference. Since A cannot be proved, $\{\sim A\}$ is a consistent set, and by the result proved earlier, that set can be extended to a saturated set. Let M be a saturated set of formulas that contains $\sim A$. $V_M(\sim A)$ then is T (since V_M makes a formula true if and only if that formula belongs to M) and thus $V_M(A) = F$. This establishes that if A cannot be proved by the given rules of inference, then it is false in at least one assignment of truth values that conforms to the given truth tables.

Exercises

1. Suppose that in a given state of affairs, p is T, q F, r T, and s F. For each of the following formulas, (i) convert it into the tree format of chapter 3, and (ii) determine its truth value in the given state of affairs, according to the standard truth tables.

   a. $\supset(\sim\supset(\vee pq, \vee qr), \supset rp)$
   b. $\wedge(\supset(p, \sim q), \supset rs)$
   c. $\sim\vee(p, \wedge(\supset qr, \supset(r, \sim p)), \supset(\sim p, \wedge qr))$
   d. $\supset(\vee(\wedge pr, \wedge qs), \sim\vee(\wedge ps, \wedge qr))$

2. For each of the formulas in exercise 1 that is T in the given state of affairs, determine whether it is valid; for each one that is F in that state of affairs, determine whether it is satisfiable.

   3. a. Show that the fragment of propositional logic having only the con-

nectives $\wedge$, $\vee$, and $\supset$ is not expressively complete with regard to the class of states of affairs defined by the standard truth tables.

b. Determine whether propositional logic with only $\sim$ and $\vee_e$ as connectives is expressively complete.

4. Show that propositional logic is not expressively complete with regard to the broader class of states of affairs that is developed in section 4.2. Suggest an addition to the object language that would make propositional logic expressively complete with respect to that class of states of affairs (i.e., for expressive completeness, what else would you have to be able to say besides what standard propositional logic lets you say?).

5.   A Digression into Set Theory

5.1. The Notion of "Set"

Under what circumstances is the sentence 5.1.1 true?

5.1.1   Most linguists like Chinese food.

Let us assume that *most* means "more than half" (this is not completely accurate, as will be shown in section 7.4, but the inaccuracy is immaterial at this point). Then 5.1.1 should be true provided that more than half of all linguists like Chinese food. This statement of the conditions under which 5.1.1 is true makes covert reference to two **sets:** the set of all linguists, and the set of all linguists who like Chinese food; it reduces the question of whether 5.1.1 is true to a comparison of the size of these two sets.

To discuss truth conditions for sentences involving quantifiers, it will be necessary to make constant reference to sets. In addition, sets often figure not only in one's metalanguage for talking about propositions and their truth conditions but as elements of content in the propositions themselves. For example, in the sentence *All of them subscribe to Newsweek* the word *them* refers to a set of persons, and the content of the sentence can only be analyzed by making reference to that set.

It will thus be appropriate if at this point we digress into the notion of set and clarify it and some related notions. The content of this chapter will be more mathematical than linguistic, but much of it will play a role in later chapters.

"Set" is one of those words for which it is impossible to give a real definition. Attempts at defining it generally consist in giving a list of synonyms, none of which is really any clearer than the word "set": class, aggregate, collection, and the like. The clearest explanation of what a set is is probably an explanation in terms of the kinds of relationships that sets can stand in toward each other and toward other things. A set consists of elements, for example, the set of all U.S. presidents in the nineteenth century consists of Adams,

135

Jefferson, Madison, Monroe, . . . , and McKinley. The mathematical notion of set makes the identity of a set purely a matter of what members it has. Thus, the set of all British naval personnel on 1 January 1965 and the set of all British naval personnel on 1 January 1975 are two different sets, even though the British navy on 1 January 1965 is in some sense the same entity as the British navy on 1 January 1975 (or at least, they are the same entity in the sense in which I am the same person that I was ten years ago: I may have grown a mustache, lost a tooth, gained some fat, and changed many of my beliefs, just as the British navy has acquired and lost personnel, closed some bases, and scrapped some ships). It is thus a mistake to think of sets as typified by such corporate bodies as the British navy, the Chicago city council, or the Juilliard String Quartet. Such bodies may "consist of" persons, but the body remains the same body even when the set of persons of which it consists changes; it is reasonable to speak of the Juilliard Quartet changing its membership by getting a new second violinist, but it is absurd to speak of the set {Robert Mann, Joel Smirnoff, Samuel Rhodes, Joel Krosnick} changing its membership: to describe that set as changing its membership when the quartet gets a new second violinist would be as absurd as describing a rise in temperature from 30° to 35° as a change of the number 30 into the number 35.

There is no restriction on what kinds of elements can be members of a set: you can talk of a set of numbers, a set of persons, a set of formulas of predicate logic, a set of sentences of Amoy Chinese, even a set of sets. A set need not be the membership of any corporate body. Indeed, its members need not even have anything in common: you can talk of such sets of highly heterogeneous elements as a set consisting of the number 38, Chester Alan Arthur, Mozart's nineteenth symphony, and the formula $\vee(p, \sim p)$. In actual fact, people do not normally refer to sets as outlandish as the one just described: you normally don't have occasion to refer to things together unless they have something significant in common. However, I will follow the standard practise of logicians and mathematicians and accept the broad conception of set that includes even such outlandish collections of heterogeneous objects.

The elements of which a set consists are called its **members,** and they are said to **belong to** the set. The symbol $\in$ is used to represent the relation of "belonging to" a set; thus, if E is used to represent the set of all even numbers, we can write $2 \in E$ to express the proposition that 2 belongs to that set, that is, that 2 is an even number. The symbol $\notin$ is used to represent the negation of $\in$, for example, $3 \notin E$ means "3 is not a member of E," that is, "3 is not an even number." To say that two sets are identical is to say that they have the same members; for example, to say that the set of all precincts in Chicago with 100 percent voter turnout is identical to the set of all precincts in Chicago that contain cemeteries is to say that every precinct in Chicago that has 100 percent voter turnout contains a cemetery and every precinct in Chicago that contains a cemetery has 100 percent voter turnout.

The notion of an element belonging to a set must not be confused with the relationship of a set being **subset** of a set. If M and N are two sets and every element that is a member of M is also a member of N, then M is said to be a subset of N. The symbol ⊆ is used to indicate the subset relation: M ⊆ N means "M is a subset of N." A set can be a member of another set without being a subset of it and can be a subset of another set without being a member of it. To see this, let us accept the standard conception of a line as a certain kind of set of points;[2] then saying that a point lies on a given line or that the line passes through the point amounts to saying that the point is a member of the line. Let P be any point, let L be any of the lines that pass through P, and let M be the set of all lines that pass through P.

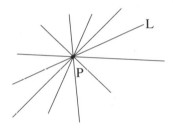

Then L is a member of M but it is not a subset of M: the subsets of M are not lines but sets of lines, and L is not a set of lines, i.e., its members are not lines but points. It is trivial to find subsets of M that are not members of it, since indeed no subset of M is a member of it. The only way that a set could have subsets that were also members of it would be for it to be inhomogeneous to the extent of having among its members not only various entities but also sets having those entities as members. For example, the set that has 1 and 2 as its members (i.e., the set that will be represented as {1, 2} in the notation to be presented below) would be both a member and a subset of the three-member set whose members were 1, 2, and {1, 2}: {1, 2} ∈ {1, 2, {1, 2}}, and {1, 2} ⊆ {1, 2, {1, 2}}.

From the example of a point, a line, and the set of all lines that pass through the point, one can readily see that the membership relation is not **transitive,** that is, from A ∈ B and B ∈ C, one is not entitled to infer that A ∈ C: note that in the above example, P ∈ L and L ∈ M, but P ∉ M. By contrast, the subset relation **is** transitive. Suppose that A ⊆ B and B ⊆ C, and suppose that a ∈ A. Since every member of A is a member of B, a ∈ B, and since every member of B is a member of C, $a \in$ C. Thus, all members of A are members of C, i.e., A $\subseteq$ C.

The relations $\in$ and $\subseteq$ differ not only with regard to transitivity but also with regard to reflexiveness. According to the definition of "subset" given above, every set is a subset of itself: this follows from the trivial fact that "if $x \in$ A, then $x \in$ A" is always true. However, the idea that a set might be a **member** of itself is fraught with paradox. To come up with a plausible example of a set that might be a member of itself, one has to get into the realm of misty abstractions such as "the set of all sets," and one can rightly question whether it makes sense to speak of such a thing as a set of all sets, since if one allows the same freedom of expression that is innocuous in the case of less all-encompassing sets, one can describe subsets of that supposed set that lead to contradictions under all circumstances. For example, if one denotes by S the "set of all sets" and defines S$'$ as the subset of S consisting of all x for which $x \notin x$, then both the proposition S$' \in$ S$'$ and the proposition S$' \notin$ S$'$ lead to contradictions (think about each of them for a minute, and you should be able to see why).[3] We thus have further reason to be sure to distinguish sharply between $\subseteq$ and $\in$: M $\subseteq$ M is as innocuous and trivial a formula as one could hope to find, obviously true of any set whatever, whereas M $\in$ M is a formula that could be truly only of rather outlandish sets, and it is not even clear that the notion of set should be interpreted so broadly as to allow for such sets.

There are a number of ways in which one can specify what set one is referring to. One way is simply to enumerate the members of the set. For example, I can describe a certain set by saying that it consists of the numbers 37, 24893, and 701 and nothing else. Curly brackets and commas are standardly used in forming expressions such as {37, 24893, 701}, which denotes the set whose members are the elements listed inside the brackets. Note that the order of the elements in the enumeration is immaterial: {37, 24893, 701} denotes exactly the same set as does {701, 37, 24893}, since in both cases the set defined by the expression has exactly the same members. Defining a set by **enumeration** is possible only when the set if **finite:** if a set has infinitely many members, then it has more members than you could possibly put into a list.

A second way of specifying a set is to give a criterion for membership in the set. This is in fact what was done in defining most of the sets that have been referred to so far in this chapter; for example, the set M of lines that we spoke of a few paragraphs earlier is defined by the condition: $x \in$ M if and only if x is a line and P $\in x$. Curly brackets and either a colon or a vertical stroke are standardly used in forming expressions that correspond to this kind of definition:

$$\{x: x \text{ is a line and } P \in x\} \quad \text{or} \quad \{x| x \text{ is a line and } P \in x\}$$

What appears to the left of the colon or stroke is a general formula for members of the set being defined. What appears to the right is the conditions that must be met for something of that general form to belong to the set. The general formula in the example just given is quite trivial; a less trivial example would be an expression such as

$$\{x^2: x \text{ is an even number}\}$$

which would define the set of all squares of even numbers. It is of course possible to do without complex expressions before the colon by employing quantifiers after the colon; for example, the following expression also serves to define the set of all squares of even numbers:

$$\{y: (\exists: x \text{ is an even number})_x(y = x^2)\}$$

That is, y belongs to the set in question if and only if there is an even number such that y is the square of that number. Nonetheless, I will retain the more general version of "definition by criterion" and allow complicated expressions to appear to the left of the colon.

There are other, less straightforward ways of specifying a set. For example, a certain set might be specified as "the smallest set which contains the numbers $\frac{1}{23}$ and $\sqrt{7}$ and which contains both the sum and the difference of any two of its members." However, there is not much point in going into the details of such types of definitions here. One thing that must be emphasized, though, is that there is nothing a priori that requires that every set be describable. Indeed, it is easy to show that there are more sets of numbers than there are possible descriptions of sets of numbers, and hence there must be sets of numbers which cannot be given a description that singles out that particular set unambiguously. Thus, "the set of all sets of whole numbers" has as members not only sets with such nice straightforward definitions as $\{1, 5, 94\}$ or $\{x: x^3 - 43x \text{ is a prime number}\}$, but also sets (necessarily, infinite sets) whose members cannot be characterized by any formula built up from the basic concepts of arithmetic. This fact is no cause for alarm: it merely reflects the fact that the ways in which sets can differ from each other greatly exceed the ways in which descriptions of sets can differ from each other. Each of the infinitely many whole numbers constitutes an independent dimension on which two sets of whole numbers can differ from each other: a set can either contain a given number or fail to contain it, independently of what other numbers it contains or fails to contain; however, the great freedom that one has in constructing formulas is limited by the fact that every formula has to be of finite length. If formulas are represented as strings of symbols, including a "period" which marks the end of the formula (and has no other typographical function), then every formula must contain a period, and there is absolutely no freedom in what can follow a period: only blank spaces can follow. The sets that cannot be described are necessarily things even more outlandish than a set consisting of a dozen randomly selected numbers. Their existence will be of importance only in connection with questions of generality: whether something can be allowed to be any set at all or must be restricted to the realm of the describable.

5.2. Operations on Sets

The operations of **union, intersection,** and **difference** (or **[relative] complement**) are defined as follows:

$A \cup B$ (the union of A and B) is $\{x: \vee(x \in A, x \in B)\}$
$A \cap B$ (the intersection of A and B) is $\{x: \wedge(x \in A, x \in B)\}$
$A - B$ (the complement of B with respect to A) is
$\{x: \wedge(x \in A, x \notin B)\}$.

Thus the union of two sets consists of everything that belongs to either or both of them, the intersection of two sets consists of those elements that are common to the two sets, and the complement of one set with respect to another consists of those elements of the latter that do not belong to the former. If sets are represented by regions in a plane, the shaded areas in the following diagrams will illustrate the results of performing these three operations:

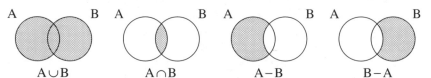

$A \cup B$ $A \cap B$ $A - B$ $B - A$

In addition, a notion of **(absolute) complement** is sometimes recognized: the absolute complement $\bar{A}$ of a set A is defined as $\{x: x \notin A\}$. The notion of absolute complement is problematic, since it commits one to belief in a "set of all objects," in that $A \cup \bar{A}$ would be such a set. If "all objects" is interpreted in the fullest generality, thus as including all sets, acceptance of a set of all objects leads one into Russell's paradox (see note 3). In actual practise, most apparent references to absolute complements really relate to relative complements: the author is referring to complements relative to some fixed "universe of discourse"[4] U, and $\bar{A}$ is used as an abbreviation for $U - A$.

With a little meditation, you should be able to see that the following equalities are true

$$\{1, 2, 3, 4, 5\} \cup \{3, 4, 5, 6, 7\} = \{1, 2, 3, 4, 5, 6, 7\}$$
$$\{1, 2, 3, 4, 5\} \cap \{3, 4, 5, 6, 7\} = \{3, 4, 5\}$$
$$\{1, 2, 3, 4, 5\} - \{3, 4, 5, 6, 7\} = \{1, 2\}$$

If M consists of those whole numbers that are multiples of 3 and N consists of the even numbers, then M $\cap$ N = the multiples of 6, and M $-$ N = the odd multiples of 3.

A consideration of how intersection and difference work forces us to be more explicit than we have been with regard to how small a set can be. Suppose that M is the set of all persons who served as president of the U.S.A. in the nineteenth century and N is the set of all persons who have served as president of the U.S.A. in the twentieth century. Then what is M $\cap$ N? The intersection is supposed to be the set consisting of all elements that belong to both of the sets. In this case, there is exactly one element common to both sets: William McKinley. If M $\cap$ N is to denote anything here, it will have to be a set that has William McKinley as its sole member. There is in fact no obstacle to allowing sets that have a single element. Note, though, that it will be necessary to distinguish between a single-element set and that single element: William McKinley is not a set whose sole member is William McKinley. The notation involving curly brackets and commas for specifying a set by enumeration is equally applicable in the case of a one-element set as in the case of a larger set (though, of course, commas will be unnecessary if the list of elements has only one entry); thus we can write

M $\cap$ N = {William McKinley}

Suppose now that M is the set of all persons who were elected president as candidates of the Whig party and N is (as before) the set of all persons who have served as president during the twentieth century. What is M $\cap$ N? In this case the sets have no element in common: the last Whig president was Zachary Taylor, who died in office in 1850. Thus, if M $\cap$ N is to denote anything here, it will have to be a set that has no members. There is in fact no obstacle to admitting an **empty set,** which has no members. Using the symbol $\emptyset$ to represent this set, we can write M $\cap$ N = $\emptyset$. Note that there can be only one empty set: two sets differ only if one has a member that the other does not, and since an empty set has no members, an empty set can be distinct only from a nonempty set; thus, the set of all Trappist monks who are members of the Interstate Commerce Commission = the set of all operas composed by Johannes Brahms. A set which has members is said to be **nonempty.** To say that M ∩ N = ∅ is to say that M and N are **disjoint,** that is, that they have no elements in common. To say that M − N = ∅ is to say that M is a subset of N. Note that the only way that M ∪ N could be ∅ is for both M and N to be ∅.

5.3. Finite and Infinite Sets

In the last section we had occasion to refer to many sets that had infinitely many members. For example, we referred to the set of all even numbers, and there are infinitely many even numbers; we referred to the set of all lines that pass through a given point, and there are infinitely many such lines.

The expression "infinitely many" should not mislead one into assuming that there is exactly one infinite number and all sets that are not finite have that many members. It turns out that infinite sets can differ in size and that it makes perfect sense to speak of distinct infinite numbers, and of one infinite number being smaller than another one. However, to show that that is the case it will be necessary first to show how the notion of the "size" of a set can be generalized so as to be applicable to infinite sets.

"Size" in the case of finite sets refers to numbers of elements. The set of all states that belonged to the U.S.A. in 1945 has the same size as the set of all preludes in Bach's Well-tempered Clavier: both sets have 48 members. To say that two finite sets have the same size is to say that if you count off the elements of the first set (i.e., point to one element and say "one," point to another element and say "two," point to yet another element and say "three," etc., until you have exhausted the set) and separately count off the elements of the second set, you will end up with the same number. However, the role of numbers in this procedure is dispensable: instead of matching elements of the two sets to numbers, you could have just as easily matched elements in the one set to elements in the other set, and the two sets would have the same number of elements provided you can match each element of the one set to a different element of the other set (in perhaps a totally arbitrary way) and have no elements of either set left over. Thus, you could establish that there were as many states in the U.S.A. in 1945 as there are preludes in the Well-tempered Clavier by matching them up in, say, the following way:

Alabama	Arizona	Arkansas	. . . Wyoming
C maj., bk. 1	C min., bk. 1	C# maj., bk. 1	. . . B min., bk. 2

The order in which the states and the preludes are listed here is in fact of no theoretical significance (though it is of practical help in making sure that you haven't left anything out); a totally random pairing such as the following would equally well show that there were as many states in 1945 as there are preludes in the Well-tempered Clavier:

Montana	Ohio	New Mexico	. . . Indiana
A min., bk. 1	C min., bk. 2	E maj., bk. 1	. . . F# min., bk. 2

This notion of "same size" is applicable regardless of whether the sets are finite or infinite. For example, you can justify the claim that there are as many positive even numbers as there are positive odd numbers by showing that there is a one-to-one correspondence between the two sets, for example, the correspondence in which every positive odd number corresponds to the even number that is one greater than it:

1	3	5	7	9	11	13	. . .	847	849	. . .	17,891	17,893	. . .
2	4	6	8	10	12	14	. . .	848	850	. . .	17,892	17,894	. . .

The only qualification that needs to be imposed in applying this notion of same size to infinite sets is that while for finite sets it made no difference **how** you matched up the elements of the two sets (i.e., how you arrange the members of the two sets will have no bearing on whether any elements are left over), it can make a difference in the case of infinite sets, and thus it is somewhat harder to prove that two infinite sets **differ** in size than it is to prove that two finite sets differ in size. For example, from the fact that you can match each positive even number to a positive whole number (namely, itself) and still have positive whole numbers left over (see below), it does not follow that there are more positive whole numbers than there are even numbers, since by matching every positive whole number with the even number that is twice that whole number (b) one can match the two sets in such a way that nothing is left over:

```
a. 1   2 3    4  5    6  7    8  9      . . .
   —   2 —    4  —    6  —    8  —      . . .
b. 1 2 3  4   5    6    7    8    9      . . .
   2 4 6  8  10   12   14   16   18      . . .
```

In fact, it is easy to show that a set is infinite if and only if it can be matched up one-to-one with a proper subset of itself.

The positive whole numbers are the smallest infinite set. Smallest, that is, with respect to the notion of size that was just introduced. There are, of course, infinite sets which are smaller than the positive whole numbers in the sense of being proper subsets of that set; however, those sets have the same size as the positive whole numbers: they can be put into a one-to-one correspondence with the positive whole numbers, with no element of either set left over. To see why the positive whole numbers should be the smallest infinite set, suppose you are given an infinite set. Pick any member of that set and call it x_1. There will be other elements of the set, since if x_1 were its only member it would not be infinite. So pick another element of the set and call it x_2. There will still be elements left in the set, since if x_1 and x_2 were all the elements it had, it would not be infinite; thus you can pick another element of the set and call it x_3. This can continue without limit. But this procedure gives you a one-to-one correspondence between the positive whole numbers and a subset (not necessarily a proper subset) of the given set:

$$1 \quad 2 \quad 3 \quad 4 \quad 5 \quad \ldots$$
$$x_1 \quad x_2 \quad x_3 \quad x_4 \quad x_5 \quad \ldots$$

There may be some elements of the given set that aren't included in the second line, but all of the positive integers will appear in the first line. Thus the positive integers are the smallest infinite set: it can be put into a one-to-one correspondence with a subset of any other infinite set.[5]

If every size is to be represented by a number, there must be a number corresponding to the size of the set of all positive integers, and that number will be the smallest infinite number. The symbol $\aleph_0$ is standardly used to denote that number (the Hebrew letter used here is aleph; the whole symbol is read "aleph sub zero," "aleph zero," "aleph naught"). The question must now be raised: are there any infinite numbers that are larger than $\aleph_0$, or is $\aleph_0$ the only infinite number? If a set is to have more than $\aleph_0$ members, it will have to be larger than the set of all positive whole numbers, indeed a lot larger than it: note, for example, that the set of all whole numbers (positive, zero, and negative) won't be big enough to have more than $\aleph_0$ members, since the same kind of one-to-one correspondence can be set up between all whole numbers and the positive ones as was set up between all positive whole numbers and the positive even numbers:

$$\ldots \quad -4 \quad -3 \quad -2 \quad -1 \quad 0 \quad 1 \quad 2 \quad 3 \quad 4 \quad 5 \quad \ldots$$
$$\ldots \quad 8 \quad 6 \quad 4 \quad 2 \quad 1 \quad 3 \quad 5 \quad 7 \quad 9 \quad 11 \quad \ldots$$

That is, the odd numbers are matched with zero and the positive whole numbers, and the even numbers are matched with the negative whole numbers, and nothing is left over.

What about the rational numbers, then—all numbers that can be expressed as fractions with whole numbers for numerator and denominator? It turns out that despite the fact that between any two whole numbers there are infinitely many rational numbers, there are still the same number of rational numbers as there are positive whole numbers. To show this, it suffices to show that the rational numbers (let's only talk about the positive rational numbers here—bringing in the negative ones wouldn't change anything, though it would make the discussion slightly more complicated) can be arranged into a sequence of r_1, r_2, r_3, . . . which is exhaustive, that is, every rational number turns up somewhere or other in the sequence. To construct such a sequence, arrange all fractions in order of the sum of numerator and denominator: first the fractions whose numerator and denominator add up to 2 (since only positive rational numbers are under consideration here, they couldn't add up to less than 2), then those for which the sum of the numerator and denominator is 3, then those for which it is 4, and so on:

$$\tfrac{1}{1};\ \ \tfrac{2}{1},\ \tfrac{1}{2};\ \ \tfrac{3}{1},\ \tfrac{2}{2},\ \tfrac{1}{3};\ \ \tfrac{4}{1},\ \tfrac{3}{2},\ \tfrac{2}{3},\ \tfrac{1}{4};\ \ \tfrac{5}{1},\ \tfrac{4}{2},\ \tfrac{3}{3},\ \tfrac{2}{4},\ \tfrac{1}{5},\ \ldots$$

There are duplications in this list; for example, $\tfrac{1}{2}$ represents the same number as does $\tfrac{2}{4}$. The desired sequence can be obtained by correcting that deficiency: delete all entries in the above sequence which duplicate earlier entries:

$$\tfrac{1}{1},\ \tfrac{2}{1},\ \tfrac{1}{2},\ \tfrac{3}{1},\ \tfrac{1}{3},\ \tfrac{4}{1},\ \tfrac{3}{2},\ \tfrac{2}{3},\ \tfrac{1}{4},\ \tfrac{5}{1},\ \tfrac{1}{5},\ \tfrac{6}{1},\ \tfrac{5}{2},\ \ldots$$

Every rational number will occur somewhere or other in this sequence, since every rational number can be represented as a fraction a/b and there will be only finitely many rational numbers whose numerator and denominator add up to $a + b$ or less.

If we go significantly beyond the set of all rational numbers and consider the set of all real numbers, we finally get a set that demonstrably has more than $\aleph_0$ members. The real numbers include not only the rational numbers but also "irrational numbers" such as π and $\sqrt{2}$, which do not correspond exactly to any ratio of whole numbers. Every real number can be represented in decimal form, for example, $\pi = 3.14159...$, $\sqrt{2} = 1.414....$ In the case of a rational number, the decimal form either terminates ($\tfrac{1}{4} = 0.25$) or repeats ($\tfrac{1}{11} = 0.090909...$); in the case of an irrational number, the decimal form continues for infinitely many places, with no group of figures repeated more than a finite number of times in succession. If we treat terminating decimals as having repeated zero at the end ($\tfrac{1}{4} = 0.250000...$), all real numbers can be represented as nonterminating decimal forms. We have to show that there is no way to arrange all real numbers into an exhaustive sequence. Let's concentrate on the real numbers between 0 and 1; it is easy to show that there are as many of them as there are real numbers altogether, and it will simplify things if we can forget about what comes before the decimal point. Suppose that the real numbers between 0 and 1 could be arranged into an exhaustive sequence:

$$a^1 = .a^1_{\ 1}a^1_{\ 2}a^1_{\ 3}a^1_{\ 4}\ \dots$$
$$a^2 = .a^2_{\ 1}a^2_{\ 2}a^2_{\ 3}a^2_{\ 4}\ \dots$$
$$a^3 = .a^3_{\ 1}a^3_{\ 2}a^3_{\ 3}a^3_{\ 4}\ \dots$$
$$a^4 = .a^4_{\ 1}a^4_{\ 2}a^4_{\ 3}a^4_{\ 4}\ \dots$$
$$\dots$$

If I can show that a contradiction follows, I will have shown that the real numbers between 0 and 1 cannot be arranged into an exhaustive sequence, and that will establish that the real numbers between 0 and 1 (and thus the real numbers altogether) form a set with more than $\aleph_0$ members. I will show that there is a contradiction by showing that, regardless of what numbers appear in the various places in that sequence, it is possible to construct another real number between 0 and 1 that does not appear in the sequence, which will contradict the assumption that the sequence was exhaustive. I will construct such a number by giving a procedure for constructing each of the digits in its decimal form. If $a^1_{\ 1} = 5$, let $x_1 = 4$, and if $a^1_{\ 1} \neq 5$, let $x_1 = 5$. If $a^2_{\ 2} = 5$, let $x_2 = 4$, and if $a^2_{\ 2} \neq 5$, let $x_2 = 5$. If $a^3_{\ 3} = 5$, let $x_3 = 4$, and if $a^3_{\ 3} \neq 5$, let $x_3 = 5$. In general, if $a^i_{\ i} = 5$, let $x_i = 4$, and if $a^i_{\ i} \neq 5$, let $x_i = 5$. This procedure defines a real number between 0 and 1 whose decimal form is $.x_1 x_2 x_3 x_4 \dots$. This number, call it x, is different from all the numbers a^i: its first digit was picked so as to insure that $x \neq a^1$, its second digit was picked in such a way as to insure that $x \neq a^2$, its third digit was picked in such a way as to insure that $x \neq a^3$, and in general, its ith digit was picked in such a way as to insure that x was different from a^i. But this means that no matter how a sequence of real numbers between 0 and 1 was arranged, it could not contain all of them: it is always possible to construct a number that does not appear in the sequence. But that means that there is no one-to-one correspondence between the positive whole numbers and the real numbers between 0 and 1.

A set which has $\aleph_0$ elements is called **countable** or **denumerable**.[6] An infinite set which has more than $\aleph_0$ elements is called **uncountable** or **nondenumerable**. The set of all real numbers is thus an uncountable set. Note that if M is any finite set of symbols and M* is the set of all **finite** sequences of symbols of M, then M* is countable. (This can be shown the same way that we showed that the set of all rational numbers was countable: you can arrange them into a sequence by listing first the sequences of length 1, then those of length 2, then those of length 3, etc.) Let us assume that all descriptions of sets of whole numbers can be expressed as formulas in some finite alphabet (for example, the alphabet might consist of curly brackets, commas, quantifiers, logical connectives, digits with which to write specific numbers, etc.) Then there are only countably many descriptions of sets of whole numbers. If

I can establish that there are uncountably many sets of whole numbers, I will have established a point stated in the last section: that there are more sets of whole numbers than there are descriptions of sets of whole numbers, and thus that there are sets of whole numbers that literally cannot be singled out by any description.

For any set M, let P(M) (the **power set** of M) denote the set of all subsets of M. We will now prove that P(M) has more members than M, not only in the special case where M is the set of all positive whole numbers, but indeed no matter what set M is. Proving that P(M) has more members than M amounts to showing that there is a one-to-one correspondence between M and a subset of P(M) but there is no one-to-one correspondence between M and the whole of P(M). The first part of this result is trivial: the correspondence which matches each element a of M to the set $\{a\}$ (i.e., the set whose only members is a) is a one-to-one correspondence between M and a subset of P(M). Thus, all we have to prove is:

Theorem. For any set M, there is no one-to-one correspondence between M and P(M).

Proof. The proof of this theorem is very similar to the proof that there is no one-to-one correspondence between the positive integers and the real numbers between zero and 1: any correspondence between M and P(M) will fail to exhaust P(M), since no matter what the correspondence is, it will always be possible to construct a member of P(M) which is not included in the correspondence. Suppose that we have a set M and a function f which associates to each element x of M an element $f(x)$ of P(M). Since the elements of P(M) are the subsets of M, $f(x)$ will be a subset of M. For each element x one can then raise the question of whether x is a member of $f(x)$ and define a set N as consisting of those x's for which the answer is negative, that is, $N = \{x: x \notin f(x)\}$. Then the function f does not associate N to any element of M. For suppose that it did, that is, suppose that there is some element a of M such that $f(a) = N$. There are two possibilities: either a belongs to N or it does not. Suppose $a \in N$; then $a \notin f(a)$ (since that is the criterion for membership in N); but since $f(a) = N$, that means $a \notin N$, which contradicts the supposition. Now suppose that $a \notin N$; since $N = f(a)$, that means that $a \notin f(a)$, which means that a meets the criterion for membership in N, and thus $a \in N$, which contradicts the supposition. Thus f cannot exhaust M, since the assumption that it does implies a contradiction ($a \in N$ and $a \notin N$). Thus there can be no one-to-one correspondence between M and P(M), no matter what set M is.

This shows that there are more infinite numbers than you can shake a stick at. The set of all sets of real numbers has more members than does the set of all real numbers; the set of all sets of sets of real numbers has more members than does the set of all sets of real numbers; and so on. The theorem also establishes that there is no largest infinite number.

5.4. Relations and Functions

Consider an expression such as *is taller than* or *went to the same school as* which expresses a relationship. For any given pair of objects, one can ask whether that pair of objects stands in the given relation, for example, whether the pair (Sigourney Weaver, Michael Jackson) stands (stand?) in the relationship "is taller than" (i.e., whether Sigourney Weaver is taller than Michael Jackson) or whether the pair (Chomsky, Kissinger) stand/stands in the relationship "went to the same school as" (i.e., whether Chomsky went to the same school as did Kissinger). Ordinary English would dictate the use of the form *stand* rather than *stands* in the last sentence, that is, the verb is chosen to fit the plural *Sigourney Weaver and Michael Jackson* rather than to fit the singular *the pair*. However, it has become common among logicians and mathematicians to conceive of things in a way which would make the singular form more appropriate, that is, to think of a (two-place) relationship as identical with the set of pairs of objects that stand in that relationship, with the members of that set thus being (ordered) pairs such as (Weaver, Jackson) rather than individuals such as Weaver and Jackson.

Identifying a two-place relation with the set of pairs that it is true of is essentially the same thing as identifying a one-place predicate with the set of individuals that it is true of. In either case,[7] an element of meaning is being identified with the set of things that it is true of, its **extension,** to use a widely accepted term. While I do not actually believe that predicates can be identified with their extensions, in the remainder of this section I will speak as if they could, which will allow me to use simple locutions such as "the converse of a relation R" in place of more cumbersome locutions such as "the converse of a relation whose extension is R." In any event, it will be the extensions of predicates that will figure centrally in the discussion in chapter 6 of the truth conditions for complex propositions.

The extension of a two-place (or "binary") relation between members of a set A and members of a set B is thus a subset of the set of all pairs of a member of A and a member of B. The latter set, written AxB, is known as the **Cartesian product** of A and B:

5.4.1   a. $AxB = \{(a,b): \wedge (a\in A, b\in B)\}$, or more generally,
        b. $A_1 x A_2 x \ldots A_n = \{(a_1, a_2, \ldots, a_n): \wedge (a_1\in A_1, a_2\in A_2, \ldots,$
            $a_n\in A_n)\}$

Thus, if H is the set of all human beings and T is the set of all times, then the relation of human beings to the times at which they were born will have as its extension a subset of HxT.

Many of the notions in terms of which relations are often classified can be described in terms of properties of the extension of the relation. For example, a **partial ordering** on a set A is a two-place relation R such that:

5.4.2   a. R is a subset of AxA;
        b. (Antisymmetry) For all members a, b of A, if $(a,b)\in R$, then
            $(b,a)\notin R$; and
        c. (Transitivity) For all members a, b, c of A, if $(a,b)\in R$ and
            $(b,c)\in R$, then $(a,c)\in R$.

Extensions provide an easy way to define various derived and composite relations from given relations. The **converse** of a two-place relation R is a relation R^{-1} for which:

5.4.3 $R^{-1} = \{(a,b): (b,a)\in R\}$

If two two-place relations R and S are respectively subsets of AxB and BxC (i.e., the domain for the second place of R is the same as that for the first place of S), their **composition** is the relation R∘S is defined as follows:

5.4.4 $R\circ S = \{(a,c): (\exists x\in B)\wedge((a,x)\in R, (x,c)\in S)\}$

That is, two entities stand in the relation R∘S if they are "linked" by something to which the first element stands in the relation R and which stands in the relation S to the second element. Thus, if R is the relation "has insulted" and S is the relation "is a parent of," then $(a,b)\in R\circ S$ if and only if a has insulted one of b's parents.

A relation R between members of a set A is called an **equivalence relation** if it has the following properties:

5.4.5   a. ("Reflexive") $(\forall: x\in A) (x,x)\in R$
        b. ("Symmetric") $(\forall: x\in A)(\forall: y\in A) \supset((x,y)\in R, (y,x)\in R)$
        c. ("Transitive") $(\forall: x\in A)(\forall: y\in A)(\forall: z\in A) \supset(\wedge((x,y)\in R,$
            $(y,z)\in R), (x,z)\in R))$

The defining characteristics of an equivalence relation can be recast in an alternative form that makes use of the notions introduced earlier in this section.

For any set A, let I_A be the "identity relation" on A: the set of all pairs (a,a), for all elements a of A. Then 5.4.5 can be recast as:

5.4.6   a. ("Reflexive") $I_A \subseteq R$
         b. ("Symmetric") $R = R^{-1}$
         c. ("Transitive") $A \circ A \subseteq A$

The notions of operation and function can to a large extent be explained away in terms of the notion of relation. For example, the operation of addition of real numbers can be eliminated from an account of arithmetic if one instead talks in terms of the three-place relation "a and b add up to c." Using s to stand for that relation, one can replace $a + b = c$ by $s\,(a,b,c)$. The only respect in which that translation is questionable is that $a + b$ occurs in other contexts than as the left half of an equation. For example, it occurs in such formulas as

5.4.7 $a + (b + c) = (a + b) + c$
         $a + (b + c) > (a + b) + d$

It takes a bit of circumlocution to eliminate the $+$'s from 5.4.7 in favor of s's; specifically, it is necessary to bring in quantifiers, as in

5.4.8 $(\exists{:}s(b,c,x))_x(\exists{:}s(a,x,y))_y(\exists{:}s(a,b,z))_z(\exists{:}s(z,c,w))_w\ y = w$
         $(\exists{:}s(b,c,x))_x\exists{:}s(a,x,y))_y(\exists{:}s(a,b,z))_z(\exists{:}s(z,d,w))_w\ y > w$

While the formulas in 5.4.8 are in fact true under the same conditions as the corresponding formulas of 5.4.7, they have little more than that in common with them. In fact, formulas like 5.4.7 illustrate a respect in which the intuitive notion of an "operation" as something that is "performed on" **operands** and yields a **result** makes sense: "operations" can be iterated and complex formulas built up in which each of the constituents is not a proposition but an expression denoting an "object."

In any event, though, the extension of a two-place operation is the extension of the corresponding three-place relation, for example, the extension of the operation of multiplication is a complete multiplication table. There is no sharp distinction between the notions of "operation" and "function." "Function" is sometimes used as a more general term than "operation": an n-place function is anything which associates to a sequence of n operands a single value, that is, anything whose extension is a set of $(n + 1)$-tuples $(a_1, a_2, \ldots, a_n, b)$ such that for any choice $(a_1, \ldots, a_n)$ there is exactly one b such that $(a_1, \ldots, a_n, b)$ is in the set. One particularly well-known kind of function is that which provides a way of getting from the operands to the value by performing specific operations, for example, the function f defined by $f(x, y, z)$

$= x^2 + 2y^3 + 3z^4$ associates to any triple of numbers (x, y, z) the value obtained by squaring the first, cubing the second and multiplying the result by 2, and so on. The term "operation" is most commonly used for the functions corresponding to the elementary steps in such a computation: one speaks of an operation of addition and an operation of multiplication, though not of an operation of dividing the square of one number by the cube of a second number. To a certain extent, however, it is arbitrary what computational steps one takes as basic (as one can easily convince oneself by comparing some of the popular computer programming languages with each other), and it is to an equal extent arbitrary how one would distinguish operations from functions in general.

The operands and result of a function need not be numbers. For example, one can speak of a function "$PB(x)$" for which the operand is a person and the value is that person's place of birth, that is, the function which associates to each person his place of birth. A propositional function is also a function; for example, $(\exists: z \text{ Person})_z \wedge (x \text{ Parent } z, z \text{ Parent } y)$ is a propositional function which associates to each pair of objects the proposition that the one is a parent of a parent of the other, that is, is a grandparent of the other. A function thus need not be expressible as a sequence of arithmetic operations. Indeed, a function can be a completely arbitrary association of members of one set to members of the same or another set, as in the functions discussed in section 5.2, which associated to each state that belonged to the U.S.A. in 1945 one of the preludes of Bach's Well-tempered Clavier. There are in fact $48 \times 47 \times 46 \times \ldots \times 2 \times 1$ different functions which associate to each state a different prelude (i.e., functions which establish that there are as many states as there are preludes) and 48^{48} different functions which associate to each state a prelude, with no restriction against the same prelude being associated to different states; among those 48^{48} functions there is for example a function which associates to Kentucky the $C\#$ minor prelude of book two and to all other states the D major prelude of book one.

5.5. Ensembles

The set theory that we have developed so far in this section will play a central role in the semantics for predicate logic that will be presented in chapter 6: the denotations of one-place predicates such as "Linguist" will be sets of entities, and the denotations of two-place predicates such as "Admire" will be sets of pairs of entities. However, there is an important and ubiquitous class of predicates that cannot plausibly be treated as denoting sets, namely **mass predicates** such as are expressed by mass nouns (*water, blood, bread, furni-*

ture, poetry, . . .). This section will be devoted to elaborating a notion that is broader than that of set, namely the notion of what we will call **ensembles,** that will be of use in working out a semantics for mass predicates.

An ensemble (Bunt 1976, 1979, 1985) is an object that is structured around a part-whole relation that shares many properties with the subset relation among sets and which will indeed be written with the same symbol $\subseteq$ that is used for the subset relation. The subset relation was defined in terms of the membership relation $\in$: one set is a subset of an other if all its members are members of the other set. However, it will not be possible to define the part-whole relation among ensembles in terms of a membership relation, since ensembles need not even have anything analogous to members, and to the extent that one can speak of members of an ensemble, saying what members an ensemble has does not suffice in order to say what the ensemble consists of. The reason for this is that while a set is the union of its minimal parts (the one-member subsets of a set are its minimal parts, in the sense that a one-member set has no subsets other than itself and the empty set), an ensemble need not even have minimal parts and can be larger than the union of its minimal parts, if it has any. Accordingly, in ensemble theory, the part-whole relation $\subseteq$ is taken as a primitive notion, axioms are given for $\subseteq$ that repeat many familiar properties of the subset relation but do not require an ensemble to have minimal parts, let alone to be their union, and an analog to the notion of "membership" is introduced in conjunction with the notion of "minimal part." It is easy to construct an object that will satisfy Bunt's axioms for "ensemble" but which has no minimal parts. Suppose we take the "parts" of a line to be "half-open intervals": sets $[a, b)$ consisting of all real numbers x such that $a \le x < b$ (note that the left end point is included but the right end point is not) and unions of finitely many half-open intervals.[8] Clearly, none of these parts is minimal, since every half-open interval contains still smaller half-open intervals; note in particular that a one-member set $\{a\}$ is not a half-open interval and is thus not a part of the ensemble under discussion.

Bunt introduces the notion of membership in two stages. According to one of his axioms, for every "atomic" ensemble b, that is, every nonempty ensemble that has no parts other than itself and the empty ensemble, there is an entity a that is the "contents" of b, in the same sense in which an element c is the contents of the one-member set $\{c\}$. Bunt symbolizes the relation between the contents of an atomic ensemble and the ensemble with $\underline{\in}$: $a \underline{\in} b$, or equivalently with curly brackets: $b = \{a\}$. A member of an ensemble is the contents of one of the atomic parts of the ensemble, i.e., $a \in b$ if and only if there is an ensemble c such that $a \underline{\in} c$ and $c \subseteq b$, or equivalently, if and only if $\{a\} \subseteq b$. An ensemble can perfectly well have no members and still be nonempty, as was the case with the example above in which the parts of a line were taken to be unions of half-open intervals.

The notion of ensemble is set up in such a way as to provide for possible states of affairs in which, even if all rings are made of gold and all gold exists in the form of rings, something can still be gold without being a ring (e.g., half a ring would be gold but would not be a ring).[9] "Ring" will correspond to an ensemble R that is a union of minimal parts (i.e., R will in effect be the set of all rings) while "gold" will correspond to an ensemble G that does not have minimal parts. A given ring r will be a part of G but not a part of R, though $\{r\}$ will be a part of R:

5.5.1 $r \subseteq G$

             $\{r\} \subseteq R$

Even though, by assumption, all of the gold that comprises G makes up the rings that comprise R, G is not equal to R but is rather the **union** of R: the ensemble whose parts are parts of members of R or are "sums" of parts of members of R.[10] More generally, to every ensemble A there corresponds an ensemble ∪A, the union of A, which is the minimal ensemble that has among its parts all of the members of A. This takes in the special case of a union of two ensembles, E_1 and E_2: the union (which can be written $E_1 \cup E_2$, just as in the case of unions of sets) will be $\cup\{E_1, E_2\}$, where $\{E_1, E_2\}$ is the minimal ensemble having E_1 and E_2 as members. In the above example, each of the rings that are members of R will be a part of ∪R, and, since (by one of Bunt's axioms) the relation $\subseteq$ is transitive, each of the parts of each of the rings will be a part of ∪R; ∪R will in fact consist of all entities that are made up of parts of rings that belong to R, but since in the given state of affairs the gold is precisely what makes up the rings, the parts of ∪R will be precisely the entities that are made up of gold, i.e., $\cup R = G$.

Bunt's axioms likewise provide for intersections of ensembles: the minimal ensemble that contains all common parts of the given ensembles. Another analog to a set operation that Bunt's axioms provide for is a **difference** $E_1 - E_2$ between two ensembles E_1 and E_2: a maximal part of E_1 whose intersection with E_2 is empty.

Another of Bunt's axioms extends to ensembles the device that we have for picking out from a set the subset defined by a given predicate, as in expressions such as $\{x: \wedge(x \in M, P(x))\}$, or, to replace that notation with one that separates out the role of M as the set from which the condition "P(x)" is allowed to select members, $\{x: P(x)\}_{x \in M}$. He gives an axiom according to which, for every ensemble E and every predicate P that includes all parts of E in its domain, there is an ensemble $\{x: P(x)\}_{x \subseteq E}$ that (i) has among its parts all of the parts of E that have the property P and (ii) is minimal: it is contained in every ensemble that contains all parts of E that have the property P. One important difference between "set descriptions" such as $\{x: P(x)\}_{x \in M}$ and "ensemble descriptions" such as $\{x: P(x)\}_{x \subseteq E}$ should be noted: since the former operates in terms of $\in$ while the latter operates in terms of $\subseteq$, all members of $\{x: P(x)\}_{x \in M}$ have the property P, but there may well be parts of $\{x: P(x)\}_{x \subseteq E}$ that do not have the property P: $\{x: P(x)\}_{x \subseteq E}$ has among its parts not only all of the parts of E that have the property P, but also all unions of those parts, and if P is a property that two ensembles can have without their union having it (that is, if P is not what we will eventually call a "cumulative" property), then $\{x: P(x)\}_{x \subseteq E}$ may have parts that do not have the property P. For example, the property "weighs less than one gram" is not a cumulative property (two entities can each weigh less than a gram while their union weighs more than one gram), and if one uses that property in the role of P one will usually thereby define an ensemble having parts that do not have the property P. The most obvious alternatives to Bunt's treatment of $\{x: P(x)\}_{x \subseteq E}$ are unsatisfactory. If one took $\{x: P(x)\}_{x \subseteq E}$ to be an entity whose parts were precisely the parts of E that have the property P, the result would not necessarily be an ensemble, because the union of two parts of E having the property P need not itself have it, and if one took it to be a maximal part of E whose parts all have the property P, one would not define a unique entity, since there can be more than one maximal part of E whose parts all have the property P (for example, if P were "weighs no more than one gram," then all of the one-gram parts of E would be maximal parts of E that have the property P). I will accordingly stick with Bunt's treatment of $\{x: P(x)\}_{x \subseteq E}$.

5.6. Valuations

In our informal discussion of "states of affairs" in section 4.2, I took the significant differences among states of affairs to be differences in what propositions were true in each state of affairs. The state of affairs can then for all practical purposes be identified with a specification of what propositions are true and what ones false in that state of affairs. We can thus identify a state of affairs with a function that associates to each proposition a truth value. The term **valuation** is commonly used for such a function: given a "formal language" L, a valuation on L is a function which associates to each proposition of L a value T or F. The discussion in 4.2 made clear that not all valuations are equally worthy of consideration. If one is to develop a coherent notion of state of affairs, it will be necessary to exclude such absurd assignments of truth values as the one in which all propositions are assigned the value "true," or the one in which "God is dead and Cincinnati is in Mongolia" is assigned the value T and all other propositions (including the proposition that God is dead) the value F.

The most widely discussed restricted class of valuations is the **classical** valuations: those valuations which assign to complex propositions values that are predictable by the classical truth tables from the values that they assign to the constituents of those propositions (e.g., if v is a classical valuation and $v(p) = $ F, then $v(\sim p)$ must be T). In 4.2 we considered a somewhat broader set of valuations than the classical valuations, namely, the valuations that conformed to the rules of inference of chapter 3, in the sense that if a set of propositions are true according to the given valuation, then anything deducible from them by the given rules of inference will also be assigned the value T by the given valuation.

This notion of valuations conforming to a system of rules of inference can be generalized so as to be applicable with regard to any system of rules of inference. Specifically, suppose that for any formal language L and any system R of rules of inference, we define V(L, R) as consisting of those valuations f with respect to which R leads from true premises to true conclusions, that is, $f \in$ V(L, R) if and only if for all $A_1, \ldots, A_n, B \in$ L, if $f(A_1) = \ldots = f(A_n) = $ T and B is provable from $A_1, \ldots, A_n$ by the rules of R, then $f(B) = $ T. In 4.2 we proved that if L is a language of propositional logic and R is the rules of inference of chapter 3, then the set of all classical valuations on L is a proper subset of V(L, R): V(L, R) contains all classical valuations, but it also contains nonclassical valuations, in which there are cases where a proposition and its negation are both assigned the value F.

By referring to V(L, R), we can make sense out of a perplexing problem posed by Prior (1960). Prior, objecting to the common practise of speaking of the logical connectives as being "defined by" their rules of inference, pointed out that if we allow connectives to be defined by any imaginable rules of inference, there is nothing to prevent us from defining a connective *tonk* as that connective which obeys the rules

Tonk-introduction: A
                         A *tonk* B

Tonk-exploitation: A *tonk* B
                         B

Of course, these rules would allow any proposition to be inferred from any proposition at all; for arbitrary propositions A and B, the proof would be:

1	A	supp
2	A *tonk* B	1, *tonk*-intro
3	B	2, *tonk*-expl

Consider, now, V(L, R), where R includes the two rules for *tonk*. V(L, R) would contain at most two valuations: that which assigns to every proposition the value T and that which assigns to every proposition the value F. (Proof: suppose a valuation f does not assign all propositions the same value, say, $f(A) = T$, $f(B) = F$; B is inferrable from A by R; therefore $f \notin$ V(L, R), since f does not assign T to all propositions that are inferrable from propositions to which it assigns T). While there is nothing to prevent one from defining *tonk* as above, a system of rules of inference that contained the rules for *tonk* would allow only an extremely narrow and uninteresting set of valuations. Therefore, including *tonk* in a formal language and rules of inference would defeat the logician's purposes.

5.7 Proof by Induction

There is an important principle, ostensibly a principle of arithmetic, but in fact of much greater applicability, which will figure in some proofs to be given in later chapters. Since this principle is commonly formulated in terms of sets of numbers, this chapter is as good a place as any to include a brief discussion of it.

The **principle of mathematical induction** is one of the axioms that Peano formulated in his attempt to derive all of arithmetic from a conceptual minimum. Peano's axioms involve two positive notions: "1" and "successor." The successor of a particular positive whole number (or **natural number,** to use the terminology generally employed in this context) is the next higher natural number, for example, the successor of 3 is 4, and the successor of 794 is 795. Using S to stand for "successor," natural numbers greater than 1 can be given definitions such as "2 = S1," "3 = SS1" (i.e. S(S(1))), and so on. Among Peano's axioms was one which asserted that the natural numbers were precisely those things that could be constructed from "1" by iteration of S: if a set contains 1, and if for every element n that it contains, it also contains Sn, then it contains all of the natural numbers. This formulation is equivalent to the following, perhaps more familiar, formulation of the principle of mathematical induction:

> For any property $f(x)$, if $f(1)$ is true and if whenever $f(n)$ is true, $f(n + 1)$ is also true, then $f(x)$ is true of all natural numbers.

The latter formulation follows from Peano's since it is what you get when you apply Peano's formulation to the set $\{x: f(x)\}$; for example, to say that $f(1)$ is true is simply to say that 1 belongs to $\{x: f(x)\}$.

The following proof illustrates the way in which the principle of induction can be used in proving theorems of arithmetic:

Theorem. For any natural number n,

$$1 + 2 + \ldots + n = \frac{n(n + 1)}{2}$$

Proof. Let $f(x)$ be the proposition that the sum of the first x natural numbers is $x(x + 1)/2$. Since the sum of the first 1 natural numbers is 1, and $1(1 + 1)/2 = 1$, $f(1)$ is true. Suppose that $f(n)$ is true for some natural number n, that is, that for that particular number, $1 + 2 + \ldots + n = n(n + 1)/2$. We can find the sum of the first $n + 1$ natural numbers by adding $n + 1$ to both sides of this equation:

$$1 + 2 + \ldots + n + (n + 1) = \frac{n(n + 1)}{2} + (n + 1)$$

$$= \left(\frac{n}{2} + 1\right)(n + 1)$$

$$= \frac{n + 2}{2}(n + 1)$$

$$= \frac{(n + 1)[(n + 1) + 1]}{2}$$

But this shows that when $f(n)$ is true, $f(n + 1)$ is also true. Consequently, by the induction principle, $f(x)$ is true for all natural numbers x.

The following alternative formulation of the induction principle is equivalent to the two already given:

> If $f(1)$ is true, and for every natural number n, if all natural numbers less than n have the property f, n has it also, then $f(x)$ is true of all natural numbers.[11]

This version of the induction principle can be illustrated by the following proof.

Theorem. Every natural number is a product of prime numbers.

Proof. "Product of prime numbers" is here taken in the broad sense which allows the degenerate case in which there are no factors (i.e., $1 = 2^0$) and that in which there is only one factor (e.g., $3 = 3^1$). Suppose that every natural number less than n is a product of prime numbers. Three cases must be distinguished: (i) $n = 1$; in this case, n is a (degenerate) product of primes: $n = 2^0$; (ii) n is a prime number; in this case, n is also a (degenerate) product of primes: $n = n^1$; and (iii) n is a composite number; that is, $n = ab$, where a an b are natural numbers less than n. By the inductive hypothesis, both a and b are products of prime numbers: $a = p_1 p_2 \ldots p_i$, $b = p'_1 p'_2 \ldots p'_j$. Then n is also a product of primes: $n = ab = p_1 p_2 \ldots p_i p'_1 p'_2 \ldots p'_j$. Thus, by the induction principle, every natural number is a product of primes.

The reason that the induction principle can play a role outside of arithmetic is that nonarithmetic objects (e.g., formulas of predicate logic) allow numerical measures of "size" or "complexity": you can compare formulas as regards how many symbols long they are, or compare trees as regards how "deep" they go (where the "depth" of a node might be taken to be the number of S-nodes that one encounters in tracing from that node up to the top of the tree). It is then possible to reinterpret a statement "all formulas of predicate logic are such that . . ." as "for every natural number n, all formulas of predicate logic which are of length n are such that . . ." or "for every natural number n, all formulas of predicate logic in which Ss are embedded to at most a depth of n are such that . . .". The reinterpreted statement will be amenable to an inductive proof if it is possible to "reduce" behaviour of complex formulas to that of simpler formulas, for example, to show that if the immediate constituents of a formula have a certain property, then the whole formula will have it also.

Let us illustrate this by making explicit a proof that was sketched informally in chapter 4: the proof that a formula constructed by $\vee_e$-conjoining propositions two at a time is true if an odd number of the ultimate conjuncts are true and is false if an even number of them are true. If $f(n)$ is the proposition that all $\vee_e$-conjunctions of n ultimate conjuncts have that property, then $f(1)$ is true in the sense that "the $\vee_e$-conjunction of one proposition" can be interpreted as that proposition, and a proposition A is true if and only if an odd number of members of the set {A} are true. Suppose that for some number n, every iterated two-term $\vee_e$-conjunction with less than n ultimate conjuncts is true if and only if an odd number of its ultimate conjuncts are true. Take any iterated two-term $\vee_e$-conjunction $\vee_e AB$ which also has n ultimate conjuncts. Call m the number of ultimate conjuncts in A, in which case $n - m$ will be the number of ultimate conjuncts in B. Both m and $n - m$ are less than *n*. Thus, by the inductive hypothesis, A is true if and only if an odd number of its ultimate conjuncts are true, and B is true if and only if an odd number of **its** ultimate conjuncts are true. From the truth table for $\vee_e$, we know that $\vee_e AB$ is true if A is true and B false, or if A is false and B true, and is false otherwise. The sum of two natural numbers is odd if and only if one of them is odd and the other is even. Thus the number of true ultimate conjuncts in $\vee_e AB$ will be odd if and only if either the number of true ultimate conjuncts in A is odd and the number in B is even, or the number in A is even and the number in B is odd. By the inductive hypothesis, this will be the case if and only if either A is true and B false or A is false and B true. But we know that that will be the case if and only if $\vee_e AB$ is true. Thus $\vee_e AB$ is true if and only if an odd number of its ultimate conjuncts are true. The induction principle thus allows us to conclude that **any** iterated two-term $\vee_e$-conjunction will be true if and only if an odd number of its ultimate conjuncts are true.

For a final illustration of the principle of induction, let us prove the claim made in 3.1 that parentheses are in fact superfluous in so-called Polish parenthesis-free notation, that is, if $\wedge$ and $\vee$ are only allowed to conjoin things two at a time and all connectives are written before the items that they combine with, then the sequence of terminal symbols in a formula uniquely determines the constituent structure of the formula. Let us use the term "Polish formula" for any sequence of connectives and atomic proposition symbols without parentheses that corresponds to a logical structure conforming to rules 3.1.15 in which each occurrence of $\wedge$ or $\vee$ has exactly two conjuncts. We need to show that for every positive integer *n*, every Polish formula of length *n* has only one syntactic analysis that conforms to the rules of 3.1.15. That is trivially the case for Polish formulas of length 1: a Polish formula of length 1 can only be an atomic proposition symbol, and the formula can only be analyzed as a S consisting of that one symbol. Suppose that Polish formulas of length less than *n* never have more than one syntactic analysis. A Polish formula of length > 1 must contain a subformula of the form $\wedge pq$, $\vee pq$, $\supset pq$, or $\sim p$, with *p* and *q* atomic, since otherwise it would never come to an end. Let φ be a Polish formula of length $n > 1$, and let φ' be the formula obtained from φ by replacing a subformula of the form $\wedge pq$, $\vee pq$, $\supset pq$, or $\sim p$ by an atomic proposition *r*. Then φ' is of length $n - 1$ or $n - 2$ (depending on whether *r*, which is of length 1, replaces something of length 2 or of length 3) and thus, by the inductive hypothesis, φ' has only one syntactic analysis, and φ has only the analysis that one obtains by replacing *r* by (as appropriate) $\wedge pq$, $\vee pq$, $\supset pq$, or $\sim p$ in the unique analysis of φ': it can have no other syntactic analysis, since the subformula that *r* replaces would have to be a constituent in an syntactic analysis of φ (note that this is where the assumption that connectives precede what they are combined with is used: in a Polish formula ... $\lor pq$ ..., p and q would have to be the conjuncts that the $\lor$ is combined with, whereas in an "Italian" formula ... $p \lor q$ ..., either the p or the q could be part of a larger expression that was combined with the $\lor$) and since, by the inductive hypothesis, there can be only one syntactic analysis for the formula in which that subformula is embedded. Thus, by the principle of induction, for every positive integer n, every Polish formula of length n has only one syntactic analysis, that is, every Polish formula (of whatever length) has only one syntactic analysis.

Exercises

1. Let A be the set of all nouns listed in *Webster's Third International,* let B be the set of all three-syllable words that it lists, and let C be the set of all Greek-derived words that it lists.
    a. Is *oligarchy* a member of A ∩ B? A ∩ C? C − B?
    b. Is *persecute* a member of B − A? B ∩ C? B − (A ∪ C)?
2. For each of the following, decide whether it is true and say why:

    a. Ø ⊆ Ø.
    b. Ø ∈ Ø.
    c. q ∈{A: p, ⊃pq ⊢ A}.
    d. {A: p ⊢ A} ∩ {B: q ⊢ B} = Ø.

3. For each of the following words, determine whether the relation is denotes is reflexive, whether it is symmetric, and whether it is transitive, giving reasons for each part of your answer:

    a. brother (of)   d. adjacent (to)
    b. perpendicular (to)   e. approximately equal (to)
    c. far (from)

4. Show that
    a. For any binary relation R, R∘R^{-1} is symmetric.
    b. For any three binary relations, R, S, and T, R∘(S∘T) = (R∘S)∘T.
    c. For any two binary relations R and S, (R∘S)$^{-1}$ = S^{-1}∘R^{-1}.
5. Suppose that v and w are classical valuations. For each of the following functions, determine whether it will necessarily also be a classical valuation.

    a. The function f such that $f(A) = T$ if $v(A) = F$.
$$f(A) = F \text{ if } v(A) = T.$$

b. The function f such that $f(A) = T$ if either $v(A) = T$ or $w(A) = T$.
$$f(A) = F \text{ otherwise.}$$

c. The function f such that $f(\vee A_1 \ldots A_n) = v(A_1)$
$$f(\wedge A_1 \ldots A_n) = w(A_n)$$
$$f(A) = F \text{ if A is not an } \vee\text{-conjunction or an}$$
$\wedge$-conjunction.

6. Using the principle of mathematical induction, prove that a structure conforming to the formation rules of chapter 2 that contains n quantifiers must contain at least $2n + 1$ Ss.

6.   Predicate Logic II: Semantics

6.1 Truth in Predicate Logic

In propositional logic it was possible to get by with a very rudimentary notion of "state of affairs": a state of affairs could be taken to be just an assignment of truth values to the propositions expressible in the given system, subject to the restrictions imposed by the system of rules of inference (e.g., if A and B are T, then $\wedge$AB must be T also, since otherwise the rules of inference could draw a false conclusion from true premises). If the assumption is made that the connectives are truth-functional, then an even more rudimentary notion of state of affairs is possible: a state of affairs is any assignment of truth values to the **atomic** propositions of the system, with the truth values of the nonatomic propositions being predictable from those of the atomic propositions in accordance with the standard truth tables.

In predicate logic, it will be necessary to use a more involved notion of state of affairs. States of affairs can differ not only with regard to what propositions are true but also with regard to what objects exist. For example, the truth of the proposition that some Italians are bald will depend on whether there are bald Italians, and states of affairs can differ with regard to what individuals exist and what their properties are.

Let us assume that $\forall$ and $\exists$ are truth-functional, in the sense that the truth values of $(\forall: Fx)Gx$ and of $(\exists: Fx)Gx$ are predictable from information as to what objects Fx and Gx are true of, and also that the propositional connectives are truth-functional, and consider the question of what the closest analog in predicate logic is to the rudimentary notion of state of affairs in propositional logic that we considered above. In any state of affairs, the atomic propositions will be the propositions consisting of predicates predicated of specific things. But what specific things? To even say what atomic propositions can play a role in a given state of affairs, it is necessary to know what things there are in that state of affairs for the predicates to be predicated of. I thus provisionally take

162

one essential part of a state of affairs α to be a **domain:** the set D^α of objects which play a role in that state of affairs. The domain will be a set, possibly finite, possibly infinite.

In any given state of affairs, each element of nonlogical vocabulary (that is, each constant or predicate) will have a **denotation.** It will be convenient to indicate the denotation of an element by combining that element with a superscript, e.g., a^α will indicate the denotation of the constant a in the state of affairs α and f^α will indicate the denotation of the predicate f in that state of affairs. The denotation of an individual constant will be a member of the domain.[1] The denotation of a one-place predicate will be the **extension** of that predicate, i.e., the set of objects that have the property that it corresponds to. Thus, the denotation of a one-place predicate will be a subset of D^α. The denotation of a two-place predicate will be the set of pairs of objects that stand in the relation that the predicate corresponds to, which is to say that it will be a subset of $D^\alpha \times D^\alpha$. For example, suppose we have the one-place predicates p "is an Italian," q "is fat," and r "is a Greek," the two-place predicate s "distrusts," and the individual constant c "Carlo Genovese." A grossly simplified picture of a state of affairs α might take the following form:

6.1.1
$$D^\alpha = \{a_1, a_2, a_3, a_4, a_5\}$$
$$c^\alpha = a_1 \qquad\qquad q^\alpha = \{a_1, a_3, a_5\}$$
$$p^\alpha = \{a_1, a_2, a_3\} \qquad r^\alpha = \{a_4, a_5\}$$
$$s^\alpha = \{(a_1, a_1), (a_1, a_3), (a_1, a_5), (a_2, a_4), (a_2, a_5), (a_3, a_1),$$
$$(a_3, a_4), (a_3, a_5), (a_4, a_1), (a_4, a_2), (a_4, a_3), (a_5, a_1),$$
$$(a_5, a_2), (a_5, a_4), (a_5, a_5)\}$$

The information about the denotations of p, q, r, s given in 6.1.1 could alternatively be given in the form 6.1.2, in which the truth values of the relevant atomic propositions (e.g., the proposition that a_1 is an Italian, the proposition that a_1 distrusts a_1, etc.) serve to specify which individuals in D^α have the properties expressed by p, q, r, and which pairs of individuals have the property expressed by s:

6.1.2

	p	q	r
a_1	T	T	F
a_2	T	F	F
a_3	T	T	F
a_4	F	F	T
a_5	F	T	T

s first argument	second argument				
	a_1	a_2	a_3	a_4	a_5
a_1	T	F	T	F	T
a_2	F	F	F	T	T
a_3	T	F	F	T	T
a_4	T	T	T	F	F
a_5	T	T	F	T	T

The information given in 6.1.1 has to be supplemented by something before we can use it to determine the truth value in α of 6.1.3, which corresponds to the sentence *Some Italian is fat and distrusts all Greeks:*

6.1.3 $(\exists: px) \wedge(qx, (\forall: ry)sxy)$

It is easy enough to propose truth conditions for $\forall$ and $\exists$, e.g., we could propose that $(\forall: Fx)Gx$ is true in those states of affairs in which the denotation of Fx is a subset of the denotation of Gx, and that $(\exists: Fx)Gx$ is true in those states of affairs in which the denotation of Fx contains at least one member of the denotation of Gx. However, that is not enough, since Fx and Gx could be complex expressions, possibly containing several variables other than x, and we have not yet said what the denotation of such a thing is. Furthermore, even if F is an atomic predicate, we have so far assigned denotations only to predicates themselves and not to open sentences such as Fx, in which the predicate is combined with a variable. If we are going to use anything like the truth-conditions for $\forall$ and $\exists$ that were just suggested, we will have to provide a procedure for assigning denotations to open sentences, whereby we determine the denotation of each open sentence from the denotations of its parts. Moreover, since combinations of the same predicate with different variables can affect the truth value of a sentence (e.g., if sxy were replaced by syx in 6.1.3, the resulting formula would correspond to *Some Italian is fat and is distrusted by all Greeks* and could well have a different truth value from the original formula), such a procedure would have to give an appropriate role to the variable(s) with which each predicate is combined.

It will be convenient for me to give such a procedure in terms of **assignments** of values to variables. Let us introduce the notation $(a/x \; b/y \; c/z \ldots)$ to represent the assignment of a as value for x, b as value for y, c as value for z, etc. (Note that the order of the terms in such an expression is immaterial—all that matters is which value goes with each variable; thus $(a/x \; b/y)$ and $(b/y \; a/x)$ are merely two ways of writing the same assignment of values to x and y.) An assignment of values to variables will be said to **satisfy** an open sentence if the open sentence becomes a true proposition when the variables are given those values. For example, $(a_1/x \; a_3/y)$ satisfies sxy in the given state of affairs. It is a reasonably easy matter to give rules saying what assignments of values to variables satisfy each of the different kinds of open sentence that one can construct out of simpler open sentences. For example, if $x_1, \ldots, x_n$ are all the free variables that occur in an open sentence A, then $(a_1/x_1 \ldots a_n/x_n)$ satisfies $\sim$A if and only if it does not satisfy A.[2] We can likewise say that an assignment $(a_1/x_1 \ldots a_n/x_n)$ satisfies $\wedge$AB if and only if it both satisfies A and satisfies B, but only if we make a stipulation about a possibility that we have not considered before. It would be nice to be able to say that (Chomsky/x Cher/y) satisfies $\wedge(x$ Linguist, y Actress), but the rule given in the last sentence does not allow us to draw that conclusion from the fact that (Chomsky/x) satisfies the first conjunct and (Cher/y) satisfies the second conjunct: each of those assignments satisfies only one of the two conjuncts. What we need to do is allow extraneous variables to be included in assignments but ignored in determining whether the assignment satisfies a given open sentence. For example, we need to be able to say that not only (Chomsky/x) but also (Chomsky/x Cher/y) satisfies (x Linguist). With that stipulation, we can then say that (Chomsky/x Cher/y) satisfies both conjuncts of $\wedge(x$ Linguist, y Actress) and thus that it satisfies the conjoined sentence as a whole.

We can then give the following rules for satisfaction of quantified formulas by assignments of values to variables:

6.1.4   If $x_1, x_2, \ldots,$ and x_n include all the variables other than x that are free in one or both of the expressions A and B, then

a. $(a_1/x_1\ a_2/x_2 \ldots a_n/x_n)$ satisfies $(\forall: A)_x B$ in α if and only if for every $a \in D^\alpha$ for which $(a/x\ a_1/x_1\ a_2/x_2 \ldots a_n/x_n)$ satisfies A, $(a/x\ a_1/x_1\ a_2/x_2 \ldots a_n/x_n)$ also satisfies B;

b. $(a_1/x_1\ a_2/x_2 \ldots a_n/x_n)$ satisfies $(\exists: A)_x B$ in α if and only if for at least one $a \in D^\alpha$ for which $(a/x\ a_1/x_1\ a_2/x_2 \ldots a_n/x_n)$ satisfies A, $(a/x\ a_1/x_1\ a_2/x_2 \ldots a_n/x_n)$ also satisfies B.

This says which assignments of values to variables satisfy a formula in a given state of affairs, but it does not tell us when a formula is just plain true or just plain false in that state of affairs. However, there is a fairly straightforward way in which the satisfaction conditions of 6.1.4 can be interpreted as providing truth conditions. If x is the only variable that appears free in A or in B, we would presumably want to say that $(\forall: A)_x B$ was true if every assignment (a/x) that satisfies A also satisfies B. But according to 6.1.4a, if every assignment (a/x) that satisfies A also satisfies B, then $(\forall: A)_x B$ is satisfied by the assignment $()$ in which no value is assigned to any variable, since that is the assignment that is identical to (a/x) except for not assigning a value to x. Suppose that we in fact admit this "empty" assignment, in which no value is assigned to any variable, and say that a formula is true if it is satisfied by the empty assignment. We have then extended 6.1.4 to cover the case of $n = 0$ (that is, the case in which A and B contain no free variables other than x), and we have done it in such a way that satisfaction by the empty assignment occurs under the conditions under which we would want to take a quantified proposition to be just plain true. Moreover, overlooking the mathematicianly cute sound of the expression "empty assignment of values to variables," invoking such an idea in this case is quite plausible: it amounts to saying that a formula is true if it is satisfied without regard to assignments of values to variables.

Let us accordingly adopt the policy that:

6.1.5   a. A formula A is true in a given state of affairs α if the empty assignment of values to variables satisfies A in α.
       b. A formula A is false in a given state of affairs α if the empty assignment of values to variables satisfies $\sim$A in α.

Note that according to these rules, only a formula that contains no free variables can be true: if a formula A contains a free variable z, then only assignments that include a value for z can satisfy A, which implies that the empty assignment does not satisfy A. (In that case, the empty assignment does not satisfy $\sim$A either, since a formula and its negation have the same free variables). Thus, while a formula such as $\vee(Gxy, \sim Gxy)$ will be true relative to (i.e., satisfied by) every assignment that assigns values to its variables, it will not be true (nor false) simpliciter.[3]

Let us see what assignments of values to variables satisfy the various Ss contained in 6.1.3. From 6.1.2 we can read off that the simple propositional functions in 6.1.3 are satisfied by the following assignments of values to variables:

6.1.6 px is satisfied by (a_1/x), (a_2/x), and (a_3/x).
         qx is satisfied by (a_1/x), (a_3/x), and $a_5/x)$.
         ry is satisfied by (a_4/y) and (a_5/y).
         sxy is satisfied by $(a_1/x\ a_1/y)$, $(a_1/x\ a_3/y)$, $(a_1/x\ a_5/y)$, $(a_2/x\ a_4/y)$,
            $(a_2/x\ a_5/y)$, $(a_3/x\ a_1/y)$, $(a_3/x\ a_4/y)$, $(a_3/x\ a_5/y)$, $(a_4/x\ a_1/y)$,
            $(a_4/x\ a_2/y)$, $(a_4/x\ a_3/y)$, $(a_5/x\ a_1/y)$, $(a_5/x\ a_2/y)$, $(a_5/x\ a_4/y)$, and
            $(a_5/x\ a_5/y)$.

Then $(\forall: ry)sxy$ is satisfied by (a_2/x), (a_3/x), and (a_5/x), since those are the values for x that, when combined both with (a_4/y) and (a_5/y) yield assignments that satisfy sxy. Since qx is satisfied only by the second and third of those assignments, $\wedge(qx, (\forall: ry)sxy)$ is satisfied precisely by (a_3/x), and (a_5/x). Since the assignments that satisfy px include one, namely (a_3/x) that is on this list, 6.1.4 is satisfied by the empty assignment (), i.e., it is true.

While the tables in 6.1.2 have a visual resemblance to truth tables, the whole of 6.1.2 is in fact more analogous to a line of a truth table. Each of the entries in 6.1.2 represents part of the same state of affairs. By contrast, each line of a truth table represents a different state of affairs. In 6.1.2 we have one line for each element of the domain, whereas in a truth table, each line corresponds to a different combination of truth values for the constituent propositions. The truth conditions for the logical elements peculiar to predicate logic, that is, the quantifiers, do not lend themselves to presentation in tabular form. One could, of course, make up such tables for special cases in which there are a fixed finite number of elements in the domain, for example,

6.1.7	Fa_1	Fa_2	Ga_1	Ga_2	$(\forall{:}Fx)Gx$	$(\exists{:}Fx)Gx$
	T	T	T	T	T	T
	T	T	T	F	F	T
	T	T	F	T	F	T
	T	T	F	F	F	F
	F	T	T	T	T	T
	F	T	T	F	F	F
	F	T	F	T	T	T
	F	T	F	F	F	F
	T	F	T	T	T	T
	T	F	T	F	T	T
	T	F	F	T	F	F
	T	F	F	F	F	F
	F	F	T	T	(T)	F
	F	F	T	F	(T)	F
	F	F	F	T	(T)	F
	F	F	F	F	(T)	F

The 16 lines of this table correspond to the possible combinations of truth values of two predicates in a two-element domain. The truth values in the last four lines of the column for the universal proposition are parenthesized so as to single them out for special consideration. Those four lines correspond to the case in which nothing has the property F; there is some controversy as to what truth value should be assigned to "All Fs are G" when there are no Fs, and the parenthesized truth values correspond to the popular policy of taking universal propositions with empty domains to be "vacuously true." The notion of "vacuous truth" will be taken up in 6.3.

6.2. Predicate Logic with Identity

So far I have left completely open the question of what predicates appear in a system of predicate logic. I will now change this policy to the extent of assuming that a predicate of **identity** (written =) will always be included in the inventory of predicates. The notational conventions that I have adopted so far regarding predicates will apply to $=$; thus, I will write the expression saying that x is identical to y in the form "$x = y$" in contexts in which the constituents of logical formulas are written in an order that roughly matches English word order (cf. the English sentence X *equals* y), but in the form "$=xy$" in contexts in which predicates are otherwise being written to the left of all their arguments.

While identity is such a special notion that doubts might be raised as to whether it is appropriate to lump it together with other predicates such as "is an uncle of" or "is a divisor of," it is at least clear that it behaves like other two-place predicates with regard to the formation rules: anywhere that a coherent formula contains pxy, it could contain $=xy$ instead and be just as well formed a formula of predicate logic.

Following Thomason 1970, I will assume that there are two rules of inference relating to identity: a rule of $=$-introduction and one of $=$-exploitation. The rule of $=$-introduction allows a step $=aa$ to appear at any point in a proof, where a can be any (constant or variable) element symbol. Thus, if the system involves an individual constant symbol c, one can construct the following trivial proofs:

6.2.1   a. 1 fc _____   supp   b. 1 fc _____   supp
           2 $=cc$ $=$-intro   2 $=cc$ $=$-intro
           3 $(\exists: fx) =xc$ 2, 1, $\exists$-intro   3 $(\exists: fx) =xx$ 2, 1, $\exists$-intro

The rule of $=$-exploitation allows one to substitute one side of an equation for the other. More specifically, $=$-exploitation allows inferences of the form

6.2.1 $=xy$
           A
           B

where B is a formula obtained from A by substituting y for one or more occurrences of x. Note that it is not necessary to replace **all** occurrences of the one symbol by the other: from $=xy$ and Fxx you can infer Fyx, Fxy, or Fyy.

These two rules of inference insure that identity will have the familiar properties of being **reflexive, symmetric,** and **transitive:**

6.2.3   a. (reflexive law)   b. (symmetric law)
               1 $= uu$ $=$-intro   1 │ $= uv$ _____   supp

                                              2 │ $= uu$ $=$-intro
                                              3 │ $= vu$ 1, 2, $=$-expl
                                              4 $\supset(= uv, = vu)$ 1–3, $\supset$-intro

c. (transitive law)

1	$\wedge (= uv, = vw)$		supp
2		$= uv$	1, $\wedge$-expl
3		$= vw$	1, $\wedge$-expl
4		$= uw$	3, 2, $=$-expl
5	$\supset(\wedge(= uv, = vw), = uw)$		1–4, $\supset$-intro

Identity plays a role in the analysis of many semantically complex words. For example, *other, else,* and one sense of *but* can be treated as manifestations of clauses containing $\sim$ and $=$:

6.2.4   a. All philosophers other than Spinoza arouse Bill's suspicion.
         ($\forall$: $\wedge$(Phil x, $\sim=xs$))(x arouses b's suspicion)
     b. [John was sure he'd be hired, but] someone else got the job.
         ($\exists$: $\wedge$(Person x, $\sim=xj$))(x got the job)
     c. No one but Agnes is qualified.
         $\sim$($\exists$: $\wedge$(Person x, $\sim=xa$))(x is qualified)

Note that *else* incorporates not only $\sim$ and $=$ but also a referential index: it can be paraphrased as "other than him/her/it/them/ ...".

The semantics for $=$ is fairly trivial, except that we must be careful to distinguish between constants and variables:

6.2.5   a. If a and b are constants, then $(=ab)^\alpha$ is T if $a^\alpha = b^\alpha$ and is F if $a^\alpha \neq b^\alpha$.
     b. If a is a constant and x is a variable, then an assignment of values to variables satisfies $=xa$ (likewise, $=ax$) if $a^\alpha =$ the value that is assigned to x, and does not satisfy it if a^α is not the value that is assigned to x.
     c. If x and y are variables, then an assignment of values to variables satisfies $=xy$ if the value assigned to $x =$ the value assigned to y, and does not satisfy it if the value assigned to $x \neq$ the value assigned to y.

6.3 Vacuous Truth and Pragmatic Restrictions of Domains

Many cases arise in which a sentence is interpreted as if its bound variables had much more restricted domains than the overt form of the sentence seems to call for. Consider, for example, the interpretation of the word *always* in 6.3.1:

6.3.1   John has always loved Mary.

Always embodies a universally quantified time variable, and the present perfect restricts the time reference of the verb to an interval extending from the past up to the present. In a fairly straightforward way we can set up 6.3.2 as a logical structure that directly represents these observations:

6.3.2 $(\forall: \wedge(\text{Time } t, t \leq n))\text{Love}(j,m,t)$

Here, n is used as an ad hoc device to represent "now" and "Love" is treated as a three-place predicate, with the time serving as its third argument. According to a literal interpretation of 6.3.2, it would imply not only that John loved Mary two years ago, but also that he loved her twenty years ago (which might be before he had met her), that he loved her two thousand years ago (which would be before either of them existed), and that he loved her two trillion years ago (which would be before even the matter that makes up their bodies existed). However, 6.3.1 is normally interpreted as implying that John loved Mary only for a much narrower range of times, say, all times since he met her, or all times since he got to know her. The restriction on the values of t in this case is to values for which the question of John loving Mary arises: under normal assumptions, a person can love only persons with whom he is acquainted.

The truth conditions for $\forall$ given in 6.1 make a universally quantified proposition true when the domain of its bound variable is empty, e.g., the nonexistence of unicorns will be sufficient to make *Any unicorn drinks champagne* true. The term **vacuous truth** is often used to mean truth in virtue of emptiness of a domain. In deciding whether to accept truth conditions that commit one to allowing for vacuous truth, it will be necessary to survey the possible accounts of sentences containing constituents for which the possibility of vacuous truth arises. Let us start by comparing the following two sentences:

6.3.3   a. Any person who loves all of his children is saintly.
           b. Any parent who loves all of his children is saintly.

If these sentences are treated according to the standard policies of twentieth-century formal logic, in which *each, every, any,* and *all* are rendered as a universal quantifier $\forall$ whose truth conditions allow for vacuous truth, 6.3.3a will be interpreted as expressing a considerably more general proposition than 6.3.3b: it will imply not only that parents who love all their children are saintly but also that persons who have no children are saintly, because if a has no children, $(\forall: x \text{ is a child of } a)(a \text{ loves } x)$ will be vacuously true and thus a will be in the domain of the variable bound by *any*. That conflicts with the normal understanding of 6.3.3a, which is generally understood as synonymous with 6.3.3b, i.e., as having implications only about persons who have children.

There are at least three ways in which one might attempt to account for the way that 6.3.3a is normally understood. (i) Perhaps it is understood as referring only to parents because of the truth conditional semantics for *all*, i.e., perhaps a sentence of the form (all: Fx)Gx implies that there are values of x for which Fx, in which case identifying *all* with ∀ would get the truth conditions wrong. (ii) Perhaps *his children* carries with it a presupposition that he has children and that presupposition is responsible for the restriction of the values of the variable to persons who have children. For example, if we can identify *his children* as the bearer of a **semantic presupposition**, i.e., a condition that a proposition must meet for it to have a truth value at all, then we might be able to claim that *x loves all of x's children* is not true (and likewise, not false) for those values of x who have no children, which would mean that the domain expression for the variable bound by *any* would be satisfied by the same values of the variable in 6.3.3a as in 6.3.3b. (iii) Perhaps we can invoke the principle that was proposed in connection with 6.3.1 and say that persons who have no children are irrelevant to what 6.3.3b asserts.

Without ruling out the possibility that either (i) or (ii) might be right (there is no reason why (i)–(iii) couldn't all be right simultaneously), let us look at (iii) in some detail. If we wish to account for the interpretation of 6.3.3a in terms of relevance of entities to what is said, we will have to go beyond the particular type of relevance that was discussed in connection with 6.3.1, where the relevant values of the variable were those for which the question of the matrix being true arose. While the question of whether John loves Mary does not arise at times before John has met Mary, the question of whether a person is saintly arises irrespective of whether he has children: there can be both saintly and nonsaintly childless persons. Perhaps we should take relevance also to be affected by whether the question of the domain expression being true arises: unless a person has children, the question of whether he loves all of his children does not arise (in the sense that there is then no possible distinction between his loving all of his children and his not loving all of his children). In that case, (iii) would have the same effect as (ii): persons without children would be irrelevant to what the sentence says for the same reason that corresponding instances of the domain expression would lack a truth value. Alternatively, one might say that childless persons were irrelevant for a different reason: that the sentence would be used to assert a connection between loving one's children and being saintly, and childless persons would presumably be irrelevant to such a connection.

Alternatives (i) and (ii) provide no reason for any given universal quantifier word to vary from one case to another with regard to whether it allows for vacuous truth. The following pair of sentences, however, suggest that such variation exists, i.e., 6.3.4a would normally be interpreted as not implying that candidates who received no campaign contributions at all will be defeated, while 6.3.4b would probably be interpreted as including members who incurred no bills among those to whom the 10 percent discount is offered:

6.3.4   a. Any candidate who got all his campaign contributions from the Teamsters' Union will be defeated.
          b. Any member who paid all his bills by the fifteenth of the month was entitled to a 10 percent discount on their publications.

The difference between these two interpretations lends itself easily to a description in terms of alternative (iii): 6.3.4a would be likely to be used to express a connection between a candidate's indebtedness to the Teamsters' Union and his losing the election, and candidates who received no contributions from anyone are irrelevant to such a generalization, whereas 6.3.4b would be likely to be understood in terms of a policy of rewarding members whose accounts are fully paid up, and members who incurred no debts could plausibly be taken in under such a policy.

If some version of (iii) is accepted (and it should be emphasized that acceptance of it requires one to adopt a clearer and more comprehensive conception of "relevance" than has been developed so far in this book), it may be possible to accept the policy of most logicians that universal propositions are vacuously true when their domains are empty, while deploying the principle restricting domains to "relevant" values of the variable in such a way that few cases will arise in which a universal proposition must be judged vacuously true. Alternatively, it may be possible to leave the truth conditions of universal propositions unspecified in cases where the domain is empty and to treat the principle about relevant values of the variable as enlarging the domain in cases like 6.3.4b in which elements for which the domain proposition is vacuously true are relevant to the superordinate proposition. I will leave this issue unresolved here.

6.4. Restricted and Unrestricted Quantifiers

The quantifiers that have figured in the formulas given so far are **restricted quantifiers:** each quantifier comes with a propositional function that specifies what the **domain** of its variable is, as in $(\forall: x \text{ Man})(x \text{ Mortal})$, where "$x$ Man" specifies that the relevant objects are those which possess the property of being a man. Modern logicians have generally operated instead in terms of **unrestricted quantifiers,** that is, they have taken all variables to have the same domain and have thus taken quantifiers as not requiring a special propositional function to indicate the domain of the variable in question.[4] How then do they distinguish between, say, *All pianists admire Beethoven* and *All violinists admire Beethoven?* This has been accomplished by incorporating *pianist* and *violinist* into the propositional function that the quantifier applies to (6.4.1a and b), or to use what is in fact a more common notation for quantifiers, 6.4.1a′ and b′:[5]

6.4.1 a. $(\forall)_x \supset (x \text{ Pianist}, x \text{ Adm } b)$
  b. $(\forall)_x \supset (x \text{ Violinist}, x \text{ Adm } b)$
  a′. $(\forall x) \supset (x \text{ Pianist}, x \text{ Adm } b)$
  b′. $(\forall x) \supset (x \text{ Violinist}, x \text{ Adm } b)$

In predicate logic with restricted quantifiers, the quantifier is combined with two propositional functions: one specifying the domain of the variable bound by the quantifier, and one whose truth in that domain is at issue. In predicate logic with unrestricted quantifiers, the quantifier is combined with only one propositional function, generally a complex propositional function chosen to get the effect of a restriction on the domain of the variable.

A proposition with an unrestricted universal quantifier, $(\forall x)Px$, is supposed to be true if Px is true of every value of x. That means that $(\forall x) \supset (Fx, Gx)$ will be true if $\supset (Fx, Gx)$ is true of every value of x. Since an if-then proposition is true when either the antecedent is false or the consequent is true, $(\forall x) \supset (Fx, Gx)$ will be true if for every value of x either Fx is false or Gx is true. But that condition is equivalent to the condition that for those values of x for which Fx is true, Gx is also true: whenever Fx is false, $\supset (Fx, Gx)$ is true, and so it is precisely for the x's for which Fx is true that Gx need be true. That means that the truth condition for $(\forall x) \supset (Fx, Gx)$ coincides with what we have been taking as the truth condition for $(\forall: Fx)_x Gx$: only the x's for which Fx is true are relevant, and if for all of those, Gx is true, then the whole proposition is true; and if Gx is false for any of the x's for which Fx is true, then the whole proposition is false.

In the case of existential propositions, a theory of unrestricted quantification likewise combines the quantifier with a single propositional function, though in this case the way that the quantifier is in effect restricted to a specific domain is by applying the quantifier to an *and*-conjoined propositional function, as in the analysis of *Some men are bald* as

6.4.2 $(\exists x) \wedge (x \text{ Man}, x \text{ Bald})$

It is important to note that in a theory of unrestricted quantification, universal and existential quantifiers have to be treated differently: it takes an *if*-clause to (in effect) restrict the variable of a universal quantifier to a specific domain, but it takes an *and*-conjunct to (in effect) restrict the variable of an existential quantifier to a specific domain. An *if*-clause won't do the trick for an existential quantifier, since 6.4.3 is true just by virtue of the fact that there are objects that are not men.

6.4.3 $(\exists x) \supset (x \text{ Man}, x \text{ Bald})$

For example, $\supset(lb \text{ Man}, lb \text{ Bald})$, with *lb* a constant denoting Lake Baikal, is true, since $(lb \text{ Man})$ is false; thus there are values of *x* for which $\supset(x \text{ Man}, x \text{ Bald})$ is true, independently of whether any men are bald. However, the fact that Lake Baikal is not a man does not suffice to make *Some men are bald* true. Thus, you can't extend the $\supset$ of the universal cases to the existential cases. But you can't use an $\wedge$ to fit the domain restriction into a universally quantified proposition either, since 6.4.4 is false just by virtue of the fact that there are objects that are not politicians:

6.4.4 $(\forall x) \wedge (x \text{ Politician}, x \text{ Crooked})$

For example, $\wedge(rs \text{ Politician}, rs \text{ Crooked})$, with *rs* a constant denoting Ringo Starr, is false since Ringo Starr is not a politician (or at least, he is not one at the moment that I write this), and thus there are values of *x* for which $\wedge(x \text{ Politician}, x \text{ Crooked})$ is false, independent of whether all politicians are crooked. However, the fact that Ringo Starr is not a politician ought not to be sufficient to make *All politicians are crooked* false. Thus, you can't extend the $\wedge$ of the existential cases to the universal cases.

This means that in a system of predicate logic with unrestricted quantification, the two sentences

6.4.5   a. Some politicians are crooked.
         b. All politicians are crooked.

differ in more than the quantifier: the logical structure of the one contains an $\wedge$ where that of the other contains a $\supset$. By contrast, in a system of predicate logic with restricted quantifiers, the quantifier is the only difference in their logical structures: in both cases the quantifier ($\forall$ or $\exists$, as the case may be) is combined with the propositional function "politician *x*," which gives the domain of the variable, and the combination of quantifier and domain restriction is combined with the propositional function "crooked *x*." The following sentences provide at least a weak basis for holding that *some* and *all* fit into identical logical contexts, as in the restricted version of quantification:

6.4.6   a.   Some politicians are crooked, but not all politicians are
               crooked.

a′. Some, but not all politicians are crooked.
b. Those politicians are crooked, but not all politicians are crooked.
b′. *Those, but not all politicians are crooked.
c. Only politicians are crooked, but not all politicians are crooked.
c′. *Only but not all politicians are crooked.

Example 6.4.6a′ is evidently a variant of 6.4.6a, derived by an application of conjunction reduction that gives rise to a conjoined determiner. However, as 6.4.6b–b′ show, conjunction reduction is not applicable unless the determiner is the right type of thing. Since *those* and *all* occupy the same surface syntactic role, it must be something other than surface syntactic structure that is responsible for the difference. Logical structure is a reasonable place to look for differences to which the difference in applicability of conjunction reduction can be ascribed, and under a scheme of restricted quantification, *some* and *all* are in corresponding places in otherwise identical logical structures in 6.4.6a, whereas *those* would have a different logical role from *some* in 6.4.6b. However, under the scheme of unrestricted quantification, *some* and *all* would not appear in corresponding places in otherwise identical logical structures. Moreover, the difference between 6.4.6a′ and 6.4.6b′ cannot be ascribed to the fact that *those* has a constant reference whereas *some* is combined with a variable, since the *only* of 6.4.6c also binds a variable; as we will see in section 9.2, *only* is a combination of several logical elements, and the logical structure of *Only politicians are crooked* differs markedly from that of *Some politicians are crooked*.

In a system with unrestricted quantifiers, the closest analogs to the rules of inference given for restricted quantifiers are as follows:

6.4.7

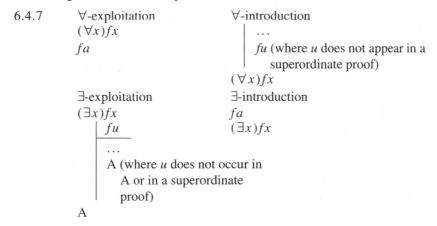

The parallelism between the proofs allowed in the two systems is illustrated by the following derivations of parallel conclusions from parallel premises:

6.4.8   Unrestricted version

1	$(\forall x) \supset (\wedge(fx, gx), hx)$	supp
2	$\supset(\wedge(fu, gu), hu)$	1, $\forall$-expl
3	$\wedge(fu, \sim hu)$	supp
4	gu	supp
5	fu	3, $\wedge$-expl
6	$\wedge(fu, gu)$	5, 4, $\wedge$-intro
7	hu	2, 6, $\supset$-expl
8	$\sim hu$	3, $\wedge$-expl
9	$\sim gu$	4–8, $\sim$-intro
10	$\supset(\wedge(fu, \sim hu), \sim gu)$	3–9, $\supset$-intro
11	$(\forall x) \supset (\wedge(fx, \sim hx), \sim gx)$	2–10, $\forall$-intro

Restricted version

1	$(\forall: \wedge(fx, gx)) hx$	supp
2	$\wedge(fu, \sim hu)$	supp
3	gu	supp
4	fu	2, $\wedge$-expl
5	$\wedge(fu, gu)$	4, 3, $\wedge$-intro
6	hu	1, 5, $\forall$-expl
7	$\sim hu$	2, $\wedge$-expl
8	$\sim gu$	3–7, $\sim$-intro
9	$(\forall: \wedge(fx, \sim hx) \sim gx$	2–8, $\forall$-intro

Note that with the unrestricted quantifier version of $\forall$-exploitation, the subordinate proof has no supposition: you simply derive conclusions "about u" without assuming anything "about u".

If *many, most, almost all* and *all but one* are treated as quantifiers themselves (rather than being decomposed into more primitive elements, as in the proposal which would analyze *Most politicians are crooks* as "There is a set M such that M consists of more than half of all politicians, and all members of M are crooks"), they will have to be restricted quantifiers. *Most Americans are right-handed* cannot be treated as a combination of a quantifier and the propositional function "x is an American and x is right-handed"; the meaning of the sentence is not that that propositional function is "true of most x," since that propositional function obviously is not true of most x: there are a billion

Chinese (to say nothing of trillions of bacteria and hydrogen atoms) of whom "x is an American and x is right-handed' is false, and they far outnumber the 200 million or so right-handed Americans of whom it is true. The sentence likewise could not be interpreted as a combination of *most* with the propositional function "if x is an American, then x is right-handed," since that propositional function is "true of most x" for reasons that have no bearing on whether most Americans are right-handed (i.e., it is true of all Chinese and all bacteria and all hydrogen atoms). *Most* doesn't mean "over 50 percent of all things": it means "over 50 percent of the kind of things being referred to."[6] Restricted quantifiers provide a natural basis for coping with *most* and other quantifiers of "relative magnitude": they provide a characteristic that defines the domain of relevant items, and the sentence is true if the other propositional function is true in an appropriate-sized subset of that domain (e.g., if "x is right-handed" is true of more than half of the x's that meet the condition "x is an American"; similarly, *Many Americans are atheists* is true if, among the x's such that "x is an American," the fraction who meet the condition "x is an atheist" is large).

Likewise, the following two sentences have different truth conditions:

6.4.9   a. Most politicians are crooks.
          b. Most crooks are politicians.

If there are one million crooks who are not politicians, 100,000 crooks who are politicians, and 50,000 politicians who are not crooks, then 6.4.9a is true (since two-thirds of all politicians are crooks) but 6.4.9b is false (since only one-eleventh of all crooks are politicians). But then the truth of *Most As are Bs* could not just be a matter of counting the x's that meet the condition "x is an A and x is a B," since "x is a crook and x is a politician" is true of exactly the same x's as is "x is a politician and x is a crook." It likewise could not just be a matter of counting the x's that meet the condition "if x is an A, then x is a B," since those are the same individuals as the x's that meet the condition "if x is not a B, then x is not an A," and *Most nonpoliticians are noncrooks* obviously can differ in truth value from 6.4.9b. (If we restrict our attention to Americans and accept the above figures, then there are more than 200 million individuals who are neither crooks nor politicians, which means that *Most nonpoliticians are noncrooks* would be true though *Most crooks are politicians* is false.)

For those quantifiers that carry an existential commitment (or, accepting the suggestion made in the last section, those quantifiers that carry a pragmatic presupposition that the domain over which the variable ranges is nonempty), one can argue that they must be treated as restricted quantifiers, since a treatment in terms of unrestricted quantification would provide no way of identifying the predicate involved in the pragmatic presupposition. In particular, treating existential quantifiers as restricted quantifiers makes the two propositional functions have different roles and thus provides a basis for identifying the difference between

6.4.10   a. Some Buddhists are vegetarians.
          b. Some vegetarians are Buddhists.

To make a real argument out of this suggestion, it is necessary to demonstrate that the existential commitment or pragmatic presupposition is not merely a conversational implicature (i.e., something that one would convey by uttering the sentence by virtue of considerations of cooperativity). Let us contrast the existential commitment of *all* with a clear case of conversational implicature: the fact that *some* usually conveys *not all*. Yes-no questions provide a good test for conversational implicature: the question calls for a *Yes* answer even in cases where the speaker does not accept the conversationally implicated proposition, for example,

6.4.11   Q. Are some politicans crooks?
          A. Yes, indeed, all of them are.
              *No, (but) all of them are.

    If the existential commitment of *all* were a conversational implicature, the question in 6.4.12 should demand a positive answer:

6.4.12   Q. Do all unicorns eat clover?
          A. *Yes, but there are no unicorns.
              *?No, indeed there are no unicorns.
              **Yes, indeed there are no unicorns.
              *?Yes, but of course there are no unicorns.

Note that the least normal answer is the one that ought to be best if universal propositions whose variable ranges over an empty domain were vacuously true and the proposition that the domain was nonempty were only a conversational implicature. A quirk of English makes it difficult to compare *all* with *any* on this point. While one can of course form the question *Does any unicorn eat clover?*, that question is most naturally interpreted as the interrogative counterpart of *Some unicorn eats clover,* i.e., an answer of *Yes* would say that there is a unicorn that eats clover. However, there is a way of requesting information using a sentence that does not have interrogative form and thus does not participate in replacement of *some* by *any*, and there *any* does not display the existential commitment that *all* does:

6.4.13   Q. Any unicorn eats clover, right?
        A. a. Yes, any unicorn eats clover. (Neutral with regard to
                whether unicorns exist.)
            b. ??No, there aren't any unicorns.

I will close this section by taking up briefly a class of sentences that seem *prima facie* to demand an analysis in terms of an unrestricted existential quantifier, namely **pure existential** sentences as in 6.4.14, which appear to call for analyses such as those indicated:

6.4.14   a.   There are some excellent philosophers.
        a'. $(\exists x)(x$ is an excellent philosopher$)$
        b.   There isn't any Santa Claus.
        b'. $\sim(\exists x)(x$ is a Santa Claus$)$

Before drawing any conclusion about the logical structures of examples such as 6.4.14a,b, however, let us consider a broader selection of existential sentences, with a view towards integrating our analysis of 6.4.14a,b with an analysis of other existential sentences:

6.4.15   a.   There is an error in your argument.
        b.   There is a mole on John's left arm.
        b'. John has a mole on his left arm.
        c.   There is still some room in the closet. (Kuno 1971: 349)
        c'. The closet still has some room in it.

The most obvious way to set up a logical form is to treat *a mole* or *an error* or *some room* as an existentially quantified NP applying to a matrix such a "*x* is in your argument" or "*x* is on John's left arm" or "*x* is in the closet":

6.4.16   a. $(\exists: x$ is an error$)(x$ is in your argument$)$
        b. $(\exists: x$ is a mole$)(x$ is on John's left arm$)$
        c.   still$[(\exists: x$ is room$)(x$ is in the closet$)]$

On reflection, however, such analyses turn out not to be as plausible as they at first seem, since they give to parts of entities an undeserved autonomy: there isn't an independently existing set of possible errors that can turn up in various arguments—the errors are errors only in virtue of their roles within various arguments; likewise, there isn't an independently existing set of possible moles, any one of which might turn upon John's left arm or on Iris's right ankle, or on Oscar's abdomen—a mole exists only as part of a particular body—and there isn't an independently existing ensemble of room: a volume of space constitutes "room" only in virtue of its relation to a larger space that it is a part of (here, the closet). Moreover, the NPs in question do not have the option of turning up in subject position without the *there*, as the postverbal NPs of many other sentences with existential *there* do:

6.4.17 a. *An error is in your argument.
        b. *A mole is on John's left arm.
        c. *Some room is still in the closet.
        d. There is a spider crawling up your leg.
        d'. A spider is crawling up your leg.
        e. There was a prisoner being tortured.
        e'. A prisoner was being tortured.

An alternative analysis is suggested by the syntactic analysis of existential sentences given in Kuno (1971). On the basis of a number of syntactic facts about English and Japanese, Kuno argues that the underlying subject of existential sentences is a locative expression such as *in your proof* or *on John's left arm*. Suppose that we were to treat those expressions, rather than the apparent subjects of locative sentences, as the domain expression for the existential quantifier:

6.4.18 a. $(\exists: x$ is in your proof$)(x$ is an error$)$
        b. $(\exists: x$ is on John's left arm$)(x$ is a mole$)$
        c. $(\exists: x$ is in the closet$)(x$ is room$)$

The domain expression now defines the domain as consisting of the parts of some structured object (perhaps a space, in the case of *in the closet*, as it is used here), with the locative preposition (*in*, *on*) indicating the relevant part-to-whole relationship, and the logical form now suggests a more plausible way to test whether the given proposition is true (e.g., one examines the surface of John's left arm to see whether any of its parts is a mole, rather than examining all of the moles in the world to see whether any of them is on John's left arm).

If 6.4.15a,b,c are to be given an analysis of this type, an alternative to 6.4.14a',b' now suggests itself: perhaps pure existential sentences such as 6.4.14a,b have a logical form of the same type, but with the domain expression given no overt expression. That suggestion is in fact directly analogous to the syntactic analysis that Kuno (1971) proposes for 6.4.14a,b: an analysis in which they have a zero locative expression in their underlying subject position, where the zero locative expression is given an interpretation suggested by the context, e.g., for 6.4.14b it might be "among (real) persons," in which case 6.4.14b would be given the same interpretation as *No (real) person is Santa Claus*. Such logical forms in fact look very like the unrestricted quantifier formulas 6.4.14a′,b′: in either case, an existential quantifier expression is combined with a matrix "*x* is an excellent philosopher" or "*x* is a Santa Claus," and the difference is in whether there is no domain expression at all or a domain expression that has no overt expression.[7]

6.5 Satisfiability and Validity

The notions of "satisfiable" (i.e., true in at least one state of affairs) and "valid" (i.e., true in all states of affairs) that were introduced in chapter 4 for propositional logic carry over unchanged to predicate logic: for any formula of predicate logic, one can reasonably ask whether there are states of affairs in which it is true and whether there are states of affairs in which it is false, and one can ask whether it is true in all of the states of affairs in which a given set of propositions are true. For example, 6.5.1a is true in all states of affairs, which means that we can say that it is valid (6.1.5a′), while 6.5.1b is true in only some states of affairs, namely those in which the denotation of F is disjoint from that of G, and in all states of affairs in which the formula before the $\vDash$ in 6.5.1c is true, the formula after it is also true, which is to say that the one formula semantically entails the other:

6.5.1   a. $\supset((\forall\colon Fx)\sim Gx, \sim(\exists\colon Fx)Gx)$
       a′. $\vDash \supset((\forall\colon Fx)\sim Gx, \sim(\exists\colon Fx)Gx)$
       b. $(\forall\colon Fx)\sim Gx$
       c. $(\forall\colon Fx)Gx \vDash (\forall\colon Fx)\wedge(Gx, Hx)$

However, since the notion of "possible state of affairs" is considerably richer for predicate logic than it is for propositional logic, it is possible to draw finer distinctions than just these. For example, some formulas can be true in a given state of affairs only if the domain of that state of affairs meets some condition. For example, each of the formulas in 6.5.2 can be true only in a state of affairs whose domain contains at least two members, since the truth of 6.5.2a depends on there being something having the property G and something else having the property ~G, and the truth of 6.5.2b, depends on there being two distinct elements having the property G:

6.5.2   a. $\wedge((\exists\colon Fx)Gx, (\exists\colon Fx)\sim Gx)$
       b. $(\exists\colon Fx)\wedge(Gx, (\exists\colon \wedge(Fy, \sim =yx)Gy))$

While these formulas impose lower limits on the size of the domain of states of affairs in which they are true, they do not impose any upper limit; for example, for 6.5.2a to be true, there could be arbitrarily many elements with the property F, as long as at least one of them had the property G and at least one had the property ~G, and there could be arbitrarily many elements with the property ~F. Indeed, it is not clear that **any** formula of predicate logic with restricted quantifiers could impose an upper limit on the size of the domains of states of affairs that satisfy it, because only those elements of the domain that satisfy the domain expressions of the quantifiers play any role in determining the truth value of the formula.

Things are very different in a system with unrestricted quantification, where, for example, it is a trivial matter to construct a formula that is true in precisely those states of affairs whose domain contains exactly one element, in virtue of the fact that what it says is that there is exactly one element:

6.5.3 $(\exists x)(\forall y) = xy$

For any finite number n, it is quite easy to construct a formula that is true in any domain which contains exactly n elements and false in any domain containing fewer or more than n elements, as illustrated by 6.5.4, which is true in precisely those states of affairs whose domain contains exactly 3 elements:

6.5.4 $(\exists x)(\exists y)(\exists z) \wedge (\sim = xy, \ \sim = xz, \ \sim = yz, (\forall w) \vee (= wx, \ = wy, = wz))$

The content of 6.5.4, of course, is that there are three distinct elements such that every element is identical to one of those three. Note the role that $=$ plays in 6.5.3–4: without using $=$, one can construct formulas that impose a lower bound on the size of domains in which they can be satisfied, but not formulas that impose an upper bound. For example, it is easy to show that for any state of affairs in which a formula (such as 6.5.2a) that does not involve $=$ is true, there is another state of affairs in which it is true that has one additional member to its domain. To construct an alternative state of affairs in which the given formula is true, pick any element a of the domain of the given state of affairs and add to the domain a "doppelgänger" of that element—an element a' such that the same predicates are true of a' as of a. The addition of this extra element will not change the truth value of any of the constituents of the given formula, though it will change the size of the domain. (Note how the assumption that the given formula does not contain $=$ is tacitly utilized here: $= aa$ and $= a'a$ can not have the same truth value if a and a' are distinct elements, and thus if formulas involving $=$ are admitted, a new element can never be a complete doppelgänger of an old one.[8]

There are indeed formulas which are satisfiable only in infinite domains, for example:

6.5.5 $\wedge((\exists:Fx)(\exists: Fy)Rxy, (\forall:Fx)(\exists:Fy)Rxy, (\forall: Fx)(\forall:Fy)\supset(Rxy,$
$\sim Ryx), (\forall:Fx)(\forall:Fy)(\forall:Fz)\supset(\wedge(Rxy, Ryz), Rxz))$

The content of 6.5.5 is that R is a partial order relation among Fs (things with the property F) and that every F is followed by an F: the first conjunct says that there are Fs that stand in the relation R, the second says that every F has the relation R to some F, the third says that R is antisymmetric (i.e., wherever R holds, its converse does not), and the fourth says that R is transitive. For 6.5.5 to be satisfied in a state of affairs, the domain must be infinite, since F must have an infinite denotation. Suppose 6.5.5 is satisfied in some state of affairs α. Then, in view of the first conjunct of 6.5.5, D^α must contain at least one element a_1 of which F is true in α. In view of the second conjunct, F^α must contain an element a_2 such that $(a_1, a_2) \in R^\alpha$. In view of the third conjunct, $a_2 \neq a_1$, since if they were identical, (a_1, a_1) would both belong and not belong to R^α. But the procedure by which we have produced a_2 can be iterated indefinitely: there will be an element a_3 of F^α such that $(a_2, a_3)\in R^\alpha$ and a_3 is distinct from a_2 and (in virtue of the transitivity of R) also from a_1. Thus, for any finite number n, we could find a sequence of distinct elements $a_1, a_2, a_3, \ldots, a_n$ of F^α such that all the pairs $(a_i, a_{i+1})\in R^\alpha$. Hence D^α must have at least n elements, for every finite number n, which is possible only if it is infinite.

There is, of course, a countable infinite domain in which 6.5.5 is satisfied: take the domain to be the natural numbers, and take Rxy to be $x < y$. Are there formulas of predicate logic that are satisfiable only in uncountable domains? Surprisingly, the answer is negative: according to the Löwenheim-Skolem theorem, a formula of predicate logic which is satisfiable in an infinite domain is satisfiable in a countable infinite domain. This is a surprising result because it shows a sharp and not at all obvious limitation on the expressive power of predicate logic: predicate logic is not capable of expressing a property that is only possessed by domains having uncountably many elements. Thus, whatever property of the real numbers that one might formulate in predicate logic will not serve to characterize the real numbers: there will be a countable domain which possesses the same property.

There is one misleading thing in the last paragraph, namely, my use of the term "predicate logic" to refer to the specific kind of predicate logic that was treated in chapter 2, which is more correctly called **first-order predicate logic.** "First-order" here means that the bound variables are individual variables rather than set variables or predicate variables. A system of logic that allowed formulas such as

6.5.6 $(\exists f)(\forall x)(\forall y) \supset (fxy, fyx)$

would be of (at least) second order. A system allowing variable predicates of predicates or variable sets of sets would be third-order predicate logic (e.g., in third-order logic, you can formulate propositions such as "for every set of sets of real numbers, there is a set of real numbers such that every member of the latter is a member of a member of the former"). The Löwenheim-Skolem theorem has to do only with first-order predicate logic.

A semantic completeness theorem for first-order predicate logic can be proved: a formula of first-order predicate logic is true in all states of affairs if and only if it is provable relative to the rules of inference of chapter 2. The proof of this theorem is a simple extension of the proof of the completeness theorem for propositional logic.

Exercises

1. Consider the following state of affairs:

Domain = $\{1, 2, 3, 4, 5\}$

	f	g	h		1	2	3	4	5
1	T	F	1		T	F	T	F	T
2	F	T	2		F	F	F	F	T
3	T	F	3		F	F	F	T	F
4	F	F	4		F	T	F	F	F
5	F	T	5		F	F	F	F	T

Determine the truth value of each of the following formulas in this state of affairs:

a. $(\forall: fx)_x (\exists: gy)_y hxy$
b. $(\forall: fx)_x hxx$
c. $(\forall: (\exists: hxy)_y fy)_x gx$
d. $(\forall: (\exists: fy)_y hyx)_x \vee (\sim fx, hxx)$

2. For each of the formulas in exercise 1, give its nearest equivalent in a system of logic with unrestricted quantification.

3. For each of the formulas involving unrestricted quantification (and "connectives" written between the component formulas), give a formula in

terms of restricted quantification (and the notation used in this book) that a charitable reader might take the author to have intended:

a. $[(\forall x)(fx \supset gx)] \supset [(\exists x)(fx \land hxx)]$
b. $(\exists x)((fx \land (\forall y)(hyx \supset kxy)) \land \sim kxx)$
c. $(\forall x)[(\exists y)(fy \land hxy) \supset (\exists z)(gz \land \sim hxz)]$

4. Assume that *No linguist admires no linguist* is ambiguous as to which *no* has higher scope (it's ambiguous for some people but not for others; act as if you're the former kind of person) and treat *no* as $\sim$ plus $\exists$. Show that the two interpretations can differ in truth value (i.e., show how it could happen that one interpretation was true while the other was false).

5. For each of the following sentences, construct a formula of predicate logic with identity that represents its meaning:

a. Any person who admires another person is sane.
b. Sam denounced every linguist but Chomsky.
c. No person who respects himself ridicules anyone else.
d. Every philosopher admires no one but himself.
e. Every philosopher hates all of every other philosopher's relatives.
f. Every donkey is owned by a man who beats no donkey but it.

6. Construct an analysis of *all but one* in terms of $\forall$, $\exists$, $=$, and propositional connectives, and show how the following sentence would be analysed under your proposal:

All but one poet hated himself.

7.   Further Topics in Predicate Logic

7.1. Linguistic Justification for S: Q'S

The logical forms that were proposed in section 2.2 differ in an important respect from the surface forms of the corresponding English sentences, namely, that the quantifier and the noun that it goes with are outside of the clauses which, in the surface form of the sentence, they are inside of. This aspect of the proposed logical forms can be justified by demonstrating that there are linguistic phenomena which can be given a satisfying description only by making reference to the propositional function that figures in the logical form. If these grammatical phenomena are to be described in terms of grammatical transformations, those transformations will have to apply to a structure in which that propositional function is separate from the quantifier and the noun, as in logical structure, rather than containing them, as in surface structure.

Consider the conditions under which reflexive pronouns may be used. Reflexive pronouns in English are quite restricted in distribution: they must refer to an antecedent that occurs in the same clause, and the antecedent may not be part of a larger noun phrase (though the reflexive may be)[1]

7.1.1   a. John admires himself.
        b. *John$_i$ thinks that most people admire himself$_i$.
        b'. *John thinks that himself deserved the prize.
        c. John asked Shirley$_i$ about herself$_i$.
        d. John$_i$ asked Shirley about himself$_i$.
        e. John gave Shirley$_i$ a picture of herself$_i$.
        f. *A picture of John$_i$ rarely resembles himself$_i$.
        g. *John$_i$'s mother loves himself$_i$.

In many works by transformational grammarians, an analysis has been proposed whereby this skewed distribution is attributed to a transformation which creates reflexives out of something nonreflexive. The detail of this analysis that was controversial from the outset is that of **which** nonreflexive NP underlies a reflexive pronoun: a full NP identical to the antecedent?, a simple pronoun counterpart of the antecedent?, a NP that is completely unspecified with regard to form? Whichever answer is given to this question, the analysis will have to be set up in such a way that the purported reference of the various NPs is taken into account, since it is only when NPs purport to refer to the same entity that any need to put one of them into a reflexive form arises, e.g., *John talked to John* and *John talked to him* are perfectly normal sentences as long as two different persons are referred to, even if both of them are called John. Thus, whichever form of the Reflexivization transformation is adopted, it will be necessary to take it as applying to syntactic structures in which NPs bear indices specifying their purported reference and as applicable only to a pair of NPs that bear the same index.

It is not immediately obvious how a Reflexivization transformation would apply in the derivation of sentences such as 7.1.2, in which the antecedent of the reflexive is a quantified NP:

7.1.2   Every American admires himself.

One difficulty is raised by the fact that one can speak of *every American* as having a reference only by stretching the latter term considerably; moreover, if one stretches the notion of reference in the one obvious way and speaks of *every American* as referring to the set of all Americans, then such sentences as 7.1.3a become problematic, since they then would contain two coreferential NPs and thus ought to be as unacceptable as sentences like 7.1.3b–b′, in which a NP is coreferential with a nonreflexive NP:

7.1.3   a.   Every American admires every American.
           b.   *John$_i$ admires John$_i$.
           b′. *John$_i$ admired him$_i$.

Suppose that the syntactic **derivation** of sentences such as 7.1.2, in whose course Reflexivization and perhaps other transformations apply, has as the deep structure something approximating the logical structures that were proposed in chapter 2, rather than a structure in which *every American* appears as a syntactic unit and in a NP position. Suppose further that transformations apply according to the principle of the **cycle**, which says that when one S is contained in another (say, S_2 is contained in S_1), any application of transformations with S_2 as domain precedes any application of transformations with S_1 as domain, where the **domain** of a particular application of a transformation is the lowest S that contains all of the material that is relevant to the transformation.[2]

Under these assumptions, there will then have to be a transformation (called **Q′-lowering**) which moves a Q′ into a position in the matrix S where the variable that it binds occurs.[3] The presumable logical structures of 7.1.1 and 7.1.2 are:

7.1.4   a. (every: x American)(x Adm x) [= 7.1.2]
            b. (every: x American)(every: y American)(x Adm y) [= 7.1.3a]

The derivation of 7.1.2 will then be as in 7.1.5, where subscripts indicate the domain to which the transformation applies in each step, e.g., Reflexivization$_2$ means "the application of Reflexivization with S_2 as domain":

7.1.5

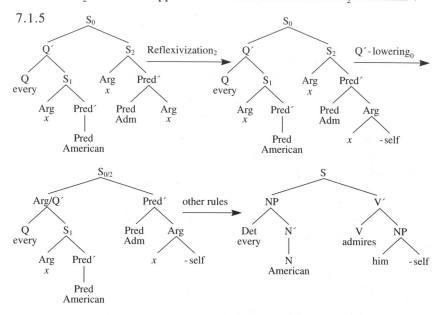

That is, Reflexivization gets a chance to apply to S_2 at a level of structure in which *every American* is external to S_2 and thus S_2 still contains two coreferential NPs; only after the second of those NPs has been made reflexive is *every American* moved into S_2. By contrast, in the derivation of 7.1.3, the conditions for reflexivization are not met at any point in the derivation:

7.1.6

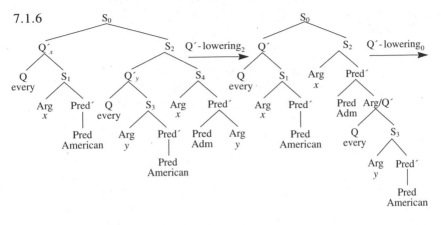

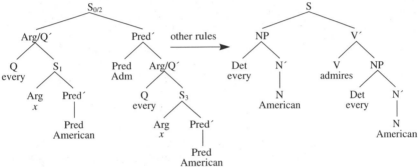

In the deep structure in 7.1.6, no S contains two coreferential NPs (note that the variables *x* and *y* count as referentially distinct irrespective of the fact that they range over the same set of values and indeed are assigned the same value by some assignments of values to variables), and no other stage of 7.1.6 contains two coreferential NPs except perhaps for the two occurrences of *every American* in the output of Q'-lowering$_0$ and subsequent stages. However, even if the variables *x* and *y* were ignored and those two NPs were counted as identical, Reflexivization would still not be applicable at that stage of the derivation: after the applications of Q'-lowering to S$_2$ and S$_0$, all of the material of S$_0$ is inside S$_4$, and hence the application of Reflexivization would violate the cyclic principle: a transformation would be applying with S$_4$ as its domain subsequent to the application of transformations to higher domains (namely S$_2$ and S$_0$).

The proposed underlying structures let one solve in a similar way a similar problem involving **Equi-NP-deletion**, the tranformation which deletes the subject of a nonfinite subordinate clause if it is coreferential with a certain NP of the main clause, as in 7.1.7:

7.1.7   a. Alice wants to spend the summer in Mauritius.
           [<Alice$_i$ wants (she$_i$ spend the summer in Mauritius)]
        b. The court forced Nixon to hand over the tapes.
           [<The court forced Nixon$_i$ (he$_i$ hand over the tapes)]
        c. Bill promised Marge to wash the dishes.
           [<Bill$_i$ promised Marge (he$_i$ wash the dishes)]

Some such transformation is needed to represent the relationship between sentences with and sentences without an overt subject of the infinitive (compare 7.1.7a with *Alice wants her husband to spend the summer in Mauritius,* which in this analysis differs from 7.1.7a only with regard to what the subject of the embedded clause is) and between sentences with a *that*-clause and sentences with a subjectless infinitive (compare 7.1.7c with *Bill promised Marge that he would wash the dishes*).[4]

Consider now the two sentences

7.1.8   a. Every American wants to get rich.
        b. Every American wants every American to get rich.

The two differ sharply in meaning; note that if every American desires wealth for himself and poverty for everyone else, 7.1.8a will be true and 7.1.8b false. Example 7.1.8a cannot plausibly be derived by deletion of a repetition of *Every American,* since coreferentiality is as much a condition for **Equi-NP-deletion** as it is for Reflexivization (note, e.g., that 7.1.7a refers to a trip to Mauritius by the same Alice that the subject of *want* refers to). Even if it made sense to speak of two instances of *every American* as being coreferential, that condition ought to be met in 7.1.8b and the structure underlying 7.1.8b ought to yield 7.1.8a instead.

The problem of providing syntactic derivations of 7.1.8a and 7.1.8b such that Equi-NP-deletion applies only in the former derivation evaporates if the deepest stage of the derivations is logical structures of the sort that conform to the proposals of this chapter:

7.1.9   a. (every: x American)(x want (x get rich))
        b. (every: x American)(x want((every: y American)(y get rich)))

In the derivation of 7.1.8a, Equi-NP-deletion would apply to "x want (x get rich)," and then Q′-lowering would replace the remaining x by (every: x American). In the derivation of 7.1.8b, Equi-NP-deletion would never be applicable, since at no stage of the derivation would there ever be two identical NPs.[5]

An analysis in which Q's are outside their host Ss in deep structure, in conjunction with the cyclic principle, implies not only that Reflexivization and Equi-NP-deletion interact with quantification in the way described above, but also that **all** transformations that apply to a domain without regard to the content of quantified expressions must apply before any transformations that are sensitive to quantifiers; the latter generalization accounts correctly for the interactions between, on the one hand, transformations such as Passive, *Tough*-movement, and Conjunction Reduction, and on the other hand, transformations such as Quantifier-float and *There*-insertion.

Quantifier-float (henceforth, Q-float) is the transformation that optionally detaches *all, both,* or *each* from a subject NP and adjoins it as a left sister of the predicate phrase:[6]

7.1.10   a. The guests all have gone home.
          b. His hands both had scars on them.
          c. Smith's partners each hated him for a different reason.

If these sentences have deep structures in which the quantifier is part of a quantified NP that is outside the host S, as in 7.1.11a, then Q-float will have to apply not as commonly thought as in 7.1.11b, but rather to a structure in which the quantified NP is still outside its host S (7.1.11b'):

7.1.11

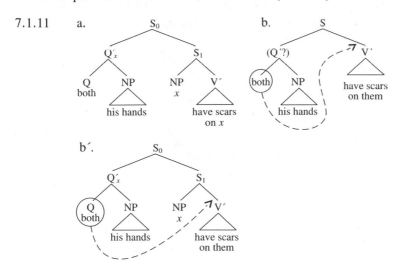

The reason for this is that if the deep structure has the Q' external to the host S, as in 7.1.11a, then a structure such as 7.1.11b could be derived only through the application of Q'-lowering with S_0 as domain; but then the cyclic principle would rule out the step indicated by the arrow in 7.1.11b, since once Q'-lowering has applied to S_0, all the material of S_0 is in S_1, and thus the domain to which the movement indicated in 7.1.11b would apply would be S_1; the cyclic principle would be violated, since a transformation would be applying with a domain lower than a domain to which a transformation had already applied. (More generally, no transformation can apply after Q'-lowering on any domain, since otherwise the cyclic principle is violated.) The only way to have a Q-float transformation without giving up either the deep structures posited here or the cyclic principle is to have it apply before Q'-lowering, as in 7.1.11b'. The appropriate version of Q-float can then be stated as in 7.1.12:[7]

7.1.12   a.

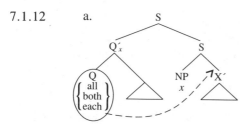

Note that this formulation makes Q-float sensitive to the scope of the floated quantifier: for quantifier float to apply as indicated here, the scope of the floated quantifier must be the S to whose predicate phrase it is adjoined. The treatment of Q-float adopted here thus implies that it should be possible for Q-float to disambiguate scope ambiguities: there should be cases in which a sentence that is ambiguous with regard to the scope of a quantified subject becomes unambiguous if the quantifier is floated. That is precisely what happens in examples such as 7.1.13a:

7.1.13   a.   All the students appeared to be cheating.
          a'.   ($\forall$: $x \in$ M) Appear(x is cheating)
          a".   Appear[($\forall$: $x \in$ M)(x is cheating)]
          b.   The students all appeared to be cheating. ($=$ a')
          b'.   The students appeared to all be cheating. ($=$ a")

Appear is a "Raising-to-subject" verb: it combines with an underlying embedded S, and the subject of the embedded S is converted into a derived subject of *appear*. Both the main S and the embedded S are possible scopes of a quantifier in such a S, and 7.1.13a is in fact ambiguous with regard to which of the two Ss is the scope of the quantifier in the subject. Depending on which S is the scope of the quantifier, Q-float will have a different domain of application, according to the treatment of Q-float proposed here: with the main clause as scope (7.1.13a′), it will adjoin *all* to the V′ of the main S, thus yielding *all appear to be cheating,* as in 7.1.13b, and with the embedded S as scope (7.1.13a″), it will adjoin *all* to the V′ of the lower S, thus yielding *all be cheating,* as in 7.1.13b′; 7.1.13b–b′ do in fact have the meanings that this analysis predicts they should have.

Essentially the same account can be given of why separating *only* from its focus can remove an ambiguity in the scope of *only:*[8]

7.1.14   a.   John allows Mary to drink only wine.
         b.   John only allows Mary to drink wine.
        b′.   John allows Mary to only drink wine.

When *only* appears in direct combination with its focus, as in 7.1.14a, it can be ambiguous with regard to its scope: 7.1.14a can be interpreted either with the main S as its scope (in which case it says that wine is the only thing that John allows Mary to drink: he doesn't allow her to drink beer, he doesn't allow her to drink whisky, . . .) or with the subordinate S as its scope (in which case it says that it's all right with John if Mary drinks only wine: he doesn't require her to also drink beer, whisky, etc.). When *only* occurs within a predicate phrase, it can be separated from its focus and put at the beginning of the predicate phrase, as in 7.1.14b–b′, and the result is unambiguous with regard to its scope: 7.1.14b, in which *only* is an adjunct to the main V′, has the main S as the scope of *only,* while 7.1.1b′, in which *only* is an adjunct to the subordinate V′, has the subordinate S as its scope. Suppose that *only* is given a treatment like that proposed for quantifiers here, say, one in which the combination of *only* and its focus is an underlying adjunct to the S that is its scope. (The question of whether *only* can in fact be decomposed into more ordinary quantifiers will be touched on in sections 7.2 and 9.2.) In that case, the two interpretations of 7.1.14a will have deep structures as in 7.1.15, and those two structures will afford different possibilities for the domain to which *Only*-separation applies:

7.1.15

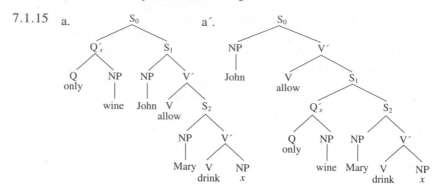

With such underlying structures, the cyclic principle will rule out the commonly assumed version of *Only*-separation in which it raises *only* out of an expression such as *drink only wine:* to avoid violation of the cyclic principle, it will be necessary to reformulate *Only*-separation as applying prior to the application of Q'-lowering that moves *only* and its focus into the host S. The only difference between Q-float and *Only*-separation will then be that whereas Q-float requires that the bound variable be the subject of the host S, *Only*-separation requires that the bound variable be contained in the predicate phrase of the host S; in either case, the transformation detaches *only* or the quantifier from the external quantified expression and makes it an adjunct of the predicate phrase of the host S. Accordingly, the output of *Only*-separation is unambiguous with regard to scope for the same reason that the output of Q-float is: with 7.1.15a as deep structure, the domain to which *Only*-separation applies is S_0, and the *only* is thus adjoined to the V' of S_1; with 7.1.15a' as deep structure, the domain to which it applies is S_1, and the *only* is thus adjoined to the V' of S_2; thus, the predicate phrase to which the *only* gets attached is that of the S that is its scope, and the result is thus unambiguous with regard to scope.

In conjunction with an analysis in which auxiliary verbs are also external to their host sentences and have essentially the syntax of *appear* (as is argued for in McCawley 1988a: chap. 8), this treatment of Q-float implies that floated quantifiers should be able to appear not only before the main V' but also before any auxiliary verbs, and that the auxiliary verbs that precede the floated quantifier are outside its scope while those that follow it are within its scope. With one important qualification, that prediction is also fulfilled:

7.1.16 a. The students all must have been cheating.
        b. The students must all have been cheating.

c. The students must have all been cheating.
d. The students must have been all cheating.

The qualification is that sentences such as 7.1.16b, in which the floated quantifier immediately follows the tense-bearing auxiliary verb (in standard English, the first auxiliary, here *must*, is a tensed form and the following auxil-
iaries are in infinitive or participial forms), are ambiguous with regard to
whether the tense-bearing auxiliary is in the scope of the floated quantifier
(i.e., 7.1.16b has an interpretation like that of 7.1.16a, as well as one in
which *must* is not in the scope of *all*); this deviation from pristine parallelism
between the position of floated quantifiers and their scope can be explained in
terms of the rule for combining tenses with auxiliary verbs, which can raise
an auxiliary verb over material that is higher than it in logical structure (see
McCawley 1988a:596–97 for details).

The version of Q-float given in 7.1.12 also solves the well-known puzzle
of why Passive cannot apply to the output of Q-float:

7.1.17   a.   All the workers denounced the manager.
         b.   The workers all denounced the manager.
         c.   *The manager all was denounced by the workers.
         c'. *The manager was all denounced by the workers.

The result of applying Passive to the output of Q-float (7.1.17b) would be
either 7.1.17c or 7.1.17c', depending on where exactly the passive auxiliary
would go in relation to *all*, but in any event the result is ungrammatical (as
contrasted with a sentence such as *The workers all were criticized by the manager*, in which Q-float applies to the output of Passive). According to the
7.1.12 treatment of Q-float, the deep structure of 7.1.17a would be 7.1.18:

7.1.18

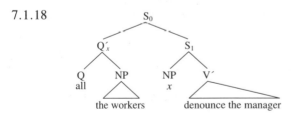

The only domain to which Passive could apply in 7.1.18 is S_1, since S_0 is not
of the form to which Passive applies until Q-float applies to it, after which the
cyclic principle would make Passive (or anything else) inapplicable. But once
Passive has applied to S_1, Q-float can no longer apply, since the bound variable
x is no longer the subject of S_1 (the output of Passive on S_1 is of the form *the*

manager be denounced by x); consequently the combination of rules and principles that we are assuming here would rule out any possible derivation for 7.1.17c–c'.

In 7.4, we will draw conclusions about *There*-insertion that are parallel to those drawn here with regard to Q-float: if underlying structures are adopted in which quantified expressions are external to the Ss that are their scopes, the cyclic principle will require that *There*-insertion be treated as applying to structures in which the existentially quantified NP is outside its host S, and that will make *There*-insertion sensitive to the scope of that quantifier.

Let us turn now to another transformation that interacts in an interesting way with quantifier scope, namely Conjunction Reduction. Consider the following sentences, taken from Partee 1970:

7.1.19 a. Few rules are both correct and easy to read.

b. Few rules are correct, and few rules are easy to read.

The expression *easy to read* in 7.1.19 presumably requires the same syntactic analysis as in such sentences as *USA Today is easy to read,* in which the surface subject of *easy* is an underlying constituent of the infinitive V' (i.e., the deep structure is something like [(*for one to read USA Today*) *is easy*]) and the transformation of **Tough-movement** moves a NP out of the dependent V' into the position of the main subject. Examples 7.1.19a and 7.1.19b obviously can differ in truth value: if many rules are correct but few of the correct ones are easy to read, then 7.1.19a is true and 7.1.19b false. The problem that 7.1.19a poses is that of providing a syntactic derivation for it without incorrectly treating it as merely a variant of 7.1.19b. That problem can be solved by identifying the deep structures of these sentences with their logical structures, in which one has a single quantifier with a conjoined S in its scope and the other is a conjunction of two Ss, each of which is the scope of a separate quantifier:

7.1.20 a. (Few: x Rule)$\wedge$(x Correct, (one Read x) Easy)

b. $\wedge$((Few: x Rule)(x Correct), (Few: y Rule)((one Read y) Easy))

In the derivation of 7.1.19a, *Tough*-movement converts "(one Read x) easy" into "x (easy (for one to read))"; since the quantified NP is outside the conjoined S, the domain to which Conjunction Reduction applies will not involve the quantified NP but only the bound variable: it will convert $\wedge$(x correct, x(easy (for one to read))) into "x $\wedge$ (correct, easy (for one to read))"; finally Q'-lowering puts (few: x rule) in place of the last formula, yielding ultimately 7.1.19a. One can derive *correct and easy to read* without falsely identifying 7.1.19a with 7.1.19b, thanks to the possibility of having a deep structure in which *few rules* is outside what underlies *x is correct and easy to read* and thus of having *Tough*-movement and Conjunction Reduction apply to domains that do not contain *few rules*.

One important problem remains: why is there not, in addition to the derivation of 7.1.19a just sketched, an alternative derivation of it involving the deep structure 7.1.20b and an application of Conjunction Reduction to a structure essentially identical to 7.1.19b? Ruling out such a spurious derivation will not be as easy as showing why Reflexivization and Equi-NP-deletion were inapplicable in derivations having the deep structures of 7.1.3a and 7.1.8b, in which it was enough to note that the logical structures of those sentences had to involve two distinct variables and thus the conditions for application of the transformations were not met, since x and y did not count as coreferential. In 7.1.20b there is nothing to prevent both variables from being called x: the part of the structure that the first Q' commands and the part that the second one commands are disjoint from each other, and hence no incoherence would result if the same letter were used for both variables. Thus, while the difference between x and y would prevent Conjunction Reduction from applying in any derivation with the deep structure 7.1.20b, nothing that has been said here so far would prevent it from applying in a derivation with the equivalent deep structure in which both variables were called x. We could, of course, exclude the latter derivation ruling by fiat that different variables must have different names, but that fiat would create a new problem, since it would prevent Conjunction Reduction from applying in some cases where it ought to: 7.1.21a ought to have the same logical structure as 7.1.21b and their derivations ought to differ only to the extent that Conjunction Reduction applies in the derivation of the former but not of the latter:

7.1.21   a. Both Tom and Dick admire few authors.

   b. Tom admires few authors, and Dick admires few authors.

If we are required to call the two variables in 7.1.21b by different names, then Conjunction Reduction ought to be inapplicable, since the two occurrences of *few authors* will then count as nonidentical.

A way out of the dilemma posed by 7.1.19 and 7.1.21 might be sought in terms of what has come to be known as the **sloppy identity** principle, that is, the principle that allows the difference in reference of the two pronouns in 7.1.22a to be ignored and thus allows 7.1.22b to be derived from a structure that also underlies 7.1.22a:[9]

7.1.22   a. John$_i$ loves his$_i$ wife, and Bill$_j$ loves his$_j$ wife too.

   b. John$_i$ loves his$_i$ wife, and Bill does too.

If the sloppy identity principle can be formulated in such a way that one can ignore the difference between the two variables in 7.1.21a but not between the two variables in 7.1.21b, then we could in fact impose the fiat restriction that variables bound by different Qs must have different names. In section 8.2, a specific proposal will be made that provides the basis for a sloppy identity principle that will allow one to ignore the difference between the variables in 7.1.21a but not in 7.1.19b.

Certain facts about the acceptability and interpretation of quantifiers in complex sentences can be explained in terms of general constraints on syntactic movements serving to rule out various applications of Q'-lowering that the examples in question would require but which would violate the constraints. Consider, for example, 7.1.23–24:

7.1.23   a. John had a fight with Bill.
         b. John had a fight with each of my teachers.
         c. John and Bill had a fight.
         d. ??John and each of my teachers had a fight.

7.1.24   a. John and Bill despise each other.
         b. John despises many of my friends, and many of my friends
            despise John.
         c. *John and many of my friends despise each other.

The oddity of 7.1.23d and 7.1.24c can be attributed to violations of the **Coordinate Structure Constraint** (**CSC**. Ross 1967), which rules out derivations in which material is moved into or out of one conjunct of a coordinate construction without it being moved into or out of all of them together:[10]

7.1.25   a. *Who did John denounce Reagan and praise?
         a'. Who did John first denounce and later praise?
         b. *The brand of beer that John drinks and smokes cigars is
              Budweiser.
         b'. The brand of beer that John drinks himself but forbids his
              children to drink is Budweiser.

The CSC rules out the step in the derivation of 7.1.25a in which the interrogative pronoun is moved to the front of the sentence (and thus out of the conjoined V' *denounce Reagan and praise who(m)*), while not excluding the corresponding step in the derivation of 7.1.25a', which moves *who* simultaneously out of both conjuncts of the conjoined V' *denounce whom$_i$ and praise whom$_i$*); similarly, it excludes the step in the derivation of 7.1.25b in which the understood relative pronoun is moved out of one conjunct of *drink which* *and smoke cigars,* while allowing the corresponding step in the derivation of 7.1.25b' in which it is moved simultaneously out of both conjuncts. In his original formulation of the CSC, Ross gave it as a restriction on moving material **out of** a coordinate structure and did not even raise the question of whether the same constraint applies to derivational steps that move something **into** a coordinate structure. There are not many transformations for which the latter possibility arises, but there are some, Conjunction Reduction being a case in point, since in the output of Conjunction Reduction the conjunction is lower in the structure than it was in deep structure, and Conjunction Reduction in fact appears to respect the CSC:

7.1.26   Quine denounced either Chomsky or Davidson, and Hockett denounced either Chomsky or Postal ⊹→ *Quine and Hockett denounced either Chomsky or Davidson and Postal, respectively.

The oddity of 7.1.23d and 7.1.24c can then be attributed to the violation of the coordinate structure constraint which takes place when the quantifier is moved into "John and x had a fight" or "John and x despise each other."

Interactions between quantifiers and the transformation of **Negative Raising**, which has been proposed in connection with sentences such as those in 7.1.27, provide the basis for a further argument (Carden 1973) for underlying structures in which quantifiers are external to their clauses.

7.1.27   a. Bill doesn't want Sam to finish the report until Friday.
            b. Lucy doesn't think that Phil will give her a red cent.

The negations in 7.1.27 appear to have the complement clauses as scope, that is, in 7.1.27a, Bill's desire is that Sam does not finish the report until Friday, and in 7.1.27b, Lucy's belief is that Phil will not give her a red cent, even though the *n't* appears in the main clause rather than the subordinate clause. The judgment that the scope of the negative is the subordinate clause is strengthened by the fact that here the subordinate clause contains a **negative polarity item**, which can only occur in the scope of a negation:[11]

7.1.28   a. *Sam finished the report until Friday.
            b. *Phil will give Lucy a red cent.

Negative Raising moves a negation out of the complement of an appropriate verb or adjective (e.g., *want, expect, think, believe, likely*) and into the clause containing that verb or adjective.

Consider now the interpretation of the sentences 7.1.29:

7.1.29   a. Victor doesn't want many people to know about his past.
          a'. Victor wants many people not to know about his past.
          b. Tim doesn't expect practically everyone to vote for him.

Example 7.1.29a allows the interpretation in which what Victor wants is that not many people know about his past, but not the interpretation that what he wants is that many people not know about his past. In 7.1.29a', however, the situation is exactly the reverse. In 7.1.29a the negation is in the main clause in surface structure, whereas in 7.1.29a' it is in the complement, as is clear from the corresponding "tag questions":[12]

7.1.30   a. Victor doesn't want many people to know about his past, does/
              *doesn't he?
          a'. Victor wants many people not to know about his past, doesn't
               he?

Thus Negative Raising has applied in 7.1.29a but not 7.1.29a'. This means that the relative scopes of the *n't* and the *many* determine whether negative transportation can apply: in 7.1.29a, where the negative is "higher than" the quantifier, Negative Raising can apply, but in 7.1.29a', where the negative is "lower than" the quantifier, Negative Raising cannot apply. Example 7.1.29b does not allow an interpretation "Tim expects that practically everyone won't vote for him": it can only be interpreted as "Tim expects that it is not the case that practically everyone will vote for him" or as "It is not the case that Tim expects that practically everyone will vote for him." Again, what determines whether Negative Raising can apply is the logical form of the complement (i.e., whether it is logically of the form $\sim$S) rather than the syntactic form that it would have if Negative Raising did not apply.

I turn finally to two classes of facts relating to **anaphora** (pronouns and other elements that take their interpretation at least in part from an **antecedent** elsewhere in the sentence or discourse). The host Ss that quantified expressions are combined with in the underlying structures posited here can serve as the antecedents of pronouns, as in the sentences 7.1.31a,b, which have the respective paraphrases 7.1.31a',b':

7.1.31   a. Most linguists admire most philosophers; that's true even of
              Hockett.
          a'. The linguists who admire most philosophers are a majority of
               linguists; even Hockett admires most philosophers.
          b. Most linguists admire most philosophers; that's true even of
              Sartre.

  b'. The philosophers who most linguists admire are a majority of
       philosophers; even Sartre is admired by most linguists.

In 7.1.31a the interpretation involves the propositional function "*x* admires
most philosophers," and *that* refers to that propositional function: the second
clause means that even Hockett satisfies the propositional function "*x* admires
most philosophers." In 7.1.31b the interpretation involves the propositional
function "most linguists admire *y*", and *that* refers to that propositional function: the second clause means that even Sartre has the property "most linguists
admire *y*." Moreover, if one pronoun refers to the one propositional function,
it is not possible for another pronoun to refer to the other propositional function:

7.1.32   Most linguists admire most philosophers; that's true even of
              Hockett, though that isn't true of Halliday/*Sartre.

In the first version of 7.1.32, both *that*'s refer to "*x* admires most philosophers" and the sentence is normal (meaning ". . . though Halliday doesn't
admire most philosophers"); however, the second version, in which one *that*
is supposed to refer to "*x* admires most philosophers" and the other one to
"most linguists admire *y*," is decidedly abnormal. This observation provides
syntactic confirmation for an analysis in which *Most linguists admire most
philosophers* has two distinct underlying structures, one in which *most linguists* is combined with "*x* admires most philosophers," and one in which *most
philosophers* is combined with "most linguists admire *y*." The availability of
the one propositional function to serve as antecedent for a pronoun implies the
nonavailability of the other, as would be predicted by an analysis in which two
distinct structures underlie the sentence, one containing the one propositional
function and the other containing the other one. It is interesting to note that
everything that I have said in this paragraph about sentences with two *most*'s
applies equally to parallel sentences with two *all*'s or two *every*'s. Thus facts
about the interpretation of *that* also provide reason for distinguishing between
(all: *fx*)(all: *gy*)*hxy* and (all: *gy*)(all: *fx*)*hxy*, notwithstanding their deductive
equivalence. It follows from this observation that there are deductively equivalent structures that must be treated as distinct.

    In conjunction with the analysis of restrictive relative clauses adopted in
2.5, the positing of structures in which the material of the quantified NP is
outside its surface clause yields a simple solution to a puzzle about zero V's
(as in *If Mary buys a new car, John will ∅ too*, in which the zero V' stands for
a repetition of *buy a new car*). Sentences in which a zero V' is contained in

its apparent antecedent were first noted by Bouton 1970 and have subsequently received attention in such works as Grinder 1976:

7.1.33   Tom kissed a woman who had ordered him to Ø.

Such sentences pose a serious problem for any syntactic analysis that restricts itself to syntactic structures in which NPs are within their host clauses. If the zero V′ of 7.1.33 is to be derived by a transformation of **V′-deletion**, which applies to a structure containing two identical V′s, deleting one of them,[13] the zero V′ in 7.1.33 would have to be derived by deletion of an occurrence of either *kiss a woman who had ordered him to* or *order him to,* since those would then be the only V′s in any available syntactic structure. But neither of those two possibilities would provide for a derivation of 7.1.33, since a structure with either of those expressions in place of the zero V′ would still not contain a V′ identical to the one that is to be deleted, e.g., in *John kissed a woman who had ordered him to* <u>kiss a woman who had ordered him to,</u> none of the V′s is identical to the underlined part. Worse, the latter sentence means something quite different from 7.1.33: it has the woman not ordering John to kiss her but ordering him to kiss a woman who had ordered him to (kiss her?). In any case, the underlying structure thus obtained would still contain a zero V′ that would have to be derived from another V′, and only an infinite underlying structure (*John kissed a woman who had ordered him to kiss a woman who had ordered him to kiss a woman who had ordered him to . . .*) would contain the requisite identical V′s, since only an infinite structure can be identical to one of its proper parts.

These problems disappear if 7.1.33 is assigned as its deep structure the sort of logical structure that was adopted in section 2.5, with the restrictive relative clause construction analyzed as a coordinate structure in which the head noun is in predicate position in one conjunct:

7.1.34 $(\exists:\wedge(x \text{ Woman}, x \text{ Ordered Tom (Tom Kiss } x)))_x \text{ (Tom Kiss } x)$

In virtue of the cyclic principle, the domain to which V′-deletion applies would be the whole structure (since nothing smaller contains the two identical occurrences of the V′ *kiss x*), and V′-deletion could apply only before Q′-lowering moved the quantifier expression into the position of the variable in the matrix S. In principle, V′-deletion might delete either occurrence of *kiss x,* but in this case only the one in the relative clause is a live option for deletion, since deleting the one in the matrix S would remove the only occurrence in the matrix S of the variable for which the Q′ must be substituted. Thus, V′-deletion applies to a finite structure in which there are two identical V′s, neither contained in the other, and only a subsequent application of Q′-lowering creates a structure having the peculiar form noted by Bouton, in which an anaphoric device is contained in its antecedent. Such a structure can arise only when the anaphoric device is of a type that must normally be derived from a copy of its antecedent (zero V', *so* as in *do so* or *I think so,* and S-denoting personal pronouns as in *I doubt it,* but not ordinary personal pronouns),[14] and only when the anaphoric device is inside a relative clause that is contained in its antecedent. The analysis proposed here explains why this phenomenon should be restricted to that class of cases.

7.2 Russell's Analysis of *the*

Bertrand Russell (1905) argued that an expression such as *the king of France* does not correspond to a constituent of logical structure: rather it represents a complex logical structure containing a predicate ("*x* is king of France") and various connectives and quantifiers, embodying the proposition that that predicate is true of one and only one element. Specifically, Russell proposed that the logical structure of 7.2.1a was 7.2.1b:[15]

7.2.1   a. The king of France is bald.
          b. $(\exists x) \wedge (KFx, (\forall y) \supset (\sim = yx, \sim KFy), Bx)$,

where KF*x* stands for "*x* is king of France" and B*x* for "*x* is bald." The content of 7.2.1b is that there is an individual such that he is king of France, no one but him is king of France, and he is bald. Russell's principal reason for proposing this analysis was to allow coherent discussion of sentences such as 7.2.1a even when there is no individual in existence who meets the description given (in this case, when there is no king of France). Thus, for Russell, 7.2.1a is true when there is one and only one king of France and that individual is bald; it is false in each of the three cases in which that fails to be so: when there is one and only one king of France and that individual is not bald, when there is no king of France, and when there is more than one king of France.

Discussion of Russell's analysis, both by Russell himself and by his critics and commentators, has been concerned almost exclusively with the second of these three cases. Thus, in the first serious attack on Russell's proposals, which had stood essentially unchallenged for forty-five years, Strawson (1950) devoted much space to arguing that 7.2.1a is not false when there is no king of France, that rather the question of truth or falsehood simply does not arise in that case; however, Strawson did not even mention the question of what should be said about 7.2.1a when there is more than one king of France. Odd as it is to say that 7.2.1a is false when there is no king of France, it is far odder to say that *The senator from Illinois is bald* is false merely because there are two senators from Illinois. This judgment of a difference between the two cases is confirmed by a difference in the naturalness of a common device for expressing disagreement; it is normal to respond *Bullshit* to a sentence that Russell's analysis would make false for reasons of nonexistence but it is quite bizarre to do so in a case of nonuniqueness:

7.2.2   a. A: The king of France is bald.
               B: Bullshit! There isn't any king of France!
          b. A: The senator from Illinois is bald.
               B: *Bullshit! There are two senators from Illinois!

Russell's analysis builds into the logical structure of sentences with *the* two stringent criteria for the successful use of *the X:* that there is an *X* and that no more than one thing is an *X,* and it builds them in in exactly the same way, so that failure of either criterion results in the same thing, namely falsehood of the proposition expressed by the sentence. Actual use of definite NPs in ordinary language is not nearly so constrained; for example, one can say *The restaurant on Clark Street is excellent,* even knowing that there are easily a hundred restaurants on Clark Street, provided that one restaurant on that street is prominent relative to the linguistic or extralinguistic context in which one utters the sentence (e.g., you have just been talking about five Korean restaurants, exactly one of which is on Clark Street), and it will express the proposition that that restaurant is excellent. See section 10.6 for an alternative account of *the* in which this context-dependence plays a central role, and section 10.1–2 for discussion of the possibility that (as proposed by Strawson 1950) when there is no king of France, 7.2.1a expresses a proposition that is neither true nor false.

For the time being, however, let us stick within Russell's framework, which did not allow truth value gaps or interactions between logical form and context, and take 7.2.1a to have precisely the truth conditions that correspond to 7.2.1b, a policy that is not too hard to live with as far as the first conjunct in 7.2.1b is concerned though quite hard to swallow as regards the second conjunct: if there is no king of France, 7.2.1a clearly does not express a true proposition, and if one takes a broad conception of falsehood, according to which everything that is not true is false, the proposition that it expresses is then false; however, the multiplicity of restaurants on Clark Street does not make *The restaurant on Clark Street is excellent* express a false proposition but at most makes it unclear what (possibly true) proposition it expresses.

What about the apparent negation of 7.2.1a, namely 7.2.3a? Russell held that 7.2.3a was ambiguous between an interpretation in which negation applied to an expression containing *the* (7.2.3b) and one in which *the* applied to an expression containing negation (7.2.3c):

7.2.3   a. The king of France is not bald.
         b. $\sim(\exists x)\wedge(KFx, (\forall y)\supset(\sim=yx, \sim KFy), Bx)$
         c. $(\exists x)\wedge(KFx, (\forall y)\supset(\sim=yx, \sim KFy), \sim Bx)$.

Example 7.2.3b denies that there is one and only one king of France and that individual is bald; 7.2.3c says that there is one and only one king of France and that that individual is not bald. Thus, in the controversial cases, those in which there is no king of France and those in which there is more than one king of France, 7.2.3b is true and 7.2.3c is false. Example 7.2.3a is a simple (and not all that convincing) illustration of the point that a **definite description** such as *the king of France* has a scope, just like a quantifier, and may be involved in scope ambiguities. Russell proposed a notation involving $(\imath x: KFx)$ as an abbreviation of the combination of quantifiers and connectives into which he analyzed *the king of France*. We will adopt a variant of Russell's notation and represent the content of 7.2.1a and 7.2.3a as follows, thus displaying the scope of the definite description more transparently than in 7.2.3b–c:[16]

7.2.4   a. $(\imath: KFx)_x Bx$ $(= 7.2.1b)$
         b. $\sim(\imath: KFx)_x Bx$ $(= 7.2.3b)$
         c. $(\imath: KFx)_x \sim Bx$ $(= 7.2.3c)$

While some doubt might be raised as to whether 7.2.4b is a legitimate interpretation of 7.2.3a, on the grounds that it may involve not ordinary negation but "metalinguistic" negation such as is described in Horn 1985, 1989, and McCawley 1991, there are clear examples where a definite description can be interpreted as within the scope of other elements or even as having scope between those of two other elements, as in the following examples taken or adapted from Neale (1990):[17]

7.2.5   a.   Every man admires the woman who raised him.
         a$'$. $(\forall{:}x \text{ Man})_x(\imath{:}\wedge(y \text{ Woman}, y \text{ Raised } x))_y (x \text{ Admires } y)$
         b.   Mary wants Bill to marry the richest debutante in Dubuque.
         b$'$. $m \text{ Want } ((\imath{:} y \text{ Richest-debutante-in-d})_y(b \text{ Marry } y))$
         c.   Each teacher heard the rumor that the best student in his class had cheated.
         c$'$. $(\forall{:} x \text{ Teacher})_x (x \text{ heard the rumor that } ((\imath{:} y \text{ Best-student-in-}x\text{'s-class})_y (y \text{ Cheated})))$

    d.   Each woman wanted the man who had deceived her to apologize for every lie he had told her.

    d'. $(\forall: x \text{ Woman})_x$ (x Want $((\iota:\wedge(y \text{ Man}, y \text{ Deceived } x))_y$ $(\forall:\wedge(z \text{ Lie}, y \text{ Told } z \text{ to } x)_z$ (y apologize to x for (y told z to x))))

Thus, it is in any event necessary to allow a definite description operator to have a determinate scope in order to account for the possible interpretations of sentences such as those in 7.2.5. I will in fact use the notation of 7.2.4 not only in the parts of this book that are concerned with Russell's analysis but even in those parts of the book in which I wish to assume a non-Russellian treatment of definite descriptions: while Russell's specific analysis can be contested on several quite serious grounds, his idea that a definite NP can be treated as a type of quantified expression having a determinate scope in relation to other elements of logical structure has stood up well, and a notation that indicates the scope of definite descriptions is desirable irrespective of whether one accepts Russell's specific analysis.

Russell's analysis of *the* has figured in a large number of semantic analyses that have been constructed from 1905 through the present. While most of these use Russell's analysis as a stopgap measure to allow the author to set *the* aside and get on to matters that really interest him and are thus not worth discussing in this book, there are a few in which Russell's analysis does serious semantic work. Before surveying some of the problems with Russell's analysis, I will make a substantial digression in order to sketch an influential application of Russell's analysis to a class of sentences that not only are of considerable linguistic interest but which have indeed figured prominently in some highly publicized controversies in syntax and semantics, namely so-called **Bach-Peters sentences** such as 7.2.6:[18]

7.2.6   The pilot that shot at it hit the MIG that chased him.

The underscoring indicates the intended pronoun-antecedent relationships: the *him* is supposed to refer to *the pilot that shot at it* and the *it* to *the MIG that chased him*. The importance of this sentence was that it showed the untenability of the popular analysis of personal pronouns as being derived from copies of their antecedent NPs: if each of the pronouns in 7.2.6 was derived from a copy of its antecedent, then the deep structure of 7.2.6 would have to contain infinitely much material (as can be seen if one tries to replace each pronoun by a copy of its antecedent and continue until no pronouns remain).

Lauri Karttunen (1971a) discovered an important characteristic of 7.2.6 that had been missed in previous discussion of it, namely, that it is ambiguous. In one interpretation, 7.2.6 refers to the pilot that shot at the MIG that chased him and says that that pilot hit that MIG; in the other interpretation, 7.2.6 refers to the MIG that chased the pilot that shot at it and says that that pilot hit that MIG. Karttunen showed the two interpretations to be distinct, in that (i) the conditions for the appropriateness of the one definite description can be met without the conditions for the appropriateness of the other one being met, and (ii) even in cases where the appropriateness conditions for both are met, the one may single out a different pilot-MIG pair than the other one does. The appropriateness conditions for the two definite descriptions are as follows:

7.2.7   a. the pilot that shot at the MIG that chased him
                There is exactly one pilot *x* such that (*x* shot at the MIG that
                chased *x*).
          b. the MIG that chased the pilot that shot at it
                There is exactly one MIG *y* such that (*y* chased the pilot that
                shot at *y*).

Consider a restricted set of MIGs and pilots and let diagrams like those given below indicate who shot at whom and who chased whom:

7.2.8   pilot   MIG   pilot
                  shot at   chased

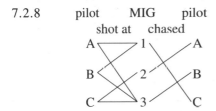

In the state of affairs represented by 7.2.8, the appropriateness conditions for 7.2.7a are met: 1 is the MIG that chased C, 2 is the MIG that chased A, 3 is the MIG that chased B, and since B shot at 3 but C did not shoot at 1 and A did not shoot at 2, B is the only pilot having the property "*x* shot at the MIG that chased *x*." However, the appropriateness conditions for 7.2.7b are not met: C is the pilot that shot at 2, but since two pilots shot at 1 and three pilots shot at 3, no one can be described as "the pilot that shot at 1" or "the pilot that shot at 3"; since 2 did not chase C, no MIG has the property "*y* chased the pilot that shot at *y*." Thus, under the one interpretation, 7.2.6 says, relative to this state of affairs, that B hit 3 and it will be true or false depending on whether B did in fact hit 3; however, under the other interpretation, 7.2.6 is vacuously false regardless of who hit whom: it is false in precisely the same way that *The king of France is bald* is false. By interchanging the roles of the MIGs and the pilots in 7.2.8, one obtains a state of affairs in which the appropriateness condition for 7.2.7b is met but not that for 7.2.7a:

7.2.9   pilot   MIG   pilot
                shot at   chased

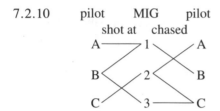

Relative to the state of affairs 7.2.9, there is exactly one MIG having the property "*y* chased the pilot that shot at *y,*" namely, 2; however, there is no pilot having the property "*x* shot at the MIG that chased *x.*"

In the state of affairs 7.2.10, 2 is the MIG that chased A, 1 is the MIG that chased B, but no MIG can be described as *the MIG that chased C,* since two MIGs chased C:

7.2.10   pilot   MIG   pilot
                shot at   chased

A──────7 1 ╲ ╱ A
B ╱ 2 ╲ B
C ╱ ╲ 3 ──────7 C

Since B shot at 1 but A did not shoot at 2, B is the only pilot having the property "*x* shot at the MIG that chased *x,*" and in the 7.2.7a interpretation, 7.2.6 says that B hit 1. B is the pilot that shot at 3, C is the pilot that shot at 2, but, since two pilots shot at 1, no pilot can be described as "the pilot that shot at 1"; since 2 chased C but 3 did not chase B, 2 is the only MIG having the property "*y* chased the pilot that shot at *y,*" and thus in the 7.2.7b interpretation, 7.2.6 says that C hit 2. This means that in the state of affairs 7.2.10, the two interpretations of 7.2.10 say different things: one of them says that B hit 1 and the other one says that C hit 2.

According to Karttunen's discussion of 7.2.6, its two interpretations should have logical structures involving stacked definite descriptions corresponding to 7.2.7a and 7.2.7b:

7.2.11   a. (ʔ: ∧(*x* Pilot, (ʔ: ∧(*y* MIG, *y* Chase *x*))$_y$ (*x* Shoot *y*)))$_x$
              b. (ʔ: ∧(*y* MIG, (ʔ: ∧ (*x* Pilot, *x* Shoot *y*))$_x$ (*y* Chase *x*)))$_y$

But what exactly are 7.2.11a and 7.2.11b combined with? It won't do to say that they are combined with "*x* Hit *y,*" since a combination of either of them with "*x* Hit *y*" would be incoherent: one of the two variables in "*x* Hit *y*" would be outside the scope of the definite description operator that binds it, for example,

7.2.12

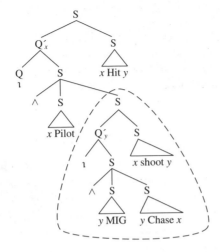

Only the part of the tree inside the dotted line is commanded by the quantifier that binds *y*.[19] The best that can be done using standard logical formulas is to analyze both interpretations of 7.2.6 as involving more definite description operators than are apparent in the surface, that is, take 7.2.11a as applying not to "*x* Hit *y*" but to "*x* hit the MIG that chased *x*" and take 7.2.11b as applying not to "*x* Hit *y*" but to "the pilot that shot at *y* hit *y*." The resulting structure appears to have appropriate truth conditions and satisfies the coherence conditions, for example, the logical structure of the 7.2.7a interpretation of 7.2.6 would be given not by the incoherent 7.2.12 but by

7.2.13

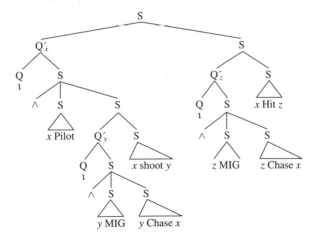

In the alternative approach to be discussed in section 10.6, the coherence conditions are weakened in such a way as to allow expressions such as 7.2.12, and the truth conditions provided for such expressions in fact turn out to be appropriate for 7.2.6.

I turn now to a survey of some problems with Russell's analysis. I begin with one that can be solved in a fairly simple fashion and then turn to others that will require more radical deviations from Russell's general approach. Discussions of Russell's treatment of *the* have rarely devoted any attention to definite predicate NPs, as in 7.2.14:

7.2.14   a. Michael Moskowitz is the mayor of Hoople, South Dakota.
         b. Sheila Ostrovsky is the student who did the best exam paper.

There are two ways in which one might fit such sentences into a Russellian analysis: either apply the Russellian analysis directly to them, taking them to involve constituents "Michael Moskowitz is x" and "Sheila Ostrovsky is x," with *is* taken as meaning $=$, or give an analysis of predicate definite NPs as corresponding to parts of formulas such as 7.2.1b. Under the former approach, 7.2.14a would be analyzed as in 7.2.15a, and under the latter approach it would be given an analysis such as 7.2.15a′, involving constituents similar to the first two conjuncts in 7.2.1b:

7.2.15   a. $(\imath\colon x \text{ Mayor } h)_x \, (m \,=\, x)$
             i.e. $(\exists x)\wedge(x \text{ Mayor } h, \, (\forall y)\supset(\sim(y \,=\, x),\sim(y \text{ Mayor } h)),$
             $m \,=\, x)$
         a′. $\wedge(m \text{ Mayor } h, \, (\forall y)\supset(\sim(y \,=\, m), \, \sim(y \text{ Mayor } h)))$

The two analyses have different implications for the possible interpretations of sentences involving predicate definite NPs: according to the analysis in 7.2.15a, such sentences should potentially be ambiguous with regard to the scope of the definite description, whereas according to that in 7.2.15a′, there should be no possibility of a scope ambiguity, since the sole quantifier in 7.2.15a′ has to have the second conjunct as its scope. We are thus led to compare the possible interpretations of sentences in which a predicate definite NP is embedded in a larger structure and of otherwise parallel sentences in which the definite NP is not in predicate position, for example:

7.2.16   a. Michael Moskowitz wants to be the mayor of Hoople, SD.
         b. Michael Moskowitz wants to meet the mayor of Hoople, SD.

There is a clear scope ambiguity in 7.2.16b: it can be interpreted either with the whole sentence as the scope of the definite description (this is the *de re* interpretation, which picks out a certain person as the mayor of Hoople,

SD, and says that Moskowitz wants to meet that person, with the fact that that person is the mayor of Hoople not being a condition on the fulfillment of that wish—he could be thrown out of office and Moskowitz would still want to meet him), or with the definite description having only the embedded "Michael Moskowitz meets x" as its scope (this is the *de dicto* interpretation, in which Moskowitz's wish is fulfilled if he meets whoever is mayor of Hoople, regardless of who that happens to be). The most obvious interpretation of 7.2.16a is a *de dicto* one in which Moskowitz's wish is fulfilled if he holds the office of mayor of Hoople. With a little strain one can find an extra interpretation of 7.2.16a, indeed, two extra interpretations. Both refer to Moskowitz changing his identity rather than his occupation. One is *de re:* there is a certain person who is the mayor of Hoople, SD, and Moskowitz wants to be him; the other is *de dicto:* Moskowitz desires that, regardless of who is mayor of Hoople, SD, he should become that person. The only way that I can see to accommodate the three-way ambiguity of 7.2.16a in an essentially Russellian analysis is to adopt **both** 7.2.15a and 7.2.15a′ in analyses of 7.2.14a and represent its three senses as:

7.2.17 a_1. $(\imath{:}\ x\ \text{Mayor}\ h)(m\ \text{Want}\ (m\ =\ x))$
         a_2. $m\ \text{Want}\ ((\imath{:}\ x\ \text{Mayor}\ h)(m\ =\ x))$
         a'. $m\ \text{Want}\ (\wedge(m\ \text{Mayor}\ h,\ (\forall\ y)\supset(\sim(y\ =\ m),\sim(y\ \text{Mayor}\ h))))$

This discussion provides grounds for distinguishing between a *be* of identity and a copula *be,* with a definite NP after the *be* of identity analyzed as in 7.2.15a and a definite NP after a copula *be* as in 7.2.15a′. Only in the latter case, then, is the NP strictly strictly speaking a **predicate** NP. If an adherent of the Russellian analysis accepts this argument for an analysis of predicate definite NPs as in 7.2.15a′, the one way that he could retain some sort of uniformity in his analysis of definite NPs in general would be to treat nonpredicate definite NPs as analysed in terms of predicate definite NPs; for example, 7.2.1a could be analyzed as in 7.2.18a, which would amount to 7.2.18b, in view of the suggested analysis of predicate definite NPs, which would agree with Russell's analysis except for having two of the conjuncts grouped together:

7.2.18   a. $(\exists x)\ \wedge\ (x$ is the king of France, x is bald$)$
         b. $(\exists x)\ \wedge\ (\wedge(\text{KF}(x),\ (\forall y)\supset(\sim\ =\ yx,\sim\text{KF}(y))),\ \text{B}(x))$

In this modified Russellian analysis, it is not strictly speaking the *the* that has a scope but rather the existential quantifier that is combined with the *the;* for example, under that proposal 7.2.3b–c would be reanalyzed as:

7.2.19   b. $\sim(\exists x)\wedge(x$ is the king of France, x is bald)
        c. $(\exists x)\wedge(x$ is the king of France, $\sim(x$ is bald))

A problem with Russell's analysis that is much harder to remedy is that there is no apparent way in which it can be generalized so as to cover plural definite NPs, as in:

7.2.20   a. The operas of Mozart are delightful.
        b. The dogs are barking.

It is occasionally suggested that plural definite NPs be analyzed as universally quantified, e.g., that 7.2.20a be assigned the same logical form as *All operas of Mozart are delightful*. However, that suggestion is highly unsatisfactory, not only because it gives *the* a different analysis when the NP is plural than when it is singular, but also because it misrepresents the truth conditions of sentences as in 7.2.20: it can be true that the dogs are barking even if it is false that all of them are barking, and a speaker who utters 7.2.20a is not thereby committing himself to the proposition that such an obscure Mozart opera as *Ascanio in Alba* is delightful, as he would be if he were to say *All the operas of Mozart are delightful*. Likewise, in saying that the dogs are barking, one is not saying that **all** dogs are barking: the sentence refers only to whatever dogs are being referred to as *the dogs* (perhaps the dogs that my upstairs neighbor keeps in his apartment), not to dogs in general, and does not even say that all of **those** dogs are barking.

This last point is similar to a problem that arises with singular NPs, namely that, despite what the "uniqueness" term of Russell's formula says to the contrary, a sentence such as 7.2.21 does not imply that there is only one dog:

7.2.21   The dog is barking.

Adherents of Russell's analysis occasionally attempt to reconcile it with the interpretation of such banal sentences as 7.2.21 by exploiting the indeterminacy of the "universe of discourse": if the universe of discourse is taken to contain only one dog, namely the one that 7.2.21 is supposed to refer to, the Russell analysis yields a defensible interpretation of it. The problem with that response is that a Russellian universe of discourse is supposed to provide the values of **all** bound individual variables, not just the ones bound by a definite description operator, and it is easy to construct sentences in which a definite NP is used in combination with a quantified NP that could not receive a plausible interpretation unless the universe of discourse contained more dogs (or whatever) than the one that the definite NP was supposed to refer to:

7.2.22   a. The dog barked at another dog.
       b. The postman likes all postmen.

The Russellean formula corresponding to 7.2.22a is self-contradictory (the uniqueness term implies that there isn't such a thing as "another dog"), and the interpretation that would normally be assigned to 7.2.22a requires a universe of discourse containing at least two dogs; the Russellean formula corresponding to 7.2.22b would have the same truth conditions as that for *The postman likes himself,* though that sentence clearly can differ in truth value from 7.2.22b. The problem that these examples bring out is that while Russell's formal language requires that all individual variables take their values from a single "universe of discourse," the variable bound by a definite description operator often seems to take its values from a different and much smaller set. In the alternative treatment of definite descriptions that will be given in section 10.6, there will in fact be a different domain for variables bound by ꟼ, and sentences like 7.2.22 will cease to be problematic.

    I turn finally to a much less widely noted difficulty with Russell's analysis. There is a pattern of inference (7.2.23a) that Russell's analysis implies is valid but which in fact has numerous apparently invalid instances such as 7.2.23b–c:

7.2.23   a. The X is a
         $\sim(a - b)$
        Therefore, the X is not b.
       b. Leonard Linsky's office address is Dept. of Philosophy,
          University of Chicago.
         Dept. of Philosophy, University of Chicago $\neq$ 1010 E. 59th St.,
          Chicago 60637.
         Therefore, Linsky's office address is not 1010 E. 59th St.,
          Chicago 60637.
       c. The place where Edward Koch lives is New York.
         New York $\neq$ Manhattan.
         Therefore, the place where Koch lives is not Manhattan.

In both of these cases, the premises are true but the conclusion is false. What makes it possible for the premises to be true while the conclusion is false is that the a and b of the second premise are distinct but not disjoint. The philosophy department and several other departments have their offices at 1010 E. 59th St., and accordingly "1010 E. 59th St., Chicago 60637" is the office address both of many persons whose office address is "Dept. of Philosophy,

University of Chicago" and of many persons whose office address is not. Manhattan is distinct from New York in virtue of being a proper part of it; a person who lives in New York (City) might live in Manhattan or in any of the other four boroughs, and the proposition that he lives in New York gives no information about whether Manhattan is the borough in which he lives. The Russellian analysis makes 7.2.23a valid only because the "uniqueness" term is formulated in terms of identity versus nonidentity rather than overlap versus disjointness: if "$\sim(y = x)$" in the Russell formula were replaced by the more restrictive condition "y is disjoint from x," it would no longer imply that 7.2.23a was valid, since "$\sim(a = b)$" would no longer be enough to let one draw any inference. I conjecture that the invalidity of 7.2.23a has so long gone unnoticed only because philosophers working in the Russellian tradition have restricted their attention to entities that overlap only if identical, e.g., persons and numbers.[20]

7.3. Sets in the Object Language; Extended Predicate Logic

The "grammar" for predicate logic that we constructed in section 2.2 allowed as arguments only **individual** constants and individual variables, that is, constants that denoted an object (rather than a set) and variables whose values were individual objects rather than sets. If our system of logical form is to be rich enough to accommodate sentences such as *One of them killed Lefty* or *He's one of them,* propositions of the form "$x \in M$" will have to be admitted into logical structure. $\in$ will fit into logical structure as a two-place predicate having an individual in its first place and a set in its second place.

There are in fact many expressions of natural language which can reasonably be interpreted as predicates which have a set as argument:

7.3.1   a. The king and the queen are an amiable couple.
      b. Tom, Dick, and Harry conspired to assassinate the Postmaster General.
      c. Your friends are similar in that they are all canasta freaks.
      d. Bob and Carol met Ted and Alice at O'Rourke's Pub.
      e. The boys carried the piano up the stairs.
      f. Sammy, Mike, and Billy ganged up on George.

The analysis of these examples is controversial. First of all, it is not completely clear that it is the set of persons rather than some entity associated with that set that serves as argument. For example, one might hold that the "couple" consisting of the king and the queen was not identical to the set consisting of the king and the queen but was rather some object of a different type (more like, say, a club or a partnership) though it also consists of members. Second, it has been suggested (e.g., Gleitman 1965) that sentences such as 7.3.1b and 7.3.1c have an understood reciprocal pronoun (cf. *Tom, Dick, and Harry conspired with each other to assassinate the Postmaster General*) and really involve individual variables or constants as the arguments of the predicates, just as in *Tom, Dick, and Harry hate each other.*

The first of these objections to positing set arguments in 7.3.1 is implausible, since the composite entities that figure in 7.3.1 are not of the sort that, like a string quartet or an army, retains its identity even when its membership changes: when Henry VIII had Ann Boleyn beheaded and married Jane Seymour, a couple did not simply change its membership—rather, one couple ceased to exist and a new couple came into existence. Moreover, an expression that refers to a couple made up of two given persons can simultaneously refer to some other sort of composite entity that they make up. Suppose, for example, that there is a palace softball team on which the king is the pitcher and the queen the catcher; the king and the queen then form their team's battery, and the expression *the king and the queen* can be used in simultaneously referring to them as a couple and as a battery:

7.3.2   The king and the queen are both an amiable couple and an
          excellent battery.

The acceptability of sentences such as 7.3.2 argues that "amiable couple" and "excellent battery" are predicated of the same thing, which would presumably be the set consisting of the king and the queen.

The correctness of the second objection can be evaluated only on the basis of facts about reciprocal pronouns and about the sentences in which a supposed understood reciprocal occurs. It should be noted at the outset that not all candidates for an analysis with set arguments are open to an analysis with individual arguments and an understood reciprocal; for example, 7.3.1a does not allow any paraphrases along the lines of

7.3.3   a. *The king and the queen are an amiable couple to each other.
        b. *The king is an amiable couple to the queen and the queen is an
           amiable couple to the king.

For the sentences for which an analysis involving an understood reciprocal is plausible, two questions must be raised: (i) do they mean the same as corresponding sentences containing reciprocals? And (ii) can the sentences with reciprocals be analyzed as having only individual arguments? The most obvious first approximation to an analysis of reciprocals is to say that a sentence with *each other* involves universal quantifiers that range over all pairs of distinct elements of the given set:[21]

7.3.4   They hate each other.

$(\forall{:}x{\in}M)_x(\forall{:}\wedge(y{\in}M, \sim = yx))_y(x \text{ Hate } y)$

This is only a first approximation and will not work as an analysis of some of the more interesting examples of reciprocals, such as

7.3.5   a. Linguists are always insulting each other.
        b. They spent the afternoon taking group photographs of each other.
        c. Those boys have a tendency to gang up on each other.

However, let's accept it for the time being and see how it would work as an analysis of reciprocal analogues of 7.3.1b–c:

7.3.6   a. Tom, Dick, and Harry conspired with each other to assassinate the Postmaster General.
        b. Your friends are similar to each other in that they are all canasta freaks.

Example 7.3.6a does in fact seem to be an accurate paraphrase of 7.3.1b, but it resists analysis along the lines of 7.3.4: it doesn't say that each of the three men conspired with each of the others (i.e., that Tom conspired with Dick, Dick conspired with Harry, etc.) but rather that there was a single conspiracy in which all three participated (as opposed to, say, three different conspiracies, each involving two of them). The only obvious alternative to allowing a set as the first argument of *conspire* is to recognize a strange type of entity, a "conspiracy," and analyze 7.3.1b as asserting the existence of a conspiracy such that Tom, Dick, and Harry all participated in it and such that its goal was the assassination of the Postmaster General. Essentially the same alternatives are available in some examples (such as 7.3.1e) to which no reciprocal sentence corresponds: in the interpretation of 7.3.1e which refers to an event in which the boys jointly carry the piano (as opposed to the interpretation which is paraphraseable as *Each of the boys carried the piano up the stairs*), one must either allow a set as subject of *carry* or analyze the sentence in terms of auxiliary notions like "an act" and "participate": there was an act x such that each of the boys participated in x and x consisted in carrying the piano up the stairs. However, the latter analysis still has to contend with the problem of what the subject of *carry* is. Example 7.3.6b would fit into the mold of 7.3.4 if it weren't for the problem of how to fit in the *in that S*. You could of course construct the formula

7.3.7 $(\forall: x \in M)(\forall: \wedge(y \in M, \sim = yx))[x$ is similar to y in that $(x$ is a canasta freak and y is a canasta freak$)]$

However, 7.3.7 does not accord with the *all* that occurs in the surface form of the *in that* clause. If *all of them are canasta freaks* is to be a logical constituent of 7.3.1c, as it presumably has to, 7.3.7 will have to be rejected, and the remaining alternatives are as before: either *similar* has a set subject or the analysis makes reference to "a similarity" which all the individuals participate in.

The proposal that the predicates involved in 7.3.1 have set arguments thus withstands the more obvious objections to it and deserves to be treated seriously. Let us then see what revisions have to be made in the grammar of section 2.2 in order to accommodate set arguments. It will be necessary to draw a distinction between set-type and individual-type constants and variables. It will not do just to use the brute force ploy of different typography (using capital letters for set indices and small letters for individual indices), since the rules giving the contexts in which each predicate may be used will have to distinguish between the two types. For the moment, let me use close to brute force and take the grammar to have a rule which adds to each argument (Arg) node a feature specification "+ Set" or "− Set" and have those feature specifications play a role in the remainder of the grammar. These features specifications correspond not to extra nodes dominated by the Arg nodes but to extra labels **on** the Arg nodes:

7.3.8   Arg is $+$ Set or $-$ Set
$\text{Arg}_{+\text{Set}}$: M $\text{Arg}_{+\text{Set}}$: M_1 ... $\text{Arg}_{-\text{Set}}$: x $\text{Arg}_{-\text{Set}}$: x_1 ...
$\text{Arg}_{+\text{Set}}$: M $\text{Arg}_{+\text{Set}}$: N_1 ... $\text{Arg}_{-\text{Set}}$: y $\text{Arg}_{-\text{Set}}$: y_1 ...

...   .

Pred: Love / $\text{Arg}_{-\text{Set}}$ —— Arg
Pred: Couple / $\text{Arg}_{+\text{Set}}$ ——
Pred: Gang-up / $\text{Arg}_{+\text{Set}}$ —— Arg
Pred: $\in$ / Arg —— $\text{Arg}_{+\text{Set}}$

The rule for "love" given here restricts the first argument to being an individual but imposes no restriction on whether the second argument is $+$ Set or $-$ Set. I have formulated it this way in accordance with my feeling that only an individual can love, though the objects of his love may be either individuals or sets of individuals, and loving a set is not the same thing as loving each of its members; for example, you can love the Marx brothers without it necessarily being the case that you love Groucho, love Chico, and love Harpo.

Since the sets that figure as the arguments of the predicates in 7.3.1 are described in natural language by expressions that correspond to specification by enumeration and specification by description (*Tom, Dick, and Harry carried the piano* vs. *The boys who live in the next apartment carried the piano*), the grammar ought to be further modified to allow $\text{Arg}_{+\,\text{Set}}$ to dominate expressions that serve to define sets. An obvious proposal to make here is that we incorporate into our formal language, structures corresponding to the devices for describing sets that were given in section 5.1, namely describing them by enumeration and by giving conditions for membership in the set:[22]

7.3.9 a. $\text{Arg}_{+\,\text{Set}}$: Arg^n $(n \geq 2)$
   b. $\text{Arg}_{+\,\text{Set}}$: Arg S

There is a terminological inconsistency in 7.3.9, namely, that we now have "Arg" appearing in positions other than "argument positions." For example, if *Tom, Dick, and Harry* is the subject of *conspire,* then neither *Tom* nor *Dick* nor *Harry* is an argument of *conspire: conspire* is predicated of the set, not of each of its members. Terminological purism would demand that we distinguish between the **relational** notion of "argument" (i.e., the notion of being an argument *of* something) and the **categorial** notion that we have been calling "Arg." Since the linguist's category "noun phrase" (NP) has been used in a way that corresponds closely to our "Arg" (i.e., items of types that "fill argument positions" are all labeled "NP"), a terminological purist might prefer to write "NP" where we have been writing "Arg," as in 7.3.10, and we will in fact henceforth adopt that notational policy:[23]

7.3.10

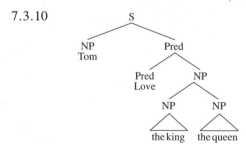

7.4. Other Quantifiers

The only quantifier words that we have discussed in any detail so far are those that correspond roughly to the ∀ and ∃ of standard logic. In this section I wish to take up other words that appear in the same syntactic positions as do

all, each, some, and the like and which play a role in the binding of a variable:
the numerals *one, two, three,* . . . , vague numerals such as *several, a couple,*
a few, and perhaps *many,* approximate numerals such as *roughly one hundred,*
over fifty, and *between fifty and a hundred,* near-universal quantifiers such as
almost all and *all but one/two/* . . . , negative quantifiers such as *no* (= *not*
any), few, and *not many,* and the unclassifiable *most.*

There is a syntactic test that allows one to identify some of these items as
'existential', namely, the possibility of using existential *there* when the subject NP has the given quantifier:

7.4.1   There are some people who think Daley was a saint.

There are $\left\{\begin{array}{l}\text{many}\\ \text{a lot of}\\ \text{a large number of}\\ \text{a great many}\end{array}\right\}$ Americans who like baseball.

There are $\left\{\begin{array}{l}\text{a few}\\ \text{a couple/number of}\\ \text{three/several}\\ \text{at least/most 30}\\ \text{few}\\ \text{not many}\\ \text{(almost) no}\\ \text{*most}\end{array}\right\}$ books that I'd never recommend to a student.

There aren't any hangers in the closet.
*There are (almost) all of the books on the table.

These facts pose the problem of how to analyze the various expressions in
such a way that something can be identified that is shared by quantifiers that
according to this test are "existential" but is absent from the other quantifiers.

It is easy to come up with an analysis in which the various "existential"
quantifiers all correspond to logical structures in which an existential quantifier binds a set variable; for example, one might analyze 7.4.2a as 7.4.2b:

7.4.2   a. Many Americans like baseball.
         b. $(\exists{:}\wedge(\text{M Large}, (\forall{:}x{\in}\text{M})_x(x \text{ is an American})))_M[(\forall{:}x{\in}\text{M})_x \,(x$
            Likes baseball)]

That is, there is a large set of Americans such that the members of that set all
like baseball. What is not so easy is to exclude similar analyses of the nonex-
istential quantifiers. For example, unless we can exclude the fairly plausible
analysis of 7.4.3a as 7.4.3b, we cannot take the existentially quantified set
variable of 7.4.2b as being responsible for the existential character of *many:*

7.4.3   a. Most Americans like baseball.
         b. $(\exists{:}\wedge(\text{M more than half of } \{x{:} x \text{ is an American}\}))_M [(\forall{:}x{\in}\text{M})_x$
            $(x \text{ Likes baseball})]$

However, we should not be too hasty in accepting 7.4.3b as an analysis of 7.4.3a. Note that there are other expressions that correspond more directly to 7.4.3b, and those differ from *most* in allowing existential *there*, at least according to many speakers' judgments:[24]

7.4.4   a. There are more than half/50 percent of all Americans who
              distrust politicians.
         b. There are over half/50 percent of all Americans who distrust
              politicians.
         c. There are a/*the majority of (all) Americans who distrust
              politicians.
         d. *There are most Americans who distrust politicians.

Let us hold the analysis of *most* in abeyance until later in this section, noting here simply that the approach to existential *there* adopted here requires that an analysis of *most* be justified in which it (unlike such supposed paraphrases as *a majority of*) is not represented as an existential quantifier plus the sort of material that appears in 7.4.2b.

    Let us attempt to set up logical forms for the various quantifiers other than *most,* starting with what looks like the simplest case, that of numerals. If we are going to follow the general scheme of 7.4.2b, we will need to give an analysis containing a term that says the numeral is the number of members in the set. Accordingly, let us introduce a two-place predicate No, with "M No n" to be interpreted as "M is n in number," i.e., "There are (exactly) n members in M." We can then propose 7.4.5b as an analysis of 7.4.5a:

7.4.5   a. Three linguists were drunk.
         b. $(\exists{:}\wedge((\forall{:}x{\in}M)_x(x \text{ is a linguist}), M \text{ No } 3))_M(\forall{:}y{\in}M)_y(y$ was
              drunk)

Suppose that we provisionally accept 7.4.5b and ask how such a semantic structure might be related to the surface form 7.4.5a on the basis of the most general rules possible. Since expressions such as $(\forall{:}x{\in}M)(x \text{ Drunk})$ are the means that we have chosen to represent that "they" are drunk, where "they" are the members of the set M, and since set indices such as M are analogs to plural pronouns the way that individual indices such as x are analogous to singular pronouns, I propose that the syntactic derivation of such a sentence as 7.4.5a involves a transformation (henceforth called **Aggregation**) by which $(\forall{:}x{\in}M)fx$ is replaced by fM, i.e., a universal proposition about the members of a set is replaced by a sentence in which the index of that set appears in place of the bound individual variable.[25] Some such rule will probably be necessary anyway in virtue of sentences such as those in 7.4.6 in which a set-denoting subject is combined with a conjoined V' whose conjuncts are a set predicate and an individual predicate:

7.4.6   a. The persons in the next room are linguists and are three in
                number.
            b. The persons in the next room are linguists and met at a
                conference on bilingualism.

The proposed rule of Aggregation makes possible the application of Conjunction Reduction even though in logical structure one of the two V's has an individual variable as its subject and the other has a set variable: it yields a derived structure in which both have the set variable M as subject. The conversion of $\wedge((\forall{:}x{\in}M)_x(x$ be a linguist, M No 3)) into (M be 3 linguists) can be accomplished by Aggregation in conjunction with independently motivated transformations. Let us assume that "M No 3" can be realized as "M is 3" or "M is 3 in number," just as "x is blue" and "x is blue in color" would be alternative realizations of a proposition "x Col blue" expressing a relation between objects and colors.[26] The coordinate structure in the domain expression is, after the application of Aggregation, of the form that we took in section 2.5 to underlie restrictive relative clauses. That structure can undergo Relative-clause Formation (RCF), which adjoins the second conjunct to a predicate N' in the first conjunct, the relative clause can undergo Relative-clause Reduction (RCR), which optionally deletes a subject relative pronoun, reducing a relative clause to its predicate phrase, and if we treat numerals as belonging to the category "adjective," that step can be followed by Adjective-preposing, which puts an adjective before an N' when it has become an adjunct to that N' through RCR. The derivation of 7.4.5a can then be sketched as in 7.4.7:[27]

7.4.7

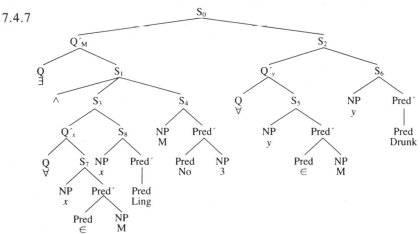

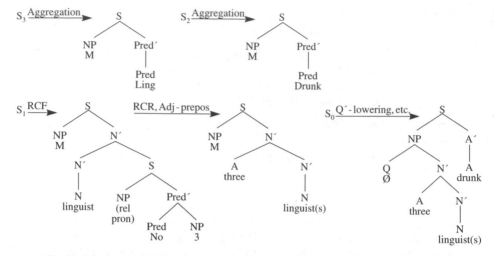

(Omitted from this derivation are steps that insert the copula *be* in S₂, mark the noun *linguist* as plural, combine *be* with the present tense element that would be in an additional S of the underlying structure, and make the tense element agree with the subject *three linguists* by marking it third-person plural.)

One noteworthy feature of this derivation is that it makes the numeral not, strictly speaking, a quantifier but rather a modifier. This detail of the analysis has the important implication that numerals fit into the syntactic structure of NPs differently than true quantifiers do. In particular, such a treatment of numerals, in conjunction with an analysis of restrictive relative clauses as adjuncts of N's, implies that while a quantifier can only be higher in the structure of a NP than a restrictive relative (7.4.8a), a numeral can appear either higher (7.4.8b) or lower (7.4.8b') than a restrictive relative, and I have argued (McCawley 1981a) that NPs of both of the latter shapes are attested in English:

7.4.8   a.   b.

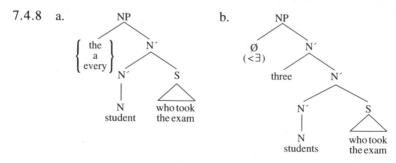

b′.

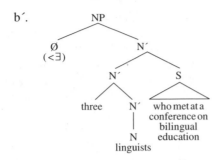

The restrictive relative clause in each case is derived from a conjoined clause containing an index that appears in the other conjunct as the subject of a predicate N′, an individual index in the case of 7.4.8b and a set index in the case of 7.4.8b′. It is the possibility of (derived) structures in which *three linguists* is a predicate N′ that makes relative clause structures such as appear in 7.4.8b′ possible.

The syntactic distinction drawn here between numerals and true quantifiers is confirmed by the fact that relative clauses in which the relativized NP refers to a set rather than an individual are possible with numerals but not with universal quantifiers (7.4.9a), and the existence of structures like 7.4.8b′ is confirmed by the possibility of conjoining two or more numeral + noun combinations that share a restrictive relative (7.4.9b):

7.4.9   a. Three/several/*all/*any linguists who met at a conference on
              bilingual education were drinking and carousing.
          b. Three linguists, two anthropologists, and one sociologist who
              had met at a conference on bilingual education were among
              those arrested.

Moreover, while *the* can appear in quantifier position in sentences parallel to 7.4.9a, the conjuncts in sentences parallel to 7.4.9b must be all indefinite or (perhaps marginally) all definite, but combinations mixing conjuncts with *the* and conjuncts with only a numeral are excluded:[28]

7.4.10   a. The linguists who met at the conference were arrested.
          b. The linguists and (?the) anthropologists who met at the
               conference were among those arrested.
          b′. *Two linguists and the anthropologists who met at the
               conference were among those arrested.
          b″. The two linguists and (the) three anthropologists who met at
               the conference were among those arrested.

These restrictions are consequences of the approach taken here: the structure in which ∃ binds the set variable M can involve any description of M (e.g., that M consists of three linguists and two anthropologists) and the clause specifying what M consists of can be conjoined with another clause that would underlie a restrictive relative clause, say, a clause specifying that all members of M were among those arrested. A true quantifier (including a definite description operator) must command all occurrences of the variable that it binds, which means that the only way in which a true quantifier could be involved in a structure in which conjoined NPs share a restrictive relative clause would be for the sentence to have a logical structure in which the quantifier is combined with a domain expression that provides all the nouns and the relative clause, which is to say, a structure of the shape 7.4.11:

7.4.11

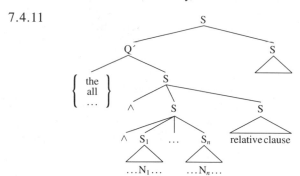

This can give rise to 7.4.10b or 7.4.10b″ if *the* is allowed to distribute itself over the conjuncts (i.e., logically there is only one *the,* but it is manifested in each of the conjuncts); any of the S*ᵢ* can itself be a coordinate structure that provides a source for a numeral. No derivation of 7.4.10b′ from anything of this form is possible, since if the *the* has the deep structure position indicated in 7.4.10, it must either be manifested on every conjunct or appear at the very beginning of the NP, applying to all the conjuncts jointly.

In the derivation proposed in 7.4.7, the logical structure is of the general shape 7.4.12a, and applications of Aggregation and the relative clause rules convert it respectively into 7.4.12b–c:

7.4.12   a.

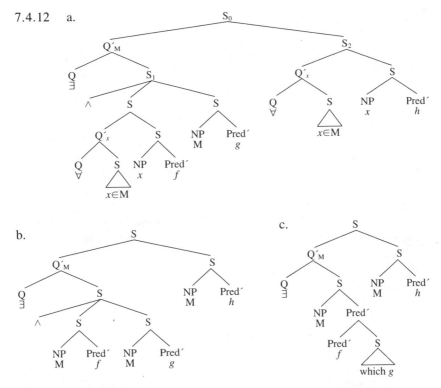

Let us ask how **There-insertion,** the transformation that inserts existential *there* and shifts the underlying subject into the V' as in 7.4.1, might fit into a derivation that involves such structures. The possibility of *There*-insertion depends on the quantifier in the subject NP, i.e., provided the V' has an appropriate form and meaning, an existentially quantified subject NP allows *There*-insertion, but a definite or universally quantified subject NP, or one with *most* does not allow it. This means that the domain to which *There*-insertion has to include the quantified subject, i.e., in a structure like 7.4.12a it would have to be S_0 and not S_2. But this means that *There*-insertion will have to apply prior to the application of Q-lowering to S_0, and will thus have to apply as in 7.4.13a rather than (as is commonly assumed) 7.4.13b:

7.4.13   a.

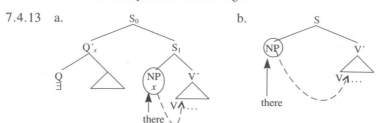

As in the case of Q-float that was discussed in 7.1, with quantified expressions outside their host Ss in deep structure, the cyclic principle would be violated if the input to *There*-insertion were a structure as in 7.4.13b that is derived by Q-lowering rather than a structure as in 7.4.13a that reflects structural relations prior to the application of Q-lowering.

But if *There*-insertion applies as in 7.4.13a, the analysis correctly predicts that, as was observed in McCawley 1970, *There*-insertion requires the S into which it inserts *there* to be the scope of an existential quantifier, as in 7.4.14, where the version without *There*-insertion is ambiguous with regard to whether the main clause or the complement clause is the scope of the quantifier, while the version with *There*-insertion unambiguously has the complement clause as its scope:

7.4.14   a. Bill thinks that some drugs are in short supply.
          b. Bill thinks that there are some drugs in short supply.

With *There*-insertion applying as in 7.4.13a, it will be applicable in 7.4.14 only if *some drugs* has narrow scope, thus deriving 7.4.14b; if *some drugs* has wide scope in a structure underlying 7.4.14a, the conditions for *There*-insertion will not be met, since the subject of the S with which *some drugs* is combined will then not be the bound variable but rather *Bill*.[29]

According to this treatment of *There*-insertion, all quantifiers that can be analyzed as in 7.4.12a ought to allow its application: with such a semantic structure, the various steps of Aggregation and Relative-clause Formation will apply with S_1, S_2, and their parts as domains, and the input to *There*-insertion will then be as 7.4.12c, which will conform to the template in 7.4.13a. The part of 7.4.12 where analyses can differ from each other is the second conjunct of S_1: for the sentences analyzed so far, that S takes the form "M No n," and replacing it by a S that gives a different property of M should yield an analysis of another possible quantified NP. One class of quantified NPs for which such a S can be found is those that specify the size of a set imprecisely, e.g., the sentences in 7.4.15 could be given analyses in which the second conjunct of S_1 takes each of the indicated forms:

7.4.15   a.   Many linguists are insane.
        a'.   ($\imath$: M No n)$_n$(n Large), i.e., the number of members of M is large.[30]
        b.   Approximately 50 students passed the exam.
        b'.   ($\imath$: M No n)$_n$(n Near 50), i.e., the number of members of M is near 50.
        c.   Over 50 students passed the exam.
        c'.   ($\imath$: M No n)$_n$($n > 50$), i.e. the number of members of M is more than 50.
        d.   Several brokerage firms went bankrupt last year.
        d'.   ($\imath$: M No n)$_n \wedge (n > 2, n < 10)$, i.e., the number of members of M is more than 2 and less than 10.[31]
        e.   A large/small/substantial number of politicians are in trouble.
        e'.   ($\imath$: M No n)$_n \wedge (n$ Number, n Large) (or n Small, n Substantial, ...)

The analysis adopted here implies that such quantified NPs can be the displaced subjects of sentences with *There*-insertion, and that implication is in fact correct:

7.4.16

$$\text{There were} \left\{ \begin{array}{l} \text{many/several} \\ \text{approximately/over 50} \\ \text{a large/small/substantial number of} \end{array} \right\} \text{students in the room.}$$

Before continuing this survey of quantified NPs, it is necessary to point out an important respect in which these analyses as they stand are inadequate. All that the analyses say is that there **is** a set having the given property, all of whose members are insane, passed the exam, etc.: it doesn't say that (in the case of 7.4.15d) the **total** number of brokerages that went bankrupt is between 3 and 9; thus, strictly speaking, the analysis offered for 7.4.15d would be assigned the value "True" even in a state of affairs in which hundreds of brokerages went bankrupt last year, because a set consisting of hundreds of bankrupt brokerages will contain subsets with smaller numbers of members, and a six-member set of bankrupt brokerages would suffice to make the formula true even if it leaves out hundreds of other bankrupt brokerages. The position that I will take here (and argue for in section 9.2) is that 7.4.15d does not express a false proposition when hundreds of brokerages went bankrupt but is just a very misleading thing to say: it tells some of the truth but leaves out a large part of the truth that would probably be of interest to anyone who wants to know about failures of brokerage firms. Some confirmation of the position that 7.4.15d suffers from a fault other than falsehood when *several* understates the number of brokerage failures is seen in the appropriateness of *Yes* in an answer to a corresponding question:

7.4.17   Did several brokerage firms go bankrupt last year?
               Yes, indeed hundreds of them went bankrupt.

In this respect, *few* differs from the quantity expressions discussed so far, and also from *a few,* since if the number of linguists who can speak Spanish is large, a statement that few linguists can speak it is not just misleading but simply false:

7.4.18   a. Can a few linguists speak Spanish?
               Yes, indeed a very large number of them can.
          b. Can few linguists speak Spanish?
               $\begin{cases} \text{No, in fact a very large number of them can.} \\ \text{*Yes, indeed a very large number of them can.} \end{cases}$

This means that *few* must not be given the same analysis as *a small number:* when you say that few linguists can speak Basque, you aren't saying that there are a small number of linguists who can speak it but rather that there aren't a large number of linguists who can speak it. Thus, if *few* is to be given an analysis in terms of negation, "Large," and the material that appears in 7.4.12a, the negation must not be inside S_1 but rather outside S_0, as in an analysis that would treat *Few linguists can speak Basque* as the negation of *Many linguists can speak Basque.* Such an analysis would correctly account for the fact that sentences with *few* are not just misleading but false when the number of elements satisfying the matrix S is large, would correctly account for the fact that *few* (unlike *a few* and *a small number*) behaves like a negative in that, e.g., it supports negative polarity items (7.4.19a), and still implies that *few* should allow *There*-insertion (7.4.19b), because the proposed underlying structure would allow *There*-insertion to apply to the S corresponding to *Many linguists were on the committee* before the step (which applies on the next higher S) that would fuse negation and *many* into *few:*

7.4.19   a.   Few linguists give a hoot about literary criticism.
          a'. *A few linguists give a hoot about literary criticism.
          a". *A small number of linguists give a hoot about literary
               criticism.
          b.   There were few linguists on the committee.

Note that the treatment of *There*-insertion in 7.4.14 does not (as a cursory look might suggest) imply that all quantified NPs that are analysed in terms of an existentially quantified set variable allow *There*-insertion: it is necessary that there be a derivation with an intermediate stage like 7.4.13a, in which the set variable bound by the ∃ appears in subject position. Thus, while hedged universal quantifiers such as *all but three* or *almost all* can plausibly be given an analysis in terms of an existentially quantified set variable, as when 7.4.20a is analyzed as 7.4.20b, a derivation with such a deep structure would not yield an intermediate stage of the type that would allow *There*-insertion to apply:

7.4.20   a. All but three presidents were crooks.
          b. (∃: ∧((∀:x∈M)$_x$(x is a president), M No 3
              (∀: ∧(y is a president, ~(y∈M)))$_y$(y was a crook)

Note that in 7.4.20b, the matrix S is not (as it was in the earlier examples) of the form (∀:x∈M)fx but rather says something about all the members of some set other than M. Since there is no way for such a deep structure to yield an intermediate stage in which M occupies the subject position of the matrix S, a quantified NP that is given an analysis as in 7.4.20b can never set up the conditions that license the application of *There*-insertion.

That, of course, does not rule out the possibility that some analysis of *all but three* **other than** 7.4.20b might allow a derivation in which the conditions for *There*-insertion were met. It is in fact quite easy to set one up whose matrix S would be of the right form for *There*-insertion, namely an analysis on the lines of "There is a set of presidents to which all but three presidents belong, such that all its members were crooks." I maintain, though that a deep structure conforming to that logical structure would not yield a derived structure containing the NP *all but three presidents:* by Relative-clause Formation and the other usual rules that relate logical structures to surface form, the quantified expression would yield *??presidents who all but three presidents are,* with a zero existential quantifier in the determiner position and with *all but three* in a relative clause that could not be reduced any further, because the relative pronoun is not the subject but rather a predicate constituent.

I now return to the problematic quantifier *most*. The widespread belief that *most* means the same as *more than half* can be shown to be false by a consideration of the following examples:

7.4.21   Most of the ladies and more than half of the gentlemen wore
         evening clothes. (Sinclair Lewis, *It can't happen here*)

7.4.22   a.   Most positive integers are greater than 10^{80}.
         a′. More than half of all positive integers are greater than 10^{80}.
         b.   Most positive integers are composite.
         b′. More than half of all positive integers are composite.

In 7.4.21, it appears as if a greater proportion of the ladies than of the gentlemen wore evening clothes. Of the four sentences in 7.4.22, only 7.4.22b is a fairly normal use of English, and it can plausibly be held to be true, while 7.4.22b' is clearly false;[32] and while 7.4.22a and 7.4.22a' can both plausibly be argued to be true, 7.4.22a' is more clearly true than 7.4.22a is.

These differences in what is conveyed by *most* and *more than half* could be accounted for in a fanciful way by describing their meanings in terms of procedures for verifying the sentence, where the procedure for *most* begins with the instruction "Look" and the procedure for *more than half* begins with the instruction "Count." The reason that 7.4.21 conveys what it does about the numbers of ladies and gentlemen wearing evening clothes is that it suggests that you can tell "by inspection" that ladies in evening clothes outnumber other ladies (i.e., just about everywhere you look, there are more ladies in evening clothes than ladies in other garb), whereas you have to count to tell that the gentlemen in evening clothes outnumber the gentlemen in less formal clothing. Since both prime numbers and composites are infinite in number, neither set constitutes "more than half of" the positive integers, and thus 7.4.22b' comes out false; but since all primes greater than three are locally outnumbered by composites (i.e., they are surrounded by composites) but composites are only occasionally surrounded by primes, "inspection" tells you (albeit wrongly) that composites outnumber primes. Example 7.4.22a is true for the trivial reason that the infinitely many integers greater than 10^{80} outnumber the 10^{80} positive integers not exceeding 10^{80}; however, integers less than 10^{80} are not surrounded by integers greater than 10^{80} and thus the procedure for verifying 7.4.2a' fails.

In the proposal of the last paragraph, the procedure for *most* involved comparing a set directly with its complement, whereas with *more than half* a set was counted and its cardinal number was compared with that of the larger domain. This can be reinterpreted as an analysis in which "Most As are B" is analyzed not along the lines of 7.4.3b but as something like "the set of As which are not B is smaller than the set of As which are B" or even "the set of As which are not B is small." This amounts to analyzing *most* as *not many not*,[33] and such an analysis in fact solves the problems with which I am grappling. Note that the lower of the two negations will inhibit the application of *There*-insertion. That is, in all sentences in which existential *there* is combined with a negated V', the negation always has the existential quantifier in its scope and not vice versa, e.g., while 7.4.23a can mean either (simplified for ease of reading) 7.4.23a' or 7.4.23a", 7.4.23b can mean only 7.4.23a":

7.4.23   a.   Many of my friends weren't at the party.
          a'.   (∃: M is a large set of my friends)$_M$~(M were at the party)
          a".   ~(∃:M is a large set of my friends)$_M$(M were at the party)
          b.   There weren't many of my friends at the party.

Suppose that to exclude such interpretations as 7.4.23a' for 7.4.23b we impose on *There*-insertion a condition requiring that the V to whose right the subject is to be moved be at the top of the matrix S, i.e., that the configuration that it affects has the shape 7.4.24a, which would exclude 7.4.24b from its application:

7.4.24   a.

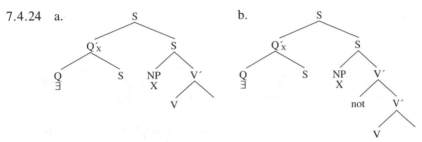

(*Not* would be a sister of the V' at the relevant stage of the derivation, in virtue of English rules for placement of negation as presented in McCawley 1988a: chap. 17). If *There*-insertion is formulated in this way, then it will be inapplicable to Ss having the form 7.4.24b, thus to sentences that are analyzed as having an existential quantifier with a negation in its scope. This will mean that the *many not* part of the *not many not* analysis of *most* will inhibit the application of *There*-insertion to the one S in the underlying structure that has an existential quantifier and thus could conceivably undergo *There*-insertion.[34] In addition, this proposal allows the vagueness of *large* to be built into an analysis of *many* and thus also into an analysis of *most* and hence can allow subjective factors to affect whether a particular subset is interpreted as making up most of the whole. The dividing line between large and not large can be below, at, or in rare cases even above 50 percent,[35] with the lower bound for *most* then being respectively above, at, or below 50 percent; it is only because 50 percent is such a natural dividing line between large and not large that *most* often conveys the same thing as *more than half*. I have framed the last sentence just in terms of what proportion of a set a subset comprises, but *large* can also be given an interpretation that is sensitive to the distribution of the members of a subset in addition to their relative numbers, and we have already seen in 7.4.21–22 that *most* can be sensitive to the distribution of elements. It is because composite numbers are relatively densely distributed and prime numbers relatively sparsely distributed that one can plausibly call 7.4.22b true, and it is because the integers greater than 10^{80} are so remote from the vantage point of the numbers that figure in ordinary experience that 7.4.22a is less clearly true than 7.4.22a′: the distribution of Xs makes a difference to the interpretation of *most Xs* but not to that of *more than half of all Xs*. It is in virtue of the way that vantage point intrudes on the interpretation of *most* that 7.4.25a is a more defensible assertion than 7.4.25a′:

7.4.25. a.   Most linguists accept some version of the X-bar conception of syntactic categories.

   a′. More than half of all linguists accept some version of the X-bar conception of syntactic categories.

There are hundreds of tagmemicists doing linguistic fieldwork in South America and New Guinea, and very few of them accept any version of X-bar syntactic categories. There are probably enough of them to clearly falsify 7.4.25a′, but it takes more than numbers to falsify 7.4.25a: from the vantage point of linguists who operate in the academic mainstreams of North America, Europe, and East Asia, the tagmemic fieldworkers are as remote as the sites of their fieldwork, and the non–X-bar tagmemicists, numerous as other linguists know them to be, do not count as falsifying 7.4.25a.[36]

7.5. Mass Expressions

The nouns in the examples in logic texts are virtually always **count** nouns: they denote properties that are predicated of individuals and they serve to define sets of individuals such as the set of all kangaroos or the set of all books on astrophysics. Natural languages contain not only count nouns but also **mass** nouns such as *water, sand, furniture,* or *prose,* which refer without regard to individuation and serve to define not sets but "masses" that need not have any minimal parts in the way that a set consisting of a single kangaroo is a minimal part of the set of all kangaroos.

There may in some cases be minimum quantities of what a mass noun refers to, but the most obvious supposed examples of that are actually less clear than they at first seem to be. For example, one might maintain that water is H_2O and thus that the minimum quantity of water is a single molecule of H_2O. However, *water* normally refers not just to any kind of H_2O but only to **liquid** H_2O, and a single molecule of H_2O (or of anything else) is not in itself in the liquid state or in the gas or solid state: the differences among the gas, liquid, and solid states are differences in the way in which molecules fit together, not differences in individual molecules themselves. Moreover, a substance need not be pure H_2O in order to be water; dirty water is a kind of water, and there is no such thing as dirty H_2O.[37] Even for words such as *carbon* that can be applied to an individual atom or molecule as well as to a macroscopic mass, it would be a mistake to gratuitously import chemical theories of the structure of matter into our semantic analysis, since the development of the molecular conception of matter did not change the way in which words such as *carbon* or *water* are used. The applicability of a mass term does not depend on whether there are minimum units of what it is applied to.

There are in fact many cases in which a mass noun refers to something that is not arbitrarily subdividable. For example, furniture comes in "pieces," and a part of a piece of furniture is not furniture: an arm of a chair or a nail in a bookcase is not furniture. Mass nouns are not restricted to unindividuated entities—they merely refer to entities without regard to whatever individuation they might have. This can be seen in the use of the word *furniture,* which is applicable even in cases of indeterminate individuation, as illustrated by modular furniture: a crateful of modules that can be put together in different ways to make up anything from two to ten pieces of furniture is a crateful of furniture even though it is not any determinate number of pieces of furniture. Pairs of nouns can be found that refer to things that are equally much individuated, but one of the nouns is a count noun, referring to those things in terms of their individuation, and the other is a mass noun, referring to things without regard to their individuation. A striking example of this type is provided by the words *brownie* and *baklava.* These words refer to two kinds of pastry that both arc bakcd in unindividuated panfuls and are not individuated until the baked pastry is removed from the oven and is cut into individual portions. The portion is a brownie in the one case and a piece of baklava in the other, and brownies are spoken of in terms of their individuation even before the baker's knife imposes that individuation, as when one says, "I have a pan of brownies baking." Similarly, *bean* is a count noun and *rice* a mass noun, even though the individuation of rice into grains is parallel to the individuation of beans. An interesting case is provided by the word *succotash.*[38] Succotash usually consists of discrete grains of corn and lima beans, and no number of lima beans and grains of corn constitutes a minimum quantity of succotash, for example, one grain of corn and one lima bean cannot be described as succotash (except when viewed as the remains of a large quantity of succotash, though note that the remains of a bowl of succotash can be called succotash even if one of the essential ingredients is missing—one can say *Johnny left some succotash in his bowl* even if what is left is three lima beans and no corn).

Mass nouns (more generally, **mass expressions**, such as *dirty water* or *footwear that has been inspected by the county clerk*) can combine with quantifiers, indeed with many of the same quantifiers that combine with count nouns:

7.5.1   a. All human blood is red.
          b. Most succotash is high in protein.
          c. Some sand is black.
          d. A lot of whiskey is under 90 proof.

Moreover, the quantifier words in 7.5.1 appear to have the same meanings as when they are combined with count nouns. In English, the quantifier words that cannot combine with mass nouns are *each, every,* numerals (including vague numerals such as *several*), and *many.*

7.5.2   a. Each poem/*poetry was discussed by the poet.
          b. Every chair/*furniture was in poor condition.
          c. Fred bought several vases/*pottery.
          d. Susan performed several compositions/*music.

The only quantifiers that do not combine with count nouns appear to be *much, little,* and *a little:*

7.5.3   a.   Much poetry is rarely read.
          a'. *Much poem(s) is/are rarely read.
          b.   Little Japanese food is eaten in Egypt.
          b'. *Little Japanese dish(es) is/are eaten in Egypt.

In view of the fact that there is no obstacle to treating *much* and *many* (likewise, *little* and *few,* and *a little* and *a few*) as meaning the same thing (at least, no more of an obstacle than there is to identifying the meaning of *most* in *most water* with that of *most* in *most kangaroos*) and that most languages in fact have the same word for "much" as for "many" (German *viel,* French *beaucoup,* Japanese *takusan;* likewise with *little* and *few* and *a little* and *a few*), I will henceforth treat *many* and *much* as being two forms of the same word (like *this* and *these*) rather than two different words. Accordingly, I recognize quantifiers (including *much/many* and *few/little*) that combine both with count and with mass expressions, and quantifiers that combine only with count expressions, but no quantifiers that combine only with mass expressions. I will attempt below to find a semantic explanation for this gap.

The rules of inference for universal and existential quantifiers seem to carry over without change to the mass noun case:

7.5.4   a. All water is wet.
             This puddle is water.
             Therefore, this puddle is wet.

          b. This puddle is water.
             This puddle is dirty.
             Therefore, some water is dirty.

It is not so easy, however, to formalize the rules of inference so that they will apply to the mass noun case and to state truth conditions for quantified propositions that will cover the mass noun case as well as the count noun case. These problems manifest themselves with the greatest vengeance if one attempts to give an account of mass terms within the framework of unrestricted quantification. Suppose that we were to symbolize 7.5.4a as 7.5.5:

7.5.5 $(\forall x) \supset (\text{Water } x, \text{ Wet } x)$
          Water p
          Wet p

The problem with this formalization is that it is far from clear what must be allowed as values of the bound variable for it to make sense. The values must include things of which "is water" can be predicated,[39] and while there are many entities of which "is water" can innocuously be predicated (puddles, pools, drops), it is not clear that any set of such entities would provide enough values for the bound variable, since the first premise of 7.5.4a implies not merely that the various discrete bodies of water are wet but also that all parts of those bodies are wet. Example 7.5.4a is valid not only for a believer in the modern atomic and molecular conception of matter but also for someone of A.D. 1700 who believed that matter is continuous and infinitely divisible, and an adequate account of mass terms must be as consistent with the latter view as with the former, since the logic of quantifiers cannot by itself establish or refute any theory of matter. Thus in any state of affairs, the "universe of discourse" would have to include all "parts" of all objects, according to whatever notion of part corresponds to the theory of matter that is true in that state of affairs; this makes for a whopping big universe of discourse, especially for states of affairs in which a preatomic conception of matter holds and all physical objects will have uncountably many parts.

There have also been analyses that attempt to do without such predicates as "is water," though, as far as I can determine, they leave quite unclear what the "universe of discourse" is to be. For example, Parsons (1970) treats mass nouns as proper names and treats quantified mass expressions as involving a relationship Q "is a quantity of"; for example, he analyzes *All water is wet* as $(\forall x) \supset (Qxw, \text{Wet } x)$, where w is the denotation of *water*. For Parsons, in effect, quantifiers only combine with count nouns, and apparent instances of a quantifier combining with a mass noun m really involve the count expression "quantity of m." I find Parsons's approach unappealing in view of two prejudices that I hold: (i) I believe that mass nouns are semantically more basic than count nouns—that the meaning of a count noun involves something over and above what goes into the meaning of a mass noun, namely, the specification of an individuation; and (ii) I think that any adequate account of the semantics of mass expressions must explain the oddity of sentences such as 7.5.2, whereas Parsons's approach provides no reason why there should be any difference in the acceptability of the various combinations of quantifier and mass noun—if you can supply an understood "quantity of" in interpreting the examples in 7.5.1, why shouldn't you be able to do the same in interpreting those in 7.5.2? In addition, Parsons's approach has no chance of coping with the semantics of *most* and *much*: to the extent that any sense can be made of a notion of "most quantities of gold," that notion has no bearing on the truth conditions of such sentences as *Most gold is still underground*. Parsons in fact makes this very point himself and adopts a quite different analysis for *most* than he has for *all* and *some*.

I will accordingly make no further attempt to reduce the semantics of mass terms to that of count terms, that is, to describe the denotations of mass terms in ordinary set theory, but will instead turn to the more general notion of **ensemble** that was introduced in section 5.5, which was in fact constructed with a view towards developing a framework for semantics that would embrace mass terms as well as count terms, with the sets that are denoted by count nouns being ensembles that are unions of their minimal parts.

Ensemble theory (Bunt 1976, 1979, 1985) allows one to take the denotation of any noun, count or mass, to be an ensemble. In the case of a count noun, the ensemble will be a set; in the case of a mass noun, it need not be (but could be) a set. Simple propositions with predicate nouns will be true if and only if the denotation of the subject is a part of the ensemble denoted by the predicate noun. Whether the predicate noun is singular or plural (*Tom is a lawyer* vs. *Tom and Dick are lawyers*) is taken here to be semantically irrelevant: its denotation is the same in either case (here, the ensemble of lawyers, that is, the ensemble having all sets of lawyers as its parts). To make this consistent it will be necessary to change one detail of the analyses accepted in chapter 6, namely, that singular count NPs that apparently refer to an individual must now be taken as referring to the set having that individual as its sole member; for example, if a is the individual that *Tom* refers to, then the subject of *Tom is a lawyer* must be taken to denote $\{a\}$ rather than a. Note that this gives equivalent truth conditions to what we had earlier: a is a member of the set of all lawyers if and only if $\{a\}$ is a part of the ensemble of lawyers. Predicate mass nouns will work in exactly parallel fashion: *This puddle is water* will be true only if the denotation of the subject is part of the ensemble that is the denotation of *water*.

Variables bound by quantifiers that combine with both count and mass nouns will take as values part of the ensemble denoted by the noun, for example, the truth of *All water is wet* depends on the truth of "x is wet" for values of x which are parts of the ensemble denoted by *water*: if "x is wet" is true of all such x, then the sentence expresses a true proposition. This analysis can be carried over to a treatment of combinations of *all* with a count noun only if two changes are made in the proposals of chapter 6. First, the noun to which the quantifier is attached must be taken as defining an ensemble, and second, the values of the bound variable must be taken to be parts of that ensemble (here, subsets of a set) rather than individuals. Otherwise preserving the analysis of chapters 2 and 6, we would then analyze 7.5.6a as 7.5.6b, where the double primes are used according to the general scheme in 7.5.6c for deriving from each predicate of individuals a corresponding predicate of ensembles:

7.5.6   a. All politicians are crooks.
         b. $(\text{All: Politician}''(M))_M \text{Crook}''(M)$
         c. $F''(M)$ if and only if $(\forall: x \in M)_x F(x)$

Thus, for any set M, Politician$''$(M) is true if and only if Politician(x) is true of all of the members of M.[40] The truth conditions for 7.5.6b proposed here agree with those of Section 6.1: all sets of politicians are sets of crooks if and only if all politicians are crooks.

Bunt notes that a distinction parallel to that between count nouns and mass nouns can be made in predicate adjectives:

7.5.7   a. Count adjectives
              This blanket is warm. (in the sense: "keeps one warm")
              This apple is red.
              The ladder is long.
         b. Mass adjectives
              This soup is warm.
              This ink is red.
              The ladder is wooden.

Mass predicates, whether nouns or adjectives, have the property of being **distributive**: a proposition with a mass predicate implies corresponding propositions about nonempty parts of what is denoted by the subject; for example, if this soup is warm, then any spoonful of it is warm, and if this ink is red, then any drop of it is red.[41] By contrast, count predicates are generally not distributive; for example, if this blanket is warm, it need not be the case that every 6-inch square of it is warm, and if this apple is red, it need not be the case that its core is red. Mass predicates are also **cumulative**: if an entity is the union of parts, each of which the predicate is true of, then the predicate is true of that entity; for example, if every spoonful of the soup is warm, then the soup is warm. By contrast, count predicates are normally not cumulative; for example, this stack of books may be heavy even though every book in it is light. Count predicates express properties of entities as wholes; mass predicates express properties that are distributed homogeneously over an entity. I note here one important property of mass predicates that will prove of some importance later in this section, namely, that the negation of a mass predicate generally is not a mass predicate. Let $\text{Yellow}_m(x)$ correspond to the mass sense of *yellow,* that is, $\text{Yellow}_m(x)$ is true if and only if every part of x (not just the surface) is yellow. Let a be an object that has both red parts and yellow parts and let b be a yellow part of a. Then $\sim\text{Yellow}_m(a)$ is true but $\sim\text{Yellow}_m(b)$ is false. Thus $\sim\text{Yellow}_m(x)$ is not distributive: it can apply to an object without applying to all parts (even to all "sufficiently large" parts) of that object.

To provide an analysis in which *many* and *much* come out semantically identical, as it was proposed earlier in this section that they are, it will be necessary to revise slightly the analysis of *many* sketched in section 7.4. If 7.5.8a and 7.5.8b are to have fully parallel analyses and if *black* in 7.5.9a is to correspond to a predicate that is predicated of ensembles, then *insane* in 7.5.8b will have to be predicated not of individuals but of ensembles, that is, in this case the relevant values will be not linguists but subsets of the set of all linguists:

7.5.8   a. Much coal is black.
         b. Many linguists are insane.

Thus, using the notation introduced in 7.5.6, *insane* will be rendered not as $\text{Insane}'(x)$ but as $\text{Insane}''(M)$, where $\text{Insane}''(M)$ is true if and only if $\text{Insane}'(x)$ is true for all x that are members of M. Thus we can tentatively represent the logical structures of 7.5.8a–b as

7.5.9   a. $(\exists:\wedge(\text{Coal(M)}, \text{Large (M)}))_M \text{ Black(M)}$
         b. $(\exists:\wedge(\text{Linguist}''(M), \text{Large(M)}))_M \text{ Insane}''(M)$

("Large" here is the count predicate that attributes great size to an ensemble; thus 7.5.9b must be interpreted "There is a large set of linguists . . .", not as "There is a set of large linguists . . .".)

Let us now see whether the analysis of *most* as "not many not" that was sketched in section 7.4 can be revised so as to be applicable to combinations of *most* with a mass term. The most direct analogue to that proposal would be an analysis in which 7.5.11a is rendered as 7.5.10b:

7.5.10   a. Most gold is yellow.
   b. $\sim(\exists{:}\wedge(\text{Gold}(E), \text{Large}(E)))_E \sim \text{Yellow}(E)$

Under the most obvious interpretation of the predicates (in particular, the interpretation of 'yellow' as a mass predicate—an ensemble will have the property 'yellow' if and only if all its parts are yellow), 7.5.10b can be false for irrelevant reasons. If there is a large ensemble E_1 of gold that is yellow and a nonempty ensemble E_2 of gold that is not yellow, then $\sim\text{Yellow}(E_1 \cup E_2)$ will be true, $E_1 \cup E_2$ will be large (I assume that an ensemble having a large ensemble as a part must itself be large), and hence 7.5.10b will be false by virtue of the existence of a large ensemble of gold (namely, $E_1 \cup E_2$) that has the property $\sim\text{Yellow}(E)$. This would have the catastrophic consequence that *Most gold is yellow* would have the same truth conditions as *All gold is yellow:* both would be false as long as there is any nonyellow gold. The closest variant of 7.5.10b that would be free of this defect would be a formula that involved not the negation of yellow(E) but a mass predicate corresponding to "not yellow," that is, a predicate that was true of an ensemble if and only if no part of the ensemble was yellow. Let us introduce an operator N, referred to as "mass negation," defined by

7.5.11 $(NF)(E)$ if and only if $(\forall{:}\wedge(E' \text{ nonempty}, E' \subseteq E))_{E'} \sim F(E')$

That is, $(NF)(E)$ if and only if no nonempty part of E has the property F. It can be proved that if F is distributive, then NF is distributive and cumulative. The analyses of sentences with *most* would then have to be as follows if *most* is to combine in the same way with count terms as with mass terms:

7.5.12 a. Most gold is yellow.
   a'. $\sim(\exists{:}\wedge(\text{Gold}(E), \text{Large}(E)))_E \ (N\text{Yellow})(E)$
   b. Most linguists are insane.
   b'. $\sim(\exists{:}\wedge(\text{Linguist}''(E), \text{Large}(E)))_E \ (N\text{Insane}'')(E)$

The truth conditions for 7.5.12a' seem to fit 7.5.12a, for 7.5.12a' will be true if and only if there is no large ensemble of gold, all of whose parts are nonyellow, that is, there is no large uniformly nonyellow ensemble of gold. The truth conditions for 7.5.12b′ also fit 7.5.12b and agree with those of the analysis of 7.4: (NInsane″)(E) is true if and only if no member of E is insane, that is, all members of E are sane, and thus 7.5.12b′ is true if and only if there is no large set of linguists who are all sane.

7.6. Polyadic Quantifiers

Logicians and mathematicians occasionally use, at least as an informal device, formulas in which a single quantifier binds two or more variables, for example,

7.6.1 $(\exists x, y)f(x, y)$

In a system of unrestricted quantification, such formulas can always be interpreted as abbreviations of formulas having multiple occurrences of the quantifier; for example, 7.6.1 would be an informal abbreviation of 7.6.2:

7.6.2 $(\exists x)(\exists y)f(x, y)$

However, in a system of restricted quantification, a possibility emerges in which a 'polyadic quantifier expression' cannot be regarded as standing for a sequence of single quantifier expressions, namely the possibility of a domain expression containing a clause in which two or more bound variables figure. Such a logical form seems like a plausible way of analyzing sentences such as 7.6.3 (taken from Perlmutter and Ross 1970; see also Link 1984 for further discussion of similar sentences), in which a restrictive relative clause is equally tied to two or more head nouns in a conjoined NP:

7.6.3   A man came in the front door and a woman came in the side
               door who had met in Vienna.

Here the relative clause is chosen so as to resist any attempt to analyze it into parts in which the two bound variables are kept separate: there is no practical alternative to having a clause "x and y met in Vienna" in the logical form of 7.6.3. I regard as implausible any attempt to squeeze 7.6.3 into the scheme of monadic quantifiers by arbitrarily treating the relative clause as combining with only one of the two head nouns in logical structure, as in 7.6.4a, a formula that corresponds more directly to 7.6.4b than to 7.6.3:

7.6.4   a. $(\exists{:}x\ \text{Man})_x\ (\exists{:}\wedge(y\ \text{Woman},\ \{x,\ y\}\ \text{met in Vienna}))_y\ \wedge(x\ \text{came in}$
               the front door, y came in the side door).
          b. A man came in the front door and a woman such that he and she
               had met in Vienna came in the side door.

While the prospect of assigning 7.6.3 a logical form involving a polyadic quantified NP may thus be attractive, it is not immediately obvious **which** such logical form we should assign to it. There is of course a formula that can easily enough be constructed and interpreted in a way that appears to account correctly for the truth conditions of 7.6.3, namely one in which expressions corresponding to the two head nouns and the relative clause are simply conjoined with each other, as in 7.6.5:

7.6.5 $(\exists{:}\wedge(x$ Man, y Woman, $\{x,y\}$ met in $v))_{x,y} \wedge(x$ came in the front door, y came in the side door)

The problem with 7.6.5 is that it seems to require new rules to relate it to its surface form, since, for example, the Q′ that 7.6.5 posits is not of the form that we have hitherto taken Q′-lowering to apply to, in which there is one bound variable and one domain expression for that variable and Q′-lowering moves the whole Q′ into a position in the matrix S where the given bound variable occurs. The task before us then is to see whether we can work out the details of a logical structure for sentences like 7.6.3 in such a way that a minimally altered version of Q′-lowering will be applicable to it and will move the various head nouns to the appropriate positions.

Let us postpone briefly the question of how the relative clause should fit into the structure and consider just how Q′-lowering might be taken to apply to polyadic Q′s. Suppose that we alter our formation rule for Q′, which allowed each Q′ to consist of one quantifier and one S (the domain expression for its single bound variable), so as to allow each Q′ to consist of one quantifier and any finite number of Ss, one for each of its bound variables. We can then assign to 7.6.6a the logical form 7.6.6b (= 7.6.6b′), in which the Q′ contains two Ss (NB: not a conjunction of those two Ss!), each defining a domain for one of the two variables:

7.6.6   a. A man came in the front door and a woman came in the side door.
    b. $(\exists{:}x$ Man, y Woman$)_{x,y} \wedge(x$ came in the front door, y came in the side door)

    b.′
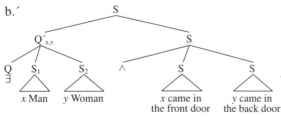

Suppose that we take Q'-lowering as applying to such a structure as 7.6.6b by simultaneously moving one copy of the Q and one S into a position occupied by each variable in the matrix S, i.e., here Q-lowering would move ∃S₁ into the position of the x into the matrix S and ∃S₂ into the position of the y in the matrix S. Q'-lowering thus applies in such a way that it will associate 7.6.6a with 7.6.6b. (This is not to suggest that 7.6.6b is a good analysis of 7.6.6a: 7.6.6a can be analyzed most straightforwardly simply as a conjunction of *A man came in the front door* and *A woman came in the side door,* with a separate ∃ in each conjunct; the point of 7.6.6b is rather to develop an approach that will be applicable to cases such as 7.6.3, in which an analysis with a separate Q in each conjunct is not available.) Suppose then that we try assigning to 7.6.3 a logical structure in which the relative clause is simultaneously in both conjuncts. This could be accomplished either by repeating the relative clause, as in the formula 7.6.7a, or by treating a single occurrence of it as belonging simultaneously to both domain expressions, as in the structure (not directly translatable into a linear formula) 7.6.7b:

7.6.7   a. (∃:∧(x Man, {x, y} met in v), ∧(y Woman, {x, y} met in v))$_{x,y}$
           ∧(x came in the front door, y came in the side door)

      b.

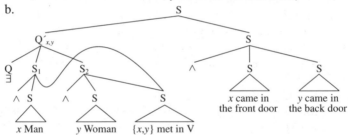

Q'-lowering, applying to one or other of these structures, will yield an output in which ∃S₁ occupies the position of x in "x came in the front door" and ∃S₂ occupies the position of y in "y came in the side door." The problem with this output, though, is that "x and y met in Vienna" does not underlie a relative clause that would be syntactically acceptable within either of the two NPs, e.g., one cannot say *a man who and she met in Vienna* or *a woman who he and met in Vienna*. The only way to get an acceptable surface structure that corresponds to the indicated logical structure is to exercise the option of extraposition of relative clauses, applying "across-the-boards" to yield a derived structure in which a single relative clause *who had met in Vienna* occupies the S-final position reserved for extraposed relative clauses and jointly modifies both nouns.

Sentences in which numerals are combined with an understood existential quantifier can also occur in combinations that demand an analysis involving a polyadic quantifier:[42]

7.6.8   a. Two linguists and three sociologists who had met at a
               conference on graffiti were among those who were arrested.

b.

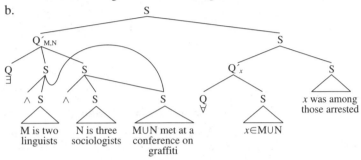

The latter analysis is slightly different from the one suggested in 7.4, which corresponded to "there is a set containing two linguists and three sociologists such that that set met at a conference on graffiti . . .". The analysis given in 7.6.8b has one important advantage over that of 7.4, namely that it can be adapted to sentences such as 7.6.9a–b as indicated in 7.6.9a'–b', where to save space, I will adopt the ad-hoc notational practise of underlining a constituent that is to be shared with one or more subsequent expressions and leaving the positions in which it is to be shared blank but underlined.[43]

7.6.9   a. Two linguists were chanting and three sociologists were
               shouting the same slogan.
         a'. ($\exists$:x is a slogan)($\exists$: M is two linguists, N is three
               sociologists)$_{M,N}$ $\wedge$(M were chanting x, N were shouting x))
         b. Tom bought and Erica sold securities totalling over a million
               dollars in value.
         b'. ($\exists$:$\wedge$(M is securities, M$\cup$N totals over \$1 million), $\wedge$(N is
               securities, ————))$_{M,N}$ $\wedge$(Tom bought M, Erica sold N)

Note that here the quantifier that binds the variables of the matrix sentence has the whole matrix sentence in its scope, whereas in an analysis of the type suggested in 7.4, the quantifier expressions binding those variables are properly contained in the domain expression of the Q' with which the matrix S is combined and thus do not themselves have the matrix S in their scope.

The examples given so far of polyadic quantifiers have all involved a two-variable existential quantifier. Examples that require a polyadic universal quantifier are much harder to construct, but at least such sentences as 7.6.10a are marginally acceptable; according to the above proposals, it ought to correspond to the logical form 7.6.10b:

7.6.10   a. ?Every man wore a gaudy shirt and every woman wore a
                matching blouse who were partners in the dance marathon.
         b. ($\forall$:$\wedge$(x is a man, $\{x,y\}$ were partners in the dance marathon), $\wedge$(y
                is a woman, _____)$_{x,y}$ $\wedge$(x wore a gaudy shirt, y wore a
                blouse matching x's shirt)

It is much easier to construct examples where a definite description operator binds multiple variables:

7.6.11   a. The man entered and the woman left who had met in Vienna.
         b. ($\imath$:$\wedge$(x is a man, $\{x,y\}$ met in Vienna), $\wedge$(y is a woman,
                _____))$_{x,y}$
            $\wedge$(x entered, y left)

A particularly interesting type of sentence in which a definite description operator binds several variables is discussed by Lakoff (1972a:644–45), who notes that 7.6.12a has multiple occurrences not only of *the* but also of *usual*, corresponding to a logical structure in which those items are represented only once each:[44]

7.6.12   a. The usual men were talking to the usual women about the usual
                subjects.
         b. ($\imath$: $\wedge$(M are men, [M talk to N about R] is usual), $\wedge$(N are
                women, _____), $\wedge$(R are subjects, _____))$_{M,N,R}$(M were
                talking to N about R)

     Let us conclude this section with a sketch of how the alterations suggested here of the formation rules for predicate logic will affect the rules of inference and truth conditions. A polyadic Q' binding the variables x_1, x_2, ..., x_n can be interpreted as saying how many n-tuples of values for those variables that satisfy the domain expressions (NB plural!) also satisfy the matrix S.[45] The truth conditions for $\forall$ and $\exists$ thus need only be revised to the extent of speaking in terms of assignments of values to all of the bound variables rather then just to one bound variable:

7.6.13   If y_1, y_2, ..., y_m are the variables that occur free in A_1, A_2, ...,
            A_n, then
         a. (c_1/y_1 c_2/y_2 ... c_m/y_m) satisfies ($\forall$:A_1, A_2, ... A_n)$_{x_1,x_2,...x_n}$ B if and
            only if, for every set of values a_1, a_2, ..., a_n such that (a_1/x_1

$a_2/x_2 \ldots a_n/x_n\ c_1/y_1\ c_2/y_2 \ldots c_m/y_m)$ satisfies all of A_1, A_2, $\ldots A_n$, it also satisfies B, and

b. $(c_1/y_1\ c_2/y_2 \ldots c_m/y_m)$ satisfies $(\exists: A_1, A_2, \ldots A_n)_{x_1, x_2, \ldots x_n}$ B if and only if at least one set of values $a_1, a_2, \ldots, a_n$ such that $(a_1/x_1\ a_2/x_2 \ldots a_n/x_n\ c_1/y_1\ c_2/y_2 \ldots c_m/y_m)$ satisfies all of A_1, A_2, $\ldots A_n$ also satisfies B.

The requisite change in the rules of inference will consist in having separate lines in the proof corresponding to each of the bound variables. For example, one might infer 7.6.3 from plausible premises as in 7.6.14a, and the version of $\exists$-intro that it uses can be stated as in 7.6.14b:

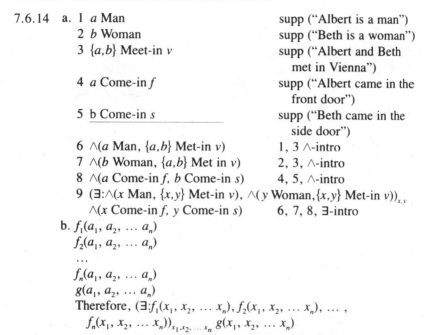

7.6.14 a. 1 a Man   supp ("Albert is a man")
           2 b Woman   supp ("Beth is a woman")
           3 $\{a,b\}$ Meet-in v supp ("Albert and Beth
                                                        met in Vienna")
           4 a Come-in f supp ("Albert came in the
                                                        front door")
           5 b Come-in s supp ("Beth came in the
                                                        side door")
           6 $\wedge(a$ Man, $\{a,b\}$ Met-in $v)$ 1, 3 $\wedge$-intro
           7 $\wedge(b$ Woman, $\{a,b\}$ Met in $v)$ 2, 3, $\wedge$-intro
           8 $\wedge(a$ Come-in f, b Come-in $s)$ 4, 5, $\wedge$-intro
           9 $(\exists{:}\wedge(x$ Man, $\{x,y\}$ Met-in $v)$, $\wedge(y$ Woman,$\{x,y\}$ Met-in $v))_{x,y}$
              $\wedge(x$ Come-in f, y Come-in $s)$ 6, 7, 8, $\exists$-intro

        b. $f_1(a_1, a_2, \ldots a_n)$
           $f_2(a_1, a_2, \ldots a_n)$
           $\ldots$
           $f_n(a_1, a_2, \ldots a_n)$
           $g(a_1, a_2, \ldots a_n)$
           Therefore, $(\exists{:}f_1(x_1, x_2, \ldots x_n), f_2(x_1, x_2, \ldots x_n), \ldots ,$
              $f_n(x_1, x_2, \ldots x_n))_{x_1, x_2, \ldots x_n}\ g(x_1, x_2, \ldots x_n)$

Similar restatements of the other rules of inference for $\forall$ and $\exists$, and of the conditions on coherent combination of variables, can be given in a straight-forward fashion.

Exercises

1. Using the $\imath$ notation, suggest logical forms for the following sentences. (Subscripts are used as an informal indication of pronoun-antecedent relationships.)

a. John loves his wife.
b. John hates his wife's boyfriend.
c. No executive$_i$ admires the person who shines his$_i$ shoes.
d. John$_i$ doesn't like the man who loves the woman who loves him$_i$.

2. *Only* has often been given an analysis rather like Russell's analysis of *the*, e.g., (i) has been analyzed as (i'):

i. Only Nixon resigned.
i'. $\wedge$(N resigned, $(\forall x)\supset(\sim\,=x\mathrm{N},\ \sim(x$ resigned)))

Give logical forms for the following sentences according to that analysis:

a. Only Lucifer pities Lucifer.
b. Only Lucifer pities himself.
c. Only Lucifer pities only Lucifer.
d. Only Lucifer pities only himself.

3. Show that no two of (a)–(d) in exercise 2 are true under exactly the same conditions.

4. a. Work out as close an analog as possible to (i') of exercise 2 that could be taken as an analysis of sentences in which *only* is combined not with a singular NP (e.g., *only Nixon*) but with a conjunction of singular NPs (e.g., *only Nixon and Agnew* or *only Nixon, Haldeman, and Ehrlichman*). Your analysis should be a conjunction of two Ss analogous to the two conjuncts in i'.

b. Show that the analysis that you have worked out in part a of this exercise, if extended in the most straightforward way to sentences in which *only* is combined with a plural indefinite NP (e.g., *only rich people*), yields implausible truth conditions for such sentences as *The FBI hires only American citizens*).

5. Suggest how the analysis suggested in exercise 2 might be adapted so as to cover the following two types of sentences, in which there is an expression (underlined) that limits the domain of the bound variable:

Of his neighbors, Bill hates only Larry.
John is the only living philosopher who admires Meinong.

6. Give analyses of the following sentences in the style of section 7.4:

a. Each executive is assisted by three secretaries.
b. Every student talked to at least five other students.
c. Many women overlook a considerable number of their husbands' faults.

7. Give the logical structure and a sketch of the syntactic derivation for each of the following sentences:

a. The candidates appear to all be greedy.
b. There were three prisoners beaten by the guards.
c. Mary gave a kiss to every boy who asked her to.
d. You shouldn't tell stories about anyone who doesn't want you to.
e. A man$_1$ committed suicide and a woman$_2$ was run over by a truck who$_{1,2}$ had conspired to kidnap the Secretary of the Treasury.

8. For each of the following predicate elements, say whether it is distributive, adding enough discussion to justify your answer:

a. heavy
b. pasta
c. noodle
d. multi-colored
e. bland

8. Sorts, Types, and Kinds

8.1. The Uniformity of the Domain; Sorts

We have so far taken a state of affairs to involve a single "domain," with no restriction on the kinds of objects in the domain or on what kinds of things a predicate can be predicated of. The subsets of that domain which are defined by the various predicates provide the domains of quantifiers. For example, if we have a formal language that is to represent the content of sentences like *You can fool some of the people all of the time,* the language will have to involve predicates like "is a person" and "is a time," and we will be particularly interested in those states of affairs which have a domain D containing both times and persons. The more heterogeneous the predicates that the formal language contains, the more heterogeneous the set D will have to be allowed to be, and that may be pretty heterogeneous: in a short nontechnical text one could very well encounter references to persons, times, events, numbers, names, biological species, routes from Chicago to Houston, and Mozart symphonies.

In our description of what a "state of affairs" is, we have said that it includes specifications of truth values for every predicate of the language combined with every possible value (in D) for its arguments. But that seems to be leading us to a rather disconcerting and bizarre prospect: for each state of affairs one now will apparently have to specify not only whether the number 11 is prime, whether Richard Nixon is Jewish, and whether the Battle of Hastings took place before the invention of the zipper, but also whether the invention of the zipper is prime, whether the Battle of Hastings is Jewish, and whether Richard Nixon took place before the number 11. We ought thus to digress at this point to see how we can modify our assumptions so as to avoid being forced into a wild proliferation of possible states of affairs in which we must distinguish states of affairs in which the Battle of Hastings is Jewish from states of affairs in which the Battle of Hastings is not Jewish.

If we wish to rule out the possibility of states of affairs differing with regard

248

to whether the Battle of Hastings is Jewish, there are basically two approaches that can be pursued: either try to set things up in such a way that the truth values of such propositions are always predictable (e.g., so that "The Battle of Hastings is Jewish" and "The invention of the zipper is prime" are false in every state of affairs) or try to set things up in such a way that such propositions are never assigned a truth value at all, that is, have a state of affairs contain not a **complete** table of truth values for each predicate but a table covering only those members of the domain for which the question of the truth of the predicate arises. Either way, for each predicate it will be necessary to draw a distinction between those members of D (or combinations of members of D) for which the predicate can differ in truth value from one state of affairs to another, and those members of D for which it cannot.

So far we have placed no restrictions on the propositional functions that appear in expressions like $(\forall: Fx)Gx$, beyond the conditions on coherent use of variables. Suppose that we adopt the first alternative of the last paragraph and try to set things up so that for any propositional functions F and G, Fx and Gx will have truth values no matter what member of the domain is substituted for x. There is then nothing to prevent us from constructing expressions in which the "F" is somewhat more outlandish than what has appeared in the examples so far, for example,

8.1.1 $(\forall: \vee(\text{Person } x, \text{ Time } x))(\text{Mortal } x)$

The truth value of 8.1.1 in any particular state of affairs will hinge upon what exactly we have chosen to impose as the truth value of "Mortal x" for the case in which x is a time rather than a person. If we have chosen to require "Mortal x" to be false in all such cases, then 8.1.1 comes out false, which is surely a more reasonable result than if it had come out true. Consider, however, the notions of "rational" and "irrational" as they figure in mathematics. It would be nice to be able to define "rational" as "is the ratio of two integers" and define "irrational" as the negation of "rational." If we are then going to assign to "x is rational" the value F when x is not a number (just as we assigned to "x is mortal" the value F is x is a time, or perhaps, more generally, when x is not a living being) and if our truth value assignments are to conform to the classical truth tables (as we have been assuming throughout this chapter), then "x is irrational" ought to get the value T whenever x is not a number, and thus 8.1.2 ought to be assigned the value T:

8.1.2 $(\forall: \vee(x$ is the square root of a prime number, x is a cigar box$))(x$
            is irrational)

Thus, if we are to maintain some fairly natural semantic analyses and retain the classical truth tables, while disallowing the bizarre profusion of possible states of affairs that we are trying to avoid, we will be forced to assign the value T to some formulas and the value F to other formulas in which ($\forall$: $\vee(F_1 x, F_2 x)$) is combined with a propositional function that makes sense only for the values of x that have the property $F_1 x$.

One way that we might avoid the problem of assigning truth values to propositions in which quantifiers have domains with bizarre definitions would be to place heavy restrictions on what the F can be in formulas of the form (Quantifier: Fx)Gx. If we attempt to impose such a restriction, we should see whether in the process we can also make it unnecessary to assign truth values to *The Battle of Hastings is Jewish* and the like. This in fact ought to be possible, since in both cases the bizarre examples that we were forced to deal with were bizarre because they mixed entities of different sorts; thus the direction that seems most promising is to seek a restriction based on the notion of "sort."

Suppose then that we posit a fixed finite inventory of sorts, each corresponding to a one-place predicate that is true of entities of that sort and false of entities that are of other sorts. We can then make the following revisions in the conception of possible state of affairs that we adopted in chapter 6. For any given state of affairs α, the "domain" D^α can now be replaced by several disjoint domains, one for each sort; thus, letting the different sorts correspond to the sort predicates F_1, F_2, ..., and F_n, the state of affairs will involve sets D_1^α, D_2^α, ..., D_n^α, with $F_i x$ being true when the value assigned to x belongs to D_i^α and false otherwise. Sort predicates will be unusual in having arguments that are not restricted to a single sort; another predicate that has this unusual property is $=$. Generally speaking, though, a predicate will impose on each of its arguments a requirement that it be filled by entities of one particular sort, e.g., *last*, as in *The meeting lasted two hours*, will require that its first argument denote an event and that its second argument denote an amount of time. For any one-place predicate f whose argument is restricted to the sort F_i, $f^\alpha \subseteq D_i^\alpha$; for any two-place predicate g whose first argument is restricted to the sort F_i and whose second argument is restricted to the sort F_j, $g^\alpha \subseteq D_i^\alpha \times D_j^\alpha$, etc.

"Sort predicates" are a very special type of "essential properties": properties that an individual could not gain or lose without ceasing to exist or losing its identity. A person may become red-headed or become bald, but he cannot become a number or a battle or a route from Chicago to Houston. In comparing alternative states of affairs, we can identify a bank president in one state of affairs with a skid-row bum in another state of affairs (as we might need to in order to make sense out of sentences like *If Schwartz hadn't inherited his uncle's chicken ranch, he'd be a bum on skid row*), but we cannot identify a bank president in one state of affairs with the invention of the zipper, or with 21 March 1844, or with an 11th symphony of Beethoven in some other state of affairs (thus, we cannot make sense out of sentences like *If Schwartz hadn't inherited his uncle's chicken ranch, he'd be Beethoven's 11th Symphony*). Sort properties, however, are not the only essential properties; for example, we could not identify the number 11 in one state of affairs with a number in another state of affairs that was divisible by 2, 7, and 31. Indeed, it is very odd even to raise the possibility of numbers differing from one state of affairs to another: we rather feel that the numbers are something outside of any state of affairs, albeit something that can be referred to in describing any state of affairs (e.g., part of a description of a state of affairs might be a specification of how many chickens each person owns).

Determining what sorts there are is a philosophical activity that has a long tradition (in which the systems of categories of Aristotle, Kant, and Hegel are particularly noteworthy), though it has fallen into disrepute and been much neglected during the twentieth century. It is an activity which will have to be revived if a useful notion of state of affairs is to be developed along the lines of the program suggested here.

Expressions like the $\vee(x$ is the square root of a prime number, x is a cigar box) of 8.1.2 are true of things of two different sorts (at least, under the plausible assumption that $\vee AB$ is true if either A or B is true, even if the other conjunct has no truth value). Similarly, if the domain expression were $\sim(x$ is odd), it would be satisfied by things of many different sorts: not only by even numbers but by all persons, events, and symphonies. Indeed, the overwhelming majority of the domain expressions that one could form by putting together open sentences, propositional connectives, and quantifiers would be satisfied by entities of more than one sort. Accordingly, if the values of each variable are to be restricted to entities of one sort (so as to make it possible for the values of the variables with which the predicates in the matrix S are combined to all be of the sort that the predicate calls for), we will need a fairly stringent restriction on the form of the domain expressions. The most straightforward way to impose such a restriction is probably to require the domain expression of a quantifier binding a variable x to be an $\wedge$-conjunction that has a conjunct Fx, where F is a sort predicate. I will adopt a version of that restriction that is aimed at allowing for domain expressions of forms that directly match the forms of the N's with which quantifiers are combined in natural languages, in which "stacked" relative clause constructions, as in 8.1.3, have a left-branching surface constituent structure as indicated, with each of the N' constituents derived by a step in which one conjunct of a [$_s$ S *and* S] structure is adjoined to a predicate N′ in the other conjunct:

8.1.3

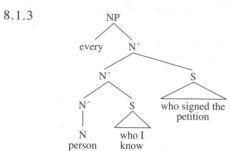

So as to provide for domain expressions having this structure, I will give a recursive definition of a notion **domain-defining expression (DDE)**, consisting of a sort predication to which expressions involving its variable are successively conjoined:

8.1.4   For any variable x, (i) for any sort predicate F_i, $F_i x$ is a DDE of sort F_i for x; and (ii) if $F_1(..., x, ...)$ is a DDE of sort F_i for x and $F_2(..., x, ...)$ is any propositional function of x and perhaps other variables, $\wedge(F_1(..., x, ...), F_2(..., x, ...))$ is a DDE of sort F_i for x.

If we adopt the additional definition 8.1.5, we can then impose the restrictions 8.1.6, which require that the domain expression for each variable be a DDE for that variable and in addition that the predicates with which that variable is combined be restricted to values of the corresponding sort for the relevant argument:

8.1.5   a. If G is an atomic predicate whose jth argument position is restricted to sort F_i, then $G(..., x, ...)$ with x in the jth argument position is of sort F_i for x.
      b. If $G_1(..., x, ...)$ and $G_2(..., x, ...)$ are of sort F_i for x, then so are $\wedge(G_1(..., x, ...), G_2(..., x, ...))$, $\vee(G_1(..., x, ...), G_2(..., x, ...))$. $\supset(G_1(..., x, ...), G_2(..., x, ...))$, and $\sim G_1(..., x, ...)$.
      c. For any quantifier Q and any variable y that is free in $G(..., x, ..., y, ...)$, if $G(..., x, ..., y, ...)$ is of sort F_i for x, then $(Q:H(..., y, ...))_y G(..., x, ..., y, ...)$ is of sort F_i for x.

8.1.6   In any expression (Quantifier: A)$_x$ B of a logical structure, there must be a sort F_i such that A is a DDE of sort F_i for x, and B is of sort F_i for x.

The imposition of these restrictions will disallow some of the inferences that conform to the rules of inference that we have been assuming so far. For example, the following inference will have to be disallowed, since even if its premise meets the restriction 8.1.6, its conclusion will not, because $\sim Gx$ is not a DDE for x:

8.1.7
1	$(\forall : Fx)\, Gx$	supp
2	$\sim Gu$	supp
3	Fu	supp
4	Gu	1, 3, $\forall$-expl
5	$\sim Gu$	2, reit
6	$\sim Fu$	3–5, $\sim$-intro
7	$(\forall : \sim Gx)\, \sim Fx$	2–6, $\forall$-intro

If we assume, as we have so far, that all inferences are subject to the condition that its various lines conform to all of the conditions that we are imposing on the well-formedness of logical structures, then there is no need to impose any special restriction on the application of $\forall$-intro: since line 7 violates 8.1.6, 8.1.7 will be excluded even though it conforms to the system of rules of inference given in chapter 2.

Note that while 8.1.7 is excluded, close counterparts of it that do not violate 8.1.6, such as 8.1.8, where F_i is a sort predicate, are not excluded:

8.1.8 $(\forall{:}\wedge(F_i x,\ Fx))Gx \vdash (\forall{:}\ \wedge(F_i x,\ \sim Gx))\sim Fx$

This would correspond to, say, an inference with premise *All animals which are dogs bite postmen* and conclusion *All animals which do not bite postmen are nondogs*. The premise in that case amounts to *All dogs bite postmen*, in that dogs are necessarily animals. Thus the inferences in 8.1.7 and 8.1.8 have essentially the same premise, but they differ in that a sort predicate is factored out of the domain expression in 8.1.8 and is retained in the domain expression of the conclusion, whereas the domain expression of the conclusion of 8.1.7 would be satisfied by things of (literally) all sorts.

8.2. Logical Types; Lambda Calculus

In section 7.3 we distinguished between predicates that took individuals as arguments and predicates that took sets of individuals as arguments. The distinction that we thereby drew was a distinction in what we will call (following Russell and Whitehead 1910–13) the **type** of the entities of which a given predicate can be predicated. In the remainder of the book, we will have occasion to refer not only to constants of all of the various types (the two types referred to so far, plus infinitely many other types that will be introduced shortly) but also to variables of each of the types, since it is generally possible to have a quantified expression appearing in whatever position a constant can appear in, and to each quantified expression there must correspond a variable whose possible values are entities of the appropriate type. For example, sentences like the premises of 8.2.1a–b require analyses in terms of a bound variable that takes propositions (8.2.1a) or properties (8.2.1b) as its values, so that the validity of those inferences can be attributed to the rule of ∀-exploitation:

8.2.1   a. Sam disagrees with everything that Lucy believes.
             Lucy believes that there is a tooth fairy.
             Therefore, Sam disagrees with [the proposition that] there is a
                tooth fairy.
         b. Napoleon had all the properties of a great general.
             Being stubborn is a property of a great general.
             Therefore, Napoleon had the property of being stubborn.

I wish tentatively to assume the following types (which will be supplemented by additional types in chapter 14):

8.2.2   a. e = Individuals.
         b. p = Propositions.
         c. For any two types A and B, <A, B> = functions that
             associate to entities of type A entities of type B.
         d. For any particular type A, [A] = sets of entities of type A.

For example, $[e]$ will be the type for sets of individuals, $<e, p>$ will be the type for propositional functions of individuals (i.e., functions that associate to an individual a proposition), $<[e], <e, p>>$ will be the type for functions that associate to each set of individuals a propositional function of individuals, and so on. Note that in view of the reference that 8.2.2c–d make to arbitrary types, each of those entries in the list covers infinitely many types. For example, for any particular type a, 8.2.2d allows us to construct a type $<a, p>$, corresponding to propositional functions with an argument of type a, i.e., functions that associate to an entity of type a a proposition.

Variables of the types provided for in 8.2.2d play a role in the analysis of sentences as in 8.2.3:

8.2.3   a. Napoleon had all the properties of a great general.
         b. Having all the properties of a great general was a property that
             Napoleon possessed.

In 8.2.3a there is a quantifier binding a variable whose values are properties that great generals possess, thus, entities of the type $<e, p>$. In 8.2.3b, there is in addition a predicate "be a property that Napoleon possessed," and it will be necessary to distinguish between properties of which that predicate is true and properties of which it is false; the predicate thus is of type $<<e, p>, p>$, that is, to a propositional function of individuals it associates a proposition.

In the remainder of this section, I will introduce and make some use of a device that allows one to construct expressions of all the types that are covered by 8.2.2d. Specifically, let ϕ be any expression of type a,[1] and let x be a variable of type u that occurs in ϕ. Then $(\lambda x)\phi$ denotes the function of type $<u, a>$ that associates to each value of x the corresponding value of ϕ, i.e.,

8.2.4 $[(\lambda x)\phi](c)$ = the result of substituting c for all occurrences of x in ϕ.

For example, $[(\lambda x) (x \text{ Bald})]$ (Aristotle) = Aristotle is bald. The λ-notation provides an easy way of expressing **properties.** Thus, 8.2.5a expresses the property of having a spouse who is older than one and 8.2.5b expresses the property of being a property of all archaeologists; these two expressions can be put together in a formula (8.2.6) that says that the property of having a spouse who is older than one is a property of all archaeologists:

8.2.5   a. $(\lambda x)((\exists: y \text{ Person})_y \wedge (y \text{ Spouse } x, y \text{ Older } x))$
         b. $(\lambda P)((\forall: z \text{ Arch})_z Pz)$

8.2.6 $[(\lambda P)(\forall: z \text{ Arch})_z Pz)] [(\lambda x) (\exists: y \text{ Person})_y \wedge (y \text{ Spouse } x,$
             $y \text{ Older } x)]$

The definition in 8.2.4 allows one to simplify formulas such as 8.2.6 through successively substituting for the various λ-bound variables the value that the formula indicates. This procedure, which is known as **λ-conversion**, enables one to obtain from 8.2.6 a formula expressing directly what 8.2.6 expresses in a roundabout way, namely that all archaeologists have spouses who are older than them:

8.2.7   a. $(\forall: z \text{ Arch}) [(\lambda P) (\exists: y \text{ Person}) \wedge (y \text{ Spouse } x, y \text{ Older } x)](z)$
         b. $(\forall: z \text{ Arch}) (\exists: y \text{ Person}) \wedge (y \text{ Spouse } z, y \text{ Older } z)$

The first formula in 8.2.7 is the result of replacing P in $(\forall: z \text{ Arch}) Pz$ by the expression in the second pair of square brackets in 8.2.6 (which, since it follows a (λP) ... expression, serves as the value of P), and the final formula is the result of substituting z for x in the preceding formula (in which a (λx) ... expression is combined with z).

In the remainder of this book, I will adopt the following policies about types: (i) I will assume that each variable or constant is of one particular type; (ii) I will assume that for every type, arbitrarily many variables of that type are available; and (iii) where the context does not make obvious what the type of a given variable or constant is, I will mark its first occurrence with a superscript indicating its type, e.g., I will use expressions such as the following alternative way of writing 8.2.5b:

8.2.8 $(\lambda P^{<e,p>})((\forall: z^e \text{ Arch})_z Pz)$

Note that z^e is not a different symbol from z: it is the same symbol, just with the addition of a reminder of its type. In addition, (iv) I will assume that the various expressions that conform to our formation rules belong to the appropriate types, and that **closed** expressions (an expression is closed if every variable that it contains is bound by a variable-binder that it contains) are to count as (complex) constants of the type in question:

8.2.9   a. $(\forall: x \text{ Ling})(x \text{ Insane})$ is a constant of type p.
   b. $(\lambda x^e)(x \text{ Admire } x)$ is a constant of type $<e,p>$.
   c. $(\lambda P^{<e,p>}) ((\forall: z^e \text{ Arch})_z Pz)$ is a constant of type
                      $<<e, p>, p>$.

This enlargement of the range of expressions that are to be admitted into our system of logic amounts to a revision of our system of formation rules: predicates are now subcategorized with regard to the type of each of their arguments, and only those predicate-argument combinations are well formed in which each argument position is filled by an expression of the type that the predicate demands.

 The rules of inference given in chapters 2 and 3 will not need to be altered, since the (revised) formation rules will suffice to impose on the quantifier rules the restriction that the constants and variables that get substituted into each position are of the right type. For example, if one is drawing a conclusion by $\exists$-intro, the variable that one introduces must be of the same type as the constant that figured in the premises, as when one draws the conclusion that some Greek is bald from the premises that Aristotle is a Greek and that Aristotle is bald: the bound variable of $(\exists: x \text{ Greek}) (x \text{ Bald})$ cannot be of type $<e,p>$ or $<<e,p>, p>$ but must be of type e. But there is no need to impose any special restriction on $\exists$-intro if we continue to require that all lines in a proof conform to the formation rules: if a variable of any other type were used in the conclusion, Greek and Bald would be predicated of a variable of the wrong type and the resulting combinations would thus not conform to the formation rules. We can then treat 8.2.1 (repeated here as 8.2.10a) as corresponding to an inference (8.2.10b) that conforms to our rules of inference:

8.2.10 a. Sam disagrees with everything that Lucy believes.
        Lucy believes that there is a tooth fairy.
        Therefore, Sam disagrees with [the proposition that] there is a
        tooth fairy.

   b. 1 $(\forall\colon lu\ \mathrm{Bel}\ X^p)_X\ (s\ \mathrm{Disag}\ X)$ supp
       2 $\underline{lu\ \mathrm{Bel}\ (\mathrm{There\ is\ a}\ tf)}$ supp
       3 $s\ \mathrm{Disag}\ (\mathrm{There\ is\ a}\ tf)$ 1, 2, $\forall$-expl

In 8.2.10b there is a tacit reference to the formation rules, in that "There is a tf" is identified as being of the type p and thus available for serving as a value of the variable X in the first premise.

One rule of inference given in 6.2 **will** have to be altered, though, namely = -exploitation. Note that the changes that we have made in our formation rules greatly enlarge the set of contexts in which a term could occur, and substitutions made in such a context as "John believes that _____ is a prime number" need not yield a true conclusion when applied to true premises. For example, even though $47 \times 91 = 4277$, it could very well be true that John believes that 47×91 is not a prime number but false that he believes that 4277 is not a prime number. I am not in a position to state the appropriate restriction on = -exploitation at this point in the book (the question will arise again in section 11.3), but will merely suggest here that the factor that makes the substitution in the given position invalid is that the substitution is made in a position that refers to "a different world" from the world in which the premises are evaluated, e.g., the complement of *believe* here purports to describe not the world as it really is but the world as John believes it to be, and what is relevant to the validity of the substitution is not whether 47×91 really is 4277 but whether $47 \times 91 = 4277$ in the world as John believes things to be. It may ultimately be possible to give an appropriate revision of = -expl in terms of a scheme of representation in which (as in section 12.1) the parts of sentences are indexed for the worlds that they purport to refer to, and = -expl is allowed only when the index of the equation matches that of the immediate context of the substitution.

Revising the truth conditions is much more problematic. Certain parts of the revision are a straightforward enough matter: we must require each constant to denote an object of the corresponding type, require each variable to range over objects of the corresponding type, and revise the truth-conditions for quantifiers so as to take into account the type of the bound variable—each assignment of values to variables must assign to each variable values of the appropriate type, and the satisfaction conditions for universally quantified or existentially quantified sentences must be in terms of all or some (respectively) of the ways of assigning values to the bound variable satisfying the sentence. There are two interrelated problems here, though: (i) under what conditions do entities of a given type count as identical (e.g., when is one justified in speaking of two different propositions, as opposed to just the same proposition presented in two different ways?), and (ii) for each type, what is the **full** range of values of a variable of that type (e.g., what counts as a possible proposition and what counts as a possible one-place predicate of individuals?)? Note that the answers to these questions can affect the truth values that will be assigned by our rules for quantifiers; for example, the answer to (i) can affect whether it is true that Sam disagrees with only two propositions that Lucy believes (if you say that there are three such propositions, you have to make sure that you are not counting the same proposition twice), and the answer to (ii) can affect what entities are available as potential counterexamples to generalizations about propositions or about properties.

Question (ii) assumes an especially large role in the more usual version of type theory in which propositions are not admitted as types but truth values (symbolized "t") are. In that version of type theory (the one assumed in Montague grammar), the denotation of a one-place propositional function of individuals is taken to be a function of type $<e,t>$, i.e., a function that associates to each entity a truth value. The problem with that is that if one takes **all** functions of that type to be possible values of a variable of that type, one admits functions that are literally indescribable, i.e., for any subset whatever of the domain, there is a function that associates "true" to all members of that subset and "false" to all other members of the domain, even when the domain is infinite and it thus has more subsets than there are possible ways of describing subsets of the domain.

For most of the remainder of this section, I will turn to an interesting application of the λ-notation proposed independently by Sag (1976) and Williams (1977), who use representations involving λs in explaining why V'-deletion fails to apply in certain cases in which its conditions for application apparently are met. V'-deletion is the transformation that deletes one of two identical V's, subject to the usual constraints on the relationship of an anaphoric device (here, the gap left by the deletion of the V') to its antecedent, as in:[2]

8.2.11 a. John didn't win a prize, but Mike did ∅. (∅ = win a prize)
        b. If Macy's lowers the price on platinum backscratchers,
           Bloomingdale's will ∅ too. (∅ = lower the price on platinum
           backscratchers)
        c. Peter is easy to talk to, and Betsy is ∅ also. (∅ = easy to
           talk to)

Consider the failure of V'-deletion to apply in such examples as:

8.2.12   a. *Peter is easy to talk to. and Betsy is easy to ∅ (< talk to)
                 also.
             b. The steak is ready to eat, and the chicken is
                 $\begin{Bmatrix} ∅ \ (< \text{ready to eat}) \\ *\text{ready to } ∅ \ (< \text{eat}) \end{Bmatrix}$ also.

Deletion of a V' that is contained in a larger potentially deletable V' (as *talk to* is contained in *easy to talk to* in 8.2.12a) is not in general excluded, since, as Sag notes, deletion of the contained V' is permissible in examples such as:

8.2.13   a. Peter is ready to give up, and Betsy is
                 $\begin{Bmatrix} ∅ \ (< \text{ready to give up}) \\ \text{ready to } ∅ \ (< \text{give up}) \end{Bmatrix}$ also.
             b. Sam wants to write a novel, and Larry
                 $\begin{Bmatrix} \text{does } ∅ \ (< \text{want to write a novel}) \\ \text{wants to } ∅ \ (< \text{write a novel}) \end{Bmatrix}$ also.

Sag also notes that V'-deletion in an ambiguous clause often is possible only on certain readings of that clause:

8.2.14   a.   Alan said that Betsy had hit him, and Peter also said that she
                  had hit him.
             a'. Alan said that Betsy had hit him, and Peter also said that she
                  had ∅.

The first *him* in 8.2.14a could refer either to Alan or to some person other than Alan and Peter. The second *him* can be given a **strict identity** interpretation, in which it refers to the same person that the first *him* refers to; if the first *him* refers to Alan (but not if it refers to any other person), the second *him* can be given a so-called **sloppy identity**[3] interpretation, in which it refers to Peter. In 8.2.14a', only two of these three interpretations are possible: it can be given either of the strict identity interpretations, but not the sloppy identity interpretation (in which the first clause has to do with Betsy hitting Alan and the second clause with her hitting Peter). However, if the higher V' is deleted rather than the lower one, the three-way ambiguity reappears, i.e., unlike 8.2.14a', 8.2.15 allows an interpretation in which the second clause refers to Betsy hitting Peter:

8.2.15   Alan said that Betsy had hit him, and Peter did ∅ also.

Similarly, the ambiguity of 8.2.16a vanishes when V'-deletion deletes *taller than he was:*

8.2.16   a.   Sam claimed he was taller than he was, and Bill claimed he
               was taller than he was too.
         a'. Sam claimed he was taller than he was, and Bill claimed he
               was ∅ too.

Each of the conjoined clauses in 8.2.16a is ambiguous between an interpretation that attributes to Sam or Bill (respectively) the self-contradictory claim that his height exceeds itself and an interpretation that attributes to him a claim that is false but not self-contradictory, namely one in which he overestimates his height.[4] However, 8.2.16a' allows only the interpretation that attributes self-contradictory claims to both Sam and Bill. Once again, deletion of the higher V' causes the lost ambiguity to reappear, i.e., 8.2.17 can be interpreted either as attributing to each of them an overestimate of his height or as attributing to each of them a self-contradictory claim:

8.2.17   Sam claimed he was taller than he was, and Bill did ∅ too.

Sag proposed an explanation of these facts in terms of logical structures in which a V' is represented in semantic structure as a λ-expression, for example, the V' *love Betsy* would be represented as $(\lambda x) (x \text{ Love } b)$. This apparently trivial notational proposal shows remarkable descriptive possibilities when it is applied to sentences involving complex V's. Consider the unreduced counterpart 8.2.18a and 8.2.11c and 8.2.12a, and the logical structure that Sag would assign to it:

8.2.18   a.   Peter is easy to talk to, and Betsy is easy to talk to also.
         b.

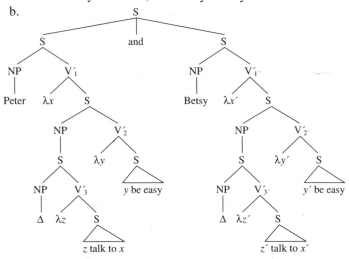

Sag suggests that the reason why $V'_{1'}$ can be deleted under identity with V'_1 but $V'_{3'}$ cannot be deleted under identity with V'_3 is that V'_1 and $V'_{1'}$ express the same property: they differ only to the extent that variables bound by operators **within** V'_1 and $V'_{1'}$ are labeled differently; but V'_3 and $V'_{3'}$ do not, strictly speaking, express properties, since they are not of the form $(\lambda x)S$, nor are they identical constituents of some larger property, and thus there is no basis for identifying the x of the one with the x' of the other.

The notion described informally in the last sentence can be made more precise by introducing the notion of **alphabetic variant:** a coherent formula α is an alphabetic variant of a coherent formula β if α differs from β at most in that there are variable-binding operators in α that correspond to occurrences of the same operator (but with a different variable) in β. Sag's proposal is then that V'-deletion is possible only if the logical structures of the two V's are alphabetic variants to each other. To get this proposal to work, it is necessary that all variables be given distinct names, as in 8.2.10b, even though the coherency conditions would not be violated if, for example, x and x' were given the same name; let us assume henceforth that different variables will be given different names. What makes V'_3 and $V'_{3'}$ fail to be alphabetic variants is that V'_3 contains a variable x bound by an operator that is not within that V', and $V'_{3'}$ contains in the corresponding position a variable bound by another operator (another operator-occurrence, that is—the fact that both operators are λs doesn't make V'_3 and $V'_{3'}$ alphabetic variants).[5]

Note that the definition of alphabetic variance allows two V's to be alphabetic variants if both are in the scope of some operator and both contain occurrences of the variable that that operator binds. Example 8.2.19 illustrates that V'-deletion is applicable in that situation:

8.2.19   Betsy greeted everyone when Sandy did.

One interpretation of 8.2.19 presents no problems: the one that refers to two acts of greeting everyone (say, by saying "Hello, everybody"), one performed by Betsy and one by Sandy. We are interested here in the other reading of 8.2.19, which says that, for every person, Betsy greeted him when Sandy did (e.g., when George entered, Betsy and Sandy both said "Hello, George," when Ellen entered, Betsy and Sandy both said "Hello Ellen," and so forth). The latter reading of 8.2.19 could be expressed by a formula along these lines:

8.2.20 $(\forall{:}x \; \text{Person})_X \; ([\text{Betsy}, (\lambda y)(y \; \text{Greet} \; x)] \; \text{when} \; [\text{Sandy}, (\lambda w)$
            $(w \; \text{Greet} \; x)])$.

Note that here the two V's are alphabetic variants: $(\lambda y)(y \; \text{Greet} \; x)$ contains two variables, one bound and one unbound (at least, not bound by anything within the V's under consideration); $(\lambda w)(w \; \text{Greet} \; x)$ likewise contains two

variables, one bound and one unbound, and the bound one differs only alpha-
betically from the corresponding variable in the first V', while the unbound
one is identical to the unbound one in the first V'.

The difference between 8.2.12a and 8.2.13a is that 8.2.12a demands a logical structure like 8.2.18b, in which the V' whose deletability is at issue contains a variable bound by the λ of a higher V', whereas such is not the case
with 8.2.13a:

8.2.21   a. Peter is easy to talk to.
              (Peter, $(\lambda x)[\Delta, (\lambda z)(z$ talk to $x))$, $(\lambda y)(y$ be easy)])
         b. Peter is ready to give up.
              (Peter, $(\lambda x)[x$ ready for $(x, (\lambda z)(z$ give up))])

The explanation of why 8.2.14a' lacks the ambiguity that both 8.2.14a and
8.2.15 have is that the logical structures for the two readings, according to
Sag, will be:

8.2.22   a. Strict identity reading:
              (Alan$_i$, $(\lambda x)(x$ said [Betsy$_j$, $(\lambda y)(y$ hit him$_i$)])) and
              (Peter, (λw) $(w$ said [she$_j$, $(\lambda z)(z$ hit him$_i$)]))
         b. Sloppy identity reading:
              (Alan$_i$, $(\lambda x)(x$ said [Betsy$_j$, $(\lambda y)(y$ hit $x)$]) and
              (Peter, $(\lambda w)(w$ said [she$_j$, $(\lambda z)(z$ hit $w)$]))

In 8.2.22a $(\lambda y)(y$ hit him$_i$) and $(\lambda z)(z$ hit him$_i$) are alphabetic variants—each
contains only one variable (here him_i is a constant, not a variable)—and are
identical aside from the naming of the variable. Thus, when the logical structure is 8.2.22a, $(\lambda z)(z$ hit him$_i$) can be deleted under identity with the corresponding V' of the first conjunct, and 8.2.14a' is derived. However, in
8.2.22b, $(\lambda y)(y$ hit $x)$ and $(\lambda z)(z$ hit $w)$ are not alphabetic variants: the x in the
former is an unbound variable and is not identical to the w that appears in the
corresponding position of the latter. Thus, V'-deletion cannot delete $(\lambda z)(z$
hit $w)$, which means that 8.2.14a' can only be derived with the "strict identity"
interpretation, which is exactly the factual observation that we set out to ex-
plain. By contrast, $(\lambda x)(x$ said [Betsy$_j$, $(\lambda y)(y$ hit $x)$]) and $(\lambda w)(w$ said [she$_j$,
$(\lambda z)(z$ hit $w)$]) are alphabetic variants, and thus in the derivation of 8.2.15 the
sloppy identity reading may serve as the logical structure. The explanation of
the difference in interpretation between 8.2.16*a* and 8.2.17 is along the same
lines.

Sag's proposal provides a solution to the problem raised in section 7.1:
why can Conjunction Reduction apply to 8.2.23a to yield 8.2.23a' when it
cannot apply to 8.2.23b to yield 8.2.23b'?

8.2.23   a.   Tom admires few authors, and Dick admires few authors.
        a'.   Both Tom and Dick admire few authors.
        b.   Few rules are correct and few rules are easy to read.
        b'.   Few rules are both correct and easy to read.

Suppose that the identity condition for Conjunction Reduction is the same as that for V'-deletion: two constituents count as identical for Conjunction Reduction only if they correspond to parts of logical structure that are alphabetic variants of each other. Then Conjunction Reduction can apply in 8.2.23a' because the underlined V's in 8.2.24 are alphabetic variants:

8.2.24   (Tom, (λx)(few author y)(x admire y))and
        (Dick, (λz)(few author w)(z admire w))

We will be able to explain its inapplicability in 8.2.23b if we can show that the constituents that must be identified (the two occurrences of *Few rules*) are not alphabetic variants. It is not immediately obvious how the definition given above of alphabetic variant should apply to a pair of constituents such as (few: x Rule) and (few: u Rule) in 8.2.25:

8.2.25   (few: x Rule)$_x$(x, (λy)(y Correct)) and (few: u Rule)$_u$(u, (λv)([Δ,
        (λz)(z Read v)], (λw)(w Easy))

However, it appears that we should not take them to be alphabetic variants, since the essential idea in "alphabetic variant" appears to be: two expressions are alphabetic variants if we could rename their bound variables (otherwise leaving things unchanged) and make them identical without changing meaning. Note that one could not change the variables in (few: x Rule) and (few: u Rule) and preserve the meaning unless one made further changes in the formula. On this understanding of alphabetic variant, then, Conjunction Reduction cannot identify the two occurrences of *few rules* in 8.2.23b. More generally, two occurrences of a quantified NP will not count as identical, though (as in 8.2.23*a–a'*), two expressions containing a quantified NP may count as identical.[6]

8.3. Kinds; Generic Propositions

The term "generic" is often applied to sentences such as the following:

8.3.1   a.   Bears hibernate in caves.
        b.   A dog has four legs.
        c.   The dodo is extinct.

    c′. Cockroaches are widespread.

    d. Fido chases cars.

In each example there are one or more NPs (*bears, caves, a dog, the dodo, cockroaches, cars*) that can be said to be "used generically," and it is common to see analyses in which generic sentences are analyzed as having logical structures in which one of those NPs has a universal or near-universal quantifier or the "sort of universal" quantifier *most*.

It should be noted at the outset that the different kinds of "generic NP" differ semantically from one another and that none of them is adequately represented as involving universal, near-universal, or "sort of universal" quantification. First, *caves* in 8.3.1a and *cars* in 8.3.1d cannot be analyzed as involving such quantifiers, since 8.3.1a does not imply that all or most or even very many caves ever have bears hibernating in them: 8.3.1a could express a true proposition even if only one cave in every thousand has ever been used as a hibernation site by a bear; and 8.3.1d can be true even if Fido has only chased a hundred or so of the hundreds of millions of existing cars.[7]

Second, "counterexamples" falsify universal propositions but not generic propositions: if there is a bear, Waldo, who does not hibernate in caves, then *All bears hibernate in caves* is false even though 8.3.1a may be true. Similarly, a freak dog that had a fifth leg or only three legs would make *All dogs have four legs* false but would not show that 8.3.1b was false. Even near-universal and "sort of universal" propositions have different truth conditions from generics. For example, sentences such as 8.3.2a–c can be true even if a corresponding sentence with *most* or *almost all* is false, 8.3.2d–e are false even though corresponding sentences with *most* or *almost all* are true, and 8.3.2f–g can be false even if corresponding sentences with *all* are true:[8]

8.3.2   a. Sea turtles lay approximately two hundred eggs at a time.

        b. Dutchmen are good sailors.

        c. Horses were first ridden by the Egyptians.

        d. Bees are female.

        e. Bees are sterile.

        f. Yellow-bellied rathawks have long tails.

        g. Yellow-bellied rathawks are male.

Only adult female sea turtles lay eggs at all, and thus it is false that most sea turtles lay eggs 200 at a time, but 8.3.2a is nonetheless true. The fact that most Dutchmen are not sailors at all and thus are not good sailors does not prevent 8.3.2b from being true. Even though most horses have never been ridden by Egyptians, 8.3.2c may well be true. Since female bees grossly outnumber males and very few bees of either sex are fertile, it is true that most bees are female and that most bees (indeed, almost all bees) are sterile, but it is false that bees are female and likewise that bees are sterile. Finally, if the yellow-bellied rathawk is a nearly extinct species whose surviving members all are males with long tails, it would be true that all yellow-bellied rathawks have long tails and that all yellow-bellied rathawks are male, but it could still be false that yellow-bellied rathawks have long tails (perhaps the gene pool includes both genes for long tails and genes for short tails, with the latter a recessive gene that is carried by some of the surviving members of the species), and it would certainly be false that yellow-bellied rathawks are male.

Third, the universal or near-universal analog to a generic sentence may not even be semantically coherent, let alone logically equivalent to it. For example, *All dodos are extinct* makes no sense (unless taken as quantifying over species rather than individuals: all species of the genus *Raphus* are extinct); only a species or other taxonomic entity can be extinct, not an individual member of the species. Likewise, *All cockroaches are widespread* makes no sense: the species is widespread, but Archie, an individual member of the species, is not widespread, even if he gets around a lot.

The plural generic and the definite generic can be used, as in 8.3.1c–c′, to refer to properties of a species as whole, whereas the indefinite singular generic can be used only with reference to properties that characterize members of the species:

8.3.3   a. *A dodo is extinct.
          b. *A cockroach is widespread.

The indefinite plural generic and the indefinite singular generic can be used for kinds that are defined by pretty much any combinations of properties, whereas the definite generic requires that the referent be a "natural" kind:

8.3.4   a. A bed that was slept in by George Washington is easy to find.
          b. Beds that were slept in by George Washington are easy to find.
          c. *The bed that was slept in by George Washington is easy to find. (OK only if it refers to a specific bed and is thus nongeneric.)[9]

Carlson lavishes attention on the indefinite plural generic, the most frequent of the three constructions and also the one that appears to be the least uniform in its semantic interpretation. He argues that indefinite plural generics are basically references to **kinds** rather than to objects or sets of objects and that they often appear to make reference to objects only because many properties of kinds are derivatives of properties of the members of the kind. The central idea of Carlson's approach is to distinguish predicates with regard to whether they are basically predicated of kinds, of individuals, or of "stages" (this term will be explained below) and to provide rules whereby under certain circumstances derived predicates can be formed that are predicated of a different type of things. For example, *run* is basically predicated of "stages," but there is also a derived usage in which it is predicated of individuals, as in the habitual present *Fido runs* (not the "narrative present" that appears in an on-the-spot report by a radio announcer, in which *run* is predicated of a "stage"), as well as a derived usage in which it is predicated of kinds, as in *Rabbits run* or *The rabbit runs.*

A "stage" for Calson is an instantiation of a kind or of an individual. For example, two hours worth of Fido (say, the two hours beginning at 4:37 P.M. Eastern Daylight time on 12 July 1971) is an instantiation of both the individual Fido and the kind "dogs." While there are predicates that are basically predicated of stages, there are no NPs that basically refer to stages. Thus predicates referring basically to stages must be combined with other semantic material that bridges the gap between kind and stage or between individual and stage. Carlson does this by having an individual subject not combine directly with a stage predicate like Bark but rather with an expression that means "there is a stage y of x for which Bark(y)." Specifically, suppose we introduce the two-place predicate I(y,x), corresponding to "y is an instantiation of x."[10] Then to combine the stage-predicate Bark with the individual variable x, we form not Bark (x), which is incoherent because an individual fills an argument position that is reserved for stages, but rather 8.3.5:

8.3.5 $(\exists{:}I(y,x))_y$ Bark(y)

More specifically, let us use superscripts on variables and constants to indicate whether they denote stages (s), individuals (i), or kinds (k), and let us use λs in representing V's. Then the V' *barked* will be represented as 8.3.6a, the latter will be replaced by 8.3.6a' when it is combined with a subject that denotes an individual, and thus the combination of that V' with a constant corresponding to *Fido* will be represented as 8.3.6b, which can be converted by λ-conversion into 8.3.6b', that is, into "There is a stage of Fido which barked":

8.3.6   a. (λy^s) Bark(y)
      a'. $(\lambda x^i)(\exists{:}Iy^sx)_y$ Bark(y)
      b. $[(\lambda x^i)(\exists{:}Iy^sx)_y$ Bark(y)](f^i)
      b'. $(\exists{:}Iyf)$ Bark(y)

Suppose we treat kinds as a special case of individuals and interpret the instantiation predicate I as covering not only the relation of stages to individuals but also the relation of stages and individuals to kinds (e.g., the various stages of Fido are also stages of the kind "dogs"). Then Carlson's approach has the happy consequence of explaining why indefinite plural NPs in certain sentences have an existential interpretation rather than the generic interpetation that is often mistaken for universal quantification; for example, *Dogs barked* can be interpreted as "There was barking by (some) dogs." For Carlson, the translation is exactly parallel to *Fido barked:*

8.3.7 $[(\lambda x^i)(\exists{:}Iy^sx)_y \text{ Bark}(y)](d^k) \rightarrow$
$(\exists{:}Iyd)_y \text{ Bark}(y)$

Since an instantiation of a kind is barking only when instantiations of individuals belonging to that kind are barking, the last formula implies that there were dogs barking.[11]

When an expression denoting a kind appears as the subject of an expression that is predicated of individuals rather than of stages, the sentence has a generic interpretation, as in 8.3.8:

8.3.8   a. Dutchmen are good sailors. (= 8.3.2b)
          b. Cats make nice pets.
          c. Rabbits have long ears.

Once again the subject expression denotes something of a different type from what the predicate expression is normally predicated of, and here again Carlson invokes a device that will convert the predicate expression into something that allows subjects of the type in question. However, the device here has to go beyond the devices of predicate calculus that were invoked in 8.3.5: what is needed is an operator (here written Gn) that applies to a one-place predicate of individuals and associates to it a one-place predicate of kinds. The conditions under which an expression G$n(f)(a)$ is true (where a denotes a kind of f a one-place predicate of individuals) amount to the conditions under which membership in a given kind can be held responsible for the relevant members of the kind possessing the property, e.g., it is because of membership in the kind "sea turtle" that those sea turtles who have an opportunity to lay eggs (a subset of the set of adult female sea turtles) do so in holes that they dig in sandy beaches, and it is because of membership in the kind "Dutchman" that the relevant members of that kind (i.e., those who engage in seafaring) are good sailors. The predicate to which the operator Gn is applied can of course be of arbitrary internal complexity.

Besides sentences that predicate something of a kind, there are also generic sentences that predicate a "habitual" property of an individual, as in *John snores* or *Ann smokes*. The term "habitual" is somewhat misleading, since habits are only one of many things that can serve as the basis for predicating a given habitual predicate of an individual. For example, the sentence *Dr. Novotny performs lobotomies* would not normally be interpreted as implying that Dr. Novotny has a habit of performing lobotomies but merely that he will perfom one when the occasion to do so arises: he is someone to whom a doctor who has recommended a lobotomy might refer the patient. The grounds for applying a habitual predicate to an individual are simply whatever grounds there are for distinguishing two varieties of individuals, those having a property that is manifested in actions of the given kind and those not having that property, and such grounds may be a habit in one class of cases, a commitment in another class of cases, and an occupational qualification in a third class of cases.[12]

Carlson (1977) describes habitual predicates in terms of an operator that derives predicates of individuals from predicates of stages, leaving it up to real-world knowledge to decide what the appropriate grounds for applying that derived predicate to an individual should be. Calling that operator "Hab," one can apply Hab to any predicate f of stages and derive a corresponding one-place predicate Hab(f) of individuals. A full description of Hab (which will not be attempted here) would have to incorporate the idea that Hab(f) is true of a given individual only in virtue of something having to do with f being true of stages of that same individual.

Carlson (1989:170–73) later altered this analysis in response to his observation there are many habitual clauses whose subjects do not denote anything that can plausibly be said to possess habitual properties, e.g.:

8.3.9   a. It rains 30 inches a year here.
         b. A computer computes the daily weather forecast.

One cannot interpret 8.3.9a as saying that *it* (even if one can assign it a denotation) has a property of (generally, normally, etc.) raining 30 inches a year; rather it says that 30 inches of rain a year is what (generally, normally, etc.) happens here. Likewise, in 8.3.9b *a computer* is interpreted as an existentially quantified NP that is embedded within a habitual sentence: it says that (on a typical/normal/... day) the weather forecast is computed by a computer (not necessarily the same computer each day; cf. *A limousine brings the governor-elect to the inauguration,* where there can be a different limousine for each inauguration). Carlson's revision of his earlier analysis is then to treat habitual clauses not in terms of an operator applying to a predicate but an operator applying to a sentence. Carlson does not say how one should then represent the meanings of habitual V's, i.e., how one should reduce the predicate operator Hab of his earlier analysis to the sentential operator HAB of the new analysis. The only coherent formula that I can construct that would correspond to "Hab(Snore)" of the earlier analysis is 8.3.10, and I will provisionally adopt such a formula as my analysis of a habitual V':

8.3.10 $(\lambda x^i) \mathrm{HAB}((\exists : \mathrm{I} y^s x)_y \, \mathrm{Snore}(y))$

Note that since the habitual V' denotes a property of individuals and not of stages, the λ has to bind an individual variable, but somehow that individual variable has to be tied to the stage variable of which Snore is predicated; the existential quantifier has to be within the scope of HAB, since what is said to occur "habitually" here is not events in which some particular stage snores (there can be only one such event) but rather events in which a stage of some particular individual snores.

Habitual predicates can occur either by themselves or in combination with references to kinds, in such sentences as

8.3.11   a. Dogs bark.
         b. Frenchmen smoke.
         c. Graduates of the University of Bimini Medical School perform
            lobotomies.

Note that the most obvious interpretation of 8.3.11b is not an existential proposition as in 8.3.7: it doesn't say that some Frenchmen smoke but rather that the members of the kind "Frenchmen" typically/commonly/... have the property that is expressed in such sentences as *Pierre smokes* or *Théophile smokes*, and the indeterminancy in the grounds for applying a habitual predicate is paralleled in sentences such as 8.3.11 that combine a habitual predicate with reference to a kind, as is seen in the difference in interpretation between 8.3.11b and 8.3.11c. Thus, the semantic interpretation of such sentences should presumably be derived simply by combining the semantic interpretation of a habitual predicate with a reference to a kind that consists of individuals of which the habitual predicate can be predicated.

Carlson's approach provides an explanation of the fact that *foxes* in the sentence *Foxes eat chickens* receives a generic interpretation while *chickens* gets rather an existential interpretation. Since *eat* is basically a predicate of stages, it will combine with ∃ and I as in 8.3.5; the habitual sense of *Foxes eat chickens* involves a V' that is predicated of individuals, derived from the latter expression as in 8.3.10:

8.3.12 $(\lambda x^i)\text{HAB}[(\exists:\text{I}w^sx)_w (\exists:\text{I}z^sc)_z \text{Eat}(w,z)]$

The result can then combine with either an individual expression or a kind expression, and if the latter, we obtain an interpretation that says of the kind "foxes" that its members (typically, generally, etc.) are such that there are chickens that they eat. Note the reason that *chickens* has an existential interpretation while *foxes* has a generic interpetation: *foxes* is substituted for a variable that is bound outside of the "HAB(S)" expression, while all the parts of the formula that are tied to *chickens* are inside the scope of HAB, and while both argument positions are bound by existential quantifiers, the one corresponding to *chickens* has to do with stages of a kind while the one corresponding to *foxes* has to do with stages of an individual.

8.4. Convergent ("Branching") Quantifiers

Certain bound variables are dependent on others. For example, when 8.4.1a has the meaning that is representable as 8.4.1b, y depends on x in the sense that the value of y that makes "x have y" true will generally vary with x: 8.4.1b tells you that for each person there is a fault that he has but that different persons need not have the same fault. A dependency could be made explicit in the notation by, say, writing a subscript x on the variable y:

8.4.1   a.   Every person has a fault.
         b. $(\forall: x \text{ Person})_x (\exists: y \text{ Fault})_y (x \text{ have } y)$
         b'. $(\forall: x \text{ Person})_x (\exists: y \text{ Fault})_y (x \text{ have } y_x)$

If one enlarges one's formal language so as to countenance second-order bound variables, that is, variables that range not over individuals but over functions or sets or predicates of individuals, one can propose something on the order of 8.4.2a, which can be abbreviated informally as 8.4.2a', as an alternative to 8.4.1b or 8.4.1b':

8.4.2   a. $(\exists: (\forall: z \text{ Person})_z (fz \text{ Fault}))_f (\forall: x \text{ Person})_x (x \text{ have } fx)$
         a'. $(\exists: \text{Person} \rightarrow \text{Fault})_f (\forall: x \text{ Person})_x (x \text{ have } fx)$

(The use of the arrow in 8.4.2a' is a makeshift device to indicate that the values of f are functions that associate to every person a fault.)

Note that this sort of dependency arises when an existential quantifier is in the scope of another quantifier but not when a universal quantifier is in the scope of an existential quantifier, as in 8.4.3a, whose meaning corresponds to 8.4.3b:

8.4.3   a. There is a fault that every person has.
       b. ($\exists$: y Fault)$_y$ ($\forall$: x Person)$_x$ (x have y)

Formula 8.4.3b corresponds to a very special instance of 8.4.2, namely that in which the value of f that makes ($\forall$: x Person)$_x$ (x have fx) true is a constant function: a function that has the same value no matter what x is. Thus, 8.4.3b clearly implies 8.4.2 but not vice versa; for example, if one-third of all people are miserly and stupid but neat, one-third are stupid and untidy but generous, and one-third are untidy and miserly but smart, and we count only miserliness, stupidity, and untidiness as faults, then 8.4.2 is true but 8.4.3b is false.

More complex dependencies are possible in logical structures containing more complicated arrangements of quantifiers. Consider, for example, 8.4.4a in the interpretation that is representable as 8.4.4b:

8.4.4   a. Every day a senator told every newspaper about a crooked
           judge.
       b. ($\forall$: x Day)$_x$ ($\exists$: y Senator)$_y$ ($\forall$: z Newspaper)$_z$ ($\exists$: u Crooked-
           judge)$_u$ (y told z about u on x)

Here u depends on both z and x: on each day a different senator may well have been talking to the press, and on any given day some talkative senator may have told each newspaper about a different judge, with each paper learning about a different judge from the one it had been told about the day before by a different senator.[13] The result of recasting 8.4.4b in the style of 8.4.2a' would be 8.4.5:

8.4.5   ($\exists$: Day $\rightarrow$ Senator)$_f$ ($\exists$: (Day, Newspaper) $\rightarrow$ Crooked-judge)$_g$
       ($\forall$: x Day)$_x$ (V: z Newspaper)$_y$ (fx tell z about gxz on x)

Suppose, however, that we wanted to set up a logical structure with different dependencies from those in 8.4.4b, say, one in which the value of the judge u that satisfies "y told z about u on x" for given x and z depended only on z and not on x (i.e., for each newspaper there would be a judge that it would be hearing about every day, though not always from the same senator, and without necessarily only that judge being gossiped about on any day). Using the notational scheme of 8.4.5, this is no problem—the second existential quantifier would simply bind a function of one variable rather than of two, and the "matrix" would be "fx tell z about hz on x":

8.4.6   ($\exists$: Day $\rightarrow$ Senator)$_f$ ($\exists$: Newspaper $\rightarrow$ Crooked-judge)$_h$ ($\forall$: x
       Day)$_x$ ($\forall$: y Newspaper)$_y$ (fx tell z about hz on x)

Can this dependency among the variables be expressed using only first-order predicate logic, as in 8.4.5b? In important but largely neglected work by Henkin, Ehrenfeucht, and Walkoe, the significance of which is pointed out in Hintikka 1974, it is shown that the unrestricted quantifier version of the general question that this illustrates has a negative answer, i.e., there is no formula of first-order predicate logic that is systematically equivalent to 8.4.7:

8.4.7 $(\exists f)(\exists g)(\forall x)(\forall z)F(x, fx, z, gz)$

Hintikka argues that there are natural language sentences involving bound variables whose dependencies are of a type not expressible in first-order logic. He points out that 8.4.8a (the simplest such example that he was able to construct) cannot be adequately analyzed with a formula such as 8.4.8b, since in the situation in which the only hatred in the population is that the eldest relative of each villager$_i$ and the relative$_j$ of each townsman who$_j$ knows the villager$_i$ best hate each other, 8.4.8b will be true and 8.4.8a false:

8.4.8   a. Some relative of each villager and some relative of each
              townsman hate each other.
         b. $(\forall: x$ Villager$)_x$ $(\exists: y$ Rel $x)_y$ $(\forall: z$ Townsman$)_z$ $(\exists: u$ Rel $z)_u \wedge (y$
              Hate u, u Hate $y)$

In 8.4.8b, u is allowed to be dependent on x, as in the state of affairs just described, where each villager could perfectly well have different relatives who stood in a relationship of mutual hatred with different relatives of each townsman. Hintikka claims (correctly, I think, though my judgment wavers) that in that state of affairs, 8.4.8a is false in its most natural interpretation. Note the difference between the second-order formulas corresponding to 8.4.8a and to 8.4.8b:

8.4.9   a. $(\exists:$ Villager$_x \rightarrow$ Rel of $x)_f$ $(\exists:$ Townsman$_y \rightarrow$ Rel of $y)_g$ $(\forall: x$
              Villager$)_x$ $(\forall: y$ Townsman$)_y$ $\wedge(y$ Hate u, u Hate $y)$
         b. $(\exists:$ Villager$_x \rightarrow$ Rel of $x)_f$ $(\exists:$ (Villager$_x$, Townsman$_y) \rightarrow$ Rel of
              $y)_g$ $(\forall: x$ Villager$)_x$ $(\forall: y$ Townsman$)_y$ $\wedge(y$ Hate u, u Hate $y)$

Hintikka (1974) elaborates on a proposal by Henkin (1950) that extends the combinatory possibilities of first-order quantifiers in such a way as to match the expressive power of second-order quantifiers. Specifically, Henkin proposed an enlarged conception of logical structure in which logical structures need not be trees—he allowed distinct chains of quantifiers to be combined with a single "matrix," in structures representable by formulas such as 8.4.10:

8.4.10. $(\forall x)(\exists y)$
$$\qquad\qquad\qquad\qquad > F(x, y, z, u)$$
$(\forall z)(\exists u)$

The term "branching quantifiers" has almost universally been adopted for structures such as are represented in formulas like 8.4.10. However, I will reject the term as misleading and will suggest an alternative that I find less objectionable. First, the branching that the terms alludes to is presumably branching from the vantage point of the matrix S, looking out or up. But that isn't what linguists mean by branching; "branching" as a linguistic term has a downward orientation: a unit branches if it splits up into two or more smaller units. What logicians have called branching is convergence in linguists' terminology. Second, it is misleading for logicians to speak as if the two branches were just disparate pieces of material that join further down but are not themselves part of a larger structure. The most obvious linguist-style structural diagram for 8.4.10 would have an S-node at the top (8.4.11a), and it may be for reasons of typographical economy rather than theory that logicians have drawn diagrams like 8.4.10 rather than 8.4.11b:

8.4.11   a.

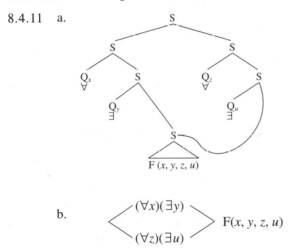

b.

These logical structures make up logical units and can be embedded in the logical structures of other sentences, as can be seen from examples such as:

8.4.12   a. If some relative of every villager and some relative of every townsman hate each other, there must be a lot of brawls when the villagers go into town to drink.

b. I strongly doubt that some product of every company is
advertised in some issue of every popular magazine.

I will henceforth avoid the standard term "branching quantifiers," substituting instead **convergent quantifiers.**[14]

The semantics that Hintikka provides for expressions like these is a version of the "game semantics" that he and his collaborators have developed in various publications (e.g., Hintikka 1973, Saarinen 1976, Hintikka and Kulas 1985, Hintikka and Sandu 1991). He defines truth and validity in terms of strategies in a game in which the goal of one player (referred to by Hintikka as "me") is to make the game end with a true atomic proposition and the goal of his opponent (whom Hintikka calls "Nature") is to make it end with a false atomic proposition. At the outset of the game, both players have full information as to which atomic propositions are true and which ones are false. Whose move it is is determined by the form of the formula on which the game is being played, e.g., Hintikka gives the following rules for $\wedge$ and $\vee$:

8.4.13   a. If the formula on which the game is being played is $\wedge AB$, then
it is Nature's move and Nature picks one or other of A, B as
the formula on which play continues.

b. If the formula on which the game is being played is $\vee AB$, then
it is my move and I pick one or other of A, B as the formula
on which play continues.

Let us illustrate how the game proceeds, using just the little that we have so far plus the assumption that p is T, q T, and r F:

8.4.14

Formula being played	Player to move	His choice
$\wedge(p, \vee qr)$	Nature	$\vee qr$
$\vee qr$	I	q
q	Game ends. I win, because q is T.	

In the first move, Nature chooses $\vee qr$, because to do otherwise would be suicide: if he picked p, the game would immediately end with me winning. But in the second move I get to bring the game to an almost as quick victory for me: I pick q, and I win.

The two rules given in 8.4.13 do the duty of the truth tables for $\wedge$ and $\vee$, in the sense that the $\wedge$-rule lets Nature win the game if he can pick a conjunct that will eventually yield a false proposition (and thus he wins only if the $\wedge AB$ proposition was false), and the $\vee$-rule lets me win the game if I can pick a conjunct that will eventually yield a true proposition (and thus, I win only if the $\vee AB$ proposition was true). If Nature and I know the truth tables for $\wedge$ and

∨, we can always make the moves that most advance our cause. Hintikka also gives rules for numerous other elements of logical structure, including not only ∼ and ⊃ but also nouns with restrictive relative clauses. (The rule for ∼ at first sounds a little bizarre, but makes sense in the context of this sort of game: if the formula in play is ∼A, neither player makes a move, and the game continues on A, with me and Nature exchanging goals.) However, I will skip over these other elements in the interests of getting to what really concerns me here, namely quantifiers.

Hintikka, not surprisingly, gives rules for unrestricted quantifiers and does not take up restricted quantifiers. His rules are as in 8.4.15:

8.4.15   a. If the formula on which the game is being played is (∃x)Fx, it is my move and I must pick an individual a; the game continues with Fa as the formula.

b. If the formula on which the game is being played is (∀x)Fx, it is Nature's move and Nature must pick an individual a; the game continues with Fa as the formula.

The parallelism with the rules for conjunctions is obvious, and likewise the rationale for having these as the rules for ∀ and ∃: if the formula in play is universal, Nature has the opportunity of putting into play any counterexample to it that he can find, and if it is existential, I have the opportunity of putting into play any verifying instance of it that I can find.

Let us see how we might take that part of the rationale for 8.4.15 and develop it into Hintikka-style rules that apply instead to formulas with restricted quantifiers. The most obvious proposal for a restricted quantifier analog to 8.4.15 is something on the lines of 8.4.16:

8.4.16   a. If the formula on which the game is being played is (∃:Fx)ₓGx, then it is my move and I must pick an individual a for which Fa is true; the game continues with Ga as the formula.

b. If the formula on which the game is being played is (∀: Fx)ₓGx, then it is Nature's move and Nature must pick an individual a for which Fa is true; the game continues with Ga as the formula.

The reference to "Fa is true" is really a fudge: to make the rules conform to Hintikka's program, this part of 8.4.16 would have to be restated in terms of games and moves; perhaps that a subsidiary game must be played on Fa at this point, which I must win before the main game is allowed to continue on Ga. I note one important difference between the game played with 8.4.16b and its unrestricted quantifier analog played with 8.4.15b, namely that in a state of affairs in which no individual has the property F, Nature would win according to 8.4.15b but either lose or draw (depending on the convention for situations in which a player has no legal move he can make) according to 8.4.16b. Of course, it is possible to alter 8.4.16b so as to remove this discrepancy, e.g., by allowing Nature to pick any individual whatever as a if there is no choice of x that lets me win the game on Fx. What I regard as significant here is not that that stipulation can be made but that some stipulation has to be made and different stipulations have different implications as to whether universal propositions can be vacuously true.

In the case of an ordinary formula such as 8.4.8b, the sequence of moves in the game is unproblematic: Nature picks a villager to substitute for x, then I pick a relative of that villager to substitute for y, then Nature picks a townsman to substitute for z (NB: in picking the townsman, Nature has full knowledge of what relative of the villager I have picked and can use that knowledge in making his choice of the townsman), and then I pick a relative of that townsman (with full knowledge of the preceding three choices). In the case of formulas with convergent quantifiers such as 8.4.10, Hintikka takes the moves as given by 8.4.15, but with each move made without any knowledge of moves involving the other branch. Thus, in 8.4.10 Nature has to pick values for x and z and I have to pick values for y and u; in picking my value for u I know what value Nature has picked for z but not what he has picked for x, and in picking my value for y I know what value Nature has picked for x but not what he has picked for z. (Here the metaphor has become a bit muddled—it sounds as if I acquire knowledge about both of Nature's moves but forget one piece of information before I make each of my moves; it would be better to speak of me and Nature as teams: I have one player on the upper branch and one on the lower branch, and each of them knows what the Nature player on his own branch has done but not what the Nature player on the other branch has done). To win playing on 8.4.10, I have to pick a value of y that will make F(x, y, z, u) true regardless of what value Nature has picked for z, and a value of u that will make F(x, y, z, u) true regardless of what value nature has picked for x. This fits quite well what Hintikka claims to be the normal interpretation of 8.4.8. The 'second-order' version of 8.4.9a can be taken as providing the basis of a strategy for me to win the game:

8.4.17 $(\exists f)(\exists g)(\forall x)(\forall z)F(x, fx, z, gz)$

If I know the functions f and g, then whatever value a that Nature picks for x, I can pick fa as the value for y, and whatever value b that Nature picks for z, I can pick gb as the value for u. Since these choices of y and u make F(x,y,z,u)

true if anything does, if I can win the game at all I can win it by making those moves.

Hintikka points out that the number of branches in structures like 8.4.10a can be arbitrarily large. For example, 8.4.18a would have a three-branch logical structure 8.4.18b, and the addition of extra conjuncts could increase the number of branches without limit:

8.4.18   a. Each player on every baseball team has a fan, each actress in every musical has an admirer, and each aide of every senator has a friend who are cousins.

b.

$(\forall: \text{Ballteam } x_1)_{x_1} \ (\forall: x_2 \text{ Player } x_1)_{x_2} \ (\exists: x_3 \text{ Fan } x_2)_{x_4}$
$(\forall: \text{Musical } y_1)_{y_1} \ (\forall: y_2 \text{ Actress in } y_1)_{y_2} \ (\exists: y_3 \text{ Admirer } y_2)_{y_3}$ —— $(\{x_3, y_3, z_3\}$
$(\forall: \text{Senator } z_1)_{z_1} \ (\forall: z_2 \text{ Aide } z_1)_{z_2} \ (\exists: z_3 \text{ Friend } z_2)_{z_3}$ ——   Cousins)

Noting that Walkoe has shown that every formula of predicate logic with branching quantifiers is equivalent to one of the form 8.4.19, Hintikka remarks that the existence of the class of sentences illustrated by 8.4.18a shows that English provides the full expressive power of predicate logic with convergent quantifiers:

8.4.19 $(\forall x_1)(\forall x_2)(\exists x_3)$
              $(\forall y_1)(\forall y_2)(\exists y_3)$
              $\dots$ $\rightarrow F(x_1, x_2, x_3, y_1, y_2, y_3, \dots, u_1, u_2, u_3)$
              $(\forall u_1)(\forall u_2)(\exists u_3)$

In certain cases a formula with convergent quantifiers is equivalent to a formula with nonconvergent quantifiers. For example, any formula of the form 8.4.20a has an equivalent nonconvergent formula 8.4.20b, in view of the fact that when the existential quantifiers precede the universal quantifiers, the variables bound by the latter are not dependent on those bound by the former:

8.4.20   a. $(\exists x_1)(\exists x_2) \dots (\exists x_m)$
                                                       $\rightarrow F(x_1, x_2, \dots, x_m, y_1, y_2, \dots, y_n)$
              $(\forall y_1)(\forall y_2) \dots (\forall y_n)$

          b. $(\exists x_1)(\exists x_2) \dots (\exists x_m)(\forall y_1)(\forall y_2) \dots (\forall y_n)$
              $F(x_1, x_2, \dots, x_m, y_1, y_2, \dots, y_n)$

Hintikka has suggested that a logical structure in terms of convergent quantifiers may be appropriate even in cases where an equivalent structure without branching is available. While his discussion (1974: 169–70) does not contain any explicit generalization, Hintikka appears to take the position that bound variables (perhaps just those bound by certain quantifiers) will be independent of other variables whenever possible, for example, the reason why the most normal interpretation of 8.4.21a appears to be 8.4.21b is that the most normal interpretation is really the one in which the variables are maximally independent, that is, 8.4.21c, and 8.4.21c happens to be equivalent to 8.b.21b:

8.4.21   a. John has shown all of his paintings to some of his friends.
         b. $(\exists: x \text{ Friend } j)_x(\forall: y \text{ Painting by } j)_y(j \text{ has shown } y \text{ to } x)$
         c. $(\exists: x \text{ Friend } j)_x$

$$(j \text{ has shown } y \text{ to } x)$$

$(\forall: y \text{ Painting by } j)_y$

Hintikka also suggests that sentences with multiple "nonstandard" quantifiers (i.e., quantifiers such as *many* or *five,* which are not translatable simply as $\forall$ or as $\exists$) have extra interpretations that are representable as convergent quantifier structures but not as structures with one of the quantifiers in the scope of the other(s). For example, recall the extra interpretation of 8.4.22 that we simply ignored in section 2.4, the one in which there was dancing involving most of the boys and most of the girls, without any boy necessarily having danced with most of the girls or any girl having danced with most of the boys:

8.4.22   Most of the boys danced with most of the girls.

Hintikka's discussion of similar examples suggests that he would analyze that reading of 8.4.22 as having a convergent quantifier structure in which the two bound variables are independent. To say exactly what that structure is, one would have to say something about the semantics of plural NPs, since the propositional function in this case would presumably have to correspond not to "he danced with her" but to "they danced with them" (i.e., the sentence does not say that there is a set consisting of most of the boys and a set consisting of most of the girls, such that each boy in the former set danced with each girl in the latter set—only that the boys in the former set all danced with girls in the latter set and that the girls in the latter set all danced with boys in the former set). Until a specific analysis of plural NPs is settled on, it will not be clear that a convergent quantifier analysis yeilds a satisfactory treatment of the extra reading of 8.4.22. But it is clear that the bound variables in that reading are independent and thus that a convergent structure will work if any nonconvergent structure does.

    Hintikka and Saarinen (1975) apply game semantics and branching quantifiers to Bach-Peters sentences. They maintain that convergent quantifier structures make available a reading other than the two that Karttunen recognized and that the Bach-Peters sentence in fact allows that reading.[15] (They also claim that Bach-Peters sentences do not have the readings that Karttunen claims they do, though I will ignore that dispute here.) Justifying such a claim will of course require paying attention to interactions of Hintikka's semantic treatment of convergent quantifier structures with the interpretation of pronouns. The relevant questions arise in connection with an existential-quantifier analogue to the Bach-Peters sentence:

8.4.23   A boy who was deceiving her kissed a girl who loved him.

Suppose that the convergent quantifier structure 8.4.24 is set up:

8.4.24

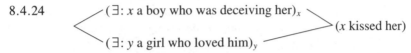

My players on both branches get to choose a value for the variable in question, neither knowing what choice the other has made. Suppose that they choose a and b respectively. Their choices are restricted by the conditions that "a is a boy who was deceiving her" must be true and that "b is a girl who loved him" must be true, but whether those conditions are met depends on the interpretation of the pronouns *her* and *him*. Let us suppose that in fact all personal pronouns in the sentence given for play have been indexed with constants (or variables, as in the case of *Every American loves his mother*, etc.) Either a or b could have been the constant assigned to one or the other of the given pronouns, and let us now suppose that b has been assigned to *her* and a to *him* in the given sentence. Then, according to Hintikka's semantics, 8.4.23 will come out true if "a is a boy who was deceiving b," "b is a girl who loved a," and "a kissed b" all come out true. (Note, by the way, that there might be several choices of the pair (a, b) that would meet this condition).

In the case of the Bach-Peters sentence 8.4.25a, the interpretation of a corresponding branching formula 8.4.25b would work similarly:

8.4.25   a. The boy who was deceiving her kissed the girl who loved him.
         b. $(\iota : x$ a boy who was deceiving her$)_x$
              $(\iota : y$ a girl who loved him$)_y$ $(x$ kissed her$)$

The only difference is that the conditions on the choice of a and b would be (following Hintikka and Saarinen) "a is a boy who was deceiving b, and no one else is a boy who was deceiving b" and "b is a girl who loved a, and no one else is a girl who loved a." In this interpretation, clearly distinct from the two that Karttunen described, there may be many pairs of a boy and a girl such that that boy and no other was deceiving the girl and that girl and no other loved the boy; the interpretation picks one such pair and says that the boy kissed the girl.

Does 8.4.25a in fact have such a reading? This question is difficult to answer, in view of the fact that cooperativity would normally demand that one use the sentence to pick out one specific boy-girl pair. The best source of evidence regarding whether the definite descriptions allow that interpretation is probably sentences in which 8.4.25a is embedded in a negative or conditional superstructure, e.g.:

8.4.26   a. If the boy who is deceiving her kisses the girl who loves him,
               I'll scream.
         b. I doubt that the boy who was deceiving her kissed the girl who
               loved him.

In a state of affairs in which there are several boy-deceiving-loving-girl pairs, can one use 8.4.26a to state that one will scream if the boy of **any** of those pairs kisses the girl? I think I would answer affirmatively, but my judgment here is shaky.

8.5. Conjunctions and Quantifiers

In many respects $\forall$ is similar to $\wedge$ and $\exists$ is similar to $\vee$. Note, for example, the parallelism between the following pairs of theorems:

8.5.1   a. $\supset(\sim\wedge(A_1, A_2, ..., A_n), \vee(\sim A_1, \sim A_2, ..., \sim A_n))$
        a'. $\supset(\sim(\forall: fx)gx, (\exists: fx) \sim gx)$
        b. $\supset(\supset(\vee AB, C), \wedge(\supset AC, \supset BC))$
        b'. $\supset(\supset((\exists: fx)gx, A), (\forall: fx)\supset(gx, A))$
        c. $\supset(\vee(\wedge AB, \wedge CD), \wedge(\vee AC, \vee BD))$
        c'. $\supset((\exists: fx)(\forall: gy)hxy, (\forall: gy)(\exists: fx)hxy)$

Indeed any theorem involving $\wedge$'s or $\vee$'s with arbitrarily many conjuncts corresponds to a theorem in which the corresponding quantifier appears in place of the conjunction (i.e., $\forall$ in place of $\wedge$, and $\exists$ in place of $\vee$) and a propositional function appears in place of the list of conjuncts. There is also an exact parallelism between the rules of inference for quantifiers and the rules of inference for conjunctions. For example, $\wedge$-exploitation allows one to infer from $\wedge (A_1, A_2, ..., A_n)$ any particular conjunct A_i, and $\forall$-exploitation allows one to infer from the general proposition $(\forall: fx)gx$ any of the propositions ga for which a meets the relevance condition f. In either case the rule of inference takes one from the "general" proposition to any of the specific cases that that general proposition covers. Similarly, $\wedge$-introduction allows one to infer $\wedge(A_1, A_2, ..., A_n)$ from the individual conjuncts $A_1, A_2, ..., A_n$, and $\forall$-introduction allows one to infer $(\forall{:}fx)gx$ from a demonstration that anything having the property f has the property g. In either case one is allowed to infer the general proposition once one has established all of the cases that the general proposition covers.

The machinery developed in section 7.3 allows one to provide a solid basis for the observation that a universal quantifier is a "big *and*" and an existential quantifier a "big *or.*" Note first, though, that one cannot just analyze quantifiers as conjunctions, since one does not always have available an enumeration of the objects that are "relevant" (the content of the sentence may indeed imply that it is not known exactly how many objects are relevant) and since the set of relevant objects may be infinite:

8.5.2   a. Everyone who has ever set foot in Saint Peter's Basilica has
          been astonished at its magnificence.
       b. Each of the approximately 100 persons interviewed expressed
          interest in emigrating to Fiji.
       c. Every number greater than 1 is less than its square.

Furthermore, even if one did have a complete list of those who have ever set foot in Saint Peter's, the content of 8.5.2a would not be represented accurately by the conjoined proposition 8.5.3:

8.5.3   Pope Pius IX was astonished at the magnificence of Saint
          Peter's, and Jacqueline Onassis was astonished at the
          magnificence of Saint Peter's, and Msgr. Umberto
          Quattrostagioni was astonished at the magnificence of Saint
          Peter's, and . . .

since 8.5.3 does not include the information that Pope Pius IX, Jacqueline Onassis, Msgr. Quattrostagioni, et al., are all the persons who have ever set foot in Saint Peter's. A person who has set foot in Saint Peter's and was not astonished at its magnificence would be a counterexample to 8.5.2a; however, he would not be a counterexample to 8.5.3 unless he happened to appear in the list. What it takes to falsify 8.5.3 is to show that one of the persons on the list was not astonished at the magnificence of Saint Peter's, irrespective of whether that person ever set foot in Saint Peter's; what it takes to falsify 8.5.2a is to show that someone who has set foot in Saint Peter's was not astonished at its magnificence, irrespective of whether that person is mentioned in 8.5.3.

The only way I know of to identify quantified propositions with conjoined propositions and get the details to work out correctly is to treat conjunctions and quantifiers as both applying to sets of propositions but differing in how the sets of propositions are specified, whether by enumeration or by description. The logical elements corresponding to conjunctions and quantifiers could then be taken as filling a gap in the framework of section 7.3. Recall that while there were numerous examples of predicates that took set arguments and predicates that took propositional arguments, no cases were cited in section 7.3 in which a predicate had an argument position that had to be filled by a set of propositions, even though the formation rules given there do not rule out that possibility. If we treat *all/and* and *some/or* as corresponding to one-place predicates of sets of propositions, we thereby fill that gap. Specifically, suppose that we introduce predicates "All" and "Some" that take a set of propositions as arguments, employing them as in the following translations:

8.5.4   a. Tom is Polish, Dick is Norwegian, and Harry is Portuguese.
              All {Tom is Polish, Dick is Norwegian, Harry is Portuguese}
          b. All men are mortal.
              All {x is mortal: x is a man}
          c. Either Bill will help Mike or Mike will ask Karen for help.
              Some {Bill will help Mike, Mike will ask Karen for help}
          d. Some linguists are insane.
              Some {x is insane: x is a linguist}

In 8.5.4a and 8.5.4b, the content expressed is that all of the propositions in the set are true; in 8.5.4a the propositions in question are simply enumerated, whereas in 8.5.4b the set of propositions is described as consisting of those propositions "x is mortal" for which x is a man. In 8.5.4c and 8.5.4d, the content expressed is that at least one of the propositions in the set is true; in 8.5.4c the propositions in question are simply enumerated, whereas in 8.5.4d the set of propositions is described as consisting of those propositions "x is insane" for which x is a linguist.[16]

The rules of inference for both quantifiers and conjunctions can now be stated in the form of rules that are applicable both to cases in which the set of propositions is specified by enumeration and cases in which it is specified by description.

8.5.5   All-exploitation All M   All-introduction | A∈M
                            A∈M | . . .
                            A | A
                                                              All M

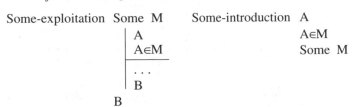

Some-exploitation Some M   Some-introduction A

$\qquad\qquad\qquad\quad$ A $\qquad\qquad\qquad\qquad\qquad\quad$ A∈M

$\qquad\qquad\qquad\quad$ A∈M $\qquad\qquad\qquad\qquad\qquad$ Some M

$\qquad\qquad\qquad\qquad$ . . .

$\qquad\qquad\qquad\quad$ B

$\qquad\qquad$ B

In cases where M is specified by enumeration, the premise A∈M will be trivial and thus need not be mentioned; for example, in the following inference,
the parenthesized premise need not be mentioned, since it is guaranteed to be
true in virtue of what curly brackets and ∈ mean:

8.5.6   All {Tom is Polish, Dick is Norwegian, Harry is Portuguese}
           (Dick is Norwegian ∈ {Tom is Polish, Dick is Norwegian,
               Harry is Portuguese})
           Dick is Norwegian

Inferences like 8.5.6 are what the rule of ∧-exploitation was for. The "All-
exploitation" rule of 8.5.5 does not only the work of ∧-exploitation but also
that of ∀-exploitation, as becomes clear if one notes that when M is given in
the form {$gx: fx$}, the proposition that $ga \in$ {$gx: fx$} is equivalent to the proposition fa, that is, a proposition belongs to {$gx: fx$} if and only if it is of the
form ga, where a has the property f. Thus, when the set of propositions is
specified by description, the inference done by All-exploitation exactly
matches an inference done by ∀-exploitation:

8.5.7   1 All {x is mortal: x is a man}   1′ (∀: x is a man)$_x$ (x is mortal)
           2 (Socrates is mortal) ∈   2′ Socrates is a man
             {x is mortal: x is a man}
           3 Socrates is mortal   3′ Socrates is mortal

The rules given in 8.5.5 are in fact not enough to do all the work that was
done by the rules for conjunctions and for quantifiers. To apply the rules in
8.5.5 to the concrete cases to which the rules of inference of chapters 2 and 3
applied, one must have rules of inference for the introduction and exploitation
of the set-theoretic apparatus that appears in 8.5.4. The following rules of
inference enable one to simulate the rules of inference for quantifiers and conjunctions with the rules 8.5.5:[17]

8.5.8   SF-intro$_1$ $a \in \{ \ldots, a, \ldots \}$
             SF-intro$_2$ Fa
                             $\varphi a \in \{\varphi x \colon Fx\}$, where φ is any function (propositional or otherwise) of a variable of the type of a

SF-expl$_1$ $a \in \{ a_1, \ldots, a_n \}$ SF-expl$_2$ $a \in \{ \varphi x \colon Fx \}$

$$
\begin{array}{l}
\quad\begin{array}{|l}
 a = a_1 \\\hline
 \ldots \\
 A
\end{array} \\
\quad \ldots \\
\quad\begin{array}{|l}
 a = a_n \\\hline
 \ldots \\
 A
\end{array} \\
A
\end{array}
\qquad\qquad
\begin{array}{l}
\quad\begin{array}{|l}
 Fu \\
 a = \varphi u \\\hline
 \ldots \\
 A
\end{array} \\
A
\end{array}
$$

As the simulation of the old rules in terms of the new proceeds, it should become clear to the reader that much of the work of the old rules of inference is now built into the rules of inference for set formation in 8.5.8. This should come as no shock: it will have to be up to the set formation rules to mediate between the highly general and abstract rules in 8.5.5 and the much more specific types of expressions that figured in the earlier rules.

Let us first attempt to simulate ∧-introduction in terms of the rules in 8.5.5 (and 8.5.8). What we need is thus a way of getting from premises A and B (or rather, A_1, A_2, ..., and A_n; for expository ease, I will discuss just the two-term case here) to the conclusion All {A, B}. Rules 8.5.5 and 8.5.8 in fact allow one to derive that conclusion, albeit by a somewhat devious path:

8.5.9
1	A		supp
2	B		supp
3		C ∈ {A, B}	supp
4			C = A supp
5			A 1, reit
6			C 4, 5, = -expl
7			C = B supp
8			B 2, reit
9			C 7, 8, = -expl
10		C	3, 4–6, 7–9, SF-expl$_1$
11	All {A,B}		3–10, All-intr

This derivation simulates the earlier rule of $\wedge$-intro, in that its premises and conclusion are the analogues in the notational system of this chapter to the premises and conclusion of the earlier rule. The simulation of $\wedge$-expl is far more straightforward:

8.5.10   1   All $\{A_1, \ldots, A_n\}$ supp
           2   $A_i \in \{A_1, \ldots, A_n\}$ SF-intro$_1$
           3   A_i 1,2, All-expl

The rules for $\vee$ can be simulated as follows:

8.5.11   a. $\vee$-intro
              1   A_i supp
              2   $A_i \in \{A_1, \ldots, A_n\}$ SF-intro$_1$
              3   Some$\{A_1, \ldots, A_n\}$ 1,2, Some-intro

          b. $\vee$-expl
              1   Some $\{A_1, \ldots, A_n\}$ supp
              2 | A   supp
              3 | $A \in \{A_1, \ldots, A_n\}$ supp
              4 | | $A = A_1$ supp
              5 | | A   2, reit
              6 | | A_1 4, 5, =-expl
              7 | | . . .   various intermediate steps
              8 | | B   (by the proof of B from A_1 in the proof being simulated)

                   . . .
              9 | | $A = A_n$ supp
              10 | | A   2, reit
              11 | | A_n 9, 10, =-expl
              12 | | . . .   various intermediate steps
              13 | | B   (by steps in the proof being simulated)
              14 | B   3, 4–8, 9–13, SF-expl$_1$
              15 B   1, 2–14, Some-expl

Note how steps 7–8 and 12–13 make reference to subproofs in the proof being replicated. It would actually take an argument by induction to demonstrate that those can always be simulated in the system of this section; I will omit details of such a proof.

The simulation of the quantifier rules is as follows:

8.5.12   a. ∀-intro

1	A ∈ {Gx: Fx}	supp
2	Fu	supp
3	A = Gu	supp
4	...	various intermediate steps
5	Gu	(by the proof of Gu from Fu in the proof being simulated)
6	A	5, 3, =-expl
7	A	2–6, SF-expl$_2$
8 All {Gx: Fx}		1–7, All-intro

b. ∀-expl

1 All {Gx: Fx}	supp
2 Fa	supp
3 Ga ∈ {Gx: Fx}	2, SF-intro$_2$
4 Ga	1, 3, All-expl

c. ∃-intro

1 Fa	supp
2 Ga	supp
3 Ga ∈ {Gx: Fx}	1, SF-intro$_2$
4 Some {Gx: Fx}	3, 2, Some-intro

d. ∃-expl

1 Some {Gx: Fx}		supp
2	A ∈ {Gx: Fx}	supp
3	A	supp
4	Fu	supp
5	A = Gu	supp
6	Gu	5, 3, =-expl
7	...	various intermediate steps
8	B	(by the proof of B from Fu and Gu in the proof being simulated)
9	B	2, 4–8, SF-expl$_2$
10 B		1, 2–9, Some-expl

The proofs involving the rules 8.5.5 and 8.5.8 are of course significantly more involved than the proofs in the earlier system that they simulate. However, while it would rarely make sense to give a proof of a concrete result in terms of the rules of this section rather than in terms of rules specific to quantifiers and conjunctions, it is of considerable significance that alternative proofs are always available in which the difference between quantifiers and conjunctions is reduced to the difference between the two species of set formation.

Humberstone (1975) has pointed out a difficulty with the proposals of this section that is worth noting here. As conjoining has normally been understood in logic, there is no constraint requiring that conjuncts be mutually distinct.[18] Indeed, logic texts customarily give proofs of results involving repeated conjuncts, for example, $\wedge AA \dashv\vdash A$. Under the approach presented here, the latter result would follow from the identity of $\{A, A\}$ with $\{A\}$. But what about sentences in which exclusive *or* has two identical conjuncts? Humberstone notes that $\vee_e AA$ is always false (since it can never be the case that only one of its conjuncts is true), and hence $\vee_e AA$ can differ in truth value from A. If an $\vee_e$-conjunction is to be true when exactly one conjunct is true and false otherwise, then $\vee_e AAB$ and $\vee_e AB$ can differ in truth value: if A is T and B is F, then $\vee_e AAB$ is F but $\vee_e AB$ is T. However, $\{A, A, B\} = \{A, B\}$, and hence $\vee_e AAB$ ought to agree in truth value with $\vee_e AB$ if $\vee_e$ is predicated of a set of propositions.

Sentences that exemplify formulas such as $\vee_e AAB$ or $\vee_e ABA$ are sufficiently bizarre that it is unclear whether they should be held to have 8.5.13a or 8.5.13b as truth table:

8.5.13 a. Truth table if $\vee_e$ is predicated of a set of propositions

A	B	$\vee_e AAB$
T	T	F
T	F	T
F	T	T
F	F	F

b. Truth table if $\vee_e (A_1, ..., A_n)$ is to be true when exactly one A_i is true

A	B	$\vee_e AAB$
T	T	F
T	F	F
F	T	T
F	F	F

For example, can one comply with the request *Play Brahms ór Brahms ór Chopin*, where the request is interpreted as involving exclusive *or*, by playing Brahms, or can one comply only by playing Chopin? The former interpretation seems less outlandish than the latter, though that may be because the request would be even more bizarre if it were interpreted the latter way than the former way, since not just one but **both** occurrences of *Brahms* would be superfluous (as would the *or*'s). I conclude tentatively that while Humberstone is correct that my position here forces $\vee_e$'s with duplicated conjuncts to be interpreted in a way that conflicts with what has usually been done in formal logic (which is not to imply that logicians have said much about exclusive *or*), it is not clear that the discrepancy constitutes a fault in this treatment.

Exercises

1. Determine the type of each of the following expressions:

a. $(\lambda P)P(x)$
b. $(\lambda R)R(P)$
c. $(\lambda Q)(\exists:P(x))_x(\forall: P(y))_y Q(y)(x)$
d. $\sim$
e. $(\exists: P(x))$
f. $\exists$

Assume that the variables are of the type indicated below:

x, y	e
P	$<e, p>$
Q	$<e, <e, p>>$
R	$<<e, p>, p>$

2. For each of the following formulas, (i) simplify by λ-conversion and (ii) provide plausible English translations for both the original formula and the simplified formula.

a. $[(\lambda x)(x\ \text{Love}\ x)](a)$
b. $[(\lambda P)(\exists: \text{Linguist}\ x)_x P(x)]\ (\lambda y)(\forall:z\ \text{Relative}\ y)_z(y\ \text{Love}\ z)$
c. $[\lambda R)(\forall: \text{Linguist}\ x)R(x,x)]\ (\lambda(y,z))(y\ \text{Admire}\ z)$
d. $[(\lambda Q)Qa]\ (\lambda x)(\forall: Pb)_p Px$

3. Determine for each of the following sentences whether the analysis given in section 8.2 implies that it should allow both a strict identity and a sloppy identity interpretation, and say whether the prediction is confirmed by the facts:

a. Mary wanted John to help her, and Ann wanted Fred to ∅.
b. Mary promised John to tell him about her experiences, and Ann promised him to ∅ also.

   c. If John is easy for Mary to force to do things he thinks are disgusting, then Bill is ∅ too.

4. Give logical forms for the following sentences, using *Gn* and HAB where appropriate, and indicating whether the various variables take stages, individuals, or kinds as their values:

   a. It rains a lot in Japan in June.
   b. Frenchmen drink wine.

5. Pick any characteristic of indefinite plural generic NPs (such as *dogs*) that was taken up in section 8.3 and determine whether it is shared by

   a. indefinite singular generic NPs (e.g., *A dog has four legs*).
   b. definite singular generic NPs (e.g., *The hyena is a fascinating animal*).

6. Give a brief sketch of the forms that generic **mass** expressions can have in English, and discuss briefly the extent to which they are parallel to the forms for generic **count** expressions given in 8.3.1a–c.

7. Give a logical form in terms of convergent quantifiers for each of the following sentences:

   a. Every linguist has made a stupid claim and every philosopher has come to a profound conclusion that are equivalent.
   b. The richer a country is, the more powerful one of its officials is (from Barwise 1979:59) [Analyze the "comparative conditional" construction of this example in terms of a formula that includes a constituent "if *x* is richer than *y*, *z* is more powerful than *w*."]

8. What would be an appropriate Hintikka-style game rule for exclusive *or*?

9. Write a brief essay on the relative expressive powers of formulas like 8.4.7 and those like 8.4.10 (i.e., does admitting formulas of the one type let you in for anything that admitting formulas of the other type doesn't?). Devote some attention to the question of whether formulas that are slightly different from one or the other of the examples taken up (e.g., a formula like 8.4.7 that had ∀*f* instead of ∃*f*) can be given a straightforward paraphrase in terms of the other kind of framework.

10. Pick any proof in chapter 3 in which rules of inference for ∧ or ∨ are used, restate the premises and conclusion in terms of the "All" and "Some" of 8.5, and redo the proof in terms of the rules 8.5.5 and 8.5.8. Say what the corresponding result with ∀ in the role of ∧ and ∃ in the role of ∨ is.

9 Speech Acts and Implicature

9.1. Speech Acts and Illocutionary Force

When people speak, they are not merely constructing a sequence of propositions but are performing actions of a wide variety of types: informing, reminding, requesting, challenging, offering, and so on. These acts generally **involve** propositions but must be kept distinct from the propositions that they involve; for example, the proposition that Lima is further east than Miami is distinct from an act of informing someone that Lima is further east than Miami or of reminding someone that Lima is further east than Miami.

The notions of truth and falsehood are strictly speaking applicable only to propositions, not to speech acts. In discussing the content of propositions, it is necessary to be able to refer both to propositions and to speech acts. Consider, for example, the following two dialogues:

9.1.1   A: The moon is owned by General Motors.
          B: That's false.

9.1.2   A: Your father is a retired pimp.
          B: That's pretty damn cheeky of you.

In 9.1.1, *that* refers to the proposition that A has just asserted. In 9.1.2, *that* refers to the act that A has just performed, that is, the act of telling B that B's father is a retired pimp, and not to the proposition that B's father is a retired pimp. An act of asserting that the moon is owned by General Motors cannot be true or false any more than an act of buying a radio or of punching someone in the nose can be true or false.

A speech act can have any of a variety of things wrong with it, as is pointed out in the insightful discussion by Austin (1962, lectures II–III). For example, if a person who has no money and does not expect to come into a large sum of money were to promise to give you a million dollars next Thursday, you could object to his act of promising on the grounds that it was irresponsible (since he thereby made a commitment that he knew he could not fulfill) or that it was misleading (since it could lead you to believe the false proposition that he would have a million dollars next week) or that it was impudent (since he was acting as if you would believe an outrageous falsehood). While these objections involve certain propositions associated with the act, they also involve considerations of morality and of etiquette. A speech act (indeed, any kind of act) can be objectionable in one of these respects without being objectionable in others; for example, one can be irresponsible without being impudent or be impudent without being misleading. Of these dimensions of objectionability, the one most closely related to the notion of falsehood is that of misleading- ness: an act is misleading if it leads one to believe a proposition which is in fact false (or at least, would so lead one if it were entirely successful). How- ever, whether an act is misleading depends not only on the act but on the circumstances under which it is performed, and the false proposition which a misleading speech act leads one to believe may have no particular connection with the meaning of the sentence that the speaker utters. For example, if an orthodox jew who is eating a corned beef sandwich says *May I have a glass of milk?* he may be leading others to the false conclusion that he is not an orthodox jew; the same is true if he says *I'm flying to Toledo tonight* on a Friday. Of course, the proposition expressed by *I'm flying to Toledo tonight* is true or false independent of whether an act of uttering it misleads the hearers about the speaker's religion. Thus, the fact that it is misleading to utter a certain sentence does not imply that the proposition expressed by that sen- tence is false. This platitude will turn out to have considerable significance later in this chapter, where an attempt will be made to clear up a number of confusions that have resulted from making the mistake of calling a proposition false merely on the grounds that the act of asserting it is (generally) mislead- ing or that a sentence expressing that proposition is "a funny thing to say."

In many cases, there is no chance of confusing a speech act with an asso- ciated proposition. For example, one could hardly confuse an act of saying *Shine my shoes* and thereby ordering someone to shine one's shoes with the proposition that the person will shine the speaker's shoes, nor could one con- fuse an act of thanking someone for a gift by saying *Thank you very much for your lovely gift* with the proposition that the speaker is grateful to that person for giving him that gift. The possibility of confusion arises principally in two classes of cases: (i) speech acts in which one asserts a proposition by uttering a sentence that expresses that proposition (as in 9.1.1, where A asserts that the moon is owned by General Motors by uttering the sentence *The moon is owned by General Motors*) and (ii) speech acts in which the speaker uses a verb **performatively,** that is, makes explicit with it the type of act that he purports to be performing, as in

9.1.3   a. I order you to shine my shoes.
         b. I christen this ship the HMS Kreplach.
         c. I promise to return this money by next Thursday.
         d. I hereby inform you that we have no more money.

In uttering 9.1.3a, the speaker is ordering the addressee to shine the speaker's shoes; in uttering 9.1.3b, he is christening the ship; in uttering 9.1.3c, he is promising to return the money; in uttering 9.1.3d, he is informing the addressee that they have no more money. The danger of confusion in these two cases comes from two common tendencies: to identify a declarative sentence with the proposition that that sentence expresses, and to identify a declarative sentence with the act that one would (normally) perform by uttering that sentence. If one succumbs to both of these tendencies, he will identify the sentence *The moon is owned by General Motors* both with the proposition that the moon is owned by General Motors and with the act of asserting that the moon is owned by General Motors and will thus by implication identify that act and that proposition with each other.

   So far in this section, I have been using an overly vague expression that had now better be replaced with more precise terminology. The objectionable expression is "what the speaker is doing" when he says X. Suppose that one of the characters in a television program that you are watching says *I have more money than I know what to do with* and you are asked what that person has just done. Given certain assumptions about what has been going on, each of the following would be a correct answer:

9.1.4   a. He said, "I have more money than I know what to do with."
         b. He said something in a very affected English accent.
         c. He said that he had more money than he knew what to do with.
         d. He indicated that he was willing to pay off Oliver's mortgage.
         e. He offered to pay off Oliver's mortgage.
         f. He displayed contempt for Oliver.
         g. He embarrassed Oliver's wife.
         h. He woke up the baby.

Sentences 9.1.4a and 9.1.4b make reference to his words and the way that he pronounced them, without regard for the meaning of the words, or the purpose for which they were uttered, or what resulted from his uttering them. Sentence 9.1.4c reports the meaning of what he said, though it is noncommittal about what words he uses in saying it, and indicates that he asserted the proposition in question. Sentences 9.1.4d and 9.1.4e bring in the purpose for which he made that assertion: by uttering the sentence that he uttered, he has offered to pay off Oliver's mortgage. Sentences 9.1.4f–h refer to various results of his uttering that sentence, with 9.1.4f and 9.1.4g having to do with the meaning and function of the utterance, whereas 9.1.4h has to do only with its acoustic nature (i.e., he would have awakened the baby if he had said anything that loud, regardless of its meaning, whereas he would not have embarrassed Oliver's wife if he had uttered exactly the same words in another context where they would not have conveyed an offer to assume Oliver's debt).

The notion of what the speaker is doing that is most relevant to the concerns of this section is one that is illustrated by 9.1.4c–e (especially clearly in 9.1.4e): an **illocutionary act,** that is, an act that the speaker performed **in** saying what he did, in the sense that he makes something be the case (e.g., he takes on an obligation, discharges an obligation, places himself on record as believing something) by saying something that normally can make it the case. Illocutionary acts are to be contrasted with a number of other types of acts: a **locutionary act** (i.e., act of using particular linguistic means), to which 9.1.4a-b refer, a **perlocutionary act** (i.e., act of bringing about some effect **by** using some linguistic means or other), to which 9.1.4g and perhaps 9.1.4f refer, and the so far unnamed type of act that figures in 9.1.4h, in which language figures only incidentally: what Oliver said (and even **whether** he said anything: he could have been babbling incoherently) is immaterial to whether he did what 9.1.4h says he did. The following are some important characteristics of illocutionary acts:

i. To almost every type of illocutionary act, there corresponds a **performative verb,** that is, a verb which can be used as an explicit indication that one is performing (or purports to be performing) an act of this type, as in 9.1.3 above.[1] By contrast, verbs referring to perlocutionary and locutionary acts cannot be used in sentences like 9.1.3 as explicit indications of the acts being performed; for example while some of 9.1.5 have normal uses, the verbs do not really indicate what the speaker is doing in uttering the sentence, even if (coincidentally) the sentence does provide a correct description of something that he is doing:

9.1.5   a. I utter these words in an affected English accent.
          b. *I wake up the baby.
          c. I embarrass your wife.
          d. I insult you.
          e. *I force you to eat this cake.
          f. *I convince you that there is intelligent life on Uranus.

For example, you may embarrass a woman by telling her husband in her presence that you embarrass her; indeed, you probably **would** embarrass her by doing that. However, 9.1.5c can only be interpreted as a "habitual present," that is, as a description not of the act that the speaker is at that moment performing but as a report of the usual state of affairs. Indeed, if you had hitherto never embarrassed that person's wife, you would be uttering a falsehood in saying 9.1.5c, even though you would thereby be embarrassing her, and the second time you uttered 9.1.5c you might very well be saying something true. Also, you could just as easily embarrass his wife by saying that you don't embarrass her as by saying that you do embarrass her; by contrast, you can't promise to return the money by saying *I don't promise to return the money soon*.

If one utters 9.1.5a in an affected English accent, one is really performing two acts: the locutionary act of uttering those words in an affected English accent and the illocutionary act of telling your interlocutor that that is what you are doing. The latter act is the same sort of thing that one does when he gives a move-by-move account of a nonverbal act that he is carrying out (e.g., *I display the inside of the box. I roll up my sleeves to show that they are empty. I reach into the box with my right hand . . .*). Actually, the present progressive would be preferable to the simple present in 9.1.5a unless it were part of a narration such as the magician's patter just quoted:

9.1.6   I am uttering these words in an affected English accent.

Verbs cannot be used performatively except in the simple present tense. For example, in uttering any of the following, the speaker is not performing the act of christening, ordering, or sentencing:

9.1.7   a.   I am christening this ship the HMS Kreplach.
          a'. I have christened this ship the HMS Kreplach.
          b.   I am ordering you to shine my shoes.
          b'. I have ordered you to shine my shoes.
          c.   I am sentencing him to 20 years of hard labor.

Either the speaker is reporting an act that he has already performed (9.1.7a', 9.1.7b') or he is commenting on another act that he is in the process of performing (but interrupts in order to say 9.1.7a, b, c); for example, 9.1.7c might be a reply given by a very cooperative judge when he is interrupted by a television reporter just as he is about to pronounce the sentence and is asked what is going on, and 9.1.7b might be said by a colonel to an uncooperative private in order to make sure that the private has understood the order just issued.[2]

ii. In uttering a sentence one sometimes performs more than one locutionary act, or more than one illocutionary act, with different parts of the sentence involved in each of the acts:

9.1.8   a. Tom, you wash the dishes, and Lucy, you empty the garbage.
          b. I order you to shine these shoes, and I warn you that if you
             don't obey that order immediately, you'll be court-martialed.
          c. Is Bill, who was standing here a minute ago, still in the
             building?

In 9.1.8a, the two conjuncts are involved in two distinct locutionary acts, one
directed to Tom and one directed to Lucy. Note that *you* refers to Tom in the
first conjunct and to Lucy in the second conjunct: a second person pronoun
refers to (or more accurately, has a reference that overlaps with) the addressee
of the locutionary act. In 9.1.8b–c, there is one locutionary act but there are
two illocutionary acts: in 9.1.8b, the speaker issues an order in the first conjunct and gives a warning in the second conjunct, and in 9.1.8c, the speaker
asks the addressee about Bill's present whereabouts in the main clause and
reminds him about Bill's recent whereabouts in the nonrestrictive relative
clause. The nonrestrictive clause is not, strictly speaking, part of the request
for information but corresponds to a separate act that the speaker performs
while in the process of asking his question.

iii. Sentences having no overt performative verb are often ambiguous with
regard to what illocutionary act they are used to perform. For example, 9.1.9a
might be used to make either a promise or a prediction, and 9.1.9b might be
used to inform, warn, or rebuke someone:

9.1.9   a. I'll be in my office until 5:30.
          b. You can get 10 years of hard labor for possession of pot in this
             state.

The term **illocutionary force** provides an alternative way of speaking
about illocutionary acts: the illocutionary force of an utterance is the type of
illocutionary act that the speaker performs in uttering it; for example, some
occurrences of 9.1.9a would have the illocutionary force of a promise and
others would have the illocutionary force of a prediction. As noted above, an
utterance may have two or more illocutionary forces, each associated with a
different part of the sentence.

An adequate account of the syntax of a natural language will have to distinguish somehow among different sentence types: declarative sentences, inter-
rogatives, imperatives, exclamative sentences, and the like. If one's scheme
of linguistic description is that which I have assumed throughout this book,
according to which a grammar of a language is a set of explicit rules that relate
the sentences of that language to their meanings, it will be necessary to draw
distinctions of meaning that correspond to the differences among the various
sentence types. I will sketch here an approach, the so-called **performative**

analysis, in which the illocutionary force of an utterance is treated as figuring in the meaning of the sentence in question as an overt or understood performative verb,[3] as in an analysis in which an imperative sentence such as 9.1.10a is assigned the same meaning as a sentence with an overt performative verb (9.1.10b), and the syntactic properties of imperative sentences are formulated in terms of the (ultimately deleted) performative verb:[4]

9.1.10   a. Open the door!
         b. I order/request you to open the door.

In the traditional classification of sentence types, 9.1.10b would generally be regarded as a declarative rather than an imperative sentence. The performative analysis thus involves deriving nondeclarative sentence types from the declarative type, but with the important twist that the nondeclarative sentence appears as the complement of the underlying declarative clause.

The term "declarative" is somewhat confusing. It is not always clear whether it is being used as a grammatical term, denoting sentences of a particular form, or as a pragmatic or semantic term, denoting sentences of a particular type of meaning or of function. The stock examples of declarative sentences are those which are declarative in both senses:

9.1.11   a. Birds eat.
         b. The cat is on the mat.

Both examples are declarative in form and serve to assert a proposition expressed by the whole sentence. Such sentences were referred to in Austin 1963 and the first few lectures of Austin 1962 as **constative** sentences and were opposed to what Austin called "performative sentences," which included sentences having an explicit performative verb, and perhaps other nonconstative sentences, though Austin was not completely clear about exactly what the term covered. In the latter part of Austin 1962 (see especially lecture XI), Austin, in accordance with his policy of "playing Old Harry" with popular dichotomies, such as the fact/value dichotomy, adopted the position that there is not a great deal of difference between constative sentences and performative sentences in which the same proposition is asserted, for example,[5]

9.1.12   a. The cat is on the mat. (constative)
         b. I assert to you that the cat is on the mat. (performative)

The performative analysis is in the spirit of the later chapters of Austin 1962 in holding that constative sentences do not have any privileged position and that whether the sentence involves an overt performative verb or not is a matter only of its superficial structure.

The presence or absence of an overt performative is not entirely a trivial matter for a number of reasons. First, there are grammatical phenomena which depend on whether a given clause is a main clause or is a subordinate clause **in surface structure** and which thus give rise to differences between a sentence without an overt performative and a corresponding complement of an overt performative verb. For example, the movement of the auxiliary verb in a question to a position before the subject takes place only in surface main clauses and thus applies in 9.1.13a but not in 9.1.13b:

9.1.13   a. Where <u>were you</u> on the night of January 15th?
         b. I hereby ask you where <u>you were</u> on the night of January 15th.

Second, as pointed out by Davison (1973), while an overt performative clause can be the antecedent of a pronoun (such as the *so* of 9.1.14a), an understood performative verb generally cannot be:

9.1.14   a. I promise to never tell any more lies, and you should do so too.
         b. *I'll never tell any more lies, and you should do so too.

However, these facts present no obstacles to identifying the meanings of non-performative sentences with those of corresponding sentences that have an overt performative verb: they simply show that there are syntactic rules that are sensitive to the configurations in which elements occur subsequent to the deletion of the performative superstructure (e.g., the *so* of 9.1.14b apparently requires an antecedent that is overtly present in surface structure, and deletion of the performative superstructure of 9.1.14a results in violation of that restriction).

In the remainder of this section, I will illustrate how the performative analysis can interact with ordinary syntax. **Super-equi-NP-deletion** deletes the subject of a complement clause under identity not with a NP of the next higher clause (as with Equi-NP-deletion, 9.1.15a) but with a NP of a still higher clause (9.1.15b–c):

9.1.15   a. [John$_i$ wanted [he$_i$ go home]] → John wanted to go home.
         b. [John$_i$ thought [[he$_i$ buy him$_i$ a new hat] would be wise]] →
             John thought it would be wise to buy himself a new hat.
         c. It appeared to John that it was unlikely that there would be any opportunity to buy himself a new hat.

In 9.1.15b the NP that controls the deletion is two clauses above the deletion site, and in 9.1.15c it is three clauses above it; there is in principle no limit to how much higher in the structure than the deletion site the controlling NP may be. William Cantrall (cited in Lakoff 1972a: 566) notes that first-person and second-person pronouns can be deleted even if there is no first-person or second-person pronoun elsewhere in the sentence to serve as antecedent, though a third-person NP cannot be deleted unless there is an antecedent in a higher clause:

9.1.16   It would be wise to buy myself/yourself/*himself a new hat.

(Examples with a reflexive pronoun as indirect object of *buy* are used here, since the deleted subject of *buy* is the only possible antecedent for the reflexive, and thus the reflexive indicates what the deleted subject is). Cantrall notes that the otherwise anomalous paradigm 9.1.16 is explained if the performative analysis is adopted: the deletions in 9.1.16 are simply instances of Super-equi-NP-deletion operating under exactly the same conditions as in 9.1.17:

9.1.17   a. I assert to you that it would be wise to buy myself/yourself/
                *himself a new hat.
          b. Bill told Frieda that it would be wise to buy himself/herself/
                ?myself/?yourself a new hat.

The controller of the deletion of the subject of *buy* is either the subject or the indirect object of *assert* (in 9.1.17a) and *tell* (in 9.1.17b). Under the performative analysis, 9.1.17b would be analyzed as having an underlying performative clause such as "I assert to you S," whose complement clause is *Bill told Frieda. . . .* The fact that the *I* and *you* of the understood performative clause in 9.1.17b are less acceptable as controllers of Super-equi-NP-deletion than are the *I* and *you* of the understood performative clause of 9.1.16 reflects a general fact about Super-equi, namely, that only the lowest possible controller is actually allowed to control the deletion:[6]

9.1.18   Frieda said that Bill had told me that it would be wise to buy
                himself/myself/?herself a new hat.

Just as the presence of *Bill* and *me* in the *tell*-clause of 9.1.18 inhibits *Frieda* from controlling deletion in the *buy*-clause, the presence of *Bill* and *Frieda* in the *tell*-clause of 9.1.17b inhibits the *I* and *you* of the understood performative clause from controlling deletion of the subject of the *buy*-clause.

Cantrall's argument illustrates the most common form of argumentation for an understood higher clause: anomalous application (or nonapplication) of some rule is explained in terms of a proportion "surface main clause is to hypothesized higher clause as complement clause is to clause of which it is complement"; for example, the deletion of *I* or *you* in 9.1.16 is to the hypothesized higher clause *I assert to you S* as the deletion of the *I* or *you* in 9.1.17a is to the overt higher clause *I assert to you S* or as the deletion of *he* or *she* in 9.1.17b is to the overt higher clause *Bill told Frieda S*.

The other common form of argumentation for an understood higher clause is that in which a higher clause is argued to be necessary in order to provide a "resting place" for an element that otherwise does not have a structural role in the sentence. The two forms of argumentation can be combined when the element that is assigned a "resting place" is one that otherwise has a syntactic function (such as modifier of some kind) and which can be treated as always having that function if there is an understood higher clause. For example, Rutherford (1970) and Davison (1973) have argued for a performative analysis on the basis of the adverbial clauses found in sentences such as 9.1.19a, b, as contrasted with those in 9.1.19a′, b′:

9.1.19 a.   In case you haven't heard, Bob and Frieda have decided to get married.
        a′. In case you aren't home by 6:00, I'll start peeling the potatoes.
        b.   Since you're so smart, what's the capital of South Dakota?
        b′. Since you're so smart, you probably know what the capital of South Dakota is.

Example 9.1.19a′ gives a condition under which the speaker will start peeling the potatoes; however, 9.1.19a doesn't give a condition under which Bob and Frieda have decided to get married. The condition given in the adverbial clause in 9.1.19a is a condition under which the utterance of the sentence will accomplish what it purports to accomplish, namely, informing the addressee that Bob and Frieda have decided to get married. In 9.1.19b, the addressee's being so smart is the (ostensible) reason for the speaker's asking his question, not the reason why the capital of South Dakota is what it is; but if 9.1.19b′ is uttered without irony, the addressee's being so smart **is** (according to the speaker) the reason why that person will probably know what the capital of South Dakota is.

The adverbial clauses in 9.1.19a, b can be interpreted as modifiers only if the sentences are analyzed as providing appropriate items for them to modify, and the performative analysis does precisely that: they would modify the understood performative clauses exactly as if the performative clauses were overtly present:

9.1.20 a. In case you haven't heard, I inform you that Bob and Frieda have decided to get married.
        b. Since you are so smart, I ask you to tell me what the capital of South Dakota is.

Sadock (1974:36–37) has given a similar argument based on the distribution of *in conclusion, once and for all,* and a number of such expressions. These items occur in two contexts: (i) where they modify a clause that describes one of the steps in a verbal presentation, and (ii) where they introduce a declarative sentence that is part of a verbal presentation:

9.1.21 a. Professor Smirk described in conclusion the mating habits of
            rotifers.
        a'. *Julia baked in conclusion a zucchini cobbler.
        b. In conclusion, the world is not ready for efficient postal
            delivery.
        b'. *In conclusion, shine my shoes!

Under the performative hypothesis, these expressions always modify a clause that denotes one of the steps of a verbal presentation whether the clause has an overtly occurring verb (as in 9.1.21a) or an understood performative (as in 9.1.21b).

9.2. Conversational Implicature: Grice Saves

'What does the sentence X imply?' and 'What could you conclude if I uttered the sentence X?' are quite different questions and have quite different answers. This point is made particularly clear by an example adapted from Grice 1967. Suppose that I am asked to write a letter of recommendation for a student of mine who is applying for a teaching position in linguistics and I write a letter which reads in its entirety: "Mr. A was always on time for classes, and in his papers he always displayed excellent penmanship." The reader of this letter could conclude that I regarded Mr. A as incompetent to teach linguistics. Nonetheless, one could hardly maintain that the proposition that Mr. A is incompetent is part of the meaning of the one sentence of which the letter consists, since if that sentence were part of a longer letter which extolled Mr. A for unusual knowledge, intelligence, and originality, the reader of the letter would not conclude that I regard Mr. A as incompetent (unless, say, the reader believed that I always extol my worst students for nonexistent virtues).

The conclusions that the hearer (or reader) draws from my uttering the sentence X depend not only on the content of X but also on (i) the fact that I uttered X, and (ii) the fact that I didn't utter any of the other sentences that I might have uttered instead. The letter is damning to Mr. A not because I extol his punctuality and penmanship but because I do not extol anything else. The conclusions drawn by the hearer/reader reflect his conclusions about why I didn't say the other things that I could have said. The fact that I didn't say that Mr. A is a marimba virtuoso can be ascribed to the fact that, even if he is one, it is irrelevant to the purpose of the communication; thus the letter does not convey that Mr. A is not a marimba virtuoso. However, the fact that I did not say that he has an excellent understanding of linguistics cannot be ascribed to my believing it to be irrelevant to a testimonial to his qualifications to teach linguistics, particularly since it is clearly more relevant than the two things that I did mention in the letter. A more plausible reason for my failure to say it is that it is false. Thus, it is reasonable for the reader to conclude that I think Mr. A does not have an excellent understanding of linguistics.

The fact that I didn't mention that Mr. A has read Bloomfield's *Language* would have to be attributed to a different reason: while it is relevant to Mr. A's capacity to teach linguistics, there are sufficiently many more important questions to answer about Mr. A that I could easily tell the reader more than he wants to know about Mr. A without mentioning whether Mr. A has read Bloomfield. Indeed, if I had added to the one-sentence letter the second sentence "He has read Bloomfield's *Language*," the reader would be justified in concluding that Mr. A has read little beyond Bloomfield's *Language*: if Mr. A knows the linguistic literature well, then there was more reason for me to say that than just to say that he has read Bloomfield, particularly since Bloomfield's *Language* is a standard reading assignment in elementary linguistics courses, and thus the fact that someone has read it is no reason to suppose that he has read other linguistic classics. By contrast, if I wrote in support of a candidate for a teaching position in Japanese that he has read the entire Genji Monogatari in the original Japanese, the reader would not be justified in concluding that the candidate has read little else: to read Genji Monogatari you need the kind of command of Japanese that you can only get by reading large quantities of less demanding stuff.

The conclusions that the hearer/reader draws from the fact that you said what you said (and didn't say what you didn't say) are based on the assumption that you are cooperating with him: that you are supplying him with information that is correct and is relevant to your/his purposes, that you are not withholding information that is important to him, and that you are not wasting his time by going into minor matters when there are more important things you could mention instead. (Or at least, this is what cooperation would consist in when you are responding to his request for information; given other purposes for the interchange, other things may constitute cooperation; for example, if a person is trying to solve a puzzle that you have posed to him, it is cooperative not to tell him the answer until he gives up).

Grice (1975) groups the principal dimensions of cooperation in communication under the following four headings, to which I have added capsule paraphrases of what he says about each. **Quantity:** you should assert neither more nor less than is appropriate for the purpose at hand. **Quality:** what you assert should be true, and you should have adequate grounds for holding it to be true. **Relation:** what you mention should be relevant to the purpose at hand. **Manner:** you should use linguistic means no more elaborate than what is needed to convey what you are asserting. Since cooperation plays a role not only in assertion but in all speech acts (indeed, in all acts that involve interaction between persons), these "maxims of cooperation" should clearly be recast in a more general form which is not restricted to acts of assertion, and Grice (1975:47) indeed provides instances of them that do not even involve speech, let alone assertion.[7] However, for the time being, let us concentrate on assertion and the way that cooperation affects what one asserts and how one asserts it.

One aspect of cooperation that does not fit clearly under any of Grice's four maxims but perhaps can be subsumed under "Manner" is that of "effort": extra effort must be justified by extra cooperation, in the sense that one must only go to extra effort in saying something if one thereby makes what one says more informative or more relevant or more intelligible (or more desirable in some other way, e.g., more polite) than it would have been without the extra effort. The interaction of effort with cooperation can be seen by comparing 9.2.1a with 9.2.1b, assuming that the speaker in 9.2.1a and the answerer in 9.2.1b know that Truman was president in 1947:

9.2.1   a. In the middle of a lecture on the Cold War, the speaker says "In 1947, the president of the United States was either Truman or Eisenhower."
        b. When asked "Was either Truman or Eisenhower the president of the United States in 1947?," a person answers
          i.   "Yes."
          ii. "Yes, either Truman or Eisenhower was president."
          iii. "Yes, as a matter of fact, Truman was president."

In 9.2.1a, the speaker has been especially uncooperative, since he not only has been less informative than he could have been (i.e., it is more informative to say that Truman was president than to say that either Truman or Eisenhower was) but he has gone out of his way to be uninformative: he could have been more informative by leaving out words (namely, the words *either* and *or Eisenhower*). In 9.2.1b, the first answerer is being somewhat uncooperative, though not nearly so uncooperative as was the speaker in 9.2.1a: to answer more cooperatively, he would have to add extra words, as in the third answer of 9.2.1b; he is being less informative than he could have been, but he is not going out of his way to be uninformative. The second answerer in 9.2.1b is being as uncooperative as was the speaker in 9.2.1a: he could have been more informative without greater effort by giving the third answer in 9.2.1b or the even shorter *Yes. Trúman was.*

A dimension of cooperation is **exploited** when the speaker chooses his words so that he will convey something other than (generally, more than) what he is, strictly speaking, saying as a result of the addressee's assuming that the speaker is being cooperative, as when a person conveys that he doesn't know (or doesn't remember) which of Truman and Eisenhower was president in 1947 by saying *Either Truman or Eisenhower was president in 1947.* While *or* usually conveys "I don't know which," its dictionary entry need not, indeed, must not make that a component of its meaning: it conveys that only because cooperativity generally demands that the speaker say something else if he does not know which alternative is true. Similarly, Searle (1969:142–46) has argued that while (as noted by Austin 1957) adverbs such as *intentionally* and *voluntarily* usually convey that something is aberrant about the action described (e.g., *John intentionally brushed his teeth* suggests that, say, he was doing it to annoy me), the fact should not be entered in their dictionary entries: if the possibility of John's action being unintentional, involuntary, or the like is not under consideration, cooperativity demands that the speaker not go out of his way to mention something that would be taken for granted if it were not mentioned. When the intentionality of normally intentional actions is mentioned, the speaker conveys that their intentionality is deserving of mention, thus that normal conditions, in which it is not worthy of mention, do not prevail.

Grice gives the following example of exploitation of "relevance":

9.2.2   A. I'm nearly out of gas.
             B: There's a filling station around the corner.

Here B conveys not merely the proposition that there is a filling station around the corner but also that it is likely to be open right now: A would be justified in being angry at B if it turned out that B knew that the filling station was closed. It conveys that because, if B did not think that the filling station was likely to be open, his utterance would be as irrelevant to A's presumable concerns as if he had said *There's a grocery store on 14th Street.*[8] The relation between B's utterance and the proposition that the filling station is probably open is not one of implication but one of what Grice calls **conversational**

implicature: an utterance "conversationally implicates" a proposition p when it conveys that p by virtue of the assumption that the speaker is being cooperative.

The above discussion of 9.2.1 accomplishes part of a major goal that Grice undertook in his study of conversational implicature: to show that the supposed discrepancies between natural language and standard formal logic are not real discrepancies but are instances of implicature, that is, the formula of logic and the corresponding sentence of a natural language really mean the same thing, but when one uses the sentence of natural language he will generally convey more than it means, as a result of the maxims of cooperation. Thus, the occasionally encountered claim that *or* is non–truth-functional, in that it implies that the speaker does not know which alternative is true, is a mistake according to Grice: "A or B" is true whenever either or both of the conjuncts is true, though asserting that true proposition will generally be a misleading thing to do if one happens to know that A is true.

Grice said the same thing of *if:* "If A, then B" does not **imply** that there is a connection between A and B, and the many strange-sounding sentences of the form "If A, then B" which should be true according to the standard truth table, but in which there is no connection between A and B, really are true, though asserting them would generally be a misleading thing to do. Specifically, suppose one were to assert any of the following, all of them true according to the standard truth tables:

9.2.3   a. If Sapporo is the largest city on Hokkaido, then Beethoven lived
               in Vienna.
          b. If Philadelphia is in Nepal, then Beethoven lived in Vienna.
          c. If Philadelphia is in Nepal, then Beethoven lived in Istanbul.

Could a person do so and still be cooperative with regard to both quantity and quality? Consider first how quality could be satisfied, that is, how one could have a reasonable ground for believing the proposition expressed by one of these sentences. Either there is a connection between the protasis and apodosis that enables one to be sure that the protasis can't be true and the apodosis false simultaneously, or there is no such connection. In the latter case, one could have reasonable grounds for believing the proposition expressed by the conditional only by having reasonable grounds for believing the protasis false or by having reasonable grounds for believing the apodosis true. But if that is the nature of one's reasons for believing the conditional proposition to be true, then, with an important exception to be discussed momentarily, one could not assert the conditional without being uncooperative with regard to quantity: if you know that Beethoven lived in Vienna, it would be more informative for you to say that than to assert 9.2.3a or 9.2.3b, and if you know that Philadelphia is not in Nepal, it would be more informative for you to say that than to assert 9.2.3c or 9.2.3b. Thus, argues Grice, a conditional usually conveys that the speaker sees a connection between the protasis and apodosis, since he would have to base his belief in the conditional on such a connection if his act of asserting the conditional is to be cooperative.

The exception alluded to in the last paragraph is that in certain cases a conditional in which there is no connection between protasis and apodosis can be used to assert the apodosis or to deny the protasis:

9.2.4　　a. If $2 + 2 = 4$, my client is innocent. (Conveys: my client is innocent)
　　　　　b. If Nixon was innocent, then geraniums grow on the moon. (Conveys: Nixon wasn't innocent)

However, mere truth of the protasis is not enough to allow a conditional to be used to assert the apodosis, nor is mere falsehood of the apodosis enough to allow a conditional to be used to deny the protasis: it must be obvious truth in the one case and blatant falsehood in the other, as one can see by comparing 9.2.4 with 9.2.5:

9.2.5　　a. If $847 \times 698 = 591{,}206$, then my client is innocent.
　　　　　b. If Nixon was innocent, then Seattle has more inhabitants than Columbus, Ohio.

Since the protasis of 9.2.4a is obviously true, the only way that the hearer could conceive of 9.2.4a being true, connection or no connection, is for its consequent to be true; and since the apodosis of 9.2.4b is blatantly false, the only way that the hearer could conceive of 9.2.4b being true, connection or no connection, is for the protasis to be false. Note that 9.2.4 does not violate the quantity maxim the way that 9.2.3 does: since the possibility of the protasis of 9.2.4a being false is ruled out, it is just as informative to assert 9.2.4a as to assert its apodosis, whereas in 9.2.5a, since the possibility of the falsehood of the protasis is not ruled out by what people would normally take for granted, asserting 9.2.5a is significantly less informative than asserting its apodosis; the comparison of 9.2.4b with 9.2.5b works similarly. If there is any lack of cooperation in the uttering of 9.2.4a or 9.2.4b, it is the less serious one of violating the maxim of manner by taking more words than are needed to say what one wants to say: foregoing the possibility of using a shorter but no less informative sentence. Actually, one could argue that in saying 9.2.3a one is being more informative than if one asserted its apodosis (and that in saying 9.2.4b one is being more informative than if one denied its protasis):

the speaker is conveying not just that his client is innocent but that his client's innocence is as clear as the obvious fact that $2 + 2 = 4$. Saying that would involve changing ground: instead of talking about the information content of the proposition that you are asserting, we are talking about the information content of the proposition that you are conveying. But what then is to prevent one from saying that 9.2.3a–c are more informative than asserting the apodosis (in 9.2.3a–b) or denying the protasis (in 9.2.3b–c), in that they convey a highly informative (though quite bizarre) proposition such as that Sapporo's being the largest city on Hokkaido is a reason why Beethoven lived in Vienna? Presumably only the fact that in that case the conveyed proposition ("informative" as it is) is false. Exploitation of the cooperative maxims is itself cooperative: one takes the speaker to have conveyed something only if it is something that it would be reasonable to take him as having intended to convey.

One particularly appealing part of Grice's argument that a "connection" between protasis and apodosis is not part of the meaning of *if* is his argument that paraphrases of conditionals in terms of *or* and *not* just as much commit one to a "connection," despite the fact that *or* is not normally held to require a "connection" between the things that it conjoins. Specifically, Grice notes that 9.2.6b is a good paraphrase of 9.2.6a:

9.2.6   a. If Labour doesn't win the next election, there'll be a depression.
         b. Either Labour will win the next election or there'll be a
            depression.

Both commit the speaker equally to the idea that there is a causal connection between Labour losing the election and a depression ensuing. Just as in the case of the conditional, knowledge of a connection between the two constituent propositions can be one's grounds for believing that some disjunctive proposition is true. My only qualm about this argument relates to the fact that conditionals do not always have an adequate paraphrase with *or;* for example, note how much less normal 9.2.7b and 9.2.8b are as paraphrases of 9.2.7a and 9.2.8a than 9.2.6b was as a paraphrase of 9.2.6a:

9.2.7   a. If Labour wins the next election, there'll be a depression.
         b. Either Labour won't win the next election or there'll be a
            depression.

9.2.8   a. If you come a step closer, I'll scream.
         b. Either you won't come a step closer or I'll scream.

On Grice's account of *if* and *or,* there is no obvious reason why 9.2.7b and 9.2.8b should sound any less normal than 9.2.6b.

Another well-known supposed discrepancy between standard formal logic and natural language that Grice's approach explains away is that *some* is normally taken as implying *not all,* whereas $(\exists: fx)gx$ does not imply $\sim(\forall: fx)gx$. Grice argues that it is misleading to say 9.2.9a when you know that all men are mortal, since you could at no extra linguistic cost say the more informative 9.2.9b:

9.2.9   a. Some men are mortal.
          b. All men are mortal.

Thus, a person who utters 9.2.9a is taken as holding that not all men are mortal (or at least, that he does not know for sure that all men are mortal).

The use of *yes* and *no* in answers to questions provides confirmation of the position that *some* means $\exists$ and that it is only because of the principles of cooperation that a speaker who utters 9.2.9a is taken to mean that not all men are mortal. Recall that in the discussion of 9.2.1b I noted that the question 9.2.10a can be answered with 9.2.10b; but 9.2.10b′ would be inappropriate as an answer:

9.2.10   a.   Was either Truman or Eisenhower president in 1947?
          b.   Yes, as a matter of fact, Truman was president.
          b′.   *No, Truman was president.

The use of *yes* and *no* accords with the idea that *Either Truman or Eisenhower was president in 1947* is true even though the speaker could not utter that sentence without being misleading: he must use *yes,* the word that indicates truth of the proposition which the question asked about,[9] rather than *no,* the word which indicates the falsehood of that proposition. The same paradigm is exhibited by sentences involving *some;* note that 9.2.11a can be answered with 9.2.11b but not with 9.2.11b′:[10]

9.2.11   a.   Are some men mortal?
          b.   Yes, as a matter of fact, áll men are mortal.
          b′.   *No, all men are mortal.

One discrepancy between standard logic and natural language cannot be explained away by Grice's cooperative maxims: the fact that while *All unicorns drive Chevrolets* commits the speaker to the existence of unicorns (and, in general, the use of *all* commits the speaker to the existence of elements in the domain over which its variable ranges), $(\forall x)\supset(fx,gx)$ does not imply $(\exists x)\wedge(fx,gx)$. In this case, the use of *yes* and *no* in the answer to questions such as 9.2.12a does not accord with the claim that *All unicorns drive Chevrolets* is (vacuously) true:

9.2.12   a.   Do all unicorns drive Chevrolets?
         b.   *Yes, indeed, there are no unicorns.
         b′. ?No, there are no unicorns.
         b″. *Yes, but there are no unicorns.

Grice's account of the alleged discrepancies between standard logic and natural logic has been challenged by L. J. Cohen (1972). Cohen objects that Grice's discussion covers only the cases where *If A, then B* (or *Either A or B* or *Some A's are B's*) is asserted and ignores the cases where it is a constituent of a larger logical structure or is involved in a speech act of another type. He holds that in many such cases a sentence of English does not mean what in Grice's account it ought to mean. For example, does 9.2.13 really attribute to Frank a belief of the form $\supset AB$, where $\supset$ is the standard truth-functional connective?

9.2.13   Frank believes that if God is dead, then everything is permitted.

Cohen argues that it does not, on the grounds that 9.2.13 attributes to Frank a belief about a connection between God being dead and everything being permitted and that, for example, 9.2.13 would be false if Frank did not believe in such a connection but merely believed that everything is permitted. One might retort that in that case 9.2.13 would be a misleading thing to say: you could be more informative at less cost by saying that Frank believes that everything is permitted. However, that retort skirts the issue of whether 9.2.13 is **true** in such a case. The use of *yes* and *no* does not accord with the position that 9.2.13 is true:

9.2.14   a.   Does Frank believe that if God is dead, everything is
              permitted?
         b.   ??Yes, indeed he believes that everything is permitted.
         b′. No, but he does believe that everything is permitted.
         b″. Yes, and he also believes that everything is permitted.
         b‴. No, but he does believe that God is not dead.

If 9.2.13 attributed to Frank a belief $\supset AB$, then 9.2.14b′ and 9.2.14b‴ ought not to be possible answers: a belief that everything is permitted ought to be a special case of a belief that if God is dead, everything is permitted.

It might be objected that 9.2.13 and 9.2.14 are beside the point, since they involve "belief contexts" and strange things happen in belief contexts. Let us then take an example involving as innocuous a context as can be imagined, namely, mere negation:

9.2.15   It is not the case that if God is dead, everything is permitted.

According to classical logic, 9.2.15 implies that God is dead (i.e., from $\sim\supset AB$ you can infer both A and $\sim B$); however, ordinary speakers do not accept arguments such as *It is not the case that if God is dead, everything is permitted; therefore, God is dead.* One could know the premise of that argument to be true either on the basis of knowledge of the truth values of the constituent propositions (i.e., knowing that God is dead and that not everything is permitted) or on the basis of some connection between those propositions. In the former case, one could hold that the argument was circular (i.e., its conclusion is something that you used in establishing its premise) and that that fact was responsible for the fact that people reject the argument. However, what basis could there be for rejecting the argument in the case where you know the premise on the basis of some connection between the proposition that God is dead and the proposition that everything is permitted? Doesn't the fact that it is odd in that case to say *Therefore, God is dead* (or *Therefore, not everything is permitted*) point to a real discrepancy between formal logic and natural language? The only apparent alternative to admitting a real discrepancy is to deny that the premise is really of the form $\sim\supset AB$, for example, to hold that there is a covert quantifier ("It is not the case that for every state of affairs, if God is dead in that state of affairs, then everything is permitted in that state of affairs"). However, that analysis is at least very close to the analysis that Cohen was arguing for: that *if* is not just the standard truth-functional connective but makes reference to a connection between the antecedent and consequent, for example, a connection such as could be formulated as "In every state of affairs in which God is dead, everything is permitted."[11]

While Gricean conversational implicature has commonly been used as a device for defending classical analyses of logical elements, it has also occasionally been deployed to defend nonclassical analyses, as in Stalnaker's (1975) defense of a non–truth-functional analysis of *if* against an argument that appears to show that *if* must be assigned the classical truth table. Specifically, the following inference appears to be valid, and its validity would mean that *If not A, B* would have to be true whenever *Either A or B* was:

9.2.16   Either the butler did it or the gardener did it.
           Therefore, if the butler didn't do it, the gardener did.

Stalnaker argues that 9.2.16 is not valid but merely "reasonable," where a **reasonable inference** is one such that "in every context in which the premisses could appropriately be asserted or supposed, it is impossible for anyone to accept the premises without committing himself to the conclusion." The notion of "context" that Stalnaker assumes defines a set of worlds that are taken to be "epistemically possible," in the sense that for all one knows the real world might be any of those worlds. Within Stalnaker's framework, the Gricean account of sentences of the form (*Either*) *A or B* amounts to the requirement that one assert such a sentence only when worlds in which A but not B is true and worlds in which B but not A is true are epistemically possible. The premise says that worlds in which neither the butler nor the gardener did it are not epistemically possible, which means that after the premise has been asserted the epistemically possible worlds in which the butler didn't do it are worlds in which the gardener did do it, and according to Stalnaker's analysis of conditionals, that makes the conclusion true.

But note that this derivation of the conclusion depended not just on the truth of the premise but on the fact that someone asserted it. Stalnaker shows that there can also be cases in which *A or B* is true but in which one could deny that *If not A, then B* was true (and in which, according to Stalnaker's treatment of conditionals, it is indeed false). Suppose that I know that I didn't do it. Then whether *Either the butler did it or I did it* is true or false depends just on whether the butler did or didn't do it. Even if I believe that the butler did it and thus that the proposition expressed by that sentence is true, I can still deny that *If the butler didn't do it, then I did it,* and that sentence expresses a false proposition if one treats *If A, then B* as true when B is true in all epistemically possible worlds in which A is true. (This is not exactly Stalnaker's proposal, but it will do for present purposes.) In the given situation, there are epistemically possible worlds in which the butler didn't do it and I didn't do it either, and thus not all epistemically possible worlds in which the butler didn't do it are worlds in which I did it, irrespective of whether in fact the butler did it. If the butler in fact did it, then it will be true that either the butler did it or I did it, but the mere truth of that proposition is not (according to Stalnaker) sufficient grounds to make it true that if the butler didn't do it, then I did.

I will now turn to brief sketches of a number of analyses in terms of conversational implicature. Let us begin with the question of what the word *pink* means. A reasonable first approximation to the meaning of *pink* is "pale red": pink differs fom red in having relatively low "saturation" (i.e., it is pale rather than deep), though its "hue" is in the range covered by *red*. However, it is much harder to think of a normal use for the expression *pale red* than for such combinations as *pale blue/yellow/green,* which have obvious uses. Fred Householder (1971:75) has proposed an explanation of these facts in terms of a principle that when there is a single word equivalent of a multiword phrase, the single word must be used instead: *pale red* is odd because you have to say *pink* instead, whereas there is no alternative to saying *pale blue/yellow/ green*.[12] However, the expression *pale red* in fact is occasionally encountered, not merely in a definition such as *"Pink" means "pale red,"* but to indicate what color some object is, and moreover, it does not refer to the same range of color as *pink* does; specifically, *pale red* is used to refer to a color that is pale in comparison with true red, but not so pale as to be pink. Some sense can be made of these facts if the Householder and Gruber proposal is reinterpreted in terms of conversational implicature. When a person calls something *pale red,* he had the alternative of calling it *pink* but chose to call it *pale red* instead. His choice of words implies that the color is red in hue but is pale in comparison with true red, and his rejection of *pink* as the designation of the color would have to be because *pink* did not apply to it. Since the most obvious way that these conditions could be fulfilled is for the color to be somewhat pale but not very pale (i.e., not so pale as to be unqualifiedly pale), the use of *pale red* conveys that the color is deeper than pink but paler than red. Note that an analysis in terms of implicature thus allows one to define *pink* as "pale red" but still admit cases where *pink* and *pale red* designate different colors.

Second, consider the difference between 9.2.17a and 9.2.17b:

9.2.17   a. Only Muriel, Lyndon, and Ed voted for Hubert.
         b. Only Southerners voted for Hubert.

While a person who utters 9.2.17a will be taken to hold that Muriel, Lyndon, and Ed all voted for Hubert, a person who utters 9.2.17b will not be taken as holding that all Southerners voted for Hubert (he will be taken as holding that at least some Southerners voted for Hubert, perhaps even that persons who voted for Hubert were widely distributed in the South, but not that **all** Southerners voted for Hubert). By the same token, *Only American citizens are employed by the FBI* does not imply that all American citizens are employed by the FBI.

If one of the persons enumerated in 9.2.17a is known by the speaker not to have voted for Hubert, then the speaker is being misleading: he could have been more informative by leaving that person out of the list. Thus, 9.2.17a could be uttered cooperatively only if for each of the three persons enumerated, either the speaker knows that the person voted for Hubert or he does not know whether that person voted for Hubert. But if he doesn't know, say, whether Ed voted for Hubert, cooperativeness would demand that he indicate that (say, by saying *Only Muriel, Lyndon, and perhaps Ed . . .*), since it is so easy for him to indicate that his knowledge about Ed is incomplete, and since his addressee presumably cares who voted for Hubert (if he doesn't, then why utter the sentence at all?). Thus a speaker could utter 9.2.17a cooperatively only if he holds that Muriel, Lyndon, and Ed all voted for Hubert. However, since 9.2.17b does not involve an enumeration, it takes extra effort to exclude people rather than to include them (e.g., *Only Southerners other than Johnny Cash and George Wallace voted for Hubert*), and an expression indicating what Southerners were excluded would be misleading unless either it were complete (and thus incredibly long) or made explicit about the way in which it was incomplete (e.g., *Only Southerners other than Johnny Cash, George Wallace, and many others too numerous to mention* . . .). Thus the reason why a person who utters 9.2.17b does not explicitly say that not all Southerners voted for Hubert need not be that that is false—it could as easily be that a nonmisleading qualification would take more effort than it was worth. These considerations suggest that an analysis of *Only Muriel voted for Hubert* as "Muriel voted for Hubert, and no one other than Muriel voted for Hubert" is incorrect: only the second conjunct is really part of the meaning of an *only*-sentence, with the first conjunct being conveyed by virtue of the assumption that the speaker is being cooperative. That implicature can be **suspended** by adding the appropriate words:

9.2.18.   Only Muriel voted for Hubert, and maybe even she didn't vote for him.

The analysis of *only* in terms of implicature is important, since it makes it possible to associate *only* with the same logical analysis in 9.2.17b as in 9.2.17a, namely, to treat all instances of 'Only *f*'s are *g*'s' as $(\forall: \sim fx)_x \sim gx$, where *fx* can be either an "ordinary" propositional function such as "*x* is a Southerner" or a function such as "*x* $\in$ {Muriel, Ed, Lyndon}".[13]

For a third example, consider reduced passives (passives without a *by*-phrase, often misleadingly called "agentless passives"). Reduced passives have sometimes been treated by transformational grammarians as having a deep structure with *someone* or *something* as subject, as in an analysis in which 9.2.19a is assigned the same deep structure as 9.2.19b and its derivation involves passivization followed by deletion of *by someone:*

9.2.19   a. Bill was mugged.
         b. Someone mugged Bill.

However, an indefinite pronoun is not indefinite enough to serve as the underlying subject. First of all, as has often been pointed out, reduced passives are possible even with verbs that demand a semantically plural subject and which thus do not admit *someone* (which can only be singular) as underlying subject:

9.2.20   a.   The fort was being surrounded.
   a′.   *Someone was surrounding the fort.
   b.   A compromise was agreed on.
   b′.   *Someone agreed on a compromise.

Second, consider what the following sentences imply about the authorship of
Syntactic Structures:

9.2.21   a.   Chomsky's *Syntactic Structures* was written in 1955.
   a′.   Someone wrote Chomsky's *Syntactic Structures* in 1955.

While 9.2.21a can be uttered by someone who believes Chomsky to be the
author of *Syntactic Structures* (though it could also be uttered by someone
who believes the author to be Bernard Bloch but who persists in calling it
"Chomsky's *Syntactic Structures,*" just as many people persist in speaking of
"Purcell's Trumpet Voluntary" even though they know it is by Jeremiah
Clarke), 9.2.21a′ would only be appropriate if the speaker believes that the
author was not Chomsky.

 Nevertheless, a reconsideration of these examples in terms of conversational implicature provides a way of preserving the essence of the proposal to
derive 9.2.19a and 9.2.19b from the same deep structure. I wish to propose
that 9.2.21a and 9.2.21a′ have the same logical form and that their difference
in appropriateness conditions stems rather from the choice of words by which
that common logical form is expressed. Note in particular that the *someone* of
9.2.21a′ may serve as the antecedent of a pronoun, whereas the underlying
subject of 9.2.21a may not:

9.2.22   a.   *Chomsky's *Syntactic Structures* was written in 1955, but his
     identity has not been revealed. (* if *his* refers to the subject
     of *write*)
   a′.   Someone wrote Chomsky's *Syntactic Structures* in 1955, but
     his identity has not been revealed.

I will argue in section 10.6 that "existential" NPs such as *someone* and *some
linguist* serve a dual function: they both quantify a bound variable and create
a constant that can play a role in subsequent discourse (a constant corresponding to the individual that the quantified proposition says exists). Or at least,
existential NPs that have overt linguistic manifestation have that dual function: as examples like 9.2.22a suggest, an existential quantifier (assuming that
there is one in the logical structure of 9.2.22a) that does not appear overtly
does not have the function of creating a constant.[14] However, in accordance
with the maxim of quantity, constants are interpreted as distinct unless the

speaker signals that they are or may be identical. Whether entities are the same or different will be relevant to virtually any discourse in which one refers to those entities, and since one can refer to identical entities by treating them as identical (that is, by using the same name for them, or by using anaphoric devices such as *he* or *that bastard*), one would be saying less than is relevant if one failed to advise the addressee that the constants were or might be identical. And since uncertainty about whether two entities are identical is far less common than certainty that they are distinct, it is the former and not the latter that requires comment. Reduced passives like 9.2.21a allow one to remain noncommital about whether the understood underlying subject is identical to some other individual that is referred to, since nothing corresponding to the understood subject is added to the "cast of characters" that are available to the subsequent discourse.

Consider next the division of labor between the transitive and intransitive uses of such verbs as *open:*

9.2.23   a. I opened the door
         b. The door opened.

The analysis of transitive *open* as a causative of intransitive *open* (e.g., analyzing 9.2.23a as "I did something which caused the door to open") might be objected to on the grounds that there are cases where it is appropriate to say 9.2.23a but not appropriate to say 9.2.23b. In particular, it would be quite irresponsible for a person to say 9.2.23b in response to the question *How did the dog get out of the house?* when he had opened the door and thereby let the dog out. Note, though, that there are cases where 9.2.23b may be embedded in a larger context in which it is made clear that a particular agent is responsible for the door's opening:

9.2.24   I pulled and pulled at the door, and finally it opened.

Fillmore (1978) observes that 9.2.25a (the first sentence of Hemingway's "The Killers") differs from 9.2.25b not only in the location of the narrator (with *came,* the narrator views things from inside the lunchroom, and with *went,* he views things from outside), but also in who opens the door: 9.2.25a suggests that the two men opened the door, whereas 9.2.25b suggests that the door was opened from inside the lunchroom:

9.2.25   a. The door of Henry's lunchroom opened, and two men came in.
         b. The door of Henry's lunchroom opened, and two men went in.

As Fillmore notes, however, 9.2.25a is really noncommittal about who opened the door (you could use 9.2.25a even when a third person opened the door from outside for the two men, or when Henry pushed a button on some electronic door-opening device, thus causing the door to open), and the suggestions of both sentences would change radically if it had been established that Henry's lunchroom had an all-glass exterior, so that a person inside it could see what people outside it were doing, and vice versa.

The generalization about when you can use intransitive *open* and when you must use transitive *open* appears to be: you may use intransitive open when no agent is responsible for the event (e.g., the door just opens by itself), or when the agent is not yet part of the scene that you are describing (as in the most obvious understanding of 9.2.25a), or when you are referring to an event that is part of an action and have otherwise indicated the agent's involvement in that action (as in 9.2.24, where the agent's activity and the eventual consequence of that activity are split between two clauses). What this amounts to is that you must expressly indicate an agent's involvement in an event as soon as you know of the agent's involvement in it. Witnessing an agent performing an action is the case par excellence of knowing of an agent's involvement in an event. If you are outside the lunchroom and see the two men open the door, or if you are inside looking through a glass door and see the two men open it, you have witnessed their act of opening the door; if you are inside the lunchroom and the doors and walls are opaque, or if you are looking in some other direction when the men open the door and you hear but do not see the men and the door, you have witnessed the event of the door opening, but not the men's act of opening the door, and you have only inferred, not witnessed, that such an act took place. This pattern reflects an interaction of the maxims of quantity, quality, and relevance: the existence of an act as the cause of a given event and the identity of the agent of that act will generally be relevant to a discourse in which that event is referred to, and it is misleading to leave out information about the existence of the act and identity of the agent, provided that one's information is of sufficient quality. Thus, "verbs of change" such as the intransitive *open* at most suggest, rather than imply, that no agent was involved. This should be contrasted with agentive verbs of change such as intransitive *dress*, which imply agency on the part of the subject. Transitive *dress* (similarly, *shave, wash*) cannot be a causative of intransitive *dress*, since it refers to only one agent, not two; for example, in *Wilbur dressed the baby,* the baby need not be an active participant in the dressing. Of course, an alternative analysis of the relationship between transitive and intransitive *dress* is available: treat the transitive as basic, and the intransitive as having an understood reflexive object.

For a final example of an analysis based on conversational implicature, let us turn to the supposed "exclusive" sense of *or.* Pelletier (1977) challenges the view that there are two *or*'s, an inclusive *or* that combines propositions into a complex proposition that is true if and only if at least one of the conjuncts is true, and an exclusive *or* that combines propositions into a complex proposition that is true if and only if exactly one of the conjuncts is true. Pelletier notes that many of the supposed examples of exclusive *or* are merely cases in which, for reasons having nothing to do with *or*, it is impossible for more than one of the conjuncts to be true:

9.2.26   a. Today is either Monday or Tuesday.
    b. Either there is a God or there isn't.

Such examples are irrelevant to the question of whether there is a distinction between exclusive or inclusive *or*, since the case in which the two *or*'s are supposed to differ does not arise in these examples. Of considerably more interest are such examples as[15]

9.2.27   a. On the $4.95 lunch you get either a soup or a dessert.
    b. You can use either the hall closet or the attic to store your
     books.

While there is no logical impossibility about a state of affairs in which you get both a soup and a dessert for your $4.95 or in which you store books in both the hall closet and the attic, nonetheless these sentences at least suggest that you don't get both the soup and the dessert and that you aren't entitled to store books in both places. This does not mean, however, that an exclusive *or* is involved in the permissions that the sentences in 9.2.27 report, any more than the fact that 9.2.28 leaves one free to take only soup or only dessert or neither means that 9.2.28 involves a constituent "You get a soup % you get a dessert," where % is a connective such that *p*%*q* is true regardless of the truth values of *p* and *q:*

9.2.28   On the $4.95 lunch you get a soup and a dessert.

Similarly, the fact that 9.2.29 leaves one free to take only one vegetable does not mean that 9.2.29 involves a special sense of *two* that includes *one* as a special case, distinct from the ordinary sense of *two* found in *John and Mary have two children:*

9.2.29   On the $7.50 dinner you get two vegetables.

When one is offered a package deal, one is not normally required to accept all the items in the package: in exchange for your money, you receive the entitlement to all the items in the package, but you still have the option of not exercising that entitlement in the case of items that you do not want. Thus, 9.2.28

reports a more generous offer than 9.2.27a: an offer in which the customer has all the options that are available to him in 9.2.27a plus the additional option of having both soup and dessert. While what is offered has the form of a proposition, the offer need not entitle the recipient to make that proposition true in whatever way he pleases: the generosity of the offer is only broad enough to make the recipient entitled to more than what linguistically simpler alternatives entitle him to. For example, 9.2.27a entitles the hearer to take a soup and entitles him to take a dessert (since if he were not entitled to one of them, a linguistically simpler alternative such as *On the $4.95 lunch you get a soup* would express the full generosity of the offer) but does not entitle him to take both, any more than it entitles him to take two soups or two desserts. The illusion of an exclusive *or* in sentences like 9.2.27 results from the fact they relate to the transfer of entitlements from one person to another and that entitlements do not change unless some act of the current owner causes them to change; only as little entitlement is transferred as is consistent with the statement of what is transferred, interpreted in light of the maxims of quantity, manner, and relevance.

9.3. Conventional Implicature

In developing the notion of conversational implicature, Grice drew two major distinctions: what a sentence says versus what an occurrence of that sentence conveys or "implicates," and what it conveys in virtue of principles of cooperativity (**conversational implicature**) versus what it conveys in virtue of conventions for the use of words and syntactic constructions that it contains (**conventional implicature**). Having discussed the former kind of implicature at some length, we now turn to the latter kind.

Let us begin by noting some differences between conventional implicatures and the two things that Grice's taxonomy opposes it to, namely meaning in a narrow sense and conversational implicature. (i) A conventional implicature plays no role in the truth conditions of a sentence, whereas the various details of meaning in the narrow sense do affect truth conditions. For example, Grice takes *but* as differing from *and* in that *but* carries a conventional implicature that the truth of the second conjunct is remarkable, given the truth of the first conjunct, e.g., 9.3.1a and 9.3.1b are true under exactly the same conditions, but 9.3.1b conveys (in virtue of a convention about the use of *but*) that it is remarkable for a person who has inherited a million dollars not to quit his job:

9.3.1   a. Smith inherited a million dollars and he didn't quit his job.
          b. Smith inherited a million dollars but he didn't quit his job.

(ii) Conventional implicatures are borne by particular linguistic units (e.g., *but* in 9.3.1b), whereas conversational implicatures result from interactions among the words that the speaker used, the words that he could have used but chose not to, and diverse contextual factors, and there usually is no one linguistic unit that can be held responsible for the implicature. This observation holds even for implicatures that are commonly spoken of as associated with a particular word, e.g., the implicature "The speaker doesn't know which" that is commonly generated by sentences with *or:* not only *or* but also the potentially irrelevant additional conjunct plays a role in creating the implicature. (iii) Conversational implicatures can be **canceled** but conventional implicatures cannot. For example, *lack* can usually be paraphrased as "not have," and sentences with *not have* and *lack* generally both convey that the person in question ought to have the thing in question (9.3.2a–b), but the implicature that Joan ought to have a tennis racket is a conversational implicature in the case of *not have* and a conventional implicature in the case of *lack,* since it can be cancelled in the former but not in the latter case (9.3.3):[16]

9.3.2   a. Joan doesn't have a tennis racket.
           b. Joan lacks a tennis racket.

9.3.3   a. Of course Joan doesn't have a tennis racket—there's no earthly
              reason for her to have one.
           b. ??Of course Joan lacks a tennis racket—there's no earthly
              reason for her to have one.

The noncancellability of the conventional implicature borne by *but* is illustrated by 9.3.4:

9.3.4   a. ?John is rich but stupid, though there's nothing remarkable
              about rich people being stupid.
           b. ?John is rich but stupid, though I expect rich people to be
              stupid.

One widely cited supposed example of conventional implicature (indeed, a favorite example of Grice himself) actually may not involve conventional implicature at all and in any event involves a subtle but serious error. Grice treated *therefore,* as in 9.3.5, essentially the same way that he treated *but*—he assigned it the same meaning as *and* but treated it is bearing a conventional implicature (here, the implicature that the truth of the first of the two component sentences is a reason why the second would be true also):

9.3.5   a. He is an Englishman; he is, therefore, brave. (Grice's actual
              example)

      b. He is an Englishman, therefore he is brave. (an alternate version
          that will figure in the discussion below)

Grice's proposal is more plausible for 9.3.5b, in which *therefore* appears to occupy the same position where *and* could occur, than for 9.3.5a, in which it appears in a clearly adverbial position. In any event, though, neither version involves conjoining, and the example indeed is not even a sentence but rather a **paratactic** combination of two sentences, as can be seen from the fact that it cannot be embedded in a larger sentence:

9.3.6   a. *I doubt that [John is an Englishman, therefore he is brave].
       b. *It is not the case that [John is an Englishman; he is, therefore,
          brave].

Therefore is not a conjunction but rather a S-modifying adverb (meaning roughly "because of that," where "that" has an antecedent elsewhere in the sentence or discourse), and it makes its own contribution to the meaning of the clause in which it occurs, irrespective of whether that clause is conjoined with anything else. One can of course convert 9.3.6 into acceptable sentences by putting *and* before the second of the paratactically combined sentences, but it is then *and* and not *therefore* that is combining the two component sentences into a single larger sentence; the truth conditions of a sentence with *and therefore* will of course reflect those of *and*. To determine whether the contribution of *therefore* to the meaning of a sentence of the form *A and therefore B* is a conventional implicature, we must ask whether it can be false not only in virtue of the falsehood of A or of B but also in virtue of the failure of the connection between A and B that *therefore* refers to. Let us accordingly consider sentences such as:

9.3.7   a. John isn't English and therefore brave—he's Hungarian.
       b. John isn't English and therefore brave—Englishmen aren't all
          brave, though John in fact *is* brave.

There is no problem with 9.3.7a: there, *A and therefore B* is false simply because A is false, as the truth conditions for *and* dictate. If 9.3.7b, the speaker is not denying the conjunction ∧(John is English, John is brave) but rather the proposition that John is brave in virtue of his being English. If my judgment (not one that I make with great confidence, I admit) is correct that 9.3.7b is a perfectly normal thing to say, I can conclude that *A and therefore B* is false when the connection between A and B that *therefore* alludes to is absent; the proposition that there is such a connection is then not a conventional implicature but part of the meaning in the narrow sense.

Another word whose interpretation involves a conventional implicature is *even*, as in 9.3.8:

9.3.8   Even Los Angeles sometimes gets cold weather.

This sentence says that Los Angeles sometimes gets cold weather and conveys that it is more remarkable that Los Angeles sometimes gets cold weather than that other places do. A sentence with *even* can thus serve as an indirect answer to a question:

9.3.9   A: Do you ever get cold weather here in Atlanta?
             B: Hell, even Los Angeles sometimes gets cold weather.

The answer given by B says that Los Angeles sometimes gets cold weather and indirectly conveys that Atlanta does too by creating a context in which Atlanta is one of the places that Los Angeles is contrasted with, which get cold weather sometimes, but where that isn't so remarkable as that Los Angeles sometimes gets cold weather. The use of *Yes* and *No* corresponds to the claim just made that the meaning in the narrow sense is that the **focus** (the item contrasted with alternatives, here *Los Angeles*) has the property in question and that there is an implicature that it is more remarkable for the focus to have that property than for the things it is contrasted with to have it:

9.3.10   a. Does even Montreal sometimes have cold weather?
                 Yes, and any fool should know that it sometimes has cold
                    weather.
                 *No—any fool should know that it sometimes has cold weather.
              b. Does Smith even drive a car?
                 No, he doesn't drive, though I don't see what would be strange
                    if he did.

Saying what exactly the conventional implicature associated with *even* is is not easy. Most of the proposals say either too little, e.g., that something else has the property in question, which would wrongly imply that 9.3.11a was a normal thing to say, or too much, e.g., that the focus is the least likely member of the contrast set to have the property, which would incorrectly make 9.3.11b abnormal:

9.3.11   a. Even Hitler sent millions of people to their deaths.
              b. Even Houston has some good Chinese restaurants.

The most satisfactory proposal that I have seen for the conventional implicature of *even* is that of Kay (1990), namely that "the [clause] in which it occurs expresses, in context, a proposition which is more informative (equivalently, 'stronger') than some particular distinct proposition taken to be already present in the context." Kay explicates this notion of "more informative" in terms of "scalar models" that rank elements on such scales as how likely it is or how widely believed it is or how significant it is that, say, a given city will have some good Chinese restaurants. In Kay's framework, likeliness or expectedness does not have the privileged role that it has had in some accounts of what is conveyed by *even:* it is simply one of a number of notions that define scales that can be used in the interpretation of particular tokens of *even.* For an example where something other than likeliness or expectedness figures in the interpretation of *even,* note that the following dialog is quite normal even if the lieutenant governor is someone known to be hard to please while the governor happily goes along with everything:

9.3.12   A: Did the lieutenant governor like our idea?
          B: Hell, even the governor thought it was a great idea.

Here all that is required to make the interchange normal is a scale on which the governor's approval is more significant than the lieutenant governor's; while the governor's approval is not more informative from the point of view of classical information theory, it is more informative from the point of view of what it implies about future events (the governor can get things done, but the lieutenant governor can't).

Conventional implicature plays a major role in the interpretation of an important class of predicate elements, namely so-called **implicative** predicates. An implicative predicate is an element such as *manage, happen,* or *have the impudence to* that has the property in 9.3.13:

9.3.13   A one-place predicate $f(p)$ is implicative if and only if, for all relevant values of p, $f(p)$ implies p and $f(\sim p)$ implies $\sim p$.
          A two-place predicate $f(x, p)$ is implicative if and only if, for all relevant values of x and p, $f(x, p)$ implies p and $f(x, \sim p)$ implies $\sim p$.

For example, "John managed to pass the exam" implies that John passed the exam, and "John didn't manage to pass the exam" implies that John didn't pass the exam; "There happened to be a cow in the back yard" implies that there was a cow in the back yard, and "There didn't happen to be a cow in the back yard" implies that there wasn't a cow in the back yard. This might seem at first to make implicative predicates semantically vacuous, since the truth value of a sentence with an implicative predicate then is the same as the truth value of its argument sentence.[17] However, a sentence with an implicative predicate always conveys something that need not be conveyed by a corresponding sentence without that predicate, e.g., the examples with *manage* convey that whether John passed the exam depended on whether he overcame obstacles to his passing it, and the examples with *happen* convey that whether there was a cow in the back yard depended on matters of chance. This extra thing that is conveyed is a conventional implicature (it has to be a conventional and not a conversational implicature, since it is what distinguishes the various implicative predicates from each other and thus must at least involve conventions for the use of each of them), and it is precisely that conventional implicature that renders the implicative predicates nonvacuous semantically. More specifically, the conventional implicature of each implicative predicate is of the form "Whether S takes place depends on whether X is the case", and the different implicative verbs differ with regard to what X is: for *manage*, X is "(the person in question) overcomes an obstacle to S," for *happen*, X is "random factors bring S about," for *have the impudence/foresight/. . .*, X is "(the person in question) has sufficient impudence/foresight/. . .".

Remarkably little attention has been devoted to the **projection problem** for conventional implicatures: the problem of determining what the conventional implicatures of a complex sentence are from the conventional implicatures borne by the various units of which it is made up. The only detailed treatment of that problem that I know is that of Karttunen and Peters 1979, who treat sentences as having a two-part semantic representation: one part is a formula representing the meaning in the narrow sense, and the other part is a formula in which the various conventional implicatures of the sentence are combined (e.g., conjoined).

Determining what is conventionally implicated by a sentence is not always just a matter of conjoining contributions made by the various elements that make up the sentence. As an illustration of the way in which conventional implicatures of a part of a complex sentence sometimes figure only in a transformed form as conventional implicatures of the whole sentence, consider what the conventional implicatures of a conditional sentence *If A, B* are. Karttunen and Peters note that the conventional implicatures of the protasis A carry over to the whole conditional sentence, e.g., 9.3.14a conventionally implicates that whether John opens the door depends on whether he overcomes an obstacle to his opening it, and 9.3.14b conventionally implicates that John is located towards the noteworthy or informative end of a scale on which his passing the exam is contrasted with other persons' passing it:

9.3.14   a. If John manages to open the door, he'll take the money we've
             left on the table.
         b. If even John passed the exam, we've made the exam too easy.

However, conventional implicatures of the apodasis B do not automatically become conventional implicatures of the whole conditional sentence, e.g., 9.3.15 does not conventionally implicate that whether John opens the door will depend on whether he overcomes an obstacle to his opening it:

9.3.15   If John loses his key, he'll (still) manage to open the door.

Rather what it conventionally implicates is that if John loses his key, then whether he opens the door will depend on whether he overcomes an obstacle to his opening it. Karttunen and Peters thus propose the following treatment of conventional implicatures of a conditional sentence. Suppose that, following Karttunen and Peters, we use A^e and A^i to represent the two parts of the meaning of a sentence A ('e' stands for 'entailment,' 'i' for 'implicature'). Then the conventional implicature of a conditional sentence can be given by the following formula:

9.3.16 $(\text{if } A, B)^i = \wedge(A^i, \supset(A^e, B^i))$

For details of their treatment of the conventional implicatures of other types of complex sentences, see Karttunen and Peters (1979).

Exercises

1. In each of the following cases, identify whether the proposition indicated in parentheses is a logical implication, a conversational implicature, or a conventional implicature of the given sentence, or none of the preceding.

   a. There was a package on the table. (there was only one package on the table)
   b. There were packages on the table. (there was more than one package on the table)
   c. Tom is a linguist, but he doesn't smoke pot. (linguists usually smoke pot)

2. Give accounts in terms of Gricean conversational implicature of:

   a. Why the slogan *Serving Chicagoland at over twenty locations* conveys that the company in question has fewer than 30 locations in the Chicago area.
   b. Why the sentence *He had a large nose, bushy eyebrows, and a thick black beard* suggests that he had a mustache, while *He had a large nose, bushy eyebrows, and a thick black mustache* suggests that he did not have a beard.

    c. Why *The king and the queen are an excellent battery* is most easily interpreted as implying that the king is the pitcher and the queen the catcher and not vice versa.

    d. Why *a number*, as in *I've been to India a number of times,* conveys "at least three or four," even though 1 is a number, as is 0.

    3. a. Could a proposition simultaneously be logically implied and conventionally implicated by a given sentence? If so, give an example; if not, say why.

    b. What about a proposition being simultaneously logically implied and conversationally implicated by a given sentence?

    4. Sadock (1978) has offered **reinforceability** as a test for conversational implicature: if a proposition is conversationally implicated but is not logically implied by or conventionally implicated by it, one can assert the conversationally implicated proposition without redundancy. For example, there is no redundancy in saying *Some but not all of the culprits were arrested.*

    a. Pick three examples of conversational implicatures and make up examples that will verify whether material can be added (without redundancy) that reinforces the implicature.

    b. Pick three examples of sentences that imply or conventionally implicate (but do not conversationally implicate) some proposition, and make up examples that will verify whether the addition of material that asserts the latter proposition makes the sentence redundant.

    5. Horn (1989:225) argues that *or* usually conveys "exclusive *or*" as a result of conversational implicature: if a speaker utters a sentence *A or B,* he chose to say *or* rather than *and,* and he thus conveys that A and B are not both true, since if they were, cooperativity would have demanded that he say so. Show that this argument is fallacious: that if this reasoning is applied to the full range of *or*-conjoining, the implicature generated by the speaker's choice of *or* rather than *and* will not in general agree with exclusive *or.*

    6. In the discussion of cancellability in note 11, it was stated that *but I'm not going to tell you which* cancels from *Either Truman or Eisenhower was president in 1947* the conversational implicature that the speaker doesn't know which of them was president then. The cancellation here is indirect: the proposition that the speaker knows which one was president isn't part of the meaning of the added clause but is itself a conversational implicature of that clause. Make up examples that will test whether in general it is possible for conversational implicatures of S_2 in S_1 *but* S_2 to cancel out conversational implicatures of S_1.

    7. What is wrong with the following analysis (Grice 1975:53), in which a

conveyed proposition is treated as a conversational implicature resulting from exploitation of the maxim of quality:

> X, with whom A has been on close terms until now, has betrayed a secret of A's to a business rival. A and his audience both know this. A says *X is a fine friend.* (Gloss: It is perfectly obvious to A and his audience that what A has said or has made as if to say is something that he does not believe, and the audience knows that A knows that this is obvious to the audience. So, unless A's utterance is entirely pointless, A must be trying to get across some other proposition than the one he purports to be putting forward. This must be some obviously related proposition; the most obviously related proposition is the contradictory of the one he purports to be putting forward.)

Compare Grice's example with the following two:

a. Tom is visiting Dick's new apartment. The apartment is warm. Dick has just been complaining about the many defects of the apartment. Tom says *Can you open the window?* intending thereby to get Dick to open the window.

b. George and Martha are eating in a Chinese restaurant, talking about baseball. George says *I don't want any soy sauce,* intending thereby to get Martha to pass him the soy sauce, which is on Martha's side of the table.

8. Does a machine that takes English questions as input, chooses an answer by consulting a data base, and prints out the answer in English perform locutionary acts? illocutionary acts? perlocutionary acts? Answer this question first for a machine that is programmed to give answers as accurate as the data base allows for, then for a machine that is programmed to give systematically misleading answers to questions that relate to certain sensitive topics.

10   Presupposition

10.1. Kinds of Presupposition

The word "presupposition" has been used by both linguists and philosophers to cover a class of phenomena that is not obviously homogeneous. Sometimes one speaks of a proposition presupposing another proposition, sometimes of a sentence (in its surface form) presupposing a proposition, sometimes of a person presupposing something in uttering a sentence. Linguists also occasionally speak of a word as presupposing a proposition.

One notion of presupposition that has been studied fairly widely is that of **semantic presupposition,** which is a relation between two propositions and has to do with truth value assignments. It involves an important modification of the notion of assignment of truth values assumed so far, namely, giving up the assumption that a proposition is always either true or false. The possibility of a proposition being neither true nor false is not outlandish; indeed, it is fairly reasonable in the case of propositions like that expressed by 10.1.1a, for which the question of their truth does not arise unless some other proposition (in this case, 10.1.1b) is true:

10.1.1   a. Bush$_i$ regrets that he$_i$ named Noriega attorney general.
        b. Bush named Noriega attorney general.

Let us admit the possibility of valuations in which some propositions are assigned neither the value T nor the value F. As an aid to exposition, let us speak of a proposition having the value # (which I like to read as "Tilt") when it has neither the value T nor the value F. Just as not all assignments of T and F to a set of propositions deserve to be given serious consideration, neither will all assignments of T, F, and #. In particular, a proposition should only be assigned # for a reason, and the constraints on assigning T, F, and # must reflect the reasons for which a proposition could lack a truth value.

One obvious restriction to impose on assignments of T, F, and # is that a proposition is # if and only if its negation is #, that is, that a proposition and its negation have the same presuppositions. Assuming that we are attempting to conform as much as possible to classical logic and thus to avoid assignments in which a proposition and its negation can be simultaneously true or simultaneously false, we arrive at the following truth table for negation:

10.1.2

A	~A
T	F
F	T
#	#

What further modifications must be made in the principles of truth value assignment and in the rules of inference will for the time being be left up in the air. For the moment, I will speak vaguely of "coherent assignments of truth values," meaning roughly assignments of the truth values T, F, # for which (i) the previously presented rules of inference and principles of truth value assignment require only relatively minor modification in order that the rules of inference always lead from true premises to true conclusions even when truth value assignments involving # are allowed, and (ii) # is assigned only to propositions for which there is a reason for them to lack a "real" truth value.

The following definition of semantic presupposition has frequently been offered:

10.1.3   A semantically presupposes B if A $\models$ B and ~A $\models$ B.

That is, A semantically presupposes B if whenever A is true, B is true, and whenever ~A is true (that is, by virtue of 10.1.2, whenever A is false), B is true. "A $\gg$ B" is used to symbolize "A semantically presupposes B." This definition allows for "trivial presuppositions," that is, cases where B fits 10.1.3 because B is true in every state of affairs. For example, if B is "Either there is a Santa Claus or there isn't a Santa Claus," then no matter what A is, whenever A is true, B will be true, and whenever A is false, B will be true, and thus any proposition whatever presupposes that either there is a Santa Claus or there isn't a Santa Claus. For a proposition to have "nontrivial" presuppositions, it must have **truth value gaps,** that is, there must be states of affairs in which it is assigned #. This follows from the fact that if A $\gg$ B and in some coherent assignment of truth values, B is not true (i.e., is either F or #), then in that assignment of truth values, A cannot be either true or false, since if it were true, B would be true (since A $\models$ B), and if it were false, B would be true (since ~A $\models$ B), contrary to hypothesis that B is not true. It should be noted, though, that before we can apply 10.1.3 to any concrete cases, we must specify what is to count as a "coherent assignment of truth values." "A $\models$ B" means "in all (coherent) truth value assignments in which A is true, B is also true," and to determine whether that condition is met one will have to be able to tell whether a given truth value assignment in which B is F or # is "coherent."

There are a variety of linguistic phenomena to which the term "presupposition" has been applied which do not conform to the definition given for semantic presuppositions. For example, 10.1.4 has been said to presuppose rather than imply that the neighbor is female:

10.1.4   My neighbor has hurt herself.

This is not a case of semantic presupposition, since the falsehood of the proposition that the neighbor is female does not make 10.1.4 lack a truth value, nor does it make 10.1.4 false. If the neighbor is a male transvestite whom the speaker takes to be a woman, 10.1.4 is still true or false, depending on whether the neighbor has suffered an injury or not, despite the speaker's incorrect choice of a pronoun to refer to the neighbor. It neither says nor semantically presupposes that the neighbor is female: it rather **pragmatically presupposes** it; that is, the neighbor's being female is a condition on the appropriateness of the use of 10.1.4 rather than a necessary condition for the proposition expressed by 10.1.4 to have a truth value.

The relationship between 10.1.5 and the proposition that the person addressed is called Sam is then also a case of pragmatic presupposition:

10.1.5   You know, Sam, China is industrializing rapidly.

If the addressee is not called Sam, the utterance is inappropriate, though the proposition which it expresses is true or false depending on whether China is or is not industrializing rapidly, regardless of the name of the person to whom the utterance is addressed. Similarly with the relationship between 10.1.6 and the proposition that the speaker has the authority to order the addressee to give him the tapes:

10.1.6   Mr. President, I order you to give me all your tapes.

The proposition that he has such authority is not a necessary condition for 10.1.6 to have a truth value, since only by stretching the terms "true" and "false" could one speak of 10.1.6 as having a truth value (even the truth value #). The way in which those terms might be stretched would be to speak of an occurrence of 10.1.6 as being true if the speaker did in fact thereby order the addressee to give him all the tapes (and either false or truth-valueless otherwise). However, such usage obscures the systematic difference between the presuppositions of 10.1.4−6 and the semantic presupposition of 10.1.1: semantic presupposition is a relationship between two propositions, whereas pragmatic presupposition is a relationship between an utterance and a proposition. In ordinary usage, utterances are not said to be true or false (though propositions involved in those utterances are said to be true or false: recall the discussion of 10.1.4). While one might respond to an utterance of 10.1.5 by saying *That's false*, the *that* would refer not to the utterance but to the proposition that China is industrializing rapidly. Note that according to what has just been said, the presupposition in 10.1.7 that Bush named Noriega attorney general is only a pragmatic, not a semantic presupposition:

10.1.7   Does Bush$_i$ regret that he$_i$ named Noriega attorney general?

This fact may seem worrisome, in that the pragmatic presupposition in 10.1.7 and the semantic presupposition in the corresponding declarative 10.1.1a have exactly the same source, namely the factive predicate *regret*. However, there is no reason why a sentence by which one asserts a proposition having a semantic presupposition cannot also have a corresponding pragmatic presupposition; for example, not only does the proposition that Bush regrets that he named Noriega attorney general semantically presuppose that he named Noriega attorney general, but an utterance in which one asserts that Bush regrets that he named Noriega attorney general will pragmatically propose that Bush named Noriega attorney general.

At least two distinct notions of "pragmatic presupposition" can be distinguished. In addition to the notion that we have just been discussing ("proposition which must be true for the utterance to be "appropriate"), there is a more restricted notion, which figures prominently in Karttunen 1974: an utterance presupposes a proposition if that utterance is acceptable only at a point in a discourse where that proposition is in the set of propositions that the parties to the discourse take as established. For example, an utterance of 10.1.1a pragmatically presupposes 10.1.1b in this sense, since it is only normal for a person to assert 10.1.1a if either 10.1.1b (or propositions entailing 10.1.1b) has been asserted by one of the parties to the discourse and assented to by the others, or 10.1.1b is something that the parties to the discourse recognize as common knowledge. By contrast, *My neighbor has hurt herself* does not pragmatically presuppose that the neighbor is a woman, in Karttunen's sense, since a person can say *My neighbor has hurt herself* even if he knows that the other parties to the discourse do not know the sex of his neighbor. If one of the parties to a discourse cannot assume that the other parties assume that Bush named Noriega attorney general, he can assert that Bush regrets that he named Noriega attorney general only if he first asserts (and gets at least tacit assent from the others) that Bush named Noriega attorney general. However, a person who wishes to say *My neighbor has hurt herself* to a person who does not know the sex of the neighbor does not have to first assert that the neighbor is a woman—indeed it would be rather bizarre behavior on his part if he did. Similarly with the presupposition that the addressee is called Sam in the case of 10.1.5: if the speaker knows that one of the parties to the discourse does not know Sam's name, the speaker is not obliged to introduce that person to Sam before addressing his remark to Sam.

10.2. Some Possible Cases of Semantic Presupposition

Sentences containing *regret, realize, surprise(d), strange,* and a fairly large number of other verbs, predicate adjectives, and predicate nouns which take a clause as subject or object are widely held to presuppose that clause, as in the following pairs of sentences (10.2.1–10.2.4), where the proposition expressed by 10.2.1a can reasonably be held to semantically presuppose that expressed by 10.2.1b, that is, for the first sentence to be either true or false, the second sentence must be true:

10.2.1   a. Cecil is aware that Marcia is pregnant.
　　　　　b. Marcia is pregnant.

10.2.2   a. The Senator$_i$ didn't reveal that he$_i$ had spent the winter in Monaco.
　　　　　b. The Senator spent the winter in Monaco.

10.2.3   a. It's odd that Oliver didn't kiss Pauline.
　　　　　b. Oliver didn't kiss Pauline.

10.2.4   a. The public doesn't realize that Nauru threatens our security.
　　　　　b. Nauru threatens our security.

These elements are known as **factive predicates** and are discussed in detail in Kiparsky and Kiparsky (1970) and Karttunen (1971b, 1971c).

These examples should be contrasted with parallel examples involving other predicates, where the falsehood of the complement sentence does not remove the whole sentence from the realm of truth and falsehood:

10.2.1′   Cecil is afraid that Marcia is pregnant.

10.2.2′   The Senator didn't state that he had spent the winter in Monaco.

10.2.3′   It's likely that Oliver didn't kiss Pauline.

10.2.4′   The public doesn't believe that Nauru threatens our security.

Cecil can be afraid that Marcia is pregnant regardless of whether Marcia actually is pregnant; the Senator can state that he spent the winter in Monaco regardless of whether he actually spent the winter there, and so on. Thus the falsehood of the complement of *afraid, state,* and the like has no direct bearing on whether the whole proposition has a "real" truth value.

Since the publication of Strawson 1950, 10.2.5 has been widely held to lack a truth value, given that there is at present no king of France:

10.2.5   The present king of France is bald.

Example 10.2.5 is then held to presuppose that there is at present a king of France.

Example 10.2.5 is also widely held to be false, which is the position taken in Russell 1905 (whose analysis is discussed above in 7.2), the paper that made 10.2.5 one of the standard examples of the philosophical literature and which Strawson 1950 constituted an attack on. Strawson (1964) takes great care to point out that two distinct issues are raised by 10.2.5: first, is it defective in some way other than that for which the word "false" is normally reserved? and, second, whatever other defects it may have, does it (also) have the defect of falsehood? Strawson recognized that in his initial critique of Russell's theory of definite descriptions he failed to keep those issues separate and incorrectly took his positive answer to the first question as implying a negative answer to the second; that is, he accepted in 1950 but rejected in 1964 the position that all presuppositions (at least in the case of declarative sentences) are semantic presuppositions.

Strawson (1964) observes that one can perfectly consistently say that 10.2.5 is false and in addition has the defect of having a false presupposition. He also points out a number of clear cases in which the existence presupposition that accompanies a definite description is false, yet the whole sentence is false rather than lacking a truth value. For example, suppose that 10.2.6 is uttered in a locality where there is no public swimming pool:

10.2.6   Fred spent yesterday afternoon at the public swimming pool.

The presupposition that there is a public swimming pool is false; yet 10.2.6 is clearly false rather than lacking in truth value. Similarly with 10.2.7, under the assumption that Jenny is a real person:

10.2.7   Jenny is dating the present king of France.

The fact that there is no king of France makes 10.2.7 false rather than lacking in truth value, though it still presupposes (in some sense) that there is a king of France.

What distinguishes cases like 10.2.5, which it is at least reasonable to say lack a truth value, from cases like 10.2.6 and 10.2.7 which are clearly false, cannot be just the fact that the relevant definite description is the subject in 10.2.5 but has another grammatical role in 10.2.6 and 10.2.7. Note that contrastive stress can change the behavior of these examples; for example, in a context in which it has been established that someone is bald, 10.2.8 is false rather than lacking in truth value:

10.2.8   The kíng of Fránce is bald.

This point becomes even clearer if one notes that contrastive stress here has the same function as the "cleft" construction, as in 10.2.9, which has a "real" truth value (namely, false) provided that the presupposition contributed by the cleft construction (that someone is bald) is true:

10.2.9   It's the kíng of Fránce that is bald.

I conjecture that it is the notion of **topic** rather than that of **subject** that determines whether the failure of a presupposition makes a proposition lack a truth value: in 10.2.5, one is saying of the present king of France that he is bald, whereas in 10.2.7, one is saying of Jenny that she is dating the king of France rather than of the king of France that Jenny is dating him, and in 10.2.9 and 10.2.8 one is saying of the propositional function "x is bald" that the king of France is the one element of the given domain that satisfies it. In 10.2.5, one is predicating something of a nonexistent entity, whereas in 10.2.7 one is predicating something (a property which in fact no real object has) of the real person Jenny. However, I will drop this conjecture without making any concrete proposal on how the notion of "topic" fits into logic.

It is worth remarking that the falsehood of the complement of a factive predicate likewise does not always make the whole sentence #:

10.2.10   What Bush$_i$ regrets is that he$_i$ named Noriega attorney general.

Under the assumption that Bush regrets something and that Bush did not name Noriega attorney general, 10.2.10 is false.[1]

Another possible case of semantic presupposition is provided by **implicative predicates** such as *manage, happen, have the foresight/impudence/ . . . , get to,* and the like (Karttunen 1971b, 1971c), which were taken up briefly in 9.3. An alternative way of formalizing the property that characterizes implicative predicates is to say that a predicate f with a sentential argument is implicative if for all propositions A, $f(A) \vDash A$ and $\sim f(A) \vDash \sim A$ (and correspondingly with two-place predicates). For example, if John managed to open the window, it must be the case that he opened it, and if he didn't manage to open the window, it must be the case that he didn't open it. This does not mean that "X managed to do Y" and "X did Y" always have the same truth value: if # is admitted along with T and F as a truth value, the above condition allows A to be T or F when $f(A)$ is #, and one might well want to assign truth values in that way in cases in which the conventional implicature carried by *manage* (roughly, that the person will perform the action if and only if he overcomes some obstacle to performing it) is false. For example, if Mort is sound in mind and body and not being subjected to constraints such as a straightjacket or hypnotism, 10.2.11a would be a weird thing to say even if 10.2.11b were true:

10.2.11 a. At 7:35, Mort managed to scratch his nose.
       b. At 7:35, Mort scratched his nose.

Thus, if one so wishes, one could treat this particular conventional implicature as a semantic presupposition. Other implicative predicates would then bear different presuppositions of the same general form "A will occur if and only if B," e.g., *happen* would carry the semantic presupposition that the given event or state will come about only if chance brings it about, as illustrated in the difference between 10.2.12b, which suggests a strange situation (e.g., the waiter is incompetent at giving change), and 10.2.12a, which does not:

10.2.12 a. The waiter happened to give me the wrong change.
       b. The waiter happened to give me the right change.

Example 10.2.11a in the case where there is no obstacle to Mort's scratching his nose and 10.2.12b in the case where the waiter is willing and able to give the right change are somewhat less clear-cut cases of lack of truth value than were 10.2.5 and sentences in which the complement of a factive predicate is false, but it is still not at all unreasonable to treat them as lacking a truth value. The possibility of treating them as lacking a truth value raises important problems that will be touched on in the next section.

    I will conclude this section by noting that there is no inconsistency between treating implicative verbs in terms of a conventional implicature and treating them in terms of a semantic presupposition. If one follows Karttunen and Peters (1979) in treating sentences as having a two-part logical structure, with one part corresponding to what the sentence "says" and the other to what it conventionally implicates, there will in effect be four possible truth values: T or F for the first component, combined with T or F for the second component. To treat conventional implicatures as semantic presuppositions is in effect to identify # with two-part truth values whose second component is F:

10.2.13   truth values in
      a. scheme of Karttunen and Peters (1979)   b. scheme suggested above
                        (T, T)   T
                        (F, T)   F
                  (T, F) or (F, F)   #

10.3. Supervaluations

Van Fraassen (1969) proposed a treatment of presuppositions based on the idea that valuations in which truth value gaps occur should agree as much as possible with classical valuations: for example, if A is false, then ∧AB ought to be false no matter what truth value B has (thus, even if B is #), and ∨(A, ~A) ought to be true no matter what the truth value of A is (thus, even if A is #). As a means toward implementing this policy, van Fraassen introduced the notion of **supervaluation.** A supervaluation is an assignment of truth values according to which certain propositions are assigned "classical" truth values (T and F) and the remaining propositions are assigned T, F, or # on the basis of what the classical truth tables plus the given partial assignment of Ts and Fs forces on one. Specifically, one considers the set of all classical valuations that assign to the given propositions the agreed upon values; for any other proposition, if those valuations all assign it the same value, we assign it that value, but if those valuations do not all assign it the same value (i.e., some of them make it T and others make it F), we assign it the value #. The formal definition of supervaluation given by van Fraassen is as follows: for any consistent set of propositions X, the supervaluation v_X induced by X (i.e., the assignment of truth values which makes the propositions of X true but makes only as much else true as is forced by the classical truth tables) is the assignment of truth values such that

10.3.1   a. $v_X A$ = T if $X \vDash_c A$ (that is, if every classical valuation which makes all members of X true makes A true).
         b. $v_X A$ = F if $X \vDash_c {\sim}A$ (that is, if every classical valuation which makes all members of X true makes A false).
         c. $v_X A$ = # otherwise (that is, if some of the classical valuations that make all members of X true make A true and others of them make A false).

For example, to assign truth values in such a way that p is T, q is F, and r is #, we use the supervaluation induced by $\{p, \sim q\}$. According to that supervaluation, ∨pr will be T (since any classical valuation that makes p true will make ∨pr true), ∧qr will be F (since any classical valuation that makes $\sim q$ T will make q F and thus will make ∧qr F), and ⊃pr will be # (since, of the classical valuations that make p T and q F, those which make r T will make $\supset pr$ T, and those which make r F will make $\supset pr$ F). Alternatively, we could describe a supervaluation as an assignment of T, F, and # such that T or F is assigned to a complex proposition when those atomic constituents of the complex proposition which are # "don't matter," in the sense that if they were assigned T or F instead, the classical truth tables would assign the whole proposition the same truth value regardless of how the #s were replaced by Ts and Fs.

The notion of supervaluation is a generalization of the notion of classical valuation, in that every classical valuation is a supervaluation. Specifically, for any classical valuation v, define Y as $\{A: v(A) = T\}$. Then one can easily verify that v_Y, the supervaluation induced by Y, is identical to v: there is only one classical valuation that assigns the value T to all members of Y, namely, v, which means that $v_Y(A) = $ T if and only if $v(A) = $ T, and $v_Y(A) = $ F if and only if $v(A) = $ F. However, there are also supervaluations which are not classical valuations, that is, supervaluations in which there are truth value gaps; those will be the v_X for which, roughly speaking, X is not large enough to fix the truth values of all propositions.

Supervaluations give rise to truth tables for the propositional connectives, in the sense that if only supervaluations are allowed as assignments of truth values, only certain combinations of truth values for a complex proposition and for its pieces are possible. Trivially, van Fraassen's system yields the following truth table for negation:

10.3.2

A	~A
T	F
F	T
#	#

This follows from the fact that any classical valuation assigns A and ~A opposite truth values: if some of the classical valuations that make all members of X true make A true and some of them make A false, then the former valuations make ~A false and the latter ones make ~A true, and thus, if A is #, then so is ~A. The truth table for $\wedge$ is

10.3.3

$\wedge$ B A	T	F	#
T	T	F	#
F	F	F	F
#	#	F	F/#

Suppose that for some set X of propositions, all classical valuations that make all members of X true make A false; then all classical valuations that make all members of X true make ∧AB false, regardless of what B is (since a classical valuation makes an *and*-conjunction false whenever one of its conjuncts is false); thus any supervaluation that makes A false will also make ∧AB false, regardless of what B is. Thus Fs appear in all three cells of the second row of the table. Consider the case where some supervaluation v_x makes A T and B #; all classical valuations that make all members of X true make A true, but some of them make B true and others of them make B false; the former valuations make ∧AB true and the latter ones make ∧AB false, which means that v_x makes ∧AB #. Thus the entry in the last cell in the first row is #. In the case of A # and B #, ∧ is non–truth-functional. Consider a supervaluation v_x which makes A # and B #; some of the classical valuations that make all members of X true make A true and some of them make A false, and some of them make B true and some of them make B false. It can't be the case that all classical valuations that make all members of X true will make ∧AB true, since that could happen only if they all made A true and all made B true, which is not the case here. Whether they all make ∧AB false will depend on details of A and B; if A happens to be inconsistent with B, for example, if it is the negation of B, then ∧AB will be false under all classical valuations (even those which don't make all members of X true); however, if A and B are unrelated (e.g., if A is "Bush regrets that he named Noriega attorney general" and B is "The commander-in-chief of the Nebraskan navy plays the bassoon"), some classical valuations will make both true (and thus make ∧AB true) and others will make one or both of them false (and thus make ∧AB false). Thus both F and # are possible values for ∧AB in supervaluations that make A # and B #.

The truth tables for ∨ and ⊃ that emerge from van Fraassen's treatment are as in 10.3.4, which the reader should verify for himself:

10.3.4

In the notion of supervaluation developed in the last couple of pages, no particular restriction has been placed on what propositions can fail to have a truth value: aside from tautologies (which will be true under any supervaluation, since they are true under any classical valuation) and contradictions (which will be false under any supervaluation, since they are false under any classical valuation), any proposition is a potential truth value gap. This may allow too free a use of truth value gaps. In particular, what has been said so far does not require that truth value gaps have **sources** (e.g., factive predicates and other presupposition bearers such as were discussed in section 10.2), nor does it require that sources of presuppositions yield truth value gaps when the presupposed propositions are not true. For example, nothing said so far rules out supervaluations in which propositions corresponding to 10.3.5a–b are assigned the value #, or supervaluations that assign the proposition that Nixon is Jewish the value F but nonetheless assign the propositions corresponding to 10.3.5c–d the value T rather than the # that we would expect:

10.3.5   a. There are unicorns.
         b. If all human beings are mortal, then Socrates is mortal.
         c. Everyone regrets that Nixon is Jewish.
         d. No newspaper reporter realizes that Nixon is Jewish.

Some of these unwanted occurrences of # can be eliminated by supplementing the system of logic with a set of **meaning postulates** for those semantic elements that can be responsible for semantic presuppositions and restricting the class of supervaluations to those that respect those meaning postulates. For a reason that will be made clear shortly, van Fraassen takes these meaning postulates to have the form $A \vDash B$, e.g. the meaning postulates for *regret* might be as in 10.3.6:

10.3.6   a. Regret$(x, p) \vDash p$
         b. ~Regret$(x, p) \vDash p$

Restricting the class of supervaluations to those that respect the given meaning postulates will mean that for any meaning postulate $A \vDash B$, all supervaluations in which A is true but B is either false or # will be excluded from the class of supervaluations that are **admissible** relative to the given set of meaning postulates, and supervaluations that assign a proposition the value # will be allowed only if the meaning postulates and the propositions that are assigned the values T or F force it to have the value #.[2] The suggested meaning postulates for *regret* rule out four of the nine combinations of truth values for Regret(x, p) and p that would otherwise be possible:

10.3.7

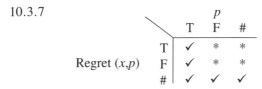

Regret (x,p)	p		
	T	F	#
T	✓	*	*
F	✓	*	*
#	✓	✓	✓

The second and third cells of the first line are excluded by 10.3.6a, which excludes supervaluations in which Regret(x, p) is T and p is not T, and the second and third cells of the second line are excluded by 10.3.6b, which excludes supervaluations in which ~Regret(x, p) is T, i.e., Regret(x, p) is F (cf. 10.3.2), and p is not T.

These meaning postulates guarantee that there will be admissible supervaluations in which p is F and Regret(x, p) is #, since there is nothing to prevent a F proposition from serving as the object of Regret, and 10.3.6a–b respectively exclude T and F as possible truth values of Regret(x, p) in that case. The possibility of p being T and Regret(x, p) being # is not excluded by these meaning postulates, and in fact Regret(x, p) might have other presuppositions besides p and hence other conditions whose failure could make it #. For example, one might wish to recognize a meaning postulate such as Regret(x, p) ⊨ Exist(x) that would allow only existing beings to have regrets. Then a sentence such as 10.3.8 could be held to be # in virtue of the nonexistence of Santa Claus, even though the complement proposition is T:

10.3.8   Santa Claus regrets that Johnson sent more troops to Vietnam.

The ⊨ in the meaning postulates should not be confused with something that it could be mistaken for, namely ⊃. Suppose that we had instead taken the meaning postulates to be as in 10.3.9, that is, suppose we had taken them as allowing only supervaluations in which the corresponding ⊃-propositions were true:

10.3.9   a. ⊨⊃(Regret(x, p), p)
           b. ⊨⊃(~Regret(x, p), p)

The meaning postulates would then exclude precisely the supervaluations that we need to allow if our account of semantic presupposition is to have any substance. Recall the truth table for ⊃ in 10.3.4. If we take Regret(x, p) in the role of A and p in the role of B, then 10.3.9a would exclude not only supervaluations in which A is T and B is not T (i.e., supervaluations corresponding to the second and third cells in the first line) but also the other two classes of supervaluations in which ⊃AB is not true, i.e., those that have the value # in the third line. That would mean that supervaluations in which p was F and Regret(x, p) was # would be excluded. But those are the very supervaluations that we have to allow if Regret(x, p) is ever to have the value # for the reason that is commonly taken to make it #, and thus if we were to accept 10.3.9 rather than 10.3.6 as our meaning postulates, we would rule out a large part of what a theory of semantic presupposition is supposed to account for. It is thus for a good reason that we will follow van Fraassen in taking $\vDash$ rather than $\supset$ as the relation between the formulas that figure in the meaning postulates.

I turn now to a comparison of the relations of entailment that correspond to different classes of valuations and supervaluations. The full set of all supervaluations makes exactly the same propositions valid and makes exactly the same entailments hold as does the set of all classical valuations. Let $\vDash_c$ stand for validity and entailment relative to the classical valuations (i.e., $\vDash_c$ A means that A is true in all classical valuations—"is classically valid"—and X $\vDash_c$ A means that in all classical valuations which make all propositions of X true, A is true—X "classically entails" A), and let $\vDash_s$ stand for validity and entailment relative to the set of all supervaluations. It can easily be shown that $\vDash_c$ A if and only if $\vDash_s$ A. Note first that it is trivially true that if $\vDash_s$ A, then $\vDash_c$ A (every classical valuation is a supervaluation, and thus, if every supervaluation makes A true, then in particular, every classical valuation does), so we need only prove that if $\vDash_c$ A, then $\vDash_s$ A. Suppose that $\vDash_c$ A, and consider any supervaluation v_X. Every classical valuation makes A true, so in particular, every classical valuation that makes all propositions of X true makes A true; but that means that $v_X(A) = T$. Thus, every supervaluation makes A true, that is, $\vDash_s$ A. It can be shown similarly that for any proposition A and any set of propositions X, X $\vDash_c$ A if and only if X $\vDash_s$ A. As before, it is trivially true that if X $\vDash_s$ A, then X $\vDash_c$ A, so all that needs to be shown is that when classical entailment holds, supervaluation entailment holds. Suppose that X $\vDash_c$ A, and let v_Y be any supervaluation that makes all members of X true. Let v be any classical valuation that makes all members of Y true. Then v makes all members of X true (since any classical valuation that makes all members of Y true makes all members of X true—that's what it means to say that v_Y makes all members of X true), and hence $v(A) = T$ (since any classical valuation that makes all members of X true makes A true). But that implies that $v_Y(A) = T$, and thus all supervaluations that make all members of X true make A true, that is, X $\vDash_s$ A.

Van Fraassen distinguished two types of presuppositional system: **conservative** systems, in which only those truth value gaps that are forced on one by the meaning postulates are allowed, and **radical** systems, in which that requirement is not imposed and thus, e.g., 10.3.5d might be # even in a state of affairs in which it is true that Nixon is Jewish. It is conservative rather than radical systems that have clear relevance to linguists' concerns, and aside from this paragraph, I will pay no attention here to radical systems. I note, though, that the supervaluations of any radical presuppositional system form a subset of the set of all supervaluations, and the supervaluations of any conservative presuppositional system form a subset of the set of supervaluations of the corresponding radical presuppositional system; consequently, if $\vDash_S$ A, then $\vDash_{M_r}$ A, and if $\vDash_{M_r}$ A, then $\vDash_{M_c}$ A, where $\vDash_{M_r}$ means "valid relative to the supervaluations of the radical presuppositional system defined by the system of meaning postulates $\mathbf{M}$" and $\vDash_{M_c}$ means "valid relative to the supervaluations of the conservative presuppositional system defined by the system of meaning postulates $\mathbf{M}$." It is not obvious that the converse of either of these statements holds; that is, it is not obvious that validity in a conservative presuppositional system implies validity in the corresponding radical system or that validity in a radical system implies validity relative to supervaluations in general (and thus, classical validity). However, it is difficult to show that those converses fail, since the most obvious candidates for propositions valid relative to one system of supervaluations but not relative to a less restricted system turn out not to be valid in either system. For example, given a system of meaning postulates containing 10.3.6, one might expect a proposition of the form $\supset(\text{Regret}(x, p), p)$ to be valid in the (radical or conservative) presuppositional system but not relative to supervaluations in general. However, $\supset(\text{Regret}(x, p), p)$ turns out to be invalid relative to either of the presuppositional systems, because the presuppositional systems allows for supervaluations in which p is F and $\text{Regret}(x, p)$ is $\#$. Relative to any supervaluation, a conditional whose antecedent is $\#$ and whose consequent is F is $\#$, and hence $\supset(\text{Regret}(x, p), p)$ is not assigned the value T by all supervaluations of the presuppositional system.

While it is hard to determine whether the same propositions are valid relative to a conservative presuppositional system, the corresponding radical system, and supervaluations in general, it is easy to show that the entailments in a presuppositional system are generally not the same as entailments relative to supervaluations in general. For example, for a system of meaning postulates $\mathbf{M}$ that contains 10.3.6, we have $\text{Regret}(x, p) \vDash_{M_c} p$ but not $\text{Regret}(x, p) \vDash_S p$, because while supervaluations in general are not constrained to make p T when $\text{Regret}(x, p)$ is T (indeed, relative to supervaluations in general, those two propositions count as unrelated atomic propositions and thus could be assigned any combination of truth values at all), the assumed system of meaning postulates $\mathbf{M}$ restricts the supervaluations of the corresponding (conservative or radical) presuppositional system to those which make $\text{Regret}(x, p)$ T only if they also make p T.

There is such a discrepancy between what can be proved about validity and what can be proved about entailment because the relationship which linked entailment to validity in the classical case fails in presuppositional systems: $\vDash_{M_c} \supset AB$ is a stronger condition than $A \vDash_{M_c} B$ (and correspondingly with $\vDash_{M_r}$), since for the conditional to be valid there must be no admissible valuation that makes A# and B F, whereas for A to entail B it is immaterial whether such a case exists. Put another way, to say that A entails B in a given presuppositional system is to say that the boxed cases in the following table never arise, whereas to say that $\supset$AB is valid in that system is to say that neither the boxed cases nor the circled cases ever arise:

10.3.10

$\supset$	B		
A	T	F	#
T	T	F	#
F	T	T	T
#	T	#	T/#

The kinds of considerations just discussed make it clear that there are significant discrepancies between classical logic and presuppositional systems with regard to what entailments follow from other entailments. For example, in classical logic, if A $\vDash$ B, then $\sim$B $\vDash$ $\sim$A. This follows from the facts that in classical logic the one entailment is equivalent to $\vDash\supset$AB and the other to $\vDash\supset(\sim$B, $\sim$A) and that in classical logic $\supset$AB always has the same truth value as $\supset(\sim$B, $\sim$A). However, in a presuppositional system (conservative or radical) with meaning postulates **M** as described above, there are formulas A and B such that A entails B but $\sim$B does not entail $\sim$A. For example, we have seen that Regret$(x,$ B) $\vDash_M$ B; however, it is not the case that $\sim$B $\vDash_M$ $\sim$(Regret$(x,$ B), since (assuming that B is not a tautology) there will be supervaluations for which B is F, and with respect to any such supervaluation, $\sim$B is T, but $\sim$Regret$(x,$ B) is #, from which it follows that $\sim$Regret$(x,$ B) is not entailed (relative to the presuppositional system) by $\sim$B.

The last observation is important in understanding a set of facts that might at first glance seem to demand an analysis in which there is a pattern of truth value gaps other than what would correspond to a supervaluation. Recall the discussion of "implicative verbs" in 10.2, where it was suggested that *manage* has a presupposition that an obstacle must be overcome for the subject to carry out the action, and thus that, for example,

10.3.11 a. John managed to put milk in his coffee.
      b. John didn't manage to put milk in his coffee.

would lack a truth value in a state of affairs in which there was no obstacle to John's putting milk in his coffee. The following combinations of truth values would then be possible, using A to stand for "John put milk in his coffee" and mA for "John managed to put milk in his coffee":

10.3.12

A	mA
T	T/#
F	F/#
#	#

(Note that when A is #, mA must be # also; if mA were T or F, then A would be T or F, respectively). The following sentence looks as if it expresses an unassailable proposition:

10.3.13   If John managed to put milk in his coffee, then he put milk in
                his coffee.

However, according to the truth tables for supervaluations, $\supset(m$A, A) does not always come out true:

10.3.14

A	mA	$\supset(m$A, A)
T	T	T
T	#	T
F	F	T
F	#	#
#	#	#[3]

Moreover, if $\supset$AB is true in a given supervaluation, so is $\supset(\sim$B, $\sim$A); this follows from the fact that that is true of classical valuations. However, 10.3.15 does not have the ring of truth to it that 10.3.13 does in that the protasis can clearly be true without the apodosis being true:

10.3.15   If John didn't put milk in his coffee, then he didn't manage to
                put milk in his coffee.

   There are several ways that one might react to these observations. (i) One might reject the idea that *manage* carries with it a semantic presupposition, and thus maintain that the cases where mA is # do not arise. (ii) One might take the facts about implicative verbs as showing that T, F, and # must be assigned in ways other than those which a system of supervaluations allows: that $\supset(m$A, A) must always be T but $\supset(\sim$A, $\sim m$A) need not always be T, in spite of the fact that in a supervaluation treatment, not only is $\supset(m$A, A) not always T, but when it is T, so is $\supset(\sim$A, $\sim m$A). (iii) One might challenge the interpretation of 10.3.13 as $\supset(m$A, A) and instead interpret it as meaning mA $\vDash$ A. I am inclined to rate the third as the most attractive of the three alternatives, and in chapter 15 I will develop a treatment of conditionals along those lines. Note that while the truth of $\supset(m$A, A) insures the truth of $\supset(\sim$A, $\sim m$A) in a presuppositional system, mA $\vDash$ A does not insure $\sim$A $\vDash$ $\sim m$A.

According to 10.3.14, $mA \vDash A$ is true (i.e., in the one case where mA is T, A is also T), but $\sim A \vDash \sim mA$ is not true, since the two cases in which $\sim A$ is T (the third and fourth lines of 10.3.14) include a case in which $\sim mA$ is not T (the fourth line). Thus, the fact that $mA \vDash A$ but not $\sim A \vDash \sim mA$ parallels the fact that one would more readily call 10.3.13 true than 10.3.15.

It is worth recalling that in the preceding chapter we also encountered considerations that suggested that *if* should be interpreted as $\vDash$ rather than as $\supset$. Recall the discussion of example 9.2.15 and the suggestion that, to account for the fact that *It is not the case that if God is dead, then everything is permitted* is not normally taken to imply that God is dead, it may be appropriate to analyze the example as having an understood quantifier in it: "It is not the case that for all states of affairs *w*, if God is dead in *w*, then everything is permitted in *w*." But that suggestion is essentially identical to the suggestion that *if* be interpreted as $\vDash$: the suggested analysis is equivalent to "It is not the case that in all states of affairs in which God is dead, everything is permitted"; that is, it is not the case that "God is dead" semantically entails "everything is permitted" (with the understanding, of course, that this entailment is with regard to some restricted class of possible states of affairs and not with regard to the whole set of classical valuations).

If one were to adopt position ii, however, it would be necessary not only to devise something other than supervaluations as the system for assigning T, F, and # to complex propositions, but also to change the rules of inference so that $\supset(\sim B, \sim A)$ was not in general inferrable from $\supset AB$. The most obvious derivation of $\supset(\sim B, \sim A)$ from $\supset AB$ is the following:

10.3.16

1	$\supset AB$		
2		$\sim B$	supp
3			A	supp
4			B	1, 3 $\supset$-expl
5			$\sim B$	2, reit
6		$\sim A$	3–5, $\sim$-intro
7	$\supset(\sim B, \sim A)$		2–6, $\supset$-intro

The step in 10.3.16 that it seems most reasonable to disallow if nontrivial presuppositions are allowed is step 6, since under the assumptions about implicative verbs which go with proposal ii, there are coherent assignments of truth values fitting the following scheme:

10.3.17

$$\begin{array}{ll} \supset AB & \text{T} \\ \sim B & \text{T} \\ \sim A & \# \end{array}$$

Steps 1 and 2 set up hypotheses that are true relative to such an assignment of truth values. However, step 6 derives a nontrue conclusion from those true premises. One obvious way to weaken the suspect rule of inference, $\sim$-intro, would be to change it from 10.3.18a to 10.3.18b:

10.3.18 a.

$$
\begin{array}{|l}
A \\
\;\cdots \\
B \\
\sim B
\end{array}
$$
$$\sim A$$

b.

$$
\begin{array}{|l}
A \\
\;\cdots \\
B \\
\sim B
\end{array}
$$
$$\sim tA$$

where tA means "A is true" and has the truth table

10.3.19

A	tA
T	T
F	F
#	F

Note that $\sim tA$ would have been innocuous as a deduction from lines 1 and 2 of 10.3.16: it would likewise be true. However, it would not have allowed the deduction of line 7 but only of $\supset(\sim B, \sim tA)$, since there is no way to get from $\sim tA$ to $\sim A$ if nontrivial presuppositions are allowed: $\sim tA$ is true not only when A is F but also when it is #.

10.4. Pragmatic Presupposition

This section is devoted to the notion of a presupposition of a sentence as a proposition which the speaker "takes for granted" when he utters the sentence, that is, a proposition which either has been established in the preceding discourse or the speaker can assume that the parties to the discourse will agree to. I will begin by describing an approach to presupposition which was in fact originally framed in terms of semantic presupposition (i.e., in terms of conditions under which a proposition will lack a truth value), but which developed in a natural way into an account of pragmatic presupposition which can be divorced entirely from considerations of truth value gaps.

Karttunen 1973 is devoted to the question of the conditions under which a proposition of the form $\wedge AB$, $\vee AB$, or $\supset AB$ shares the presuppositions of the constituent propositions A and B. Let us begin with Karttunen's treatment of $\wedge$. Karttunen claims that $\wedge AB$ shares any presuppositions of A; for example, 10.4.1a and 10.4.2a presuppose 10.4.1b and 10.4.2b, respectively:

10.4.1   a. John regrets that he beats his wife, and he intends to reform.
         b. John beats his wife.

10.4.2   a. The king of France is bald and the archbishop of Mt. Isa is deaf.
         b. There is a king of France.

However, Karttunen maintains that whether $\land AB$ shares the presuppositions of B depends on how A and B are related, as illustrated by the difference between 10.4.3 and 10.4.4:

10.4.3   Bush has named Trump secretary of the treasury, and he regrets that he named Noriega attorney general.

10.4.4   Bush has named Noriega attorney general, and he regrets that he named Noriega attorney general.

Example 10.4.3 clearly presupposes that Bush named Noriega attorney general, at least in the sense that it would be improper to say 10.4.3 in a context where one could not take it for granted that Bush named Noriega attorney general. Since Karttunen at that time recognized only semantic presupposition, he accordingly took the position that 10.4.3 was # in any state of affairs in which Bush did not name Noriega attorney general. (Note, of course, that in a supervaluation treatment, the falsehood of the first conjunct of 10.4.3 would make the whole conjoined proposition false rather than #.) By contrast, he took 10.4.4 to be false rather than # when it is false that Bush named Noriega attorney general, despite the fact that, just as in 10.4.3, the first conjunct is false and the second conjunct involves a factive predicate with a false complement. While it is not clear that Karttunen was correct in taking 10.4.3 and 10.4.4 to differ in truth value, they clearly differ with regard to pragmatic presupposition: one could say 10.4.4 even when the proposition that Bush named Noriega attorney general (the presupposition of the second conjunct) was new to the discourse.

Karttunen noted that the behavior of examples like 10.4.4 is shared by examples like 10.4.5a, in which the presupposition of the second conjunct is not identical to but is merely entailed by the first conjunct:

10.4.5   a. Many people admire Nixon, and Nixon is happy that there are people who admire him.
         b. There are people who admire Nixon.

In accordance with his policy that the pragmatic presupposition of 10.4.3 was also a semantic presupposition, Karttunen formulated the following statement of the presuppositions of $\land AB$:

10.4.6 $\wedge$AB $\gg$ C if and only if either
      i. A $\gg$ C or
      ii. B $\gg$ C and it is not the case that A $\vDash$ C.

Karttunen accordingly spoke of *and* as a **filter:** it allows some, but not necessarily all, of the presuppositions of the constituent propositions to be presuppositions of the whole proposition. He contrasts filters with "holes" and "plugs." A **hole** is an element of logical structure that allows all presuppositions of whatever proposition it combines with to be presuppositions of the derived proposition; more explicitly, an element h that combines with propositions is a hole if hA $\gg$ C whenever A $\gg$ C; factive predicates and negation are clear examples of holes. A **plug** is an element p such that the presuppositions of a proposition A that it combines with are immaterial to what (if anything) the presuppositions of pA are; Karttunen considered verbs of saying to be plugs, e.g., *John says that Nixon regrets that he is Jewish* presupposes that John exists, but not that Nixon is Jewish or even exists. Karttunen's claim that these verbs are plugs will be disputed in section 12.1.

The conditions 10.4.6 imply that $\wedge$ has the following truth table:

10.4.7

$\wedge$	B		
A	T	F	#
T	T	F	#
F	F	F	F/ⓗ
#	#	ⓗ	ⓗ

The encircled entries in 10.4.7 are those for which Karttunen's 1973 treatment of presuppositions implies different truth values than does a supervaluation treatment. The entry in 10.4.7 for A T, B # would have to be #, since for B to be #, some semantic presupposition of B would have to fail, and that presupposition would not be entailed by A, since A is true. Note that according to Karttunen's treatment, $\wedge$ is not truth-functional: when A is F and B is #, further details about A and B have to be known in order to tell what the truth value of $\wedge$AB is. In a supervaluation treatment, $\wedge$ is also non–truth-functional, but the deviation from truth-functionality is in a different place: not the case of A F, B #, but the case of A #, B #. When A and B are both # but are mutually contradictory, supervaluations make $\wedge$AB false (because every classical valuation does), but Karttunen's treatment makes it # because of the presuppositional failure in the first conjunct.

Karttunen argued that the same conditions determine what the presuppositions of $\supset$AB are:

10.4.8 $\supset AB \gg C$ if and only if either

    i. $A \gg C$ or

    ii. $B \gg C$ and it is not the case that $A \models C$.

This is supported by the parallelism between 10.4.3–5 and 10.4.9–11:

10.4.9   If Bush has named Trump secretary of the treasury, he regrets that he has named Noriega attorney general.

10.4.10   If Bush has named Noriega attorney general, he regrets that he named Noriega attorney general.

10.4.11   If many people admire Nixon$_i$, then he$_i$ is happy that there are people who admire him$_i$.

Consequently, for Karttunen 1973, $\supset$ has the following truth table:

10.4.12

$\supset$ A	T	F	#
T	T	F	#
F	T	T	T/#
#	#	#	#

Karttunen found it somewhat less clear what the presuppositions of $\vee AB$ were. If one were to hold that $\vee AB$ must have the same presuppositions as $\supset (\sim A, B)$, its presuppositions would be given by

10.4.13 $\vee AB \gg C$ if and only if either[4]

    i. $A \gg C$ or

    ii. $B \gg C$ and it is not the case that $\sim A \models C$.

This rule would imply that 10.4.14a does not presuppose 10.4.14b but that 10.4.14a′ does:

10.4.14 a.   Either Nixon belongs to the Elks or he regrets that he doesn't belong to the Elks.

    a′. Either Nixon regrets that he doesn't belong to the Elks or he belongs to the Elks.

    b.   Nixon doesn't belong to the Elks.

However, $\vee AB$ does not show the striking asymmetry between the conjuncts that $\wedge AB$ does, with regard to presupposition: 10.4.14a′ is not an extremely odd thing to say in a context where one cannot take it for granted that Nixon does not belong to the Elks, though 10.4.15 is an extremely strange thing to say in that (or indeed any other) context:[5]

10.4.15   Nixon regrets that he doesn't belong to the Elks, and he doesn't
           belong to the Elks.

In a later paper (1974) Karttunen leans more toward the policy that $\vee$ is symmetric with regard to presupposition (i.e., that in both 10.4.14a and 10.4.14a′, "Nixon belongs to the Elks" filters out the presupposition of "Nixon regrets that he doesn't belong to the Elks"). Karttunen gives the following example, which more clearly involves such symmetry:

10.4.16 a. Either Bill didn't write any letters, or all of his letters were
            intercepted.
         b. Either all of Bill's letters were intercepted, or he didn't write
            any.

(the presupposition at issue is the presupposition that there were letters from Bill: Karttunen takes *all* as carrying an existence presupposition). Accordingly, Karttunen gave the following alternative to 10.4.13:

10.4.17 $\vee$AB $\gg$ C if and only if either
           i. A $\gg$ C and it is not the case that ~B $\vDash$ C, or
           ii. B $\gg$ C and it is not the case that ~A $\vDash$ C.

The truth tables corresponding to 10.4.13 and 10.4.17 are 10.4.18a and 10.4.18b, respectively:

10.4.18 a.

$\vee$ B / A	T	F	#
T	T	T	T/#
F	T	F	#
#	#	#	#

b.

$\vee$ B / A	T	F	#
T	T	T	T/#
F	T	F	#
#	T/#	#	#

   The following sort of example, which Karttunen 1973 discusses briefly but which plays a more central role in his later papers, creates a problem for the approach just outlined that can be solved only by dealing more explicitly with the relationship of utterances to the contexts in which they are uttered. Given assumptions that the readers of this chapter are likely to share, 10.4.19a no more presupposes 10.4.19b than 10.4.5a presupposes 10.4.5b:

10.4.19 a. Bush has appointed Noriega attorney general, and he regrets that
            he has appointed a deposed dictator to the cabinet.
         b. Bush has appointed a deposed dictator to the cabinet.

However, if the $\vDash$ of 10.4.5 is classical entailment, then in 10.4.19a the condition for "filtering out" the presupposition of the second conjunct is not met:

the proposition that Bush has appointed Noriega attorney general does not classically entail the proposition that he has appointed a deposed dictator to the cabinet, since classical logic and the proposition that Bush has appointed Noriega attorney general do not rule out states of affairs in which Noriega is not a deposed dictator or in which attorney general is not a cabinet post, and in those states of affairs, it need not be the case that Bush has appointed a deposed dictator to the cabinet. The reason that 10.4.19a is normally interpreted as not presupposing 10.4.19b is that people do not determine entailments in a vacuum but bring in any facts that it is reasonable to assume, in this case, the facts that Noriega is a deposed dictator and that attorney general is a cabinet post.

There are two closely related ways in which one might revise 10.4.6 (as well as 10.4.8 and 10.4.13 or 10.4.17 to accommodate the last observation. Either one replaces classical entailment by a more restricted relationship (say, restricting the valuations to those in which the assumed facts are all assigned the value T), or one replaces $A \vDash C$ by the less stringent condition $X \cup \{A\} \vDash C$, where X is the set of propositions that the parties to the discourse can take for granted at that point in the discourse.

Karttunen in fact adopted the latter of these alternatives, though he shortly revised it further by divorcing his account of presupposition from the notion of truth value gap. Specifically, in Karttunen 1974, he restates 10.4.6 and the other conditions in terms of the notion "is acceptable relative to context X," which no longer commits him to saying that utterances with presuppositional failure must lack truth values; that is, his notion of "acceptable relative to context X" is such that a sentence can be unacceptable relative to a context without necessarily lacking a truth value. Note that Karttunen's initial revision, in which he replaced $A \vDash C$ by $X \cup \{A\} \vDash C$, could hardly be an account of semantic presupposition anymore, since, depending on what the speakers take as "established" when 10.4.19a is uttered, the revised condition can be met or fail to be met (and thus, if the account were one of semantic presupposition, 10.4.19a be respectively F or #) even though there is no difference in terms of who appointed whom to what post and who regrets what.

Karttunen (1974) also discusses cases which show that the rules 10.4.6, 10.4.8, and 10.4.13 or 10.4.17 fail to account for the presuppositions of more complex propositions (e.g., propositions in which a $\supset$ and a $\wedge$ are combined) but their failure is readily correctible in a treatment which makes explicit reference to "context." Note that 10.4.20 does not presuppose that Nixon is Jewish and loves his mother:

10.4.20   If Nixon is Jewish, then he loves his mother and he regrets that
           he is Jewish and loves his mother.

However, according to 10.4.6 and 10.4.8 it ought to presuppose that: the apodosis presupposes that Nixon is Jewish and loves his mother (since that is not entailed by the proposition that Nixon loves his mother), but the protasis does not entail the presupposition of the apodosis: the proposition that Nixon is Jewish does not entail that he is Jewish and loves his mother. The fact that 10.4.20 does not presuppose that Nixon is Jewish and loves his mother is due to the fact that the protasis of a conditional provides "extra context" for the apodosis. With the term **context** having the technical meaning of "the set of propositions taken for granted by the participants in a discourse at a given point in the discourse," a sentence A will be acceptable relative to a context X if and only if X entails all propositions that must be taken for granted for it to be normal to utter A.[6] Using "A/X" to indicate that this condition is met, one can restate 10.4.6, 10.4.8, and 10.4.17 as follows:

10.4.21 a. $\wedge AB/X$ if and only if A/X and $B/X\cup\{A\}$.
       b. $\supset AB/X$ if and only if A/X and $B/X\cup\{A\}$.
       c. $\vee AB/X$ if and only if $A/X\cup\{\sim B\}$ and $B/X\cup\{\sim A\}$.

With 10.4.21 it is easy to show that 10.4.20 is acceptable relative to any context that contains (or entails) the propositions that Nixon exists and that Nixon has a mother. The condition $\supset(A, \wedge BC)/X$ is met if and only if A/X and $\wedge BC/X\cup\{A\}$, and $\wedge BC/X\cup\{A\}$ if and only if $B/X\cup\{A\}$ and $C/X\cup\{A, B\}$ (i.e. $C/(X\cup\{A\})\cup\{B\}$). Here, A demands of a context only that it entail that Nixon exists, and the context X, by assumption, meets that demand; B demands of a context only that it entail that Nixon exists and that he has a mother, and the context $X\cup\{A\}$ meets that demand. Proposition C demands of a context only that it entail that Nixon exists and that Nixon is Jewish and loves his mother (this demand being by virtue of the "basic presupposition" carried by *regret*), and the context $X\cup\{A, B\}$ meets those demands, since X meets the first demand and $\{A, B\}$ meets the second.

The condition 10.4.21a corresponds to the observation that the first conjunct of an *and*-conjoined proposition "provides context for" the second conjunct; that is, that what is at issue in considering the acceptability of the second conjunct is not acceptability relative to the context of the entire conjoined sentence (i.e., relative to the propositions that are taken for granted at the moment one begins to utter the sentence) but relative to that context supplemented by the first conjunct. Condition 10.4.21b corresponds to a similar observation about conditionals: that the protasis provides context for the apodosis.

This is as good a place as any to remark on the distinction between "indicative" and "counterfactual" conditionals. In a counterfactual conditional, the protasis usually is inconsistent with the context (i.e., it conflicts with what you are taking for granted). Condition 10.4.21b thus applies only to indicative, not to counterfactual conditionals. The closest analogue to 10.4.21b that would make sense in an account of counterfactual conditionals would be a condition $B/Y \cup \{A\}$, where Y is a maximal subset of X that is consistent with A (i.e., Y is what you get by throwing out as little of X as is necessary to achieve consistency with A). Of course, there will generally be many nonequivalent ways of throwing out propositions so as to achieve consistency with A (for example, if X contains both $\sim p$ and $\sim q$, and $A = \vee pq$, then one could either throw out $\sim p$ or throw out $\sim q$ to attain consistency with A), and how one chooses the Y can affect whether $B/Y \cup \{A\}$. In 13.1 I will briefly discuss an account of counterfactuals along these lines by Rescher (1964) in which the choice of Y is made on the basis of the "degree of confidence" or "degree of attachment" that the speaker has for the various propositions. In Rescher's account, Y is chosen so that not only is it a maximal subset of X consistent with A but the "degree of confidence" in the propositions of Y is maximized (for example, if one had more confidence in $\sim p$ than in $\sim q$, then $\sim q$ would be thrown away and Y would contain $\sim p$).

The "basic presuppositions" associated with the "atomic propositions" may be but do not have to be semantic presuppositions. However, even if they are semantic presuppositions, the pragmatic presuppositions that they contribute to complex sentences need not also be semantic presuppositions; for example, one can take the truth conditions of conjoined sentences to be given by van Fraassen's tables and still take the pragmatic presuppositions of conjoined sentences to be determined by 10.4.21a. In addition, one can take items as contributing pragmatic presuppositions without being committed to ever allowing them to contribute semantic presuppositions; for example, one can take *The king of France is bald* to pragmatically presuppose that there is a king of France regardless of whether one takes it to be false or truth-valueless when there is no king of France. Moreover, while items that contribute semantic presuppositions generally also contribute pragmatic presuppositions, there is a class of factive verbs (the so-called semifactives) that not only are not accompanied by a pragmatic presupposition of the complement but indeed are commonly used to introduce that complement as "new information":

10.4.22 a. I was about to get on the bus when I <u>realized</u> that I had left my briefcase in the office.
   b. After he graduated from college, Bill <u>discovered</u> that most of what he had been taught was nonsense.

10.5. Broad and Narrow Conceptions of Falsehood

In 4.2, we considered the possibility of nonstandard valuations, that is, assignments of truth values which do not conform to the standard truth tables. It was shown there that if a nonstandard valuation is to fit the rules of inference for propositional logic that were given in chapter 3, that is, if the rules lead to true conclusions (relative to the given valuation) whenever applied to premises that are true relative to the given valuation, then there must be false propositions whose negations are false relative to the valuation. I suggested there that the possibility of a proposition and its negation being simultaneously false was not at all outlandish and that it might be reasonable to assign F to both a proposition and its negation when the proposition has a false semantic presupposition. That policy would amount to taking a broader conception of falsehood than is normally taken. Normally a proposition is taken to be false if and only if its negation is true; thus, under that narrow conception of falsehood, if neither a given proposition nor its negation is true, then neither it nor its negation is false, and both the proposition and its negation 'lack any truth value'. The policy suggested in 4.2 involved the broader conception of falsehood, according to which a proposition was false whenever it was not true; under the broad conception of falsehood, if a proposition and its negation both fail to be true, then both are false.

There is thus a precise scheme for translating between valuations involving a narrow conception of falsehood (with possible "truth value gaps") and valuations involving a broad conception of falsehood (where a proposition is false whenever it is not true, and a proposition and its negation may be simultaneously false). Using T, F, # to represent "truth", "falsehood", and "lack of truth value," under the narrow conception of falsehood, and using t, f, to represent "truth" and "falsehood" under the broad conception of falsehood, the correspondence is given by:

10.5.1

Narrow		Broad	
A	~A	A	~A
T	F	t	f
F	T	f	t
#	#	f	f

An interesting question can now be raised. If the truth tables for "broad falsehood" that were established in 4.2 are translated into the narrow conception of falsehood, how will they compare with the truth tables that follow from van Fraassen's supervaluations? Alternatively, how does the set of valuations that conform to the rules of inference of chapter 3 compare with the set of super-valuations defined by the "classical" valuations?

Let us start by translating the truth table for $\wedge$ that was given in 4.2, using only the two truth values t and f,[7] into a truth table involving T/F/#. The "narrow" truth table here takes the same form as the "classical" table:

10.5.2
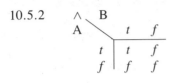

However, that appearance is slightly misleading, since this table covers a broader class of situations than the classical table was envisioned as covering: it covers even cases where A and ~A are both assigned the value f. The translation of this table will be a 3 × 3 matrix of the form

10.5.3
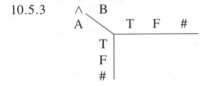

Filling in the nine blanks will involve determining for each situation not only whether $\wedge$AB is "true with a small t" or "false with a small f" but also whether ~$\wedge$AB is "true with a small t" or "false with a small f." The upper left cell will of course be filled by T, since a proposition is true with a small t if and only if it is true with a capital T: when A and B are both T, they are both t, thus $\wedge$AB is also t, and thus $\wedge$AB is T. Let us now turn to the second cell in the top row, that is, the case where A is t, B is f, and ~B is t. The proposition $\wedge$AB will then be f, which means that it will be either F or #, depending on whether ~$\wedge$AB is t or f, respectively. Since ~$\wedge$AB is deductively equivalent to $\vee$(~A, ~B) and by assumption, ~B is t, $\vee$(~A, ~B) will also be t (as a consequence of the rule of $\vee$-introduction) and hence so will ~$\wedge$AB. Thus, the second cell in the top row must contain F. Now let us turn to the last cell in the top row, that corresponding to the case where A is t, B is f, and ~B is also f. Again, $\wedge$AB is f, and thus will be F or # depending on whether its negation is t or f, respectively. At first glance it might appear that both possibilities can occur, since ~$\wedge$AB is deductively equivalent to $\vee$(~A, ~B) and an $\vee$-conjunction of f propositions can be either t or f. However, in this case it can't be t, since if it were, the following inference would lead from true premises to a false conclusion:

10.5.4   1 A   supp
           2 $\vee$(~A, ~B)   supp
           3 | ~A   supp
           4 | A   1, reit
           5 | ~B   3, 4, 3.2.8e
           6 | ~B   supp
           7 | ~B   6, reit
           8 ~B   2, 3–5, 6–7, $\vee$-expl

Thus, when A is T and B is #, $\wedge$AB will be #.

The first line of the truth table under construction thus agrees with the corresponding line of van Fraassen's truth table. In fact the remaining entries also agree with van Fraassen's table; a proof of this is left as an exercise to the reader. Note in particular that both F and # are possible truth values for $\wedge$AB in the case where both A and B are #. This follows from the fact that among the cases where A, ~A, B, and ~B are all f, there are both instances in which ~$\wedge$AB is t (for example, cases where $\wedge$AB is a contradiction and its negation is thus a theorem and hence true, for example, the case of $\wedge(p, \sim p)$) and instances in which ~$\wedge$AB is f (for example, under the valuation which assigns t to all theorems and f to everything else, ~$\wedge pq$ will be f if p and q are atomic propositions).

In fact, the same is true of the truth tables for $\vee$ and $\supset$, as the reader should attempt to verify for himself. (The truth table for ~ of course agrees with van Fraassen's since we set up the correspondence between T/F/# and t/f in such a way that the truth tables for negation would agree). Thus the notion of semantic presupposition that van Fraassen's system formalizes coincides exactly with the notion of semantic presupposition obtained by admitting all valuations that conform to the standard rules of inference and taking a proposition to have failure of semantic presupposition relative to a given valuation if and only if both it and its negation are false relative to that valuation. This perhaps surprising result becomes less surprising if one notes that the valuations that conform to the given rules of inference can be characterized in a way that is parallel to van Fraassen's characterization of supervaluations. Let X be any set of propositions. Define a valuation w_X as follows:

10.5.5   If X $\vdash$ A, then $w_X(A) = t$ (i.e., w_X assigns t to those
           propositions that can be inferred from the premises X by the
           given rules of inference). Otherwise $w_X(A) = f$.

Every valuation that conforms to the rules of inference is a w_X for some choice of X. Specifically, let v be any valuation that conforms to the given rules of inference, and define X as $\{A: v(A) = t\}$. It can easily be verified that $v = w_X$. If the above definition is translated into the T/F/# system, the result is:

10.5.6   If $X \vdash A$, then $w_X(A) = $ T.
              If $X \vdash \sim A$, then $w_X(A) = $ F.
              Otherwise, $w_X(A) = \#$.

This definition is quite parallel to van Fraassen's definition of v_X. They differ only in that where the above definition has "A is deducible from X by the standard rules of inference," van Fraassen's definition has "A is true under all classical valuations that make all members of X true." But the completeness theorem for propositional logic implies that those two conditions are equivalent and thus that $v_X = w_X$: the completeness theorem implies that a proposition is true whenever given premises are true, if and only if it is inferable from them, where the admissible valuations are the classical ones and the rules of inference are those of chapter 3.

10.6. Discourse Referents

In section 7.2, where I criticized Russell's analysis of definite descriptions, I sketched an alternative analysis that made use of a notion of **contextual domain (CD):** the set of entities whose identities are treated as knowledge shared by the participants in the discourse. The notion of contextual domain is in fact quite parallel to the notion of **context** that was introduced in the discussion of pragmatic presupposition in section 10.4. The context and the contextual domain both consist of things that are taken as "known" by the participants in the discourse (propositions in the one case and entities in the other case), both are enlarged as the discourse progresses (propositions that are asserted and not challenged are added to the context, and entities that are referred to are added to the CD), and, I will claim, just as the propositions expressed by the antecedents of conditionals or the first conjuncts of conjoined sentences serve as "extra context" for the consequents or the second conjuncts, so also do the entities that are referred to in the antecedents of conditionals or the first conjuncts of conjoined sentences serve as "extra contextual domain" for the consequents or the second conjuncts. Consider, for example, the sentence:

10.6.1   Last week I went to a concert and a play, and I enjoyed the
              concert much more than the play.

I wish to propose that just as the second conjunct is interpreted relative to a context to which the proposition that last week I went to a concert and a play has been added, it is likewise interpreted relative to a contextual domain to which entities have been added that correspond to the concert and play that 10.6.1 says I saw last week. Specifically, if X is the context and C the CD relative to which 10.6.1 is uttered, then the context and CD relative to which its second conjunct is interpreted will be:

10.6.2   · Context: X ∪ {*a* is a concert, *b* is a play, last week I went to *a*
                       and went to *b*}
          CD:·   C ∪ {*a*, *b*}

Then the referent that will be picked out for *the concert* will be *a* and the referent picked out for *the play* will be *b*.

In this sketch of the interpretation of 10.6.1, I have assumed that the existential quantifiers in the first conjunct will have only the first conjunct as scope, that is, I have assumed a logical form of the type of 10.6.3a and rejected a logical form of the type of 10.6.3b:

10.6.3   a. $\wedge((\exists$: concert $x)(\exists$: play $y)$(last week I saw x and y), I liked the
             concert better than the play)
         b. $(\exists$: concert $x)(\exists$: play $y)\wedge$(last week I saw x and y, I liked x
             better than y)

Since logicians have usually regarded the second conjunct of sentences like 10.6.1 as involving the variables that are bound by the quantifiers that appear in the first conjunct, they have usually adopted logical structures that, as in 10.6.3b, have quantifiers outside of the coordinate structure and binding variables that appear in both conjuncts. The question of the logical form of 10.6.1 is complicated considerably by the presence of the definite descriptions in the second conjunct, and to develop the two suggestions in 10.6.3 into concrete proposals, it would be necessary to supplement 10.6.3a by a concrete suggestion for the logical form of definite descriptions and to supplement 10.6.3b by an account of how the definite descriptions that figure in the surface form of the sentence relate to the variables that logicians wish to have in the logical form of the sentence.

To separate for the moment the question of the scope of the quantifiers from the question of the definite descriptions, consider a sentence in which the second conjunct contains not a definite description but a pronoun having an existential NP in the first conjunct as antecedent:

10.6.4   Last week someone asked me to contribute to the Ku Klux
          Klan, and I told him to go to hell.

Logicians have generally assigned to such sentences a logical form as in 10.6.5a rather than one as in 10.6.5b, in which the repetition of the variable is outside the scope of the quantifier that binds it:

10.6.5   a. (∃: person x)∧(last week x asked me to contribute to the KKK, I told x to go to hell)
         b. *∧((∃: person x)(last week x asked me to contribute to the KKK), I told x to go to hell)

Nonetheless, the suggestion made above about CDs allows one in effect to adopt 10.6.5b as the logical form of 10.6.4, notwithstanding the fact that it violates one of the standard constraints on coherent combination of quantifiers with variables. Strictly speaking, what the policy on CDs allows one to adopt is not 10.6.5b but rather something having in place of the second x a constant that the existential NP in the first conjunct allows one to add to the CD, but one can alternatively simply interpret formulas such as 10.6.5b that way: if a quantified NP allows a corresponding constant to be added to the CD, occurrences of the variable outside the scope of the quantifier are to be interpreted as instances of the corresponding constant when they are interpreted relative to a CD that contains that constant. This policy, incidentally, conforms to the popular informal usage of mathematicians, who will use the same letter for a bound variable in the existential proposition and for a corresponding constant in subsequent propositions, as in the following formulation of the postulates for the notion "group":

10.6.6   A set G with a binary operation · is a group if and only if:
         a. (∀: $x \in G$)$_x$ (∀: $y \in G$)$_y$ ($x \cdot y \in G$) (Closure)
         b. (∀: $x \in G$)$_x$ (∀: $y \in G$)$_y$ (∀: $z \in G$)$_z$ ($x \cdot (y \cdot z) = (x \cdot y) \cdot z$)
            (Associativity)
         c. (∃: $e \in G$)$_e$ (∀: $x \in G$)$_x$ ($x \cdot e = e \cdot x = x$) (Identity element)
         d. (∀: $x \in G$)$_x$ (∃: $x' \in G$)$_{x'}$($x \cdot x' = x' \cdot x = e$) (Inverses)

Note that the quantifier that binds e in 10.6.6c has only 10.6.6c as its scope; the occurrence of e in 10.6.6d figures as a constant (if it were an instance of the same bound variable as in 10.6.6c, it would be a blatant violation of the coherency conditions on bound variables), though in some sense it corresponds to the bound variable of 10.6.6c.

More purist mathematicians will not accept 10.6.6 as it stands: they will insist that before a constant such as the e of 10.6.6d can be employed, a proper baptismal ceremony must be performed, in which defining characteristics of the putative constant are given and it is proved that only one element has those characteristics. In this case, the purist's demands can easily be satisfied: it is easy to show that if a set with an associative operation contains an identity element, then it contains only one identity element. However, the informal practise of less purist mathematicians is of inherent interest, since it corresponds closely to the way that people (mathematicians or not) use existential propositions regardless of whether the uniqueness theorem that a purist would demand can be proved.

In 10.6.6d, the existence and identity of the item written as e are treated as known. The existence of such an element has in fact just been vouched for, that is, 10.6.6c says that there is such an element. The identity of that element need not, strictly speaking, be known, but the participants in a (mathematical) discourse containing 10.6.6 nonetheless take it as known. In doing so, they are doing essentially the same thing as when they participate in a discourse in which one of the participants says 10.6.6:

10.6.7   One day last week a strange person visited me at my office. He wanted me to give money to a home for unemployed philosophers.

The persons who hear 10.6.7 have no idea who the strange fund-raiser is, and the speaker might indeed be unable to identify him in a police lineup. Nonetheless, the hearers cooperate with the speaker by acting as if he could provide a specific referent for his words if called upon to do so and the speaker in effect guarantees referential backing for the *he* of 10.6.7 even though he might not be able to supply it in a form satisfactory to a less charitable interrogator.

The use of the economic term "backing" in the last paragraph is intentional. The relationship between discourse referents and entities is closely parallel to that between paper money and the gold or silver that it originally was redeemable for: discourse referents are issued by someone who commits himself (perhaps irresponsibly or insincerely) to redeem them on demand, they facilitate transactions, and they are traded on a par with the things that they purportedly are redeemable for. This section will be devoted principally to exploring ways in which discourse referents "facilitate transactions" and indeed make possible a broad range of transactions that would otherwise be impossible. Specifically, we will explore ways in which discourse referents can serve to make sense out of certain logical formulas that we have hitherto dismissed as incoherent but which fit certain linguistic facts better than their logically coherent alternatives, and we will show in some detail how a treatment of definite descriptions in terms of discourse referents avoids all of the more serious defects in Russell's treatment.

In 2.4, we considered the proposal (Quine 1960) that *any* is a universal quantifier with wide scope. In the alternative proposal of Klima 1964 and Horn 1972, the *any* that appears in conditional and negative clauses is an existential quantifier with "narrow" scope and arises through a transformation of "*some-any* conversion" that converts an existential quantifier into *any* if it is commanded by an appropriate triggering element such as negation or *if*. Thus, according to Quine's proposal, 10.6.8a has the logical structure 10.6.8b, and according to Klima and Horn's the structure 10.6.8c:

10.6.8   a. If anyone objects, I'll resign.
         b. $(\forall x) \supset (x$ objects, I resign$)$
         c. $\supset ((\exists x)(x$ objects$)$, I resign$)$

That both 10.6.8b and 10.6.8c should be serious candidates for the title of logical structure of 10.6.8a is not surprising, since, as was shown in chapter 3, they are deductively equivalent.

For sentences such as 10.6.9a, Quine's proposal appears to have a decisive advantage over Klima and Horn's, since the pronoun referring back to the quantified NP is inside the scope of the quantifier in Quine's proposal but outside the scope of the quantifier in Klima and Horn's proposal, which thus leads to a violation of the coherency conditions:

10.6.9   a. If any student asks me, I'll tell him the answer.
         b. $(\forall: x$ student$)_x \supset (x$ asks me, I tell x the answer$)$
         c. $*\supset ((\exists: x$ student$)_x(x$ asks me$)$, I tell x the answer$)$

There are, however, linguistic facts that provide support for the Klima and Horn analysis over Quine's and raise some question about whether formulas such as 10.6.9c should be admitted despite their violation of the coherency conditions.

First, there are instances in which an anaphoric device demands as its antecedent the existential clause that figures as a constituent of the Klima and Horn analysis but does not appear in the Quine analysis:

10.6.10   If you find any copies of *Fanny Hill,* I'll give you $10 for one,

but if $\begin{Bmatrix} \text{not} \\ \text{you don't} \end{Bmatrix}$, I'll buy a copy of *Lady Chatterly's Lover.*

The deleted sentence in the first version of 10.6.10 must be "You find copies of *Fanny Hill,*" and the deleted V′ in the second version must be "find copies of *Fanny Hill,*" and each of those constituents demands an existential quantifier in its logical structure.[8] Thus, if the ellipsis in the two versions of 10.6.10 is accomplished through transformations that delete constituents under identity, the two conjuncts of 10.6.10 must both contain occurrences of "You find copies of *Fanny Hill*" in their underlying structure, in which case 10.6.10 has an underlying structure that conforms to Klima and Horn's proposal but not to Quine's.

Second, consider such sentences as

10.6.11 a. If a war breaks out in Uganda, it will spread to Tanzania.
      b. If we have a son, we'll name him Oscar.
      c. Whenever Jack writes a story, he submits it to Playboy.
      d. If blisters develop on the patient's body, you should bandage
          them.

It makes no sense to speak of these sentences as being universal quantifications of "If x breaks out in Uganda, x will spread to Tanzania," "If we have x, we'll name x Oscar," and so on. In each of the sentences of 10.6.11, the *if*-clause involves a verb of coming into being and demands an analysis in which an existential clause ("There is a war," "We have a son," with the stative sense of *have* that figures in *Tom and Betty have three sons*, etc.) is the complement of a predicate such as "come about," and the existential quantifier of that complement clause does not even have the whole *if*-clause in its scope, let alone the main clause as well.[9]

Karttunen's notion of discourse referent can be adapted to the analysis of sentences such as 10.6.9–11 by taking the pronoun in the apodoses of these sentences to correspond not to a repetition of the bound variable of the protasis but to a discourse referent associated with that variable. The discourse referent here is only a temporary addition to the set of constants, or contextual domain: it is available only in the apodosis of the given conditional.[10] The contextual domain then behaves very much the way that the context did in Karttunen's treatment of pragmatic presupposition: the apodosis of a conditional is interpreted relative to a temporarily augmented context (the protasis is temporarily added to the context) and a temporarily augmented contextual domain (discourse referents corresponding to entities that the protasis says exist are temporarily added to the CD).

I turn now to definite descriptions and the defects in Russell's analysis of them. The innocuous-looking definite description in 10.6.12a corresponds to the Russellian analysis in 10.6.12b:

10.6.12 a. The dog is barking.
      b. $(\exists x)\wedge(\text{Dog } x, (\forall y)\supset(\sim = yx, \sim \text{Dog } y), x \text{ is barking})$

One point about 10.6.12b is immediately suspicious: it logically implies that there is only one value of x that makes "Dog x" true, whereas 10.6.12a does not imply that there is only one dog. An adherent of Russell's analysis might counter that observation by saying that Russell's analysis allows the universe of discourse to be chosen in any way and 10.6.12b is unobjectionable as an analysis of 10.6.12a as long as one interprets it relative to a universe of discourse containing only one dog. However, that response is unsatisfactory, since it is possible to use *the dog* in combination with expressions whose normal interpretation would require a universe of discourse that contains more than one dog:

10.6.13 a. The dog likes all dogs.
      b. The dog was barking at another dog.

The Russellian formula for 10.6.13a has the same truth conditions as that for *The dog likes himself,* even though 10.6.13a obviously says something very different, and the one for 10.6.13b is self-contradictory (since it contains a term implying that there is no dog other than the given one and a term implying that there **is** a dog other than that one), even though 10.6.13b says something that could easily be true. Restricting the universe of discourse so that it contains only one dog allows one to make *the dog* pick out the one dog that one intends it to refer to, but it prevents one from saying anything about that dog's relationship to other dogs.

The problem with Russell's analysis that 10.6.13 reveals is that in Russell's framework, all bound variables have the same domain and thus the variables that serve to identify a referent for the definite description (the x and y of Russell's formula) must range over exactly the same values as does a variable that is bound by a normal quantifier such as the universal quantifier of 10.6.13a and the existential quantifier of 10.6.13b. The most obvious alteration in Russell's treatment that would avoid that problem would be to allow the variables that figure in the analysis of the description to have a different domain from "normal" variables, and if one supplements the Russellian analysis with the notion of contextual domain, taking the CD to be the domain over which the x and y of Russell's formula range, while normal variables continue to range over the universe of discourse, the problem raised by 10.6.13 is solved: even if the CD contains only one dog, the universe of discourse can contain arbitrarily many dogs.

Russell's analysis of definite descriptions cannot be adapted in any straightforward way to plural definite descriptions (as was noted in 7.2) nor to mass definite descriptions:

10.6.14 a. The dogs are barking.
      b. The milk is in the refrigerator.

For example, if one were to apply Russell's analysis to 10.6.14b in the most obvious way, with "*x* is milk" in the role of "*x* is king of France" and "*x* is in the refrigerator" in the role of "*x* is bald," the resulting formula would be false for a reason that has nothing to do with the truth of 10.6.14b, namely the fact that quantities of milk can be divided into smaller quantities of milk: if anything at all is milk, then many things are milk, namely all of the quantities that one obtains by subdividing the given quantity of milk, and thus there can't be only one value of *x* that makes "*x* is milk" true, as the Russellian formula demands. Note, though, that that problem does not normally arise if the values of *x* with which one seeks to satisfy "*x* is milk" are taken from the CD rather than from the whole universe of discourse: a given quantity of milk can be a member of the CD without any of its parts necessarily belonging to the CD, and thus one can have a CD that contains only one quantity of milk (which would be identified as the referent of *the milk* in 10.6.14b) while still recognizing that any quantity of milk can be subdivided into smaller quantities of milk.

We can say essentially the same thing about plural definite descriptions provided we say that a plural definite description has a set as its referent (in the case of 10.6.14a, a set of dogs) and that sets just as well as individuals can be members of the CD. Note that, according to our understanding of CD (namely that its members are the entities whose identities count as known at the given point of the discourse), a set can be a member of the CD without its members being members of the CD. For example, there may be a set of dogs (namely, the ones that my upstairs neighbor keeps in his apartment) whose identity counts as known in a given discourse even though there is no member of that set whose identity counts as known (I can't identify individual dogs in the set and don't even know how many of them there are). If there is exactly one set of dogs that is a member (NB, not a subset) of the CD, that set will be picked out as the referent of *the dogs*.

An important respect in which what I have said in the last few paragraphs is an oversimplification is that a definite description clearly can have a determinate referent even in cases where the CD contains more than one entity of the given kind. Indeed, as David Lewis (1979) has pointed out, it is possible for the same definite description to have different referents at different points in the same discourse, as in 10.6.15, where the first occurrence of *the dog* would normally be taken as referring to my dog and the second as referring to the other dog:

10.6.15   When I took the dog for a walk last night, he started barking at another dog. When the dog barked back at him, I was afraid they were going to have a fight.

The possibility of a definite description picking out one referent in one sentence and a different one in the next sentence suggests that the CD is not as unstructured as I have been taking it to be but that there is rather a relationship of relative "salience" among members of the CD, with more salient members of the CD being more available to serve as the referent of a definite description than less salient members. At the beginning of 10.6.15, there may be only one dog in the CD, but the main clause of the first sentence introduces a second dog into the CD and that dog is at that point more salient in the CD than the first dog. The second occurrence of *the dog* is interpreted relative to a CD that contains two dogs, and it takes the second of them as its referent.[11]

While the contextual domain has figured centrally in the discussion of the last couple of paragraphs, the context (in Karttunen's sense) has not. There is in fact one important respect in which the context plays a role in the interpretation of definite descriptions. I have spoken of the interpretation of the definite NP *the dog* as involving a search through the contextual domain for an entity that "is a dog." But does this mean "is a dog really" or perhaps rather "is a dog according to the context"? This difference will be important in cases where there is a discrepancy between what is the case and what is treated as established, as in Donnellan's (1966) celebrated example:

10.6.16   The man in the corner with the martini in his hand has just been hired at Stanford.

One could very well interpret 10.6.16 as picking out a certain person and saying that that person has just been hired at Stanford, even if that person really had a daiquiri or even a glass of chicken soup in his hand. It would in fact be so interpreted as long as the speaker and addressee(s) take as established (most likely, as background knowledge) that that person has a martini in his hand. If the utterer of 10.6.16 and his hearers later discover that Schwartz, the person whom they had taken to have a martini in his hand, was really drinking a daiquiri and that another person in the same corner, Gonzalez, whom they had taken to be drinking coffee, was really drinking a martini out of a coffee cup, they would not then take the speaker to have asserted that Gonzalez had been hired at Stanford, and the speaker would not be expected to recant 10.6.16. Thus, at least in some cases, for an element a of the contextual domain to be picked out as referent of a definite description ($\imath x\colon fx$), what is necessary is not that fa be true but that $X \models fa$, where X is the context. For the moment, subject to later revision, let us assume that that is always the case.[12]

According to what was said about temporary augmentation of the contextual domain, it ought to be possible to get not only pronouns, as in 10.6.9–10.6.11, but also definite descriptions in the apodosis of a conditional sentence that refer back to an existential NP in the antecedent, since the discourse referent temporarily added to the contextual domain is then there to be found in the search for a referent for a definite description. Sometimes the definite description is awkward, probably because a simple personal pronoun would have done as well, but in many cases it is perfectly natural, especially in cases where it would not be clear which of two or more NPs would be the antecedent if a pronoun were used, as in 10.6.17c:

10.6.17 a. ?If a student asks me, I'll tell the student the answer.
          b. If a war breaks out in Uganda, the war will spread to Tanzania.
          c. If a motorcycle collides with a truck, the motorcycle is usually damaged worse than the truck.

Even if 10.6.17c is uttered relative to a CD that contains no motorcycles or trucks, it is still interpretable, in virtue of the temporary addition to the CD of two entities, one a motorcycle and the other a truck, that are available for the interpretation of the definite descriptions in the consequent of 10.6.17c. Specifically, the interpretation will proceed as follows. Prior to the uttering of 10.6.17c, there will be some context X and some CD C. The interpretation of the consequent will be relative to the following context and CD:

10.6.18   Context: X $\cup$ {a is a motorcycle, b is a truck, a collided
                          with b}
        CD: C $\cup$ {a, b}

The referent that will be picked out for *the motorcycle* will then be a and the referent picked out for *the truck* will be b. If C does contain a motorcycle and/or a truck (as it might if 10.6.17c were a father's admonition to his biker son to be careful when sharing the road with trucks), the interpretation will proceed in the same way, provided we make one stipulation about the relation of relative salience, about which we have so far made no explicit assumptions: let us stipulate that temporary additions to a CD (such as the a and b of 10.6.18) count as more salient than all elements hitherto belonging to the CD. Then a and b will be the most salient motorcycle and the most salient truck in the CD relative to which the definite descriptions are evaluated and will thus be picked as their referents. The same treatment covers 10.6.19:

10.6.19   If a Kawasaki collides with a three-axle semi, the motorcycle is usually damaged worse than the truck.

Provided that X contains the proposition that Kawasakis are motorcycles and the proposition that three-axle semis are trucks, a and b will be the most salient elements of the enlarged contextual domain for which the enlarged context entails that the one is a motorcycle and that the other is a truck, and thus they will be picked out as the referents of the two definite descriptions.

Since the treatment in 10.6.18 covers any choice of *a, b* that makes "a motorcycle collides with a truck" true, it implies that no matter what motorcycle and truck collide, the motorcycle is damaged worse than the truck. Thus, this treatment implies that 10.6.17c has truth conditions similar to those of the universally quantified formula (e.g. $(\forall: \text{Motorcycle } x)(\forall: \text{Truck } y) \supset (x$ Collide y, x is damaged worse than y)) that logicians commonly give as its logical form. The correspondence is not exact, because of the word *usually,* which I have so far ignored. *Usually* incorporates a quantifier whose domain is possible events, i.e., 10.6.17c means something like "Among events in which a motorcycle collides with a truck, it is usual for the motorcycle to be damaged worse than the truck." Thus, strictly speaking, it is inaccurate to follow the common practise of logicians and assign to sentences like 10.6.17c a logical form as a universally quantified proposition in which the domains of the universal quantifiers are, say, motorcycles and trucks: the apparent universal interpretation of *a motorcycle* and *a truck* is merely a side effect of the near-universal quantifier (*usually*) whose domain is one of possible events. Moreover, it is necessary to posit a narrow scope existential quantifier in order for the V' *collide with a three-axle semi* to meet the identity condition for V'-pronominalization in sentences such as *If a Kawasaki collides with a three-axle semi, as my cousin's bike did last week, the motorcycle is usually damaged worse then the truck,* in which the understood repeated V' has to be interpreted as containing an existential rather than a universal quantifier.

The discussion so far has been confined to cases where the discourse referent corresponds directly to an existentially quantified variable. In fact, in many cases the discourse is related only very indirectly to entities that have been explicitly introduced in prior discourse. Consider, for example, the sentences

10.6.20 a. The last time I ate here, I had to wait 15 minutes before the waiter brought me the check.
      b. Whenever I teach freshman algebra, the girls do better than the boys.
      c. If there's a war between Kenya and Uganda, the winner will probably invade Tanzania.

To utter 10.6.20a, it is not necessary that there have been any prior mention of a waiter or of a check. The relevant background information relates not to the specific waiter and the specific check to which 10.6.20a refers but to the way in which a waiter and a check figure in typical events of eating in a restaurant. Such information is referred to by Schank and Abelson (1977) as a **script,** and in many cases it does in fact take the form of a skeletal scenario, giving the normal sequence of events and a description of the roles of the various persons and objects that figure in those events. By virtue of one's knowledge of a "restaurant script," one will know that a waiter and a check figured in the event described as *the last time I ate here.*[13] The reference to teaching freshman algebra in 10.6.20b makes available a discourse referent corresponding to the pupils in the class. The two NPs *the girls* and *the boys* refer to subsets of that set. The participants in the discourse need not have established yet that in any algebra class taught by the speaker of 10.6.20b there will be both boys and girls. By contrast, if 10.6.20b had ended with *the Zulus do better than the Fijians,* it would have to have been established previously that the classes contain both Zulus and Fijians. Clearly the fact that it is normal for a high-school class to contain both girls and boys is responsible for the acceptability of 10.6.20b.

In this section I have ignored entirely those examples that seem to fit Russell's analysis best—those that involve no reference to an entity whose existence and identity have been established in the discourse but do involve commitment on the part of the speaker to the proposition that there is one and only one entity fitting the given description:

10.6.21 a. The solution to this equation is greater than 43 and less than 107.
　　　　 b. The person who wrote these instructions is an imbecile.
　　　　 c. I'm still looking for the person who stole my guitar.

There is a way of dealing with sentences like 10.6.21 within the framework of this chapter that is in some respects close to Russell's approach. Suppose that we generalize the notion of "relative salience" so as to turn the members of the universe of discourse that do not otherwise belong to the CD into peripheral members of the CD: they will count as belonging to the CD but as being less salient than all elements that belong to the CD as we have hitherto understood that notion. Then if a search for the referent of a definite description fails to find one in the CD proper, it will continue to search for one in the remainder of the universe of discourse. This suggestion agrees with Russell's analysis to the extent that, when the CD proper does not provide a referent for a given definite description, a referent is found if and only if exactly one member of the universe of discourse has the given property; it differs from Russell's account in that it provides no truth value for the proposition in cases where that search fails, that is, where no element or more than one has the property (e.g., where there is no king of France or there is more than one).

Russell's treatment of definite descriptions would then take on the status of a default mechanism that is activated when definite descriptions are not interpretable in terms of the CD proper. It should be added that the treatment of definite descriptions presented here is close to the spirit of much work in "procedural semantics" (e.g., Miller and Johnson-Laird 1976), in which meanings are given in the form of algorithms (not always deterministic algorithms) for identifying objects and determining truth values, typically algorithms involving searches through structured domains.

I turn finally to a class of sentences, first dealt with by Geach (1962:143) but not widely discussed in the linguistic literature until the 1980s, in which, as in the examples above that were used to motivate the notion of "discourse referent," the most obvious logical form to propose is one in which the variable bound by an existential quantifier is outside the scope of that quantifier:

10.6.22 a.   Any man who owns a donkey beats it.
         a′. $(\forall: \wedge(x \text{ Man}, (\exists: y \text{ Donkey})_y(x \text{ Own } y))_x (x \text{ Beat } y)$
         b.   Some man who owns a donkey does not beat it.
         b′. $(\exists: \wedge(x \text{ Man}, (\exists: y \text{ Donkey})_y(x \text{ Own } y))_x \sim(x \text{ Beat } y)$

Much of the literature on such **donkey sentences,** as they have come to be called, is concerned with the question of their truth conditions, especially in connection with the question of what a sentence like 10.6.22a implies about a man who owns more than one donkey (does a man who owns three donkeys have to beat all three of them for 10.6.22a to be true?). I will sidestep that question, noting that the availability of such alternatives as *Any men who own donkeys beat them,* which more clearly allow for an owner owning multiple donkeys, may cause 10.6.22a to suggest that each owner owns only one, which would increase the difficulty of deciding what 10.6.22a implies about situations in which there are individuals who own more than one donkey.[14] Once again, analyses in the spirit of Quine's treatment of *any* in examples like 10.6.9a as a wide-scope universal quantifier have occasionally been proposed, e.g., an analysis of 10.6.22a with *a donkey* as a wide-scope universal quantification (10.6.23a′), but such a proposal is not viable, first, because it conflicts with the fact that for the purposes of such rules as V′-deletion, as in 10.6.23b, *own a donkey* in 10.6.22a counts as identical to occurrences of *own a donkey* that have a narrow-scope existential quantifier, and second, because the resulting formula has hopelessly incorrect truth conditions if the quantifier on *man* is not universal or existential (10.2.23c):

10.6.23 a.   Any man who owns a donkey beats it. (= 10.6.22a)
         a′. $(\forall: y \text{ Donkey})_y (\forall:\wedge(x \text{ Man, x Own } y))_x(x \text{ Beat } y)$

    b.   Any man who owns a donkey beats it, and any man who doesn't $\emptyset$ beats his wife.

    c.   Most men who own donkeys beat them.

    c.$'$ $(\forall{:}y \text{ Donkey})_y \text{ (most: } \wedge(x \text{ Man, } x \text{ Own } y))_x \text{ } (x \text{ Beat } y)$

For example, for 10.6.23c to be true, sufficiently many men who own donkeys have to beat them, but 10.6.23c$'$ says for each donkey, most of the men who own it beat it, irrespective of how many donkey-owners beat their donkeys.

    What we need to assimilate these examples to the treatment of definite descriptions given here is essentially what we did with examples 10.6.17 and 10.6.19, though spelling it out will require adopting an explicit policy as to how the context and CD function in the interpretation of quantified sentences. Consider interpreting, relative to a context X and a CD C, any quantified sentence of the form $(Q{:} Fx)_x \text{ } Gx$, where Fx and/or Gx may well be complex, e.g., Fx might itself be existentially quantified and Gx might contain a definite description operator. For each value of x that meets the domain condition Fx, an interpretation has to be given to Gx. Suppose that we treat Gx as being interpreted relative to the context X and the contextual domain C, supplemented by whatever Fx would cause to be added to a context and to a CD if it were simply asserted. In terms of 10.6.22a$'$, this would mean that "x Beat y" would be interpreted relative to the following context and CD:

10.6.24   Context: $X \cup \{x \text{ Man, } a \text{ Donkey, } x \text{ Own } a\}$
           CD: $C \cup \{x, a\}$

To obtain from this a plausible interpretation of 10.6.22a$'$, all we need now is a convention that, in cases such as that of 10.6.22a$'$, where the matrix S (here, "x Beat y") involves a variable that is existentially quantified in the domain expression, the matrix S will be given an interpretation in which that variable is interpreted as the counterpart of the existentially quantified variable that was added to the CD (thus, "x Beat y" will be interpreted as saying that x beats a). Where there is a definite description in the matrix S, the definite description will then be interpreted relative to the enlarged context and CD, as in the case of 10.6.23b, where for each value of x the CD will contain a donkey and a goat that will have been added temporarily to the CD, and *the donkey* and *the goat* will be assigned those two entities as referents. This proposal comes very close to that of Neale (1990), who gives a treatment of donkey sentences that is very like Karttunen's treatment of Bach-Peters sentences, with the pronoun treated as derived by a pronominalization process from an underlying definite description (e.g., 10.6.22a is treated as an optional variant of *Any man who owns a donkey beats the/whatever donkey he owns*); it at least is set up in such a way that it insures that 10.6.22a will imply that any man who owns a donkey beats whatever donkey he owns. The main difference is that the approach sketched here allows the normal procedure for the interpretation of definite descriptions to apply automatically to donkey sentences in which the problematic element is not a pronoun but a definite description.[15]

Exercises

1. In each of the following pairs, sentence (i) has at some time or other been claimed to "presuppose" the proposition expressed by sentence (ii). In each case, identify what sort(s) of presupposition, if any, is/are involved, and justify your claim. (Underlines indicate elements that have been held responsible for the alleged presupposition):

    a. (i) John has <u>stopp</u>ed beating his wife.
        (ii) John used to beat his wife.
    b. (i) The vacuum cleaner is working <u>again.</u>
        (ii) The vacuum cleaner once was working and subsequently was not working.
    c. (i) <u>Have</u> you visited the Monet exhibition?
        (ii) It is possible for you to visit the Monet exhibition.
    d. (i) Tom <u>ordered</u> Mary to shine his shoes.
        (ii) Tom has the authority to give Mary orders.
    e. (i) Mary <u>accused</u> Bill of writing the letter.
        (ii) It was bad to write the letter.

2. It is sometimes stated (Horn 1969) that the following example presupposes that Muriel voted for Hubert:

Only Muriel voted for Hubert.

Write about one page on the question of what is presupposed by sentences involving *only,* mentioning all examples of *only* that appear in section 9.2 and the exercises for chapter 9, with attention to the question of whether it is possible to give a uniform statement of what is presupposed by *only-*sentences.

3. A definition of "presupposition" that figures in some linguistic literature is that a *sentence* S presupposes a proposition *p* if uttering S and uttering the

negation of S both commit the speaker to p. Write one to two pages comparing this notion of presupposition with the others discussed in this chapter, with regard to (a) the circumstances in which the criterion can be applied, (b) which of the well-known supposed instances of presupposition it would classify as being presuppositions, and (c) any other important issues.

4. According to the supervaluation that assigns the values p T, q F, r #, what is the truth value of

  a. $\supset(\wedge\, pr, \vee qr)$
  b. $\wedge(\supset rq, \supset(\sim p, \sim r))$
  c. $\vee(\supset(p, \wedge(\sim q, r)), \supset(q, \wedge(\sim p, r)))$

5. Making obvious assumptions about what pragmatic presuppositions the component sentences have, determine for each of the following sentences according to 10.4.21 what a context must contain in order for it to be a normal thing to say relative to that context:

  a. If Bush managed to seduce Thatcher, then he's proud that he seduced her.
  b. Nixon was a KGB agent during the 50s, and if he has stopped working for the KGB, he is secretly proud that he is a former KGB agent.

6. For each of the following sentences, suggest what background knowledge could **plausibly** be part of a context relative to which the sentence would be acceptable relative to 10.4.21:

  a. It rained this morning and the roads are <u>still</u> wet.
  b. John has written a sonnet, and he's put a stupid pun in <u>the 13th line</u>.
  c. If Bob has any children, it's <u>appalling</u> that none of them visited him while he was in the hospital.

The underline indicates the element whose presupposition is at issue (NB: *appalling* is a factive predicate). In doing this exercise, pay particular attention to considerations of plausibility, e.g., it is plausible that the mutual knowledge of the parties to a discourse would include the proposition that the United States consists of 50 states, but it is not plausible that it would include the proposition that the United States consists of at least 37 states, even though that is something that, in a sense, everyone who knows that the United States consists of 50 states would know.

7. Fill in the missing parts of the partial proof given in section 10.5 that supervaluations yield the same truth tables as does the approach given in section 4.2 in terms of a broad conception of falsehood.

8. Describe informally how scripts figure in the interpretation of the following sentences:

   a. When a pronoun has a quantified NP as its antecedent, logicians generally represent it as a repetition of the bound variable.
   b. When Ted was driving home yesterday, he had to step on the brake suddenly and his head went through the windshield.

9. For each of the following sentences, sketch its logical form (going into no more detail than is relevant) and say what the context and CD are that figure in the interpretation of each of the component Ss, assuming that it is uttered relative to a context X and a CD C:

   a. If someone tells scandalous lies about you, you should demand that he retract them in public.
   b. If two lawyers collaborate on a lawsuit and one of them has just lost an important case, the other one will try to get him to take a smaller fee.

11 Modal Logic

11.1. Notions of Necessity

The term "modal logic" takes in the logic of notions of "necessity" and "possibility," but there is no real consensus on what else it takes in; it is sometimes used so broadly as to take in the whole of logic that is not taken in by predicate logic and sometimes so narrowly as to take in nothing more than "necessity" and "possibility" (in combination with the expressive material of propositional logic and predicate logic). In any event, notions of necessity and possibility have been of central interest in everything that has been called modal logic, and it is thus fitting for us to start our treatment of modal logic by concentrating on those notions.

The terms "necessity" and "possibility" are in fact used in quite a large number of ways. The following is a sample of the notions of necessity that can be distinguished:

A proposition is **logically** necessary if the given system of logic insures that it will be true; for example, the proposition that there either is a planet made of green cheese or is no planet made of green cheese is logically necessary.

A proposition is **epistemically** necessary if it has to be true, given what we already know. Thus, the proposition that J. S. Bach was 40 years old in 1725 is epistemically necessary, given that we know that Bach was born in 1685 and did not die until 1750, though it is not logically necessary. If we consider the constraints imposed not by the whole of our knowledge but by some specific area of our knowledge, we obtain other notions of "necessity" that are basically variants of "epistemic necessity," such as "physical necessity," which applies to propositions that have to be true, given what we know about the laws of physics and about the physical makeup of the world. The proposition that if a person jumps off the Empire State Building he will fall is physically necessary; the proposition that if a sane adult jumps off the Empire State

Building he will expect to die from the fall is epistemically necessary but not physically necessary.

A proposition is **morally** necessary for a given person if he will be at fault unless he sees to it that that proposition is (or becomes) true.

A proposition can be (though usually is not) called "**temporally** necessary" if it is true at all times.

While these notions of necessity obviously are not equivalent, they nonetheless have a lot in common. If asked to say what they have in common, the best answer I could come up with at the moment would be: in each case, to say that the proposition is necessary is to say that something would be anomalous if that proposition were not the case. The different notions of necessity correspond to different notions of anomaly: the anomaly of a breakdown in the assumed system of logic, the anomaly of a proposition being true which conflicts with what we already know, the anomaly of a state of affairs prevailing even though it conflicts with our code of morality, or the anomaly of something which is always true not being true. Any notion of "anomaly" divides "states of affairs" into two types: anomalous states of affairs and nonanomalous states of affairs. In section 4.2 we have already made use of a distinction between anomalous and nonanomalous states of affairs: we consider an extremely broad notion of state of affairs (i.e., any assignment of the values T and F to all propositions of the given language was a "state of affairs") and distinguished between those states of affairs which conformed to the given rules of inference (i.e., those states of affairs such that any conclusion obtained by applying the rules of inference to premises that are true in that state of affairs is also true in that state of affairs) from those that did not conform (i.e., those states of affairs in which there was a false conclusion that could be inferred from true premises by the given rules of inference). To say that some proposition fails to be true only in an anomalous state of affairs is to say that it is true in all nonanomalous states affairs. Thus, for example, a system R of rules of inference determines a notion of necessity N_R: a proposition is necessary relative to R if and only if it is true in all states of affairs that conform to R.

To say that a proposition is necessary if it is true in all nonanomalous states of affairs is essentially to repeat a characterization of necessity popularly attributed to Leibniz: a proposition is necessary if it is true in all possible worlds.[1] Our "nonanomalous" corresponds to Leibniz's "possible" and our "state of affairs" corresponds to Leibniz's "world." Since the publication in 1959 of Saul Kripke's remarkable paper, "A Completeness Theorem in Modal Logic," the term "possible world" has been reinstated in the normal vocabulary of logicians, and I will in fact from now on feel free to use the term, keeping in mind, however, that it is composed of the two words "possible" and "world" and that "possible" means "nonanomalous," and thus its interpretation varies, depending on what notion of "anomaly" one might happen to be discussing.

Let us adopt the standard practise of writing □ to stand for "necessary," irrespective of the specific kind of "necessity" that is at issue. We can then form expressions containing □ and ask under what interpretations of □ those expressions will be true. For example, consider the formula

11.1.1   ⊃(□A, A)

If □ is "logic necessity," then 11.1.1 will be true in any (logically nonanomalous) state of affairs, regardless of what A is: it could be false in a given state of affairs only if A were false in that state of affairs but A were true in all nonanomalous states of affairs, which is impossible since A is false in the given nonanomalous state of affairs. Suppose, however, that □ stands for "moral necessity"; unless the assumed moral code is vacuous (or effectively vacuous, e.g., the only thing that is prohibited is trisecting a 30° angle with a compass and straightedge), 11.1.1 can be false, that is, there can be a state of affairs in which something morally necessary fails to be the case (e.g., I may fail to love all my fellow human beings even though I am morally obliged to do so). Thus, in the case of moral necessity, the actual state of affairs may be anomalous, though in the case of logical necessity, the actual state of affairs will not be anomalous.

But wait a minute—how can I get away with saying that? When I was talking about logical necessity, I considered all and only those states of affairs that were logically nonanomalous and said that in any such state of affairs 11.1.1 was true; but I ruled out by fiat any consideration of states of affairs that are logically anomalous (e.g., the state of affairs in which all "atomic" propositions are true and all complex propositions are false). When I was talking about moral necessity, instead of restricting myself to morally nonanomalous states of affairs, I considered the broader class of all **logically** nonanomalous states of affairs; but couldn't I just as well have exercised my fiat and ruled out of consideration all morally anomalous states of affairs? I could have, but in that case I would have ruled out of consideration a large part of the subject matter of moral philosophy, whereas in the case of my earlier fiat, I ruled out only states of affairs in which no one has any particular interest. The point is that one cannot always restrict one's attention to nonanomalous states of affairs. The question to ask about 11.1.1 is: for the given interpretation of □, how anomalous would a state of affairs have to be in order for 11.1.1 to be false? In the case of logical necessity, the answer is "extremely," indeed, so anomalous that the states of affairs that would make 11.1.1 false can just as well be forgotten about, as indeed they usually are. In the case of "moral necessity," however, 11.1.1 could be false in a state of affairs that had nothing much anomalous about it beyond the fact that some moral principle was being violated, and thus a huge class of states of affairs that make 11.1.1 false cannot very well be forgotten about.

11.2. Syntax and Semantics for Modal Propositional Logic

So far, for each of the notions of necessity under discussion, I have spoken of various states of affairs being anomalous and others nonanomalous. In some cases, however, it makes more sense to speak of a state of affairs as being anomalous relative to other states of affairs rather than absolutely. In the case of epistemic necessity, a state of affairs is anomalous if it is inconsistent with what is known. But one state of affairs can differ from another with regard to "what is known." For example, there might be two states of affairs such that in both there are nine planets, but in only one of the two states of affairs is it **known** that there are at least nine planets: in the other state of affairs it is only known that there are at least six planets. A state of affairs in which there are eight planets would be inconsistent with what is known in the one state of affairs but not with what is known in the other. Similarly with moral necessity. Suppose one takes a state of affairs to be morally anomalous relative to a given state of affairs if there is a violation of some moral principle in that state of affairs that does not occur in the given state of affairs. Let w_1 be a world in which Simon Legree owns slaves and beats his slaves, let w_2 be a world in which Legree owns slaves but does not beat them, and let w_3 be a world in which Legree owns no slaves and beats no one, assuming there to be no further differences of relevance to a moral code that forbids both slavery and beatings. Then w_2 would be morally anomalous relative to w_3 but not relative to w_1.

Thus, to distinguish between the different kinds of "necessity," we will have to refer to more than just different ways of classifying worlds into "anomalous" and "nonanomalous" worlds. Rather, it will be necessary to bring in a relationship of "relative nonanomaly" or (to use terms that have become fairly standard) **accessibility** or **alternativeness** among worlds. Suppose that we consider a binary relation R among the worlds that come into consideration. Rw_1w_2 is to mean "w_2 is possible relative to w_1" (or, figuratively, "from w_1 you can get to w_2"). In the case of logical necessity, the relation R is very simple: if w_1 and w_2 both conform to the rules of inference, then Rw_1w_2, and otherwise it is not the case that Rw_1w_2. In this case, R has the important properties:

11.2.1   Symmetry: if Rw_1w_2, then Rw_2w_1
            Transitivity: if Rw_1w_2 and Rw_2w_3, then Rw_1w_3

Whether it possesses the further property 11.2.2, the remaining criterion that it would have to fulfill to be an **equivalence relation,** depends on a technicality, namely, whether we consider "all worlds" to be literally "all worlds" (i.e., all assignments of truth values to the propositions of the given language L, even assignments which fail to conform to the assumed rules of inference) or to be a more restricted class of worlds (such as the set of all worlds that conform to the assumed rules of inference, or the set of worlds that conform to the "classical" truth tables):

11.2.2   Reflexivity: For all worlds w, Rww

Since the only way that Rww could be false in this case is for w not to conform to the rules of inference, the only way that the R corresponding to the notion of logical necessity could fail to be an "equivalence relation" is for worlds to be allowed that do not conform to the rules of inference.

The assessibility relation R appropriate to other notions of necessity may fail to be symmetric or to be transitive or to be reflexive. For the notions of necessity that are most widely discussed, it will be reasonable to take R to be reflexive. However, it is not clear that it should be taken as reflexive if it is to be appropriate to a notion of moral necessity. Two possibilities suggest themselves for that case: one could either take Rw_1w_2 to mean that w_2 is morally no worse than w_1, in which case R would be reflexive, or take Rw_1w_2 to mean that bringing about (or maintaining) the state of affairs w_2 is morally desirable if one is in the state of affairs w_1, in which case R would not be reflexive.

Let us allow ourselves the power of fiat to decide what set of worlds we will allow into consideration in a particular discussion. We can then consider the full range of necessity relations that can be defined by choosing a set of worlds and an accessibility relation among those worlds, where $\Box A$ is to be true in a world w provided that A is true in all worlds accessible from w. We thus require the following definition and rule for truth value assignment:

11.2.3   A modal system M consists of
            i. a language L,
            ii. a set W of "worlds" (= assignments of truth values to the propositions of L), and

iii. a binary relation R between the worlds of W.

$\Box$A is true in a world w of a modal system M if and only if for all w' such that Rww', A is true in w'.

For the purposes of this chapter, we will also stipulate that L must contain the propositional connectives $\wedge$, $\vee$, $\supset$, $\sim$, and that only worlds that conform to the classical truth tables will be admitted.

Note that according to this truth condition, $\Box$A may be true in one world and false in another world of the given system. That characteristic is all to the good: otherwise we could not adequately accommodate the notions of epistemic necessity and moral necessity within the framework of modal systems. It will be useful to define a notion of **validity** in a modal system M: A is valid in M (symbolized $\vDash_M$ A) if A is true in every world of M. Note that if a formula does not contain the modal operator $\Box$, whether it is true in a particular world will depend only on what is true in that world, but if it does contain $\Box$, its truth in a particular world will generally depend at least in part on what is true in other worlds. We are now in a position to prove some theorems about modal systems.

Theorem.   For any modal system M and any formulas A and B, 11.2.4 is valid in M:

11.2.4 $\supset(\Box\supset AB, \supset(\Box A, \Box B))$

Proof. Pick any world w of any modal system M; what we must show is that 11.2.4 is true in w. Suppose that $\Box\supset AB$ is true in w. We must now prove that $\supset(\Box A, \Box B)$ is true in w. Suppose that $\Box A$ is true in w, and let w' be a world such that Rww'. Since $\Box\supset AB$ is true in w, $\supset AB$ is true in w', and since $\Box A$ is true in w, A is true in w'; consequently (by $\supset$-exploitation), B is true in w'. But that establishes that B is true in all worlds accessible from w, that is, that $\Box B$ is true in w. We have thus established that $\supset(\Box A, \Box B)$ is true in w. But this establishes that 11.2.4 is true in w.

Formula 11.2.4 is one of a number of formulas that have appeared among axioms for some variety or other of modal logic. These systems of axioms have also included formulas which are not valid in all modal systems, though they are valid in these modal systems whose accessibility relations have certain characteristics. For example, 11.2.5 is valid in all modal systems in which R is reflexive:

11.2.5 $\supset(\Box A, A)$

Suppose that R is reflexive, and pick some world w in which $\Box A$ is true. Thus A is true in all worlds w' for which Rww'. But, by assumption, R is reflexive, and thus we have Rww. Consequently, A is true in w. This establishes that 11.2.5 is true in any world of the modal system.

It is easy to find examples of modal systems in which R is not reflexive and 11.2.5 fails to be valid. For example, consider the trivial case of a modal system in which no world is accessible from any world. Then $\Box A$ will be (vacuously) true in every world, no matter what A is (since for any given world w, A is true in all of the no worlds that are accessible from w); but any world has false propositions, and by choosing A such that A is false in w, we will have chosen A such that $\supset(\Box A, A)$ is false in w. In section 11.5, a proof is given that under certain conditions, the validity of 11.2.5 in a modal system implies that its accessibility relation is reflexive, and thus that, under those conditions, the validity of 11.2.5 is equivalent to reflexiveness of R.

The following formula is valid in any modal system whose accessibility relation is transitive:

11.2.6 $\supset(\Box A, \Box\Box A)$

Suppose that R is transitive and that $\Box A$ is true in world w. Let Rww'. If we can show that $\Box A$ is true in w', we will have established that $\Box A$ is true in any world accessible from w and thus that $\Box\Box A$ is true in w, which will establish that 11.2.6 is true for any world w. Consider any world w'' such that $Rw'w''$. Because Rww' and $Rw'w''$ and R is transitive, we have Rww''. But A is true in all worlds accessible from w, and A is hence true in w''. Thus A is true in all worlds accessible from w', and hence $\Box A$ is true in w', as we were attempting to prove. In section 11.5, we will prove a converse of this result: under certain conditions, if 11.2.6 is valid in a modal system, then the accessibility relation of that system is transitive.

So far I have been speaking only of notions of "necessity." Corresponding to any notion of "necessity" there is a related notion of "possibility"; for example, there is a notion of "logical possibility" (something is logically possible if the rules of inference do not force it to be assigned the value "False"), "epistemic possibility" (something is epistemically possible if it is consistent with what is known), "moral possibility" (something is "morally possible" if it does not conflict with the moral code in question; in this case one usually says "permissible" rather than "possible"). Let us use the symbol $\Diamond$ to denote the notion of "possibility" that goes along with whatever notion of necessity that we happen to be using $\Box$ as a symbol for. I will assume that $\Box$ and $\Diamond$ are related by the conditions:

11.2.7   a. □A if and only if ~◇~A.
            b. ◇A if and only if ~□~A.

(Think about each of the notions of possibility in turn, and verify for yourself that 11.2.7 is reasonable in each case). The following is a reasonable way to set up truth conditions for ◇ so that 11.2.7 comes out true:

11.2.8   ◇A is true in a world w of a modal system M if and only if
            there is a world w' of M such that Rww' and A is true in w'.

That is, ◇A is true if A is true in some "possible world"—possible, that is, in the sense of accessible from the world that you are talking about. You should verify for yourself that under the assumption 11.2.8, the conditions of 11.2.7 come out true.

The following formula is equivalent to 11.2.5 and is thus valid in any modal system whose alternativeness relation is reflexive:

11.2.9   ⊃(A, ◇A)

If 11.2.5 is true in every world of a modal system, for every formula A, then so is ⊃(□ ~A, ~A) (the result of substituting ~A for A in 11.2.5), and thus so is ⊃(A, ~□~A), which (by virtue of 11.2.7b and the principle of substitution of deductive equivalents) is true under the same circumstances as ⊃(A, ◇A). This establishes that if 11.2.5 is valid, then 11.2.9 is. All of the steps in this argument can be reversed, yielding a proof of the converse: that if 11.2.9 is valid, 11.2.5 is also. Of course, 11.2.9 can fail to be valid in a modal system, as in the trivial case of a system whose alternativeness relation does not hold of any pair of worlds: in that system, ◇A will always be false, and if we choose A so that it is true in a given world w (which is always possible, since in any world there are true propositions), ⊃(A, ◇A) will be false in w for that choice of A.

Consider now whether the formula 11.2.10 could be false under any conditions:

11.2.10   ⊃(□A, ◇A)

For 11.2.10 to be false in a world w, □A would have to be true and ◇A false in w; that is, A would have to be true in all worlds that are accessible from w but not be true in any world accessible from w. The only way in which that could be the case would be for there to be no worlds that are accessible from w. Thus 11.2.10 is valid in all modal systems that meet the condition 11.2.11:

11.2.11   For any world w, there is a world w' (not necessarily distinct
            from w) such that Rww'.

In talking about ethics, one might want to consider modal systems that do not meet condition 11.2.11. For example, if one took the accessibility relation R to be such that Rww' whenever w' is a morally more acceptable state of affairs that can be reached from a state of affairs w by performing a physically possible act, one might have to admit situations in which 11.2.11 was violated— situations in which one had painted himself into a moral corner: immoral situations from which one could do nothing to extricate himself. However, in the case of logical possibility and epistemic possibility, 11.2.11 will hold, since in that case an even stronger condition than 11.2.11 holds: the R for logical possibility or epistemic possibility is reflexive.[2]

The following formula, the so-called Brouwer formula,[3] is valid in modal systems whose alternativeness relation is symmetric:

11.2.12 $\supset$(A, $\square\lozenge$A)

To see this, suppose that A is true in some world w of a modal system whose alternativeness relation is symmetric. Let Rww'. By the symmetry of R, we then have R$w'w$. But A is true in w, and thus A is true in a world accessible from w', that is, $\lozenge$A is true in w'. But since w' can be any world accessible from w, this establishes that $\square\lozenge$A is true in w. We have thus established that 11.2.12 is valid in any modal system whose R is symmetric. In section 11.5 we will prove a converse of this result: under certain conditions, if 11.2.12 is valid in a modal system, then the R of that system is symmetric.

Suppose that we restrict ourselves for the moment to systems in which 11.2.9 is valid. Then the following, since it has a "weaker" protasis than does Brouwer's formula, will be valid only under more stringent conditions than those under which Brouwer's formula is valid:

11.2.13 $\supset$($\lozenge$A, $\square\lozenge$A)

One clear set of circumstances under which 11.2.13 would be valid in a modal system is that in which the alternativeness relation is symmetric **and** transitive. Suppose that $\lozenge$A is true in some world w of a modal system whose alternativeness relation is both symmetric and transitive. Then there is a world w' such that Rww' and A is true in w'. Let us now try to prove that $\square\lozenge$A is true in w, that is, that $\lozenge$A is true in all worlds accessible from w. Let w'' be accessible from w, that is, Rww''. Then, since R is symmetric, we have R$w''w$. But since Rww' and R is transitive, we then have R$w''w'$, and since A is true in w', we have A true in a world that is accessible from w'', that is, $\lozenge$A is true in w''. Since this is true of any world w'' that is accessible from w, $\lozenge$A is true in all worlds accessible from w, that is, $\square\lozenge$A is true in w, as we set out to prove.

So far I have been talking about "semantics" of modal systems, that is, about the assignment of truth values to propositions involving "modal operators." Let us turn now to "syntactic" treatments of modal logic, that is, to systems of rules of inference[4] that have been proposed for various kinds of modal logics. There are in fact a bewildering array of axiomatic systems of modal logic and an extremely rich literature on their logical properties and their mutual relationships. Most of these systems relate to notions of necessity that "include" logical necessity, that is, they have a rule of inference that if A is provable, then □A is a theorem of the modal system;[5] this rule of inference is known as **necessitation.** One particularly rudimentary axiomatic system is the one (variously called T, t, and M; T seems to be the most popular name) that has the following rules of inference:

11.2.14   System T
              a. The rules of propositional logic.
              b. □-introduction:

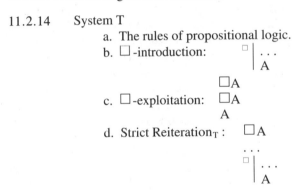

              c. □-exploitation: □A
                                  A

              d. Strict Reiteration$_T$:   □A

This is in fact not the form in which the rules of inference of T are usually presented but rather an alternative form (proposed in Fitch 1952) that conforms to the style in which the rules of inference for predicate logic and propositional logic have been given here, with rules of introduction and exploitation for each "logical" element. A more common way of characterizing T is in terms of the rules in 11.2.15, two of which are "axioms" (i.e., rules of inference without premises):

11.2.15   System T (traditional formulation)
              a. The rules of propositional logic
              b. Necessitation: if ⊢A, then ⊢□A
              c. ⊢⊃(□A, A)
              d. ⊢⊃(□⊃AB, ⊃(□A, □B))

While it is not immediately obvious that 11.2.14 and 11.2.15 are equivalent (in the sense of allowing one to draw the same conclusions from the same premises), it is in fact fairly easy to show that they are, by showing that each rule of inference in one of the two versions can be simulated using rules in the other version. For example, 11.2.14c and 11.2.15c each can simulate the other's application as follows:

11.2.16   a. 1 $\Box$A   supp
              2 $\supset$($\Box$A, A)   11.2.15c
              3 A   2, 1, $\supset$ -expl
           b. 1 | $\Box$A   supp
              2 | A   1, $\Box$-expl (11.2.14c)
              3 $\supset$($\Box$A, A)   1–2, $\supset$ -intro

The one part of 11.2.14 that requires special comment is 11.2.14d. As will emerge shortly, different types of modal logic differ substantially with regard to the importations that they allow into the subordinate proofs that are used to establish modal propositions. (Such subproofs are indicated by $\Box$ at the top of the vertical line.) While ordinary reiteration applies to those parts of the proof that rely only on propositional logic, only under restricted circumstances can propositions be imported into the specifically modal parts of the proof. (It may be helpful to think of the main proof as having one particular world as its frame of reference, and a subordinate proof by which one establishes a proposition $\Box$A as relating to all worlds that are possible relative to the given one; since not all propositions that are true in a given world need be true in all worlds that are possible relative to it, not all of them can be imported into the modal subproof.) While 11.2.14d has little if anything in common conceptually with 11.2.15d, it nonetheless plays a significant role in deriving 11.2.15d as a theorem in the 11.2.14 version of T:

11.2.17   1 | $\Box$$\supset$AB   supp
           2 | | $\Box$A   supp
           3 | | $\Box$ | $\supset$AB   1, SR_T
           4 | | | A   2, SR_T
           5 | | | B   3, 4, $\supset$ -expl
           6 | | $\Box$B   3–5, $\Box$ -intro
           7 | $\supset$($\Box$A, $\Box$B)   2–7, $\supset$ -intro
           8 $\supset$($\Box$$\supset$AB, $\supset$($\Box$A, $\Box$B))   1–8, $\supset$ -intro

If we treat 11.2.7a not just as giving truth conditions for $\Diamond$ but as a definition of it (i.e., $\Diamond$A is **defined as** $\sim$$\Box$$\sim$A), we will have the deductive equivalences 11.2.18 not only in T but indeed in all systems of modal logic:

11.2.18 a. $\Box{\sim}A \dashv\vdash {\sim}\Diamond A$.

  b. $\Diamond{\sim}A \dashv\vdash {\sim}\Box A$.

Despite my objections to taking one of $\wedge$, $\vee$ and $\supset$ as basic and defining the other two in terms of it and negation, I see nothing at all objectionable or counterintuitive about defining $\Diamond$ in terms of $\Box$ and negation (i.e., saying that "possible" means "doesn't have to not be the case"), and I will henceforth follow the usual practise of modal logicians in defining one or other of $\Box$ and $\Diamond$ in terms of the other and negation, and thereby committing myself to accepting the deductive equivalences in 11.2.18. This will thus allow $\Diamond$ to be added to the vocabulary of T and will allow such theorems as those in 11.2.19 to be proved in T:

11.2.19   a. $\supset(A, \Diamond A)$

    b. $\Diamond(\vee AB)$ if and only if $\vee(\Diamond A, \Diamond B)$

    c. $\supset(\Diamond\wedge AB, \wedge(\Diamond A, \Diamond B))$

    d. $\supset(\wedge(\Box A, \Diamond B), \Diamond\wedge AB)$

An extensive hierarchy of systems of axioms for modal logic was developed by C. I. Lewis (Lewis 1918; Lewis and Langford 1932) and expanded by numerous subsequent logicians. The various sets of axioms have names like S2, S4, S4.2, and S4.3.3; S1, S2, S3, S4, and S5 are the original Lewis hierarchy, and the others are later interpolations into the hierarchy.[6] The most widely known of these systems are S4 and S5. From the vantage point of this book, these systems differ from T in that they have "stronger" versions of strict reiteration, which allow the importation into subordinate proofs of formulas that SR_T would not allow to be imported into them:

11.2.20   System S4

      a.–c. (as in 11.2.14)
      d. Strict Reiteration$_{S4}$ $\Box A$
                                          . . .
                                      $\Box$ | . . .
                                          | $\Box A$

11.2.21   System S5

      a.–c. (as in 11.2.14)
      d. Strict Reiteration$_{S5}$ $\Box A$ and ${\sim}\Box A$
                                          . . .   . . .
                                      $\Box$ | . . . $\Box$ | . . .
                                          | $\Box A$ | ${\sim}\Box A$

Each of the last two versions of Strict Reiteration can do all the work of the preceding version. Since SR_{S5} consists of SR_{S4} plus something additional, it obviously can do everything that SR_{S4} can, and it is quite easy to replicate SR_T using SR_{S4}, e.g., in 11.2.22, the application of SR_{S4} in line n and the application of $\Box$-expl in line $n + 1$ have jointly the effect of an application of SR_T:

11.2.22   1 ...
           i $\Box A$

           n $\Box A$ i, SR$_{S4}$
           $n + 1$ A n, $\Box$-expl

Since SR is the only difference in the rules of inference for T, S4, and S5, this shows that whatever follows from given premises in T follows from them in S4, and whatever follows from given premises in S4 follows from them in S5.

As these two systems are conceived of more traditionally, they differ from T (11.2.15) by the addition of one axiom:

11.2.23   System S4 (traditional formulation)
           a.–d. The rules of T (11.2.15)
           e_4. $\vdash \supset(\Box A, \Box\Box A)$ (= 11.2.6)

11.2.24   System S5 (traditional formulation)
           a.–d. The rules of T (11.2.15)
           e_5. $\vdash \supset(\Diamond A, \Box\Diamond A)$ (= 11.2.13)

It is trivial to show that in the versions of S4 and S5 adopted here, the distinctive axioms of S4 and S5 are theorems:

11.2.25   a. 1 $\Box A$ supp
               2      $\Box A$ 1, SR$_{S4}$
               3      $\Box\Box A$ 2–2, $\Box$-intro
               4 $\supset(\Box A, \Box\Box A)$ 1–3, $\supset$-intro

           b. 1 $\sim\Box\sim A$ (i.e., $\Diamond A$)   supp
               2      $\sim\Box\sim A$ 1, SR$_{S5}$
               3      $\Box\sim\Box\sim A$ (i.e., $\Box\Diamond A$)   2–2, $\Box$-intro
               4 $\supset(\Diamond A, \Box\Diamond A)$ 1–3, $\supset$-intro

In the interests of conserving space, I will omit the remainder of the demonstration of the equivalence of the two versions of the rules of inference of each of these systems and will turn to an interesting property of S5, namely that in that system any string of modal operators ($\Box$s and $\Diamond$s) can be simplified by canceling all but the last of the operators. That is, the following are theorems of S5:

11.2.26 a. ⊃(□□A, □A)   a′. ⊃(□A, □□A)
       b. ⊃(□◇A, ◇A)   b′. ⊃(◇A, □◇A)
       c. ⊃(◇□A, □A)   c′. ⊃(□A, ◇□A)
       d. ⊃(◇◇A, ◇A)   d′. ⊃(◇A, ◇◇A)

The proofs of 11.2.26a and 11.2.26b are trivial, since both theorems are special cases of the first axiom of T: one gets 11.2.26a from the axiom ⊃(□A, A) by substituting □A for A, and 11.2.26b by substituting ◇A for A. Thus, 11.2.26a and 11.2.26b are theorems not only of S5 but also of T and of S4. To establish some of the other parts of 11.2.26, it will be necessary first to demonstrate that the principle of "substitution of deductive equivalents" applies in S5; that is, that if X is a constituent of A, X ⊣⊢ X′, and A′ is something obtained by substituting X′ for X in A, then A ⊢A′, where the ⊢s refer to proof in S5. Since the propositional connectives allow substitution of deductive equivalents for constituent propositions (which remains the case even if the extra deductive machinery of S5 is added to propositional logic), it suffices to show that such substitutions can be made in the scope of □, that is, that if X ⊣⊢X′, then □X ⊣⊢ □X′. This can be established as follows:

11.2.27   1 X ⊢ X′   supp
           2 ⊢ ⊃XX′   1, ⊃-intro
           3 ⊢ □⊃XX′   2, necessitation
           4 ⊢⊃(□X, □X′)   3, T axiom
           5 □X ⊢ □X′   4, ⊃-expl

By the same derivation, if X′⊢X, then □X′⊢□X, and thus if X ⊣⊢X′, then □X ⊣⊢ □X′. Substituting X′ for X in more complicated expressions such as ~□X or □⊃(∨XY, □∧XZ) will also produce a result that is deductively equivalent to the original. For example, the deductive equivalence of ~□X and ~□X′ follows from the deductive equivalence of □X and □X′ and the fact that the negations of deductive equivalents are deductively equivalent. We are now able to prove 11.2.26c:

11.2.28   1 ⊃(◇~A, □◇~A)   11.2.13 with ~ A for A
           2 ⊃(~□A, ~◇~◇~A)   1, 11.2.18a, 11.2.18b, SDE
           3 ⊃(◇~◇~A, □A)   2, contraposition
           4 ⊃(◇□A, □A)   3, SDE

Let us now turn to 11.2.26d. Since 11.2.26d is obviously equivalent to the S4 axiom, proving that it is a theorem of S5 will establish a point that had been implicit in our choice of terminology, namely, that S5 is a special case of S4. To prove 11.2.26d, I will substitute a proof of the S4 axiom. First, however, I must justify a couple of steps that appear in the proof. Since 11.2.26b′ is the S5 axiom, it is trivially a theorem of S5, and thus we have

11.2.29   □◇A and ◇A are deductively equivalent in S5.

One can also easily establish 11.2.26c′: substitute ~A for A in 11.2.26b and then perform a couple of obvious steps. Thus we have:

11.2.30   ◇□A and □A are deductively equivalent in S5.

Finally, the following is a theorem of T and thus also of S5:

11.2.31   Theorem (T): ⊃(A, ◇A)
    1 ⊃(□~A, ~A)   T axiom with ~A for A
    2 ⊃(~~A, ~□~A)   1, contraposition
    3 ⊃(A, ~□~A)   2, SDE
    4 ⊃(A, ◇A)   3, 11.2.7b

We are now ready to prove the S4 axiom, and then 11.2.26d.

11.2.32   1 ⊃(□A, ◇□A)   11.2.31 with □A for A
    2 ⊃(□A, □◇□A)   1, SDE (11.2.29 with □A for A)
    3 ⊃(□A, □□A)   2, SDE (11.2.30)

11.2.33   1 ⊃(□~A, □□~A)   11.2.32 with ~A for A
    2 ⊃(~□□~A, ~□~A)   1, contraposition
    3 ⊃(◇◇A, ◇A)   SDE, applied several times

In the course of proving 11.2.26d, we have already proved 11.2.26a′. As noted before, 11.2/16b′ is the S5 axiom and thus trivially a theorem of S5. Theorems 11.2.26c′ and 11.2.26d′ are both special cases if 11.2.19a, which is a theorem of T and thus also a theorem of S5. These theorems imply that any formula beginning with a sequence of modal operators is deductively equivalent in S5 to the formula obtained by deleting all but the last of the modal operators; for example, □□◇□◇A is deductively equivalent to ◇A in S5.

11.3. Modal Predicate Logic

The formulas of modal logic that were discussed in the last section involved no quantifiers. This deficiency will have to be remedied, since modal logic will have to contend with perfectly ordinary sentences in which both modal operators and quantifiers appear, for example,

11.3.1   a. All men are necessarily mortal.
         b. Many linguists may beat their spouses.

These examples are in fact ambiguous as regards the scope of the quantifier and the modal operator. The different interpretations possible for each could be expressed as follows:

11.3.2   a.   (All: Man x)□Mortal x
         a'. □(All: Man x)(Mortal x)
         b.   (Many: Linguist x)◇(x beats x's spouse)
         b'. ◇(Many: Linguist x)(x beats x's spouse)

Note that 11.3.2a and 11.3.2a' (likewise, 11.3.2b and 11.3.2b') need not have the same truth values: if one allows for alternative states of affairs in which there are not only ordinary men but also supermen who, unlike actual human beings, will live forever, then one could reasonably hold 11.3.2a to be true and 11.3.2a' to be false: every actual man has the property that of (physical) necessity he will die, but there are alternative worlds in which there are men who will not die and in which it is thus not the case that "all men are mortal."

There are two important respects in which 11.3.2a' and 11.3.2b' are less problematic than 11.3.2a and 11.3.2b. First, 11.3.2a and 11.3.2b involve the propositional functions "□(Mortal x)" and "◇(x beats x's spouse)." In both of those propositional functions, a modal operator is applied not to a self-contained expression but to an expression containing a variable. It thus associates to each object the property "is necessarily mortal" or "possibly beats his/her spouse." At least some doubt can reasonably be entertained about whether an **object** can coherently be said to have (or lack) that sort of property. For example, Quine (1943, 1953) has maintained that it makes no sense to speak of "□($x > 7$)" as being true or false of particular objects; rather, Quine holds that only expressions such as "□($9 > 7$)" (presumably true) or "□(the number of planets > 7)" (presumably false), in which particular linguistic expressions appear in place of the variables inside the scope of the modal operator, can reasonably be assigned truth values and that different names for the same object (e.g., "9" vs. "the number of planets") can yield different truth values when employed in a given modal context. Second, if one is to analyze 11.3.2a and 11.3.2b in terms of systems of possible worlds, it will be necessary to identify individuals in one world with individuals in another: to decide whether "□(Mortal x)" is true of Ringo Starr, it is necessary to identify the Ringo Starr (if any) in each alternative world and determine whether he is mortal. But how do you tell which individual in an alternative world is Ringo Starr and not just another individual who happens, confusingly, to have the same name and to practise the same trade as the Ringo Starr that we all know? This problem also arises in connection with "9" and "the number of planets": if the number of planets in w' is smaller than the number of players on a baseball team in w', can we identify either of those numbers nonarbitrarily with the number 9 of w? We might attempt to do it by looking at the arithmetic properties of these numbers, for example, the number of planets in w' is prime, so it can't be 9; but why does that show that that number can't be identified with 9 and not just that 9 has different arithmetic properties (such as being a prime number) in w' than in w?

One can react to the problems just mentioned either by avoiding them or by meeting them head on. Quine has chosen the former course and has rejected formulas such as 11.3.2a and 11.3.2b on the grounds that one can do philosophy adequately without making use of such formulas and that the philosopher has no compelling reason to get his hands (and mind) dirty wrestling with the problems that they raise. I am not convinced that one in fact **can** do philosophy adequately without allowing logical structures in which a quantifier outside the scope of a modal operator binds a variable inside the scope of that operator, as in 11.3.2a and 11.3.2b. However, be that as it may, it is at least clear that one cannot do linguistics adequately without recourse to such formulas, since they correspond to real meanings that may be exactly what the speaker intends in the given utterance. For example, 11.3.1b can perfectly well occur in a context where it is parallel to a sentence with a meaning of the form (Many: Fx)Gx and thus itself demands a meaning of that form:

11.3.3   a. A: Chomsky beats his wife, Fromkin beats her husband, Bach
                    beats his wife, Partee beats her husband, . . .
               B: Yeah, many linguists beat their spouses.
           b. A: Chomsky may beat his wife, Fromkin may beat her husband,
                    Bach may beat his wife, Partee may beat her husband, . . .
               B: Yeah, many linguists may beat their spouses.

Example 11.3.4a, which figures importantly in Quine's discussion of his doubts about formulas like 11.3.2a appears to be ambiguous between 11.3.4b and 11.3.4c, as was pointed out in Smullyan's (1948) reply to Quine 1943:

11.3.4   a. Necessarily, the number of planets > 7.
           b. $\Box$(ı: x is the number of planets) $(x > 7)$
           c. (ı: x is the number of planets) $\Box(x > 7)$

Formula 11.3.4b is false, since there are alternative worlds in which there are 7 or fewer planets, but 11.3.4c is presumably true, since the number of planets is 9 and 9 is necessarily greater than 7. Quine was worried about the possibility that a propositional function "$\Box(x > 7)$" might make no sense, since one could have $a = b$ and yet "$\Box(a > 7)$" true but "$\Box(b > 7)$" false, with "$\Box(9 > 7)$" being an instance of the former and 11.3.4a an instance of the latter. However, 11.3.4a is ambiguous and neither of its interpretations has "the number of planets" in the position of the variable in the suspect propositional function.

Nonetheless, one of the interpretations of 11.3.4a does involve a constituent $\Box(x > 7)$, and Quine (1969) has contested the claimed ambiguity of 11.3.4a on the grounds that one of the putative two interpretations, namely 11.3.4c, is something whose coherence has not been adequately established.[7] Let us thus take up the question of whether 11.3.4c allows a coherent assignment of truth conditions (or, better yet, whether a coherent assignment of truth conditions can be achieved without incorrigible arbitrariness). The scheme for assigning truth conditions that is developed in this section provides a way of determining the truth value of 11.3.4c in any modal system whose language includes the vocabulary of 11.3.4c. However, that is not saying much, since we have so far left wide open the question of what modal systems are to be admitted. If we admit a modal system in which 9 is the prime minister of Ethiopia (and Dan Quayle is the square root of Michael Jackson, though 9 is still the number of planets), and that world is accessible from the real world, sure enough that will make 11.3.4c false in the real world. But is there any nonarbitrary way of ruling out such bizarre modal systems and thus making 11.3.4c come out true, as I said it should be? For example, if we are admitting an alternative world in which there are only 6 planets (or better, in which there are $1 + 1 + 1 + 1 + 1 + 1$ planets, since it is at issue whether we should identify that number with 6 in the alternative world), should we identify $(1 + 1 + 1) \times (1 + 1 + 1)$ of that world with the 9 of the real world, or should we identify the number of the planets of that world with the 9 of the real world? If we can find a principled basis for rejecting the latter identification and accepting the former, we will then have a basis for calling 11.3.4c true. But if not, then we do not.

Thus, the question of what sense can be made of formulas like 11.3.4c reduces to the question of how one can identify the individuals of one world with the individuals of another world. Quine (1953) observed that if one allows formulas like 11.3.4c, one must distinguish between **essential properties** (properties an individual must have if it is to retain its identity) and **accidental properties** (properties an individual could acquire or lose without changing its identity). For example, the property of being $1 + 1$ would be an essential property of 2, but the property of being the maximum number of terms that a person may serve as president of the United States is an accidental property of 2.[8] In the case of numbers, there is in fact a consensus as to essential properties that identify them: 1 is the unique "identity element" for multiplication ($1 \cdot x = x \cdot 1 = x$, no matter what x is), 2 is the unique element that equals $1 + 1$, etc.; more generally, numbers can be identified by their arithmetic properties. One indeed need not take numbers as belonging to the various worlds with which a modal logician deals: one can follow David Lewis (1983:40) in holding that "Numbers et al. are no more located in logical space than they are in ordinary time and space" and that they do not exist **in** any particular world, though they do exist **from the standpoint of** every world. Or at least, one need not if one assumes, as I have throughout this book, that there are only **restricted** quantifiers, and as I have assumed from section 8.1 onwards, that the expression that restricts the domain of any individual variable must restrict its values to things of a single **sort**; from that point of view, bound variables that take numbers as their values have nothing to do with bound variables that include among their values entities whose identification across worlds might be problematic, and any problems that the latter sorts of entities pose need not prevent one from adopting a policy according to which numbers do not differ from one world to another. Things are different, though, if one adopts **unrestricted** quantification and requires numbers to be values of all individual variables if they are to be values of any individual variables: from that point of view, it is not so easy to separate the (fairly trivial) problem of identifying numbers across worlds from the more general problem of cross-world identification for entities of whatever sort, since the variable of an expression such as $\Box(x > 7)$ would always have among its values not only numbers but also more problematic objects of other sorts.

While the notion of "essential properties" as applied to numbers seems fairly unproblematic, it is far less clear that essential properties will suffice to identify entities across worlds in general. There is in fact reason to say that many entities can be viewed in different ways that give rise to different ways of identifying them across worlds and different conceptions of what their essential properties are. Suppose that one takes a completely materialistic view of organisms, according to which an organism consists of the molecules (and atomic particles, etc.) that make up its body, and nothing more. (Even if one does not hold that view, it would at least be nice if one's system of logic did not deny one the option of holding such a view, and I will aim at adopting policies on logic that neither force such an option on one nor rule it out.)

Holding such a materialistic view does not prevent one from making sense of such sentences as 11.3.5:

11.3.5   If John had gone on the diet that I had recommended, he'd be at least 20 pounds lighter than he is.

In that sentence, one is identifying the real-world John with alternative world entities that weigh over 20 pounds less than John does in the real world, and since the matter making up a body determines its mass, one is identifying John with entities in the other worlds that are made up of different assemblages of molecules than the one that currently makes him up. Materialist or not, one can identify John across worlds (and across times) in terms of his status as a person or in terms of his status as (being, if one is a materialist, being associated with, if one is not) an assemblage of molecules, and the two **principles of identity** (to use the terminology of Gupta 1980) correspond to different ways in which an entity can be involved in a modal proposition such as 11.3.5.

According to the approach developed by Gupta, Quine's worries about quantified modal logic are right in one sense and wrong in another. They are right in the sense that expressions in which a variable or an individual constant occurs free within the scope of a modal operator do not have a determinate interpretation. They are wrong in that the indeterminacy can generally be resolved by supplying each individual variable or constant with something that is arguably part of the interpretation of corresponding sentences anyway, namely a principle of identity. Gupta localizes principles of identity in **common nouns** and accordingly rejects the practice of most logicians since Frege, who treat common nouns along with words of most other parts of speech as corresponding to a single logical category ("predicates"). For Gupta, not only are quantifiers restricted rather than unrestricted, but the restricting expression must be a "common noun expression" (the logical counterpart of what in syntax is called an N': a common noun along with its adjuncts and modifiers), and the common noun that is in a sense the core of the restricting expression determines how values of the variable are to be identified not only with entities in other worlds but also with entities at other times. In fact, it is with identifications across time that we find the clearest contrasts between different principles of identity, e.g.,

11.3.6   a. The same person occupies that chair now as occupied it exactly
                  a year ago.
             b. The same assemblage of molecules occupies that chair now as
                  occupied it exactly a year ago.

Under normal conditions, the set of molecules making up a person's body would change considerably in the course of a year, and thus in a state of affairs in which 11.3.6a was true (which it well could be, even from the point of view of a materialist who thinks that an organism is made up of nothing but its molecules), 11.3.6b would surely be false, because the common noun expressions *person* and *assemblage of molecules* identify things differently across time: a change in the set of molecules that make up a body is not accompanied by a change in personal identity. According to Gupta's view, an expression $\Box Fx$ is uninterpretable not because it is ill-formed but because it is incomplete: interpreting it involves determining what values of x satisfy it, but to determine whether any given value of x satisfies it, one must know what that value of x is to be identified with in the relevant alternate worlds, and to know that, one must have a principle of identity for values of x.

Gupta's notion of "principle of identity" does not provide a general solution to the question of what element in the domain of w' should be identified with what element in the domain of w; rather, it specifies what kinds of identifications can be made in combination with a given common noun. Its application is clearest with regard to identification across time and identification across worlds that are related in terms of a shared past (as in 11.3.5, where one is comparing different continuations of a certain past state of affairs), since the principle of identity for a given common noun C determines what changes can affect a C while allowing it to remain the same C. However, the notion does not always yield clear results when applied to alternate worlds that are not related in terms of a shared past. Consider, for example, worlds that represent the (possibly false) beliefs of a person, and the problems involved in interpreting sentences containing a subordinate clause referring to such a world, as in the complements of verbs and adjectives of "propositional attitude":

11.3.7   a. John realizes that Bernard Ortcutt is a spy. (example adapted
                from Quine 1956)
         b. Commissioner Gordon knows that Batman is a millionaire.

John may have realized that the sinister-looking bearded man that he has seen lurking near the Institute of Strategic Seismology is a spy, without realizing that that person is identical to the charming, clean-shaven pillar of the community, Bernard Ortcutt, who lives down the block from John. Is 11.3.7a true or false in that case? And does one's difficulty in deciding imply that "x realizes that y is a spy" is not a well-formed propositional function? Commissioner Gordon knows that Bruce Wayne is a millionaire but does not know that Batman and Bruce Wayne are the same person and has no information about Batman's financial status. Does this mean that "x knows that y is a millionaire" is not a proper propositional function, since substituting different proper names of the same individual in place of y can result in different propositions?

Suppose that Batman/Wayne is lying on the ground, totally naked and with his head in a brown-paper bag, and someone points at him and says,

11.3.8   Commissioner Gordon knows that that man is a millionaire.

Has he expressed a true proposition? Is it even clear what proposition he has expressed? The reason that 11.3.8 is problematic is that the **deictic** use of *that* requires an interpretation based on the same world w with respect to which the whole sentence is being interpreted: *that man* must be interpreted as referring to the man in w that is picked out by the gesture. But since *that man* occurs in the complement of *Commissioner Gordon knows . . . ,* the man in w to whom it refers must be identified with an entity in the world w' that corresponds to the way that the commissioner believes things to be. (To say that someone knows something is, roughly, to say that a certain proposition that is true in his belief world can be identified with a proposition that is true in the real world.) But in w', there are two separate men, Batman and Wayne, and no single man in w' combines the Batman and Wayne identities as does the man in w that is picked out here by *that man*. Gupta's approach offers no solution to the problem of the interpretation of 11.3.8, but perhaps it is unreasonable to expect any approach to assign it a determinate interpretation: perhaps one should instead say that 11.3.8 has no determinate truth value, since its interpretation requires a given entity in w that has no determinate counterpart in w' to have one.

I have just spoken in terms of entities in one world having **counterparts** in another world. Such a notion is central to an approach to quantified modal logic developed by David Lewis (1968), in which a relation of counterparthood is taken as a primitive notion. Lewis takes the domains of different worlds to be disjoint, that is, he takes individuals of one world never to be, strictly speaking, identical to their counterparts in other worlds,[9] a policy comparable to that of treating the Gerald Ford of 30 November 1975 and the Gerald Ford of 11 April 1937 as distinct individuals, though connected by an important relation, namely, that the latter individual is a "temporal ancestor" of the former. He restates the truth conditions in terms of the counterpart relation. For example, for the truth conditions of $\Box fa$ (where a is an individual belonging to the domain of w), Lewis gives not 11.3.9a but 11.3.9b:

11.3.9   a. $\Box$ *fa* is T in *w* if and only if for all *w'* such that R*ww'*, *fa* is T
             in *w'*.
          b. $\Box$ *fa* is T in *w* if and only if for all *w'* such that R*ww'* and all *a'*
             such that *a'* is a counterpart in *w'* to *a*, *fa'* is T in *w'*.

According to 11.3.9b, incidentally, if there is a world accessible from the real
world in which Gerald Ford has two counterparts (a world in which he doesn't
just **have** a twin but **is** twins), then both of them would have to like sports for
Gerald Ford necessarily likes sports to be true.

One fairly obvious proposal for identifying the counterparts of a given element turns out to be grossly unsatisfactory, namely the proposal that one take
as the counterpart in *w'* of a given individual *a* of *w* the individual of *w'* that
is most similar to *a*.

Over and above the objection that any measure of similarity is doomed to
arbitrariness, this proposal is open to two fatal objections. First, as Feldman
(1971) has pointed out, there are perfectly intelligible sentences which presuppose cross-world identities between an individual of the one world and
some individual other than the one most like him in the other world, for example:

11.3.10 a. If Nixon had received the education that I did and I had received
            the education that Nixon did, I would be a ruthless
            megalomaniac and Nixon would be a pure-hearted anarchist.
        b. If I had been brought up by your parents and you had been
            brought up by my parents, I'd be just like you and you'd be
            just like me.

In either case the speaker is comparing the real world with an alternative
world in which he is not the person in that world who has the most in common
with the real him. Second, as Lewis (1968) himself points out, if an individual
in the one world had to be identified with the individual in the other world that
is most similar to him, the notion of identity would be neither symmetric nor
transitive.

Suppose, for sake of concreteness, that we measure similarity between individuals by the number of properties that they have in common on a fixed
checklist of properties, and that we have individuals as follows in three
worlds:

	Waldo$_1$	Oscar$_1$	Walter$_2$	Otto$_2$	Otokar$_3$	Waldemar$_3$
trustworthy	+	−	+	+	−	+
loyal	+	−	−	−	−	+

brave	+	−	−	−	−	+
reverent	+	+	+	−	+	+
kind	+	+	+	+	−	−

etc.

Here the subscript indicates the world to which the individual belongs. The names are purely for our convenience—it is not to be assumed that "Waldo," is called "Waldo," and I will indeed assume that all of these individuals are called "Charlie." Let us suppose that these individuals agree on all the other properties on the checklist (including the property of being called Charlie) and that there are no other individuals that are "closer" to any of them. Then the individual of w_2 who is most similar to Waldo is Walter, but the individual of w_1 who is most similar to Walter is not Waldo but Oscar, and thus identity is not symmetric if an individual of one world is identified with the most similar individual of another world. The individual of w_2 who is most similar to Waldo is Walter, and the individual of w_3 who is most similar to Walter is Otokar, but the individual of w_3 who is most similar to Waldo is not Otokar but Waldemar; thus identity is not transitive if an individual of one world is identified with the most similar individual of another world.

This, however, does not mean that quantified modal logic is doomed to admitting the full range of imaginable cross-world identifications in the case of entities whose identity cannot be established on the basis only of essential properties. Recall that modal logic is applied in highly diverse ways and that many of the applications of modal logic carry with them a particular cross-world identification, as in the case of such sentences as 11.3.11a, which are commonly interpreted as referring to alternative worlds that share with the real world a past that provides the basis for the cross-world identification:

11.3.11 a. Gerald Ford could have been an insurance executive.
        b. Gerald Ford could have been identical twins.
        c. Gerald Ford could have been the daughter of a Nigerian goatherd.

One would normally interpret 11.3.11a as saying that one could trace back in the real history of the world to some point (say, Ford's graduation from the University of Michigan) and then trace forward again along a different chain of events, with the events being restricted to what we take to be possible events and with individuals retaining their identities through these changes, except where events bring new individuals into being, eliminate old individuals, or bring about the fission or fusion of old individuals. In interpreting 11.3.11b one would push this identification to what most persons would probably regard as its limit, tracing Ford back to a point when he consisted of a single cell, and tracing forward along a possible history in which that cell split into two separate individuals that developed into identical twins. What is bizarre about 11.3.13c is that to trace Gerald Ford back to a point in time when different events could have given rise to a daughter of a Nigerian goatherd, you would have traced back to a point when there was no Gerald Ford and thus nothing to identify with the Nigerian goatherd's daughter that came into being later: from the moment that Gerald Ford first existed, he was the son of two Americans. (Of course, different assumptions about how persons come into existence would change things: if you believe in reincarnation, with a free-floating soul being incorporated into each new body at the moment of conception, 11.3.11c would become intelligible: you could interpret it as meaning that if the actual conception of Gerald Ford had not taken place, Ford's present soul might have been infused into the body of a Nigerian goatherd's daughter.)

There is no reason to expect that any general criterion of identity of elements in different worlds will make sense for all the kinds of quantified modal logic that one might want to do. The theory of quantified modal logic developed in this section can be combined with any system of identifying elements in different worlds. Whether one must operate with a modal system in which 11.3.11c comes out true will depend on what kind of modal logic one is doing (and on what auxiliary nonlogical assumptions one makes, for example, the assumption that a person starts to exist at the moment of conception). Any "modal" sentence must be supplied with an indication of what notion of necessity or possibility it involves. For a particular modal system to be of any use in analyzing the given sentence, one will have to establish that that system (including the way that elements of different worlds are identified) adequately represents the particular notions of possibility and necessity that play a role in the given sentence.[10]

I will turn now to one other difficulty in interpreting a formula such as 11.3.12a, namely the indeterminacy in how to apply truth conditions such as 11.3.12b in a case in which some individual satisfying the domain expression of the quantifier does not exist in some accessible alternative world:

11.3.12 a. ($\forall$: Man x) $\square$(Mortal x)
          b. For every element a of the domain of w, and every world w'
              such that Rww', (Mortal a) is true in w'.

For example, suppose that w_{89} has in its domain all men of the real world except Ringo Starr. In that case, should (Mortal RS) count as true in w_{89}? And if it doesn't, should that be grounds for saying that 11.3.12a is not true in the real world? There are three sets of answers to these questions that immediately spring to mind as worth considering: (i) The proposition (Mortal RS) should be held not to be true (whether F or # is immaterial) in w_{89}, and that fact should be sufficient to make 11.3.12a false in w, since what the truth conditions for 11.3.12a require to be true for every element of the domain of w and every accessible w' is not true for every element and every accessible world. (ii) It should be taken to lack a truth value in w_{89}, and 11.3.12a should be considered # in the real world (assuming that no real man is immortal in any alternative world) on the grounds that # is the lowest truth value that "Mortal RS" takes in any world accessible to the real world. (iii) In interpreting □(Mortal RS), one should ignore worlds in which there is no Ringo Starr, and accordingly one should take 11.3.12a to be true on the grounds that, for any real world man, in any alternative world in which he exists, he is still mortal.

I lean strongly to the last alternative on the grounds that under the other two alternatives an object would have to have necessary existence before it could have any other necessary atomic properties. Under either (i) or (ii), □fa could be true in w only if □(a exists) were true in w. However, necessary existence is too stringent a prerequisite to impose on anything—it would make □fa virtually always F or # for an uninteresting reason. It should be noted that policy (iii) may amount to a special case of a proposal that I made in discussing whether universally quantified propositions with empty domains should always be considered (vacuously) true. In connection with examples 6.3.4 I suggested that it may not be possible to impose a general policy on whether "vacuously true" instances should contribute to the truth value of a complex proposition and that the only thing common to the interpretation of the examples discussed there was that in each case only those elements that were relevant to the presumable purpose of the utterance were taken into consideration.

I conclude this section by taking up briefly some further problems involving individuation that have a bearing on cross-world identification. Suppose that one utters 11.3.13 (= 11.3.8) not in the circumstances discussed above but while pointing at Batman/Wayne dressed in his Bruce Wayne clothes and appearing at a public function at which he is clearly identified as Bruce Wayne:

11.3.13   Commissioner Gordon knows that that man is a millionaire.

Even relative to a world in which Batman and Wayne are the same person but Commissioner Gordon thinks that Batman and Wayne are two distinct persons, 11.3.13 can be given a plausible interpretation, provided that *that man* is interpreted as referring to the Wayne role of the Batman/Wayne person and that role is identified with the person Batman (distinct from the person Bruce Wayne) in the commissioner's belief world. This would involve distinguishing the Wayne role and the Batman role of Batman/Wayne, but one will need to draw that distinction anyway in order to provide for an interpretation according to which 11.3.14a is true and 11.3.14b false:

11.3.14 a. Batman always wears a mask and a cape.
        b. Bruce Wayne always wears a mask and a cape.

More generally, it will be necessary to distinguish between different "manifestations" of an entity in order to provide accurate interpretations of the expressions *the morning star* and *the evening star.* While the morning star and the evening star usually [11] are both manifestations of the planet Venus, the two expressions need to be distinguished not only in sense but also in reference, since the morning star and the evening star have distinct properties. For example, a comparison between the morning star and the evening star is perfectly intelligible (11.3.15a), and looking at the morning star is quite different from looking at the evening star, as is shown by the bizarreness (pointed out by Roman Jakobson in a lecture in Tokyo in July 1967) of saying 11.3.15b when pointing at the evening manifestation of Venus:[12]

11.3.15 a. The morning star is more beautiful than the evening star.
        b. Look at the morning star!

The intelligibility of 11.3.15a simply reflects the fact that words like *beautiful* and *ugly* are normally predicated not of an object but of a manifestation of it (or better, a class of manifestations of it) that can be regarded as an "aesthetic object." Thus, there is no contradiction between the propositions in 11.3.16, and a person who utters 11.3.17a is not really contradicting a person who utters 11.3.17b, even though he may think he is:

11.3.16 a. Dr. Jekyll is handsome.
        b. Mr. Hyde is ugly.
        c. Dr. Jekyll and Mr. Hyde are the same person.

11.3.17 a. God, is Mount Fuji beautiful! Look at this marvelous
           photograph of it that I took from Misaka Pass.
        b. God, is Mount Fuji ugly! I climbed it last year, and there's
           nothing to see—just cinders and the garbage left by the idiots
           that climb it.

11.4. Strict Implication and Relevant Entailment Logic

The development of the hierarchy of systems of modal logic associated with the name of C. I. Lewis is intimately connected with Lewis's development of a notion of "strict implication." Lewis attempted to develop a connective that corresponded to such ordinary language words as *if* and *implies* better than the "material implication" ($\supset$) of Frege 1879 and Russell and Whitehead's *Principia Mathematica* did. Lewis's strict implication (written $\dashv3$) was to be related to necessity by virtue of $\dashv3AB$ being equivalent to $\Box\supset AB$, or alternatively, to $\Box\lor(\sim A, B)$. In the earlier works, $\dashv3$ played the major role, $\Box$ and $\Diamond$ only a peripheral role, though the balance reversed in the 1930s and 1940s.[13]

Some of the more bizarre theorems involving $\supset$ (bizarre, that is, if $\supset$ is identified with *if*) do not have analogues with $\dashv3$ as theorems in any of the Lewis systems. For example, while $\lor(\supset AB, \supset BA)$ is a theorem of standard propositional logic, $\lor(\dashv3AB, \dashv3BA)$ is not a theorem of S1, S2, S3, S4, or S5. However, in even the weakest of the Lewis systems, S1, the following so-called paradoxes of strict implication are theorems:

11.4.1   a. $\supset(\Box B, \dashv3AB)$
       b. $\supset(\sim\Diamond A, \dashv3AB)$
       c. $\dashv3(\land(A, \sim A), B)$
       d. $\dashv3(A, \lor(B, \sim B))$

These results are reminiscent of some of the so-called paradoxes of material implication, namely, the following theorems of standard propositional logic:

11.4.2   a. $\supset(B, \supset AB)$
       b. $\supset(\sim A, \supset AB)$
       c. $\supset(\land(A, \sim A), B)$
       d. $\supset(A, \lor(B, \sim B))$

Theorems 11.4.1a and 11.4.1b at least are quite different in content from their counterparts in 11.4.2: 11.4.1a can be paraphrased as "a necessary proposition is implied by anything" and 11.4.1b as "an impossible proposition implies anything," whereas it is only by quite misleading equivocation that one can give at all similar paraphrases to 11.4.2a and 11.4.2b (the common paraphrases of 11.4.2a and 11.4.2b as "a true proposition is implied by anything" and "a false proposition implies anything" are incorrect since neither says anything about implication).

Hughes and Cresswell (1968:335–39) dismiss all allegations of "paradoxicality" of 11.4.1a–d: "the 'paradoxes' seem to us on reflection not to be tiresome (though harmless) eccentricities which we have to put up with in order to have the disjunctive syllogism, transitivity of entailment, and the rest, but sound principles in their own right: a logic of entailment **ought,** for example, to contain some principle which reflects our inclination to say to someone who has asserted something self-contradictory, 'If one were to accept **that,** one could prove anything at all'—and the principle that $(p \cdot \sim p)$ entails q expresses this in just the way that a formal system might be expected to" (pp. 338–39).

Anderson and Belnap (1975), by contrast, reject 11.4.1a–d, especially 11.4.1c–d, as perversions of the notion of "entailment," maintaining instead that a proposition follows only from propositions that are relevant to it, and hold that the protases in 11.4.1c–d are blatantly irrelevant to the apodoses (and that there is a less blatant fallacy of relevance in 11.4.1a–b); they would undoubtedly accuse Hughes and Cresswell of overkill: to squelch a person who has contradicted himself, it is enough to say that if one were to accept the contradiction one could prove anything to which it is relevant, not necessarily anything at all. Anderson and Belnap hold 11.4.1a–b to be false on the grounds that the necessity of B or the impossibility of A is irrelevant to whether B follows from A: if A is irrelevant to B (say, if no atomic proposition is a constituent of both), then B does not follow **from** A, regardless of whether B is necessary and whether A is impossible.

Whether the "paradoxes of strict implication" are things that one can live with depends mainly on whether one shares the depth of Anderson and Belnap's concern for "relevance"; at least the "paradoxes" do not lead one from uncontroversially true premises to uncontroversially false conclusions (the controversial cases being inferences whose premises or conclusion are of the form "If X, then Y"). Other results that are sometimes considered paradoxical, though they are easier to live with than 11.4.1a–d, for example, are the following theorems, which hold in T and stronger systems such as S4 and S5:

11.4.3   a. $-3(\sim A, A) \dashv\vdash \Box A$
       b. $\wedge(-3AB, -3(\sim A, B)) \dashv\vdash \Box B$

Theorem 11.4.3a follows from the fact that $\supset(\sim A, A) \dashv\vdash A$ in propositional logic, and hence $-3(\sim A, A)$ (i.e., $\Box\supset(\sim A, A)$) is deductively equivalent to $\Box A$ in T, since a principle of substitution of deductive equivalents is valid in T. Theorem 11.4.3b is based in a similar way on the fact that $\wedge(\supset AB, \supset(\sim A, B)) \dashv\vdash B$ in propositional logic; it can be thought of as a variant of the idea that a proposition is necessary if and only if it follows from everything, an idea that Anderson and Belnap of course reject.

Anderson and Belnap's (1975) treatment of "strict implication" deviates far more radically from standard logic than does Lewis's. They dismiss the rationalizations usually given for identifying ⊃ with *if* as characterized by "perversity, muddle-headedness, and downright error" (p. 5) and argue for an alternative treatment of conditional propositions that rests on two ideas that play no role in the foundations of ⊃: the idea of "relevance" (i.e., that a conditional "if A, then B" should be true only if A is relevant to the drawing of the conclusion B) and the idea of "entailment" (i.e., that a conditional "if A, then B" expresses that A is grounds for drawing the conclusion B, or that B follows from A). Anderson and Belnap thus dismiss ⊃(A, ∨(B, ~B)) as embodying a fallacy of relevance (its protasis is irrelevant to its apodosis, regardless of the fact that the apodosis is guaranteed to be true), as does ⊃(A, ⊃BA), which also blatantly conflicts with an interpretation of ⊃ as involving "entailment": from A it doesn't follow that A follows from B; for example, from "2 + 2 = 4" it does not follow that "2 + 2 = 4" follows from the proposition that Beethoven's 18th piano sonata is in E♭ major.

They propose a system of rules of inference that is set up so as to respect these two characteristics that they attribute to conditionals. Their accommodation of the notion of relevance is straightforward: each supposition in a proof is provided with an index, in the proof one must keep track of the indices corresponding to the suppositions that have been used in deriving the given line, and subproofs can be made use of only if the supposition of the subproof is used in establishing the conclusion of the subproof. Their rules of inference for "entailment" (which, following Anderson and Belnap, I will write as ＞ rather than as ⊃ or ⊸3) are identical to the rules for ⊃ in chapter 3 except for the way that the indices fit in:[14]

11.4.4   → introduction

$$\begin{array}{ll} A & \{k\} \\ \cdots & \\ B & M\ (k \in M) \\ \to AB & M\text{-}\{k\} \end{array}$$

→ -exploitation

$$\begin{array}{ll} \to AB & M \\ A & N \\ B & M \cup N \end{array}$$

Here k is an index on a supposition and M and N are sets of indices that are built up in the process of keeping track of suppositions; here, as in general, in a rule involving a subproof, the set of suppositions from which the conclusion is deduced must include the supposition of that subproof (note the condition "$k \in M$" in →-intro). The conclusion that is established **by** the subproof depends on those suppositions other than the supposition of the subproof (i.e., the supposition of the subproof is "discharged"). In a rule in which a conclusion is drawn from formulas on the same "level" in the hierarchy of subproofs, the set of suppositions that the conclusion depends on is the union of the sets of suppositions on which the premises depend. There is in addition a rule of reiteration, which allows one to repeat an earlier superordinate line, preserving the set of indices of that line. Let us use $E_\rightarrow$ to denote the logical system having only the connective $\rightarrow$ plus the rules of inference in 11.4.4 and the rule of reiteration.[15] It can easily be seen that the most obvious proof of $\supset(A, \supset BA)$ fails to yield an analogous proof of the (for Anderson and Belnap) fallacious $\rightarrow(A, \rightarrow BA)$. Consider the proof of $\supset(A, \supset BA)$ given in chapter 3:

11.4.5

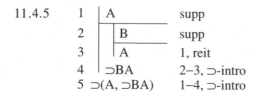

Suppose we try to construct a parallel proof using $\rightarrow$ and the $\rightarrow$-intro of 11.4.4. Call the indices of lines 1 and 2 simply 1 and 2. Line 3 will also have the index $\{1\}$, since reiteration preserves indices. But then a line 4 in which $\rightarrow BA$ is inferred will not be admissible: the index of line 2 is not a member of the set of indices of line 3, and thus $\rightarrow$-intro is not applicable.

It is in fact possible to show that $E_\rightarrow$ does not allow any proof of $\rightarrow(A, \rightarrow BA)$. The impossibility of proving that formula in $E_\rightarrow$ is a special case of the result (proven in Anderson and Belnap 1975: 34) that a formula built up from atomic propositions using only $\rightarrow$ is provable only if every atomic proposition that appears in the formula appears both as an "antecedent part" and as a "consequent part," where the notions of "antecedent part" and "consequent part" are defined as follows: (i) any formula is a consequent part of itself; (ii) if $\rightarrow XY$ is a consequent part of Z, then X is an antecedent part of Z and Y a consequent part; (iii) if $\rightarrow XY$ is an antecedent part of Z, then X is a consequent part of Z and Y is an antecedent part. The use of these terms is illustrated informally on the following:

11.4.6   a.

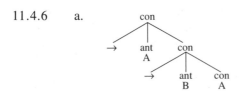

b.

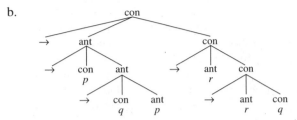

Since B occurs only as an antecedent part of →(A, →BA), the result implies that that formula cannot be proven in E_→. For the same reason, the formula in 11.4.6b cannot be proven either: r occurs only as an antecedent part and q only as a consequent part. Anderson and Belnap also prove (p. 33) that →XY is not provable in E_→ unless X and Y share an atomic proposition among their constituents. This result supports their claim that E_→ provides an account of relevance: absence of any shared atomic constituent would be a blatant instance of X being irrelevant to Y. This result also shows that there are instances in which Y is a theorem of E_→ but →XY is not, for example, it shows that →(A, →BB) is not a theorem, even though →BB obviously **is** a theorem; thus at least some of the "paradoxes of strict implication," are demonstrably not theorems of E_→.

Anderson and Belnap's approach to rules of inference requires that one make some revision in the remaining rules of propositional logic, since at the very least they will have to be revised to the extent of specifying how index sets fit into them. In carrying out that program, only a small part of which will be done here, one encounters a few surprises. For example, one might expect a relevance logician to adopt 11.4.7 as his rule of ∧-introduction, with the index set of the conclusion being the union of the index sets of the premises:

11.4.7   A   M
          B   N
          ∧AB   M ∪ N

However, that rule would have what for Anderson and Belnap is a disastrous consequence, namely that it would allow one to add spurious extra indices to lines in a proof, thereby providing proofs for many results that Anderson and Belnap want not to be provable, for example:

11.4.8   1 | A   {1}   supp
          2 | | B   {2}   supp
          3 | | ∧AB   {1,2}   1, 2, 11.4.7
          4 | | A   {1,2}   3, ∧-expl
          5 | →BA   {1}   2–4,→-intro
          6 →(A,→BA)   ∅   1–6,→-intro

That version of ∧-intro would thus rehabilitate most of the proofs that Anderson and Belnap are able to exclude on the grounds that the conclusion of a subordinate proof lacks the index that one needs in order to exit from the subordinate proof. (Recall that the analog of 11.4.5 failed to conform to Anderson and Belnap's rules because the conclusion of the subordinate proof had the index set {1}, which did not contain the index 2 of the supposition of the subordinate proof). To rule out such monkey business, Anderson and Belnap instead adopt a version of ∧-introduction that requires that the premises share their index sets, which would disallow step 3 in 11.4.8:[16]

11.4.9   ∧-introduction (Anderson and Belnap 1975)

        A   N
        B   N
        ∧AB   N

Anderson and Belnap are forced to reject the popular rule that is generally called the **disjunctive syllogism,**[17] because of its crucial role in proofs such as 11.4.11 of results that they condemn as fallacies of relevance:

11.4.10   ∨AB
             ~A
             B

11.4.11   1 | ∧(A, ~A)   {1} supp
             2 | A   {1} 1, ∧-expl
             3 | ~A   {1} 1, ∧-expl
             4 | ∨AB   {1} 2, ∨-intro
             5 | B   {1} 4, 3, disj-syll
             6 ⊃(∧(A, ~A), B)   ∅   1–5, ⊃-intro

While there is one other line in 11.4.11 on which one might want to pin the blame for the (to a relevance logician) unacceptable conclusion, namely line 4, Anderson and Belnap choose to allow free application of ∨-intro, even when it introduces "irrelevant" material into a disjunction, their rationale presumably being that all they ought to be accountable for is relevance relations **among** the lines of the proof, and the line from which line 4 is derived is surely relevant to it). Thus, they must reject the disjunctive syllogism in order to avoid having →(∧(A, ~A), B) as a theorem. More generally, if they have a rule of ∨-introduction that gives a conclusion ∨AB with the same set of indices as the premise A from which it is derived, the disjunctive syllogism will have to be excluded if one is to avoid fallacies of relevance: one will otherwise be able to deduce B from premises whose set of indices reflects only the derivational history of A and ~A.

The closest analog to the disjunctive syllogism 11.4.10 that Anderson and Belnap allow is the derived rule of inference 11.4.12:

11.4.12   If ⊢∨AB and ⊢∼A, then ⊢B.

Rule 11.4.12 will of course not justify step 5 in 11.4.11, since lines 3 and 4, from which line 5 is derived, are not theorems. Note that 11.4.12 is much weaker than 11.4.10: it is applicable only in the "main" proof, whereas 11.4.10 is applicable at any depth of subordination; that is, for 11.4.10, ∨AB and ∼A need not be things proven absolutely but can be consequences deduced from whatever set of suppositions is "operative" as the given point of the proof. The difference between 11.4.10 and 11.4.12 is the same as that between the ludicrous "rule" 11.4.13a and the perfectly respectable "law of necessitation" 11.4.13b:

11.4.13 a. A ⊢ □A
        b. If ⊢A, then ⊢□A.

In most systems of modal logic, the difference between A and □A would be wiped out by 11.4.13a, and only the most extreme fatalist could seriously propose it. By contrast, 11.4.13b embodies merely the claim that the given notion of necessity includes logical necessity as a special case, which is a reasonable condition to impose on many notions of necessity, for example, epistemic necessity.

While →(∧(A, ∼A), B) is not a theorem of Anderson and Belnap's general system E, certain special cases of it are theorems; for example, →(∧(A, ∼A), A) is a theorem, being a special case of the theorem →(∧AB, A). Anderson and Belnap prove a result that establishes a limited realm of formulas for which something akin to the dread →(∧(A, ∼A), B) is a theorem of E. Following Anderson and Belnap, let us call a formula a **manifest repugnancy** if it is of the form $\wedge(p_1, \sim p_1, p_2, \sim p_2, \ldots, p_n, \sim p_n)$, that is, if it is a conjunction of atomic propositions and their negations, with every atomic proposition that appears in it appearing both negated and unnegated. They prove that a manifest repugnancy entails every formula made up entirely of things to which it is relevant (p. 163):

11.4.14   If X is a manifest repugnancy and Y contains no atomic
               propositions other than those that appear in X, then →XY is a
               theorem of E.

Note that 11.4.14 is a good deal weaker than →(∧(A, ∼A), B), since not only is Y restricted in the way indicated, but X must be of a form "stronger" than

$\wedge(A, \sim A)$: X is not simply $\wedge(\wedge(p_1, ..., p_n), \sim\wedge(p_1, ..., p_n))$ but has all the $\sim p_i$ among its conjuncts.

Anderson and Belnap's treatment of $\rightarrow$ provides the basis of a novel treatment of necessity. They propose defining $\square A$ as $\rightarrow(\rightarrow AA, A)$. Given the interpretation that they put on $\rightarrow$, it is not too hard to get used to this at first startling formula. The proposition $\rightarrow AB$ is to be true only when B follows from A. It is occasionally held that necessary propositions follow from all other propositions, as they do in some sense in all of the Lewis systems, but for Anderson and Belnap, a formula can only follow from a formula that is relevant to it, and thus a formula could follow from everything only if everything were relevant to it. Only such formulas as the blatantly false $(\forall p)p$ (which might be read "Everything is the case") and the trivially true $(\exists p)p$ meet that condition. If less outlandish propositions are to have a chance of being necessary, a weaker criterion of necessity must be accepted. The proposition $\rightarrow AA$ is relevant to A (i.e., it contains exactly the same atomic propositions), it is a theorem of $E_\rightarrow$, and it is indeed the most trivial theorem of that system (in the sense of being both the shortest theorem and the one with the shortest proof). The Anderson and Belnap analysis of $\square A$ thus is that A follows from the most trivial necessary truth that is guaranteed to be relevant to it. They demonstrate that necessity so defined has many of the properties that they would want it to have. For example, they prove a theorem that can be paraphrased as "anything that follows from a true entailment is necessary" (they would want this to be a theorem since for them a formula $\rightarrow XY$ expresses that Y follows from X and thus ought to be true by necessity if it is true at all, and the same ought to be true of anything that follows from it). Their proof of this result is as follows:

11.4.15	1	$\rightarrow BC$	$\{1\}$	supp
	2	$\rightarrow(\rightarrow BC, A)$	$\{2\}$	supp
	3	$\rightarrow AA$	$\{3\}$	supp
	4	$\rightarrow BC$	$\{1\}$	1, reit
	5	$\rightarrow(\rightarrow BC, A)$	$\{2\}$	2, reit
	6	A	$\{1, 2\}$	4, 5, $\rightarrow$-expl
	7	A	$\{1, 2, 3\}$	3, 6, $\rightarrow$-expl
	8	$\rightarrow(\rightarrow AA, A)$ i.e., $\square A$	$\{1, 2\}$	3–7, $\rightarrow$-intro
	9	$\rightarrow(\rightarrow(\rightarrow BC, A), \square A)$	$\{1\}$	2–8, $\rightarrow$-intro
	10	$\rightarrow(\rightarrow BC, \rightarrow(\rightarrow(BC, A), \square A))$	$\emptyset$	1–9, $\rightarrow$-intro

Note the importance of step 7: while it appears to duplicate step 6, the use of $\rightarrow$AA in establishing it enlarges the set of indices, and that enlargement of the set of indices is essential if the subproof beginning at line 3 is to establish anything, since the conclusion of the subproof must involve the index 3 if the subproof is to terminate.

Anderson and Belnap (1975:29) credit Prior with calling to their attention the fact that if $E_\rightarrow$ is supplemented by certain axioms that from their point of view express plausible relations between $\square$ and $\rightarrow$, $\square$A can be shown to be deductively equivalent to $\rightarrow$($\rightarrow$AA, A). The axioms in question are

11.4.16   i. $\rightarrow$($\square$A, A)
            ii. $\rightarrow$($\rightarrow$AB, $\square$($\rightarrow$AB))
            iii. $\rightarrow$($\square$A, $\rightarrow$($\rightarrow$AB, $\square$B))

(The axiom of this set that is most controversial but also most characteristic of Anderson and Belnap's approach is axiom ii, which expresses the idea that any true entailment is true by necessity). The proof of $\rightarrow$($\rightarrow$($\rightarrow$AA, A), $\square$A) is as follows; see Anderson and Belnap (1975:29) for a proof of its converse:

11.4.17   1 $\rightarrow$AA   theorem of $E_\rightarrow$
            2 $\rightarrow$($\rightarrow$AA, $\square$($\rightarrow$AA))   axiom ii, with A
                                                                in place of B

            3 $\square$($\rightarrow$AA)   1, 2, $\rightarrow$-expl
            4 $\rightarrow$($\square$$\rightarrow$AA), $\rightarrow$($\rightarrow$($\rightarrow$AA, A), $\sqcup$A)) axiom iii, with
                                                                $\rightarrow$AA in place of
                                                                A, A in place of B

            5 $\rightarrow$($\rightarrow$($\rightarrow$AA, A), $\square$A)   3, 4, $\rightarrow$-expl

Thus, the effect of Anderson and Belnap's definition of $\square$ could be obtained equivalently by taking $\square$ as a primitive and adding the axioms 11.4.16 to the deductive apparatus of $E_\rightarrow$.

Anderson and Belnap's system $E_\rightarrow$, in which both $\sim$ and $\rightarrow$ are available as connectives and the rules of inference of $E_\rightarrow$ are supplemented by rules of inference for $\sim$, has the means available to define $\diamondsuit$ as well as $\square$ ($\diamondsuit$A is defined as $\sim$$\square$$\sim$A, that is, as $\sim$$\rightarrow$($\rightarrow$($\sim$A, $\sim$A), $\sim$A)). They are able to demonstrate a large number of deductive equivalences between formulas involving $\square$ and $\diamondsuit$, for example,

11.4.18 $\square$$\square$A $\dashv$$\vdash$ $\square$A
            $\square$$\diamondsuit$$\square$$\diamondsuit$A $\dashv$$\vdash$ $\square$$\diamondsuit$A

Using the term "modality" to denote a concatenation of □, ◇, and ~, it can be shown that E$_{\to}$ has the following 14 mutually nonequivalent modalities:

11.4.19

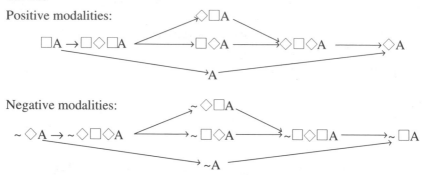

Positive modalities:

Negative modalities:

These are the same 14 "modalities" that are distinguished in Lewis's S4, though there is some problem in interpreting the word "same" here. In an extended digression into the relationship between their modal logic and the various Lewis systems, Anderson and Belnap point out that one's picture of the relationship among the various systems depends heavily on what one takes the relationship between necessity and "strict implication" to be. Regardless of whether one is operating in terms of Lewis's "strict implication" or Anderson and Belnap's "entailment," both the possibility of defining "necessary" as "implied by the proposition that it implies itself" and that of defining it as "implied by its negation" are available. Calling the first kind of necessity □ and the second kind □', one can separate the problem of determining what □-modalities a system has from that of determining what □'-modalities it has. E$_{\to}$ has the 14 □-modalities listed in 11.4.19 but has 42 □'-modalities. When it is stated that S3 has 42 modalities, what is meant is □'-modalities, and in this respect S3 and E$_{\to}$ agree completely. However, if one takes the trouble to determine what □-modalities S3 has, as apparently Anderson and Belnap were the first to do, one finds that S3, like E$_{\to}$ and S4, has the 14 modalities listed in 11.4.19. In S4 the □-modalities and the □'-modalities coincide, as a result of the fact that in S4 (though not in S3 or E$_{\to}$) □'A implies □A.

There is a large and important class of formulas X for which □X is provable in E$_{\to}$ but □'X is not provable, namely, theorems of the form →AB. Anderson and Belnap (1975:120–21) establish that **no** formula of the form →(~→AB, →CD) is a theorem of E$_{\to}$. Thus, in particular, →(~→AB,

$\rightarrow$AB), that is, $\Box'(\rightarrow$AB), is never a theorem, even though for many choices of A and B, $\rightarrow$AB is a theorem (e.g., $\rightarrow$AA is a theorem).

11.5. Appendix: Converses of the Theorems about Reflexivity, Symmetry, and Transitivity of the Accessibility Relation R

It was proved in section 11.2 that for any modal system M with accessibility relation R, and any formula A,

11.5.1   If R is reflexive, then $\supset(\Box A, A)$ is valid in M; (11.2.5)

11.5.2   If R is symmetric, then $\supset(A, \Box\Diamond A)$ is valid in M; (11.2.12)

11.5.3   If R is transitive, then $\supset(\Box A, \Box\Box A)$ is valid in M. (11.2.6)

Under the assumptions that M has only finitely many worlds and that any two worlds of M are "distinguishable," in the sense that for any two worlds there is a proposition that is true in one and false in the other, the converses of these three results can also be proved.

Theorem. Let M be a modal system that contains only finitely many worlds, any two of which are distinguishable; let R be the accessibility relation of M. Then if $\supset(\Box A, A)$ is valid in M for all formulas A, R is reflexive.

Proof. Suppose that we had a modal system M which met those conditions, but in which R was not reflexive. Since R is not reflexive, there is a world w such that $\sim Rww$. There must be some world w_1 accessible from w, since if there were not, $\Box A$ would be vacuously true for any A, and thus, since $\supset(\Box A, A)$ is valid in M, all propositions A would be true in w, contrary to the standing assumption that only a classical valuation can be a world. Since $\sim Rww$, we have $w_1 \neq w$. There is some proposition A_1 such that A_1 is true in w_1 and false in w.[18] Since A_1 is false in w and $\supset(\Box A_1, A_1)$ is true in w (being a substitution instance of a formula that is valid in M), $\Box A_1$ will be false in w. That means that there is then a world w_2 such that Rww_2 and A_1 is false in w_2. That world is not w, since $\sim Rww$, and it is not w_1, since A_1 is true in w_1 but false in w_2. There then is some proposition A_2 which is true in w_2 but false in w. Let us summarize what we have so far, using arrows to indicate the accessibility relation:

11.5.4

	w	w_1	w_2
A_1	F	T	F
$\square A_1$	F		
A_2	F		T
$\vee A_1 A_2$	F	T	T

Since $\vee A_1 A_2$ is false in w, $\square \vee A_1 A_2$ will also be false in w (by the assumption that $\supset(\square A, A)$ is valid in M for any A), and thus there is some world w_3 such that Rww_3 and $\vee A_1 A_2$ is false in w_3. Since $\vee A_1 A_2$ is true in w_1 and w_2, w_3 cannot be the same world as w_1 or w_2, and since $\sim Rww$, w_3 cannot be the same world as w. Let A_3 be a proposition which is false in w and true in w_3. We then have the following more complete description of M:

11.5.4′

	w	w_1	w_2	w_3
A_1	F	T	F	
$\square A_1$	F			
A_2	F		T	
$\vee A_1 A_2$	F	T	T	F
$\square \vee A_1 A_2$	F			
A_3	F			T
$\vee A_1 A_2 A_3$	F	T	T	T

It is now apparent that the method used in constructing w_1, w_2, w_3 can be continued indefinitely. Each time that we construct another world w_i in this sequence, we find a proposition A_i which is true in w_i but false in w. Since $\vee(A_1, A_2, ..., A_i)$ will be false in w, $\square \vee(A_1, A_2, ..., A_i)$ will be false in w, and there is then a world w_{i+1} such that Rww_{i+1} and $\vee(A_1, A_2 ..., A_i)$ is false in w_{i+1}. The world w_{i+1} will be distinct from $w_1, w_2, ..., w_i$, since $\vee (A_1, A_2, ..., A_i)$ is true in all of those worlds, and it will be distinct from w, since $\sim Rww$ but Rww_{i+1}. Thus, M will have to contain infinitely many worlds, contrary to the assumption that it contains only finitely many.

Theorem. Let M be a modal system that contains only finitely many worlds any two of which are distinguishable. Let R be the accessibility relation of M. Then if $\supset(A, \square \diamond A)$ is valid in M for all formulas A, R is symmetric.

Proof. Suppose that we have a modal system M which meets those conditions but in which R is not symmetric. Then there are two worlds w and w_1 such that Rww_1 but $\sim Rw_1w$. There is then a proposition A_1 such that A_1 is true in w and false in w_1. Then $\square \diamond A_1$ is true in w (since both A_1 and $\supset(A_1, \square \diamond A_1)$ are), which means that $\diamond A_1$ is true in all worlds accessible from w, thus in particular in w_1. Thus A_1 is true in some world w_2 which is accessible from w_1, and that world cannot be w_1, since A_1 is false in w_1 and true in w_2, nor can it be w, since Rw_1w_2 but $\sim Rw_1w$. There is then a proposition A_2 which is true in w and false in w_2. We then have the following partial description of M:

11.5.5

	w	w_1	w_2
A_1	T	F	T
$\Box\Diamond A_1$	T		
$\Diamond A_1$		T	
A_2	T		F
$\wedge A_1 A_2$	T	F	F
$\Box\Diamond\wedge A_1 A_2$	T		

Since $\Box\Diamond\wedge A_1 A_2$ is true in w, $\Diamond\wedge A_1 A_2$ is true in all worlds accessible from w, thus in particular in w_1, which means that $\wedge A_1 A_2$ is true in some world w_3 accessible from w_1. That world is distinct from both w_1 and w_2, since $\wedge A_1 A_2$ is false in both of those worlds but true in w_3, and it is distinct from w, since Rw_1w_3 but not Rw_1w. Let A_3 be a proposition that is true in w and false in w_3. Then $\wedge(A_1, A_2, A_3)$ will be true in w but false in w_1, w_2, and w_3. The proposition $\Box\Diamond\wedge(A_1, A_2, A_3)$ is then true in all worlds accessible from w, thus in particular in w_1, which means that $\wedge(A_1, A_2, A_3)$ is true in some world w_4 accessible from w_1. By the same argument as before, w_4 is distinct from w, w_1, w_2, and w_3. It is clear that this construction can be continued without limit. Having found a world w_i which is accessible from w_1 and distinct from w, w_1, ..., w_{i-1}, we know that there is a proposition A_i that is true in w and false in w_i, and $\wedge(\Lambda_1, \Lambda_2, ..., \Lambda_i)$ will be true in w but false in w_1, w_2, ..., w_i. The proposition $\Box\Diamond\wedge(A_1, A_2, ..., A_i)$ is then true in w, which means that $\wedge(A_1, A_2, ..., A_i)$ is true in some world w_{i+1} which is accessible from w_1 and which (by the same arguments as before) will be distinct from w, w_1, ..., w_i. Since this construction can be carried on indefinitely, M will have to contain infinitely many worlds, contrary to the assumption that M contains only finitely many.

Theorem. Let M be a modal system that contains only finitely many worlds of which any two are distinguishable, with accessibility relation R. Then if $\supset(\Box A, \Box\Box A)$ is valid in M for all formulas A, R is transitive.

Proof. Suppose that M meets the above conditions and that R is not transitive. Since R is not transitive, there are worlds such that Rww', $Rw'w''$, but $\sim Rww''$. Since M contains only finitely many worlds, there are only finitely many worlds accessible from w. Call those worlds w_1, w_2, ..., w_n. Since w'' is not accessible from w, w'' is not among the w_i's. For each i ($1 \leq i \leq n$) there is a proposition A_i such that A_i is true in w_i but false in w''. Let B stand for $\vee(A_1, A_2, \ldots, A_n)$. We have chosen B in such a way that it is true in $w_1, w_2, \ldots, w_n$ but false in w''. Since $w_1, \ldots, w_n$ are all the worlds that are accessible from w and since B is true in all of those worlds, $\Box$B is true in w. Since $\supset(\Box$B, $\Box\Box$B) is valid in M, $\Box\Box$B will then be true in w, which means that $\Box$B is true in all worlds accessible from w, thus in particular in w'. But that means that B is true in all worlds accessible from w', thus in particular in w''. However, we chose B in such a way that it would be false in w''. Thus the supposition leads to a contradiction, and the theorem is established.

The assumption that the worlds of M are distinguishable is essential only to the result about reflexivity. It is possible for $\supset(\Box$A, A) to be valid in a modal system without the accessibility relation being reflexive, provided some world has a "doppelgänger," in which the same propositions are true and which stands in the same accessibility relations to other worlds, except that the given world is accessible to its doppelgänger but not to itself. For example, compare the "normal" system of worlds in 11.5.6a with its close relative in 11.5.6b, which has a doppelgänger w_1' for the world w_1:

11.5.6

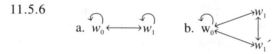

In either modal system, $\Box$A is true in a particular world if and only if A is true in all worlds, and thus $\supset(\Box$A, A) is valid in either system, despite the fact that in 11.5.6b the accessibility relation is not reflexive.

It is possible to replace a given modal system M in which some worlds have doppelgängers by an alternative modal system M* in which there are no doppelgängers and things are otherwise essentially the same. Specifically, let the worlds of M* be equivalence classes of worlds of M under the equivalence relation $\equiv$ that is defined by: $w \equiv w'$ if the same propositions are true in w as in w'. Using $w*$ to denote the equivalence class containing w (i.e., $w*$ consists of all worlds equivalent to w), let $R*w_1*w_2*$ hold if w_i* contains a world w_{1a} and w_2* contains a world w_{2a} such that $Rw_{1a}w_{2a}$. Finally, let those propositions be true in $w*$ that are true in w. We have then set things up in such a way that no world of M* has a doppelgänger, but M* is "essentially the same as" M, in that truth and accessibility in M* exactly parallel truth and accessibility in M. In particular, each of the three formulas that figure in the above theorems is valid in M if and only if it is valid in M*. R is symmetric if and only if R* is symmetric, and R is transitive if and only if R* is transitive; thus the distinguishability requirement can be dropped from the second and third theorems.

However, it is not the case that R is reflexive if and only if R* is reflexive; in fact, if R is as in 11.5.6b, then R* will be as in 11.5.6a, which shows that it is possible for R* to be reflexive without R being reflexive. Thus, the construction of M* from M allows one to prove a more general form of the symmetry and transitivity theorems, though not of the reflexivity theorem.

Exercises

1. Assume a system of possible worlds as follows ($\textcircled{i} \to \textcircled{j}$ means Rw_iw_j):

	p	q	r
w_0	T	T	F
w_1	T	F	T
w_2	F	T	F

For each of the three worlds, determine the truth value of

a. $\Box p$
b. $\Box \supset (r, \Box \wedge pq)$
c. $\supset (\Box \vee pq, \Diamond \wedge pr)$

2. If $\Box$ and $\Diamond$ are equivalent to "in all accessible worlds, . . ." and "in some accessible worlds, . . . ," then the various valid formulas of predicate logic will correspond to valid formulas of modal logic, for example,

$\supset ((\forall x) \wedge (fx, gx), \wedge ((\forall x)fx, (\forall x) gx))$ will correspond to $\supset (\Box \wedge AB, \wedge (\Box A, \Box B))$

What is the modal analog of each of the following valid formulas of predicate logic?

a. $\supset ((\exists x) \vee (fx, gx), \vee ((\exists x)fx, (\exists x)gx))$
b. $\supset (\wedge ((\forall x)fx, (\exists x)gx), (\exists x) \wedge (fx, gx))$
c. $\vee ((\exists x)(fx, (\exists x) \sim fx)$

3. Assume a modal system as in exercise 1, plus the following:

world	objects existing	philosophers	dangerous individuals
0	a, b, c	a, c	a, b, c
1	a, b, d	a, b, d	b, d
2	b, c, d	b, d	b, c, d

Determine the truth value of each of the following formulas in each of the three worlds:

   i. □(∀: Phil *x*)(Dang *x*)
   ii. (∀: Phil *x*)□(Dang *x*)

If you find yourself needing to evaluate □(Dang *e*) for an *e* that does not exist in all relevant worlds, follow policy iii of section 11.3.

   4. Suppose we admit a one-place predicate "Exist" with the following truth conditions: for any individual *a* and any world *w*, "*a* Exist" is true in *w* if *a* belongs to the domain of *w* and is false in *w* otherwise. For each of the three policies about objects that do not exist in all worlds, say what the policy's implications are for the truth conditions of (∀: *x* Man)$_x$ □(*x* Exist).

   5. a. Determine whether the proof of 3.2.4 given in chapter 3 will stand up if ⊃ is replaced by → throughout and Anderson and Belnap's rules of inference are assumed.

     b. Do the same for 3.2.5.

     c. Show that the most obvious proof of (i) can be converted in a straightforward way into a proof of an analog (with → in place of ⊃) that conforms to Anderson and Belnap's system of rules of inference, while the most obvious proof of (ii) cannot:

       i. ⊃(⊃(A, ⊃BC), ⊃(∧AB, C))
       ii. ⊃(⊃(∧AB, C), ⊃(A, ⊃BC))

   6. Suppose we were to adopt the following version of ∼-intro in relevant entailment logic:

     | A   {*i*}
     | . . .
     | B   M ⎫
     | ∼B   N ⎬ at least one of which contains *i*
      ∼A   M∪N - {*i*}

For each of the following proofs in chapter 3, determine whether an analogous proof with → replacing ⊃ throughout would conform to the rules of relevant entailment logic:

   a. 3.2.14b.
   b. 3.2.8a.
   c. 3.2.8e.

   7. Why is *b* more difficult to interpret than *a*:

   a. World War I could have ended a year earlier.
   b. World War I could have begun a year earlier.

12. Applications of Possible Worlds

12.1. "World-Creating" Predicates

An informal practise has developed among linguists of speaking of certain verbs and adjectives as "world-creating" and of speaking of the complements of those predicates as referring to various alternative worlds, for example, speaking of the complement of *believe* in 12.1.1a (i.e., the clause *I have an elder sister*) as referring to a "world of Oscar's beliefs" rather than to the "real world" and speaking of the complement of *want* in 12.1.1b (i.e., the underlying clause *Someone helps John*) as referring to a "world of John's wants":

12.1.1   a. Oscar believes that I have an elder sister.
         b. John wants someone to help him.

In this section I will develop this informal way of speaking into something more precise and in the process deal with some of the syntactic and semantic problems that have been discussed in terms of such "worlds".

Consider first the problem of specifying where pronouns can be relative to their antecedents. A NP inside the complement of a world-creating predicate can be the antecedent of a pronoun that is not inside the complement of that predicate, even of a pronoun that is in the complement of some other world-creating predicate:

12.1.2   Tom expects to catch a fish and intends to fry it for dinner.

The interpretation of 12.1.2 at issue here is the "nonreferential" one, which does not imply that there is a specific fish that Tom expects to catch. The usual treatment of nonreferential NPs (e.g., Quine 1960: 154–56), in which they are bound by existential quantifiers with narrow scope (in this case, "Tom catch x" would have to be the scope of the existential quantifier) is doomed to failure here, since the pronoun, which should presumably be just a repetition of the bound variable, is outside the scope of the quantifier that would have to bind it. But the analysis in terms of context and CD that was developed in sec.

415

10.6 as an alternative to Quine's approach meets a failure almost as ignominious: while an interpretation of 12.1.2 in which *a fish* is used referentially (i.e., one in which the first conjunct says that there is a particular fish that Tom expects to catch, just as there was a particular whale that Captain Ahab in *Moby Dick* hoped to harpoon) of course allows such an analysis, the non-referential interpretation of 12.1.2 does not, since the first conjunct then does not express an existential proposition but only something that **contains** an existential proposition. The possibility of such pronoun-antecedent relations depends on what predicates appear in the host sentences.[1]

12.1.3 a. Tom expected to inherit $50,000 and hoped/*managed to buy a
            house with it.
       b. It's certain that you'll find a job, and it's conceivable that it
           will be a good-paying one.
       b'. ??It's conceivable that you'll find a job, and it's certain that it
           will be a good-paying one.
       c. Gladys intends to buy an apartment building and is
           considering turning it into a condominium.
       c'. ??Gladys is considering buying an apartment building and
           intends to turn it into a condominium.

Following Lakoff (1972a: 615ff.), I will ascribe these differences to differences in the relationships that the various predicates allow between their complements and the various "worlds" that come into consideration.

A second problem that has led linguists to discuss world-creating predicates in terms of worlds is that of determining the presuppositions of a complex sentence, especially determining the relationship between presuppositions of the constituents of a sentence and the presuppositions of the entire sentence. This includes such questions as why the presupposition of the *regret* clause (that Mary's parents have only one child) is a presupposition (in some sense) of the main clause in 12.1.4a but not in 12.1.4b:

12.1.4 a. Mary is sure that her parents regret that they have only one
            child.
       b. Mary thinks that she has no brothers and sisters, and she is sure
           that her parents regret that they have only one child.

I will sketch below an extension of Karttunen's (1974) treatment of pragmatic presuppositions that is suggested by ideas of Morgan (1973) and use it to provide an account of presuppositional phenomena in relation to world-creating predicates.

In addition, there is an important problem relating to the grammatical feature of person that has occasionally been analyzed in terms of worlds. Normally, two occurrences of *I/me/myself* in the same sentence must be coreferential, and, accordingly, processes such as reflexivization that are contingent on coreferentiality are obligatory when the items in question are both first-person singular:

12.1.5   a. I kicked myself/*me.
          b. Marge asked me about myself/*me.

However, it is possible to get noncoreferential first-person pronouns in such sentences as 12.1.6:

12.1.6   a. I dreamed that I was Brigitte Bardot and that I kissed me.
          b. If I were you, I'd kiss me.
          c. If we were the bosses, we wouldn't hire us either. (example
             from Reis 1974:158)

Multiple references for first-person pronouns arise when the sentence alludes to an alternative world in which the speaker (or a set of persons including the speaker, in plural cases such as 12.1.6c) is presented as experiencing something from someone else's vantage point.[2]

I have put the word "world" in quotation marks in much of the above discussion for two reasons. First, in many cases the complement of the world-creating predicate refers not to a single world but to an open-ended class of worlds, as in 12.1.1b, where the complement refers indiscriminately to any of the many worlds in which someone helps John. Second, the so-called belief worlds, wish worlds, dream worlds, and the like are not simply worlds but entire modal systems. Mark's beliefs have to do not only with what he takes to be the real world but with his conception of what the alternatives to that world are. When I ascribe to Mark belief in a modal proposition, I am ascribing to him a belief about what for him are the alternatives to his "real world," not a belief about what for me are the alternatives to my "real world." This point is brought out by such examples as

12.1.7   a. Mark believes that Bill, whom I know to already be in
             Pittsburgh, can't possibly be in Pittsburgh yet.
          b. Pythagoras thought that π was a rational number.
          c. Oliver thinks it's possible that John F. Kennedy, who we all
             know was killed in 1963, is still alive in a secret location in
             Texas.

The "belief worlds" may involve objects that the speaker not only does not take as existing in the real world but may take as not existing in any alternative worthy of consideration:

12.1.8   a. Larry thinks I have an elder sister named Mary.
         b. Janet is convinced that there is a largest prime number.
         c. My neighbor's son is worried that there may be a three-headed
            fire-breathing monster lurking under his bed.

The belief worlds may also lack objects that exist in the real world, and a belief proposition may be false simply by virtue of the alleged belief being about an object that the person does not have in his belief world for him to have a belief about. Thus, since Plato (like ancient Greeks in general) had no conception of zero as a number, 12.1.9a is false and, indeed, is false for exactly the same reason that 12.1.9b is false, namely, that neither Chomsky nor the proposition that $0 \times 7 = 0$ existed for Plato:

12.1.9   a. Plato believed that $0 \times 7 = 0$.
         b. Plato admired Chomsky.

This does not mean that $0 \times 7 = 0$ was false in the world of Plato's beliefs: the proposition simply did not exist for him. Thus, if one adopts a treatment of belief as in Hintikka (1969a), in which "a believes S" is true if and only if S is true in all worlds in which a's beliefs are true, one cannot assume the standard conception of a world as a **complete** specification of truth values of propositions, since to allow 12.1.9a to be false one should not be required to accept the absurdity of worlds in which all of Plato's beliefs are true but $0 \times 7 = 0$ is false: 12.1.9a is false not because Plato's beliefs allow 0×7 to be something other than zero but rather because that proposition that $0 \times 7 = 0$ is not provided for by Plato's beliefs.

Belief worlds may even conform to a different version of logic than the real world is taken to be subject to; such worlds would be appropriate devices for analyzing such sentences as those in which an adherent of standard logic accurately attributes beliefs to an intuitionist (or vice versa).

Let us see how the account of pragmatic presuppositions given in section 10.4 might be adapted to sentences like those in 12.1.4. The pragmatic presupposition associated with *regret* is satisfied in 12.1.4b even though the presupposed proposition (that Mary's parents have only one child) clearly need not be part of the context. The sentence can indeed be acceptable relative to a context that contains mutual knowledge that conflicts with that proposition, say, the proposition that Mary's parents have two children. Suppose, though, that we take into account not only mutual knowledge about the (presumable) real world but also mutual knowledge about the various other worlds that figure in the discourse. From 12.1.4b we receive information not only about the real world (namely that Mary has the beliefs in question) but also about the world as Mary believes things to be (namely that in that world Mary has no brothers and sisters and that her parents regret that they have only one child). Let us thus posit not just a single context and a single contextual domain but a context and a CD for each world that is referred to in the discourse and in addition assume that pragmatic presuppositions are demands on the context and CD that are relevant to the clause in which the bearer of the presupposition occurs, e.g., that in 12.1.4b the pragmatic presupposition of *regret* relates to the world in which Mary's parents are said to have the regret, that is, the world of Mary's beliefs. Since the first conjunct of the complement of *think* adds to the context of Mary's belief world the proposition that Mary has no brothers and sisters, the second conjunct is interpreted relative to that context, and thus the demand that *regret* makes on its context is satisfied: the belief world context entails that Mary's parents have only one child.

The same approach solves the problem raised by 12.1.2, provided an important stipulation is made about the relationship among the worlds that figure in a discourse. In 12.1.2 three worlds are referred to: the real world, the world as it will be if Tom's expectation is fulfilled, and the world as it will be if Tom carries out his intention. The intention, however, is contingent on the fulfillment of the expectation: only if Tom catches a fish does the possibility arise of his frying whatever fish he catches. Thus, the intention world here is dependent on the expectation world in a way that it would not be if we were talking about an intention that was unrelated to the expectation. I will take this dependency as implying that the context and CD of the "governing" world carry over to the dependent world, except to the extent that the dependent world is set up so as to differ from the governing world. Thus, for example, Tom will be a member of the CD for the expectation world, and all propositions in the real world context will also belong to the expectation world context, except where they conflict with the proposition that Tom will catch a fish (e.g., if the proposition that Tom is incapable of catching a fish belongs to the real context, it will not carry over to the expectation world context).[3]

Let us call the context and CD relative to which 12.1.2 is uttered X and Y respectively, and the three worlds w, w', w'', and let us determine what the context and CD for each world are at the various relevant points in 12.1.2. The interpretation of *it* (or of *the fish*, which could be substituted for *it* in 12.1.2 without altering the interpretation) is made relative to the context and CD for w'', since w'' is the world that the complement of *intend* refers to. Since the w''-CD contains an element (namely, a) that is identical to the element of the w'-CD that corresponds to the antecedent (and since the proposition that that element is a fish belongs to the w''-context), the pronoun or definite description can be interpreted as having the given antecedent.

12.1.10 $_a$ Tom expects to catch a fish and $_b$ intends to fry it for dinner. $_c$

	Context/CD at a	Context/CD at b	Context/CD at c
w-cont	X	X $\cup$ {T expects to catch a fish}	X $\cup$ {T expects to catch a fish$_i$, T intends to fry i for dinner}
w-CD	Y	Y	Y
w'-cont	X	X $\cup$ {T catches e, e is a fish}	X $\cup$ {T catches e, e is a fish}
w'-CD	Y	Y $\cup$ {e}	Y $\cup$ {e}
w''-cont		X $\cup$ {T catches e, e is a fish}	X $\cup$ {T catches e, e is a fish, T fries e for dinner}
w''-CD		Y $\cup$ {e}	Y $\cup$ {e}

The reason that 12.1.4a appears to pragmatically presuppose that Mary's parents have only one child is that, unless prior linguistic context has provided information about the world of Mary's beliefs such as was provided by the first conjunct of the complement of *think* in 12.1.4b, the belief-world context will contain only propositions that are in the real-world context, and thus the belief-world context will not satisfy the demands of *regret* unless the real-world context does. The failure of most authors to distinguish the roles of different contexts in satisfying presuppositions is largely responsible for the fruitlessness of much of the discussion about whether various world-creating predicates are presuppositional "holes" (as claimed by Langendoen and Savin 1971) or presuppositional "plugs" (Karttunen 1973). Morgan (1973) appears to be the first author to conclude that world-creating predicates are neither unequivocal plugs nor unequivocal holes. Morgan observed, for example, that while 12.1.11a normally commits the speaker to the proposition that Alice's house is on fire, it will not so commit him if it appears in a dialogue like that in 12.1.11b:

12.1.11 a. Tom thinks Alice doesn't know her house is on fire.
    b. Betty: Tom thinks Alice's house is on fire.
       Marvin: How on earth could he think that? Surely if Alice's house was on fire, she wouldn't just be sitting in the next room doing a crossword puzzle—she'd be trying to save her collection of James Joyce manuscripts from the fire.
       Betty: Tom thinks Alice doesn't know her house is on fire.

The context in 12.1.11b appears to filter out the apparent presupposition of 12.1.11a because Betty's first remark provides the addressee with information about the alternative world that her second remark relates to. It is immaterial that both of her remarks begin with *Tom thinks;* distinct predicates can refer to the same world, as in such examples as

12.1.12   Larry thinks I have a sister named Mary. He is convinced that
            my sister Mary is working for a Ph.D. in anthropology.

The two world-creating predicates in 12.1.12 both refer to the same "world of Larry's beliefs." The first sentence in 12.1.12 informs the addressee that in that world the speaker has a sister named Mary, and the second sentence informs him that in that same world the speaker's sister Mary (not a real world person, but an individual in Larry's belief world) is working for a Ph.D. in anthropology. If the second sentence in 12.1.12 were used in a different context (say, one in which nothing has yet been said about Larry's beliefs), it would be interpreted as ascribing to Larry a belief about a real world individual and would take for granted that the speaker actually has a sister named Mary. In either case the definite description *my sister Mary* picks out an individual of Larry's belief world; that individual will be identified with a real world individual unless the context establishes the existence in the belief world of a nonreal individual that is the speaker's sister and is named Mary.

There are also cases in which a belief world CD differs from the real world CD in lacking individuals that belong to the real world CD:

12.1.13   Agnes thinks I have only one older brother and that my older
            brother regrets that I am a second son.

If 12.1.13 is spoken in a context containing the proposition that the speaker has two older brothers, with both of the brothers belonging to the contextual domain, *my older brother* will pick out a referent not from the real world contextual domain but rather from an alternative contextual domain in which either a real world brother is missing or a single entity corresponds equally to the two real world brothers.

What desires, intentions, and fears a person can have and what he can order or request depend directly not on the real world but on his beliefs. I have already adopted the practice of speaking of a world as **governing** a world that is introduced as an alternative to it, and I will continue that practice with the qualification that in the case of sentences that refer to desires, intentions, orders, etc., I will speak of the **reference world** of the complement (i.e., the world that the complement purports to describe) as governed not by the world to which the main clause refers but by the person's belief world. Thus, in analyzing a sentence such as *Arthur wants to catch a unicorn,* I will speak of three worlds: the reference world of the main clause (i.e., the world that the speaker takes to be the real world), the world of Arthur's beliefs, and the reference world of the complement: a world in which the given desire of Arthur's is fulfilled; the first world governs the second, the second governs the third, and the first only indirectly governs the third. Note that in cases such as this, the analysis of a sentence involves a world that is not the reference world of any of its parts. It is from the context and CD of the world that (directly) governs a given world that its context and CD are derived by additions, occasionally also by deletions, fissions, or fusions.

In 12.1.14, the acceptability of *it* is due to the presence in the belief CD of an object *a* such that "*a* is a unicorn" and "*a* has been eating Arthur's roses" are in the belief context, and the acceptability of *its horn* is due to the same considerations plus the presence in the belief context of the proposition "every unicorn has exactly one horn," which was carried over to the belief context from the real world context:

12.1.14   Arthur stupidly thought that a unicorn had been eating his roses, and he wanted to catch it by throwing a rope around its horn.

The difference between 12.1.14 and 12.1.15 is that the complement of an implicative verb such as *manage* has the same reference world as the superordinate clause does:

12.1.15   *Arthur stupidly thought that a unicorn had been eating his roses, and he managed to catch it by throwing a rope around its horn.

Taking the reference world of the topmost S to be the real world, we can conclude that the complement of *manage* here also has the real world as its reference world, and since the real world context and CD provide no referents for *it* and *its horn,* 12.1.15 is anomalous. The sameness of reference world for the *manage* clause and its complement is part of a more general point about implicative verbs, namely, that the complement clause shares **all** reference points with the clause of the implicative verb, for example, as Karttunen (1971b) has observed, they share the same time reference: the time at which Brenda manages to open the jar is the time at which Brenda opens the jar, and the time at which Oscar has the impudence to tell you to shine his shoes is the time at which Oscar tells you to shine his shoes.

The differences in acceptability between some of the examples in 12.1.3 can be attributed to considerations of the reference world. For example, in

12.1.3c, what Gladys is considering is contingent on fulfillment of her intention, that is, the world corresponding to what she is considering is governed by the world specifying fulfillment of her intention. The unacceptability of 12.1.3c′ reflects the fact that one's intentions can be based only on what one is sure of, not on ideas that one is merely entertaining:

12.1.16 a. Gladys intends to buy an apartment building and is considering turning it into a condominium.
   b. ??Gladys is considering buying an apartment building and intends to turn it into a condominium.

The terms "belief world" and "dream world" have been convenient in the discussion so far, largely because of the relative stability of beliefs and dreams: one has a single set of beliefs at a time (possibly inconsistent beliefs, but a single set nonetheless), and one has dreams one at a time, with a second dream not beginning until the first dream has come to an end. There is no equally convenient analogous terminology for worlds having to do with wishes and orders, since one may have independent sets of wishes or independent sets of orders in effect simultaneously. For example, you can both want to spend the summer in Greece and want to spend the summer in Mexico without necessarily having the contradictory wish to spend the summer both in Greece and in Mexico. Likewise, one can both order Patricia to play the piano and order Stan to prevent anyone from playing the piano, and one must separate the question of whether the one order is complied with from the question of whether the other one is complied with, rather than lumping those two questions together by talking about a world in which your orders are complied with. It thus makes no sense to speak of "Alice's wish world" or "Oscar's order world," although it does make sense to speak of wishes and orders in terms of alternative worlds.

A treatment in terms of alternative worlds seems to be called for in view of the fact that pronouns and definite descriptions can be used that refer not to real world entities but to entities that will be identifiable only if the wish or order is fulfilled, and they can appear in the complements of separate predicates:

12.1.17 a. Nancy wants to write a short story and hopes she can get *Playboy* to accept it.
   b. Morris ordered me to write a piano sonata and suggested that I put lots of modulations in the slow movement.

It will probably be clearest if one simply avoids such terms as "wish world," which misleadingly suggests that there is a single system of wishes whose simultaneous fulfillment is at issue, and instead simply use circumlocutions that say that a particular world corresponds to the fulfillment of a particular wish or order on the part of a given person. These worlds may serve as reference worlds for other worlds that correspond to, say, the fulfillment of wishes, hopes, and so forth, that are contingent on the fulfillment of a given wish, as in 12.1.17a, where the complement of *hope* refers to a world in which the want in the first conjunct is fulfilled.

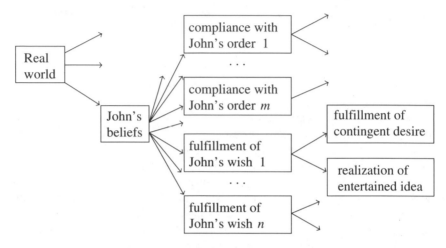

Details of the meanings of various predicates can impose various restrictions on what their complements can have as reference world. Consider, for example, what is responsible for the oddity of the sentence obtained from 12.1.17b by interchanging the two main verbs:

12.1.18   ?Morris suggested that I write a piano sonata and ordered me to
            put lots of modulations in the slow movement.

An order creates an obligation on the addressee's part to perform the action in question. But the addressee's action is performed in the real world, not in a fictitious alternative to it, and in the fictitious world in which I do not carry out Morris's suggestion that I write a piano sonata, there is no slow movement for me to put any modulations in to comply with his order. Taking the world corresponding to the complement of *suggest* as the reference world for the complement of *order* would result in an ill-formed order: an order such that whether the notion of complying with it is intelligible depends on a choice that one is ostensibly free to make. (Note that 12.1.18 is odd in a quite different way from an order that it is impossible to comply with but for which there is no problem determining what would constitute compliance, for example, ordering someone to turn a lump of lead into gold by saying magic words or to write a ten-volume history of China in half an hour.)

I have so far been describing what I want to take as the "normal" way that propositions and objects get into the contexts and contextual domains associated with the various worlds that figure in a discourse. An important class of cases in which propositions and objects get into contexts and CDs by other than the normal route was first discussed in a remarkable paper by Peter Geach (1967), which dealt with the coreferentiality relation between the underlined NPs in such sentences as

12.1.19   Jake believes that a witch has ruined his crops, and Zeke is
            convinced that she (the selfsame witch) has cursed his cows.

Geach argued that the means of standard predicate logic are insufficient to account for this coreferentiality: standard quantification theory allows *she* in 12.1.19 only to correspond to an instance of a bound variable, bound by a quantifier that both it and its antecedent are in the scope of. But since it and its antecedent are in separate conjuncts of 12.1.19, a single quantifier could bind both of them only by having the entire coordinate structure for its scope, and the resulting formula could only correspond to the referential reading of 12.1.19 (the interpretation paraphraseable as "There is a witch such that Jake believes she has ruined his crops and Zeke is convinced that she has cursed his cows"), which leaves the nonreferential interpretation unaccounted for. The proposals of section 10.6 avoid that particular difficulty, since a pronoun with an existentially quantified NP as antecedent no longer need be in the scope of the existential quantifier: it can merely be a repetition of the "discourse referent" that that quantified NP makes available. But a related difficulty immediately appears: the discourse referent here should be available only in those parts of the discourse whose reference world is (or is governed by) Jake's belief world, and the pronoun in 12.1.19 is in a part of 12.1.19 whose reference world is not Jake's belief world but Zeke's.

The problem posed by 12.1.19 arises not only in reports on the beliefs of superstitious rustics but in fact also in reports about normal science, as is shown by examples such as 12.1.20 that can easily be constructed using controversial notions of particle physics or astronomy or even linguistics:

12.1.20   Smith believes that the strange radio emission that his radio
            telescope picked up comes from a quasar, and Sakamoto is
            convinced that that quasar is responsible for the variation that
            he has observed in the spectrum of the crawfish nebula, but if

> you'll look at this calculation, you'll see that there couldn't
> possibly be a quasar in that location.

The plausibility of 12.1.19–20 depends on the ease with which we can imagine beliefs of the one person being communicated to and accepted by the other. For example, they become quite strange if one inserts *secretly* before *believes*. It is indeed such migration of beliefs and supposed objects from one person's belief world to those of others that makes it possible for scientific communities to exist. The acceptability of 12.1.19 reflects not merely the scheme of worlds and contexts developed here but also knowledge on the part of those accepting 12.1.19 and 12.1.20 of a basic mechanism in the sociology of science. Of course, 12.1.19 still fails to conform to the scheme of this section, since this principle of the sociology of science only tells one that the witch and the proposition that she ruined Jake's crops **can** migrate to Zeke's belief world: nothing in that principle or in the first conjunct of 12.1.19 tells us that they **have** migrated there.

Many world-creating predicates have negative counterparts; for example, one sense of *deny* is a negative counterpart of *think* or *believe,* and *forbid* is a negative counterpart of *order.* These items take complements involving nonreferential NPs but do not allow those nonreferential NPs to serve as antecedents for pronouns in subsequent sentences the way that "positive" world-creating predicates do:

12.1.21 a.   Arthur thinks that a unicorn has been eating his roses. He
            hopes he can catch it.
      a′.   Arthur denies that a unicorn has been eating his roses. *He
            hopes he can catch it.
      b.   Mary ordered John to paint a portrait of her and suggested that
            he hang it in the living room.
      b′.   *Mary forbade John to paint a portrait of her and suggested
            that he hang it in the living room.

This can be accounted for by treating these verbs as if they were combinations of a corresponding "positive" verb and a negation: *deny* S = believe (not S), *forbid* S = order (not S), etc. They will refer to a belief world or an order world, not to a "denial world" or a "prohibition world," and the propositions that they will cause to be added to the belief context will be the negations of the complement propositions; for example, the first sentence in 12.1.21a′ will cause the addition to Arthur's belief context of the proposition that it is not the case that a unicorn has been eating Arthur's roses; since that proposition does not imply the existence of a unicorn that has been eating Arthur's roses, no individual matching that description will be added to the contextual domain for Arthur's belief world. Of course, the negative propositions that are added to the belief context can satisfy the contextual demands made by factive predicates that refer to the belief (or other) world in question:

12.1.22 a. Arthur denies that Jennie loves him and thinks it's a shame that no one but his mother loves him.

       b. Mary forbade John to paint a portrait of her and requested that he try not to regret not being allowed to paint a portrait of her.

World-creating predicates can of course appear within the complements of world-creating predicates, for example,

12.1.23 a. Doreen dreamed that Bruno thought she admired him.

       b. Jonathan hopes that I'll want to try to believe that he has reformed.

       c. Maxine thinks Billy believes that peanut butter is a carcinogen.

Just as Maxine's beliefs about Henry Kissinger need not agree with the facts about Kissinger, her beliefs about Billy's belief world need not agree with the facts about Billy's belief world: Billy may in reality have no opinion on whether peanut butter is a carcinogen or may believe that it is not a carcinogen. It is thus necessary (following Morgan 1973) to distinguish the real belief world of Billy from Billy's belief world according to Maxine, Billy's belief world according to Jake according to Samantha, and so on. It is possible to construct sentences in which several such versions of "Billy's belief world" coexist and figure in the satisfaction of the contextual demands made by different definite descriptions and factive predicates later in the discourse:

12.1.24 a. Samantha is convinced that Jake believes that Billy thinks she snorts coke and is sure that Jake regrets that someone who thinks she uses illegal drugs is a friend of the Chief of Police, but actually Jake thinks Billy believes no one in town uses any drugs and is ashamed that Billy hasn't realized that Samantha is taking coke, when in fact Billy believes that everyone but Samantha is taking drugs.

       b. Tom thinks that Alice doesn't know me and that she regrets that none of her friends are anarchists; but Alice and I are actually very good friends and she's delighted that at least one of her friends, namely me, is an anarchist.

I will conclude this section by saying a little about an important class of cases in which sentences not necessarily involving complement clauses can refer to multiple worlds, namely, sentences making reference to "fictions," taken in the broad sense that includes pictorial representations.[4] Neither Santa Claus nor Batman exists. Nonetheless, one must distinguish between Santa Claus and Batman, since a picture of Batman, even a picture of Batman disguised as Santa Claus, is not a picture of Santa Claus. The context "a picture of _____" has often been held to be an "opaque context" because ∃-introduction would derive the supposedly false 12.1.25b from 12.1.25a when 12.1.25a was true:

12.1.25 a. This painting is a picture of Santa Claus.
　　　　　b. There is someone of whom this painting is a picture.

I maintain that the fallacy in going from 12.1.25a to 12.1.25b is not really in the inferential step but in the interpretation that one tends to (but really need not) put on the conclusion, in which the variable is interpreted as ranging over an irrelevant domain, namely, that of real world persons. The blank in "a picture of _____" need not be filled by real world persons,[5] and *someone* can be given an interpretation in which the variable that it binds has a gloriously open-ended domain, encompassing all persons, past, present, or future, real or fictitious, perhaps even from fictitious fictions (fictions that have not actually been composed, such as the play within *Hamlet*) as well as from real fictions (such as *Hamlet* or the myth of Orpheus). *Someone* is in fact ambiguous in terms of whether it ranges over that gloriously open-ended domain or only over real persons. If interpreted the former way, 12.1.25b is true, if interpreted the other way, it is false. The same ambiguity may be seen more clearly in the range of possible answers to questions like 12.1.26a; the choice between *yes* and *no* indicates that on one interpretation *This painting is a painting of someone* is true and on another interpretation is false:

12.1.26 a.　Is this painting a picture of someone?
　　　　　b.　Yes, it's a picture of Santa Claus.
　　　　　b'.　No, it's a picture of Santa Claus.

As with belief worlds and dream worlds, fictional worlds take over propositions and objects from the real world (or better, from the reference world— you can have thoughts or dreams about fictions, too). Thus, a painting can depict real world events involving real world participants, fictitious events involving real world participants, or fictitious events involving fictitious participants (or a mixture of real world and fictitious ones):

12.1.27 a. He painted a picture of George Bush conferring with
             Gorbachev.
        b. He painted a picture of George Bush leading a cavalry regiment
             into Iraq.
        c. He painted a picture of a nineteenth-century American president
             named Simon Saddlesores leading an invasion of a Balkan
             republic called Ruritania.

Kripke (1973 lecture at the University of Western Ontario) has made the important point that fictions exist in specific worlds rather than by themselves in some limbo, and thus it makes sense to speak of paintings by Rembrandt and by Picasso as depicting the same myth. Here there is a bound variable ranging over real myths (that is, myths that exist as myths in the real world, which is not to say that the things that figure in the myths exist in the real world: there is a real myth of Sisyphus but no real person Sisyphus). A bound variable ranging over real myths is no more objectionable than a bound variable ranging over real languages: the problems involved in individuating myths (i.e., in deciding whether two actual instances of myth are instances of the same myth) are of essentially the same type and complexity as the problems involved in individuating languages.

Persons, objects, and events in fictions may be represented by real world items (e.g., by actors, props, and actions in the staging of a play). The real items and the fictitious items need not be individuated the same way; for example, a single actor may play several roles, a single fictitious person may be played by a different actor in each act, and a single fictitious event may be represented by several different real world events (as in *Rashomon*, where the killing of the husband is enacted several times). Bound variables may range over either the fictitious objects or the real objects that represent fictitious objects:

12.1.28 a. In the banquet scene, the king promises a fortune to the same
             woman that he had insulted in the battle scene.
        b. In the banquet scene, the same actor is killed as is killed in the
             battle scene.

In 12.1.28a, the variable ranges over characters of the particular play, and it is immaterial whether the same character might be played by different actors in different scenes; in 12.1.28b, the variable ranges over actors in a given performance, and it is immaterial whether a given actor might have played a different role in the battle scene than in the banquet scene. Moreover, as the use of the word *kill* in 12.1.28b illustrates, one can refer to a character that a performer is portraying by mentioning the performer: 12.1.28b refers not to the death of the actor but to the deaths of the characters that he portrayed, and since he portrayed different characters in the two scenes, a different character is (indirectly) referred to in each clause. More generally, one can refer to an entity that figures in events that are being enacted by mentioning its counterpart in the enactment, and vice versa. As long as one is careful about distinguishing between the enactment and the enacted events, one can treat the various lines in a play as the orders, questions, statements, and curses that they purport to be. In the Shakespeare play, Richard III offers to exchange his kingdom for a horse; in a performance in which Dustin Hoffman plays the role of Richard, Hoffman of course does not offer to make such an exchange, though one can seemingly speak as if he did, by referring indirectly to Richard's (illocutionary) act in terms of the actor enacting it on stage:[6]

12.1.29   When Hoffman offered his kingdom for a horse, someone in the balcony started giggling.

12.2. Tense Logic

In discussing the various examples taken up so far, we have paid no attention to the tenses of the verbs or to auxiliary verbs such as *have* and *will* that have some relation to time. In this section I wish to remedy this omission partially and to suggest ways that considerations of time reference may be incorporated into logical structure and related to linguistic means of indicating time reference.

The most basic time notion is probably that of "preceding" or "being earlier than." One time precedes another time if the passage of time takes one from the former time to the latter. A second, almost equally central notion is that of "now" or "the present." The notions of "past" and "future" are put together out of these two more basic notions: the past is what is prior to now and the future is what now is prior to. Many languages express propositions differently, depending on whether they refer to the present, to the past, or to the future. However, there is not a straightforward correspondence between linguistic forms and the present, past, or future time reference of sentences in which they are used. For example, the present tense in English often refers to future events (*Bill's plane arrives at 2:00; I'm cooking red-cooked pig tripe tomorrow*)[7] and *will* may be used with reference to past or present events (*Bill will be in Baltimore by now*). The conditions under which the various tenses and auxiliary verbs may be used involves not only temporal factors but notions such as necessity and possibility and the current information of the speaker and addressee.

There are a number of ways that time considerations might be brought into logical structure. A first possibility is simply to have time appear as an extra argument in the various propositional functions that we have so far considered; for example, instead of having a predicate "Bald(x)" we would have a two-place predicate "Bald(x, t)" expressing that x is bald at time t. A second possibility is to have "operators" R_t expressing that the proposition they are combined with is true at the indicated time; for example, we would have R_t(Bald(x)) instead of Bald(x, t). A third possibility is to treat time as "indices": just as a proposition is not flatly true or flatly false but is true in certain worlds and false in others, a proposition would be true at some times and false at other times. "Now" would have the same special role among the time indices that "the actual world" has among the world indices; that is, unless something indicates the contrary, a proposition is "evaluated" relative to the "actual" indices: it is taken as referring to the present time, to the actual world, to the place where it is uttered, and so forth. These three possibilities can of course be combined with each other. For example, one can treat propositions as being evaluated at times, rather than always involving times as arguments, and still employ R_t in formulating propositions that refer to times other than "now."

Under the third approach, moments in time assume a status like that of worlds in modal logic, and both the relation of temporal precedence and its converse (the relation of temporal subsequence) assume a status like that of an alternativeness relation. For example, if "t_1 precedes t_2" (henceforth written Pt_1t_2) were taken as an alternativeness relation, then according to the truth conditions for modal operators, "necessary" would amount to "at all future times" and "possible" to "at some future time." The bulk of work done on tense logic since the 1950s has in fact developed tense logic as a variety of modal logic, with temporal relations playing the role of "alternativeness."[8] What I propose to do in this section is not to survey "standard" tense logic but rather to survey the various linguistic considerations that I regard as important and sketch a specific variant of tense logic that ties in with them as closely as possible.

The first of these considerations is that English[9] normally separates factors of time from factors of modality; for example, in 12.2.1, *possible* relates to a choice among alternative future histories, whereas *will* relates to future time within a given future history:

12.2.1   It is possible that Bill will finish his novel.

In existing work on tense logic, "branching time" is generally allowed by letting the relation P of temporal precedence be a partial ordering rather than a strict ordering: there can be distinct worlds w' and w'' such that Pww' and Pww'' with w' and w'' not standing in any temporal relation to one another (i.e., $w' \neq w''$, but neither $Pw'w''$ nor $Pw''w'$):

12.2.2

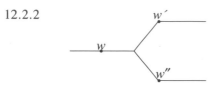

With P taken to represent a relation as in 12.2.2 and used as the alternativeness relations of a modal system, the truth conditions for $\diamond$ will not strictly speaking define a temporal notion but will rather conflate the notions that are separated into the *possible* and the *will* of 12.2.1. If we wish to have an element of logical structure that can be identified with a linguistic notion of futurity and to define that element in terms of an alternativeness relation, we will have to require that it deal with time branches one at a time: *possible* in 12.2.1 will have to be taken as saying that there is a time branch in which . . . , and the *will* of the proposition that *possible* is combined with will have to be taken as saying simply that "Bill finish his novel" is true at some future point on that time branch.

Suppose that the embedded sentence in 12.2.1 is used as an independent sentence:

12.2.3   Bill will finish his novel.

The meaning of 12.2.3 is clearly not that in some world w' such that Pww' (with P as in 12.2.2 and w taken to be the actual present world) Bill finishes his novel, since then it would only mean that there is **some** time branch containing a future point at which Bill finishes his novel, which is not the meaning of 12.2.3 but of 12.2.1 or of *Bill may finish his novel*. Nor does 12.2.3 mean that on **all** branches leading into the future from the present there is a point at which Bill finishes his novel, since 12.2.3 does not embody such a strong assertion: it only says that at some point in the **actual** future Bill will finish his novel and leaves it open whether there are other possible but nonactual futures in which Bill does not finish the novel. An extra index must thus be brought into the analysis of future sentences: one must evaluate the sentence relative not only to the actual world and the actual time but also to the actual future.

The notion of "actual future" may give one a queasy feeling, in that one normally has very little conception of which of the infinitely many possible futures is the actual one; one's knowledge of the past, which involves knowledge of innumerable details that could have turned out otherwise but in fact did not, is far richer than one's knowledge of the future, which consists merely in what can be predicted from one's knowledge of the present via general laws. Nonetheless, speakers of natural languages frequently indulge in the rashness of making statements that purport to describe the actual future. That such statements as 12.2.3 are interpreted as referring to the actual future is confirmed by a consideration of how one applies words like *right, wrong, true,* and *false* in talking about previous statements about the future. For example, 12.2.4 can be a report of George's having said *Mary will finish her thesis by January,* and the speaker's use of *wrong* indicates that the actual future was not what George said it would be:

12.2.4   George said in June that Mary would finish her thesis by
              January, but he was wrong.

The speaker is not attributing to George the proposition that Mary would finish her thesis by January in every possible future: if Mary actually finished her thesis by January but was in grave danger of not finishing it by then, one could not say 12.2.4 to indicate that George made a rash assertion; 12.2.4 is a remark about the correctness of a statement about the actual future, not a comment on a statement about all possible futures. I accordingly take 12.2.3, both as an independent sentence and when it appears embedded in a larger sentence as in 12.2.1, as involving a time variable that ranges over only one time branch at a time, with the time branch over which it ranges being either the actual time branch (if it is an independent sentence) or a variable time branch bound by a quantifier such as I would suggest is involved in the *possible* of 12.2.1 ("there is a time branch in which . . .").

So far it appears that the best temporal analogues to $\Diamond$ and $\Box$ will be operators $\Diamond_f, \Box_f, \Diamond_p, \Box_p$, with the following truth conditions:[10]

12.2.5 $\Diamond_f$ A is true at t on time branch B if and only if there is a t' such
              that Ptt' for which A is true at t' on branch B.
              $\Box_f$ A is true at t on time branch B if and only if for all t' such
              that Ptt', A is true at t' on branch B.
              $\Diamond_p$A is true at t if and only if there is a t' such that P$t't$ for
              which A is true at t'.
              $\Box_p$A is true at t if and only if for all t' such that P$t't$, A is true
              at t'.

However, these four operators do not fit at all closely any devices of the English language. First of all, the bound time variables that figure in the meanings of English sentences typically range over restricted segments of time, rather than over the whole past or the whole future; the language provides a great profusion of devices for indicating the limits of the domains of bound time variables (*since he was three years old, until November,* and the like), and such devices are of very frequent use. Second, in sentences referring to the future, *will* (or *'ll*) is used regardless of whether the future time is constant (12.2.6a), existentially quantified (12.2.6b), or universally quantified (12.2.6c):

12.2.6 a. The concert will begin at 2:00.
       b. I'll phone you some time before I leave.
       c. There'll always be an England.

Third, the conditions for the use of the devices for referring to the past, namely, the past tense, the present perfect, and the past perfect, are in terms of factors other than the one ($\exists$ vs. $\forall$) that distinguishes $\Diamond_p$ from $\Box_p$: they have to do with what the "reference point" is and what relevance the past event has to the present (e.g., it is normal to say *I've sprained my ankle* only as long as the injury still interferes with your activities). Thus, if we are to use temporal analogues of $\Diamond$ and $\Box$ in logical structures, we will have to expect that (i) in addition to the operators defined in 12.2.5 we will need "restricted" versions of those operators, for example, an operator $\Diamond_f^t$ such that $\Diamond_f^t A$ is true if and only if there is a future time between now and t at which A is true; and (ii) it will be necessary to go beyond what can be expressed with these temporal operators in order to distinguish among the relevant natural language devices.

Before I take up in some detail these natural language devices, it will be useful if I first bring in the important notion of an **interval** in time. Many predicates or combinations of predicates and arguments refer to things that are spread over time rather than concentrated at an instant:

12.2.7 a. John has read *War and Peace.*
       b. Elsa hitchhiked across Europe last summer.
       c. J. Paul Getty amassed one of the finest art collections in the world.

To express the meaning of 12.2.7a, it is absurd to say that there is a time instant at which John's reading of *War and Peace* took place, since it is physically impossible for there to be such an instant—reading *War and Peace* isn't something that can be accomplished in an instant. Nor can one reduce the analysis of 12.2.7a to sentences referring to instantaneous events such as that of finishing reading *War and Peace,* since any time adverbials combined with the sentences in 12.2.7 refer to the entire process and not to, say, its termination. For example, 12.2.8a implies that the entire reading took place yesterday, whereas 12.2.8b strongly suggests that the reading did not begin yesterday—John could have read *War and Peace* one sentence a day and have read only the last sentence yesterday:

12.2.8   a. John read *War and Peace* yesterday.
         b. John finished reading *War and Peace* yesterday.

Nor can one analyze *read "War and Peace"* as a conjunction such as "begin reading *War and Peace* and finish reading *War and Peace,*" since in 12.2.9 the reading that began yesterday need not be the same reading that finished yesterday—John might have begun a second reading of the book in the morning and then devoted the evening to finishing his first reading:

12.2.9   John began reading *War and Peace* and finished reading *War and Peace* yesterday.

I would like to propose that not only points in time but also intervals figure in the logical structures of sentences and that the logical structures of examples like 12.2.7 all involve time intervals. Example 12.2.7a will then not say that there is a past time at which John read *War and Peace* but that there is a past time interval such that he read it on that interval. I maintain, though, that propositions that must be evaluated on intervals do not comprise whole sentences but are only constituents of larger sentences that are evaluated at points in time, as in the case of 12.2.7a, in which "John read *War and Peace*" is embedded in the scope of a generalized version of $\Diamond_p$, which is evaluated at the present moment.

The progressive aspect is another common device for deriving point propositions from interval propositions. For example, 12.2.10a can be taken as saying that the point at which Tom enters Agnes's office is contained in an interval occupied by Agnes's writing a letter, formalized provisionally in 12.2.10b:

12.2.10 a. When Tom entered Agnes's office, she was writing a letter.
         b. ($\imath$: R_t(T enter A's office)) ($\exists$: $t \in I$)$_I$(A write a letter)

The interval need not be wholly within the actual time branch; for example, Agnes might have stopped writing when Tom entered and never resumed the task. However, not just any interval leading into a possible future will do, since in describing a roll of fair dice that was interrupted (say by a police raid or an earthquake), it is not correct to say any of *I was rolling* 2/3/4/ . . . /12, even though there were possible futures in which the dice turned up 2, 3, . . . , or 12. The interval must lead into either the actual future or a "normal" future: one in which things turn out as they were supposed to. If we introduce an operator Pr (= "progressive") such that Pr(A) is true at t if and only if A is true on an interval that contains t and is an actual or "normal" continuation of events then in progress,[11] then 12.2.10b can be restated as

12.2.11   ($\imath$: R_t(T enter A's office)), R_t(Pr(A write a letter))

One important thing is still missing from 12.2.11, namely, any indication that the event of Tom's entering Agnes's office is in the past rather than the future. Note that there is no way of employing $\Diamond_p$ or $\Box_p$ to incorporate that information into 12.2.11: there are no more time variables available for them to bind. The minimum application for brute force that would fit in the information that the value of t is past is probably to conjoin Ptn, where n stands for "now," with R_t(T enter A's office) in the definite description operator.

Intervals figure in the logical structure not only of propositions involving events and states that are spread over time but also in propositions in which an instantaneous event is located inexactly. It is often either impossible or not worth the effort to specify the exact moment of an event's occurrence, and one will be satisfied with sentences such as 12.2.12 as specifications of the time at which something happened:[12]

12.2.12 a. Mozart died in 1791.
       b. I ran into Marge yesterday.

The use of *in* in 12.2.12a is directly analogous to spatial uses of *in:* the point at which Mozart died is in the interval 1791; indeed, except for the idiosyncracy of *on* rather than *in* being used with days (*on/*in Tuesday*), the use of prepositions for temporal relations matches very closely the use of the same prepositions for spatial relations (see Bennett 1975).

Natural languages provide a great profusion of devices for referring to times. Besides expressions referring to the present time (*now, at present*), there is a system of "dates" that are in effect proper names for points and periods in time (12.2.13a), there are devices for describing times in terms of things that happened or were the case at those times (12.2.13b), and there are devices for describing times in terms of their distances from other times (12.2.13c), and these devices can be combined in numerous ways:

12.2.13 a.   Darwin was born on February 12, 1809.
       a'. The explosion occurred at 4:22 P.M. Eastern Daylight Time.

    b.   When I started teaching here, housing was fairly easy to find.

    b′. Darwin was born on the day that Lincoln was born.

    c.   Bill left the party one hour after he arrived.

    c′. I'll phone you five minutes before I leave.

    c″. Janet left ten minutes ago. (= ten minutes before now)

These can be analyzed as combinations of R_t with either a constant or a definite description operator, provided one enriches the formal language by the addition of n for "now" and machinery for defining time intervals by giving their endpoints ($[t_1, t_2]$ will denote the [closed] time interval that starts at t_1 and ends at t_2) and their lengths (if I is an interval, /I/ will be the length of I):

12.2.14 b.   (ı: R_t(I start teaching here))$_t$ R_t(housing be fairly easy to find)

         c.   (ı: (ı: $R_{t'}$(b arrive))$_{t'}$(∃: ∧(P$t't$, /[t', t]/ = 1 hr)))$_t$ R_t(b leave the party)

         c′. (ı: ∧(Ptn, /[t, n]/ = 10min))$_t$ R_t(j leave)

In the remainder of this section, I will abbreviate expressions such as ∧(P $t't$, /[t', t]/ = 1 hr) as "t' = t − 1 hr" (read "t' is one hour before t"). The same devices as 12.2.13 are used in specifying the endpoints of time intervals:

12.2.15 a.   Since 1 January 1971, it has been illegal to broadcast cigarette commercials.

         a′. Genevieve worked here from 20 October 1968 until 19 May 1974.

         b.   The job will be ready by Tuesday.

         b′. Since I started teaching here, I've gone to the opera many times.

         b″. The office will be closed until the radiator is repaired.

         c.   I'll be here until an hour from now.

         c′. Between graduating from high school and getting his Ph.D., Bill made three trips to Europe.

When only one endpoint of the interval is mentioned, either the interval extends indefinitely far away from the present (*until last Wednesday*) or the other endpoint is the present (or rather, the "reference time": in such examples as *When I ran into Bill, he had been out of work since the previous April,* it is not up to the present but only up to the time when you ran into Bill that you are saying he was out of work; the sentence is noncommittal about whether he remained out of work after that).

In this discussion, Reichenbach's (1947) notion of "reference point" or "reference time" has raised its head a couple of times. It would be worthwhile at this point to say something about that notion and to sketch Reichenbach's justly influential analysis of tense and time reference. Since the notion of reference point is manifested most clearly in the past perfect, I will begin with a discussion of that relatively uncommon form. A past perfect typically involves a time adverb referring to some past time, combined with a clause that refers to a still earlier time:

12.2.16 a. When John married Amy, he had met Cynthia five years earlier.
  b. When John married Amy, he had already read *War and Peace* three times.

Example 12.2.16a is the past of a past and 12.2.16b the past of a present perfect, in the sense that the content of the main clause, if expressed at the time of John's marriage to Amy, would be expressed by a past tense (*John met Cynthia five years ago*) or a present perfect (*John has already read War and Peace three times*), respectively. The time referred to by the time adverbial serves as a reference point for the main clause, in the sense that the choice of time adverbials and auxiliary verbs and their interpretation depends on relations to that reference time; for example, *earlier* in 12.2.16a means "earlier than [reference time]," and *already* in 12.2.16b means "in the interval ending at [reference time]." Reichenbach represented the various combinations of tense and auxiliary verb in terms of diagrams that specified the relative positions of the speech time, the reference time, and the event reported (S, R, and E, respectively) and took the simple past and the present perfect to differ from the past perfect by virtue of two of the times coinciding that are kept separate in the past perfect:

12.2.17   a. past perfect   b. present perfect   c. past

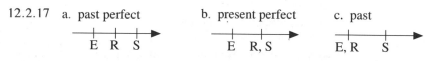

Reichenbach's assignment of reference points in present perfect and past clauses is easiest to justify when one considers not isolated sentences but entire stretches of narrative or other text, in which a single reference point extends over several sentences that differ in time reference:

12.2.18 a. When Mark got off the plane, he felt apprehensive. He hadn't seen Geraldine since her wedding and had no idea how she felt about him. . . .
  b. Tom is in a lot of trouble. He $\left\{ \begin{array}{c} \text{has received} \\ \text{received} \end{array} \right\}$ several complaints about his party, and the landlord is threatening to evict him.

In 12.2.18a, *when Mark got off the plane* provides the reference time for the entire stretch of discourse, both the past tense clause of the first sentence and the past perfect clause of the second sentence. (But why is *Mark got off the plane* itself in the past tense? What is **its** reference point? See below for an attempt at an answer to these questions, which raise serious problems for Reichenbach's approach.) In 12.2.18b, there is a constant present reference point, covering both sentences.

Since Reichenbach's book is filled with formal analyses of sentences of ordinary language, it is remarkable that in his entire section on "The tenses of verbs" (pp. 287–98), he gives only diagrams in the style of 12.2.17 and does not present a single formula that would indicate what logical structure such a diagram is supposed to correspond to.[13] Let us see how closely we can mimic Reichenbach's diagrams using the descriptive apparatus that we have developed so far. The following are fairly obvious candidates for the logical structures of 12.2.16a–b:[14]

12.2.19 a. $(\imath: R_t(j \text{ marry } a))_t (\imath: t' = t - 5 \text{ years})_{t'} R_{t'}(j \text{ meet } c)$
   b. $(\imath: R_t(j \text{ marry } a))_t (\exists_3: PIt)_t R_I(j \text{ read } W\&P)$

In both of these formulas, the time corresponding to Reichenbach's R corresponds to the value of t picked out by the definite description operator. However, only indirectly can we identify that time as serving the function of a reference point in what follows: the values for the bound variables t' and I are in fact defined in terms of t, though the component formulas (such as "$t' = t - 5$ years") do not explicitly indicate which variable is being defined in terms of the other. Moreover, if the reference time were given not by a *when*-clause but by an expression such as *in 1981* or *at that time,* there would not be a quantifier expression that defines one variable in terms of another but rather an operator R_a, with the reference time a being a constant. Strictly speaking, in formulas like 12.2.19, one could insert an otherwise unnecessary R_t after the first definite description, which would allow one to treat the reference point for a sentence as the subscript on an R_t with which that sentence is combined, but that would mean resorting to considerable arbitrariness in order to give Reichenbach's R a canonical role in logical structures.

Alternatively, one might attempt to choose something other than *Pab* and R_a as the elements by which time notions are to be expressed in logical structures. Suppose that we in fact recognize elements of logical structure that will conform more closely to the devices that appear overtly in natural language by (i) having determinate temporal directions, i.e., there will be different operators corresponding to the past and the future relative to any given time, and (ii) carrying within them their dependence on a reference time (the way that, e.g., *10 minutes afterwards* picks out a time in relation to a reference time that need not be mentioned overtly). Specifically, let us set up the following elements of logical structure and give analyses in terms of them:

12.2.20 $C_p(a)$ = "at the past time a"; for example, $C_p(2:00)$(I take the cake out of the oven) will represent "I took the cake out of the oven at 2:00."

$C_f(a)$ = "at the future time a"; for example, C_f(Christmas)(*ug visit us*) will represent "Uncle George will visit us at Christmas."

$D_p(m)$ = "m units into the past"; for example, D_p(5 years)(*e buy a piano*) will represent "Ethel bought a piano 5 years ago."

$D_f(m)$ = "m units into the future"; for example, D_f(2 years)(*c get out of prison*) will represent "Charlie will get out of prison in 2 years."

$T_p(B)$ = "at the past time at which B"; for example, $T_p(j$ meet $d)(j$ be a student) will represent "When John met Dora, he was a student."

$T_f(B)$ = "at the future time at which B"; for example, $T_f(r$ arrive)(*r call you*) will represent "When Roger arrives, he will call you."

The following can serve as rules for determining the truth value of a formula involving the semantic elements posited in 12.2.20. Each rule says how to determine the truth value of a formula of one of the forms in 12.2.20 at a time a, and I follow the practise of writing the time at which a formula is to be evaluated as a superscript, i.e., A^a will mean A evaluated at time a:

12.2.21 $[T_p(B)(A)]^a \rightarrow (\iota: \wedge(Pta, B'))_t$ A^t
$[T_f(B)(A)]^a \rightarrow (\iota: \wedge(Pat, B'))_t$ A^t
$[D_p(m)(A)]^a \rightarrow (\iota: \wedge(Pta, /[t, a]/ = m)_t$ A^t
$[D_f(m)(A)]^a \rightarrow (\iota: \wedge(Pat, /[a, t]/ = m))_t$ A^t
$[C_p(b)(A)]^a \rightarrow A^b$ if Pba, undefined otherwise
$[C_f(b)(A)]^a \rightarrow A^b$ if Pab, undefined otherwise
A^a $\rightarrow R_a(A)$ if A is not one of the above forms

(The arrow here means "is translated into" or "is reduced to"; the notation is borrowed from Montague grammar and will recur in section 14.1). If 12.2.16a is given the plausible logical structure 12.2.22a, then the above rules allow one to derive what is essentially 12.2.19a by the steps in 12.2.22b:

12.2.22 a. $T_p(j$ marry $a)D_p(5$ years$)(j$ meet $c)$
        b. $[T_p(j$ marry $a)D_p(5$ years$)(j$ meet $c)]^a$
        → $(\imath\colon \wedge(Pta, (j$ marry $a)^t)), [D_p(5$ years$)(j$ meet $c)]^t$
        → $(\imath\colon \wedge(Pta, R_t(j$ marry $a)), (\upsilon\colon t' = t - 5$ years$)_{t'}[j$ meet $c]^{t'}$
        → $(\imath\colon \wedge(Pta, R_t(j$ marry $a)), (\upsilon\colon t' = t - 5$ years$)_{t'} R_{t'}(j$ meet $c)$

The symbols introduced in 12.2.20 are direct analogs of natural language devices for referring to times, as sketched in connection with 12.2.13. The translation scheme in 12.2.21 allows one to take the reference point for a constituent of logical structure to be simply the time that it is evaluated at; that is, t is the reference point for A if A^t appears in the course of the translation according to the rules 12.2.21. This is a considerably broader conception of "reference point" than corresponds to Reichenbach's use of the term, since, for example, it makes t' rather than t the reference point for "John meet Cynthia" in 12.2.22, whereas Reichenbach used his symbols E and R in such a way that when E is John's meeting Cynthia in 12.2.22a, the corresponding R is t. Nonetheless, the relationships that Reichenbach talked about are recoverable from 12.2.22, that is, t' is dependent on t, in the sense that the range of values for t' depends on the value for t, which can be said to make t "indirectly" a reference point for "John meet Cynthia."

The proposal embodied in 12.2.20 and 12.2.21 provides an explanation for a lack of correspondence between Reichenbach's diagrams and the English tense system that would otherwise appear (and to Reichenbach apparently did appear) to be simply an idiosyncracy of English, namely, that while the relationship between S and R and the relationship between R and E are relevant to the choice among linguistic expressions, the relation between S and E is not. Reichenbach remarks (1947:297) that the "posterior past" as in 12.2.23a and the "anterior future" as in 12.2.23b cover all possible relationships between S and E, though for each the relationship between S and R and between R and E is fixed:

12.2.23 a. I didn't expect that he <u>would win</u> the race.

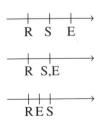

b. Mary <u>will have finished</u> her novel by the time you read this.

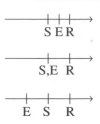

The clause expressing E is embedded in a structure that provides R, and it is evaluated relative to R; it is only the entire structure (which provides both R and E) that is evaluated relative to S, and the steps that evaluate the whole structure relative to S yield intermediate stages in which the E clause is evaluated relative to R (or relative to one of a chain of Rs), as can be seen from the superscript t's and b's (never a) that appear to the right of the arrows in 12.2.21.[15]

My discussion of Reichenbach's analysis has been in terms that suggest that S, R, and E are all constant times. I wish to take up at this point the question of how Reichenbach's scheme and the formalization of it proposed above can be extended to cases in which the time reference of a clause is a bound variable. One of the examples discussed in fact involved a bound time variable, namely 12.2.16b, and a bound time variable appeared in the analysis of it given in 12.2.19b. I spoke of 12.2.16b as being the past of a present perfect, and so presumably the sentence of which it is a past will have an analysis that also involves a bound time variable. It is easy enough to give the sentence a plausible analysis in terms of the basic temporal notions P, n, and R_t, namely 12.2.24a′, but not so easy to give one in terms of the vocabulary (12.2.20) that is supposed to correspond more directly to the devices that natural languages provide for referring to time; one way to analyze it in the style of 12.2.20 is to provide a predicate "is a time" that is true of both points in time and intervals in time and allow it to combine with C_p or C_f (12.2.24a″):

12.2.24 a.   John has (already) read *War and Peace* three times.
   a′.   ($\exists_3$: PIn)$_t$ R$_t$(j read *WP*)
   a″.   ($\exists_3$: Time I)$_t$ C$_p$(I)(j read *WP*)

The present perfect is used not only for existentially quantified past time variables, as in 12.2.24a, but, at least in English,[16] also for universally quantified past time variables, as in 12.2.25:

12.2.25 a. Mary has always lived in Milwaukee.
   b. Mary has lived in Milwaukee since she was six years old.

Analyzing these sentences in terms of P, n, and R_t is a fairly easy matter, but once again, giving analyses in the style of 12.2.20 is much harder, and this time the trick that I resorted to in 12.2.24a″ is much less plausible, since here a universally quantified variable whose values could in principle include future as well as past times would be combined with an operator (C_p) that bears a presupposition that whatever value it is combined with is in the past. Here, clearly, the information that the values of the time variable are in the past belongs in the domain expression of the quantifier. We are thus motivated to supplement the vocabulary of 12.2.20 by predicates "Past" and "Fut" with truth conditions given by the following translation rules:

12.2.26 a. $[\text{Past } t]^a \rightarrow Pta$
   b. $[\text{Fut } t]^a \rightarrow Pat$

That is, they are interpreted as saying that the time that they are predicated of is respectively before or after the time at which they are evaluated. We can then give 12.2.25a–b the following analyses:

12.2.27 a. $(\forall: \text{Past } t)_t\, C_P\, (t)(m \text{ live in Mw})$
   b. $(\imath: C_p(t')(m \text{ be } 6))_{t'}\, (\forall: \wedge(\text{Past } t, t \in [t', n]))_t\, C_p(m \text{ live in Mw})$

Clauses involving a quantified past time variable are not always in the present perfect, e.g., a present perfect would be deviant in the following examples:

12.2.28 a. George Washington (*has) slept in this house several times.
   b. George Washington $\left\{ \begin{matrix} \text{drank} \\ \text{*has drunk} \end{matrix} \right\}$ Madeira every day until
      he died.

The difference between the quantified past time variables that correspond to a present perfect and those that correspond to a simple past appears to be that the set of times at which the quantified propositional function could be true includes present and future times in the former case but is entirely in the past in the latter case, i.e., the reason that only the past tense is allowed in 12.2.28b is that the expression *until he died*, in combination with the background knowledge that only a living being can drink Madeira, implies that the values of t for which R_t(Washington drink Madeira) could be true are in the past, indeed far in the past. While 12.2.28a contains no such expression, the background knowledge that George Washington died in 1799 and that only a living being can sleep in a bed implies that R_t(Washington sleep in that bed) can be true only of values of t that are in the past. To put this point another way, cooperativity demands that the domains of bound variables be interpreted as containing only values of the quantified propositional function for which the question of its truth arises (as in 12.2.25a, which is not taken as implying that Mary lived in Milwaukee before she was born and before Milwaukee was founded, but only that she has lived there ever since her birth).

The acceptability of 12.2.24a in a given context will depend on whether that context still allows for the possibility of John reading *War and Peace;* for example, the past tense would have to be used in place of the present perfect if the parties to the discourse take it as established that John is dead, or that he suffers from a degenerative disease that will prevent him from reading again. Leech (1969) and McCawley (1971) make similar observations about the conditions for the acceptability of 12.2.29a–b:

12.2.29 a. Have you seen the Monet exhibition?
    b. Did you see the Monet exhibition?

For 12.2.29a to be acceptable, it is necessary that the context still allow for the possibility of your seeing the Monet exhibition: it would be unacceptable (and 12.2.29b acceptable) if the parties to the discourse take it as known that the exhibition has already closed, or that it is still running but the addressee will have no opportunity to see it (e.g., he will not be released from the hospital or from prison until after the exhibition closes). Both 12.2.29a and the relevant interpretation of 12.2.29b (it also has an interpretation in which the past tense refers to an already established reference point and the speaker is asking whether the addressee saw the exhibition at that time) involve a past time variable bound by an existential quantifier; they differ with regard to whether that variable's domain, interpreted cooperatively, is entirely in the past or spans the present, and contextual conditions determine whether that is the case.

In the last paragraph, I have talked in terms of the context allowing for the possibility of such-and-such a thing happening now or in the future. I wish to emphasize that I mean this locution to be interpreted in exactly the way in which I paraphrased it in the last paragraph: to say that the context allows for the possibility of something happening is to say that the context (the mutual knowledge of the participants in the interchange) does not imply that it can't still happen. This means that something that is known by the speaker but is not mutual knowledge between him and his interlocutors has no bearing on what "possibilities" the context allows for, and something that the speaker knows can no longer happen can indeed still be a possibility that the context allows for. What I have just described is a situation in which one can utter what I have called (McCawley 1971) the "hot news" present perfect. Thus, one can say 12.2.30a in informing someone of a birth, and in bringing up to date someone who has been marooned on a remote island since 1962 one could even say 12.2.30b:

12.2.30 a. Lucy has given birth to her first child.
         b. President Kennedy has been assassinated.

Once Lucy delivers her first child, it is no longer possible for her to give birth to her first child, but if the shared knowledge when 12.2.30a is uttered does not include the proposition that Lucy has given birth, it does not exclude the possibility of future events in which she gives birth to her first child; similarly with 12.2.30b: once Kennedy was assassinated it was no longer possible for anyone to assassinate him, but in the situation described, the mutual knowledge does not contain the proposition that Kennedy is dead and thus does not exclude the possibility of someone assassinating him in the future.

In my discussion of Reichenbach's scheme of analysis, I have so far followed him in treating his S, R, and E as being points. However, there are clear cases in which one or more of them has to be an interval. While it is anything but clear what should be taken as R for 12.2.28a (it is not even clear that it really has a past reference time, since it fits quite naturally into a discourse that is not set into the eighteenth century but deals with the house as it exists at present), one might hold that the appropriate R is the interval providing the values for the bound time variable, in which the appropriate diagram would not be 12.2.17c but rather 12.2.31a. If we treat the interval giving the values of a bound time variable as fulfilling the role of R, the existential and universal uses of the present perfect would correspond not to 12.2.17b but rather 12.2.31b:[17]

12.2.31 a.   b.

A generalization could then be made that would cover both quantified pasts as in 12.2.28 and constant pasts as in *John left at 2:00:* the past is used if E is contained in R (not necessarily as a proper part) and S is not contained in R.

There is another use of the present perfect that does not conform to the discussion of 12.2.24 and 12.2.25, namely, the so-called stative present perfect:

12.2.32 a. I've sprained my ankle (so I can't go skiing with you).
   b. John's gone to the library (but he should be back by 8:00).
   c. The reason you can't say "The Brooklyn Dodgers have won
      several pennants" is that the Dodgers have moved to Los
      Angeles and so the Brooklyn Dodgers can't win any more
      pennants.

Here the sentence refers to a change and the present perfect conveys that the change remains in effect (e.g., my ankle is not yet healed; John is not here, the Dodgers are in Los Angeles).[18] The difference between "stative" and "existential" present perfects is brought out in such pairs as:

12.2.33 a. Why are you limping? Have you sprained your ankle?
   b. I wonder if you know what discomfort I'm going through.
      Have you ever sprained your ankle?

Since they convey something different from what an existential present perfect does, they can't be semantically identical to existential present perfects. I conjecture that they differ from existential present perfects in carrying a conventional implicature that has to do with the state that results from events of the type in question.[19]

To identify that implicature correctly, it would be worthwhile here to see whether a stative present perfect can be negated, and if so, what implicature of the positive version of the sentence is preserved in the negative version. It is not easy to find sentences in which a stative present perfect is negated, e.g., in such an example as 12.2.34a, the negation may well be in the scope of the stative present perfect (it says that the state that results from the Vietnamese troops not pulling out of Cambodia is still in effect, i.e. the troops are still there); but at least 12.2.34b does seem to be a genuine example of a stative present perfect in the scope of the negation—it says that there isn't any event of your breaking your arm such as would result in your presently being in the state of having a broken arm:

12.2.34 a. The Vietnamese troops haven't pulled out of Cambodia.
   b. Don't be alarmed by these bandages—I haven't broken my arm.

If this informal paraphrase of 12.2.34b is correct, we can propose that a stative present perfect *X has Y-ed* conventionally implicates that if an event of X Y-ing had occurred in the relevantly recent past, the state that results from events of that type would still be in effect (here, that of the speaker having a broken arm). This conventional implicature survives embedding under other time operators; for example, the past perfects in 12.2.35 have a past reference time and the conventional implicature is that the resulting state would still be in effect at that time:

12.2.35 a. When I talked to John, he had sprained his ankle and so he couldn't come along on the skiing trip.
   b. I phoned Mary at 2:00, but she had gone to the library and so I wasn't able to talk with her.

I turn now to another matter involving the relative scopes of time operators and other elements. It has long been recognized that sentences that refer to past or future time and include a quantifier can be ambiguous with regard to whether the quantifier is inside or outside the scope of the time operator and that this ambiguity correlates with a difference in the domain of the variable bound by the quantifier. For example, Buridan (1300–1358) discussed the ambiguity of the Latin equivalent of

12.2.36   Everything at some time was God.

In the interpretation in which *everything* has higher scope than *some time*, the variable bound by *everything* ranges over all objects now existing, for example, it would imply that the World Trade Center was once God, that Prince Charles was once God, and that all the pornographic movie houses on 42d Street were once God. In the other interpretation, in which *some time* has higher scope, 12.2.36 says only that there was a past time such that everything that existed **then** was God, that is, that there was a past time at which only God existed.

The rules in 12.2.21 can be extended in a fairly natural way to quantifiers, with this relationship between domain and scope as a natural consequence. It will be necessary to distinguish between quantifiers binding time variables and quantifiers binding other variables. Specifically, I propose the following rules:

12.2.37 a. $[(Q: B)_t A]^a \rightarrow (Q: B^a)_t A^t$, for any quantifier Q and any time variable t.
   b. $[(Q: B)_x A]^a \rightarrow (Q: B^a)_x A^a$, for any quantifier Q and any non–time variable x.

The rationale for these rules can be seen by going through their application to logical structures for the two interpretations of 12.2.36:

12.2.38 a. $[(\forall: \text{Thing } x)_x (\exists: \text{Past } t)_t (\text{God } x)]^a \rightarrow$
       $(\forall: (\text{Thing } x)^a)(\exists: (\text{Past } t)^a)_t (\text{God } x)^t) \rightarrow$
       $(\forall: R_a(\text{Thing } x))(\exists: Pta)R_t(\text{God } x)$

   b. $[(\exists{:}\ \text{Past}\ t)_t\ (\forall{:}\ \text{Thing}\ x)_x(\text{God}\ x)]^a \to$
      $(\exists{:}\ (\text{Past}\ t)^a)_t\ [(\forall{:}\ (\text{Thing}\ x))(\text{God}\ x)]^t \to$
      $(\exists{:}\ \text{P}ta)_t(\forall{:}\ (\text{Thing}\ x)^t)_x(\text{God}\ x)^t \to$
      $(\exists{:}\ \text{P}ta)_t(\forall{:}\ \text{R}_t(\text{Thing}\ x))_x\text{R}_t(\text{God}\ x)$

Thus, when a quantifier binds a time variable, the proposition to which it applies is evaluated at each value of the variable, as in the second reading of 12.2.36, where what is at issue is whether there is a past time such that *Everything is God* is true of that time.

   Similar ambiguities are found in the following slightly less contrived examples:

12.2.39 a. The pope has always been a Catholic.
        b. Many linguists have always been insane.

These sentences have readings formalizable as follows, and convertible as indicated into formulas involving P and R_t:

12.2.40 a. $[(\imath{:}\ \text{Pope}\ x)(\forall{:}\ \text{Past}\ t)(\text{Catholic}\ x)]^a \to$
           $(\imath{:}\ \text{R}_a(\text{Pope}\ x))(\forall{:}\ \text{P}ta)\text{R}_t(\text{Catholic}\ x)$
      a'. $[(\forall{:}\ \text{Past}\ t)(\imath{:}\ \text{Pope}\ x)(\text{Catholic}\ x)]^a \to$
           $(\forall{:}\ \text{P}ta)(\imath{:}\ \text{R}_t(\text{Pope}\ x))\text{R}_t(\text{Catholic}\ x)$
      b. $[(\text{Many:}\ \text{Linguist}\ x)(\forall{:}\ \text{Past}\ t)(\text{Insane}\ x)]^a \to$
           $(\text{Many}\ x{:}\ \text{R}_a(\text{Linguist}\ x))(\forall{:}\ \text{P}ta)\text{R}_t(\text{Insane}\ x)$
      b'. $[(\forall{:}\ \text{Past}\ t)\ (\text{Many:}\ \text{Linguist}\ x)(\text{Insane}\ x)]^a \to$
           $(\forall{:}\ \text{P}ta)(\text{Many}\ x{:}\ \text{R}_t(\text{Linguist}\ x))\text{R}_t(\text{Insane}\ x)$

Thus, the first interpretation of 12.2.39a implies that John Paul II has always been a Catholic (even before he was ordained, let alone crowned pope) but says nothing about Innocent V or Pius IX; the second interpretation implies that John Paul II, Innocent V, and Pius IX were Catholics while they were pope but implies nothing about their religion before becoming pope (e.g., it is consistent with the proposition that John Paul II was a Buddhist until he was eighteen). The first interpretation of 12.2.39b is a proposition that could be argued for by showing that Chomsky has always been insane, that Hockett has always been insane, that Keenan has always been insane, and so on through a large number of current linguists, but the insanity of persons who were linguists in 1950 but are not linguists any longer would be irrelevant to establishing that proposition. The second interpretation of 12.2.39b could be argued for by showing that many of those who were linguists in 1935 were insane in 1935, that many of those who were linguists in 1945 were insane in 1945, and so on, but whether Chomsky was insane before he became a linguist would be irrelevant.

It is interesting to ask whether these sentences have any additional interpretations. For example, if we were to replace the first occurrence of R_t in 12.2.40b′ by R_a, would the resulting formula be a possible interpretation of 12.2.39b?

12.2.41 $(\forall: Pta)(\text{Many}: R_a(\text{Linguist } x))_x R_t(\text{Insane } x)$

This would say that at every past time, many of those who now are linguists were insane. I am inclined to say that this is not a possible interpretation of 12.2.39b, but my judgment is not clear here and I have not found other examples in which it is easier to say whether an interpretation like 12.2.41 is possible. It will be of considerable interest if such interpretations are systematically excluded, since that would mean that the narrower expressive possibilities of the system of logical structures with T_p, D_p, and the like were sufficient to specify the meanings of English sentences, rather than the broader expressive capacity of the system with P and R_t, which allows distinctions in the subscripts on R that cannot be drawn purely in terms of the notions of past and future that are the basis of the system with operators such as T_p (12.2.20).

12.3. More on the Structure of Proofs

In section 3.2, I gave 12.3.1 as an illustration of a natural language argumentative text in which an inference is drawn by $\vee$-exploitation:

12.3.1   Creepy Calabresi got off the plane in either Chicago, Kansas City, or Las Vegas.
Suppose he got off in Chicago. Then he would have called his brother. But his brother wants to get rid of Creepy and he would have tipped off the feds.
Suppose Creepy got off in Kansas City. Then he would have called his girlfriend. But his girlfriend is working for the IRS now, and she would have tipped off the feds.
Suppose Creepy got off the plane at Las Vegas. Then he would have called the Fettucini Kid. But the Fettucini Kid has been arrested and the fuzz would have a stoolie taking the phone calls, and he would have tipped off the feds.
So someone has tipped off the feds.

The most straightforward way in which 12.3.1 could be recast as a proof conforming to the rules of inference of chapter 3 is 12.3.2, which is given in somewhat schematic form through the use of p'', q'', etc., to refer to various intermediate inferences ("he would have called his brother") whose details are peripheral to the questions that will be addressed in this section:

12.3.2

1	$\lor(p, q, r)$	
2	p' (= Creepy's brother wants to get rid of Creepy)	
3	q' (= Creepy's girlfriend is working for the IRS)	
4	r' (= The Fettucini Kid has been arrested)	
5	p	supp
6	p''	
7	p'	2, reiteration
8	a tipped off the feds	
9	($\exists$: person x)(x tipped off the feds)	8, $\exists$-intro
10	q	supp
11	q''	
12	q'	3, reiteration
13	b tipped off the feds	
14	($\exists$: person x)(x tipped off the feds)	13, $\exists$-intro
15	r	supp
16	r''	
17	r'	4, reiteration
18	r'''	
19	c tipped off the feds	
20	($\exists$: person x)(x tipped off the feds)	19, $\exists$-intro
21	($\exists$: person x)(x tipped off the feds)	1, 5–9, 10–14, 15-20, $\lor$-expl

There are two major respects in which 12.3.2 deviates in form from 12.3.1. First, *Someone tipped off the feds* appears only once in 12.3.1, whereas the corresponding formula appears four times in 12.3.2 (once at the end of each of the three subproofs and once as the conclusion of the main proof). Second, each of the segments of text that corresponds to a subproof in 12.3.1 contains at least one sentence that is presented as a fact rather than as an inference from the supposition of that subproof, e.g., *His brother wants to get rid of Creepy* is not an inference from the supposition that Creepy got off in Chicago but is something that the speaker is asserting categorically. In particular, the proposition that Creepy's brother wants to get rid of him (likewise the proposition that Creepy's girlfriend is working for the IRS and the proposition that the Fettucini Kid has been arrested) can serve as premises for later inferences in the main proof, whereas of course the suppositions of the subordinate proofs and the subsequent lines of the subordinate proofs that have been inferred from these suppositions (such as the proposition that Creepy's brother has tipped off the feds) cannot. This aspect of the status of those propositions has been accounted for in 12.3.2 by making those propositions premises of the main proof and introducing them into the subordinate proofs through Reiteration; but this makes the lines of 12.3.2 appear in a different order from those of the corresponding clauses of 12.3.1, which appear in the middles of the subordinate stretches of text rather than at the beginning of the whole text.

There is a trivial way in which the structure of proofs in the system of chapter 3 could be altered so as to remove these discrepancies between the formal proof and the natural language text. Recall that, as I argued in section 3.6, proofs are **trees** in the graph-theoretic sense. More specifically, they are ordered labeled continuous trees in which the terminal nodes are sentences and the nonterminal nodes dominate proofs (or subproofs), with the sentences of any proof distinguished as to whether they are suppositions or not. Thus, using the labels Proof and S, marking suppositions and premises by a $+$, and using numerals to identify the various propositions that appear in 12.3.2, the structure of 12.3.2 can be alternatively represented as 12.3.3:

12.3.3

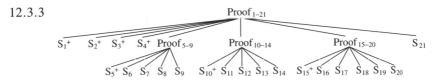

A graph with ordered terminal nodes is **continuous** if and only if whenever a node dominates two terminal nodes it also dominates all nodes that are between those two nodes. Let us consider a modified version of 12.3.3 that will fail to be continuous and will also fail to be technically a tree, in that certain nodes will have more than one mother (i.e., the graph will "branch upwards" as well as branch downwards). Specifically, let us collapse into a single node all occurrences of any given proposition in 12.3.3, while retaining the domination relations of 12.3.3 and the linear ordering of the propositions given by the natural language text 12.3.1:

12.3.4

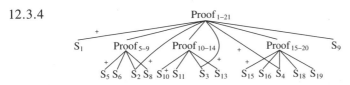

The rules of inference can be regarded as conditions under which a proposition of a given form may occur in a given position in a proof. The entire proof is well-formed according to the given rules of inference if and only if (i) every line of the proof either is a supposition or conforms to one or other of the rules of inference, and (ii) the last line of the proof is directly dominated by the topmost Proof node, i.e., the proof must terminate in a line that is a conclusion of the main proof and not just of one of the subproofs. Subject to three minor revisions, the same can be said even if the system is altered so that proofs are not trees but the more general sort of graph illustrated by 12.3.4. The minor revisions are: First, the rules of inference must now be taken as giving conditions on the logical acceptability not of nodes of the graph (= lines of the proof) but of arcs connecting the nodes, i.e., the different arcs terminating at a given node correspond to the different roles of the given proposition, and if a given proposition plays several roles in the same proof, it must play all of those roles correctly for the whole proof to be well-formed. Second, the status of a proposition as a supposition must accordingly be taken as a feature of an arc rather than of a node, since a proposition can be a supposition of only one proof at a time, e.g., in 12.3.4, S_3 is a constituent of both the main proof and the second subproof but is a supposition only of the former. Accordingly, in 12.3.4 the + 's are marked on arcs rather than on nodes. Third, whereas rules of inference in the pristine system specify what a given proposition must be preceded by if it is to be an acceptable inference, the propositions forming the justification for a given conclusion must now be allowed to either precede or coincide with it, e.g., the rule of ∨-exploitation now is taken as allowing proofs like 12.3.4, in which the various occurrences of B in the subordinate proofs coincide with the conclusion of the superordinate proof.

The justifications of the various steps (= arcs) in 12.3.4 are the same as those of the corresponding steps in 12.3.2. In particular, it is the rule of Reiteration that allows S_2, S_3, and S_4 to belong simultaneously to the main proof and to the subordinate proof. It is not clear, though, that those propositions need be regarded as belonging to the subordinate proofs at all. They are used in the subordinate proofs, and the possibility of uttering them in the middles of the stretches of text corresponding to those subordinate proofs is effective in making clear that they are used in those subproofs, but since propositions of the main proof remain "operative" in the subproofs, they need not actually belong to a subproof in order to be used there. Some discussion of the rule of the rule of Reiteration is in order here. What use need be made of that rule depends on an important detail of the interpretation of the other rules of inference. I have tacitly assumed a policy that renders unnecessary many invocations of Reiteration that would otherwise be needed. Specifically, I have assumed that the lines of proof that give the justification of a given step may be in a superordinate proof; for example, if the first premise of the main proof is $\supset AB$ and a subordinate proof begins at line 4 with the supposition A, line 5 can be B, inferred by $\supset$-exploitation:

12.3.5   1 $\supset AB$ ___   supp

             2 . . .

             3 . . .

             4 | A ___   supp

             5 | B   1, 4, $\supset$-expl

                . . .

It is legitimate to cite line 4 in the justification of line 5, because the premises of the main proof remain operative in the subproof. The alternative policy would be to require the propositions from which a given proposition is inferred to be immediate constituents of the same (sub-)proof that it belongs to and to import additional propositions from superordinate proofs, as needed, by Reiteration. These two policies are equivalent with regard to what conclusions they allow one to derive from given premises. I have chosen the former policy because of the closer correspondence that it allows between formal proofs and natural language argumentation, in which superordinate steps are repeated (often in such a form as a *since*-clause) only for the sake of clarity much in the way that one often may use a proper name in places where a pronoun would otherwise suffice. Under this policy, there is only a highly restricted class of proofs in which Reiteration need be used (or simulated by combinations of other rules of inference),[20] namely those involving $\sim$-introduction (reductio ad absurdum proofs) in which one of the two contradictory propositions B and $\sim$B that figure in the subproof is imported from a superordinate proof:

12.3.6 $\sim$-introduction

               | A ___

               | . . .

               | B

               | $\sim$B

            $\sim$A

In the rule as formulated in 12.3.6, B and $\sim$B are not premises of the whole proof but must occur within the subproof. Moreover, it will not do to replace 12.3.6 with a rule 12.3.7 in which one of B and $\sim$B is a premise, since that rule is weaker than 12.3.6, e.g., it does not allow a proof of the law of non-contradiction:

12.3.7   B

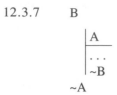

~A

Thus, one could dispense with Reiteration (and simulations of it, cf. note 20) only by generalizing 12.3.6 so that it covered both inferences that conform to the template given in 12.3.6 and inferences that conform to something on the order of 12.3.7, in which one of B and ~B is in the superordinate proof. As what can be regarded for the moment as a brute-force measure to stretch present notation to cover this generalized form of ~-introduction, I will adopt the device of putting square brackets around symbols that can be matched indiscriminately to lines of the proof in which they appear or to lines of a superordinate proof:

12.3.8 | A
              |‾‾‾‾‾‾
              | . . .
              | [B]
              | ~B
          ~A

[B] in 12.3.8 means in effect "B has already been established," in that what is established in a given proof remains established in discourse that is subordinate to that proof. This talk of propositions counting as already established at a given point in a proof is reminiscent of Karttunen's treatment of pragmatic presupposition as a demand that that sentence makes on its context, in the technical sense of context that figured in sections 10.4 and 12.1: the set of propositions that are taken as "already established" for the purposes of the given discourse, at the given point of the discourse. The context consists of background knowledge that the participants in the discourse can take as shared by all of them, plus whatever propositions have been asserted by one or other of them and not challenged or withdrawn, i.e., the assertion of a proposition causes it to be added to the context (cf. Stalnaker 1978) as long as the participants at least tacitly consent to its being added. Recall that in section 12.1 I extended Karttunen's treatment to sentences such as *Mary is sure that John never married and she thinks that he regrets that he never married* by positing multiple contexts, one for each world to which reference is implic-

itly made, and proposing that the pragmatic presuppositions are demands on
the context associated with the world that serves as reference point for the
linguistic item that bears the pragmatic presupposition, e.g., the pragmatic
presupposition borne here by *regret* demands that the context for Mary's belief
world entail that John never married, and that condition is met here because
the speaker has caused the proposition that John never married to be added to
the belief-world context in asserting that Mary is sure that John never married.

This notion of context is applicable to texts in which proofs are presented.
Let us make the following assumptions: (i) each (sub-)proof has a "context,"
consisting of a set of Ss and changing in the course of the (sub-)proof; (ii) at
the beginning of any proof, its context consists of (iia) the context of the
immediately superordinate proof or (iib) if there is no immediately superordinate proof (i.e., when a "main" proof is at issue), the context consists of a set
of "background assumptions"; as each line is added to a (sub-)proof, it is also
added to the context of that (sub-)proof. For example, let us use B to denote
the set of background propositions that provide the initial context for 12.3.2;
the contexts immediately prior to the various steps in the proof are then as
follows:

12.3.9		context for main proof	context for Proof_{5-9}
	1	B	
	2	$B \cup \{\vee pqr\}$	
	3	$B \cup \{\vee pqr, p'\}$	
	4	$B \cup \{\vee pqr, p', q'\}$	
	5	$B \cup \{\vee pqr, p', q', r'\}$	$B \cup \{\vee pqr, p', q', r'\}$
	6	$B \cup \{\vee pqr, p'; q', r'\}$	$B \cup \{\vee pqr, p', q', r', p\}$
	7	$B \cup \{\vee pqr, p', q', r'\}$	$B \cup \{\vee pqr, p', q', r', p, p''\}$

As the contexts are built up in this way, the context at any point in a (sub-)-
proof will consist of precisely those propositions that are operative at that
point (e.g., p and p'' are never operative in the main proof, but they are operative in Proof_{5-9} starting at the point where they are introduced into that
proof).

The requirement that the lines of a proof that provide the justification for a
particular step be in either the same proof or a superordinate proof can then be
restated as a requirement that those steps be in the context of the given step.
This restatement is more than a mere change of terminology, in virtue of condition (iib), which allows inferential steps to depend not just on earlier steps
of the proof but also on propositions that are taken as background knowledge.
A large proportion of textbook examples of the various rules of inference in
fact involve exactly that. Consider, for example, everyone's favorite example

of a reductio ad absurdum proof, namely the classical demonstration that $\sqrt{2}$ is an irrational number. Several propositions of number theory figure in the derivation of a contradiction from the supposition that $\sqrt{2}$ is rational: the proposition that every rational number is a ratio of two integers that have no common factor, the proposition that $(2c)^2 = 4c^2$, the proposition that if $x = y$, then $x/2 = y/2$, etc. As much of "elementary" number theory as one chooses to employ is taken as already established for the purposes of this proof. Since those propositions of number theory are cited in the proof that $\sqrt{2}$ is irrational in much the same way that p', q', and r' are cited in 12.3.1 (the proposition that Creepy's brother wants to get rid of Creepy is simply mentioned as an established fact in the middle of the first subordinate proof), one could then perfectly well recast 12.3.4 (= 12.3.2) with p', q', and r' being treated not strictly speaking as premises of the main proof but as background assumptions.

In this brief section, I have pointed out some ways in which our scheme for proofs can be altered so that, while leaving unchanged the conclusions that can be derived from given premises, we are able to keep to a minimum the discrepancies between natural language argumentative texts and formal proofs that purport to reconstruct the inferential structure of those texts. I regard the elaboration of such variants of natural deduction systems as important for the contribution that they can potentially make to a better understanding of the relationship between formal logic and the psychology of reasoning. The closer that the formalization of a system of logic can be made to agree with the structure of natural language texts, the fewer irrelevant distractions there will be for the scholar who seeks to identify the principles and structures that figure in psychological processes of reasoning.

Exercises

1. For each of the following verbs, discuss whether it is in any sense "world-creating," bringing in any considerations relevant to how similar to or different from the world-creating verbs given in section 12.1 it is:

   a. *ask* as in "He asked me to open the door"
   b. *say*
   c. *see* as in "I saw him open the window"
   d. *seem*

2. Determine whether the pragmatic presuppositions of the underlined expressions in the following stretches of discourse are satisfied in the relevant contexts and contextual domains. Give details of how the contexts and CDs

for each world are constructed. If acceptability requires that the context contain something that could plausibly be regarded as "common knowledge" (e.g., that robots have motors, in the case of (b)), indicate what that common knowledge might be.

   a. Edgar is sure that he'll win the lottery, and he plans to spend the prize money on women and good food.
   b. John thinks his father is a robot and is afraid that his father's motor will break down.
   c. John is under the delusion that he is married and has three daughters. He is convinced that his wife hates his youngest daughter and that the daughter thinks that her sisters hate her more than her mother does.

3. Write a short paragraph giving some reason why *dream/imagine/* . . . more easily allow items in their complements to be made heads of relative clauses than do the other kinds of world-creating verbs, for example:

   The woman I dreamed about last night had red hair. (where the woman does not exist outside of your dream)
   *The witch I hope will curse Sam's cow has bony fingers. (as an allusion to your hoping that a witch [nonreferential] will curse Sam's cow).

4. Give Reichenbach-style diagrams indicating the temporal relations expressed in each of the following sentences, with enough accompanying prose to make clear what time each point (or interval) in the diagram corresponds to:

   a. After you get home, we'll have dinner together.
   b. Two weeks before you arrived, Lucy was going to leave next Tuesday, and one week before you arrived, she was going to leave next Friday.
   c. When I talked to George, he had already decided that he wouldn't help us.

When it is immaterial whether one of the points precedes, coincides with, or follows another of the points, make an arbitrary choice among those alternatives and state explicitly that you are doing so.

5. Give explicit logical forms for the following sentences:

   a. Many linguists won't always remain honest.
   b. There haven't been many times at which all linguists were sane.
   c. Since he was a child, Sam has believed that no one took him seriously.

If the sentence is ambiguous, treat all of its meanings.

13   Many-Valued and Fuzzy Logic

13.1. Values between True and False

While the vast bulk of the literature of logic adheres to the traditional idea that there are only two truth values, "true" and "false," with occasional deviations to the extent of allowing some propositions to "have no truth value" and thus in effect have a third truth value, there also exists a sizeable though not widely known literature in which more than two truth values are assumed, and rules of inference and principles of truth value assignment are formulated and investigated for the set or sets of truth values in question. An excellent survey of this literature is given by Rescher 1969.

Before I begin a survey of some ideas and results in the area of "many-valued logic," I should point out that the term "truth value," while firmly established and thus hard to avoid, is misleading in one important respect, namely, that the "values" assigned to propositions need not be **truth** values per se but can be values for other parameters or combinations of parameters. For example, Belnap (1977) has investigated a four-valued system of logic in which the four values are the four possible information states that one could be in with respect to a proposition P:

13.1.1   0 (I have not been informed that P; I have not been informed that not P)

           T (I have been informed that P; I have not been informed that not P)

           F (I have been informed that not P; I have not been informed that P)

           B (I have been informed both that P and that not P)

This system of four values is of practical importance in designing a computer question-answering system, since the information that has been provided to the computer could put it into any of these four states with respect to a given proposition; in particular, it might be given inconsistent inputs and thus be in state B with respect to certain propositions. Another example of values that,

458

strictly speaking, are not truth values would be an assignment to each proposition of a real number (greater than or equal to 0 and less than or equal to 1) which expresses one's degree of confidence that that proposition is true. A third such example is the treatment of tense logic in which the value of a proposition in a given temporal model is the set of times at which it is true in that model; the set of values in this case is a partially ordered set whose maximum member is the set of all times and whose minimal member is the empty set. Many-valued logic is concerned with assignments of values to propositions, without regard to whether those values are appropriately called truth values, though the values will normally have some relation to inference (for example, if the values are degrees of confidence in the propositions, one would be interested in developing rules of inference such that the conclusions deserve at least the degree of confidence that the premises do, or perhaps, such that each rule of inference yields conclusions whose confidence level can be only a limited amount below that of the premises). Of course, it will often not particularly matter whether one considers the values to be truth values. For example, there need be no formal difference between the logic with which one formalizes a conservative approach in which every proposition is either true or false and one assigns a confidence level to propositions about whose truth he is not completely sure, and the logic with which one formalizes an "avant garde" approach in which there are only degrees of truth, with no particularly privileged place assigned to the maximum degree of truth.

One of the best known three-valued logics is that proposed by Łukasiewicz in 1920 (described in Rescher 1969:22ff.). Łukasiewicz held that future contingent propositions (such as Aristotle's celebrated example of the proposition that there will be a sea battle tomorrow) cannot properly be called either true or false (at least, not by someone speaking now) and thus deserve a different truth value, intermediate between truth and falsity. He proposed the following assignments of truth values, where "I" denotes the "intermediate" truth value:

13.1.2

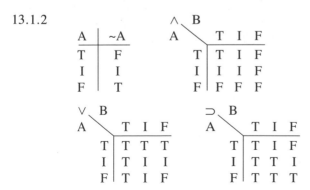

Łukasiewicz sought to fit I into a system of truth value assignment which was truth-functional and which agreed as closely as possible with the classical truth tables. The rationale for his table for ~ is obvious: the cases where A is T and where A is F agree with the classical truth table, and in the case where A is I, ~A must also be I, since the negation of a future contingent proposition is equally future and equally contingent. The rationale for most of the entries in the tables for ∧ and ∨ is also obvious. The falsehood of one conjunct of an ∧-conjunction suffices to make the conjunction false, thus the Fs in the bottom line and rightmost column; the truth of one conjunct of an ∨-conjunction suffices to make the conjunction true, thus the Ts in the top line and the leftmost column of the table for ∨. If one conjunct of an ∧-conjunction is true and the other future contingent (e.g., *Goethe is buried in Weimar and the Anchorage Braves will win the 2008 World Series*), the whole thing will turn out true if the future contingent conjunct turns out true and will turn out false if the future contingent conjunct turns out false; thus, it is itself future contingent. Similarly, an ∨-conjunction is future contingent if one conjunct is false and the other one future contingent (e.g., *Either Goethe is buried in Zanzibar or the Anchorage Braves will win the 2008 World Series*): the whole thing will turn out true if the future contingent conjunct turns out true and will turn out false if the future contingent conjunct turns out false.

The entry in the middle of both tables, however, is problematic. If both conjuncts are future contingent, then normally their ∧-conjunction and their ∨-conjunction will also be future contingent (13.1.3a–b); however, if the conjuncts are mutually contradictory, the ∧-conjunction would generally be held to be not contingent at all but out and out false (13.1.3c), and the ∨-conjunction true (13.1.3d):

13.1.3   a. There will be a sea battle tomorrow, and the Anchorage Braves will win the 2008 World Series.
b. Either the United States will annex Israel, or Saudi Arabia will invade Myanmar.
c. There will be a sea battle tomorrow and there won't be a sea battle tomorrow.
d. Either the United States will annex Israel or it won't annex Israel.

Łukasiewicz's truth tables thus conflict blatantly with the normal understanding of the term "contingent," since they require that one treat ∧-conjunctions such as 13.1.3c and ∨-conjunctions such as 13.1.3d as future contingent; one can avoid this anomaly only by letting ∧ and ∨ be non–truth-functional when both conjuncts are I, so that the middle entry in the table would be I/F in the table for ∧ and I/T in the table for ∨.

Łukasiewicz's table for ⊃ has Ts in the leftmost column and the bottom row, following the classical tables, in which falsehood of A or truth of B is sufficient to make ⊃AB true. The Is that he has in the cases of ⊃TI and ⊃IF are reasonable if one identifies "future contingent" with "could turn out either true or false, depending on future events." If A is T and B is I, then if B turns out to be true, ⊃AB also turns out to be true (by the classical truth table), and if B turns out to be false, ⊃AB also turns out to be false. The case of ⊃IF works similarly. However, by that rationale, both I and T should have been allowed as possible truth values in the case of ⊃II. If A logically implies B, then ⊃AB will turn out true even when A is future contingent, since A then cannot turn out true unless B does also. But if A and B are logically independent (i.e., either could turn out true or turn out false, irrespective of which way the other turns out, as in the case of *If there is a sea battle tomorrow, the Anchorage Braves will win the 2008 World Series*), then ⊃AB will be future contingent: it will turn out false if A turns out true and B turns out false but will turn out true otherwise. Thus, if I is really supposed to correspond to future contingent, the table should be non–truth-functional, with I/T rather than T as the entry in the middle of the table. Łukasiewicz's reason for having T rather than I is that he wanted both for the truth tables to be truth-functional and for ⊃AA to remain a valid formula, and the only way he could do that was to take all instances of ⊃II to be T.[1]

Suppose that we consider an alternative interpretation of the third truth value: let I now be interpreted not as future contingent but as "sort of true," in the sense that a sentence like *Dukakis is fat,* in which an inexact predicate is predicated of an individual of which it is neither unqualifiedly true nor unqualifiedly false, is "sort of true" but not unqualifiedly true. Some of the anomalies of Łukasiewicz's truth table now become less anomalous; for example, 13.1.4 (which would receive the value I according to 13.1.2 if *Dukakis is fat* is I) is not such an absurd thing to say as 13.1.3c:

13.1.4   Dukakis is fat and he isn't fat.

Indeed, 13.1.4 is a perfectly normal way of expressing the idea that Dukakis is sort of fat but not extremely fat. If we do not take 13.1.4 as being just a strange idiomatic expression but interpret it literally, and take *Dukakis is fat* as having the truth value I, 13.1.4 will also get the truth value I. The only remarkable thing about 13.1.4 is that it is used to convey the proposition that Dukakis is sort of fat, not the sort-of-true proposition that Dukakis is and isn't fat. This fact calls for an explanation in terms of conversational implicature, though it is a little tricky to explain why 13.1.4 is normally taken as saying that the proposition that Dukakis is somewhat fat has an intermediate truth value, while 13.1.5, which has the same truth value in the given case, according to 13.1.2, is normally taken not as saying that but indeed as conveying the speaker's unwillingness to admit intermediate truth values:

13.1.5   Either Dukakis is fat or he isn't fat.

Perhaps the key to this difference lies in the fact that 13.1.5 can have a truth value of at most I, while 13.1.5 is of a form that admits the truth value T, coupled with the idea that cooperativity demands that one assign as high a truth value as possible to the propositions that one's interlocutor asserts: 13.1.4 takes on its highest truth value when *Dukakis is fat* is I, while 13.1.5 takes on its highest truth value when that proposition is T or F.

The only entry in Łukasiewicz's tables that is pretty unreasonable if I is interpreted as "sort of true" is the value of I for ⊃IF. That assignment of truth values implies that "If Dukakis is fat, then $2 + 2 = 85$" is "sort of true." I find that result sufficiently bizarre that for the remainder of the discussion I will replace Łukasiewicz's table by one that has F rather than I in that case:[2]

13.1.6

⊃	B		
A	T	I	F
T	T	I	F
I	T	T	F
F	T	T	T

Note that neither 13.1.6 nor Łukasiewicz's original table assigns exactly the same values to ⊃AB as to ∨(~A, B): under either truth table, when A and B are both I, ⊃AB is T but ∨(~A, B) is I. Under either truth table for ⊃, some valid formulas of classical logic will cease to be valid; for example, when A and B are both I, ⊃(⊃AB, ∨(~A, B)) will have the value I both according to Łukasiewicz's original truth tables and according to 13.1.6.

The reinterpretation of I as "sort of true" can be generalized in a natural way to systems in which there is more than one "degree of truth" between T and F. In particular, it can be generalized to allow arbitrary numbers in the interval from 0 to 1 as truth values (0 corresponds to F, 1 to T, and the numbers in between to various greater and lesser degrees of truth).[3] A system with this range of truth values is useful in coping with inexact concepts such as "fat," "obnoxious," and "uncomfortable." Rather than having to draw arbitrary distinctions by assigning to every proposition of the form "*x* is fat" either the value T or the value F, even in borderline cases one can assign the value 1 to propositions in which the inexact concept is applied to something that is in its core of applicability, and smaller truth values to propositions in which the concept is only peripherally applicable. For example, one might assign truth values as follows, where /p/ is used to indicate the truth value of p in the given assignment:

13.1.7   /Dummett is fat/   = 1
          /Quine is fat/   = 0.8
          /Dukakis is fat/   = 0.5
          /Gorbachev is fat/ = 0.2
          /Chomsky is fat/   = 0

Note that "the extent to which it is true that x is fat" is not the same thing as "the extent to which x is fat": to say that "x is fat" has the truth value 0 is to say that x is not at all fat, not that x is at the extreme lower end of the fat/thin scale. This point is clearer in the case of "x is tall": you can speak of one person being taller than another (i.e., of the extent to which the one is tall exceeding the extent to which the other is tall) even when neither is at all tall, that is, when neither is at or above "normal height." Thus I spoke of "Chomsky is fat" as having the truth value 0 rather than some positive truth value, even though Chomsky is nowhere near the limit of thinness.

Let us try to generalize Łukasiewicz's truth tables so as to get something applicable to the case where the truth values are numbers on the interval from 0 to 1. Suppose that we replace T, I, and F by 1, 1/2, and 0, respectively (which in fact is what Łukasiewicz originally called them). Then Łukasiewicz's truth tables for $\sim$, $\wedge$, and $\vee$ can be summarized as follows:

13.1.8   /$\sim$A/   = 1 − /A/
          /$\wedge$AB/   = min(/A/, /B/) (i.e., the lesser of /A/ and /B/)
          /$\vee$AB/   = max(/A/, /B/) (i.e., the greater of /A/ and /B/)
          /$\supset$AB/   = 1 if /A/ ≤ /B/
                    = /B/ if /A/ > /B/

No simple formula gives the truth table in 13.1.6 for $\supset$; the best one can do is to divide it into two cases along the lines of the above.[4]

Suppose that we allow arbitrary numbers from 0 to 1 as truth values and assign them according to the formulas in 12.1.8. For example, if A and B have the truth values given below, $\wedge$AB, $\vee$AB, and $\supset$AB will have the indicated truth values:

13.1.9

/A/	/B/	/$\wedge$AB/	/$\vee$AB/	/$\supset$AB/
1	0.5	0.5	1	0.5
0.3	0.5	0.3	0.5	1
0.9	0.2	0.2	0.9	0.2
0	0.3	0	0.3	1

Before taking up the question of what formulas of propositional logic will be valid according to the truth conditions given by 13.1.8, however, it is necessary to clarify an important point about the notion of "validity." When there are only two truth values, the notion of "valid" is unproblematic: a formula is valid if it has the value 1 ($=$ T) under all admissible assignments of truth values. When there are more than two truth values, however, one has the possibility of taking more than one truth value to be **designated,** in the sense that a formula will count as valid if it is always assigned a designated truth value and is invalid if it is possible to assign a nondesignated value to it. Allowing more than one truth value to be designated need not constitute a perversion of the notion of validity: as Dummett (1958:61) points out, the different designated values can be conceived of as "different ways in which a statement may be true" and the nondesignated values as "different ways in which it may be false." Thus, if one adopted Łukasiewicz's truth tables 13.1.2 and took not only T but also I to be designated, then $\lor(A, \sim A)$ would be valid, while if one took only T to be designated, then it would be invalid. In this case, it would be counterintuitive to take both I and T to be designated, since then it would be possible for both a proposition and its negation to be true, i.e., they could simultaneously have a designated truth value; thus, the only plausible notion of validity in a three-value logic is one in which there is only one designated truth value. In what follows, I will in fact take only 1 to be a designated truth value, though it is important to keep in mind that many-valued logic is not generally subject to any restriction that there be only one designated truth value.

As we noted above for the special case of three-valued logic, not all formulas that are valid in classical propositional logic remain valid in many-valued logic with the truth conditions 13.1.8:

13.1.10   Classically valid formulas that are valid with respect to 13.1.8
      a. $\supset AA$
      b. $\supset(A, \supset BA)$
      c. $\supset(\sim\land AB, \lor(\sim A, B))$, and the other de Morgan laws
      d. $\lor(\supset AB, \supset BA)$

13.1.11   Classically valid formulas that are not valid with respect to 13.1.8
      a. $\lor(A, \sim A)$
      b. $\sim\land(A, \sim A)$
      c. $\supset(\land(A, \sim A), B)$
      d. $\supset(B, \lor(A, \sim A))$
      e. $\supset(\supset AB, \supset(\sim B, \sim A))$

    f. $\supset(\wedge(\vee AB, \sim B), A)$
    g. $\supset(\supset AB, \vee(\sim A, B))$
    h. $\supset(\vee(\sim A, B), \supset AB)$

For example, 13.1.10b can be shown to be valid as follows. The only way a conditional formula can fail to be valid is for there to be cases where its protasis has a greater truth value than its apodosis. Thus 13.1.10b is invalid only if a case can arise in which $/A/ > /\supset BA/$. In such a case, $/\supset BA/$ would have to be less than 1 (since $/A/$ can be at most 1), which would mean that $/\supset BA/$ $= /A/$ (i.e., the only way that the truth value of a conditional can fail to be 1 is for it to equal the truth value of the apodosis). This means that $/\supset(A, \supset BA)/$ can be less than 1 only if $/A/ > /A/$; thus $/\supset(A, \supset BA)/$ always equals 1. Demonstrations of the other claims embodied in 13.1.10 and 13.1.11 are left as an exercise. It is interesting to note that under the truth conditions adopted here, $\supset AB$ and $\vee(\sim A, B)$ not only do not always have the same truth value but indeed generally differ in truth value. In the following diagram, the vertically cross-hatched area is the region in which the truth value of $\supset AB$ exceeds that of $\vee(\sim A, B)$ (the former equals 1, the latter is less than 1 in that region), and the horizontal cross-hatching indicates the region where $\supset AB$ is lower in truth value than $\vee(\sim A, B)$ (in that region, $/\supset AB/ = /B/$ and $/B/ < 1$ $- /A/$):

13.1.12

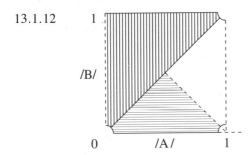

(The diagonal and the upper edge belong to the vertically cross-hatched region, the lower edge to the horizontally cross-hatched region.)

    If fewer formulas are going to be valid than in classical propositional logic, then a different system of rules of inference will have to be developed to fit the "fuzzy logic" whose truth conditions are given by 13.1.8, since otherwise we would be in the anomalous position of having theorems that need not always be true. Before we can say anything further along these lines, however, we must reexamine the question of what it means to say that a system of rules of inference and a set of conditions on truth value assignment "fit." The criterion of fit in the two-valued case was that, for any admissible assignment of truth values, the conclusions that can be inferred from premises that are true (in that assignment) are also true. This criterion, in conjunction with the specific rules of inference that we considered in chapter 3, imposed very heavy constraints on how truth values could be assigned to complex propositions. The constraints were so heavy largely because we had only two truth values. For example, we noted that since ∧-exploitation allows you to infer A from ∧AB, ∧AB has to be false if A is false, since if it were true you would be able to infer a false conclusion (A) from a true premise (∧AB). However, if truth values can be any number from 0 to 1 and "true" is identified with 1, then the most that ∧-exploitation would force on us is that if /A/ < 1 (likewise, if /B/ < 1), then /∧AB/ < 1.

Or at least, that is the most that it would force on us if our criterion of fit is merely that conclusions inferred from true premises must be true. Suppose we were to adopt a more stringent criterion of fit, namely, that the conclusion of an inference can't be less true than the premises, or more precisely, that the conclusion must be at least as true as at least one of the premises. In that case, ∧-exploitation would impose a much tighter constraint on truth value assignment, namely, that /∧AB/ ≤ min(/A/, /B/). Since you can infer A from ∧AB, its truth value must be at least that of ∧AB; since you can infer B from ∧AB, its truth value must also be at least that of ∧AB. Since /A/ and /B/ are both greater than or equal to /∧AB/, the lesser of them is greater than or equal to /∧AB/, that is, /∧AB/ ≤ min (/A/, /B/). The rule of ∧-introduction imposes the constraint that /∧AB/ ≥ min (/A/, /B/): since you can infer ∧AB from the premises A and B, ∧AB must have a truth value at least that of the weaker premise. Putting these two results together, we reach the conclusion that in fuzzy logic with a system of rules of inference that includes both ∧-exploitation and ∧-introduction, /∧AB/ must be exactly what 13.1.8 says it is: it is neither greater than nor less than min(/A/, /B/) and thus must be equal to it. Note that according to this criterion of fit, Łukasiewicz's original truth table for ⊃ would be inconsistent with ⊃-exploitation: by ⊃-exploitation, from ⊃AB and A you can infer B; but Łukasiewicz's table makes /⊃AB/ = 1 when /A/ = 0.5 and /B/ = 0, thus allowing you to infer a conclusion with truth value 0 from premises whose truth values are both at least 0.5. Since ⊃-exploitation is something that we could not possibly give up if our account of ⊃ is to fit a normal understanding of "if," Łukasiewicz's table cannot be admitted unless a less stringent criterion of fit is adopted.

The truth conditions given in 13.1.8 are clearly consistent with the rules of ∧-introduction, ∧-exploitation, ∨-introduction, ⊃-exploitation, and ∼-exploitation. One rule that 13.1.8 is clearly not consistent with, under this criterion of fit, is ~-introduction. Note that if $/A/ = 0.5$ and $/B/ = 1$, ~-introduction would allow one to perform the following inference, in which a conclusion with truth value 0 is deduced from premises with truth value 0.5:

13.1.13   1 A   0.5
           2 ~A   0.5
           3 │ B   supp   1
           4 │ A   1, reit
           5 │ ~A   2, reit
           6 ~B   3–5, ~-intro   0

It should be noted that ~-introduction plays a role in the most obvious proofs of all of the nonvalid formulas listed in 13.1.11. Thus, if a system of rules of inference is to be developed which will make the present version of fuzzy logic "semantically complete" (i.e., which will insure that what is provable is exactly what is valid), it ought to differ from the rules of chapter 3 at least to the extent of having a weaker form of ~-introduction.

The remaining rules from chapter 3 (∨-exploitation and ⊃-introduction) also fit 13.1.8 in that if they are involved in an unsound inference, that is, an inference in which a conclusion is drawn that is less true than any of the premises, some other rules of inference must be responsible for that anomaly. For example, suppose that ∨-exploitation were to yield a conclusion that had a truth value less than that of any of the premises. Let $/A/ = a$, $/B/ = b$, $/C/ = c$, and let d be the minimum truth value of any other premises:

13.1.14   . . .
           ∨AB   max(a, b)
           │ A a
           ├
           │ . . .
           │ C c
           │ B b
           ├
           │ . . .
           │ C c
           C c

Suppose that C has a lower truth value than any of the premises, that is, $c < \min(d, /\vee AB/)$. Then one of the steps in the subproofs must lead to a conclusion with truth value less than that of all the operative premises. Since $c < \min(d, /\vee AB/) = \min(d, \max(a,b)) = \max(\min(d,a), \min(d,b))$, we have either $c < \min(d,a)$ or $c < \min(d,b)$. But that means that one of the steps either in the inference of C from A or the inference of C from B yielded a conclusion whose truth value was less than that of all the operative premises, since min(d,a) is the truth value of the weakest premise operative in the one subproof, and min(d,b) the truth value of the weakest premise operative in the other. Thus, some step other than the application of ∨-exploitation in the last line is responsible for the failure of 13.1.14 to fit the principles of truth value assignment in 13.1.8. A similar argument can be given to show that ⊃-introduction is not responsible for any inferences in which conclusions are worse than premises. Thus, a system of rules of inference that fits 13.1.8 can include all of the rules of chapter 3 except for ∼-introduction.

13.2. Fuzzy Predicate Logic

Let us turn to the question of how logic may be extended to cover combinations of "fuzzy predicates" with quantifiers, as in

13.2.1 a. All fat persons are jolly.
        b. Some tall persons are obnoxious.

If these are analyzed in terms of unrestricted quantifiers, we must find a way to extend the classical truth conditions for $(\forall x)fx$ and for $(\exists x)fx$ so as to make them cover the fuzzy case. The most obvious such proposal, and the one which is in fact adopted in Lakoff (1972b), is to take the truth value of $(\forall x)fx$ to be the minimum truth value that fx has (allowing x to range over the universe of discourse) and to take the truth value of $(\exists x)fx$ to be the maximum truth value that fx has:[5]

13.2.2 a. $/(\forall x)fx/ = \min_x /fx/$
        b. $/(\exists x)fx/ - \max_x /fx/$

If these are the truth values for quantified expressions, and if ⊃ and ∧ have the truth values proposed in section 13.1, then in an analysis with unrestricted quantification, the truth values of 13.2.1 will be given by:[6]

13.2.3 a. $\min_x /⊃(\text{Fat } x, \text{ Jolly } x)/$
        b. $\max_x /∧(\text{Tall } x, \text{ Obnoxious } x)/$

The truth values that the expressions in 13.2.3 yield are often counterintuitive. Suppose that /Kissinger is fat/ $= 0.3$ and /Kissinger is jolly/ $= 0.2$. Then /⊃(Kissinger is fat, Kissinger is jolly)/ $= 0.2$, and hence 13.2.3a can be at most 0.2. But this is counterintuitive: Kissinger is at most a weak counterexample to the proposition that all fat persons are jolly, yet under the proposal considered here, his existence would take an enormous bite out of the truth value of that proposition. Moreover, as things are set up here, a weak counterexample like Kissinger does not reduce the truth value of that proposition any less than does a strong counterexample, such as a person (the name of Marlon Brando comes to mind) for whom /Fat x/ $= 0.9$ and /Jolly x/ $= 0.2$. In this case, just as in the case of Kissinger, /⊃(Fat x, Jolly x)/ comes out to be 0.2, and thus Brando makes no more of a dent in the truth value of *All fat persons are jolly* than does Kissinger.

The truth values given in 13.2.2b for the existential quantifier create a similar problem. Suppose there are three persons whose tallness and obnoxiousness are as in 13.2.4:

13.2.4		Bill	Sam	Mike
	/tall x/	0.9	0.6	0.6
	/obnoxious x/	0.6	0.6	0.9

The truth value of /∧(tall x, obnoxious x)/ in each of the three cases is 0.6, and thus each of the three persons should make the same contribution to the truth value of the proposition that some tall persons are obnoxious. However, the three persons in fact differ in how well they illustrate the proposition that some tall persons are obnoxious: Bill is the best example of the three, Sam the worst example, and Mike somewhere in between. Bill's tallness makes him more relevant to the proposition that some tall persons are obnoxious than either Sam and Mike, and Mike's obnoxiousness does not counterbalance his relative irrelevance to the proposition.

It thus appears that the truth values of quantified expressions ought to take account of the relevance of various members of the domain to the proposition: in the case of a universally quantified proposition, an item should reduce the truth value only to the extent that it is a real counterexample to the proposition (thus, Brando ought to reduce the truth value of 13.2.1a more than Kissinger does), and in the case of an existentially quantified proposition, an item should count more heavily as an instance of the proposition if it partakes more strongly of the property defining the domain of the quantifier.

One possible way of coping with these difficulties is to do fuzzy predicate logic in terms of restricted rather than unrestricted quantification, and set up the truth values so as to accord with some reasonable measure of "degree of counterexamplehood" or "degree of relevance." As a first approximation to a measure of counterexamplehood, I propose that an element be a counterexample to "all f's are g's" (i) in proportion to the degree to which it is an f, and (ii) in proportion to the degree to which its f-ness exceeds its g-ness. Thus, we can propose that the degree to which a is a counterexample to $(\forall: fx)_x \, gx$ is given by $/fa/(/fa/ - /ga/)$. This measure is reasonable[7] in that it rates as the best counterexamples those elements for which $/fa/ = /fa/ - /ga/ = 1$, that is, $/fa/ = 1$ and $/ga/ = 0$, and those elements are in fact the best possible counterexamples (e.g., persons who are unqualifiedly fat but are not at all jolly). In the case discussed above, Kissinger would be a counterexample to degree 0.3×0.1 $(= 0.03)$ to the proposition that all fat persons are jolly, whereas Brando would be a counterexample to degree 0.9×0.7 $(= 0.63)$. This sounds pretty reasonable: it would mean that the existence of Kissinger would be consistent with *All fat persons are jolly* having a truth value as high as 0.97, whereas the existence of Brando would mean that it could have at most the truth value 0.37.

The truth value of a universally quantified proposition could then be taken to be 1 minus the maximum extent to which anything is a counterexample to it:

13.2.5 $/(\forall: fx)_x \, gx/ = 1 - \max_x(/fx/(/fx/ - /gx/))$
$= \min_x(1 - /fx/(/fx/ - /gx/))$

Note that 13.2.5 requires that the analysis of quantified propositions be in terms of restricted rather than unrestricted quantification, in that the expression given in 13.2.5 cannot be resolved into the contributions of a universal quantifier and a conditional. At least, if "$\min_x$" were to be the contribution of the universal quantifier, the remainder could not be identified with the contribution of $\supset$, since if $/\supset AB/$ were $1 - /A/(/A/ - /B/)$, then $\supset$-exploitation could lead to conclusions weaker than the premises:

13.2.6 $\supset AB \; 0.86 \; (= 1 - 0.7(0.7 - 0.5))$
       A   0.7
       B   0.5

Condition 13.2.5 has the desired property of being an extension of the classical truth conditions: if we apply 13.2.5 to a classical case (i.e., a case in which $/fx/$ and $/gx/$ can only take on the values 0 and 1), then a universal proposition will have the value 0 if there is a counterexample (i.e., an instance in which $/fx/ = 1$ and $/gx/ = 0$) and will have the value 1 otherwise, which is precisely the classical truth conditions.

Let us now turn to the existential quantifier. If we want the truth conditions for existential propositions and for universal propositions to remain connected by the de Morgan laws (e.g., if the truth value of *All fat persons are jolly* is to be the same as that of *There isn't any fat person who isn't jolly*), then the truth conditions for the existential quantifier will have to be chosen in a way that conforms to the truth conditions that we have assigned to the universal quantifier. Specifically, $\max_x/fx/(/fx/ - /gx/)$ would have to be the truth value of

"Some f's are not g's," and, by replacing gx by $\sim gx$, we would get 13.2.7 as the truth value of "Some f's are g's":

13.2.7 $/(\exists{:}\,fx)gx/\ =\ \max_x/fx/(/fx/\ +\ /gx/\ -\ 1)$

This proposal distinguishes between Bill, Sam, and Mike in the case discussed in 13.2.4 above: $/fx/(/fx/\ +\ /gx/\ -\ 1)$ is $0.9(1.5\ -\ 1)\ =\ 0.45$ for Bill, $0.6(1.2\ -\ 1)\ =\ 0.18$ for Sam, and $0.6(1.5\ -\ 1)\ =\ 0.3$ for Mike, which means that Bill makes the most contribution to the truth of the existential proposition and Sam makes the least contribution, which is in accordance with the considerations of the earlier discussion.

Condition 13.2.7 has the noteworthy feature that it allows *Some f's are g's* to have a different truth value than *Some g's are f's*. Note that in the last example, Bill would make more of a contribution to the truth value of *Some tall persons are obnoxious* (namely, 0.45) than he would to the truth value of *Some obnoxious persons are tall* (namely, 0.12); thus, in a world peopled by Bills and Sams but not by Mikes, *Some tall persons are obnoxious* would be more true than *Some obnoxious persons are tall*. On reflection, I find this difference reasonable: Bill is of much more relevance to a statement about tall persons than to a statement about obnoxious persons. Like 13.2.5, 13.2.7 includes the classical truth conditions as a special case: in the classical case, $\max_x/fx/(/fx/\ +\ /gx/\ -\ 1)$ has the value 1 when there is an individual such that $/fx/\ =\ /gx/\ =\ 1$ and has the value 0 otherwise.

Of the four rules of inference for quantifiers given in section 2.5, only two, namely, ∃-expl and ∀-intro, fit the truth conditions 13.2.5 and 13.2.7, in the sense that they do not yield a conclusion that is less true than all of the operative premises unless the subordinate proof does, and thus the blame for the "unsoundness" of the inference can be shifted onto some step of the subordinate proof and thus off of the application of ∃-expl or ∀-intro. The rules of ∃-intro and ∀-expl obviously do not fit the truth conditions, as is shown by picking truth values that make the conclusion have lower truth value than either premise:

13.2.8   a. Let $/fa/\ =\ 0.8$, $/ga/\ =\ 0.8$, and a be the best example of "an f which is a g"

fa	0.8
ga	0.8
$(\exists{:}\,fx)gx$	0.48

     b. Let $/fb/\ =\ 0.4$, $/gb/\ =\ 0.2$, and b be the best example of "an f which is not a g"

$$(\forall: fx)gx \qquad 0.92$$
$$fb \qquad\qquad 0.4$$
$$gb \qquad\qquad 0.2$$

It is dismaying that of the four rules for quantifiers, the two that clearly do not fit the truth conditions proposed above are the two that a logician would be most willing to stake his life on. A dilemma now arises. If $\forall$-expl is to yield conclusions of truth value not less than that of any premise, then a universal proposition can have at most the value that Lakoff's proposal (see 13.2.3) would assign to it. If $/fa/ > /ga/$, then for the truth conditions to fit $\forall$-expl, $/(\forall: fx)gx/$ can be at most $/ga/$, since otherwise both premises in the inference via $\forall$-expl would have a greater truth value than the conclusion. Since in that case $/\supset(fa,ga)/ = /ga/$, and since $/\supset(fa,ga)/ = 1$ when $/fa/ \leq /ga/$, the truth value of the universal $\leq /\supset(fa,ga)/$, no matter what a is, which is to say

13.2.9 $/(\forall: fx)gx/ \leq \min_x/\supset(fx,gx)/.$

But then $\forall$-expl can only fit truth conditions that make a universal proposition less true than I've argued it ought to be in cases like the Kissinger case. This means that if universal propositions are to have as high a truth value as I have argued for, I will have to either give up $\forall$-expl in favor of some weaker rule of inference or accept some less stringent criterion of fit between rules of inference and principles of truth value assignment than the criterion that the conclusion must be at least as true as the weakest premise. While I find giving up $\forall$-expl by far the less attractive of these alternatives, I also feel quite uneasy about the other alternative, especially in view of the fact that it was not particularly difficult to find truth conditions for the propositional connectives which fit virtually all of the natural deduction rules of classical propositional logic, under this stringent criterion of fit.

Propositions $(\forall: fx)gx$ in which f can take on nonclassical truth values constitute one of the few cases where I can see some point in a normative attitude which would either condemn some natural language usages as logically incoherent or maintain that in all supposed instances of those usages the speaker really means something else. The difficulty with applying $\forall$-exploitation or $\exists$-introduction is that both rules hinge upon the notion of "special case" or "particular instance," but when f is a fuzzy predicate it is not clear what should count as "instances" of fx for which gx. Here a striking difference between quantification and conjunction appears. Quantifiers can be thought of as "big conjunctions" (or conjunctions as little quantifiers; cf. section 8.5). However, in any conjunction, no matter how fuzzy the constituent propositions are,

there is no fuzziness about what constituent propositions the conjoined proposition is made up of: any particular proposition either is one of the conjuncts
or is not one of the conjuncts, and the possibility of its being "sort of a conjunct" does not arise. By contrast, in the case of $(\forall: fx)gx$ or of $(\exists: fx)gx,$
where fx is "fuzzy," the proposition can be regarded as a "big conjunction"
only by admitting fuzziness regarding what the conjuncts are. Does *All fat
persons are jolly* cover the case of Marlon Brando? Of Kissinger?

Not only can an absolute answer of *yes* or *no* not be given here, but an
answer of *sort of* or *somewhat* would be quite bizarre, as well as not being
true. Whether a given special case *a* for which $/fa/ < 1$ is taken in depends on
what the speaker intended to be taken in. If he intends the universal proposition to be taken broadly enough to include Brando, fine. If he intends it to be
taken even more broadly, so as to include Kissinger, also fine. However, it is
up to him to decide what is to be taken in, and for any particular decision on
his part, the truth value of the quantified proposition will be determined by
the values that $/gx/$ takes within the domain that he has taken the quantified
proposition to cover. If the truth value of the quantified proposition is taken to
be $\min_x/gx/$ for the universal, and $\max_x/gx/$ for the existential, we will have the
truth conditions that would arise were we to replace $/fx/$ by a function that
takes the values 0 and 1 in accordance with the broadness of the speaker's
conception of "special case" and then assign truth values in accordance with
Lakoff's proposal. This treatment is merely a terminological variant of the
normative logician's suggestion that a person who says *All fat persons are
jolly* really means something else, namely, that all persons whose fatness exceeds some fixed degree are jolly. (It should be emphasized that fuzziness in
gx creates no problems whatever: thus a normative logician can demand that
All fat persons are jolly be supplied with something more precise than *fat
person* as a specification of the domain of the quantifier, without his necessarily having any scruples about fuzzy predicates in general). Under this approach, the difference between Marlon Brando and Kissinger is not that they
reduce the truth value of *All fat persons are jolly* by different amounts. In any
case in which they both affect its truth value (i.e., in any case in which the
speaker interprets *all fat persons* so broadly as to take in not only Brando but
also Kissinger), they place the same upper limit on its truth value. The difference is that it takes a much less broad interpretation of *all fat persons* for
Brando to have this effect than for Kissinger to have it.

This approach differs from those discussed previously with regard to cases
such as that of $/$Kissinger is fat$/ = 0.5$ and $/$Kissinger is jolly$/ = 0.6$. In that
case, for $x =$ Kissinger, $/\supset(fx,gx)/ = 1$ and $/fx/(/fx/ - /gx/) = -0.05$. Thus,
under both of the proposals considered earlier, Kissinger would not reduce the

truth value of *All fat persons are jolly* (i.e., it could still have the value 1 despite the existence of Kissinger). Under the proposal sketched in the last paragraph, either the intended domain is so narrow as to exclude Kissinger and he thus plays no role in the determination of the truth value of the universal proposition, or it would be broad enough to include him, and since he would then be a member of the domain for which $/gx/ = 0.6$, the truth value of the universal would be at most 0.6.

The problems discussed in this section in connection with fuzzy predicate logic also arise in fuzzy modal logic. Suppose we allow the alternativeness relation to be fuzzy, that is, allow Rww' to have truth values between 0 and 1.[8] I do not intend for the degree to which w' is an alternative to w to be a measure of its similarity to w. It might be, say, a measure of the extent to which the history leading up to w would have to be different for it to have resulted in w' rather than w being "the present world," given that a minor change in the past (such as better aim by an assassin) can result in major differences in the present. The truth value of $\square$A in w might be taken to be the minimum truth value of A in the worlds w' that are alternatives to w. But how much of an alternative to w does a world w' have to be for a low truth value of A in w' to force a low truth value on $\square$A in w? Suppose, for example, that in all worlds that are unqualified alternatives to the real world, the truth value of *Tokyo is congested* is 1, but in some world that is only weakly alternative to the real world, /Tokyo is congested/ $= 0.2$. Should that mean that /Necessarily, Tokyo is congested/ in the real world must be 0.2 or less? If not, then we have essentially the same problem as with the status of Kissinger as a counterexample to the proposition that all fat persons are jolly, and the range of solutions to that problem will be essentially parallel to the range of solutions to the Kissinger problem.

Proof that $\forall$-intro fits the truth condition 13.2.5. Suppose we have a proof whose conclusion is drawn by $\forall$-intro and whose conclusion is of lower truth value (according to 13.2.5) than the weakest operative premise:

13.2.10   Premises

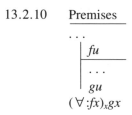

$(\forall :fx)_x gx$

Let d be the truth value of the weakest of the premises, and let a be the value of x which maximizes $/fx/(/fx/ = /gx/)$.[9] Let $b = /fa/$ and $c = /ga/$. Then the truth value of the conclusion is $1 - b(b - c)$, and that is by assumption less than d. Suppose that the steps of the proof other than its last step are sound in the sense that no instance of that step leads to a conclusion of lower truth value than the weakest premise that is operative in that step. Then 13.2.11 is sound, and thus $c \geq \min(b, d)$:

13.2.11 fa b

            Premises d
            _____

            . . .

            . . .

            ga c

Case 1. Suppose that $c \geq b$. Then $b - c \leq 0$, and so $1 - b(b - c) \geq 1$. But $d > 1 - b(b - c)$, and thus $d > 1$, which is impossible, since d is a truth value. *Case 2.* Suppose that $c < b$. Then $c \geq d$ (since $c \geq \min(b, d)$). Since $d > 1 - b(b - c)$, we then have

13.2.12 $c > 1 - b^2 + bc$

            $c - bc > 1 - b^2$

            $c(1 - b) > (1 + b)(1 - b)$

If $b = 1$, then the last line becomes $0 > 0$, which is false. We can thus assume that $b < 1$, which means that $1 - b$ is greater than 0 and thus can be canceled from both sides of the inequality. This yields $1 + b < c$. But $c < b$ and thus $1 + b < b$, which is impossible. Thus, the assumption that unsoundness comes in only in the final step of the proof leads to a contradiction, hence there must have been an unsound step somewhere earlier in 13.2.10.

Proof that ∃-expl fits the truth conditions 13.2.7. Suppose we have a proof whose conclusion is inferred by ∃-expl and whose conclusion is of lower truth value than any of the operative premises:

13.2.13   Premises

            . . .

            $(\exists{:}fx)_x gx$

            $\Big|\ \begin{array}{l} fu \\ gu \end{array}$
            _____

            $\Big|\ \ . . .$

            $\Big|\ \ A$

            A

Let e be the element which maximizes $/fx/(/fx/ + /gx/ - 1)$, and let $a = /A/$, $b = /fe/$, $c = /ge/$, and $d = $ the truth value of the weakest of the premises.

Then the truth value of the existential according to 13.2.7 is $b(b + c - 1)$, and if the application of ∃-expl is what is responsible for the unsoundness of the whole argument, we have $a < d \leq b(b + c - 1)$. If the unsoundness of the whole proof is due only to the final step, then the following proof is sound:

13.2.14   Premises d
             fe b
             ge c

             . . .
             . . .
             A a

Since b and c are both at most 1, $b(b + c - 1)$ is less than or equal to both b and c. Since we have $d \leq b(b + c - 1)$, we thus have $d \leq b$ and $d \leq c$, and hence the weakest premise of 13.2.14 has truth value d. But since $a < d$, that means that 13.2.14 has a conclusion of lower truth value than its weakest premise and is thus unsound. Since the steps in the latter argument are merely the steps prior to the final step in 13.2.13, we have shown that any unsoundness in 13.2.13 must be attributable to some step other than its final step.

13.3 Fuzzy Sets

A predicate in fuzzy logic can be said to have as its extension a "fuzzy set": an entity that has not only unqualified members but also members that belong to it to varying degrees between 0 and 1. The notion of "fuzzy set" [10] can be made more precise by defining it in terms of the notion of **characteristic function.** In ordinary (nonfuzzy) set theory, any set A can be characterized in terms of a function μ_A that specifies what its members are:

13.3.1 $\mu_A(x) = 1$ if $x \in A$
                    $= 0$ if $x \notin A$

Suppose we take characteristic functions rather than sets as basic. Then a fuzzy set A will be identifiable with a function μ_A whose values are real numbers in the interval from 0 to 1; for any object x in the universe, $\mu_A(x)$ will be the degree to which x is a member of A.

To describe a fuzzy set is to specify what its characteristic function is. Thus, to specify what the complement of a fuzzy set is or to specify what the union or intersection of two or more fuzzy sets is, it suffices to say how the characteristic function of the complement or union or intersection is related to the characteristic function(s) of the fuzzy set(s) from which it is derived. The following definitions are widely accepted

13.3.2   a. $\mu_{\bar{A}}(x) = 1 - \mu_A(x)$
         b. $\mu_{A\cup B}(x) = \max(\mu_A(x), \mu_B(x))$
         c. $\mu_{A\cap B}(x) = \min(\mu_A(x), \mu_B(x))$

These definitions are generalizations of the relationship of nonfuzzy sets to their complements, unions, and intersections; for example, if A and B are nonfuzzy sets, then $x \in A\cup B$ if and only if $x \in A$ or $x \in B$, that is, if and only if $\mu_A(x) = 1$ or $\mu_B(x) = 1$, that is, if and only if the greater of $\mu_A(x)$ and $\mu_B(x)$ is 1; and $x \notin A\cup B$ if and only if neither $x \in A$ nor $x \in B$, that is, if and only if $\mu_A(x) = \mu_B(x) = 0$, that is, if and only if the greater of $\mu_A(x)$ and $\mu_B(x)$ is 0. The notion of subset can be extended to fuzzy sets as follows:

13.3.3   A $\subseteq$ B if and only if for all x, $\mu_A(x) \leq \mu_B(x)$.

That is, A is a subset of B if and only if, to whatever extent any object is a member of A, it is to at least that extent a member of B.[11]

Just as a relation can be identified with a set of ordered pairs, a fuzzy relation can be identified with a fuzzy set of ordered pairs; if R is a fuzzy relation, then $\mu_R(a, b)$ will be the extent to which the pair (a, b) stand in the relation R, that is, the extent to which a stands in the relation R to b. Various notions having to do with relations can be generalized so as to cover fuzzy relations. For example, the notion of "fuzzy partial ordering" can be defined as follows:

13.3.4   A fuzzy relation R on a domain U is a fuzzy partial ordering if and only if
           i. R is antisymmetric: for all $x,y \in U$, if $\mu_R(x, y) > 0$, then $\mu_R(y, x) = 0$, and
           ii. R is transitive: for all $x,y,z \in U$, $\mu_R(x, z) \geq \min(\mu_R(x, y), \mu_R(y, z))$.

If U is the positive integers and R is the relation of "much greater than" and μ_R is defined so that $\mu_R(x, y)$ is 0 if $x \leq y$ and $\mu_R(x, y)$ comes closer to 1 the more that x exceeds y, then R will be a fuzzy partial ordering.

The **composition** R°S of two nonfuzzy relations R and S has the definition: $x(R°S)y$ if and only if there is a z such that xRz and zSy; for example, if R is "is mother of" and S is "is parent of," then R°S is "is grandmother of." The fuzzy version of composition will then be defined as follows:

13.3.5 $\mu_{R°S}(x, y) = \max_z(\min(\mu_R(x, z), \mu_S(z, y)))$

The extent to which x has the relation R°S to y is the maximum extent to which x has the relation R to some individual and that individual has the relation S to y. If we compare 13.3.4 (ii) and 13.3.5, we can easily see that R is transitive if and only if R°R $\subseteq$ R.

13.4. Degrees of Truth

Truth values between 0 and 1 have been proposed in a number of works as an appropriate device for dealing with inexact concepts. With intermediate truth values one is not forced to draw an arbitrary distinction between tall individuals and not-tall individuals but can recognize individuals who are somewhat tall, slightly tall, and so on without being unqualifiedly tall or unqualifiedly not tall. There are still arbitrary decisions (e.g., it will be arbitrary how one distinguishes between those who are unqualifiedly tall and those who are not so tall as to be unqualifiedly tall), but the effects of these arbitrary decisions are more attenuated: they affect whether the truth value of p will be 1.0 or 0.9, not whether it will be 1 or 0.[12]

In the case of adjectives that refer to a magnitude, such as *tall* or *heavy* or even *obnoxious,* there is no direct correspondence between values of that magnitude and truth values of propositions "x is tall," and the like. What "x is tall" expresses depends on what x is being judged as: a tall six-year-old is shorter than most short adults, and a tall Japanese may be at the same time a short basketball player. An entity is thus not tall absolutely but only relative to a standard for a class to which it belongs, and different standards may prevail for different classes to which something belongs. Each standard for tallness provides a standard for being very tall, for being somewhat tall, for being a little tall; given the relationship between x's height and the truth value of "x is tall" relative to a given standard, one is in a position to know also the relationship between x's height and the truth value of "x is very tall" relative to that standard.

There are a number of ways that the truth value of "x is very tall" could conceivably be related to the given standard. One possibility is that the truth value of "x is very tall" might be completely determined by the truth value of "x is tall" without any direct reference to x's height, as in Zadeh's proposal (1972) that

13.4.1   /x is very tall/ $=$ /x is tall/^{2}

This particular suggestion has the desirable feature that /x is very tall/ $\leq$ /x is tall/; that is, you can't be very tall to a greater degree than you're tall. However, it has the counterintuitive characteristic of making exactly the same individuals unqualifiedly very tall as are unqualifiedly tall and making exactly the same individuals unqualifiedly not very tall as are unqualifiedly not tall, since $1^2 = 1$ and $0^2 = 0$. Another possibility would be to make the truth value of "x is very tall" depend both on heights and on truth values in some fashion such as the following:

13.4.2   /x is very tall/ = /x' is tall/, where height(x') = height(x) − 3″

This proposal avoids the last difficulty: to be unqualifiedly very tall, you would have to be at least 3″ taller than is needed in order to be unqualifiedly tall. The arbitrarily chosen figure of 3″ could of course be replaced by some characteristic of the height distribution, say, some fixed multiple of the standard deviation from the mean, so as to allow 13.4.2 to be generalized to adjectives referring to magnitudes other than heights. A third possibility is that the truth values for "x is very tall" depend directly on the distribution of magnitudes and not on the truth values, as in 13.4.3a or some "fuzzified" analog of it such as 13.4.3b:

13.4.3   a. /x is very tall/ = 1 if x's height exceeds the median height by
              more than 3″, /x is very tall/ = 0 otherwise.

$$\text{b. } /x \text{ is very tall} / = \begin{cases} 0 \text{ if } t(x) \le 0.7 \\ 5(t(x) - 0.7) \text{ if } 0.7 < t(x) < 0.9 \\ 1 \text{ if } t(x) \ge 0.9, \end{cases}$$

              where $t(x)$ is the fraction of members of the domain that x is at
              least as tall as (e.g., $t(x) = 1$ if x is the tallest individual in
              the domain; $t(x) = 1/2$ if x has median height).

The truth values for "x is very tall" according to the different proposals are given in 13.4.4, under the assumption that height in the given population has a normal distribution with the mean 5′9″ and that /x is tall/ increases linearly from a value of 0 when x's height is 5′6″ to a value of 1 when his height is 6′:

13.4.4   /x is very tall/ according to

a. 13.4.1   b. 13.4.2

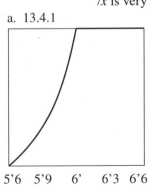

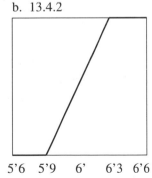

5'6 5'9 6' 6'3 6'6   5'6 5'9 6' 6'3 6'6

c. 13.4.3b

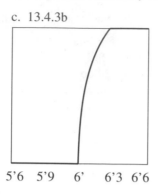

5'6   5'9   6'   6'3 6'6

The ideas embodied in the different proposals have different implications for what *very* can be combined with in a semantically coherent way. According to 13.4.1, *very* should be combinable with all inexact concepts, according to 13.4.3 it should be combinable with all adjectives that express magnitudes, and according to 13.4.2 it should be combinable with those adjectives that are both inexact and express magnitudes. A test case for choosing among these approaches will be inexact concepts that do not represent magnitudes. A good example of this type is notions like "very tall" themselves: "very tall" is an inexact concept (any sharp distinction regarding who is "very tall" is arbitrary) but there is no corresponding scale of very-tall-ness. Thus the proposals in 13.4.2 and 13.4.3 (or better, 13.4.2 and 13.4.3b, since a "fuzzy" version of 13.4.3 is called for here) imply that *very* should not be combinable with *very tall,* whereas the proposal in 13.4.1 implies the opposite. The fact that we can say things such as *very, very tall* or *very, very, very stupid* seems at first to support approaches like 13.4.1 and refute those like 13.4.2 and 13.4.3. But that conclusion is premature. Here *very* does not modify *very tall* or *very, very stupid* but rather combines with the other *very* to yield a complex degree expression, as can be seen from the fact that the relationship of *very tall* to *tall* · is not mirrored in the relationship of *very, very tall* to *very tall:*

13.4.5   a. How tall is Fred? Véry tall.
                     Very, véry tall.
          b. *How very tall is Fred? *Véry very tall.
                             (Cf. *Extrémely very tall, *Quíte very
                             tall.)

These facts suggest that for *very* an approach like 13.4.2 or 13.4.3 stands a chance of being correct whereas one like 13.4.1 must be wrong. The same is the case for many other "hedges," including *quite, somewhat, rather, pretty,* and *a little*. These hedges, like *very*, normally combine only with adjectives referring to magnitudes[14] and do not combine syntactically with one another:

13.4.6 a. $\left\{ \begin{array}{l} *\text{very} \\ *\text{quite} \\ *\text{somewhat} \\ *\text{rather} \\ *\text{pretty} \\ *\text{a little} \\ *\text{a bit} \end{array} \right\}$ $\left\{ \begin{array}{l} \text{dead} \\ \text{striped} \\ \text{two-legged} \end{array} \right\}$

b. *quite rather tall
    *a bit somewhat small
    *pretty quite unlikely

There are also hedges that combine with nonmagnitude adjectives, and at least one of them is marginally combinable with hedged adjectives:[15]

13.4.7 a. more or less dead
            pretty well impossible
        b. ?Jack is more or less very tall

In making proposals along the lines of 13.4.2 or 13.4.3 for the semantics of hedges, it is important to separate the semantic content of the sentences from what they convey by virtue of cooperativeness. While "x is pretty tall" conveys that x is tall but not very tall, that does not imply that "x is pretty tall" should have a low truth value when x is very tall. *Wilt is pretty tall* will convey that Wilt is not extremely tall by virtue of the fact that if he were extremely tall there would be more informative alternatives to *pretty tall* that involve the same amount of linguistic effort (*very tall*) or less (*tall*). Question-answer pairs such as 13.4.8 indicate that *pretty tall* conversationally implicates but does not logically imply that the individual is not extremely tall:

13.4.8   Is Wilt pretty tall?
            Yes/*No, he's over 7 feet tall.

Thus the relation between heights and the truth value of "x is pretty tall" relative to a given standard should not correspond to a curve that rises and then falls, as in Zadeh's 1972 proposal (the lower branch of the barbed curve), but to one that rises and remains at its maximum point (the upper branch):

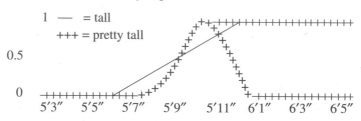

By contrast, *a little* not merely conveys but really *implies* that the truth value of the predicate is greater than 0 and less than 1 (in fact, is much less than 1). For example, if Jane weighs 400 pounds, it is not only misleading but outright false to say that she is a little fat:

13.4.9   Is Jane a little fat?
          ??Yes/?No, she weighs over 400 pounds.

Sadock (1977, 1981) gives a detailed account of what is conveyed by another important class of hedges, namely **approximations,** and argues that most of what is conveyed is a matter of conversational implicature. Sadock notes that the correctness of a sentence involving *approximately n* depends not simply on the difference between *n* and the real value but on the amount of precision suggested by the expression by which *n* is specified and the amount of precision that the context calls for. Thus, if the population of Odessa is 979,793, example 13.4.10a is more "correct" than 13.4.10b even though in 13.4.10b the number given is closer to the actual population of Odessa:

13.4.10 a. The population of Odessa is approximately one million.
         b. The population of Odessa is approximately 990,000.

The use of 990,000 in 13.4.10b suggests that the figures are given to two significant digits, and with that standard of precision 980,000 is a closer approximation that is no more costly in linguistic effort than the figure actually mentioned; thus cooperativity would demand that one say *approximately 980,000* in preference to *approximately 990,000*. By contrast, *one million* requires a minimum of linguistic effort and is closer to the actual population figure than is the next cheapest alternative, 900,000. Thus 13.4.10a is not misleading whereas 13.4.10b is. *Approximately 6 feet tall* is less correct when applied to a 5′8″ man than when applied to a 5′8″ tall fence or (to use Sadock's example) a 5′8″ tall mutant cockroach, and it is less correct with reference to a 5′8″ man than *approximately 8 feet tall* is with reference to a 7′8″ man. Normal adult human beings have heights in a fairly narrow range, within which we normally expect estimates to be accurate within a couple of inches;

but those standards of precision are dropped when one is talking about things other than human beings or about human beings of abnormal (not just unusual) height.

Sadock proposes that simple sentences containing *approximately n, roughly n,* and the like are true under virtually all conditions, that is, that *John is approximately 6' tall* is true as long as John's height is greater than 0, even if it is 4' or 8', and that what it conveys about John's height is determined purely by considerations of cooperativity. Some doubt is shed on that proposal by the fact that *no* can be an appropriate answer to questions about approximations:

13.4.11   Is John approximately 6 feet tall?
               No/*Yes, he's four foot eight.

However, considerations of cooperativity suggest that the *yes-no* test might be inappropriate here: if a proposition is guaranteed to be true, a yes-no question ostensibly about that proposition may be reinterpreted as a question about something else (here, about the proposition conveyed by the given sentence) since otherwise the question would be pointless. I accordingly suspend judgment on Sadock's suggestion. The most viable alternative to Sadock's proposal is probably the treatment in which propositions involving approximations are assigned truth values that reflect not only the discrepancy between the actual value and the approximation but also the standards of accuracy being observed (which is to say that a sentence involving an approximation expresses different propositions depending on the assumed standards of accuracy). The proposition involving the best approximation relative to the given standards should receive the truth value 1, and those involving other approximations should receive other truth values, perhaps even 0 in all cases. I know of no knockdown argument supporting any of the three candidates for the truth values of approximation sentences with less than optimal approximations: (i) that they have the truth value 1, (ii) that they have the truth value 0, (iii) that they have truth values that are lower the more that the approximation differs from the best approximation at the given standard of accuracy. One consideration pointed out by Sadock may ultimately provide an argument against (iii), namely, the fact that words like *approximately* cannot be iterated:

13.4.12   *The population of Odessa is roughly approximately one
               million.

Whether it does provide such an argument will depend on whether (iii), when worked out as best as it can be, will provide a scale of "approximate one million-hood" that *roughly* could be combined with.

13.5. Dimensions of Truth

Let us suppose that *some* and *most* make the same contribution to the meanings of the sentences in 13.5.1 as they do to sentences such as *Some/ Most linguists are insane:*

13.5.1   a. In some respects, Warren Harding was a good president.
         b. In most respects, FDR was an atrocious president.

What then is the variable that the quantifiers in 13.5.1 bind? The only plausible answer that I can think of to this question is that the "respects" over which the variable ranges are dimensions of truth (in this case, particular criteria of what a good president is). Example 13.5.1a then says that there are criteria of being a good president on which Harding was a good president, and 13.5.1b that on most criteria of being a good president, FDR was atrocious. If this conjecture is correct, then to such a sentence as 13.5.2 there should correspond not a single truth value but rather a complex of truth values, one for each of the criteria (or at least, each of the ones that come into consideration in the discourse in question) of what a good president is:

13.5.2   Warren Harding was a good president.

But wait, doesn't 13.5.2 have just a single truth value rather than some complex of truth values? Or at least, don't we treat it that way when someone utters it? I conjecture that the relation of 13.5.2 to a normal (one-dimensional) truth value is the same as that of 13.5.3 to such a truth value:

13.5.3   Scandinavians are tall.

In the type of generic construction illustrated by 13.5.3, in which the bound variable corresponds to a plural indefinite noun phrase, the speaker is not asserting the corresponding universal proposition (i.e., he is not saying something that you could refute by exhibiting a Scandinavian who wasn't tall) but is rather saying that it is "typical" of Scandinavians to be tall. Example 13.5.2 is given a similar interpretation: not that in every respect Harding was a good president, but only that the values for Harding on the dimensions of goodness as a president are typically high. I thus conjecture that when 13.5.2 is a constituent of a larger proposition it has a complex of truth values rather than a one-dimensional truth value, but a sentence in which it appears to be used as an independent proposition is actually interpreted as a generic construction, with "dimensions of goodness as president" as the domain over which the bound variable ranges.

Lakoff 1972b has discussed a number of words that serve to pick out particular dimensions of propositions that have multiple dimensions of truth. Consider the sentences

13.5.4   a. Technically, Richard Nixon is a Quaker.
         b. Esther Williams is a regular fish.
         c. Strictly speaking, the tomato is a fruit.
         d. Loosely speaking, whales are fish.

Someone who is a regular fish is not a fish but possesses some property popularly associated with fish, particularly that of swimming with such naturalness that one seems at home in the water.[16] *Technically,* by contrast, excludes such "connotational" dimensions of meaning in favor of precise definitional dimensions. *Technically* is thus inappropriate where no precise definition has any status:

13.5.5   a. ?Technically, this soup is icky.
         b. ?Technically, your brother is a creep.
         c. ?Technically, Quayle is a klutz.

While the examples given so far have involved combinations of *technically* with something of the form "NP be Adj/NP," it is possible to combine it with more complex sentences:

13.5.6   a. Technically, Nixon isn't a criminal.
         b. Technically, any student using profanity can be expelled.
         c. Technically, you're related to every other human being.
         d. Technically, there are infinitely many nouns in English.

These sentences allow analyses in which *technically* imposes a "precise definitional" interpretation on one of the predicates, though in the case of 13.5.6b the only apparent such analysis (that in which *technically* qualifies *can*) may be somewhat counterintuitive, and in 13.5.6d it is not clear whether *technically* qualifies *infinite* or *noun* or both. In fact it strongly suggests that *technically* really qualifies the whole sentence rather than some particular predicate or predicates in it; after all, there really isn't any nontechnical interpretation of *infinite* or of *noun* that 13.5.6d could be taken as contrasting with, given that 13.5.6d is used as a way of expressing that the means for forming compound nouns in English can be iterated without limit. Note, though, that the use of *technically* does not force all words in the sentence to be given a "technical" interpretation:

13.5.7   Technically, any idiot who shoots his mouth off in public can get
              pushed around by the cops.

Here clearly no "technical" interpretation is imposed on *idiot, shoot one's
mouth off,* or *push around.* Perhaps *technically* merely warns the hearer that
he is to give a "precise" interpretation to all terms in the sentence that can
plausibly be given one.[17]

Lakoff has observed that *technically* and *strictly speaking* are far from
being synonymous. For example, given that Ronald Reagan owns cattle and
is able to deduct their expenses on his income tax but is not actively concerned
with their breeding and feeding, 13.5.8a but not 13.5.8b would be an appropriate thing to say:

13.5.8   a. Technically, Reagan is a cattle rancher.
          b. Strictly speaking, Reagan is a cattle rancher.

By contrast, for a person who thinks that Chomsky's research on language is
more philosophy than linguistics, 13.5.9b would be a more appropriate thing
to say than 13.5.9a:

13.5.9   a. Technically, Chomsky is a philosopher.
          b. Strictly speaking, Chomsky is a philosopher.

Lakoff observes that while *technically* picks out "definitional" criteria, *strictly
speaking* picks out "important" criteria, and for a criterion of X-hood to be
important, it is neither necessary that it be "definitional," as is illustrated by
13.5.10, nor is it sufficient, as illustrated by the contrast between 13.5.8a and
13.5.8b:

13.5.10   Strictly speaking, Quayle is a klutz.

The contribution of *loosely speaking* to a sentence is somewhat harder to
pin down than that of *strictly speaking.* It is not the case that *loosely speaking*
picks out the "unimportant" criteria, since examples 13.5.11 do not express
true propositions, notwithstanding the fact that Esther Williams and Lou
Brock possess properties (though not definitional criteria) that are associated
with fish and gazelles, respectively.

13.5.11   ?Loosely speaking, Esther Williams is a fish.
               ?Loosely speaking, Lou Brock is a gazelle.

While *regular* picks out "connotational" criteria to the exclusion of anything
else, *loosely speaking* gives "secondary" criteria more than usual weight relative to "important" criteria. For something to be loosely speaking a fish, it

has to be a fish under a permissive interpretation of that term, that is, an interpretation that makes it easier for something to qualify as a fish than would normally be the case, though an interpretation that still leaves *fish* being interpreted as a "natural kind": a class of objects that go together in a category for reasons that depend on their nature rather than on the technicalities of legal systems and the like. Connotations such as those picked out by *regular* are irrelevant to membership in a natural kind and are thus ignored by *loosely speaking*.[18] *Loosely speaking* also lowers "thresholds" for primary criteria. For example, while there is nothing that could be called a "secondary" criterion for being a rectangle, still one can say 13.5.12:

13.5.12   Loosely speaking, this is a rectangle.

The reference here is presumably to something that counts as a rectangle if one lowers one's standards of when lines are perpendicular (i.e., a four-sided figure whose angles are loosely speaking right angles) or of when the sides are coplanar or of whether the sides are straight-line segments (i.e., a four-sided figure with crooked sides could be loosely speaking a rectangle) or of whether the sides are continuous and intersect (e.g., a four-sided figure with a gap in one side or a missing corner could be loosely speaking a rectangle; Gestalt psychologists have shown that figures of this type are usually perceived **as** rectangles). Note that this discussion raises the possibility of combining multidimensional truth values with "fuzziness," that is, of allowing the component truth values of a multidimensional truth value to be intermediate between truth and falsehood.

So far, I have avoided the question of how the complexes of truth values that I have been alluding to so vaguely relate to traditional questions of logic such as how the truth values of $\wedge AB$, $\vee AB$, and $\supset AB$ depend on those of A and B. There is in fact no clearly satisfying answer to the question of how propositions having complex truth values determine truth values of larger propositions of which they are constituents. We have already noted that different elementary propositions need not have the same dimensions of truth: a predicate may have no technical criteria of applicability or may have no secondary criteria. Also, there is no reason to expect any one-to-one match between criteria of being a good president and criteria of being a good Catholic. We could, of course, render the various propositions comparable by giving them "vacuous" values for any missing dimensions and then set up truth conditions such as, say, that if $/A/ = (a_1, a_2, \ldots, a_n)$ and $/B/ = (b_1, b_2, \ldots, b_n)$ then $/\wedge AB/ = (\min(a_1, b_1), \min(a_2, b_2), \ldots, \min(a_n, b_n))$; that is, you compute the truth value component by component. However, I will refrain from presenting a detailed proposal of that type here, since it is not clear that the truth values of complex propositions work that way. It might very well be, for example, that each of the conjuncts of a conjoined proposition is assigned a "one-dimensional" truth value (either by interpreting it as a generic proposition about the various dimensions of truth, or on the basis of an explicit or implicit hedge) and the truth values of the complex propositions are computed via the truth conditions proposed in 13.1.

The treatment of dimension hedges sketched in this section explains some of their combinatory restrictions. For example, 13.5.13a is deviant because *regular fish* has no connotative dimensions for another occurrence of *regular* to pick out (the connotative dimensions of *fish* are literal dimensions of *regular fish*) and 13.5.13b is deviant because combinations with *regular* are non-technical:

13.5.13 a. *Esther Williams is a regular regular fish.
       b. *Technically, Esther Williams is a regular fish.

Certain degree hedges can be taken to have an effect on various dimensions of truth; for example, regardless of what dimensions an adjective A has, *very A* and *quite A* will have no "technical" dimension. Thus, while *strictly speaking* can be combined with such expressions, *technically* cannot:

13.5.14 a. Strictly speaking, Lyndon Johnson was very tall.
       b. *Technically, Lyndon Johnson was very tall.

Certain combinatory restrictions are grammatical in nature, for example, each of the various hedges belongs to a particular part of speech and can only appear where items of that category are permitted by the syntax of the language:

13.5.15 a. Sam is a regular pig.
       b. *Sam is regular(ly) filthy. (acceptable only with irrelevant sense)
       c. *Regular(ly) Sam is filthy.

However, there remain several combinatory restrictions that do not appear to be grammatical in nature and do not seem to follow from the rough account given above of the semantics of dimension hedges:

13.5.16 a. Sam is a regular (*stingy) bastard.
          Sam is a regular tightwad.
          (Cf. Sam really is a stingy bastard)
       b. Nixon is virtually a criminal.
          Technically/*Virtually, Gandhi was a criminal.
       c. Technically/Nominally, Asimov was a professor.
          Technically/*Nominally, Nixon isn't a crook.

The literature includes a number of works in which other uses of multidimensional truth values are proposed. Herzberger (1975a, 1975b) has proposed treating semantic presuppositions in terms of two-dimensional truth values, where the first component of a truth value evaluates the proposition on the dimension true versus false and the second component evaluates it on the dimension of satisfaction versus failure of presuppositions. Suppose that each of these components can take the value 1 or 0 and that we define symbols T, F, t, f as follows:

13.5.17 $T = (1, 1)$ $t = (1, 0)$
 $F = (0, 1)$ $f = (0, 0)$

Note that there are then two different truth values, t, and f, for the case of presuppositional failure, rather than the single truth value #. There are a number of ways that truth tables might be set up involving these four values. We would presumably want the first component to obey the classical truth tables (e.g., $\wedge AB$ should have 1 as the first component of its value if both A and B have 1 as first component, and should have 0 as its first component if either A or B has 0 as first component). What the second component should be depends on what the relationship is between the presuppositions of complex sentences and the presuppositions of their pieces. Suppose, for the moment, that we take all the propositional connectives to be "holes," that is, we take a complex proposition as having presuppositional failure whenever any of its constituents has presuppositional failure. We then obtain the following truth tables.

13.5.18

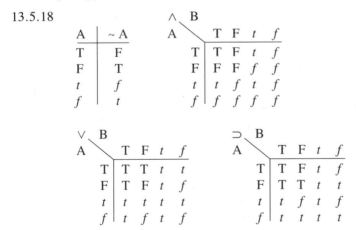

These truth tables have certain nice properties. For example, they assign reasonable truth values to $\wedge(A, \sim A)$ and $\vee(A, \sim A)$ in the cases where A suffers presuppositional failure: there $\wedge$(A, ~A) comes out f and $\vee$(A, ~A) comes out t. Thus, $\wedge$(A, ~A) will always have one of the "false" values (F or f), and $\vee$(A, ~A) will always have one of the "true" values (T or t). It is not quite so nice that $\supset$AA will have the value t whenever A is t or f; thus, $\supset$AA, the formula which ought to be a tautology if anything is, can have a value less than T.[19] Obviously, if a tautology is to be a formula that can take only the value T, no matter how truth values are assigned to its constituents, then in the system described by 13.5.18 there are no tautologies: assigning a value of t or f to one of the constituent propositions will result in the whole formula receiving a value whose second component is 0, that is, t or f.

Lakoff (1972b) has proposed a somewhat different multidimensional treatment of presupposition, in which a truth value is a complex (a, b, c) of three nonnegative numbers such that $a + b + c = 1$, where a represents the degree to which the proposition is true, b the degree to which it is false, and c the degree to which it is "nonsense." Note that this proposal is not merely a fuzzy analog of Herzberger's treatment, since Herzberger allows different truth values to be assigned to propositions that have "total" presuppositional failure, whereas for Lakoff, if $c = 1$, then $a = b = 0$ and thus there is only one truth value having total presuppositional failure.

Lakoff notes that there are expressions which cancel out failing presuppositions. For example, he maintains that 13.5.19a has a failing presupposition that 13.5.19b does not have:

13.5.19 a. J. L. Austin was a good linguist.
　　　　　b. To the extent that J. L. Austin was a linguist, he was a good
　　　　　　　linguist.

J. L. Austin was not really a linguist, but some of his research on language could be regarded as linguistics, indeed as very good linguistics. Lakoff accordingly assigns to 13.5.19a a truth value such as (0.3, 0, 0.7) and to 13.5.19b a truth value (1, 0, 0), in which the nonsense value of 13.5.19a has been reduced to zero and the truth and falsity values have been multiplied by a factor that will keep the sum of the components equal to 1. A similar treatment is available in a fuzzy analog to Herzberger's two-dimensional truth values: 13.5.19a would have a truth value such as (1, 0.3) and 13.5.19b would have a truth value in which the first component remains the same but the second component is increased (thus, (1,1)).

The system of "information values" (Belnap 1977) discussed at the beginning of section 13.1 can also be viewed as two-dimensional values: one component indicates whether you have been told that the proposition is true and a second component indicates whether you have been told that it is false. Using square brackets, to avoid confusion with the two-dimensional truth values discussed so far, we can represent the four information values as

13.5.20   B = [1, 1] (= you have been told that A and have been told
                  that ~A)
            T = [1, 0] (= you have been told that A but not that ~A)
            F = [0, 1] (= you have been told that ~A but not that A)
            0 = [0, 0] (= you have been told neither that A nor that ~A)

Belnap's system is, like the relevant entailment logic that he and Anderson have developed (see section 11.4 and Anderson and Belnap 1975), an attempt to set logic up in such a way that the effects of contradictions are localized: instead of a contradiction causing all hell to break loose (i.e., forcing all propositions to be assigned the value T), it should only cause some hell to break loose. Belnap's treatment, which is framed in terms of a computer system for storage and retrieval of (not necessarily consistent) information, allows a proposition to have the value B without all propositions having to receive that value. Consider, for example, two atomic propositions p and q, where you have been told both that p is true and that it is false and have been told that q is false but not that it is true. The conflicting information that you have been given about p has no bearing on the information you have been given about q: p has the value B and q the value F in this case. Moreover, $\wedge pq$ should be assigned the value F; your information about q is sufficient to make $\wedge pq$ F regardless of which of your contradictory pieces of information about p you believe.

Belnap's information values are non–truth-functional with a vengeance. They are sensitive to the order in which pieces of information are acquired, and to whether two pieces of information come in together or separately. For example, suppose that an information-gathering system is in state F with regard to p and state T with regard to q, and that the information that p is true and $\sim q$ is true come in together. Prior to this input, the system was in state F with regard to $\wedge pq$: we had information that p was false and no information to the contrary, and that was enough to make $\wedge pq$ false. The new information puts us into state B with regard to both p and q. That might seem to put us into state B with regard to $\wedge pq$: our information that p is false and our information that q is false are each sufficient to make $\wedge pq$ false, but our information that p is true and that q is true would make it true. However, the old information had p false and q true, making $\wedge pq$ false, and the new information has p true and q false, again making $\wedge pq$ false, and there is no reason to allow the combination of "p true" from the new information and "q true" from the old information to come into the picture. Thus, we can take $\wedge pq$ to be F in this case, though in other circumstances in which p is B and q is B, $\wedge pq$ will be B.

In addition, there are cases in which none of the four values provides an adequate statement of the state that you are in with regard to information about the proposition in question. Consider, for example, the case where you have been told both that p is true and that it is false but have been given no information about q. What then is the information value of $\wedge pq$? Since the information that p is false suffices to make $\wedge pq$ false even in the absence of information about q and since the information that p is true does not suffice to give any conclusion about the truth value of $\wedge pq$ unless one has the information that q is true, one might conclude that $\wedge pq$ is F: we have been given information implying that it is false, but we have not been given information implying that it is true. Yet our information that p is true, combined with our lack of information about q, is consistent with $\wedge pq$ being true and indeed puts us halfway to the information that $\wedge pq$ is true; thus we are not in the same position with regard to $\wedge pq$ as if we had only been told that p is false (and had no information about q), in which case our information would be unequivocally that $\wedge pq$ is false. Ought we to distinguish between these two situations by admitting extra values? We might, for example, allow the components to range over not two but three values, say, 1 ($=$ we have been told the proposition is true), 1/2 (we have information relevant to it, but not enough to tell whether it is true or false), and 0 (we have no information relevant to it). Or ought we just to be happy calling the information value F in both cases? Or perhaps say that the value is 0 when p is B and q 0, on the grounds that we do not have enough of an asymmetry in our information about $\wedge pq$ to justify giving it a value in which the two components differ? I will not attempt to choose among these alternatives here.

Exercises

1. Assume the truth conditions given in 13.1.8. What range of truth values would have to be designated for $\vee(A, {\sim}A)$ to be valid? Would that choice of designated truth values have any undesirable consequences for what counts as valid?

2. Compute the truth values of the following formulas according to 13.1.8, assuming that the atomic propositions have the truth values $/p/ = 0.8$, $/q/ = 0.6$, $/r/ = 0.3$:

  a. $\supset(\wedge pq, {\sim}\vee(\vee pr, q))$
  b. $\wedge(\supset pq, \supset(r, {\sim}p))$
  c. $\vee(\supset(p, {\sim}q), \supset(q, {\sim}r)$

3. Assume the truth conditions given in 13.1. State informally how the truth value of each of the following expressions is related to the truth values of its constituents:

a. $\supset(A, \sim A)$
b. $\supset(\wedge(A, \sim A), B)$
c. $\wedge(\vee(A, \sim B), \vee(B, \sim A))$

4. a. Pick any two formulas in 13.1.10 and verify that they are valid according to 13.1.8.

b. Pick any two formulas in 13.1.11 and verify that they are invalid according to 13.1.8.

5. In 13.1.13, it was shown that the rule of $\sim$-introduction given in chapter 3 is unsound according to the truth conditions 13.1.8. Determine whether the same is true of the following alternative version of $\sim$-introduction:

$$
\begin{array}{l}
A \\
\quad \left| \begin{array}{l} B \\ \hline \cdots \\ \sim A \end{array} \right. \\
\sim B
\end{array}
$$

6. Recall that the Cartesian product of two sets A and B is the set of all ordered pairs (a, b) for which $a \in A$ and $b \in B$. Presumably the Cartesian product of two fuzzy sets should be a fuzzy set of ordered pairs. Say **what** fuzzy set it would be (i.e., give a rule for the degree to which each pair (a, b) belongs to it), choosing your answer so as to fit uses that you might want to make of Cartesian products in doing semantics (i.e., think about what sorts of expressions might have Cartesian products as their denotations).

7. Suggest a definition of "fuzzy equivalence relation" and go through an example that will illustrate the consequences of your definition.

14. Intensional Logic and Montague Grammar

14.1 Intensional Logic

The notion of **intension** that figures in much modern work in logic is, in a sense, a compromise between the traditional notions of meaning and reference. The notion is framed in set-theoretic terms rather than in terms of concepts, but is set up in such a way as to distinguish many expressions from other expressions that have the same reference, e.g., *the first pope* and *Saint Peter* will have different intensions, as will *Beethoven's choral symphony, Beethoven's Ninth Symphony,* and *Beethoven's opus 125.* The intension of an expression is a function giving the reference of that expression in each world; that is, the intension of an expression is a function that associates to each world the **extension** of that expression in that world. Thus, expressions differ in intension if and only if it is **possible** for them to differ in extension, whether or not they actually do.[1]

The truth value of a proposition is taken to serve as the extension of the proposition. The intension of a proposition is thus a function that associates to each world the truth value that the proposition has in that world. For any two sets A and B, it is customary to write A^B to stand for the set of all functions having B as domain and having values in A. (The reason for the notation A^B is that if A has m elements and B has n elements, the number of functions that belong to A^B is m^n; for example, there are $2^3 = 8$ different functions that have the domain $\{a, b, c\}$ and have the values in the set $\{0,1\}$). Thus, the intension of a proposition is a member of the set V^I, where I is the set of worlds under consideration and V is the set of truth values, here assumed to be $\{T, F\}$. The intension of an individual constant symbol is a function that associates to each world the individual that that constant refers to in that world. Suppose that we use U to indicate the set of all individuals that figure in any of the worlds. Then the intension of an individual constant symbol is a member of U^I, since, for any world i, the extension of the constant symbol in i is a member of U.

The extension of a one-place predicate in a given world can be taken to be the set of individuals of which it is true in that world. Alternatively, it can be taken to be the **characteristic function** of that set: the function associating to each element a truth value indicating whether that element belongs to the set. It is customary in intensional logic to take the latter interpretation, and we will do so here. Accordingly, for any world i, the extension of the predicate in i is a member of V^{A_i}, where A_i is the domain of i: the set of individuals that figure in determining what universal or existential propositions are true in i. The intension of a one-place predicate is thus a function that maps each i onto a member of V^{A_i}. Since A_i will generally vary from one world to the next, and since the functions in V^{A_i} will generally not belong to V^U (U will generally contain elements that are not in A_i, and a function belonging to V^{A_i} will thus not be defined on all elements of U), we cannot say that the intension of a one-place predicate belongs to $(V^U)^I$, nor to any other such expression that we can construct. Suppose, however, that to simplify our discussion we assume that the same individuals figure in each world. Then, calling that set of individuals U, we can say that the intension of a one-place predicate belongs to $(V^U)^I$.

I have been assuming so far that what a predicate is predicated of is an individual. In various works, Richard Montague argued that predicates are predicated of the kind of thing that we have taken to be the intension of an individual constant. For Montague, thus, the extension of a one-place predicate is a member not of V^U but of $V^{(U^I)}$, and the intension of a one-place predicate belongs to $(V^{(U^I)})^I$.

The extension of a two-place predicate will be a function that associates a truth value to each **pair** of elements of U, or (if one accepts Montague's conclusions) each pair of elements of U^I. Thus, symbolizing the Cartesian product (see sec. 5.4) of two sets A and B by A $\times$ B, we can say that the extension of a two-place predicate will belong to $V^{U \times U}$ (or to $V^{U^I \times U^I}$, if one accepts Montague's conclusions; let us for the moment ignore this alternative and take predicates to be predicated of elements of U). Consequently, the intension of a two-place predicate will belong to $(V^{U \times U})^I$: the intension of a two-place predicate is a function that associates to each world the function that specifies which pairs of elements the predicate is true of in that world.

A two-place predicate can also be thought of as a one-place predicate whose values are one-place predicates, for example, the two-place predicate "Love(x,y)" can be reinterpreted as $(\lambda y)[(\lambda x) \text{Love}(x, y)]$, which associates with any individual a the propositional function "x loves a." Under the reinterpretation, the extension of a two-place predicate is a member of $(V^U)^U$, and the intension of a two-place predicate is a member of $((V^U)^U)^I$.

The notion of intension can also be applied to higher-order expressions, in which variables range over predicates or over sets. If F(P) stands for "P is true of Henry Kissinger," then the extension of F will be a function that associates a truth value to the extension of each one-place predicate. Suppose we take a permissive view of what can be an extension of a one-place predicate and allow it to be any member of V^U. It should be noted that this will allow not only functions that might be the extensions of normal predicates such as "has long hair" or "knows the *Philosophical Investigations* by heart," but also such bizarre functions as the one that associates Richard Nixon, the number 94, and Mozart's C Minor Mass with the value T and everything else with the value F. Then the extension of F will belong to $V^{(V^U)}$, and the intension of F will be a member of $(V^{(V^U)})^I$. It is customary in intensional logic to apply the term "property" not to the extension of a predicate but to its intension; that is, a "property" of individuals denotes a member of $(V^U)^I$: a function that associates to each world the extension of a predicate. Under this terminology, an object *a* has a property P if and only if the extension of P is true of *a*.

In work by or inspired by Montague, the notion of logical **type** (cf. sec. 8.2) is interpreted as follows: (i) there are two "atomic" types, *t* ("truth value") and *e* ("entity"); (ii) for any two types, *a* and *b*, there is a type $\langle a, b \rangle$; and (iii), for any type *a*, there is a type $\langle s, a \rangle$ (*s* here stands for "world"),[2] i.e., intensions of things of type *a*. For any given type, one can speak of the meaningful expressions of that type and of the possible denotations of meaningful expressions of that type. The meaningful expressions of type *t* have truth values as their possible denotations, and those of type *e* have entities as their possible denotations. The meaningful expressions of type $\langle a, b \rangle$ have as possible denotations functions whose argument ranges over possible denotations of type *a* and whose values are possible denotations of type *b;* for example, an expression of type $\langle e, t \rangle$ denotes a function that associates a truth value to each entity. A meaningful expression of type $\langle s, a \rangle$ denotes a function that associates to each world a possible denotation of type *a;* for example, an expression of type $\langle s, \langle e, t \rangle \rangle$ denotes a function that associates to each world a function from entities to truth values. A variable ranging over objects of a given type is also a meaningful expression of that type; for example, a variable ranging over individuals is a meaningful expression of type *e*. In the Montague tradition, variables of type $\langle a, b \rangle$ or $\langle s, a \rangle$ have generally been taken to range over **all** objects of the given type. This means that variables of types other than *e* generally have far more possible values than an outsider would be likely to expect them to have, for example, a variable of type $\langle s, e \rangle$ has as values not only "ordinary" objects of that type (such as the function that associates to each world the person who is pope in that world) but also bizarre functions such as one that associated a prime number to w_1, an archbishop to w_2, a Mozart string quintet to w_3, and an attack of diarrhea to w_4.

We can thus restate some of the conclusions of the earlier paragraphs. An individual constant or variable is of type e. The intension of such an expression is of type $\langle s, e \rangle$. Montague's position on intransitive verbs is that their arguments are of type $\langle s, e \rangle$ (i.e., they are predicated of "objects in intension" rather than of objects pure and simple); thus, for Montague, the translation of an intransitive verb into intensional logic must be an expression of type $\langle \langle s, e \rangle, t \rangle$. Or at least, the denotation in any world of an intransitive verb is of type $\langle \langle s, e \rangle, t \rangle$; if intransitive verbs are taken to denote functions associating denotations of that type to each world, as they are by Montague, intransitive verbs are of type $\langle s, \langle \langle s, e \rangle, t \rangle \rangle$.

If u is a variable of type a and φ is an expression of type b, then $(\lambda u)\varphi$ will be of type $\langle a, b \rangle$: it can be combined with things of type a (i.e., things that can be substituted for u), and the result of substituting anything of the appropriate type for u will still denote something of type b. Thus, within the Montague tradition the expression $(\lambda P)P(j)$ (corresponding to, say, "is a property of Michael Jackson") would be of type $\langle \langle \langle s, e \rangle, t \rangle, t \rangle$: j would be of type $\langle s, e \rangle$ (i.e., it would be a function specifying what entity in each world is Michael Jackson), P would be of type $\langle \langle s, e \rangle, t \rangle$, P($j$) would be of type t, and thus $(\lambda P)P(j)$ would be of the type $\langle \langle \langle s, e \rangle, t \rangle, t \rangle$.

In the next section, we will consider a number of analyses in which it is held that the extension of a complex expression depends on the intension of one or more of its constituents. In discussing such cases, it will be convenient to be able to use an expression whose extension in every world is the intension of the given constituent. In addition, it will often be convenient, when an expression of intensional logic denotes an intension, and thus is of some type $\langle s, a \rangle$, to have a way of referring to the entity of type a that that intension associates to a given world. Thus, we wish to introduce operators ˆ (intension) and ˇ (extension)[3] such that, for example, ˆ(the pope) will be a function mapping worlds onto individuals, with [ˆ(the pope)](i) = the individual that is the pope in i, for each world i; and if f is the intension of *dog* (i.e., if f associates to each world i a function $f(i)$ such that $f(i)(u)$ = T if and only if u is a dog in i), then ˇf must be a function mapping individuals onto truth values, such that for any individual u and any world i, (ˇf)(u) = T in i if and only if $f(i)(u)$ = T, that is, if and only if u is a dog in i.

To clarify the difference between f and ˇf, which the last sentence may have left somewhat unclear, and to put the informal definitions of the last paragraph on a somewhat firmer footing, we must get slightly more precise about the systems that we are discussing. By a **system of intensional logic,** let us understand a formal language which includes the operators, quantifiers, and variables of predicate logic (not just first-order predicate logic—we will allow for variables that range over predicates, and for quantifiers that bind such variables), λ-expressions, as outlined in section 8.2, and further modal and intensional operators (such as $\Box$, ^, and ˅) as needed. By an **interpretation** of a system of intensional logic, we will mean something consisting of (i) a set I of possible worlds, (ii) a set U of possible individuals, and (iii) an assignment of a denotation in each world of I to each individual constant or predicate constant of the system. For any interpretation Q and any world i, it is possible to determine the denotation in i, relative to the interpretation Q, of any expression X of the system of intensional logic. Using $X^{Q,i}$ to stand for the denotation of X in i relative to Q, we see from (iii) what $X^{Q,i}$ is in case X is either an individual constant or a predicate constant. In case X is a more complex expression, $X^{Q,i}$ can be determined from the denotations of the constituents of X by means of various rules. For example, if X is a conjoined proposition $\wedge X_1 X_2 \ldots X_n$, then $X^{Q,i} = T$ if $X_1^{Q,i} = X_2^{Q,i} = \ldots = X_n^{Q,i} = T$, and $X^{Q,i} = F$ otherwise (i.e., if one or other of $X_1^{Q,i}, \ldots, X_n^{Q,i}$ is F). I will not go through the details of the rules for determining $X^{Q,i}$ from the denotations of the constituents of X for all the other possibilities of what X might be; any one who wishes to see the details spelled out should consult Montague 1973: sec. 2. I will confine myself to giving the rules for the case where X is of the form ^Y or ˅Y.

Let Y be any expression of the system of intensional logic. We have to determine $(^Y)^{Q,i}$ for every i. This can be done as follows:

14.1.1 $(^Y)^{Q,i}$ is the function mapping worlds onto things of the type of
               Y, such that for every world j, $(^Y)^{Q,i}(j) = Y^{Q,j}$

Note that i does not appear on the right-hand side of this equation. Thus, $(^Y)^{Q,i}$ is the same no matter what i is. This is as it should be: the reason for having such expressions as ^Y is to allow one to refer in one fell swoop to what goes on in all worlds, independently of what world one is operating in at the moment. The denotation of ˅Y in any world with respect to any interpretation can be determined as follows. Let Y be of type $\langle s, a \rangle$ for some a. (If Y is not of such a type, then ˅Y will make no sense.) Then,

14.1.2 $(˅Y)^{Q,i} = Y^{Q,i}(i)$

It is fairly easy to show that for any expression X, $˅(^X) = X$. For any interpretation Q, any world i, and any expression X, $(˅(^X))^{Q,i} = (^X)^{Q,i}(i) = X^{Q,i}$. Thus, $˅(^X)$ and X have the same denotations in any world, relative to any interpretation, that is, $˅(^X) = X$. It is not true in general that

$^\wedge(^\vee X) = X$. First of all, unless X is of type $\langle s, a \rangle$ for some a, $^\vee X$ makes no sense and thus the equality fails. However, even if X is of a type that allows one to form $^\wedge(^\vee X)$, that expression denotes what X does only under a very stringent condition, namely, that X is of the form $^\wedge Y$. A simple example will illustrate how $^\wedge(^\vee X)$ can fail to be identical with X. Consider a rudimentary system of intensional logic in which there is a constant c of type $\langle s, e \rangle$ and two worlds 1 and 2 (it won't matter what happens in any other worlds, so we can act as if these were the only worlds). Suppose that a and b are two distinct objects and that in 1 c denotes the function mapping 1 onto a and 2 onto b, but in 2 c denotes the function mapping 1 onto b and 2 onto a. Then $^\vee c$ denotes a both in 1 and in 2, which means that $^{\wedge\vee}c$ (in either world) will designate the function mapping both 1 and 2 onto a. But since c does not designate that function in either world, $^{\wedge\vee}c \neq c$.

It is easy to show that $^{\wedge\vee}X = X$ if and only if $X = {}^\wedge Y$ for some Y. That X's being of the form $^\wedge Y$ is a necessary condition for $^{\wedge\vee}X$ to equal X is trivial: if $X = {}^{\wedge\vee}X$, then X is the intension of $^\vee X$. To show that it is a sufficient condition, let $X = {}^\wedge Y$ and let us see what $^{\wedge\vee}X$ is. Let i and j be any two worlds and Q any interpretation. Then $(^\wedge(^\vee X))^{Q,i}(j) = (^\vee X)^{Q,j} = X^{Q,j}(j) = (^\wedge Y)^{Q,j}(j) = (^\wedge Y)^{Q,i}(j)$ (since an intension has the same denotation in every world), and that equals $X^{Q,i}(j)$. Thus $(^\wedge(^\vee X))^{Q,i}$ and $X^{Q,i}$ denote the same mapping of worlds into objects, and since this is the case for any interpretation Q and any world i, we have $^\wedge(^\vee X) = X$.

14.2 Montague's Approach to Syntax and Semantics

An important tradition of logical and linguistic research has developed out of Montague's work.[4] His approach is characterized by the following features: (i) the goal of research on a given language is to provide truth conditions for all the sentences of that language, that is, to provide the conditions under which each sentence is true in any given possible world relative to any given choice of denotations for **indexical** elements such as *here, you,* and *this;* (ii) this goal is accomplished by providing a **syntax** and a **semantics** for the language; (iii) the syntax is formulated in terms of a system of **categories,** a **lexicon** listing the **basic** members (if any) of each category, and a system of **syntactic rules,** which specify how derived members of a given category can be constructed from members (basic or derived) of various categories; (iv) the semantics for the language is formulated not directly in terms of the sentences of the language but in terms of the **analyses** that the syntax provides for each sentence; (v) the semantics consists of an intensional logic, which provides means of determining the intension of any expression of the intensional logic, and **translation rules,** which associate an expression of intensional logic to each expression that appears in a syntactic analysis; (vi) the translation rules construct the translation of any derived expression out of the translations of the constituents from which it is derived; and (vii) the syntactic analyses must be in terms of the syntactic units that figure in the surface phrase structures of the given language.

For example, in terms of the rules given in Montague (1973), Montague would assign to the sentence *Every man loves some woman* the following syntactic analysis (as well as a couple of other possible analyses):

14.2.1

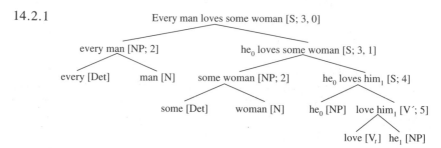

The material given in square brackets at the end of each constituent indicates the syntactic category of the constituent and (in the case of derived expressions) the rule of Montague's syntax which derives it from the expressions that it directly dominates in the tree. The category names that appear in 14.2.1 are not Montague's: for clarity's sake, I have substituted more familiar category names that correspond fairly closely to Montague's categories.

Some of Montague's syntactic rules amount to phrase structure rules. For example, his rule 5 amounts to the statement that a V' may be formed by putting a V_t before a NP, and thus it has the content of the phrase structure rule V': V_t NP. However, some of his syntactic rules correspond to transformations or to combinations of a transformation and a phrase structure rule. For example, his rule 4 says not merely that a S may be formed by putting a NP before a V' but also that the V of the V' must be put into the appropriate person and number: thus, it is a composite of the phrase structure rule S: NP V' and an agreement transformation. Likewise with his rule 3, which forms a S by replacing an occurrence of he or him_i in a given S by a given NP.[5] Its effect is thus a composite of the phrase structure rule S: NP S and the transformation of Q'-lowering (discussed in section 7.1), which applies to a S of the form [[Quantifier S] S] and inserts the Quantifier + S constituent in place of an occurrence of a variable in the remaining S; for example, it converts (every: x Man)(x be Mortal) into ((every: x Man) be Mortal).

Let us now sketch the parts of Montague's semantics that figure in his treatment of 14.2.1. He_0 and he_1 correspond to individual variables. For Montague, a basic member of the category V_t, such as *love*, corresponds to a two-place predicate[6]—a function love$'(x, y)$ that in any world associates a truth value to each pair of individuals (x, y). For the sake of making the predicate-argument structure completely clear, I will in fact take the translation of *love* into intensional logic to be not that two-place propositional function but the related function $(\lambda y)(\lambda x)$love$'(x, y)$, which in any world associates with each individual a one-place propositional function. The translation of a V' that is formed from a V_t and a variable can be taken from combining the translations of the two constituents. The V_t in 14.2.1 is translated as $(\lambda y)(\lambda x)$love$'(x, y)$ and the NP that it is combined with is translated as the variable x_1, and thus the V' is translated as $[(\lambda y)(\lambda x)$love$'(x, y)](x_1)$, which is convertible into (λx)love$'(x, x_1)$. The translation of the S formed by rule 4 is constructed similarly: the translation of the V', here (λx)love$'(x, x_1)$ is applied to the translation of the NP, here x_0, and the result, (λx)love$'(x, x_1)(x_0)$, is converted into love$'(x_0, x_1)$.

This may seem like a round-about way of arriving at love$'(x_0, x_1)$—you could have obtained that just by plugging x_0 and x_1 directly into love$'(x, y)$, without bringing in all those λ's. However, the use of λ's in deriving love$'(x, y)$ is dictated by condition (vii): in English there is a surface phrase consisting of a verb and its object(s), and Montague's approach forces one to treat such phrases as making direct semantic contributions themselves, rather than being purely syntactic constituents that have no direct role in semantics.

As we continue with the translation of 14.2.1 into intensional logic, we encounter a much less trivial use of this ploy. A quantified NP, such as *every man*, must make its own semantic contribution to the sentence, and that contribution must be something that can be combined with the translation of the expression that the quantified NP is combined with. Here Montague's solution is to take the quantified NP to represent a propositional function not of individuals but of propositional functions; that is, *every man* is translated as the propositional function $f(P)$ which is true of any property that every man has and false of any property that not every man has. Specifically, he takes the translation of *every man* to be[7] $(\lambda P)(\forall x) \supset (man'(x), Px)$. The propositional function which that expression is combined with is the propositional function obtained by prefixing (λx_i) to the S that the quantified NP is combined with, where x_i is the bound variable (thus, here x_0). Similarly, the translation of *some woman* is $(\lambda P)(\exists x) \wedge($woman$'(x), Px)$. Thus, the translation of he_0 *loves some woman* is 14.2.2a, which is convertible to 14.2.2b and then to 14.2.2c:

14.2.2   a. $[(\lambda P)(\exists x) \wedge(\text{woman}'(x), Px)][(\lambda x_1)\text{love}'(x_0, x_1)]$
         b. $(\exists x) \wedge(\text{woman}'(x), (\lambda x_1)\text{love}'(x_0, x_1)(x))$
         c. $(\exists x) \wedge(\text{woman}'(x), \text{love}'(x_0, x))$

The translation of *Every man loves some woman* will then be 14.2.3a, which is convertible to 14.2.3b, and then to 14.2.3c:

14.2.3   a. $[(\lambda P)(\forall y) \supset(\text{man}'(y), Py)][(\lambda x_0)(\exists x) \wedge(\text{woman}'(x), \text{love}'(x_0, x))]$
         b. $(\forall y) \supset(\text{man}'(y), [(\lambda x_0)(\exists x) \wedge(\text{woman}'(x), \text{love}'(x_0, x))](y))$
         c. $(\forall y) \supset(\text{man}'(y), (\exists x) \wedge(\text{woman}'(x), \text{love}'(y, x)))$

Let us now start to correct a number of oversimplifications that were made in the above illustrative sketch. The categories that figure in Montague grammar are not those of linguistic syntax but derive from the categorial grammar of Ajdukiewicz (1935). Ajdukiewicz recognized two basic categories, called *s* and *n* (standing for "sentence" and "noun" or "name"). From the two basic categories, an infinite number of derived categories can be constructed: if X and Y are any two categories, then X/Y is the category of expressions that combine with expressions of category Y to yield expressions of category X.[8] Thus, for Ajdukiewicz, *s/s* was the category of things that combine with sentences to yield sentences (thus, sentence modifiers such as *necessarily* and *supposedly*), *s/n* was the category of things that combined with names to yield sentences (thus, intransitive verbs, or more generally, V's of any internal structure), and *(s/n)/(s/n)* was the category of things that combined with V's to yield V's, thus V'-modifiers such as *quickly* or *with an axe*.

Montague also recognized two basic categories, though not exactly the same two that Ajdukiewicz did. Montague's category *t* (standing for "truth value"—Montague named his categories after the types of their denotations) does in fact amount to Ajdukiewicz's category *s*. However, his other category, *e* (standing for "entity"), differed from Ajdukiewicz's category *n* in that no expressions, whether basic or derived, belong to it: in Montague's syntax, *e* figures only as a constituent of more complex category names, and it owes its existence to the role that it plays in the translation of syntactic analyses into formulas of intensional logic. For Montague, an intransitive verb (or, more generally, a V' of any internal structure) is of category *t/e,* that is, it is of the category of things that combine semantically with entities to yield truth values. The things that V's combine with syntactically, however, that is, NPs, are not of category *e* but of category *t/(t/e)*. This choice of category for NPs is due in part to Montague's desire to have proper names and quantified NPs be of the same category, which would be impossible if proper names were of the category *e*. (As will be made clear shortly, while proper names for Montague are not of the syntactic category *e* and thus do not have denotations of the semantic type *e*, Montague set up his system so that their denotations are determined by something of type *e;* thus, he took proper names as **indirectly** referring to entities.)

In a number of instances, Montague set up two or more distinct categories that combine with items of some category B to yield results of some category A. For example, he treated V's and common nouns (more accurately, N's) both as combining with an entity to yield a truth value. However, these categories must still be distinguished, since they are not interchangeable in the syntactic rules; for example, the rule for forming quantified NPs allows a quantifier to be combined with an N' but not with a V'. Montague used multiple slashes as an arbitrary way of distinguishing such pairs of categories; for example, he represented V's as *t/e* and N's as *t//e*.[9] While *t*, *e*, and slashes are the total of Montague's official vocabulary for naming syntactic categories, he introduced several abbreviations for common categories, and his followers have in fact proliferated informal names for syntactic categories. It will be useful to follow Montague in adopting the following abbreviations: IV for *t/e*, T for *t/(t/e)*, and TV for IV/T, i.e., *(t/e)/(t/(t/e))*. "T" stands for "term" and "IV" and "TV" for "intransitive verb" and "transitive verb"; the latter mnemonics are misleading, since IV takes in V's in general, not only those consisting of just an intransitive verb, and TV takes in not only simple transitive verbs (such as *eat, seek, worship*) but also complex expressions (such as *give to Ted* and *force to apologize to you*) that Montague grammarians regard as combining with a T into an IV.

One must distinguish between syntactic categories such as *t/e* and types in intensional logic such as $\langle e, t \rangle$. The only relation between categories and types is that the category of a given expression determines the type of its translation into intensional logic. Specifically, Montague maintained that syntactic category and logical type are related by a function *f* defined as follows:

14.2.4	Syntactic category *a*	Corresponding semantic type *f(a)*
	t	*t*
	e	*e*
	a_1/a_2	$\langle \langle s, f(a_2) \rangle, f(a_1) \rangle$

Thus the expressions of any syntactic category *a/b* denote functions whose arguments are intensions of the type of object that expressions of category *b* denote and whose values are objects of the type that expressions of category *a* denote. For example, *t/e* corresponds to the semantic type $\langle \langle s, e \rangle, t \rangle$, that is,

V's denote functions from intensions of entities to truth values. In the correspondence 14.2.4, multiple slashes are ignored; that is, $t//e$ corresponds to the same semantic type as does t/e.

Montague took predicates to be predicated of intensions because it is impossible to do semantics that is both completely extensional and completely "compositional," in the sense that the translation of an item depends only on the extensions of its immediate constituents. For example, since the extension (= truth value) of *John believes that the world is round* depends on the content and not just the truth value of *the world is round* (e.g., John may believe that true proposition without believing many other true propositions), the extension of *John believes that the world is round* is not predictable from the extensions of *John, believe,* and *the world is round.* Actually, it is not clear that it can be predicated from the intensions of those constituents either. Thus, one might argue that two propositions can have the same intension and yet not make the same contribution to the intensions of propositions of which they are constituents, since any two self-contradictory propositions have the same intension (namely, the function f such that $f(i) = F$ for all worlds i) and yet a person can believe one self-contradictory proposition without believing another one. There is an alternative to intensions and extensions as the items of which predicates are predicated in a translation scheme such as Montague's, namely, expressions of a formal language themselves. There is likewise the alternative (considered in Cresswell 1973 and Hintikka and Rantala 1976) of generalizing the notion of "world" so as to admit "impossible worlds" and thus allow the possibility that two propositions are true in the same **possible** worlds without being true in the same worlds. However, rather than exploring these possibilities here, I will confine myself to the specific framework within which Montague was operating, in which the intension of a proposition is a function specifying what possible worlds it is true in, and items with the same intensions are assumed to make the same contribution to the intensions of items of which they are constituents.

Montague generalized his treatment of sentential objects to a policy about V's involving **any** kind of object. Thus, for Montague, the translation of *John loves Mary* involves not simply an individual constant m but rather a constant function $^\wedge m$ (i.e., if m denotes the same individual c in every world, then $^\wedge m$ will be the function f such that $f(i) = c$ for every world i). It might be conjectured that Montague did this in order to allow for proper names that have unusual referential properties, for example, proper names that do not have denotations in all worlds, as in 14.2.5a and a', or that have different denotations in different worlds, as in 14.2.5b, which involves a name that has been assigned to different dogs, as each holder of the name has retired or died and been replaced by a new one:

14.2.5   a.   John worships Zeus.
         a'. John worships Zoroaster.
         b.   John petted Lassie.

For example, one might want to say that 14.2.5a could be true and 14.2.5a' false in a given world in which neither *Zeus* nor *Zoroaster* denotes anything and treat *worship* as denoting a relation between persons and intensional objects, with *Zeus* and *Zoroaster* having different intensions (say, there is an alternative world in which Zeus exists but Zoroaster does not). Montague in fact did not give any account of such proper names. The partial grammars that figure in Montague 1970a, 1970b, and 1973 involve proper names that are **rigid designators** (i.e., they denote the same entity in every world)[10] and contain meaning postulates to the effect that those names are rigid designators; but he did not exclude the possibility that other proper names might not be rigid designators. For the moment, let us not take a position on how best to analyze examples like 14.2.5 within Montague's framework, a question that I would like to postpone until I have discussed verbs such as *seek,* which it will be important to contrast with *worship.*

Montague generalized his treatment of sentential objects into an even more general policy than one requiring that every object NP contribute an intension to the translation of the VP. Indeed, he adopted an exactly analogous policy for all combinations of something of category A/B (or A//B, etc.) with something of category B. We can state this policy as in 14.2.6, using primes to indicate the translations of expressions into formulas of intensional logic (as in Montague's informal practise of writing love' for a predicate of intensional logic that serves as the translation of *love*):

14.2.6   If β is of category B, γ is of category A/B (or A//B, etc.) and α is an expression of category A constructed from β and γ by some syntactic rule, then $\alpha' = \gamma'(\hat{}\beta')$.

For example, if α = *Probably John is sick,* β = *John is sick,* and γ = *probably,* then α' = probably'($\hat{}$(John is sick)'); probably' is a function which in any world maps intensions of sentences onto truth values, and the translation of *Probably John is sick* is the image under that function of the intension of the translation of *John is sick.* There is of course more to Montague's translation scheme than 14.2.6, since an expression need not be put together out of items of categories A and A/B; for example, a sentence (member of category t) may be constructed not only out of items of categories t/e and $t/(t/e)$ (by rule 4) but also out of items of categories $t/(t/e)$ and t, that is, out of a NP and a S, by rule 3. Thus there are additional translation rules to cover cases not included in 14.2.6.

The scheme 14.2.6 has a peculiar consequence which plays a central role in Montague's treatment of NPs. Recall that NPs are of the category $t/(t/e)$. Taking A $= t$ and B $= t/e$, we can derive from 14.2.6 that if α is a S consisting of a NP γ and a V′ β, say, $\gamma = $ *John* and $\beta = $ *sleep*, then

14.2.7   (John sleeps)′ $= $ John′(ˆ(sleep′))

Note that John′ is here the function and ˆsleep′ its argument, rather than vice versa. The only way to make this coherent is to take John′ to be a function that maps one-place predicates into truth values. The way that Montague accomplished that was to take John′ to denote not an individual but the property of being a property of that individual; the translation of *John sleeps* would then amount to: sleeping is one of John's properties.

As a first try at formalizing this proposal, we might write

14.2.8   John′ $= (\lambda P)P(j)$

where j is an appropriately chosen individual constant, but that would conflict with two of Montague's policies. First, Montague wanted the variable P to be of the same type as the translations of ordinary intransitive verbs such as *walk*. However, in accordance with 14.2.6, such verbs must be translated as one-place predicates whose arguments are of type $\langle s,e \rangle$ rather than e; that is, they are predicated not of ordinary entities but of "intensional entities." We can remedy this first conflict by replacing j with ˆj in 14.2.8; ˆj is a function from worlds to individuals, and if *John* is an ordinary proper name, we can take ˆj to be a constant function: it has the same value in all possible worlds. Second, Montague wanted P to range over "properties in intension": its values are not to be of type $\langle e,t \rangle$, that is, functions associating a truth value to each individual, but rather of type $\langle s, \langle e,t \rangle \rangle$, that is, functions associating to each world a function of the latter type. This second discrepancy can be corrected by replacing P by its extension. Thus, we arrive at 14.2.9a, which allows the translation of *John sleeps* to proceed as in 14.2.9b:[11]

14.2.9   a. John $\Rightarrow (\lambda P)([ˇP](ˆj))$
    b. John sleeps$\Rightarrow (\lambda P)([ˇP](ˆj))(ˆ(\lambda x)(sleep′(x)))$
            $\rightarrow$ ˇˆ$(\lambda x)(sleep′(x))(ˆj)$
            $\rightarrow$ ˇˆ$(sleep′(ˆj))$
            $\rightarrow$ sleep′$(ˆj)$

Montague took not only proper names but all NPs to have translations of this type: $\langle\langle s, \langle e,t\rangle\rangle, t\rangle$. This is the case even when the NP corresponds to a variable. Thus, for Montague, the translation of 14.2.10a is not 14.2.10b but 14.2.10c, though 14.2.10b is obtainable by λ-conversion, as indicated:

14.2.10 a. he_0 walks.

b. $walk'(x_0)$

c. $[(\lambda P)(\check{}P)(x_0)](\hat{}(\lambda x)walk'(x))$

$\rightarrow (\check{}\hat{}((\lambda x)walk'(x))(x_0)$

$\rightarrow (\lambda x)walk'(x)(x_0)$

$\rightarrow walk'(x_0)$

Since for Montague, transitive verbs are of the category $(t/e)/(t/(t/e))$, that is, they combine with NPs to yield V's and since Montague followed the policy given in 14.2.6, the translations of transitive verbs into intensional logic must have type $\langle\langle s, a\rangle, b\rangle$, where a is the type of the translation of NPs and b is the type of the translation of V's. Since $a = \langle\langle s, \langle\langle s, e\rangle, t\rangle\rangle, t\rangle$, and $b = \langle\langle s, e\rangle, t\rangle$, transitive verbs have translations of the type $\langle\langle s, \langle\langle s, \langle\langle s, e\rangle, t\rangle\rangle, t\rangle\rangle, \langle\langle s, e\rangle, t\rangle\rangle$. This means that the translation of a transitive verb will not be an expression of the form $(\lambda y)(\lambda x)f(x, y)$ involving a function f whose arguments are both of the same type (here, $\langle s, e\rangle$): rather, it will be of the form $(\lambda \mathscr{P})(\lambda x)g(x, \mathscr{P})$, involving a function whose first argument is of the type $\langle s,e\rangle$ but whose second argument is of a higher type, namely, $\langle s, \langle\langle s, \langle\langle s, e\rangle, t\rangle\rangle, t\rangle\rangle$.

The translation of *John kicked Bill* thus can proceed as follows:

14.2.11 $kick \Rightarrow (\lambda \mathscr{P})(\lambda x)kick'(x, \mathscr{P})$

$Bill \Rightarrow (\lambda P)[\check{}P](\hat{}b)$

$kick\ Bill \Rightarrow (\lambda \mathscr{P})(\lambda x)kick'(x, \mathscr{P})[\hat{}(\lambda P)[\check{}P](\hat{}b)]$

$\rightarrow (\lambda x)kick'(x, \hat{}(\lambda P)[\check{}P](b))$

$John \Rightarrow (\lambda Q)[\check{}Q](\hat{}j)$

$John\ kicked\ Bill \Rightarrow (\lambda Q)[\check{}Q](\hat{}j)\hat{}(\lambda x)kick'(x, \hat{}(\lambda P)[\check{}P](\hat{}b))$

$\rightarrow \check{}\hat{}(\lambda x)kick'(x, \hat{}(\lambda P)[\check{}P](\hat{}b))(\hat{}j)$

$\rightarrow kick'(\hat{}j, \hat{}(\lambda P)[\check{}P](\hat{}b))$

The final line of 14.2.11 is disconcerting. Can't we arrive at something that is closer to the usual formalization of *John kicked Bill* as something on the order of $kick(j,b)$? We in fact can, but only by invoking a meaning postulate that Montague provides for verbs (such as *kick*) whose objects are extensional, that is, verbs such that the truth value of "*a* V-ed *b*" in any given world depends on only the extension of b in that world, not on b's intension (its extension in other worlds).

To lead up to the meaning postulate, let us first note that there is a natural correspondence between things of the type we would like for the second argument of the predicate and a subset of the set of functions over which the second argument of kick′ ranges. To see this, note that for any object m of type a, there is a closely related function of type $\langle\langle a, b\rangle, b\rangle$, namely, $(\lambda F)F(m)$, where F is a variable of type $\langle a, b\rangle$. This function maps any function F into the value of that function at m. Thus, if we take P to be a variable of type $\langle s, \langle\langle s, e\rangle, t\rangle\rangle$ (i.e., a function that associates to each world a one-place predicate of 'intensional entities') and m to be of type $\langle s,e\rangle$, then $(\lambda P)(\check{}P)(m)$ will be a function of type $\langle\langle s, \langle\langle s, e\rangle, t\rangle\rangle, t\rangle$. Let us denote that function by m^*:

14.2.12 $m^* = (\lambda P)(\check{}P)(m)$

Note that the second argument of kick′ is of the same type as $\hat{}(m^*)$. Accordingly, we can derive from kick′ a function kick″ whose arguments are both of type $\langle s, e\rangle$:

14.2.13 $kick''(x, y) = kick'(x, \hat{}(y^*))$.

Definition 14.2.13 allows us to construct kick″ from kick′ but not to go in the reverse direction: the behavior of a function $f(x, \mathcal{P})$ need not be predictable from its behavior for those values of $\mathcal{P}$ that are of the special form $\hat{}(y^*)$. Montague provided a meaning postulate to the effect that kick′ is predictable from kick″. Specifically, the postulate given by Montague says that when a predicate is the translation of an "extensional" verb such as *kick* or *find*, the function that is in its second argument position may be "exported" from that position and the predicate replaced by a predicate taking extensions as its arguments:[12]

14.2.14   For each δ in the list *kick, find, kiss*, . . . (NB: the list does not include *seek* or *imagine*), there is a function S_δ such that
$(\forall x)(\forall \mathcal{P})\Box[\delta'(x, \mathcal{P}) \leftrightarrow \check{}\mathcal{P}(\hat{}(\lambda y)\check{}S_\delta(\check{}x, \check{}y))]$

On the basis of 14.2.14, one can easily establish the following correspondence between δ′ and δ″ for each verb δ in the above list:

14.2.15   For δ = *kick, find, kiss*, . . . (but not *seek, imagine*, . . .),
$(\forall x)(\forall \mathcal{P})\Box(\delta'(x, \mathcal{P}) \leftrightarrow \check{}\mathcal{P}(\hat{}(\lambda y)\delta''(x,y)))$

To prove 14.2.15, consider first what 14.2.14 says about the special case where $\mathcal{P}$ is $\hat{}(m^*)$. In any world and for any m and n of type $\langle s, e\rangle$, by 14.2.14 we will have

14.2.16 $\delta'(n, \hat{}(m^*)) \leftrightarrow \check{}\hat{}(m^*)(\check{}(\lambda y)\check{}S_\delta(\check{}n, \check{}y))$

Using 14.2.12, the right-hand side of 14.2.16 can be converted into

14.2.17 $(\check{}\hat{}(\lambda y)\;\check{}S_\delta(\check{}n,\;\check{}y))(m)$
        $\to\;\check{}S_\delta(\check{}n,\;\check{}m)$.

But the left-hand side of 14.2.16 is $\delta''(n,\;m)$; thus, in any world and for any n and m, $\delta''(n,\;m)$ has the same truth value as $\check{}S_\delta(\check{}n,\;\check{}m)$. Substituting $\delta''(x,\;y)$ for $\check{}S_\delta(\check{}x,\;\check{}y)$ in 14.2.14, we obtain 14.2.15.

We are now in a position to continue the translation of *John kicked Bill* (14.2.11) as follows:

14.2.18 $\mathrm{kick}'(\hat{}j,\hat{}(\lambda P)[\check{}P](\hat{}b))$
        $\to\;\check{}\hat{}(\lambda P)[\check{}P](\hat{}b)[\hat{}(\lambda y)\mathrm{kick}''(\hat{}j,\;y)]$
        $\to\;\check{}\hat{}(\lambda y)\mathrm{kick}''(\hat{}j,\;y)(\hat{}b)$
        $\to\;\mathrm{kick}''(\hat{}j,\;\hat{}b)$

We thus end up with the formula that we might have expected as the translation of *John kicked Bill*, given that argument positions are to be filled by intensions, though we are only able to arrive at it by employing a meaning postulate that expresses the "extensionality" of the object of *kick*.

The translation of *John kicked Bill* given in 14.2.11 and 14.2.18 corresponds to the analysis tree 14.2.19a; the sentence of course allows other analyses, such as 14.2.19b and 14.2.19c:

14.2.19 a.

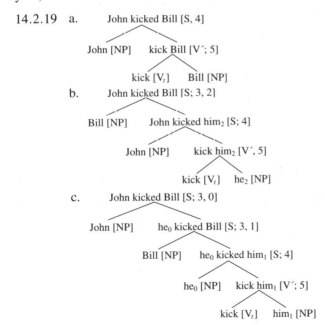

The translations corresponding to 14.2.19b and 14.2.19c yield the same formula as appears in the last line of 14.2.18, via a slightly different route, for example, for 14.2.19b:

14.2.20   John $\Rightarrow (\lambda P)(^\vee P)(^\wedge j)$; Bill $\Rightarrow (\lambda Q)(^\vee Q)(^\wedge b)$;
             he$_2 \Rightarrow (\lambda R)(^\vee R)(x_2)$
             kick him$_2 \Rightarrow (\lambda \mathscr{P})(\lambda x)$kick$'(x, \mathscr{P})^\wedge(\lambda R)(^\vee R)(x_2)$
             $\rightarrow (\lambda x)$kick$'(x, {}^\wedge(\lambda R)(^\vee R)(x_2))$
             $\rightarrow (\lambda x)^{\vee \wedge}(\lambda R)(^\vee R)(x_2)[^\wedge(\lambda y)$kick$''(x, y)]$(by 14.2.15)
             $\rightarrow (\lambda x)(\lambda R)(^\vee R)(x_2)^\wedge(\lambda y)$kick$''(x,y)$
             $\rightarrow (\lambda x)^{\vee \wedge}(\lambda y)$kick$''(x, y)(x_2)$
             $\rightarrow (\lambda x)$kick$''(x, x_2)$
     John kicked him$_2 \Rightarrow (\lambda P)(^\vee P)(^\wedge j)^\wedge(\lambda x)$kick$''(x, x_2)$
             $\rightarrow {}^{\vee \wedge}(\lambda x)$kick$''(x, x_2)(^\wedge j)$
             $\rightarrow (\lambda x)$kick$''(x, x_2)(^\wedge j)$
             $\rightarrow$ kick$''(^\wedge j, x_2)$

To continue the translation in an acceptable fashion, we will have to make a change in the translation rule for quantified sentences that is forced on us by the policy on NPs developed in the last few pages. Specifically, we must introduce $^\wedge$ into the translation rule corresponding to the rule that forms a S from a (quantified, in general) NP and a S:[13]

14.2.21   If α is a NP, β is a S, and γ is the S formed from β by
             substituting α for an occurrence of he$_n$/him$_n$ and
             pronominalizing all other occurrences of he$_n$/him$_n$,
             then $\gamma' = \alpha'(^\wedge(\lambda x_n)\beta')$

14.2.22   John kicked Bill $\Rightarrow (\lambda Q)(^\vee Q)(^\wedge b)^\wedge(\lambda x_2)$kick$''(^\wedge j, x_2)$
             $\rightarrow {}^{\vee \wedge}(\lambda x_2)$kick$''(^\wedge j, x_2)(^\wedge b)$
             $\rightarrow (\lambda x_2)$kick$''(^\wedge j, x_2)(^\wedge b)$
             $\rightarrow$ kick$''(^\wedge j, {}^\wedge b)$

The derivation of kick$''(^\wedge j, {}^\wedge b)$ for the analysis corresponding to 14.2.19c works essentially the same way.

      Let us now consider a sentence with a "nonextensional verb," with an object that is genuinely ambiguous with regard to an "extensional" or "nonextensional" interpretation:

14.2.23   a. John sought a unicorn.

b.   John sought a unicorn [S; 3, 1]

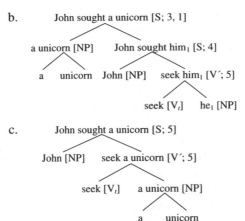

c.   John sought a unicorn [S; 5]

John [NP]   seek a unicorn [V´; 5]

seek [V$_t$]   a unicorn [NP]

a   unicorn

By all rights, 14.2.23b ought to correspond to the interpretation of 14.2.23a in which there is a unicorn such that John is looking for **it**; 14.2.23c is a reasonable candidate for an analysis corresponding to the sense of 14.2.23c in which John's search for any unicorn at all, not for some specific unicorn, and Montague so interpreted it. Let us see if we can make the translations corresponding to these two analyses correspond to these two understandings of 14.2.23a. The translation corresponding to 14.2.23b is as follows:

14.2.24   seek him$_1$ $\Rightarrow$ (λx)seek$'(x,$ $^\wedge(\lambda R)(^\vee R)(x_1))$
John sought him$_1$ $\Rightarrow$ seek$'(^\wedge j,$ $^\wedge(\lambda R)(^\vee R)$ $(x_1))$

While we cannot employ the meaning postulate 14.2.14 to "export" $^\wedge(\lambda R)(^\vee R)$ from the second argument, we can still replace the last formula by one involving seek″, since the definition of ″ depended only on the type of the second argument, not on whether that position was extensional. Thus we can replace the last formula in 14.2.24 by seek″$(^\wedge j, x_1)$ and continue as follows:

14.2.25   John sought a unicorn
$\Rightarrow (\lambda P)(\exists x)$ $\wedge$(unicorn$'(x),$ $^\vee P(x))^\wedge(\lambda x_1)$seek″$(^\wedge j, x_1)$
$\rightarrow (\exists x)$ $\wedge$(unicorn$'(x),$ $^\vee{}^\wedge(\lambda x_1)$seek″$(^\wedge j, x_1)(x))$
$\rightarrow (\exists x)$ $\wedge$(unicorn$'(x),$ seek″$(^\wedge j, x))$

Consider now the translation corresponding to the analysis in 14.2.23c:

14.2.26   seek a unicorn $\Rightarrow (\lambda x)$seek$'(x,$ $^\wedge(\lambda P)(\exists y)$ $\wedge$(unicorn$'(y),$ $^\vee P(y)))$
John sought a unicorn $\Rightarrow$
seek$'(^\wedge j,$ $^\wedge(\lambda P)(\exists y)$ $\wedge$(unicorn$'(y),$ $^\vee P(y)))$

Note that we cannot replace the last formula in 14.2.26 by anything involving seek": the second argument of seek' is not of the special form that figures in the definition of seek", and the meaning postulate that might lead to something of that form is inapplicable because *seek* is not among the verbs to which it applies.

We thus end up with two distinct formulas corresponding to the two analyses of *John sought a unicorn.* The formula that we obtained for the analysis 14.2.23b fits perfectly the interpretation that it is supposed to represent: the last line of 14.2.25 corresponds directly to "there is a unicorn that John seeks." It is less obvious that the last formula in 14.2.26 adequately represents the other interpretation of 14.2.23a, since we as yet have no policy regarding when seek'$(x, \mathcal{P})$ should be assigned the value T for those $\mathcal{P}$ that are not of the special form ^$(y*)$. Montague gave a meaning postulate that amounts to the proposal (Quine 1960: 154) that *seek* is analyzable as *try to find:*

14.2.27 $\Box$(seek'$(x, \mathcal{P}) \leftrightarrow$ try'$(x, {}^\wedge$find'$(x, \mathcal{P})))$

Since *find* is one of the verbs for which the meaning postulate 14.2.14 is applicable, 14.2.27 amounts to 14.2.28, which would yield 14.2.29 as an equivalent of the last formula of 14.2.26:

14.2.28 $\Box$(seek'$(x, \mathcal{P}) \leftrightarrow$ try'$(x, {}^{\smile\smile}\mathcal{P}({}^\wedge(\lambda y)$find"$(x, y)))$

14.2.29   try'$({}^\wedge j, {}^{\smile\smile\smile}(\lambda P)(\exists y) \wedge($unicorn'$(y), {}^\smile P(y)) {}^\wedge(\lambda z)$find"$({}^\wedge j, z))$
            $\rightarrow$ try'$({}^\wedge j, {}^\wedge(\exists y) \wedge($unicorn'$(y), {}^{\smile\smile}(\lambda z)$find"$({}^\wedge j, z)(y)))$
            $\rightarrow$ try'$({}^\wedge j, {}^\wedge(\exists y) \wedge($unicorn'$(y),$ find"$({}^\wedge j, y)))$

If the second argument of try' is to be filled by a proposition indicating the condition for the attempt to be successful, then 14.2.29 fits the intended interpretation of 14.2.23a very well: John's attempt is successful if there is a unicorn which he finds.

It should be remarked, though, that Montague rejected the idea that **all** nonreferential objects could be explained away in terms of meaning postulates such as 14.2.28: "Such a proposal, however, would not be naturally applicable, for want of a paraphrase, to such intensional verbs as *conceive* and such intensional prepositions as *about;* and I regard it as one of the principal virtues of the present treatment . . . that it enables us to deal directly with intensional locutions" (1973: 267). Montague was thus willing to regard 14.2.30a as having a translation such as 14.2.30b that irreducibly involved a "higher-order" function as an argument:

14.2.30 a. John conceived of a unicorn.
        b. conceive'$({}^\wedge j, {}^\wedge(\lambda P)(\exists y) \wedge($unicorn'$(y), {}^\smile P(y)))$

Let us now turn to the question of how another type of "nonreferential" NP might be accommodated in Montague grammar, namely, proper names such as *Zeus* and *Santa Claus* that do not denote objects that exist in the real world. Montague dealt in detail only with the more garden variety of proper names whose designation both exists and is always the same. In the fragmentary grammar given in Montague 1973, this characteristic of the relevant proper names was embodied in the following meaning postulate (1973: 263):

14.2.31 $(\exists u) \; \Box(u = \alpha)$, where α is j, m, b, or n.

The grammar contained no proper names other than *John, Mary, Bill,* and *ninety,* and the individual constants j, m, b, and n denote the entities to which those names refer; u is a variable of type e. The postulate 14.2.31 thus asserts for each of the four names that there is an entity that is the denotation of that name in all worlds, that is, that the name is a rigid designator. Montague set up the semantics of his system in such a way that the variables of type e range over exactly the same domain in every world. One fairly plausible way in which Montague's system could be modified so as to accommodate proper names such as *Zeus* would be to relax this last condition as follows: (i) to each world i there corresponds a set of A_i of objects that exist in that world, and the truth in that world of a quantified formula $(\exists u)\varphi(u)$ depends on whether there is a member a of A_i for which $\varphi(a)$ is true; (ii) "intensional objects" (i.e., objects of type $\langle s, e \rangle$) can have nonexistent extensions: an "intensional object" is a function associating to each world a "possible object" (i.e., a member of the union of the A_i's), and the object that it makes correspond to a given world need not exist in that world. Thus, under this policy, *Santa Claus* could be translated by a constant sc of type $\langle s, e \rangle$ having the same extention in every world, but with the object that serves as its extension existing in only some worlds, the real world not among them.

Consider now the sentences 14.2.32a and 14.2.32b; by the same steps as in 14.2.20, we will be able to obtain the translations:

14.2.32 a.   John sought Santa Claus
     a′. seek″(ˆj, sc)
     b.   John worships Zeus
     b′. worship″(ˆj, zs)

There is a sense in which ∃-introduction can be applied to the second argument position of these formulas and a sense in which it cannot be. We can derive the following consequences, which involve a variable ranging over intensional entities:

14.2.33 a. $(\exists x)\text{seek}''(\hat{}j, x)$
   b. $(\exists x)\text{worship}''(\hat{}j, x)$

However, we cannot derive corresponding formulas in which an existential quantifier binds a variable that ranges over entities:

14.2.34 a. $(\exists u)\text{seek}''(\hat{}j, \hat{}u)$
   b. $(\exists u)\text{worship}''(\hat{}j, \hat{}u)$

This follows from the fact that while 14.2.32a and 14.2.32b involve constants of type $\langle s, e \rangle$ and thus of the type over which x ranges, there is no way to insure the existence of a corresponding object of the form $\hat{}a$ (where a is an existing object of type e), since seek$'$ and worship$'$ are not subject to the meaning postulate 14.2.14. According to this treatment, the "referential" interpretation of *John is looking for a unicorn* ought not, strictly speaking, to imply that a unicorn exists. I think that in fact it does not. In support of this judgment, I offer the fact that 14.2.35 has a noncontradictory interpretation:

14.2.35   John is looking for someone who does not exist, namely, Santa Claus.

This is noncontradictory as long as *someone who does not exist* is taken as having the whole sentence for its scope, its variable is taken as ranging over intensional objects, and *exist* is taken to mean "exist as a real world entity." Note also the possibility of saying 14.2.36 even if one believes that no such things as gods exist:

14.2.36   Oscar worships the same god that Lucille does.

This fact is consistent with the treatment suggested in the last paragraph provided that gods are intensional objects that need not have a real world extension.

Montague likewise did not provide an analysis for proper names such as *Lassie* or *Miss America* that have denoted different individuals at different times. He gave a meaning postulate that would prevent such a proper name from functioning as the subject of the more ordinary common nouns:

14.2.37 $\Box[\supset(\delta(x), (\exists u)(x = \hat{}u))]$, where δ is any basic (as opposed to derived) member of the category $t//e$ (i.e., common noun) other than price$'$, temperature$'$, . . .

This postulate would force *Lassie is a dog* to be assigned the value "false": if l is the intensional individual whose denotation at each moment is the Lassie of that moment, then l is not of the form $\hat{}u$ (i.e., it is not a constant function, mapping each world onto the same individual), and thus dog$'(l)$ must be false if 14.2.37 is to be maintained.

While Montague's analysis did not provide for such an individual as "Lassie," it did allow for intensional individuals whose denotations changed through time, and indeed, the provision for such individuals is essential if Montague's treatment of such sentences as *The temperature is rising* is to work. Since Montague's discussion of that example rests heavily on his treatment of the verb *be,* it will be necessary first to digress into that matter. Montague treated *be* as a transitive verb (thus, of the same syntactic category as *kick*), with the translation:

14.2.38   be $\Rightarrow (\lambda\mathcal{P})(\lambda x)^{\vee}\mathcal{P}^{\wedge}((\lambda y)(^{\vee}x = {}^{\vee}y))$

As an illustration of 14.2.38 in action, consider the following translation:

14.2.39 a.   Bill is Mary

      Bill   be Mary

           be   Mary

    b. Bill $\Rightarrow (\lambda Q)(^{\vee}Q)(^{\wedge}b)$
      Mary $\Rightarrow (\lambda P)(^{\vee}P)(^{\wedge}m)$
      be Mary $\Rightarrow (\lambda\mathcal{P})(\lambda x)^{\vee}\mathcal{P}^{\wedge}((\lambda y)(^{\vee}x = {}^{\vee}y))^{\wedge}(\lambda P)(^{\vee}P)(^{\wedge}m)$
      $\rightarrow (\lambda x)^{\vee \wedge}(\lambda P)(^{\vee}P)(^{\wedge}m)^{\wedge}((\lambda y)(^{\vee}x = {}^{\vee}y))$
      $\rightarrow (\lambda x)((\lambda y)(^{\vee}x = {}^{\vee}y)(^{\wedge}m))$
      $\rightarrow (\lambda x)(^{\vee}x = {}^{\vee \wedge}m)$
      $\rightarrow (\lambda x)(^{\vee}x = m)$
      Bill is Mary $\Rightarrow (\lambda Q)(^{\vee}Q)(^{\wedge}b)^{\wedge}(\lambda x)(^{\vee}x = m)$
      $\rightarrow {}^{\vee \wedge}(\lambda x)(^{\vee}x = m)(^{\wedge}b)$
      $\rightarrow {}^{\vee \wedge}b = m$
      $\rightarrow b = m$

It can also be shown that *Bill is a man* leads to the translation man$'(^{\wedge}b)$. I will not go through the derivation here; the interested reader is referred to Partee (1975: 290–91) for details. Note thus that in Montague's treatment, *be* plays a role in the translation of *Bill is a man* into intensional logic, but the translation of *be* is set up in such a way that it will "cancel out"; that is, it will yield the same result as if there were no *be* and the predicate noun were treated as an intransitive verb.

Or at least that is the case when the predicate noun is an ordinary noun such as *man.* The derivation of man$'(^{\wedge}b)$ from *Bill is a man* depends on the meaning postulate 14.2.37 and thus cannot be carried out if the predicate noun is *price* or *temperature*. Let us now look at an example involving one of those nouns and see if, in the process, we can solve the puzzle of why the following argument is invalid:

14.2.40   The temperature is rising.
           The temperature is 90.
           Therefore, 90 is rising.

The translation of *The temperature is 90* is as follows:

14.2.41   be 90 $\Rightarrow$ [($\lambda\mathcal{P}$)(λx)$^\vee\mathcal{P}^\wedge$(λy)($^\vee x$ = $^\vee y$)]$^\wedge$(λP)($^\vee$P)($^\wedge$90)
           $\rightarrow$ (λx)$^{\vee\wedge}$[(λP)($^\vee$P)($^\wedge$90)]$^\wedge$(λy)[$^\vee x$ = $^\vee y$]
                                                  (conversion of $\lambda\mathcal{P}$)
           $\rightarrow$ (λx)[(λP)($^\vee$P)($^\wedge$90)]$^\wedge$(λy)[$^\vee x$ = $^\vee y$] ($^{\vee\wedge}$ cancellation)
           $\rightarrow$ (λx)$^\vee$($^\wedge$(λy)[$^\vee x$ = $^\vee y$]($^\wedge$90)) (conversion of λP)
           $\rightarrow$ (λx)((λy[$^\vee x$ = $^\vee y$]($^\wedge$90)) ($^{\vee\wedge}$ cancellation)
           $\rightarrow$ (λx)[$^\vee x$ = $^{\vee\wedge}$90] (conversion of λy)
           $\rightarrow$ (λx)[$^\vee x$ = 90]
           the temperature $\Rightarrow$ (λP)($\exists y$)[$\wedge$(($\forall z$)(temp$'$(z) $\leftrightarrow$ z = y),
           ($^\vee$P)(y))]
           the temperature is 90 $\Rightarrow$ (λP)($\exists y$)[$\wedge$ (($\forall z$(temp$'$(z) $\leftrightarrow$ z = y),
           ($^\vee$P)(y))]$^\vee$(λx)$^\vee$ [$^\vee x$ = 90]
           $\rightarrow$ ($\exists y$)[$\wedge$ (($\forall z$)(temp$'$(z) $\leftrightarrow$ z = y), $^{\vee\wedge}$(λx) [$^\vee x$ = 90](y))]
           $\rightarrow$ ($\exists y$)[$\wedge$ (($\forall z$)(temp$'$(z) $\leftrightarrow$ z = y), (λx) [$^\vee x$ = 90](y))]
           $\rightarrow$ ($\exists y$)[$\wedge$ (($\forall z$)(temp$'$(z) $\leftrightarrow$ z = y), [$^\vee y$ = 90])]

The translation of *The temperature is rising* can easily be shown to be

14.2.42   The temperature is rising
           $\Rightarrow$ ($\exists y$)[$\wedge$(($\forall z$)(temp$'$(z) $\leftrightarrow$ z = y), rise$'$(y))]

No conversion of 14.2.42 to anything involving $^\vee y$ is possible, since the meaning postulate that Montague gives for intransitive verbs specifically excludes rise$'$ and that for nouns excludes temperature$'$. The translations of the two premises of 14.2.40 thus do not share anything that would justify the inference in 14.2.40: while the same (intensional) object is picked out as "the temperature" in 14.2.42 as in 14.2.41, example 14.2.42 predicates something of that object but 14.2.41 only predicates something of the extension of that object. Thus, according to Montague's treatment, 14.2.40 is invalid in exactly the same way as is the inference:

14.2.43   The janitor is sleeping.
           The janitor's brother is the archbishop.
           Therefore the archbishop is sleeping.

The meaning postulate 14.2.37 provides the difference between the invalid 14.2.40 and the valid 14.2.44:

14.2.44   The balloon is rising.
            The balloon is a manufactured object.
            Therefore, a manufactured object is rising.

Because Montague grammar requires that there be a semantic interpretation for every surface syntactic constituent and that every syntactic rule be accompanied by a semantic rule that derives the semantic interpretation of its output from the semantic interpretations of its inputs, there is a very different division of labor between syntax and semantics in Montague grammar than in most other syntactic frameworks; as we will see shortly, the framework often forces one to adopt analyses in which a nearly vacuous syntactic rule is combined with a semantic rule that does work that in another framework might be done by, say, a movement transformation. Consider, for example, how one might describe passive sentences in Montague grammar. Since there are distinctively passive syntactic constituents that make up less than a sentence (for example, *given the money* and *given the money by Ann*), the Montague framework precludes an analysis in which a rule applies to an active clause (here, say, *Ann give Ted the money*) and derives a corresponding passive clause from it: there have to be separate steps deriving each of the parts of the passive clause, and a passive clause is derived by combining its subject with its V', exactly the same way that an active clause is derived.

While there are a number of ways in which a Montague grammarian might conceivably derive an expression such as *given the money,* one particular approach is now generally accepted by Montague grammarians, namely one in which such expressions are derived from a TV. Recall that TV means an expression that combines with a NP to yield a V' and that TVs include not only single words such as *kill, worship,* and *seek,* i.e., "transitive verbs" in the narrow sense, but also complex expressions such as *give the money, sweep under the rug,* and *take for granted.* The rule combining a TV with a NP does not simply concatenate the TV with the NP but rather puts the NP immediately after the verb of the TV: *give the money + Ted = give Ted the money; sweep under the rug + the dust = sweep the dust under the rug.*[14] Note that this conception of TV allows one to identify as TVs expressions that, except for the inflection of the verb, are identical to passive V's: *given the money, swept under the rug, taken for granted.*

The passive rule of such works as Dowty 1978 and Bach 1980 applies to a TV and does nothing syntactically other than put the TV in its past participle form. What gives the rule its passive character is the associated semantic rule, which is set up in such a way that the subject of the passive V' that it derives is interpreted as if it were the direct object of the TV:

14.2.45   If α is a TV, then $EN(\alpha)$ is a passive verb phrase,[15] where $EN(\alpha)$ is obtained from α by putting its verb in the past participle form. If $\alpha \Rightarrow \alpha'$, then $EN(\alpha) \Rightarrow (\lambda x)(\exists y)[\alpha'((\hat{\ }x^*))](y)$

The semantic rule in 14.2.45 is set up in such a way that the subject with which the passive V' is combined, which will provide the expression that is substituted for the λ-bound variable x, is tied to the semantic position that corresponds to the object when α is used in an active sentence; the semantic position corresponding to the subject of α in an active sentence is bound by an existential quantifier; thus *Ted was given the money* will receive the same translation as *Someone/Something gave Ted the money.* (The reason that α' is combined not with x but with $\hat{\ }(x^*)$ is Montague's policy on the types of the various argument positions: x is the right type to serve as a subject argument, but something of a higher type is needed to fill the semantic object position.)[16]

The resulting treatment of passives differs considerably from the standard treatments in transformational grammar, since the passive rule applies not to a whole clause (moving a NP out of the V' into subject position) but to a TV. This means that when a class of sentences do not have acceptable passives, a Montague grammarian may be able to argue that the corresponding active expression is not a TV and thus that it does not come under the purview of his passive rule. This is the account that Bach (1980) gives of such differences as the following:

14.2.46 a. We persuaded John to help them.
       a'. John was persuaded to help them.
        b. We promised John to help them.
       b'. *John was promised to help them.
        c. They regard Bill as dangerous.
       c'. Bill is regarded as dangerous.
        d. Bill strikes them as dangerous.
       d'. *They are struck (by Bill) as dangerous.

According to Bach, *persuade to help them* and *regard as dangerous* are TVs but *promise to help them* and *strike as dangerous* are not (rather, *promise Bill* is of category IV//IV—it combines with a V' complement into a V'—and *strike them* is of category IV/(t///e)—it combines with an A' complement into a V'). Bach offers a number of observations in support of this distinction in the internal structure of complex V's, the most striking of which is a correlation (originally noted by Visser) between the possibility of passive and the "control" properties of a V'. Specifically, the understood subject of the infinitive is the object of *persuade* but the subject of *promise;* likewise, the understood subject of the A' is the object of *regard* but the subject of *strike*. Visser's generalization is that a verb cannot be passivized if its subject is the "controller" of an understood subject. Bach's treatment explains why there should be such a restriction: under his analysis, *promise Bill* combines with a V' the same way that a simple verb with an infinitive complement does (e.g., *try*), and it should accordingly share the control properties of such verbs (thus, the subject as controller); but if a verb is part of an expression that combines with a V' into a V', the latter V' is not formed from a TV and a T and thus the possibility of passivization is precluded.

Consider now the alternative forms of dative constructions:

14.2.47 a.   Ann gave Ted the money.
       a'.   Ann gave the money to Ted.

Give is one of a large number of verbs that can be used in sentences of both these forms. However, there also are many verbs that combine only into V's of the shape V NP P', and a few verbs that combine only with V's of the shape of V NP NP:

14.2.48 a.   *Ann reported the police the accident.
       a'.   Ann reported the accident to the police.
        b.   The judge spared the defendant any further humiliation.
       b'.   *The judge spared any further humiliation to/of/ ... the
              defendant.

Dowty (1978) accordingly maintains that two separate categories of verbs must be recognized, those that fit into the one frame like *report* and those that fit into the other like *spare,* and that *give* simply belongs to both categories, or more accurately (since the two different uses of *give* could not be assigned exactly the same translation into intensional logic) that there are two homophonous verbs *give,* having distinct but related meanings, one belonging to the one category and one to the other. In Dowty's formalization, *spare* and the *give* of 14.2.47a belong to the category TV/T, and *report* and the *give* of 14.2.47a' belong to the category TV//T. In both cases, the TV that results from combining the verb with a T is combined by Right-wrap into a V':

14.2.49   give the money + Ted = give Ted the money
           spare any further humiliation + the defendant = spare the
              defendant any further humiliation
           give to Ted + the money = give the money to Ted

report to the police + the accident = report the accident to the
police

The rules for combining the two classes of verbs with a T into a TV differ in
that the two elements are simply juxtaposed when the verb is a TV/T, while a
preposition is inserted before the T if the verb is a TV//T.[17] The fairly systematic relationship between pairs of homophonous verbs such as the two *give*'s
is described by Dowty in terms of a rule that derives a verb of the one category
from a verb of the other. Once again, the syntactic rule is trivial and the substance of the relation is given by the associated semantic rule:

14.2.50   If δ is a TV//T, then δ is a TV/T. If $\delta_{TV//T}$ translates as δ', then
$\delta_{TV/T}$ translates as $(\lambda\mathcal{P})(\lambda\mathcal{Q})(\lambda x)[\delta'(\mathcal{Q})(\mathcal{P})(x)]$.

The semantic rule interchanges the roles of the two objects that the verb is
combined with: the object that *give*$_{TV/T}$ is combined with (yielding e.g., [*give
the money*]$_{TV}$) is substituted for the λ-bound variable corresponding to the
object with which a TV such as *give to Ted* would combine, and the object
that a TV such as *give the money* combines with is substituted for the λ-bound
variable corresponding to the object with which a TV//T would combine in
the formation of a TV such as *give to Ted*. Thus, 14.2.50 insures that *give the
money to Ted* and *give Ted the money* receive equivalent translations.[18]

As 14.2.50 stands, it would allow every TV//T to be used as a TV/T, which
would incorrectly predict, for example, that 14.2.48a should be acceptable.
Whether a TV//T can also be used as a TV/T is at least partly a matter of
lexical idiosyncracy, since it is a point on which near synonyms diverge; for
example, while *give* can be used as a TV/T, *donate* cannot be (**I donated the
library my books*). Dowty accordingly gives 14.2.50 and a number of other
rules a different status from the rules we have discussed so far: they are **lexical
rules,** which apply only to individual lexical items (and not to complex
expressions of the given category) and whose applicability can vary from one
lexical item to another. Thus, Dowty's analog to the "Dative-movement"
transformation of early transformational grammar is a rule expressing a pattern of relatedness among lexical items, in which only certain lexical items
participate; the semantic interpretation of the related homophonous lexical
item is predictable, but its existence is not.

Since the categories TV/T and TV//T give rise to different TVs, they
should give rise to different passive sentences. All the resulting positive predictions are correct (that is, the passive clauses that are predicted to be grammatical are grammatical), but some of the negative predictions are inaccurate

(that is, some of the passive clauses that are predicted to be ungrammatical are, in different dialects, either perfectly acceptable or nearly so):

14.2.51 a.   Ted was given the money.
     a′.   The money was given to Ted.
     a″.   ?The money was given Ted.
     a‴.   **Ted was given the money to.
     b.   The accident was reported to the police.
     b′.   *The police were reported the accident.
     b″.   **The police were reported the accident to.
     c.   The defendant was spared any further humiliation.
     c′.   ?Further humiliation was spared the defendant.

The problematic case is V′s of the form [V NP_1 NP_2] in which not only NP_1 is acceptable as the subject of a passive (as in 14.2.51a, c) but also NP_2 (as in 14.2.51a″, c′, which are generally rated as acceptable by British speakers and as only slightly odd by American speakers). I will leave up in the air the question of what determines the conditions under which a NP contained within a V′ can be the subject of a corresponding passive clause. The Montague approach sketched here makes many false negative predictions, while a transformational approach under which a NP is simply extracted from a V′ makes many false positive predictions; Bach 1980, Davison 1980, and Rice 1987 discuss insightfully the conditions that affect the acceptability of passive clauses.

14.3 "Generalized Quantifiers"[19]

Since about 1980, an approach to quantified expressions has been developed in which notions of set theory have been combined with Montague's conception of the denotations of NPs in such a way as to facilitate the formulation and testing of generalizations about what the range of possible determiners in natural languages is. Suppose that, as in Montague grammar, we take the denotation of a predicate phrase to be the set of individuals that that predicate phrase is true of (for the purposes of this section, it will not matter whether the members of such a set are taken to be intensional individuals, as in orthodox Montague grammar, or individuals plain and simple, and I will speak in the latter terms in order to simplify the exposition). Then the denotation of a NP will be a set of sets of individuals, e.g., the denotation of 14.3.1a will be 14.3.1a′, where X ranges over sets of individuals:

14.3.1   a.   every linguist
         a'. $\{X: (\forall: \text{Linguist } x)(x \in X)\}$

I will leave open the question of whether one should allow as values of X any set of individuals at all (including the highly heterogeneous sets that are unlikely to serve as the denotation of any natural language predicate phrase) or whether one should restrict the values of X to a range that will correspond more closely to the notion of "possible denotation of a (natural language) predicate phrase"; the former, broad conception of the values of X is the prevalent one in the relevant literature, and I will henceforth assume it. In that case, the members of 14.3.1a' are the sets of which the set of all linguists is a subset. To avoid encountering some form of "Russell's paradox" (cf. sec. 5.1), we will need to restrict X to subsets of some particular "universe" E. If we then use L to denote the set of all linguists, we can recast 14.3.1a' in the form of 14.3.2, that is, the denotation of *every linguist* is the set whose members are those subsets of E of which L is a subset:

14.3.2 $\{X: \wedge(X \subseteq E, L \subseteq X)\}$

The construction of the last paragraph can be carried out for any quantified NP, yielding the following as the denotations of some simple NPs:[20]

14.3.3   a.   some linguist $\{X: \wedge(X \subseteq E, L \cap X \neq 0)\}$
         b.   two linguists $\{X: \wedge(X \subseteq E, |L \cap X| \geq 2)\}$
         c.   no linguist $\{X: \wedge(X \subseteq E, L \cap X = \varnothing)\}$

To recast the truth conditions of quantified sentences in terms of denotations as in 14.3.3, the most obvious proposal is to say that a quantified sentence is true if the denotation of the predicate expression is a member of the denotation of the quantified expression with which it is combined, e.g., if one represents by C the denotation of *likes cats,* then 14.3.4a will be true if and only if the condition 14.3.4a' is met:

14.3.4   a.   Every linguist likes cats.
         a'. $C \in \{X: \wedge(X \subseteq E, L \subseteq X)\}$, i.e., $\wedge(C \subseteq E, L \subseteq C)$, which
              amounts to $L \subseteq C$, since the various sets of individuals that
              figure in the discussion are assumed to be subsets of E.

One can then factor out of expressions as in 14.3.3 the contribution that the quantifier makes to the truth conditions of sentences in which it appears. Let D represent any quantifier or other determiner (such as an article or a demonstrative), A the denotation of any N', and B the denotation of any predicate phrase. Then DA will represent a set of subsets of E, and the sentence in question will be true if and only if B $\in$ DA. Alternatively, since A and B are both subsets of E, one can treat D as a two-place relation between subsets of E and recast the above truth conditions as in 14.3.5, using [] to indicate the denotation of the element enclosed in the brackets:

14.3.5 a. [every]AB if and only if A $\subseteq$ B
    b. [some]AB if and only if A $\cap$ B $\neq$ $\varnothing$
    c. [two]AB if and only if $|A \cap B| \geq 2$
    d. [no]AB if and only if A $\cap$ B $=$ $\varnothing$

We are now in a position to identify some properties of relations between sets of individuals that will play a role in restricting such relations in ways that will reflect actual restrictions on the determiners of natural languages and in categorizing natural language determiners in ways that reflect linguistically significant distinctions among a language's determiners. First, let us briefly introduce a possible difference among determiners simply for the sake of stating the generalization that it is not a dimension on which natural-language determiners can differ from one another. In 14.3.5, we have given analyses in which A and B played a direct role but the universe E did not. One could conceive, though, of determiners whose truth conditions also depended on E, i.e., conceivably there could be a determiner D_E such that the truth of $D_E AB$ would depend not just on the relationship of A and B to each other but also on their relationship to E (imagine, for example, D_E being such that the truth condition for $D_E AB$ was that $|A| < |B|$ if E is finite and that A be a proper subset of B if E is infinite). A determiner is called **constant** (following Westerståhl 1985) if it excludes that possibility (that is, if the truth value of $D_E AB$ can't be changed by enlarging the universe while holding A and B constant), and 14.3.6b expresses the plausible claim that natural language determiners never allow that possibility to arise:[21]

14.3.6 a. A determiner D is constant if for all sets A, B, E_1, E_2 for which
     A, B $\subseteq$ E_1 $\subseteq$ E_2, $D_{E_1}AB$ if and only if $D_{E_2}AB$.
    b. Every natural language determiner is constant.

I will henceforth restrict my attention to determiners that are constant.

A second characteristic that has been proposed as a property of natural language determiners is that the truth value of DAB depends only on which members of A are and which ones are not members of B, e.g., to determine whether most linguists like cats, it is enough to know which linguists like cats and which linguists don't like cats—it is immaterial how any nonlinguists feel about cats. A determiner with this property is **conservative** (Barwise and Cooper 1981), as defined in 14.3.7a:

14.3.7   a. A determiner D is conservative if for all sets A and B, DAB if
          and only if DA(A ∩ B).
          b. Every natural language determiner is conservative.

Various determiners can be shown to be conservative by showing that the truth
value of any sentence with that determiner is the same as that of a corresponding sentence in which a conjunct is added that restricts the matrix to the given
domain:

14.3.8   a.   Every linguist likes Chinese food.
          a′. Every linguist is a linguist and likes Chinese food.
          b.   Most politicians are crooks.
          b′. Most politicians are politicians and are crooks.

There is in fact a word that might in fact be held to be a nonconservative
determiner, namely, *only.* If the *only* of such NPs as *only linguists* is treated as
a determiner, then the truth conditions for [only]AB would presumably be
given as in 14.3.9a, and it would not be conservative, because conservativity
would mean that 14.3.9a was equivalent to 14.3.9b, which it clearly is not:

14.3.9   a. (∀: ~(x ∈ A)) ~(x ∈ B)
          b. (∀: ~(x ∈ A)) ~(x ∈ A ∩ B)

Regardless of what A and B are, 14.3.9b is always true (it merely says that
something that is not a member of A is never a member of A ∩ B), while
14.3.9a is not automatically true (it is false that only linguists like Chinese
food, though it is of course trivially true that only linguists are linguists and
like Chinese food). But *only* is a not a determiner: it combines not just with
N′s but with constituents of a broad range of categories, and it cannot satisfy
the requirement that an English NP have a determiner:

14.3.10 a.   Mary only insulted John—she didn't hit him.
         a′. John gets angry only if people keep him waiting.
         b.   *Tom drank only glass of water.

Thus the universal proposed in 14.3.9b has teeth to it: it implies that a far
from rare misconception of the syntax and semantics of *only* not only does not
fit that English word but does not fit any word of any natural language.

     Another plausible universal about determiners is that they have to be non-
trivial with regard to both the domain and the matrix: the truth value of DAB
can't be completely independent of A or completely independent of B. Oddly,
though, that universal turns out to be false. Keenan (1987:310) has pointed
out that there are acceptable sentences involving determiners that guarantee

the truth of DAB, irrespective of any information about A and B, and with determiners that guarantee its falsehood:

14.3.11 a. All that your argument shows is that at least zero Fermat
             equations have integral solutions.
         b. If your proof is valid, it establishes that there are fewer than
             zero nonconservative determiners in any language. Do you
             think you might have made an error?

However, one can probably get a correct version of the universal by restricting it to syntactically **simple** determiners; sentences as in 14.3.11 probably owe their acceptability to the fact that certain semantically nonvacuous patterns for forming complex determiners (*at least n,* etc.) have semantically vacuous special cases and that the latter are available to any speaker who wishes to exploit them for humorous or ironic purposes.

Certain determiners have various properties of **monotonicity:**[22]

14.3.12   A determiner D is
         a. left monotone increasing if for all sets A, A', B such that
             A ⊆ A', if DAB, then DA'B.
             Example: If several senators are ex-convicts, then several
             elected officials are ex-convicts.
         b. left monotone decreasing if for all sets A, A', B such that
             A' ⊆ A, if DAB, then DA'B.
             Example: If all Christians believe in the resurrection, then all
             Presbyterians believe in the resurrection.
         c. right monotone increasing if for all sets A, B, B' such that
             B ⊆ B', if DAB, then DAB'.
             Example: If all senators accept huge bribes, then all senators
             accept bribes.
         d. right monotone decreasing if for all sets A, B, B' such that
             B' ⊆ B, if DAB, then DAB'.
             Example: If no atheists worship a god, then no atheists worship
             Zeus.

Notions of monotonicity have figured in some proposed universals about natural language determiners. Barwise and Cooper (1981:187) have proposed that a simple determiner in a natural language must have a meaning that is either right monotone or a conjunction of right monotone determiners. An example of a determiner that is not right monotone but whose meaning is a conjunction of right monotone determiners is *exactly five:* it is not right monotone (*Exactly five senators accept huge bribes* does not imply *Exactly five senators accept bribes,* so it isn't right monotone increasing, and it likewise doesn't imply *Exactly five senators accept huge bribes from drug dealers,* so it isn't right monotone decreasing), and it is equivalent to the conjunction of the right monotone increasing *at least five* with the right monotone decreasing *at most five.* Barwise and Cooper's proposal implies that determiners such as *an even number of* or *all but one,* which are not equivalent to a conjunction of right monotone determiners, can be expressed only by syntactically complex means in any natural language (though what exactly the universal rules out is not completely clear, in view of some indeterminacy as to what should count as a "simple" determiner). Another universal that Barwise and Cooper (1981: 197) propose is that only right monotone increasing determiners have negated counterparts, e.g., the expressions in 14.3.13a are acceptable NPs, but those in 14.3.13b are not:

14.3.13 a. not every linguist   b. *not some linguist
     not a person   *not most persons
     not a few companies   *not few companies
     not many universities   *not no universities

This is intended, of course, only as a necessary condition, not a sufficient condition for the acceptability of negated quantifiers: there are a number of right monotone increasing determiners (e.g., *each, several*) without negated counterparts.

Exercises

1. Suppose the following symbols are variables of the indicated type:

u e
x $\langle s, e \rangle$
P $\langle \langle s, e \rangle, t \rangle$

What is the type of:

  a. $\hat{}u$
  b. $(\lambda P)P(x)$
  c. $(\lambda u)P(\hat{}u)$
  d. $(\lambda P)(\lambda u)P(\hat{}u)$

2. In Montague's system of syntactic categories, what would be the category of:

  a. The *if* of *If you come near me, I'll scream.*
  b. The *almost* in *almost all.*

c. The *'s* in *This is Bill's hat.*
d. The *'s* in *This hat is Bill's.*

3. The following analysis tree is consistent with the syntactic rules alluded to in this chapter. Determine whether the translation based on this analysis has the same truth conditions as that corresponding to the more obvious analysis, in which each quantifier has a single conjunct as scope:

Every dog barks and every bird sings

every dog He_0 barks and every bird sings

         every bird He_0 barks and he_1 sings

                  He_0 barks He_1 sings

4. Sketch a possible Montague grammar analyses (both syntactic rules and semantic rules) for expressions of the following forms:

a. Conjoined sentences of the form *S and S*. (Treat the *and* as combining with the second S into a unit of the form *and S*. Ignore the possibility of conjoining more than two Ss at a time.)

b. "*Tough*-movement" A's as in *This schedule is hard to get used to.* (Suggestion: give separate rules for dependent V's such as *to get used to* and for the combination of such a V' with an A such as *hard*.)

c. Supplement your answer to part *b* with a lexical rule that relates As such as *hard* (*easy, difficult,* etc.) as they are used in *Tough*-movement sentences to their uses in such sentences as *To get used to this schedule is hard.*

5. Determine what monotonicity properties, if any, each of the following determiners has:

a. at least three
b. exactly three
c. all but one
d. most
e. between five and ten

15.   Conditional Propositions

15.1 Counterfactual Conditionals

In this chapter, I will take up a considerably broader class of conditional propositions than I have covered in the preceding chapters and will exploit notions of possible world semantics in developing analyses of conditionals. The conditional propositions that we have considered so far have been of the kind that are expressed with the indicative mood, as in 15.1.1, rather than the subjunctive mood (15.1.2):

15.1.1   If Bill left at 2:00, he's in Pittsburgh by now.
           If Susan was born in Iceland, she can't run for President of the
           U.S.

15.1.2   If Solti had been conducting, I would have gone to the concert.
           If Kennedy hadn't been assassinated, he would have been
           impeached.

Counterfactual conditionals, as in 15.1.2, have quite different logical properties from the **indicative conditionals** of 15.1.1. For example, as noted by Stalnaker (1969), indicative conditionals satisfy a law of transitivity but counterfactuals do not; that is, inferences like 15.1.3 are valid but inferences like 15.1.4 are invalid:

15.1.3   If Bill left at 2:00, he is in Pittsburgh by now.
           If Bill is in Pittsburgh by now, Lefty has tipped off the feds.
           Therefore, if Bill left at 2:00, Lefty has tipped off the feds.

15.1.4   If Bush had been born in Palestine, he would be a PLO agent.
           If Bush were a PLO agent, he would be sending American
           defense secrets to Saddam.
           Therefore, if Bush had been born in Palestine, he would be
           sending American defense secrets to Saddam.

528

The reason that 15.1.4 is invalid is that the two premises do not relate to the same possible worlds. The first premise has to do with worlds in which, other things being as close as possible to the way things actually are, Bush was born in Palestine rather than in the U.S., and consequently he would not have been president, since he would not meet the constitutional requirement that the U.S. president be a native born U.S. citizen. The second premise has to do with worlds in which, other things being as close as possible to the way things actually are, Bush was a PLO agent, say, Bush became president despite secret membership in the PLO. Since the "other things" aren't the same in the two cases, the worlds that the first premise has to do with do not overlap with those that the second has to do with: if Bush were a Palestinian, he wouldn't be president of the United States and thus presumably would not have access to American defense secrets.

A similar difference is found when one considers the putative rule of **strengthening of the protasis** (more commonly called "strengthening of the antecedent"), which licenses inferences as in 15.1.5, in which one infers from a conditional proposition a conclusion obtained by conjoining material to the protasis:

15.1.5   If Betty was at the party, Bill enjoyed the party.
          Therefore, if Betty was at the party and they served guacamole,
          Bill enjoyed the party.

While this rule is widely regarded as valid for indicative conditionals,[1] it is clearly invalid for counterfactuals, as is illustrated by such invalid inferences as 15.1.6:

15.1.6   If Betty had been at the party, Bill would have had a good time.
          Therefore, if Betty had been at the party and Bill had broken his
          leg, Bill would have had a good time.

It is invalid for a reason similar to that advanced for the invalidity of 15.1.4: those states of affairs that the premise in 15.1.6 has to do with, namely those in which Betty came to the party but other things are as close to the way they really are as possible, are not those that the conclusion has to do with, in which some of those other things are otherwise, in particular, that Bill broke his leg.

In addition, inferences drawn by contraposition, as in 15.1.7, are usually regarded by logicians as valid for indicative conditionals (see, though, sections 3.4 and 15.2 for doubts that it is generally valid even for indicative conditionals), but their counterfactual analogs, as in 15.1.8, clearly are not valid:[2]

15.1.7   If today is Tuesday, then tomorrow is Wednesday.
Therefore, if tomorrow isn't Wednesday, today isn't Tuesday.

15.1.8   If Willie Mays had played in the American League, he would
have been elected to the Hall of Fame.
Therefore, if Willie Mays hadn't been elected to the Hall of
Fame, he wouldn't have played in the American League.

This example is harder to judge than the other ones, because counterfactual
conditionals usually involve both a false protasis and a false apodosis, and
contraposition of counterfactuals forces one to consider counterfactuals in
which one or other of the protasis and the apodosis is true. At any rate,
though, here the premise could plausibly be argued to be true (as it might be
by someone who claims that no matter what major league teams Mays played
for, his playing would have been good enough to warrant election to the Hall
of Fame), but the conclusion could be false even in cases where the premise
is true (e.g., perhaps circumstances leading to Mays not being elected to the
Hall of Fame could have come about equally well irrespective of what league
he played in).

David Lewis (1973) treats counterfactuals by imposing additional structure
on modal systems such as were discussed in chapter 11. Instead of merely an
accessibility relation connecting different worlds, there must be some relation
of "relative closeness," so that one can speak of w_1 being closer to w than w_2
is. This notion of relative closeness could be expressed through a numerical
measure of distance between worlds. However, it is not necessary to treat
closeness in terms of distance: it suffices to assume that there is a three-place
relation $Cxyz$ ("y is at least as close to x as z is") which satisfies the conditions

15.1.9   For all worlds w, w', w'', w''' of the given system,
a. ("connectedness") If Rww' and Rww'', then either $Cww'w''$ or
$Cww''w'$.
b. ("transitivity") If $Cww'w''$ and $Cww''w'''$, then $Cww'w'''$.
c. ("centering") If Rww' and $w' \neq w$, then $Cwww'$ and $\sim Cww'w$.

Condition 15.1.9a says that for any two worlds that are accessible from the
given world, one of them is at least as close to the given world as the other
one is[3] (of course, it might be that both $Cww'w''$ and $Cww''w'$, i.e., w' and w''
might be equally close to w). Condition 15.1.9b says that if one world is at
least as close to the given world as is a second world, which is in turn at least
as close to the given world as is a third world, then the first world is at least as
close to the given world as is the third world. Condition 15.1.9c says that the
world closest to any world is that world itself.[4]

Lewis adds to the language of modal propositional logic a connective $\Box\!\!\rightarrow$ (which, for reasons that will soon be obvious, can be read "locally entails") that is to represent the content of counterfactual conditionals. The truth conditions for $\Box\!\!\rightarrow$ AB are given by Lewis as:

15.1.10 $\Box\!\!\rightarrow$AB is true in a world w if either (i) there is a world w' such that A is true in w' and for every world w'' such that C$ww''w'$ and A is true in w'', B is also true in w''; or (ii) there is no world in which A is true.

That is, for $\Box\!\!\rightarrow$AB to be true in w, it is necessary and sufficient that if there are worlds in which A is true, B is true in those which are closest to w. Lewis formulates the truth conditions as in 15.1.10 rather than in terms of "the closest world to w in which A is true," since he wants to allow for the possibility that no world is the closest of all those in which A is true. This will cover both the case where several worlds in which A is true are equally close to the given world and the case where there is an infinite series of worlds that "converge on a limit"; for example, if A is "David Lewis is over 7 feet tall" and worlds in which Lewis's height is closer to his real height are closer to the real world (other things being equal), there could be an infinite sequence of worlds (one in which his height is 7'1", one in which it is 7'0.1", one in which it is 7'0.01", . . .), where A is true in all of them but none of them is the closest such world to the real world.

Note that this analysis accords with the failure of transitivity noted in 15.1.4 and the failure of strengthening the protasis in 15.1.6. If the closest worlds to the real world in which A is true are pretty remote worlds and the closest worlds to the real world in which B is true are relatively close worlds, then it could perfectly well be the case that B was true and C false in the former worlds while C was true in the latter (see diagram, p. 532). The plane represents the whole set of worlds of the given modal system, distances in the diagram are to correspond to the relative closeness of the worlds, and the regions marked represent sets of worlds in which the various propositions are true. In this case, $\Box\!\!\rightarrow$AB is true (i.e., in the closest worlds to w in which A is true, B is also true), $\Box\!\!\rightarrow$BC is true (i.e., in the closest worlds to w in which B is true, C is also true), but $\Box\!\!\rightarrow$AC is not true (i.e., in the closest worlds to w in which A is true, C is false). The same diagram illustrates the failure of the argument in 15.1.6: here B is true in the closest worlds to w in which A is true but not in the closest worlds to w in which $\wedge$AC is true. The broken lines in the diagram indicate **spheres** around w: a set W of worlds is a sphere around w if and only if for every world w' that belongs to it, all worlds that are at least as close to w as w' is belong to it, i.e., for any two worlds w' and

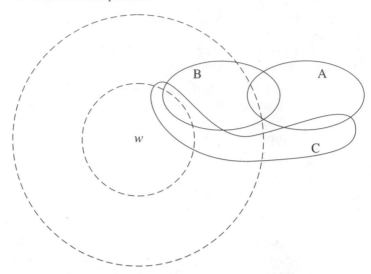

w'', if $w' \in W$ and $Cww''w'$, then $w'' \in W$. The diagram makes clear the reason for the term "local entailment": for $\Box \!\!\rightarrow AB$ to be true in w, it need not be the case that A entails B (i.e., there can be worlds in which A is true and B false, as in the diagram)—all that is necessary is that there be some sphere around w within which A entails B nontrivially (the entailment would be trivial if there were no worlds in the sphere in which A is true).

There are a number of cases in which Lewis's truth conditions could be held to make it too easy for $\Box \!\!\rightarrow AB$ to be true, i.e., where it comes out true according to 15.1.10 but where the corresponding sentence "If A were the case, B would be the case" could plausibly be held to be either false or lacking in a truth value. I will list a number of such cases and then attempt to determine whether they point to defects in Lewis's proposals or merely to interactions among natural language, Lewis's system of logic, and other factors such as Grice's principles of cooperation. The first case is that in which A is true in the given world w. Since (by 15.1.9c) w is the closest world to w, if A is true in w, then $\Box \!\!\rightarrow AB$ will be true in w if and only if B is also true in w. However, examples such as the following, in which the protasis and apodosis both are clearly true sound quite bizarre:

15.1.11 a. ?If 6 were an even number, 12 would be a multiple of 4.

 b. ?If London were in England, the Queen of England would live in London.

    c. ?If Nixon had resigned in 1974, Ford would have become
       president.

    d. ?If 6 were an even number, Kathmandu would be in Nepal.

A second case in which some doubt arises about the correctness of Lewis's assignment of truth values to $\square\!\!\rightarrow\!AB$ is that in which there is no accessible world in which A is true. Here, the truth conditions 15.1.10 make $\square\!\!\rightarrow\!AB$ "vacuously true" and thus fail to distinguish among the following sentences:

15.1.12 a. If 3 were an even number, 4 would be an odd number. (true)

        b. If 3 were an even number, 4 would be a multiple of 3. (false?)

        c. If 3 were an even number, Charles de Gaulle would be the
           bastard son of Chester Alan Arthur. (false?)

A third case in which $\square\!\!\rightarrow\!AB$ is true but "If A were the case, B would be the case" could well be false was discovered by Nollaig MacKenzie (as reported in Harper 1981:9). Recall the discussion above of counterfactual conditionals whose protasis is "David Lewis is over 7′ tall." Suppose that we apply what was said about them to sentences whose apodosis is "David Lewis would be under 7′1″ tall" or "David Lewis would be under 7′0.1″ tall," or in general, "David Lewis would be under $7' + \varepsilon$ tall," where ε is any positive length. As Lewis has set up the semantics of $\square\!\!\rightarrow$, $\square\!\!\rightarrow\!AB$ would then be true: no matter how small ε was, worlds in which Lewis's height was $7' + \varepsilon/2$ would be closer to the real world than worlds in which his height was $7' + \varepsilon$, and there thus would be a sphere around the real world (namely, those worlds in which Lewis's height is $7' + \varepsilon/2$ or less) containing worlds in which his height is over 7′, but in all worlds of that sphere in which his height is over 7′, it is under $7' + \varepsilon$, and thus $\square\!\!\rightarrow$(Lewis is over 7′, Lewis is under $7' + \varepsilon$) is true. But this seems to mean that if Lewis's height exceeded 7′, it would not exceed 7′ by any amount, a rather bizarre result.

A fourth case in which 15.1.10 may let counterfactuals be true too easily is illustrated by a type of example discussed by Nute (1984:407–8). Suppose that you have an economy class seat on a flight on which the economy class section is badly overbooked but there are two unsold first class seats. When you check in, you are assigned the last remaining unassigned economy seat; a person who joined the line a split second after you did and the person immediately behind him are given upgrades to first class, taking the previously unsold seats. When you learn that that has happened, you might say 15.1.13:

15.1.13   Damn it! If I had checked in later, I would have gotten an
         upgrade.

You would be wrong if you said that: if you had checked in more than about a minute later, you wouldn't have even gotten onto the flight, let alone gotten an upgrade. But 15.1.13 would come out true according to 15.1.10, at least if the more you had delayed your checkin the further the world would be from the real world: in the worlds in which you checked in after one or two of the persons behind you in line, but not after three or more of them, you would have gotten an upgrade, and those worlds are closer to the real world than those in which you postponed your checkin long enough for three or more people to get ahead of you and thus didn't even get a seat on the plane. Lewis's truth conditions allow one to ignore the latter worlds, but it is doubtful that one is entitled to dismiss them as counterexamples to the proposition expressed by 15.1.13.

A fifth case in which Lewis's assignment of truth values is questionable is illustrated by the contraposition argument 15.1.8. Given that Willie Mays actually played only in the National League and not also in the American League, and that the sorts of changes in the actual past that could have resulted in Mays not being elected to the Hall of Fame (say, an injury that shortened his playing career) wouldn't have been sufficient in themselves to result in his playing in the American League, Lewis's approach to truth value assignment would presumably make the conclusion of 15.1.8 true: the closest worlds to the real world in which he wasn't elected to the Hall of Fame are worlds in which (as in the real world) he didn't play in the American League. To the extent that one can make clear judgments about 15.1.8, this is counterintuitive: the very consideration that suggests that the conclusion of 15.1.8 is false, namely, one's belief that there is no connection between whether something would have happened that prevented him from becoming a Hall-of-Famer and which of the major leagues he played in, would be grounds for applying Lewis's truth conditions in such a way that the conclusion comes out true.

Finally, a sixth case in which $\square\!\!\rightarrow AB$ comes out true according to 15.1.10 but in which the corresponding English sentences could well be held not to be true arises in attempts to analyze statements of causation in terms of counterfactuals. In the sort of situation in which a statement of causation such as 15.1.14a would be agreed to be true, it is usually plausible to assert the counterfactual 15.1.14b, but totally bizarre to assert its converse 15.1.14c:

15.1.14 a. George's eating those mushrooms caused him to die.
          b. If George hadn't eaten those mushrooms, he wouldn't have died.
          b'. $\square\!\!\rightarrow(\sim$(George ate those mushrooms), $\sim$(George died))

c. ??If George hadn't died, he wouldn't have eaten those
    mushrooms.

c′. □→(∼(George died), ∼(George ate those mushrooms))

The normalness of 15.1.14b and the bizarreness of 15.1.14c reflect respectively the preservation and the reversal of the normal temporal and causal connections: 15.1.14b, like 15.1.14a, implies that the eating of the mushrooms
preceded and caused the death, while 15.1.14c suggests that the death preceded and caused the eating of the mushrooms. Nonetheless, 15.1.14c′ would
come out true for a reasonable possible world structure that makes 15.1.14a
true: 15.1.14c′ implies that in the closest-to-real states of affairs in which
George did not die, he did not eat the mushrooms, and one would not normally say that George's eating the mushrooms caused him to die unless that
condition were met.

Let us now decide how to deal with these examples. The oddity of the
examples 15.1.11 sounds like a good candidate for an explanation in terms of
conversational implicature, in view of the fact that the constituent propositions are not merely true but are known true, and a person who knew that they
were true would be in a position to assert something more informative than
those conditionals. What is relevant to evaluating Lewis's policy of making
□→AB have the truth value of B in any world in which A is true is not
whether A is known to be true but simply whether it **is** true in the given world.
Facts about the use of *Yes* and *No* in answers to questions provide evidence
that sentences like those in 15.1.11 do indeed express true propositions:

15.1.15 a. If London were in England, would the Queen of England live in
        London?
        Yes, and as a matter of fact, London *is* in England.

    b. If London were in England, would the Queen of England live in
        Istanbul?
        No/*Yes—London *is* in England, and the Queen lives in
        London.

    c. If 6 were an even number, would Kathmandu be in Nepal?
        Yes, and of course, 6 *is* an even number.

While it has often been claimed (e.g., by Lakoff 1972a:571) that a counterfactual conditional semantically presupposes the falsehood of its protasis, the
following example (adapted from Anderson 1951) shows that it does not:

15.1.16   If the patient were suffering from yellow fever, he would be
        displaying exactly the symptoms that we have observed.

This sentence can be uttered by a doctor who is attempting to convince his colleagues that the patient has yellow fever (i.e., that the protasis is true) and can perfectly well express a true proposition in states of affairs in which the patient actually is suffering from yellow fever. At first, this may seem to confirm Lewis's policy of making counterfactuals with true protasis and true apodosis true. However, a closer look suggests that Lewis's policy, which makes the truth value of a counterfactual with true protasis depend only on the given world, may be wrong, i.e., that the truth of $\square\!\!\rightarrow$AB in a world w in which A is true might depend not only on w but also on other worlds in which A is true. Suppose, for example, that the patient has an extremely atypical case of yellow fever, in which he is displaying symptoms that yellow fever patients rarely display; my inclination is to say that in that case 15.1.16 expresses a false proposition, in virtue of the fairly unexotic (though not actual) worlds in which the patient has yellow fever but displays quite different symptoms. If that contention is correct, then Lewis's truth conditions make it too easy for $\square\!\!\rightarrow$AB to be true in a world in which A is true: because a set consisting of a single world is a (degenerate) sphere around that world, Lewis's truth conditions mean that in a world in which A is true, no other world will play any role in determining the truth value of $\square\!\!\rightarrow$AB. Here, as in the third and fourth of the above examples, Lewis's truth conditions exclude as counterexamples worlds that are intuitively relevant to the evaluation of the counterfactual but which don't come into the picture because of still closer worlds to w in which A is true.

A fairly natural response to these three objections, and one which preserves the rationale for Lewis's approach, is the one adopted by Nute (1975a, 1975b), in which the relation of local entailment is replaced by what might be called **uniform local entailment,** in which the protasis determines what worlds are "sufficiently close" to w to be rendered "reasonable alternatives to w" by the supposition A, and all of those worlds come into the picture in evaluating the counterfactual. To make this precise, let us introduce a function $\psi(w, A)$ that picks out a sphere around w that is large enough to take in not only some worlds in which A is true but indeed the (possibly fairly large) set of worlds that are worth considering as serious possibilities if A is regarded as a serious possibility. Nute's truth conditions for "If A were the case, B would be the case" then can be given as:

15.1.17   "If A were the case, B would be the case" is true in w if and only if B is true in all worlds w' such that $w' \in \psi(w, A)$ and A is true in w'.

These truth conditions allow one to preserve Lewis's account of the invalidity of the arguments in 15.1.3–4. They also agree with Lewis's in allowing for an infinite sequence of worlds in which A is true that are closer and closer to w but do not converge on a world in which A is true, but they avoid Mac-Kenzie's problem: $\psi(w$, Lewis is over 7′ tall) will contain worlds in which Lewis is over 7′ tall by various amounts, and hence there will be values of ε for which $\psi(w$, Lewis is over 7′ tall) contains worlds in which "Lewis is over 7′ tall" is true and "Lewis is under 7′ + ε tall" is false, and for those values of ε, "If Lewis were over 7′ tall, he would be under 7′ + ε tall" will be false. (It should be noted, though, that ψ depends on context in an indeterminate way, and thus which values of ε make the counterfactual false will also depend on context in an indeterminate way). Nute's truth conditions likewise enable one to assign the value F to 15.1.13, since $\psi(w$, I checked in later) can be taken to include worlds in which the unsold first class seats were assigned as upgrades before I checked in, and they allow one to say that the conclusion of 15.1.8 is false, since $\psi(w$, ~(Mays was elected to the Hall of Fame)) can be taken to be large enough as to include worlds in which he played in the American League as well as worlds in which he didn't.

The problem about the paraphrases of the causative sentences is not a peculiarity of counterfactual conditionals but relates to a characteristic that they share with indicative conditional sentences, namely that they are normally used only when the protasis is temporally and/or causally and/or epistemologically prior to the apodosis, as in the examples discussed in section 3.4 such as

15.1.18 a. If you touch me, I'll scream.
     a′. You'll touch me only if I scream.

The *if*-clause must be temporally/causally/epistemologically prior even if it is modified by *only*. No restriction on the temporal, causal, and epistemological connections between the protasis and apodosis is built into Lewis's 15.1.10, but one might want to admit 15.1.14c′ as it stands as part of an analysis of causation, while supplementing it by some condition on temporal or epistemological priority in a condition (perhaps, a conventional implicature?) on the use of conditionals. I have in fact argued (McCawley 1976a) that the formula 15.1.14c′ corresponding to the implausible counterfactual paraphrase is a more accurate analysis of causal statements than is either the plausible counterfactual paraphrase or the corresponding formula, in that, for example, the truth of 15.1.14a has to do more with the question of how easily George could have avoided death (i.e., with what is the case in the closest worlds in which

~(George died) is true) than with the question of how easily George could have avoided eating the mushrooms. Moreover, the analysis of "A caused B" as $\Box\!\!\rightarrow(\sim A, \sim B)$ has the defect of making "Smith's being black caused him to die" true in cases in which Smith was murdered because of his race, while the analysis of it as $\Box\!\!\rightarrow(\sim B, \sim A)$ lets that sentence be false. I will thus tentatively take the problem raised in connection with 15.1.14 not as an argument against analysing "If A were the case, B would be the case" in terms of $\Box\!\!\rightarrow$ but only as an argument against making $\Box\!\!\rightarrow AB$ be the **whole** analysis.

The problem raised by the counterfactuals that for Lewis are vacuously true is that his approach fails to draw a distinction among sentences that fairly clearly should be distinguished. I will digress at this point into an alternative treatment of counterfactuals that allows one to draw the distinction that Lewis's approach misses and will then comment on the extent to which this alternative approach can be reinterpreted in terms more like those of Lewis's approach. Nicholas Rescher (1964), elaborating ideas developed by Nelson Goodman (1947), proposed that the truth value of "If A were the case, B would be the case" is determined relative to a set M of propositions that a person accepts as true, ranked according to his confidence in them or reluctance to give them up. If $M\cup\{A\}$ is inconsistent (as it usually is in ordinary counterfactual propositions), then a subset M′ of M is found such that (i) $M'\cup\{A\}$ is consistent, (ii) M′ is maximal (i.e., there is no larger subset M″ such that $M''\cup\{A\}$ is consistent), and (iii) M–M′ involves propositions of minimum "confidence level"; that is, if $C_{M'}$ is the proposition in M–M′ that has the highest confidence level, then $C_{M'}$ is of lower confidence level than $C_{M''}$ for any M″ for which $M''\cup\{A\}$ is consistent and M″ is maximal. "If A were the case, B would be the case" is assigned the value T if $M'\cup\{A\} \vdash B$, and is assigned the value F otherwise, where $\vdash$ refers to provability in whatever system of rules of inference is assumed.

Thus, for Rescher, a counterfactual is true if the apodosis is implied by the consistent set of propositions that includes the protasis and is otherwise "closest to" the previously assumed knowledge, in the sense that as few propositions as possible, and propositions of as low a confidence level as possible, have been discarded in constructing the new consistent set. This informal statement is not precise enough to allow one to deal with any but the simplest cases, since it does not make clear how one chooses among different ways that one might delete several propositions so as to achieve consistency (which is worse—giving up one high-confidence proposition and three low-confidence ones or giving up two medium-confidence ones?). The following algorithm will remedy that defect:

15.1.19   Given a set M of propositions ranked in the order $p_1, p_2, p_3, \ldots$
           and given a proposition A, the maximal subset M′ of M
           consistent with A is the limit of the sequence $M_1, M_2, \ldots,$
           where the M_1 are defined as follows:
           (i) If $\{p_1, A\}$ is consistent, then $M_1 = \{p_1\}$; otherwise $M_1 = \emptyset$;
           (ii) for $i > 1$, if $M_{i-1} \cup \{p_1, A\}$ is consistent, then
               $M_i = M_{i-1} \cup \{p_i\}$; otherwise $M_i = M_{i-1}$.

Put more informally, one checks the p_i, starting from the one in which one is
most confident and working downwards; a p_i is retained for inclusion in M′ if
it plus the earlier p's that have not been discarded is consistent with A but is
discarded otherwise. In this scheme, propositions near the top of the confidence ranking will stand a better chance of being retained than will propositions further down, since they have to pass a less stringent test for inclusion in
M′ (i.e., there are fewer propositions that they must be consistent with). For
example, suppose M consists of the propositions $\lor pq$, $\lor(\sim p, r)$, p, q, ranked
in the order given, and that A is $\sim q$. (Note that it is reasonable for disjunctive
propositions to appear at the top of the list; e.g., you will be more certain
that physical space is either Newtonian or Einsteinian than that it is Einsteinian.)[5] M′ will then contain $\lor pq$ (since $\{\lor pq, \sim q\}$ is consistent); it will contain
$\lor(\sim p, r)$ (since $\{\lor pq, \lor(\sim p, r), \sim q\}$ is consistent); and it will contain p (since
$\{\lor pq, \lor(\sim p, r), p, \sim q\}$ is consistent); it will not contain q, since $\sim q$ is inconsistent with any set containing q. Relative to this M, "if $\sim q$ were the case, r
would be the case" is true, since M′ $\cup \{\sim q\} \vdash r$.

Rescher's approach to counterfactuals makes it easier for a counterfactual
to come out false than does Lewis's approach. The set M of "accepted" propositions can be incomplete; that is, there can be propositions such that neither
M $\vdash$ B nor M $\vdash$ $\sim$B, and the deletions needed to obtain M′ may leave
M′ $\cup \{A\}$ even more incomplete than was M, thus making both "if A were the
case, B would be the case" and "if A were the case, $\sim$B would be the case"
false if B is one of the propositions such that neither it nor its negation is
implied by M′ $\cup \{A\}$. For a trivial example of this, note that if M contains no
propositions having a bearing on whether Gilyak has VSO word order, then
both of 15.1.20a–b come out false:

15.1.20 a. If Kennedy hadn't been assassinated, Gilyak would have VSO
            word order.
         b. If Kennedy hadn't been assassinated, Gilyak would not have
            VSO word order.

For Lewis, one of these would generally be true, since the closest worlds to the real world in which Kennedy was not assassinated and Gilyak has the same word order that it really has would presumably be closer to the real world than any worlds in which Kennedy was not assassinated and Gilyak had some other word order; thus, depending on whether Gilyak does or does not really have VSO word order, 15.1.20a or 15.1.20b, respectively, would be true in the real world.

By the same token, Lewis's approach makes it easier for $\Box\!\!\to\!AB$ and $\Box\!\!\to\!(A, \sim\!B)$ to be simultaneously true than does Rescher's: for Rescher, A would have to be self-contradictory, while for Lewis, A would merely have to be true in no world. Thus, if one requires the true propositions of arithmetic to be true in all worlds (thus, to be necessary truths), then both of 15.1.21a–b will be true by Lewis's truth conditions, while at most one would be true for Rescher:

15.1.21 a. If 7 were an even number, 8 would be prime.

        b. If 7 were an even number, 8 would not be prime.

Rescher's approach thus allows for truth distinctions among 15.1.12a–c, which Lewis's treatment makes all true. The propositions one must delete from M to make the remainder consistent with "3 is an even number" will be propositions of arithmetic, and thus $M'\cup\{3$ is an even number$\}$ won't imply that de Gaulle was Chester Alan Arthur's son unless M itself implied it. And while it is easy to find high-confidence propositions that, added to "3 is an even number," would imply that 4 is an odd number (e.g., $4 = 3 + 1$, an even number $+ 1$ is an odd number), it is hard to think of propositions worthy of that degree of confidence that, added to "3 is an even number," would imply that 4 is a multiple of 3.

Still, the Lewis and Rescher approaches are not all that different. While Rescher's approach allows one to cope with *If 3 were an even number* without having to recognize worlds in which 3 is not an even number, it is possible to reinterpret Rescher's approach in terms of a version of Lewis's truth conditions in which the conception of world is broadened and the assumptions about the closeness relation are weakened somewhat. Suppose that we do not require every world to assign a value "true" or "false" to each proposition but allow worlds that assign no truth value to some propositions; specifically, suppose we take a world to correspond not to a valuation but to a supervaluation. Suppose further that we give up assumption 15.1.9a and thus admit the possibility of worlds being incomparable (i.e., the possibility of $Cww'w''$ and $Cww''w'$ both being false). Then any ranked set of propositions M will determine a set of worlds and a closeness relation C among them. For every proposition A, take the world w_A to be the assignment of truth values such that B is true if $M' \cup \{A\} \vdash B$, is false if $M' \cup \{A\} \vdash \sim B$, and is # otherwise, where M' is determined from M and A according to 15.1.19. Define the closeness relation as follows: $Cw_1 w_2 w_3$ if and only if $M_3 \subseteq M_2 \subseteq M_1$, where each w_i corresponds to the set M_i determined from M by deletions as in 15.1.19. A counterfactual will then be true according to Lewis's truth conditions, relative to this system of worlds, if and only if it is true according to Rescher's scheme.

In the worlds of such a system, necessary truths may lack truth values; for example, "$6 = 4 + 2$" might well lack a truth value in a world from which most of one's arithmetic information had been deleted, as in a Rescher treatment of "If 3 were an even number, 4 would be a multiple of 3." This need not be disconcerting. The worlds that one allows for the purpose of analyzing counterfactuals need not be the same worlds that figure in a treatment of epistemic necessity. To each notion of necessity there will correspond a different accessibility relation, and many of the worlds that figure in the analysis of counterfactuals can perfectly well be "inaccessible from the real world" with regard to the accessibility relation for epistemic necessity.

So far, I have been discussing only counterfactuals with *would* such as 15.1.22a and have ignored those with *might* such as 15.1.22b:

15.1.22 a. If Barbara had had an affair with Dan, George would have
divorced her.
b. If Barbara had had an affair with Dan, George might have
divorced her.

Might-counterfactuals have received relatively little attention from those logicians who have written about counterfactuals, but they have not been completely neglected. For example, Lewis (1973:21) proposes an analysis of *might*-counterfactuals in terms of an operator $\Diamond\!\!\rightarrow$ that he takes to have the same truth conditions as $\sim\!\Box\!\!\rightarrow(A, \sim B)$. Let us see how this proposal would deal with a *might*-counterfactual such as 15.1.22b. Suppose that there are three worlds in which Barbara had an affair with Dan that are the same distance from the real world and are closer to it than any other worlds in which she had an affair with him:

Then the truth of 15.1.22a would correspond to George divorcing Barbara in all three of those worlds, while the truth of 15.1.22b would correspond to his divorcing her in at least one of them. But that it would make it too hard for the *might*-counterfactual to be true: one would probably want to say that it was true if there were worlds a little bit further out from w than w_1, w_2, and w_3 in which Barbara had an affair with Dan and George divorced her, just as one might truthfully say *If you'd been convicted, the judge might have sentenced you to 20 years* even if the judge usually gives more lenient sentences but occasionally gives very severe sentences.

Let us then try a second possibility for the truth conditions of *might*-counterfactuals, namely, the proposal in which an existential quantifier appears in place of the universal quantifier of Lewis's truth conditions 15.1.10 for the *would*-counterfactual (given here without the extra clause for the troublesome case in which A is not true in any world):

15.1.23 a. $\square{\rightarrow}AB$ is true in w if and only if there is a world w' such that
              Rww', A is true in w', and for every world w'' such that
              $Cww''w'$ and A is true in w'', B is also true in w''.

        b. $\diamond{\rightarrow}AB$ is true in w if and only if there is a world w' such that
              Rww', A is true in w', and for some world w'' such that
              $Cww''w'$ and A is true in w'', B is also true in w''.

Note that these truth conditions allow one to factor out the contribution of *would* and *might* from a shared schema for the truth conditions of counterfactual conditionals: *would* corresponds to the universal quantifier expression "for every world w''," while *might* corresponds to the existential quantifier expression "for some world w''." This is thus a step in the direction of achieving an analysis of conditionals in terms of a single framework for conditional sentences of all types, which can be combined with an analysis of the indicative/counterfactual distinction and analyses of *would* and *might*. However, this version of the truth conditions would make it much too easy for 15.1.22b to be true: it would be enough that George divorce Barbara in some world in which she had an affair with Dan, regardless of how remote that world was from the real world, since w' can be taken to be any world in which A and B are both true and w'' can be taken to be w'.

Suppose, however, that we attempt to adapt not Lewis's but Nute's truth conditions in an account of *might*-counterfactuals. What we obtain by replacing the universal quantifier by an existential in Nute's truth conditions for *would*-counterfactuals is 15.1.24:

15.1.24   "If A were the case, B might be the case" is true in w if and
             only if B is true in some world w' such that $w' \in \psi(w, A)$ and
             A is true in w'.

It is now neither implausibly difficult (as in Lewis's proposal) nor implausibly easy (as in the revision of Lewis's proposal suggested in 15.1.23b) for *might*-counterfactuals to be true. Since $\psi(w, A)$ normally includes more worlds in which A is true than just the very closest ones to A, 15.1.24 allows 15.1.22b to be true in w even when the closest worlds to w in which Barbara had an affair with Dan and George divorced her are further from w, but not very much further, than the w_1, w_2, and w_3 of the above diagram. However, not just any worlds in which Barbara had an affair with Dan and George divorced her will be enough to make the *might*-counterfactual true: only worlds that belong to $\psi(w,$ Barbara had an affair with Dan) can affect its truth value. In addition, the Nutean analog of Lewis's proposal gives the same truth conditions as 15.1.24: the negation of "If Barbara had had an affair with Dan, George wouldn't have divorced her" will be true if and only if in some worlds of ψ (w, A) in which A is true, ~B isn't true, which is equivalent to 15.1.24, at least if we ignore the possibility of truth-value gaps.[6]

I turn now to counterfactual conditionals in which an element such as *only* or *even* is combined with *if A*:

15.1.25 a. Dukakis would have won only if he had replaced his advisors by competent people.
      b. Dukakis would have lost even if he had replaced his advisors by competent people.

As in the case of indicative conditionals with *only if* or *even if*, I maintain that ordinary *only* or *even* is used with *if S* as its focus and that *only* or *even* makes the same contribution to the meaning of the sentence as it does to a sentence in which it has a NP as its focus. Since the contribution of *only* to the meaning of sentences such as *Only Southerners voted for Humphrey* corresponds (cf. sec. 9.2) to a paraphrase such as *No one but Southerners voted for Humphrey*, the most obvious analysis of 15.1.25 is one according to which it says that in no worlds except ones in which Dukakis replaced his advisors by competent people was Dukakis elected, where the world variable is restricted (as in a simple counterfactual) to those worlds belonging to $\psi(w,$ Dukakis replaced his advisors by competent people):

15.1.26 "B would be the case only if A were the case" is true in w if and only if ~B is true in all worlds w' of $\psi(w, A)$ other than those in which A is true.

There is one problem with this proposal, however, namely that analyses of *only* and *would* that have been proposed here each involve a universal quantifier, but 15.1.26 contains only one universal quantifier, not one each for *only* and for *would*. I maintain that in fact 15.1.25a is ambiguous between an interpretation corresponding to 15.1.26 and a second interpretation in which there are indeed two universal quantifiers, namely one saying that only in a state of affairs in which Dukakis replaced his advisors with competent people was he assured of winning. In the latter interpretation, *would* fits into the logical form in the same way as does the *might* of 15.1.27, which says that only in a state of affairs in which Dukakis replaced his advisors with competent people did he have any chance of winning.

15.1.27   Dukakis might have won only if he had replaced his advisors
            with competent people.

The first interpretation of 15.1.25a is in fact essentially the same as the interpretation of 15.1.27.

    To distinguish among these interpretations, it will be necessary to be more critical in the use of the notion "world" than I have been so far. Hitherto, I have tacitly taken a "world" to be a complete specification of how things might have been throughout the whole of time, past, present, and future. However, the values of the world variable bound by *only* in 15.1.27 and the second interpretation of 15.1.25a specify things only up to an event of Dukakis replacing his advisors by competent people: what happens after that is entirely a matter of the "world variable" bound by *would* or *might,* whose values are different possible continuations of a given value of the first world variable. The sort of state of affairs in which 15.1.27 is true is illustrated in 15.1.28a and the sort in which its analog with *would* is true is illustrated in 15.1.28b, where each line branches at a point at which a decision to replace the advisors was made or could even have been made:

15.1.28

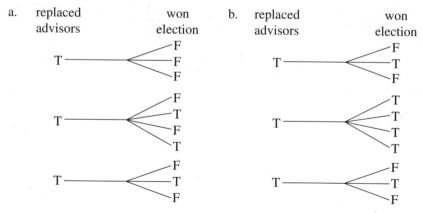

a.   replaced   won   b.   replaced   won
      advisors   election   advisors   election

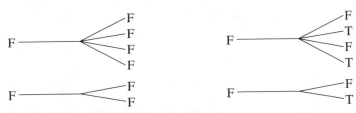

Note that in 15.1.28a, the only worlds having a possible future in which Du-kakis wins are worlds in which he replaced the advisors: in all of the worlds in which he didn't replace the advisors, there is no future in which he wins; in 15.1.28b, each of the worlds has possible futures in which he wins, but only among the worlds in which he replaces the advisors is there one whose futures all have him winning.

This suggestion requires some revision in what we have been assuming so far about worlds and the "reasonable alternative" relation ψ, since we now have to take $\psi(w, A)$ to consist of worlds that are specified only up to an event at which A becomes the case. Adopting the notational devices of $\psi'(w, A)$ to represent the latter conception of ψ and a subscript on a world variable to indicate that it is restricted to continuations of the (incompletely specified) world that corresponds to the subscript, we can sketch the interpretations of 15.1.25a (second interpretation) and 15.1.27 as follows:

15.1.29   In all worlds w' of $\psi'(w, A)$ in which A is not true, it is not true
            that [in all/some worlds $w''_{w'}$ that are continuations of w', B is
            true].

The part of 15.1.29 enclosed in square brackets corresponds to "B would/ might be true," embedded in a frame that corresponds to "only if A." With regard to the first interpretation of 15.1.25a, I conjecture that the single universal quantifier of 15.1.26 serves simultaneously as the universal quantifier encoded in *only* and the one encoded in *would*. Since the (completely specified) worlds in which Dukakis replaced his advisors with competent people are precisely the continuations of worlds that are specified only up to an event of Dukakis replacing his advisors with competent people, "Dukakis won" is true in a world of the first set only if it is true in one of the continuations of the incompletely specified world that goes up only to the event of Dukakis replacing the advisors in the former world, and consequently the interpretation of 15.1.25a given in 15.1.26 amounts to that of 15.1.27.

The analysis of *would . . . only if* sketched here brings out an important difference among three kinds of counterfactual sentences (15.1.30) whose indicative analogs (as in 15.1.31) are often claimed to be equivalent:

15.1.30 a.   Dukakis would have won only if he had replaced his advisors by competent people.
     b.   If Dukakis had won, he would have replaced advisors by competent people.
     c.   Dukakis wouldn't have won if he hadn't replaced his advisors by competent people.
    c'.   Dukakis wouldn't have won unless he had replaced his advisors by competent people.

15.1.31 a.   My pulse goes over 100 only if I do heavy exercise.
     b.   If my pulse goes over 100, I do heavy exercise.
     c.   My pulse doesn't go over 100 if I don't do heavy exercise.
    c'.   My pulse doesn't go over 100 unless I do heavy exercise.

I argued in section 3.4 that 15.1.31c is a fairly good paraphrase of 15.1.31a and that 15.1.31b, which ought also to be a good paraphrase of it according to the treatment of *only if* that is adopted in most introductory logic texts, is indeed hopelessly inaccurate as a paraphrase of it because it reverses the temporal and causal connections between the component propositions. There is equally little of a paraphrase relation between 15.1.30b and 15.1.30a, but here, interestingly, the analog to the apparently good paraphrase in the indicative case is not at all a good paraphrase of 15.1.30a, though its counterpart with *unless*, 15.1.30c', appears to be a perfect paraphrase of 15.1.30a. Note that the world variable that the above analysis of *would . . . only if* posits would take its values from three quite distinct domains in 15.1.32a–c, namely:

15.1.32 a. $\psi(w, A)$ (where A = Dukakis replaced his advisors by competent people)
     b. $\psi(w, B)$ (where B = Dukakis was elected)
     c. $\psi(w, \sim A)$

In most cases, no two of these sets will be identical, and the discrepancies between them will be enough to allow a world that belongs to one of the sets but not to another to falsify one but not the other of the corresponding sentences. For example, $\psi(w, A)$ and $\psi(w, \sim A)$ are generally distinct, because a smaller sphere will be needed to accommodate all the worlds that are made worthy of consideration by whichever of A and $\sim A$ is true in w. The above analysis, in conjunction with Geis's (1973) analysis of *unless* as *except if* (see section 15.2 for arguments in favor of Geis's analysis and against the widely but uncritically accepted analysis of it as *if not*), explains why this should be the case: the world variable for 15.1.30c' will take its values from $\psi(w, A)$, not from $\psi(w, \sim A)$, and the analyses of both 15.1.30a and 15.1.30c' amount to "$\sim B$ in all worlds of $\psi(w, A)$ other than those in which A."

The obvious candidate for truth conditions for *would . . . even if* counterfactuals such as 15.1.33a is 15.1.33b:

15.1.33 a. Dukakis would have lost even if the Republicans had nominated
                Haig.
           b. "B would be the case even if A were the case" is true in *w* if and
                only if for every world *w'* in $\psi(w, A)$, even those in which A
                is true, B is true in *w'*.

As Lycan (1984) has pointed out, asserting an *even if* conditional is not quite the same thing as simply asserting its apodosis, in that the protasis limits the class of worlds that come into the picture. Note that the role that the protasis plays in 15.1.33b is in specifying how large a class of worlds the apodosis must be true in for the conditional to be true. Thus, the reason that 15.3.33a and 15.3.34 might differ in truth value is that $\psi(w,$ the Republicans nominated Manson) is a much larger sphere than $\psi(w,$ the Republicans nominated Haig) and thus "Dukakis lost" has to be true in a much larger class of worlds for 15.1.34 to be true than for 15.1.33a to be true:

15.1.34   Dukakis would have lost even if the Republicans had nominated
                Charles Manson.

The analysis of *might even if* counterfactuals such as 15.1.35 is somewhat less obvious:

15.1.35   Bush might lose the election even if Gephart were his opponent.

The closest analog to 15.1.33b is 15.1.36, in which the parenthetical interpolation in 15.1.33b, which has no coherent direct analog, is simply left out:

15.1.36   "B might be the case even if A were the case" is true in *w* if and
                only if for some world *w'* in $\psi(w, A)$, B is true in *w'*.

But as it stands, 15.1.36 misrepresents the truth conditions of *might even if* counterfactuals: it would allow 15.1.35 to be true by virtue of Bush losing in a very close world in which not Gephart but someone else is his opponent, whereas the truth of 15.1.35 clearly hinges on the existence of a world in $\psi(w,$ Gephart is Bush's opponent) in which Bush loses and Gephart is his opponent. The best I can suggest as a way of localizing the difference between *might even if* and *would even if* in something that matches *might* or *would* is to put a redundant clause into the analysis of *would even if*:

15.1.37 a. "B would be the case even if A were the case" is true in w if and only if for every world w' in $\psi(w, A)$, including worlds in which A is true, B is true.

   b. "B might be the case even if A were the case" is true in w if and only if for some worlds w' in $\psi(w, A)$, including worlds in which A is true, B is true.

15.2. Indicative Conditionals

In section 15.1, I sketched analyses of counterfactual conditionals in terms of possible worlds, with *would*-counterfactuals being true if all worlds of some set that make the protasis true also make the apodosis true, and *might*-counterfactuals being true if some worlds of some set that make the protasis true also make the apodosis true. I also indicated the desire to develop an analysis of conditional sentences in general that would be applicable to indicative as well as to counterfactual conditionals. In this section I will endeavor to treat indicative conditionals in a way that can plausibly be integrated with the above sort of analysis of counterfactuals.

The most plausible way to broaden the analysis of counterfactuals into one that will also cover indicative conditionals is probably to treat the truth value of indicative conditionals as likewise being determined by the truth value of the apodosis in the worlds of some set that make the protasis true, but to have the relevant set of worlds be different from what it was in the case of counterfactuals, e.g., to determine whether 15.2.1a is true, we have to look at worlds differing from the real world with regard to whether Oswald was Kennedy's assassin, whereas to determine whether 15.2.1b is true, we have to look at worlds that, for all we know, may be the real world:

15.2.1   a. If Oswald hadn't killed Kennedy, then somebody else would have.
   b. If Oswald didn't kill Kennedy, then somebody else did.

Specifically, we might make use of a notion of "epistemically possible world" and adopt the truth conditions 15.2.2:

15.2.2   "If A, then B" is true in w if and only if B is true in all worlds w' such that w' is epistemically possible relative to w and A is true in w'.

For convenience, let us introduce the symbol $>$ for a 2-place connective having the truth conditions defined by 15.2.2. With the true conditions 15.2.2 for $>$, the analogs to infamous inferences from $\sim \supset AB$ to A and to $\sim B$ are unsound, because for >AB to be false in *w* it is necessary only that A be true and B not true in some epistemically possible world, not necessarily in *w* itself. So, for example, if the only epistemically possible worlds are *w*, in which A is false and B true, and *w'*, in which A is true and B false, ~>AB is true in *w*, but A and ~B are both false in *w*. It is in fact easy to see that 15.2.2 makes > non–truth-functional in all three of the cases in which the classical truth table makes ⊃AB true. Specifically, no matter what the truth values of A and B are in the given world, if there is an epistemically possible world in which A is true and B false, >AB is false. Thus, > has the following truth table:

15.2.3

A	B	>AB
T	T	T/F
T	F	F
F	T	T/F
F	F	T/F

The classical truth table for ⊃ is the degenerate case of 15.2.2 that one obtains by allowing only the actual world to count as "epistemically possible."

Quite a lot of the inferences with ⊃ that are sound according to the classical truth table have analogs with > that are sound according to 15.2.2, for example:

15.2.4   a. >AB   b. >AB
             >BC   Therefore, >(∧AC, B)
             Therefore, >AC

Note the important difference between 15.2.2 and 15.1.10 or 15.1.17 that allows these inferences to be sound while their (*would*-)counterfactual analogs are not: all epistemically possible worlds are on a par with one another in 15.2.2, whereas both Lewis's and Nute's approaches to counterfactuals presuppose a relation of relative closeness among worlds and allow the protasis to determine how close to the given world the worlds are that come into the assignment of a truth value to the conditional. Thus, 15.2.3 does not allow >AB and >BC to refer to nonoverlapping sets of worlds, the way that 15.1.10 allowed □→AB and □→BC to.

There is in fact some doubt as to the validity of Strengthening the Protasis (15.2.4b) for indicative conditionals. George Lakoff (personal communication) has suggested 15.2.5 as a possible invalid instance of it:

15.2.5   If they went to Jamaica over the Christmas break, they had a
             relaxing holiday.

> Therefore, if they went to Jamaica and to Hawaii over the
> Christmas break, they had a relaxing holiday.

As most easily interpreted, the premise of 15.2.5 would not guarantee the truth of the conclusion: it would be taken as referring to holidays in Jamaica that did not involve extraneous diversions like a side trip to Hawaii. There are several possible responses to this example. One is to say (as Braine 1978 does) that the premise of 15.2.5 simply reflects a sloppy use of *if:* it's the sort of thing that a person says when he fails to take into account the full range of ways in which it might be true that they went to Jamaica over the Christmas break. A second response would be to treat epistemic possibility the way that Lewis treated counterfactual possibility, namely, as coming in degrees, with the truth conditions of $>$ reflecting the degrees of epistemic possibility, i.e., one might take $>AB$ to be true when B is true in (as in Lewis's treatment of counterfactuals) the most epistemically possible worlds in which A is true or (as in Nute's treatment) all possible worlds in which A is true that are sufficiently epistemically possible. A third possible response would likewise recognize degrees of epistemic possibility but would treat the degrees of possibility as in the realm of pragmatics: in asserting an indicative conditional proposition, one is implicitly setting some threshold for what he will regard as an epistemically possible world, and the "sloppy" and "strict" understandings of *if* that are contrasted in the first response merely correspond to two different settings of the threshold for epistemic possibility, neither being any more virtuous than the other. This threshold would be one of the components of the "conversational score," in the sense of Lewis 1979. The fault with 15.2.5 would then consist in a tacit changing of the score in mid-argument: the threshold would have to be set relatively high if the premise is to be true, but it would have to be set much lower in order for the conclusion to be non-vacuous, that is, for it to take in at least some worlds in which its protasis is true. The second response would make transitivity for indicative conditionals simply invalid, while the third would treat it as valid and would interpret the apparent cases of invalidity as rather suffering from a pragmatic defect.

Whether contraposition is sound according to 15.2.2 depends on a detail that I have so far kept out of the discussion, namely, whether truth-value gaps are admitted. Suppose that $>AB$ is true in w. To see whether $>(\sim B, \sim A)$ then also has to be true, we need to see whether in all epistemically possible worlds in which $\sim B$ is true, $\sim A$ is also. Suppose $\sim B$ is true in an epistemically possible world w'. It is not possible for A to be true in w', because if it were, then B would be true in w' (that's what it means to say that $>AB$ is true in w), which would conflict with the supposition that $\sim B$ is true in w'. If there aren't any truth value gaps, then that means that ~A is true in w', and thus contraposition is sound; however, if truth value gaps are possible, then "A is not true in w" does not guarantee that ~A is true in w', and consequently the truth of $>AB$ in w does not guarantee the truth of $>(\sim B, \sim A)$.

Even when truth-value gaps are not admitted, certain cases of contraposition of indicative conditionals can be argued to have the same pragmatic defect as 15.2.5, provided one accepts the "conversational score" account of the latter's oddity. It is in fact not as easy to come up with examples where Contraposition would involve a surreptitious change of score as it is in the case of Strengthening the Protasis, since admitting a sufficiently broad class of epistemically possible worlds as to make $>AB$ both true and a cooperative thing to assert does not generally make $>(\sim B, \sim A)$ an uncooperative thing to say, i.e., it does not generally exclude epistemically possible worlds in which ~B is true. However, there is in fact one clear case of that type, namely that in which the truth and cooperativity of A would require that there be no epistemically possible worlds in which ~B is true, e.g.,

15.2.6   a.   If she wrote a letter to Santa Claus, she didn't get an answer
              from him.
              ??Therefore, if she got an answer from Santa Claus, she didn't
              write a letter to him.
        b.   If he said anything, he said things we can ignore.
              ??If he didn't say things we can ignore, he didn't say anything.

The premise of 15.2.6a would normally be uttered relative to a context containing the proposition that there is no Santa Claus, and thus there would be no epistemically possible worlds in which she got an answer from him; however, the conclusion would be a cooperative thing to say only relative to a "score" in which worlds in which there is a Santa Claus are admitted as epistemically possible, i.e., in going from the premise to the conclusion, the class of epistemically possible worlds would have surreptitiously been broadened to one relative to which the premise would be false.

Some possible counterexamples to the validity of Transitivity for indicative conditionals have been adduced, such as the following (discussed by Jackson 1987:83):

15.2.7   If it rained, it didn't rain hard.
            If it rained hard, it rained.
            Therefore, if it rained hard, it didn't rain hard.

The first premise of 15.2.7 is something that one would be entitled to assert in certain common circumstances (such as, that there are no puddles or other signs of a recent heavy rain); the second premise is a necessary truth; but the conclusion would always be a bizarre thing to say. There are several ways in which one might respond to 15.2.7. A defender of the classical truth table for ⊃ might say that 15.2.7 is actually a valid argument: the first premise is simply a roundabout way of saying that it didn't rain hard, and if it didn't rain hard, the conclusion is true according to the classical truth table, since the apodosis is true. An adherent of 15.2.2 might say that an indicative conditional sentence conversationally implicates that there are epistemically possible worlds in which its protasis is true, since if there are no such worlds, the conditional becomes vacuous; but then the second premise conversationally implicates something that the first premise says is not the case: the first premise (in virtue of the fact that worlds in which it rained hard are worlds in which it rained) says that there aren't any epistemically possible worlds in which it rained hard. A third response is one that agrees with the content of the second but takes the perspective of Lewis's conversational scorekeeping. For the first premise to be true, the score has to have been set so that no worlds in which it rained hard count as epistemically possible. But indicative conditionals can be asserted cooperatively only when the score is such that there are epistemically possible worlds in which the protasis is true; thus the second premise can be asserted only relative to a score that would make the first premise false. The appearance of invalidity in 15.2.6 results from the fact that such a stretch of discourse would require a midstream change of score that would suffice to make the first premise false.

The truth conditions for >AB proposed in 15.2.2 allow indicative *only if* and *even if* conditionals to be treated the way that their counterfactual counterparts were treated in section 15.1. Thus, 15.2.8a will be true if Susan will forgive you only in those epistemically possible worlds in which you admit that you were wrong, i.e., she won't forgive you in any epistemically possible worlds other than one in which you admit that you were wrong; likewise, 15.2.8b will be true if you don't go to a movie in any epistemically possible world other than one in which it got good reviews.

15.2.8   a. Only if you admit you were wrong will Susan forgive you.
          b. I go to movies only if they've gotten good reviews.

An *even if* indicative conditional is not simply equivalent to its apodosis, since its *if*-clause indicates how broad a class of worlds the speaker is treating as "epistemically possible" in his assertion that the apodosis is true in all of those worlds:

15.2.9   a. Even if you admit you were wrong, Susan won't forgive you.
        b. I go to see Clint Eastwood films even if they've gotten lousy reviews.

The truth conditions have the consequence (an unwelcome one in view of what was said in section 3.4) that "if p, q" and "p only if q" have the same truth conditions: what it takes for either of them to be true is that there be no epistemically possible worlds in which p is true and q not true.

A conditional "p only if q" can always be paraphrased accurately as "not p unless q", and sometimes but not always as "not p if not q":

15.2.10 a.   Susan will forgive you only if you admit you were wrong.
       a'.   Susan won't forgive you unless you admit you were wrong.
       a".   Susan won't forgive you if you don't admit you were wrong.
       b.   I'll excuse you from the exam only if your mother is on her deathbed.
       b'.   I won't excuse you from the exam unless your mother is on her deathbed.
       b".   ?I won't excuse you from the exam if your mother isn't on her deathbed.

While the two *only if* conditionals (15.2.10a, b) are accurately paraphrased by *not . . . unless* sentences (15.2.10a', b'), the paraphrase with *not . . . if not* is much more plausible for 15.2.10a than for 15.2.10b.

One difference between 15.2.10b" and 15.2.10b–b' is particularly worth noting: 15.2.10b" presupposes that the addressee has a (living) mother, while 15.2.10b–b' do not, i.e., 15.2.10b–b' could be addressed felicitously to a malingering student by a professor who has no idea of whether the student's mother is alive, but 15.2.10b" could not. Suppose that we go beyond the notion of possible world that we have assumed so far in chapters 11–15, according to which in each world every proposition is either true or false and the assignments of truth values conform to the classical truth tables, and admit truth-value gaps, in particular, take *your mother is/isn't on her deathbed* to be # if the addressee does not have a living mother. According to the truth conditions given above, an *only if* conditional can be true even if its protasis is #: what it takes for "p only if q" to be true is merely that p not be true in any epistemically possible worlds in which q is not true, i.e., in any epistemically possible worlds in which q is either false or #; thus, one can admit worlds in which q is # as epistemically possible without preventing "p only if q" from being true. By contrast, for 15.2.10b", the relevant epistemically possible worlds are worlds in which *your mother isn't on her deathbed* is true, which excludes worlds in which it is #.

Geis (1973) has developed an analysis of *unless* that fits the observations about 15.2.10 well. According to Geis, *unless* does not mean what logicians usually say that it means (namely, *if . . . not*) but rather *except if,* i.e., "*p* unless *q*" is true if *p* is true in all epistemically possible worlds except those in which *q* is true. Note that this makes "*p* unless *q*" stronger than "*p* if not *q*": for "*p* if not *q*" to be true, all that is required is that *p* be true in all epistemically possible worlds in which *not q* is true, whereas for "*p* unless *q*" to be true, *p* has to be true not only in those worlds but also in any others in which *q* is not true, thus also in those in which *q* is #, which are irrelevant to the truth of "*p* if not *q*." Thus, on Geis's analysis, "*p* unless *q*" implies "*p* if not *q*", **but not vice versa**. The cases in which "*p* if not *q*" seems to be a good paraphrase of "*p* unless *q*" all are cases in which the only way for *q* to fail to be true is for it to be false.

Geis in fact notes a large number of discrepancies between *unless* and *if . . . not,* and his approach explains why *unless* and *if . . . not* differ in the ways in which they do. For example, while the *not* of *if . . . not* behaves like any other negative element syntactically and semantically, *unless* does not exhibit the behavior that characterizes negative elements, such as supporting negative polarity items:

15.2.11 a.   You should complain if John doesn't give you a red cent.
        a′. *You should complain unless John gives you a red cent.
        b.   Mary will be happy if John doesn't drink a drop at the party.
        b′. *Mary will be happy unless John drinks a drop at the party.
        c.   Al will be disappointed if his blind date isn't all that pretty.
        c′. *Al will be disappointed unless his blind date is all that pretty.

Geis analyses *unless* as "except if" (or equivalently, "in worlds other than those in which"), and *except* and *other* likewise do not support negative polarity items:

15.2.12 a.   *I'll pay him any amount except a red cent.
        b.   *I'll give him anything other than a red cent.

Since, on Geis's analysis, *unless* does not contribute any syntactically negative element to the logical form of the sentence, it should not support negative polarity items, and in fact it does not.[7]

Another difference is that while sentences with *only if . . . not* generally sound normal, corresponding sentences with *only unless* sound thoroughly bizarre:

15.2.13 a. I'll put up with him only if he doesn't make unreasonable
    demands.
  a'. *I'll put up with him only unless he makes unreasonable
    demands.

If *unless* simply meant "if not," there would be no reason by 15.2.13a' should sound any less normal than 15.2.13a. Under Geis's proposal, 15.2.13a' would mean "I'll put up with him only except if he makes unreasonable demands," and one can maintain that "only except" is incoherent (cf. the bizarreness of such a sentence as *Sam works out at the gym only except on Tuesdays*) and that its incoherence is responsible for the bizarreness of 15.2.13a'.

 I turn finally to a much-discussed example that raises some doubt as to whether "epistemically possible" worlds is the right class of worlds to provide the values of the world variable in an analysis of indicative conditionals. Gibbard (1981) considers a poker game on a Mississippi riverboat, in which the sportsmanly Mr. Thomas Stone is playing against the dishonest Sly Pete. Stone, sensing correctly that one of the bystanders is secretly signaling the contents of Stone's hand to Pete, has the room cleared of everyone but himself and Pete. Outside the room, two of the bystanders make the following statements:

15.2.14 a. Al: If Pete called, he won.
  b. Bert: If Pete called, he lost.

Al does not know what cards the two players had in their hands: he bases his statement on his knowledge that Pete knows what cards Mr. Stone has and will not call unless he knows that his hand will win. Bert knows the contents of the two hands and thus can infer (from that knowledge plus the fact that three of a kind beats two pair) that Pete held a losing hand. Suppose that these two statements occur during a conversation among Al, Bert, and a third person who could not see what cards the players had and was unaware of Pete's dishonest tricks. The set of worlds that are epistemically possible relative to the mutual knowledge of these participants is then too broad to make either of the two conditionals true. Perhaps the best thing to say at this point is that in this case, both Al and Bert's statements were attempts to change the conversational score: to narrow the class of epistemically possible worlds to a set that is consistent with the speaker's knowledge and will make the corresponding conditional sentences true.

Exercises

1. a. Determine whether $\square\supset AB$ entails $\square\!\!\rightarrow\!AB$ according to Lewis's truth conditions.

b. Determine whether $\square\!\!\rightarrow\!AB$ entails $\square\supset AB$ according to Lewis's truth conditions.

c. Redo parts *a* and *b* using Nute's truth conditions instead of Lewis's.

2. For each of the following formulas, determine whether it is "valid" (i.e., true in all worlds, irrespective of what A, B, and C are) according to the Lewis semantics:

a. $\square\!\!\rightarrow\!(A, \square\!\!\rightarrow\!BA)$
b. $\supset(\square\!\!\rightarrow\!AB, \square\!\!\rightarrow\!(\wedge AB, \wedge AC))$

3. Assume the following set of beliefs, given in decreasing order of degree of confidence:

$$M = \{\vee pqr, \supset(\vee pq, \sim r), q, \sim r\}.$$

a. Using Rescher's procedure, construct the M' corresponding to a protasis $\sim q$.

b. Find one formula B for which "If $\sim q$ were the case, B would be the case" is true according to Rescher's truth conditions (other than such trivial ones as B $= \sim q$), and another for which it is false.

c. Construct English sentences corresponding to p, q, r that would make M a plausible ranking of beliefs.

4. For each of the following indicative conditional sentence forms, determine whether it is valid according to the truth conditions proposed in section 15.2:

a. If A, then (if B, A).
b. A only if (B only if A).

5. According to the classical truth table for $\supset$, the following sentence expresses a false proposition on Wednesday and a true proposition any other day of the week:

If today is Wednesday, today is Monday.

Determine for the various days of the week what its truth value is relative to the truth conditions of section 15.2, assuming that the set of epistemically possible worlds is taken to be large enough to make the sentence say something nonvacuous.

6. Can Rescher's semantics be revised to make it more like Nute's truth conditions than like Lewis's?

7. For each of the following formulas, determine whether it is valid according to the truth conditions given in 15.2.2:

   a. >(A, >BA)
   b. ∨(>AB, >(A, ~B))

Notes

Prefaces

1. I presume that reprints of earlier volumes of *Who's Who* appear under the title *Who Was Who*.

2. The chapter numbers in this sentence refer to the first edition. Otherwise, citations of chapter and section numbers in this preface have been changed to reflect the organization of the second edition. The material presented in this edition is more than will fit comfortably into a two-quarter sequence; if one wishes to cover the whole book at a not overly hectic pace, one would probably require a two-semester or three-quarter sequence of courses.

3. The recognition of such a borderline class of cases is an important feature of the 1973 Roe vs. Wade decision of the United States Supreme Court, which gave the category "human being" an appropriately fuzzy status: the Court's ruling treats a fetus up to three months from conception as having no legal status as a human being, a fetus six months or more from conception as being enough of a human being to have limited legal status as a human being, and fetuses between three and six months from conception as having an inherently unclear status that is open to arbitrary stipulations by decisions of particular state legislatures.

Chapter 1

1. According to its etymology, *ambiguous* should mean "having two interpretations." However, I will follow the general practice among linguists of using it in the sense "having more than one interpretation," since it is the latter sense that a word is needed for. There are few occasions when it is of any importance whether the number of interpretations is exactly two but many when it is important whether it is more than one.

2. Zwicky and Sadock 1975 give an excellent and thorough survey of tests for ambiguity.

3. When there is no auxiliary verb in the clause affected by V'-deletion, a semantically empty *do* is inserted to serve as bearer of the tense marker (here the *-s* of *believes* and *does*). Insertion of *do* is a general concomitant to grammatical phenomena that would otherwise leave an unattached tense marker (Chomsky 1957).

559

4. Strictly speaking, what is deleted by the process illustrated in 1.3.5 is not a noun but what linguists commonly call an N'—a unit consisting of a noun plus whatever "objects" it may have (as with *portrait of Napoleon* in 1.3.5a) or (since modifiers yield expressions of the same category as the modified expression) such an expression plus modifiers:

John owns four <u>expensive Italian sweaters</u> and Mary owns five.

The rationale for symbols such as N' and V', in which the letters N and V indicate the part of speech of the "head" of the expression (noun vs. verb, respectively) and the prime indicates "phrasal unit," will be explained in §1.5.

5. I assume here that the *one* that appears in 1.3.6 is a strong form of the indefinite article *a:* deletion of *bastard* from *a bastard* yields *a,* and *a* is pronounced *one* when it stands alone. This use of *one* should not be confused (though it usually is) with the *one* that replaces an N', as in *Maxine wore an old sweater and Frieda wore a new <u>one</u>.*

6. I ignore here the jocular use of sentences like 1.3.8c in which one adds something such as *one of each kind.* That usage requires that one add some such continuation that makes one's jocular intent explicit.

7. This test for ambiguity is discussed by Quine (1960:131).

8. For further discussion of the "autohyponymy" of words such as *Yankee,* see Horn 1984.

9. It should be noted, however, that in many cases a conjoined structure will be unambiguously one or the other. There are heavy restrictions on the occurrence of the "consecutive" interpretation. For example, the use of *respectively* forces a "symmetric" interpretation on the coordinate structure:

    i. Rocky fired at the guard and Creepy fired at the detective.
    ii. Rocky and Creepy fired at the guard and the detective respectively.

While (i) can be given either a "symmetric" or a "consecutive" interpretation, (ii) is open only to the "symmetric" interpretation, which is noncommittal regarding the temporal order of the two shots. For a detailed and well worked out argument that *and* has both symmetric and asymmetric senses, see Schmerling 1975.

10. The consensus to which I refer relates to the **kind** of information that characterizes a syntactic structure, not to the specific information that is in fact embodied in 1.5.1; there is in fact wild disagreement among linguists over, for example, what syntactic categories play a role in natural-language syntactic structure.

11. Here one of the few differences between the two constructions appears: *as* + Adjective precedes the indefinite article *a/an,* whereas *more/-er* + Adjective occupies the normal adjective position after the article. Except for this detail, though, 1.5.2b and 1.5.2b' are syntactically identical.

12. The ?? that appears at the beginning of 1.5.3b' is one of a number of **stigmata** that are used to mark examples as deviant in some way from fully normal language. The different stigmata represent in an impressionistic way the relative degree of devi-

ance or unacceptability of the example, ranging from ? for slight oddity, through ?? and ?*, to * and even ** for examples that are highly deviant.

13. I regard *as* as a preposition and thus take the combination of *as* and its "object" to be a prepositional phrase (P'). It should be emphasized that a rule excluding an *as as* combination does not warrant the deletion of one of the *as*'s; while deleting one of them happens in fact to yield an acceptable sentence (*You can earn as much money as a lawyer as a linguist*), that sentence is acceptable only with a syntactic analysis and a meaning different from those that are at issue here.

14. I have oversimplified considerably here. S, NP, and Det do not correspond exactly to the logical categories "proposition," "argument of predicate," and "quantifier" but are rather **fuzzy categories** whose core members belong to the given logical category and have the external and internal syntax that is most typical of expressions of that logical category; the periphery of the category consists of expressions that meet some but not all of these criteria for membership in the core. Thus, the category NP has a core consisting of those expressions that function logically as arguments of predicates, consist of article or quantifier + N', and appear in one of the standard syntactic positions for arguments of predicates. The periphery takes in the clausal NP of 1.5.7b, which is a NP with regard to logical category and external syntax but not with regard to internal syntax, and the predicate NP of *John is a lawyer*, which is a NP with regard to internal syntax and external syntax but not with regard to logical category (it functions logically as a predicate and not as an argument of a predicate).

15. This is one of several points on which the conception of categories adopted here deviates from the "X-bar" conception of categories found in such works as Chomsky (1970, 1981, 1986) and Jackendoff (1977), in which categories such as N″, N‴, etc., occur and addition of a modifier is supposed to yield a category one level higher (thus, A″ where I have the upper A' in 1.5.1). A second and more important difference is that in Chomsky's conception of categories, the category of any syntactic unit must remain constant throughout a syntactic derivation, so that, for example, a P' in surface syntactic structure must correspond to a P' in all levels of underlying syntactic structure. By contrast, in the approach adopted here, categories can change in the course of a derivation to the extent that the factors that define category membership can change; thus, if the P in the surface structure of *a man with a mustache* corresponds to an underlying V (as in the plausible analysis that derives this use of *with* from an underlying relative clause such as *who has a mustache*), then there is a surface P' where the underlying structure has a V', simply because that is what P' and V' mean: phrasal unit whose head is (respectively) P or V.

Chapter 2

1. The use of the terms "syntax" and "semantics" by logicians deviates considerably from linguists' use of the terms. For a linguist, "semantics" has to do with meaning rather than with truth conditions and includes at least the study of what meanings are

possible (which corresponds roughly to the logicians' formation rules, which are part of the logicians' "syntax" rather than their "semantics"). The study of the relationship between sentences and their meanings is often referred to by linguists as "semantics," though it could equally well be called syntax; the stratificational grammarians' term "semolexemics" has the advantage of avoiding an arbitrary extension of the terms "syntax" and "semantics," though it has no currency except among stratificational grammarians.

2. I am begging one important question here by assuming that all the ways of constructing complex propositions out of the three atomic propositions yield results that should be regarded as different from one another. It is not at all obvious, though, that p *and* q is a different proposition from q *and* p or that p *and* $(q$ *and* $p)$ is a different proposition from p *and* q.

The role of parentheses in the notation employed here will be clarified later in this section. I regard parentheses, like spaces between words, as not, strictly speaking, being parts of the expressions in which they appear but as a typographical convenience for conveying details of the structures of these expressions.

3. While the two formats for giving logical structures are interchangeable, there often are practical reasons for choosing one over the other. The tree diagram format of 2.2.2b makes it easier to see how the various parts of the structure fit together; thus, in constructing the logical form of a sentence (as one is asked to do in many of the exercises in this book), one usually has an easier time and is less liable to make errors if one uses the diagram format. The "parenthesized formula" format of 2.2.2a has the advantages of being much easier to typeset and of taking up much less space; the latter advantage dictates the use of the parenthesized formula format in formal proofs such as are given in 2.5 and subsequent sections, where it is much easier to see the structure of the whole proof if the various "lines" of the proof take the typographical form of single lines of type rather than diagrams.

4. The idea that quantifiers and other "determiners" are the syntactic heads of NPs was proposed by Hudson (1976) and has subsequently received wide acceptance in the "government and binding" (GB) approach to syntax (Abney 1987, Tateishi 1989).

5. In 2.2.9 and 2.2.10 we see two of the three main ways in which the arguments of a predicate can be distinguished from one another: in terms of linear order and in terms of constituent structure. The third way is by recognizing different "grammatical relations" between each argument and the predicate, as in relational grammar (Perlmutter 1982) and 2500 years earlier in the approach of the Sanskrit grammarian Panini (see Kiparsky and Staal 1969).

I have also introduced in 2.2.9 a notational practice that will recur throughout the remainder of this book, that of representing predicates and other elements of logical structure by a capitalized version of a corresponding English word: "Admire" here represents a two-place predicate that corresponds to (the assumed sense of) the English word *admire*. The choice of "Admire" as a name for this predicate is made solely for the convenience of English-reading users of this book and should not be accorded any significance.

The use of such names should likewise not be taken as implying that the corresponding English words are semantically atomic or as precluding the analysis of their meanings into semantically simpler units. For the purposes of this book, I will leave completely open the question of the extent to which the vocabulary of all languages can be analyzed in terms of a universal system of semantic units; see Wierzbicka (1980) for an impressive case that such a system of semantic primitives can be identified and Wierzbicka (1985) for a detailed analysis of the meanings of a large and important class of English verbs in terms of a putatively universal system of semantic units.

6. Interestingly, as Horn (1972) notes, *each* does not allow *almost: *Almost each student took a different examination.*

7. For further discussion of *any*, see Horn 1972, LeGrand 1975, and Carlson 1981.

8. There is one respect, however, in which *everyone, everything*, etc., behave like expressions with *every* and unlike expressions with *all*, namely, that they readily allow an interpretation in which the values of the bound variable are restricted to a contextually salient set:

$$\left.\begin{array}{l} \text{Everyone} \\ \text{Every guest} \\ \text{*All guests} \end{array}\right\} \text{ arrived between 8:00 and 8:15.}$$

9. Not all uses of *a/an* correspond to an existential quantifier. While (i) can be analyzed as indicated, (ii) allows no plausible analysis involving an existential quantifier:

    i. John insulted a policeman. $(\exists: x \text{ Policeman})_x(j \text{ insulted } x)$

    ii. A beaver builds dams.

In (ii) we have a generic construction, expressing the proposition that building dams is typical of beavers, not that there is a beaver who builds dams.

Predicate NPs, as in (iii) present a less clear case; I will argue that (iii) should be analyzed with the noun as a predicate and the article making no contribution to logical structure (iii') rather than as in the widely accepted proposal (e.g., Montague 1974:267) that such sentences are existentially quantified statements of equality (iii''):

    iii. John is a policeman.
    iii'. *j* Policeman.
    iii''. $(\exists: x \text{ Policeman})_x(j = x)$

I reject (iii'') in favor of (iii') on, among other things, the grounds that predicate NPs normally do not participate in linguistic phenomena to which identity of reference is relevant. Thus, in (iv) the antecedent of *him* can only be *Sam*, not *a policeman*, as contrasted with (iv'), in which *a policeman* is the antecedent of a pronoun whose use depends on identity of sense rather than of reference, and (iv''), in which a nonpredicate occurrence of *a policeman* may be the antecedent of an "identity of reference" pronoun:

iv. Sam is a policeman. I'm glad I'm not him.
iv'. Sam is a policeman. I'm glad I'm not that.
iv". Sue beat up a policeman. I'm glad I'm not him.

Similarly, sentences such as (v) cannot be treated as identity propositions, since the negation is not the negation of an identity proposition. What (v') says is not that Jack and Ruth's husband are not the same person but rather that Jack does not stand in the husband relation to Ruth:

v.   Jack is Ruth's husband.
v'. Jack isn't Ruth's husband. (They're only living together.)

It does not presuppose that Ruth has a husband. For further discussion of the semantics of predicate NPs, see Doron 1988.

10. Or at least, the result has the same truth conditions as the original if it is coherent, which it is if (as in 2.4.11) each of the Q's involves only one variable. However, the result of interchanging the Q's in the formula $(\forall:Fx)_x(\forall:Kxy)_yLxy$ (e.g., *All voters are disappointed in everyone that they vote for*) would be incoherent and thus the question of its truth conditions would not arise.

11. "More than half" is not completely accurate as a paraphrase of *most*, for reasons that will be made clear in section 7.4, where a more thorough treatment of *most* is given, including discussion of cases in which a paraphrase like "more than half" is implausible, e.g., cases in which a bound variable has infinitely many possible values. The argument that follows is plagiarized from a lecture given by Peter T. Geach at the University of Chicago in 1967.

12. The idea of organizing the rules of inference into introduction rules and exploitation rules was systematized by Frederic Fitch (1952), adapting an approach developed by Gentzen (1969). A system of rules organized in this fashion is called a system of **natural deduction**. I have replaced Fitch's term "elimination" by "exploitation," since "elimination" misleadingly suggests that a premise can be used only once (i.e., that an element in that premise is gone forever once it is "eliminated"), when in fact a given premise can be "exploited" any number of times.

13. For the time being, I will accept uncritically the step in line 9, which goes beyond the rules of inference that are under discussion here. This amounts to enlarging the set of rules of inference by accepting a set of "meaning postulates" for various elements of meaning, e.g., one saying that the father of someone's father is that person's grandfather.

14. Arguments for such an analysis of restrictive relative clauses are given in McCawley (1981a, 1988a). I will content my self with citing just one argument here, namely, that a restrictive relative clause can be the antecedent of a pronoun as in:
Every person who voted for Goldwater is proud of it.
What *it* means here is "that he voted for Goldwater," with *he* corresponding to the variable bound by *every;* thus, the clause that underlies the relative clause under the analysis proposed here is exactly what participates in a type of pronominalization in which (apparently) one of two identical Ss is replaced by a pronoun.

Chapter 3

1. See the list of symbols for some alternative notations that have some currency.

2. In saying this, I am taking the examples 3.1.2 to be pronounced with "neutral stress," *John dóes love his wife,* with contrastive stress on the auxiliary verb, is perfectly normal but is a different sentence from 3.1.2b. Its negation (if it can really be said to have one) is not 3.1.2a but *John dóesn't love his wife.*

3. The word "conjoin" is used in a broader sense by linguists than by logicians: logicians use "conjunction" to refer to the combining of two (or more) propositions with *and* and "disjunction" to refer to the combining of two (or more) propositions with *or*; linguists (and traditional grammarians) have generally used "conjunction" to take in both combination with *and* and combination with *or*. For the sake of convenience, I will adopt the linguist's terminology here and will use "*and*-conjunction" and "*or*-conjunction" where logicians speak of "conjunction" and "disjunction."

4. I assume throughout this book a conception of transformations as rules that associate sentences with corresponding semantic structures; it will be convenient to present transformations in terms of the popular metaphor of processes that convert a semantic structure through successive intermediate stages into a corresponding surface structure (for a more detailed and accurate presentation of this conception of transformation, see McCawley 1988a). The reader should be warned that many diverse conceptions of transformation are found in the linguistic literature, including some (e.g., Chomsky 1976, 1981, 1986) in which underlying structures need not have any direct relationship to semantic structure. (Chomsky briefly held, but has since repudiated, a conception of the deep structure of a sentence as a level of syntactic structure that determined the meaning of the sentence [e.g., Chomsky 1965, 1966]). For discussion of different conceptions of transformation and their relation to meaning, see McCawley 1975a.

Conjunction Reduction is one of several transformations whose application is restricted to coordinate structures. Besides other transformations that "simplify" coordinate structures in various ways, there are also transformations that specify how an underlying coordinating conjunction may be realized. The effects of the latter transformations can be seen in 3.1.6. An underlying *and* or *or* can be realized on one or two or all of the conjuncts: it is obligatorily realized on the last conjunct, and in addition there is the option of realizing it on the first conjunct in the form *both* (for an underlying *and,* but only if there are only two conjuncts) or *either* (for an underlying *or*), and a separate option of realizing it on all of the conjuncts between the first and the last. Both of these options are exercised in the derivations for 3.1.7c–c′, and if either or both of the options were not exercised, the following alternatives to 3.1.7c′ would be derived:

> The poem was written by either Whitman, Tennyson, or e. e. cummings.
> The poem was written by Whitman, or Tennyson, or e. e. cummings.
> The poem was written by Whitman, Tennyson, or e. e. cummings.

5. Sentences in which *and* links repeated expressions not only do not allow deriva-

tions involving Conjunction Reduction but probably should not be regarded as really involving a coordinate structure, for example:

> Alex became more and more ashamed of his past.
> I knocked and knocked on the door.

An insightful discussion of such superficially coordinate structures is given by Knowles 1979. See McCawley 1988a (chap. 9, 16) for elucidation of the notion "coordination" and arguments that syntactic structures that are coordinate on one dimension need not be coordinate on other dimensions.

6. See McCawley 1974, Partee 1974, and Ross 1976 for evidence that sentences such as *Richie wants a Mustang* have an underlying syntactic structure in which *want* has as its direct object a sentence such as *Richie have a Mustang*.

7. For reasons that have never been clear to me, authors employing "Polish notation" have generally avoided the more widely used symbols for the connectives and have instead used K for $\wedge$, A for $\vee$, N for $\sim$, and C for $\supset$.

8. Horn (1989) points out that it is only since the late middle ages that inclusive *or* has been the *or* with which logicians have mainly been concerned. The Stoic logicians (2nd c. B.C.), who did the first detailed work in propositional logic, gave rules of inference that made sense only if *or* was given an exclusive interpretation (e.g., "p or q; p; therefore, not q") and ignored the possibility of giving an inclusive interpretation to (the Greek counterpart of) *or*.

9. Rescher (1969:148–54) notes that the term "law of the included middle" has been used in several nonequivalent senses.

10. I have replaced Thomason's notation by that of this chapter.

11. To my knowledge, the first publication in which arguments are given that *A only if B* and *If A, B* are logically nonequivalent is Sharvy 1979b.

12. In constructing these examples, I have conformed to the alternation between future tense (*will* or *'ll*) in an *if*-clause and present tense in a main clause. Note that under the most normal interpretation of *If the White Sox win the World Series, I'll buy drinks for everyone*, what is at issue is not the proposition expressed by *The White Sox win the World Series* (which is in fact not a normal English sentence) but rather that expressed by *The White Sox will win the World Series*. It is necessary, however, to distinguish between the future sense of *will* and the "consent" sense of *will*. As Palmer (1965:110) has noted, only the future *will* is omitted:

> If he comes tomorrow, I'll give him these books.
> If he'll come tomorrow, I'll give him these books.

13. Jacobs and Rosenbaum (1967) give 3.5.7b not as an example of bizarre conjoining but as their stock example of conjoining. Until such works as R. Lakoff 1971 and Wierzbicka 1972, logicians and linguists had remained oblivious to the oddity of conjoining many of the things that they have merrily conjoined.

In section 11.4 we will take up an approach to logic, namely relevant entailment logic, in which the rule of ∧-introduction is restricted in a way that requires the propositions being conjoined to, in a sense, have a common subject matter.

14. This is an oversimplification, since there are additional restrictions on the occurrence of negative polarity items; for example, a negative polarity item is not acceptable as the subject when the negation is in the V′:

> *A red cent wasn't given to us by anyone.
> *Anyone didn't go home.

The unacceptability of these examples is not due merely to the negative polarity item preceding the negation, because that is acceptable in examples in which the negative polarity item is in a subject complement:

> That he'll give us a red cent isn't likely.

Chapter 4

1. Logicians commonly cite examples like *If Kathmandu is in Denmark, then I'm a monkey's uncle* as evidence for the correctness of the last line of the standard table. However, what makes such examples reasonable things to say is not just that both clauses are false but that the consequent is **blatantly** false. When the consequent is false, though not blatantly so, as in 4.1.3c, the sentence sounds quite odd. [Note: Lima is in fact slightly farther east than Miami; the west coast of South America is due south of the east coast of North America.]

2. This argument is taken from Geach (1972:196).

3. Combinations of these three possibilities also come into the picture. For example, one might maintain that 4.2.4 is ambiguous between a sense that is true and a sense that has no truth value.

4. Keep in mind that we are talking about what **can** be proved, not about what **has** been proved. The fact that no one has yet proved a certain proposition does not make it false in this assignment of truth values: if a proposition has neither been proven nor shown not to be provable, it is still either true or false, but you don't yet know which.

5. To the best of my knowledge, the problem dealt with in this section was first taken up, and the solution given here first presented, in Carnap 1943:73–94. I am grateful to Nuel Belnap and Gerald Massey for drawing my attention to the fact that Carnap anticipated by nearly forty years ideas that I had thought to be original with me.

6. Or at least, you can't prove anything in the specific system adopted here. In versions of propositional logic in which there are **axioms**, i.e., formulas, instances of which are allowed to appear anywhere in a proof, there are of course formulas that can be proved without the use of suppositions, namely, those that are instances of the axioms.

7. The rules, of course, might be redundant—perhaps the work of one of them

could be done by some combination of applications of the others. However, for our specific choice of rules, that seems pretty unlikely.

8. Since "expressive completeness" could not reasonably be demanded of a system in which the connectives were not truth-functional, the term is generally restricted to systems whose connectives are taken to be truth-functional.

9. For discussion of the possibility that all *or*'s in English are really inclusive and that supposed instances of exclusive *or* can be explained as determined by the context, see section 9.2, Pelletier 1977, and Gazdar 1979:79–83.

10. This point is made in Reichenbach 1947, but not, to my knowledge, in any other existing textbook of logic.

11. I say "a" rather than "the" since there is nothing to prevent one from using more than one metalanguage in a single discussion.

12. It will be proved in section 5.2 that those formulas can in fact be arranged into a complete enumeration, i.e., they can be arranged in a sequence in such a way that each formula turns up after a finite number of steps.

Chapter 5

1. If $M \subseteq N$ and $M \neq N$, then M is called a **proper** subset of N. The symbol $\subseteq$ is formed on the analogy of the symbol $\leq$ "less than or equal to": if $\subset$ were used to mean "is a proper subset of," then $\subseteq$ would stand for "is a proper subset of or is equal to" in the same way that $\leq$ stands for "is less than or equal to."

2. See, however, Feyerabend (1987:chap. 8), who argues that this conception of a line has been common only since Galileo's time, and that in the Aristitolean tradition a line had more structure than merely that of a set of points.

3. This disconcerting property of a "set of all sets" was discovered by Bertrand Russell and is generally referred to as "Russell's paradox."

4. Russell's term "universe of discourse" is the source of considerable confusion, since other authors such as Lyons (1977:508) have applied it to a notion much closer to what the term suggests, namely the set of objects whose identities count as shared knowledge at the given point in a discourse; for the latter notion, which figures prominently in chapters 10 and 12, I will use the term "contextual domain." The only connection between a Russellian "universe of discourse" and discourse is that for any particular subject matter a fixed set of entities that are potentially relevant to that subject matter is supposed to figure as the "universe of discourse" throughout any discourse with that subject matter; a contextual domain, by contrast, typically grows as a discourse proceeds: as new entities are introduced into the discourse, corresponding elements are normally added to the contextual domain. In the treatment of quantifiers that has been common throughout most of the twentieth century, a Russellian universe of discourse is supposed to supply the possible values of all bound individual variables; the values of bound variables will usually include entities that do not belong to the contextual domain, e.g., when one says *All dogs bark,* one is not limiting one's gen-

eralization to the (probably small, perhaps even empty) set of dogs whose identities can be taken as shared knowledge.

5. In this informal presentation, I have been cavalier about some important mathematical points. I have been assuming that "can be put into a one-to-one correspondence with a subset of" is a good analogue to the relationship "is less than or equal to" among finite numbers. To establish that, I would have to establish analogues to the propositions (i) for all x, y, if $x \leq y$ and $y \leq x$, then $x = y$; (ii) for all, x, y, either $x \leq y$ or $y \leq x$. While analogs to these propositions can in fact be proved (e.g., it can be proved that if there is a one-to-one correspondence between A and a subset of B and there is a one-to-one correspondence between B and a subset of A, then there is a one-to-one correspondence between A and B), the proofs are quite involved and rest on assumptions that, though widely accepted, are far from self-evident. One of those assumptions, the so-called **axiom of choice,** played a role in the informal argument that the positive integers are the smallest infinite set: the axiom of choice says that for any set of nonempty sets there is a function that picks one element of each of those sets, and that axiom is the basis of the claim that the sequence x_1, x_2, x_3, ... can be formed.

6. "Countable" and "denumerable" are sometimes used in a broader sense that includes finite sets. Under that terminological practise, what we are calling a "countable set" would be called a "countably infinite set."

7. The expression "either case" is somewhat misleading, since it suggests that there is a difference in meaning between "predicate" and "relation." Aside from one minor point, namely, that it is normal to speak of a "one-place predicate" but not to speak of a "one-place relation," there is in fact no difference between "predicates" and "relations."

8. I follow here the standard convention of using a square bracket to indicate that the end point is included in the interval and a round bracket to indicate that it is not. Thus [0, 1) is the set of all real number x for which $0 \leq x < 1$; [0, 1] is the set of all real numbers x for which $0 \leq x \leq 1$, and so on.

9. Similarly (this example is based on one by Bunt), it may be that all poetry is contained in poems and all poems are poetry, but while the final couplet of Milton's sonnet on his blindness is poetry, it is not a poem. And a volume that contains two-thirds of Milton's poems but not *Paradise Lost* and *Samson Agonistes* contains most of Milton's poems but not most of his poetry.

10. The notion of "sum" invoked here is that in which any two (or more) individuals (e.g., the lower half of my ring and the inner third of your ring) have a sum that is itself an "individual." The study of such individuals and the relations among them is called **mereology**, a branch of logic that can be traced from Leśniewski (1916), through the particularly influential version that Goodman and Leonard (1940) developed under the name "**calculus of individuals**," to several recent (and largely successful) attempts to give an integrated account of the semantics of mass expressions and of plurals, notably those of Link (1983) and Ojeda (1992), as well as Bunt's work.

11. Strictly speaking, "$f(1)$ is true" is superfluous here: showing that if f is true of

all natural numbers less than 1, $f(1)$ is also true, is equivalent to showing that $f(1)$ is true, since there aren't any natural numbers less than 1. I have included the superfluous clause, since in actual practise one would generally have to treat the case of $n = 1$ separately in proving that "if f is true of all natural numbers less than n, then it is true of n'.

Chapter 6

1. For the moment, I will ignore the appealing alternative possibility of allowing a constant to lack a denotation in certain states of affairs. For example, one might wish to allow a constant corresponding to "Santa Claus" to have a denotation in those states of affairs in which there is a Santa Claus and lack one in those states of affairs in which there is no Santa Claus. The version of logic in which individual constants do not necessarily have denotations is known as **free logic** (see Schock 1968 and Bencivenga 1985).

2. The clause "$x_1, \ldots, x_n$ are all of the free variables that occur in A" is important: we cannot simply say that an assignment satisfies $\sim$A if and only if it does not satisfy A, because it might fail to satisfy A simply in virtue of not providing a value for one of the variables in A. Thus, (a_1/x) does not satisfy sxy, but that fact should not mean that it satisfies $\sim sxy$; rather, it fails to satisfy $\sim sxy$ for the same reason that it fails to satisfy sxy.

3. In this respect, the conception of truth and satisfaction presented here deviates from the most widely accepted account, that of Tarski (1944). For Tarski (and most logicians since the mid-twentieth century), satisfaction is defined not in terms of assignments of values to the variables that occur in the given formula but in terms of assignments of values to the (infinitely many) variables that the language allows, and a formula is taken to be true when all assignments of values to (all) variables satisfy it. For Tarski, thus, $\lor(Gxy, \sim Gxy)$ **will** be true pure and simple. The approach adopted here (which in this respect is essentially that of Carnap 1943), unlike Tarski's approach, allows one to distinguish in truth conditions between tautologous closed sentences and tautologous open sentences, the former being true pure and simple, the latter true only relative to assignments that provide values for all free variables that occur in the formula.

4. Unrestricted quantification was first employed in Frege 1879. Its prevalence in twentieth-century logic is probably due to Bertrand Russell, who was profoundly influenced by Frege's logic and philosophy of mathematics. Frege did not give any serious consideration to any alternative to unrestricted quantification, despite the fact that predicate logic had been done in terms of restricted quantification by everyone from Aristotle to Frege's contemporaries.

5. There is a still more common notation, that in which (x) is written rather than $(\forall x)$. I have adhered to using an explicit symbol $\forall$ for the universal quantifier so as to make clear that $(\forall x)$ and $(\exists x)$ differ with regard to **what** quantifier occurs and not with regard to **whether** one occurs.

6. "Over 50 percent" is an oversimplification, for reasons that will be made clear in section 7.4.

7. If the logical form for 6.4.14–15 suggested here is accepted, the relation between logical form and surface form will be different from, indeed almost the reverse of, what it normally is in quantified sentences: the domain expression is expressed in the main clause, and the matrix appears in one of the NP positions in that clause. I maintain that there are in fact a number of kinds of existential sentences in which there is a deviation from the usual relationship between logical form and surface syntactic form. I have argued (McCawley 1981a) that there are a number of types of sentences in which an apparent relative clause is a main clause in deep structure, e.g., (i) has the same deep structure as *Many Americans like opera*:

    i.   There are many Americans who like opera.
    ii.   There's an uncle of mine who owns three houses.
    ii'. I have an uncle who owns three houses.
    iii. I've never met an American who doesn't like peanut butter.

The apparent relative clause has the internal syntax of a restrictive relative clause but does not behave like one in its external syntax, since it can more easily be separated from its supposed head by parentheticals, and it allows material to be extracted from it fairly easily:

    iv.   There are many Americans, of course, who like opera.
    iv'.   ?I sent questionnaires to many Americans, of course, who like opera.
    iv". ?Opera is an art form that there are many Americans who like very much.
    iv'''. *Opera is an art form that he is doing research on Americans who like very much.

See McCawley (1981a, 1988a; sec. 13c) for further discussion of "pseudo-relative" clauses as in (i)–(iii).

8. An additional assumption that is tacitly made here is that only ∀ and ∃ appear among the quantifiers. If other quantifiers are allowed, such as *most* or *almost all*, the addition of doppelgängers could change the truth value of a formula as by the addition to the domain of an extra element for which F but not G could be enough to change the truth value of *Almost all Fs are G* from true to false.

Chapter 7

1. As usual, subscripts indicate the intended pronoun-antecedent relationships. Thus, what is at issue in 7.1.1b is an interpretation in which *himself* refers to John. The approximate statement of the distribution of reflexives that I have just given is an oversimplification; see Jackendoff 1972 and Cantrall 1974 for a detailed treatment of this question. Languages differ considerably from one another with regard to restrictions

on where a reflexive pronoun can occur in relation to its antecedent, e.g., Japanese and Korean analogs to sentences 7.1.1b–b', in which the antecedent of the reflexive is the subject of a higher clause, are quite common. Keenan (1988) argues that linguists have grossly understated the range of possible relations between reflexive and antecedent even in such well-studied languages as English.

2. I in fact maintain (McCawley 1988a: chap. 6, 1992) that the domains to which transformations apply are not just the Ss but in fact all constituents irrespective of syntactic category. However, for the purposes of this chapter, the application of transformations to domains other than Ss plays no role and thus the inaccuracy of taking transformations to have only Ss as their domains is harmless here. The statement of the cyclic principle given here incorporates what is sometimes stated as a separate principle of **strict cyclicity**, which excludes spurious circumvention of the cyclic principle in which one takes the domain to which a particular transformation applies to be a larger constituent than the lowest one that contains all the relevant material.

One important qualification must be added to the statement of the cyclic principle given here, namely that it does not apply to a highly restricted class of **postcyclic** transformations, which apply subsequent to the application of all applicable cyclic transformations and are **local** in the sense of Emonds 1976: the elements involved in the application of the transformation must be adjacent both structurally (i.e., they are either sisters or aunt and niece) and with regard to word order (i.e., no elements intervene between them in the word order); the only postcyclic transformation that is even mentioned in this book is ***Do*-support**, which attaches the verb *do* to any otherwise unattached tense-marker. For a detailed treatment of postcyclic transformations, see McCawley 1988a: sec. 6c.

3. In such works as McCawley 1988a and the first edition of this book, this transformation is misleadingly called "Quantifier-lowering," which suggests incorrectly that the transformation moves just the quantifier rather than the whole expression consisting of the quantifier and the domain expression. In the derivations that follow, I will overlook another transformation that the treatment adopted here commits one to, namely one that reduces the S of the Q' to its predicate N', here converting (every: x American) into *every American*.

4. Not all infinitives are involved in such a parallelism. For example, there is no counterpart to 7.1.7b in which the embedded clause surfaces with a subject of its own:

> *The court forced Nixon for Kalmbach to turn over the tapes.
> *The court forced Nixon that Kalmbach would turn over the tapes.

Force is analyzed as having both an object and a sentential complement, rather than just a sentential complement, for a number of reasons. *Force* can only be followed by a NP denoting the person on whom the force was exerted, rather than just any NP that could be subject of a clause describing what the force brought about unlike *require*, which would be analyzed as having only a sentential complement:

> *The court forced the tapes to be turned over.
> *The court forced there to be separate trials for the defendants.

The court required the tapes to be turned over.
The court required there to be separate trials for the defendants.

By the same token, as pointed out by Chomsky (1965), the following sentences differ only with regard to whether the complement clause is passivized (i.e., they differ by as little as active/passive pairs otherwise do):

John wants the Yankees to beat the Orioles.
John wants the Orioles to be beaten by the Yankees.

but corresponding sentences with *force* differ as regards who the force is imposed on:

John forced Dr. Krankheit to examine Fred.
John forced Fred to be examined by Dr. Krankheit.

5. Example 7.1.8b is actually three ways ambiguous, having not only an interpretation corresponding to 7.1.9b but also interpretations corresponding to the formulas

b'. (every: x American)(every: y American)(x want (y get rich))
b''. (every: y American)(every: x American)(x want (y get rich))

Formulas b' and b'' are deductively equivalent, though they count as distinct logical structures. Each is true when for each pair of Americans, each wants the other to get rich. Example 7.1.9b means that each American has a desire that every American get rich. Note that b' and b'' could be true and 7.1.9b false in a given situation: if I have benevolent feelings toward each and every American (and if having benevolent feelings toward someone implies wanting him to get rich) though I do not have a blanket desire that all Americans be rich, I would "want every American to get rich" in a sense that appears in b' but not in the sense that appears in 7.1.9b.

6. For further details of Q-float, including justification of the claim that in the surface structure of sentences as in 7.1.10 the quantifier is a modifier of the predicate phrase, see McCawley (1998a: secs. 4, 18a). The details of Q-float vary considerably among the languages that have it, e.g., in Japanese, not only universal quantifiers but also numbers can be floated, and quantifiers can be floated from objects as well as from subjects; in English, it is slightly more general than is indicated here, since combinations of *all* with a preposed modifier (*almost all, virtually all,* but not *all but one*) also undergo it. Q-float must not be confused with "Quantifier-pronoun flip" (as in *He talked to us all*), which differs from it in several respects: it requires that the quantifier be combined with a pronoun, it does not detach the quantifier from the pronoun but merely reverses their order, and it does not apply to *each* (**He took pictures of us each*).

7. Note that 7.1.12 is formulated in accordance with the restriction that only a subject NP in English can "launch" a floated quantifier: the subject of the lower S must be the variable bound by the quantified expression that will ultimately be moved into that position by Q'-lowering. The predicate phrase is given as X' rather than V' here

so as to allow the transformation to apply not only when S_1 has a predicate V' but also when it has a predicate A', P', etc.

8. I emphasize what is at issue here is ambiguity in the **scope** of *only*, not in its **focus**. *Only* (likewise, *even, also, too*) has both a focus (a constituent that it contrasts with alternatives, here *wine*) and a scope (a S that serves as the frame for this contrast: *Mary drink x* in one interpretation of 7.1.14a, *John allow Mary to drink x* in the other), and both ambiguities of scope and ambiguities of focus occur. Prescriptive grammarians often stigmatize separation of *only* from its focus on the grounds that an ambiguity of focus is created but seem not to have realized that the device that they disparage often serves to eliminate a different ambiguity. It is only in written language, not in spoken language, that separation of *only* creates a focus ambiguity: since the focus is obligatorily stressed, sentences in spoken language are almost always unambiguous with regard to focus.

9. Example 7.1.22b is ambiguous: it can be interpreted not only like 7.1.22a but also with the meaning ". . . and Bill loves John's wife too."

10. This considerably oversimplifies the facts. See Lakoff 1986 for discussion of conditions under which it is permissible to extract material from some of the conjuncts while leaving the other conjuncts unaffected, as in the following examples:

> How many courses can you take for credit, still remain sane, and get all As in?
> Sam isn't the sort of guy you can just sit there, listen to, and not want to punch in the nose.

11. My brief remarks here do not do justice to the remarkable complexity of the behavior of negative polarity items. See Horn 1978, 1989; Linebarger 1981; and McCawley 1988a: sec. 17b for detailed discussion, including demonstrations that negative polarity items differ from one another with regard to where they can be located relative to the negative items that "license" them and how strongly negative a licensing item each negative polarity item demands. Note, for example, such differences as

> I'll be amazed if Phil gives Lucy a red cent.
> *I'll be amazed if Sam finishes the report until Friday.

12. "Reversal tag questions" such as (i)–(i') are semantically and syntactically distinct from "reduplicative tag questions" such as (ii):

> i. Victor didn't empty the garbage, did he?
> i'. Victor emptied the garbage, didn't he?
> ii. Victor emptied the garbage, did he? Well, then, all you need to do is mop the floor.

The "tag" at the end of a reversal tag question is of the opposite negative or positive form to its host, while that in a reduplicative tag question matches the positive form of its host. Reversal tag questions are real questions (i.e., they are supposed to elicit an

answer, even if it is just a confirmation of the speaker's apparent opinion), while reduplicative tags are not questions but rather "echoes": they must mimic something that
one's interlocutor has just explicitly or implicitly said, and they express the speaker's
reaction to what has just been said (in this case, that he accepts what the interlocutor
has just said and will now make some use of the proposition expressed). For further
details, see McCawley 1988a: secs. 14c, 21c.

13. The same problem arises in a slightly different form for the alternate treatment
of zero V's (Jackendoff 1972:265–72) in which a semantic interpretation rule con-
structs an interpretation for a syntactically empty V'. See McCawley 1976c for a comparison of these two approaches to zero V's.

14. On the distinction between pronouns which are and pronouns which are not
derived from copies of their antecedents, see Lakoff 1968, Hankamer and Sag 1976,
and McCawley 1988a:sec. 11c.

15. In anticipation of a point that will be discussed shortly, I have made one small
change in Russell's analysis, namely, that of replacing $\supset(KFy, = yx)$ by $\supset(\sim = yx,$
$\sim KFy)$. For the specific cases that Russell discussed, this difference is immaterial;
however, the form that I have adopted is more suggestive of a generalization of Russell's analysis, in addition to conforming more closely to idiomatic paraphrases ("no
one but him is king of France").

16. I have adopted this notation in preference to the actual notational practice of
Russell, in which the definite description operator appears in the argument position,
with or without a second instance of the operator that indicates what the scope is:

> i. $B(\imath x{:}KFx)$
> ii. $(\imath x{:}KFx)B(\imath x{:}FKx)$

Both of these ways of representing definite descriptions are objectionable: (i) does not
indicate explicitly the scope of the definite description operator, and (ii) is redundant
(the occurrence of the iota and the predicate in the argument position contributes nothing to the interpretation of the formula), especially in cases in which the matrix S
contains multiple occurrences of the bound variable (imagine either of these notations
applied to a sentence such as *The man who left his money to his mistress thought his
wife would prefer to get his house and his stamp collection*).

More importantly, (ii) has false implications about the logical structure of various
sentences. For example, consider the ambiguity of (iii), which can be interpreted either
as in iv or as in v, where $\Box$ stands for "necessary," T for "be (the) teacher of," P for
"be a person," and *a* for "Alexander," and "is a teacher" is analyzed as "is someone's
teacher":

> iii. The teacher of Alexander was necessarily a teacher.
> iv. $\Box((\imath{:} Txa)_x(\exists{:} Py)_y Txy$
> v. $(\imath{:} Txa)_x\Box(\exists{:} Py)_y Txy$

This way of representing the two interpretations of (iii) makes it clear that one of them
is true (iv says that "The teacher of Alexander was a teacher" expresses a necessarily

true proposition) and the other one false (v says about the teacher of Alexander, that is, Aristotle, that it is necessary that he was a teacher). However, if either of Russell's notational schemes were employed, the counterpart to (v) would look as if it had the same claim to truth that (iv) does, e.g., according to the notational scheme of (ii), the formula corresponding to (v) would be (v′):

$$v′. \quad (\imath x\text{: }Txa)((\Box(\exists y)T(\imath x\text{: }Txa)y)$$

Note that (v) suggests that $\Box$ applies to "the teacher of Alexander was a teacher," whereas (iv) makes clear that it applies to "x was a teacher."

17. In 7.2.5, I have sidestepped the problem of how to analyze "y is the richest debutante in Dubuque" and "y is the best student in x's class." In the logical form that I give in 7.2.5d′, I have tacitly assumed that 7.2.5d is an instance of what in McCawley 1975b I dubbed "Telescoping," i.e., *He apologized for every lie he told her* is a way of saying that for every lie that he told her, he apologized for telling it to her, with the NP *every lie he told her* standing for a complement sentence in which that NP in a sense duplicates the clause in which is appears. Another example of telescoping is (i), which provides an abbreviated way of saying (ii):

    i. I'm amazed at what they're paying Sandberg.
    ii. I'm amazed that they're paying Sandberg what they're paying him.

Note that it is the "full" rather than the "telescoped" version of the sentence that figures directly in inferences, e.g., from the premises in (iii) one is entitled to infer (iv) but not (iv′):

    iii. Bill is amazed at what they're paying Sandberg.
           They're paying Sandberg $2.5 million dollars a year.
    iv. Therefore, Bill is amazed that they're paying Sandberg $2.5 million
           dollars a year.
    iv′. ??Therefore, Bill is amazed at $2.5 million dollars a year.

18. The voluminous literature on Bach-Peters sentences includes Bach 1970, Dik 1973, Hausser 1978, Hintikka and Saarinen 1975, Hintikka and Sandu 1991, Karttunen 1971a, Kuroda 1971, May 1985, McCawley 1973b, and Wasow 1973.

19. In the alternative approach to be discussed in section 10.6, the coherence conditions are weakened in such a way as to allow expressions such as 7.2.12, and the truth conditions provided for such expressions in fact turn out to be appropriate for 7.2.6.

20. These and other problems for Russell's analysis, particularly those relating to its invocation in the philosophical literature on actions and events, are discussed at greater length in McCawley 1986; Russell's analysis is defended ably in Neale 1990, though Neale's analysis of many problematic cases relies so heavily on pragmatics that I question whether his stance is really Russellian. My statement that persons "overlap only if identical" is a considerable oversimplification, as is made clear by a reading of

such science-fiction novels as Algis Budrys's *Rogue Moon*, John Varley's *The Ophi-uchi Hotline*, and Robert Sheckley's *Crompton Divided*, in which serious questions of the individuation of persons arise.

21. The *other* of *each other* and *one another* can reasonably be identified with the clause "$\sim\ =yz$," which would also serve as an analysis of *other* in such sentences as *Edna loves no one other than Otto* or *You must be referring to some other poem of Heine's*. For detailed discussion of the analysis of reciprocals, see Fiengo and Lasnik 1973, Langendoen 1978, and Heim, Lasnik, and May 1991.

22. In combination with the rudimentary treatment that has so far been given to arguments here, 7.3.9b covers only the special case in which the Arg position is filled by a variable, not the more general case in which it is filled by a possibly complex expression involving the variable, as where the set of all squares of even numbers was represented as $\{x^2\colon x$ Even-no$\}$. To remedy this deficiency, one would need to supplement the rules given here by rules that provide for expressions built up from a variable and operation symbols.

23. The correspondence between NP and argument in fact is not exact as was pointed out in chap. 1, note 14. See McCawley 1988a: chap. 7 for exposition of a conception of syntactic category according to which each logical category determines a multi-dimensional "fuzzy category."

24. In view of the sharp difference in acceptability between the two versions of 7.4.4c, it might appear as if it is the form and not the meaning of *a/the majority* that determines whether a subject that it introduces allows *There*-insertion. However, there is some reason to dispute that *a majority* and *the majority* really mean the same thing. Suppose, for the sake of argument, that 40 percent of those who live in Africa are muslims but are not black, that 40 percent are black but are not muslims, that 15 percent are black and muslim, and that 5 percent are neither black nor muslim. That state of affairs is accurately described by (i) (since 55 percent of the people are muslims and 55 percent are black) but not by (ii):

  i. A majority of those who live in Africa are muslims, and a majority of those who live in Africa are black.

  ii. The majority of those who live in Africa are muslims, and the majority of those who live in Africa are black.

Even though there are as many majorities of a set as there are ways of dividing the set into two numerically unequal parts, *the majority* is used as if there were one special majority that deserves to be recognized, and multiple occurrences of *the majority of X* purport to refer to the same majority. If this description of the difference between (i) and (ii) is accurate, then *a majority* is existential and thus should allow *There*-insertion, but *the majority* is a definite description and thus should not allow it.

25. It should be emphasized that the conversions referred to here are syntactic transformations, not rules of inference, i.e., the output is not the logical form of a consequence of the given proposition but rather an intermediate stage in the syntactic derivation of a sentence expressing the given proposition.

26. This treatment of color words provides an immediate solution to Fodor's (1975:148–49) problem of identifying what justifies the inference from "x is blue" to "x is colored"; "x is blue" is Color(x, blue), "x is colored" is ($\exists$: y is a color) Color(x, y), and the inference from the former to the latter is an instance of $\exists$-introduction.

27. Steps in which various semantic elements are replaced by corresponding lexical items (e.g., Ling is replaced by *linguist*) are not indicated separately in 7.4.7. Since those steps do not affect the status of a constituent as a phrasal unit, replacement of the Pred of a Pred' by an adjective turns the Pred' into an A'.

28. The interpretation at issue in 7.4.10b–b" are those in which the relative clause jointly modifies both N's. Example 7.4.10b' is of course acceptable if the relative clause modifies only *anthropologists*.

29. The relation claimed here between quantifier scope and *There*-insertion casts a new light on a well-known puzzle about *There*-insertion in sentences with auxiliary verbs. When a clause has two occurrences of *be* (the possibility can arise only when the first *be* is progressive *be* and the second is either copula *be* or passive *be*), *There*-insertion can put the underlying subject only after the first *be*, not the second, even though the second *be* is something that otherwise allows the subject to come after it in a *There*-insertion construction:

  i.   There was a man being tortured.
  i'. *There was being a man tortured.
  ii. There have been several men tortured.

This fact has usually been regarded as a fact of syntax, and attempted solutions to the problem have most commonly been attempts to formulate *There*-insertion so that the subject can be moved into the position where it appears in (i) and (ii), but not that of (i'). However, if auxiliary verbs are treated as having sentential complements (as in the treatment of 7.1.16 above), (i) and (i') will differ with regard to the domain to which *There*-insertion applied: in (i), the domain to which it applies would be the whole S *A man be being tortured,* while in (i'), the domain to which it applies would be the complement of progressive *be,* i.e., *A man be tortured.* According to the treatment of *There*-insertion adopted here, this means that *a man* should have wide scope in (i) but narrow scope in (i'), which opens up the possibility of treating the anomaly of (i') as semantic rather than syntactic: progressive *be* is subject to a restriction that its complement denote an activity or process (*John was acting like his father; The temperature was rising*) and not a state (**John was resembling his father; *The temperature was being high*), and a quantified complement such as ($\exists$: x Man)(they torture x) could be claimed to denote a state, thus violating the restriction, while just plain "they torture x" would denote an activity. Whether that account of the anomaly of (i') can be maintained depends on the viability of a categorization into activities, processes, and states that applies in the way just suggested, and in the absence of a well-elaborated and well-supported scheme of categorization, I can only treat the suggestion of the last sentence as an appealing conjecture. In any event, though, the correlation between scope and *There*-insertion radically changes the character of the problem posed by (i)–(i').

30. Alternatively, one might give an analysis with "M is a large set of linguists," thus allowing for standards of largeness that vary with the kind of thing that makes up the set. See Partee 1989 for detailed discussion of the range of possible interpretations of *many*.

31. Formula 7.4.15d is a makeshift, in that there is considerable individual variation in the range of numbers covered by "several" and, in addition, all speakers of English seem to recognize "fuzziness" in the applicability of *several*: no matter what one's conception of "several" is, lowering the number of failed brokerages by one never changes 7.4.15d from unequivocally true to unequivocally false but at worst to, say, "loosely speaking, true." In chapter 13 I will deal directly with the possibility of sentences having degrees of truth rather than being simply true or simply false.

32. "Composite" is the opposite of "prime": a prime number has no factors other than 1 and itself, while a composite number is a product of two smaller whole numbers.

33. This proposal is similar to but not identical to the treatment of *most* in Peterson (1979).

34. There is actually one case in which the proposal made here would allow *There*-insertion to apply to a sentence in which an existential quantifier expression is combined with a negated matrix S, namely that in which the negation is incorporated into a lower quantified NP instead of appearing as a sister of the V′ as in 7.4.24b. Such sentences are in fact acceptable with the relevant interpretation:

> There were many of my friends in no one's debt. (= Many of my friends were not in anyone's debt.)
> There were several persons in no condition to drive home. (= Several persons were not in any condition to drive home.)

35. A case where something greater than 50 percent could conceivably count as "not large" and thus something below 50 percent count as "most" is that in which more than 50 percent of something is spread out over time in such a way as to be of relative insignificance. It is not outlandish to say *You have to pay most of the money in advance* with reference to an arrangement in which you pay 40 percent down and the remainder over the next ten years.

36. For a more comprehensive and thorough survey of English quantifiers and their meanings than is attempted here, readers are referred to Keenan and Stavi 1986.

37. By the same token, it is less of an exaggeration to describe the liquid that comes out of faucets in Philadelphia as water than to describe it as H_2O.

38. The significance of succotash for the philosophy of language was first pointed out in Sharvy 1979a.

39. "Is water" must not be confused with "is a water," which means "is a kind of water," as in *Perrier is a water that has become very popular in the United States*.

40. The definition 7.5.6c embodies essentially the same idea as the transformation of Aggregation proposed in section 7.4: from a predicate of individuals one can derive

a homophonous predicate of sets that is true of a set if and only if the original predicate is true of all the members of the set.

41. This statement will have to be qualified in that there is sometimes a lower limit on how small the part may be if the inference is still to be valid. For example, given that this stew is spicy or smelly, it is probably the case that every spoonful of it is spicy or smelly but not that every cubic millimeter of it is.

42. In the interests of simplicity, I have written "M is two linguists" and "N is three sociologists" instead of the more complicated expressions that underlie them according to the arguments of section 7.4.

43. Examples like 7.6.9 were brought to my attention by Jackendoff (1977:190–94). The intended interpretation is that in which *the same slogan* is the object of both *chant* and *shout*. As a makeshift, I have treated *the same* in 7.6.9a′ as if it were simply a wide scope existential quantifier. That treatment loses the structural parallelism between *the same* and *similar* and *different*:

> i. A linguist was shouting and a philosopher was chanting two similar slogans.
>
> ii. Several students were humming and a few professors were singing at least ten different tunes.

Second-order logic offers a means of treating these three words alike. Specifically, suppose that each of (iii), (iv), (v) has a logical structure involving a function from students to slogans, with *same, similar,* and *different* expressing characteristics of the values of that function, as in (iii′), (iv′), (v′), where M is the set of students that is referred to and "M → slogan" is an informal way of indicating that f associates a slogan to each member of M:

> iii. All the students were chanting the same slogan.
> iii′. $(\exists: \wedge (f: M \rightarrow \text{slogan}, \text{same } \{fx: x \in M\}))$ $(\forall: x \in M)(x \text{ chant } fx)$
> iv.   All the students were chanting similar slogans.
> iv′. $(\exists: \wedge (f: M \rightarrow \text{slogan}, \text{similar } \{fx: x \in M\}))(\forall: x \in M)(x \text{ chant } fx)$
> v.   All the students were chanting different slogans.
> v′. $(\exists: \wedge (f: M \rightarrow \text{slogan}, \text{different } \{fx: x \in M\}))(\forall: x \in M)(x \text{ chant } fx)$

Two difficulties must be resolved before these formulas can be accepted as logical structures of the given sentences. First, as the notion of set was developed in chapter 5, *different* cannot be taken as predicated of sets: if twelve students were chanting two slogans, (v) should be false, but (v′) would presumably be true because the two members of the set of slogans would be different from each other. A possible solution to this problem would be to replace the notion of set in these formulas by a notion that is referred to in computer science as a **bag.** A bag is an entity that is like a set except that elements can have multiple memberships in it, e.g., the bag having three instances of 1 and four instances of 2 as members is different from the bag having five instances of 1 and two instances of 2, and neither bag is the same as the set {1, 2}. A more serious problem with the formulas (iii')–(v') is that it is not obvious that they can be integrated with otherwise valid rules for the relationship of logical form to surface syntactic structure. Whether this problem can be solved satisfactorily will depend on what principles can be given for the syntactic realization of functions such as appear in the formulas.

44. Lakoff notes that complex sentences may be ambiguous as to the scope of *usual*. For example, *The usual men want to meet in the usual places* may imply either that it is usual for those men to meet in those places or that it is usual for those men to want to meet in those places.

In 7.6.12b, I have given only one of the two interpretations of 7.6.12a, namely that in which the sets of men, women, and subjects figure collectively in the various clauses. A second interpretation is that in which for various triples (m_i, n_i, p_i) of man, woman, and subject, it is usual for m_i to talk to n_i about p_i.

45. I assume that there is one domain expression for each variable, even though each of the domain expressions can perfectly well involve more than one variable, because the domain expressions must provide a sort predicate (see sec. 8.1) for each variable, and I wish to take each of these sort predicates as in a different domain expression.

Chapter 8

1. Strictly speaking, I should say "let ϕ be any expression whose denotation is of type a'," but I will henceforth use the simpler locution "expression of type a'."

2. What is called V'-deletion here actually deletes not only repeated V's but also repeated NPs, A's, and P's when they appear in combination with the copula *be*, as in 8.2.11c, where the repeated A' *easy to talk to* is deleted. Akmajian and Wasow (1975) give an explanation of why a deletion that normally affects only V's can apply to units of other categories when they are combined with copula *be*. Specifically, they argue that the derivations of the relevant examples involve a step in which *be* is extracted from its V' and moved to a higher position in the structure; in that case a predicate A' (or predicate NP, etc.) is what remains of a V' after its V has been extracted and, as such, counts as a V'.

3. The terms "strict identity" and "sloppy identity" were introduced by Ross (1967).

4. I consider here only interpretations in which the *he* of the first conjunct refers to Sam and that of the second conjunct to Bill.

5. Since every V' contributes its own λ, many examples that might at first sight be thought to involve occurrences of the same variable in two different V's really do not. For example, Sag's proposal does not imply that V' deletion is possible in (i), since the logical structure for Sag is not (ii) but (iii):

    i.   *Many linguists are neither easy to please nor hard to.

    ii.   (Many linguist u) $\wedge$ (not([Δ please u] be easy), not ([Δ please u] be hard))

iii.   (Many linguist *u*) $\land$ (not (*u*, (λx)([Δ please *x*] be easy, not (*u*, (λy)([Δ please *y*] be hard))

The Δ here and in 8.2.18b is the "unspecified subject" that has been postulated by various linguists in analyses of subjectless infinitives and reduced passives (such as *Bill was attacked*). The discussion here is neutral as to what contribution the Δ makes to the logical structure of the sentence.

6. There appear to be some syntactic rules for which Sag's conception of identity is not the appropriate one. For example, the rule of **Right-node-raising** must be allowed to identify the two occurrences of *most operas* in (i) so as to yield (ii), even though they presumably would not count as alphabetic variants according to what has just been said:

i.   Schwartz loves most operas, and Morgenstern hates most operas.
ii. Schwartz loves, and Morgenstern hates, most operas.

7. The bulk of this section leans heavily on the insightful discussion of generics by Carlson 1977, 1982, 1989.

8. Examples 8.3.2b–c are taken from Carlson 1977, 8.3.2d–e were suggested to me by Guy Carden, and 8.3.2f is adapted from an example in Dahl 1975; 8.3.2b was taken in turn by Carlson from Arnauld 1662.

9. There is actually one generic interpretation on which 8.3.4c is at least marginally acceptable: one that makes a generalization about situations (say, scavenger hunts) in which one is expected to find several things, including a bed that was slept in by George Washington.

10. Carlson actually used the letter R to represent the instantiation relation; I replace it here by "I" to avoid confusion with the alternativeness relation between possible worlds that will figure prominently from chapter 11 on.

11. A stage that instantiates the kind "dog" need not be a stage of a particular dog, since a sum of stages of several different dogs could presumably also count as a stage that instantiates that kind.

Carlson's analysis here works beautifully for English, but it seems to have false implications about many other languages. Since his derivation of the existential reading of the bare plural depends only on the semantics of the various parts of the sentence and not on their form, NPs that have the meanings of kind-denoting bare plurals ought to allow an existential reading in the analogs in other languages to *When I approached the house, dogs barked*. But Croft (1990: 251) points out that this implication is false. For example, Spanish, like many languages, uses a definite plural NP where English uses an indefinite plural generic (e.g., *Los osos inviernan en cuevas,* "Bears hibernate in caves"); however, Spanish definite plural NPs never allow an existential interpretation.

12. There is a similar range of interpretations among agent nominalizations. A murderer is any person who has ever committed murder. A killer is not anyone who

has ever killed someone but a person who can be expected to kill whoever he is hired or provoked to kill. Most murderers are not killers. An executioner is a person who is authorized to perform executions, even if he has never performed one.

13. It is not clear whether one should speak of u as depending on x and z, or on y and z, or on x, y, and z, in view of the fact that y depends on x. I will follow the practice of speaking in terms of the "most independent" variables and thus speak of u as depending on x and z.

14. One important topic that has been totally neglected in the literature on convergent quantifiers (and which will only be mentioned here) is that of the conditions under which a S can branch into nonconjoined Ss, as at the top of 8.4.11a, and under which two parts of a logical structure can share a S, as at the bottom of 8.4.11a. Is it only immediately above and immediately below quantifiers that these structural characteristics can occur? And if so, why?

Taking 8.4.11a rather than 8.4.10 as one's vantage point gives an issue raised by Barwise (1979:47) a very different character. Barwise states that the recognition of branching quantifier structures "would force us to re-examine, and perhaps re-interpret, Frege's principle of compositionality according to which the meaning of a given expression is determined by the meanings of its constituent phrases," since the meaning of an expression like 8.4.10 "cannot be defined inductively in terms of simpler formulas, by explaining away one quantifier at a time." In saying this, Barwise has ignored two expressions that are constituents of 8.4.11a but are not so obviously constituents if one represents the structure in the form 8.4.10, namely:

$$(\forall x)(\exists y)\ F(x,y,z,w)$$
$$(\forall z)(\exists w)F(x,y,z,w)$$

Is the meaning of the whole formula derivable from the meanings of these two constituents? I can't say for sure, since it isn't clear to me how one puts together meanings of two formulas in which the bound variables of the one occur free in the other, but at least I find the answer less obvious than Barwise did.

15. Karttunen in fact recognized a third reading beyond the two discussed in section 7.2, and Hintikka and Saarinen suggest that their interpretation may be identifiable with Karttunen's third reading, though Karttunen's description of the third reading is too obscure for them to be able to say for sure.

16. Exclusive *or*, if there is such a thing (see section 9.2 for arguments that English really has only an inclusive *or*), could be identified with the quantifier *one*: $one/\bigvee_e$ would be predicated of a set of propositions, and the whole proposition would be true if and only if exactly one member of that set was true.

17. As it stands, SF-intro$_2$ is perniciously overgeneral. Unless something is done to restrict the bound variable introduced by it to a specific type, it can be used to introduce the sorts of spurious "sets" that give rise to Russell's paradox; for example, we must rule out inferences like the following, in which the bound variable M is supposed to range over "all sets":

$$\sim(\emptyset\in\emptyset)$$
$$\emptyset\in\{M: \sim(M\in M)\}$$

I will tacitly assume that appropriate restrictions on this rule are in effect.

18. In Lakoff and Peters 1969 and McCawley 1970, it has been held that there is such a constraint in natural language, in view of the oddity of repeated conjuncts:

> *John is Irish, Bill is Italian, and John is Irish.
> *My mother and my mother are short and fat, respectively.

However, this oddity can be ascribed to the pointlessness of the extra conjuncts: one could be just as informative by omitting the supernumerary conjuncts. Derived coordinate constituents with repeated constituents are normal when not pointless:

> Tom, Dick, and Harry voted for Nixon, Nixon, and Humphrey/*Nixon, respectively.

Chapter 9

1. Some illocutionary act types to which no performative verb corresponds are illustrated by exclamative sentences such as *Boy, was I ever embarrassed!* or *The nerve of that bastard, asking me to patch his underwear!* and "echo questions" such as *You order me to clean the latrine with what??* For discussion of the syntax of these two types of sentences, see respectively sections 21b and 21c of McCawley 1988a.

2. In some circumstances (see Fraser 1974b and McCawley 1977a for details), a verb can be used performatively with *must* or *will:*

> In view of the gravity of your offence, I must/will hereby sentence you to 20 years of hard labor.

3. I leave aside here the illocutionary acts mentioned in note 1, for which no corresponding overt performative verb exists. For criticism of the performative analysis, see Fraser 1974a and Gazdar 1979, and for a response to the criticisms offered by those and other authors, see McCawley 1985. The literature on performative analyses has concentrated on the specific proposal of Ross 1970, in which the claim that illocutionary forces correspond to underlying performative verbs (what I refer to in McCawley 1985 as the 'pristine performative hypothesis') is combined with several untenable claims about the ways that performative verbs fit into underlying syntactic structures. I show in McCawley 1985 that most of the arguments against performative analyses that have been offered are directed not at the pristine performative hypothesis but at other claims with which it has been packaged, e.g., the claim that to be used performatively, a verb must be the topmost predicate element of a syntactic structure.

One important defect in Ross's version of a performative analysis is that it conflates the syntactic reflexes of locutionary acts with those of illocutionary acts; e.g., Ross took facts like those given in connection with 9.1.15–18 as evidence that first- and second-person elements serve as arguments of a higher **performative** verb and thus for a higher clause of the form $I\ V_{performative}\ you\ S$, but they could as well be taken as reflecting a higher **locutionary** clause of the form $I\ direct\ S\ to\ you$. I in fact maintain that a locutionary clause above the performative clause is needed to accommodate vocative expressions, which cannot always be identified with a constituent of a performative clause, in virtue of the existence of performative verbs that allow vocatives but do not allow an object that corresponds to the addressee:

Mr. Smith, I estimate (*to you) that the repairs will cost about $300.

Ladies and gentlemen, I hereby appoint Manuel Noriega Attorney General (*to you).

According to this proposal, 9.1.8a, in which there are two locutionary acts, each associated with a different illocutionary act, has underlying conjoined locutionary clauses, each containing a performative clause, and 9.1.8b, in which there is a single locutionary act associated with two illocutionary acts, has a single locutionary clause in which a conjoined performative clause is embedded.

4. For valuable comments on the syntax and semantics of imperative sentences, see Schmerling 1982; Schmerling argues for an analysis of imperative sentences very different from that which I sketch here.

5. At the end of a passage that begins with the question "What then is left of the distinction of the performative and constative utterance?" Austin says, "But the real conclusion must surely be that we need (a) to distinguish between locutionary and illocutionary acts, and (b) specially and critically to establish with respect to each kind of illocutionary act—warnings, estimates, verdicts, statements, and descriptions—what if any is the specific way in which they are intended, first to be in order or not in order, and second, to be "right" or "wrong"; what terms of appraisal and disappraisal are used for each and what they mean. This is a wide field and certainly will not lead to a simple distinction of "true" and "false"; nor will it lead to a distinction of statements from the rest, for stating is only one among very numerous speech acts of the illocutionary class" (Austin 1962: 144–46).

6. For details of the conditions under which a NP can serve as controller for Superequi, see Jacobson and Neubauer 1976. The *I* and *you* of the understood performative clause denote respectively the "principal" and the "addressee" of the illocutionary act. Goffman (1974, 1979) points out that a number of distinct notions are conflated under the popular terms "speaker" and "hearer"; for example, "speaker" conflates the roles of **author** (the person who composes the words that are uttered), **animator** (the person who produces the sound or other physical manifestation of the utterance), and **principal** (the person who makes commitments, etc., through the uttering of the sentence). While these roles commonly are played by the same person, it is not at all unusual for them to be dissociated, as when a speech writer (the author) writes a speech that is to be given by President Bush (the principal) but ends up being read in his absence by Vice President Quayle (the animator). In McCawley 1985b, I survey linguistic rules and definitions that have been stated in terms of "speaker" and/or "hearer" with a view

towards identifying the precise role or combination of roles that is relevant in each case; for example, it is the roles of principal and addressee that are relevant to the use of first- and second-person pronouns.

7. An illustration of the way in which cooperativity influences the interpretation of things other than speech is provided by the difference between how one interprets a painting and how one interprets a photograph. Everything in the painting is of significance, since the artist took the trouble to put it there; but the very same details in a photograph are often of no significance, since the photographer controls only a limited range of features of the things that he photographs.

8. Of course, even that utterance could be interpreted in such a way as to exploit "relevance": B's utterance might convey that A should get his groceries at the nearby store rather than at the store on the other side of town that he had been planning to go to, or even that A should give up the trip that he was about to embark on and should buy the groceries that he will need to hold him over until morning. Of course, for it to convey any of these things, it is necessary that A and B share appropriate assumptions: in the one case, that A's trip is to buy groceries and that 14th Street is nearby, in the other case, that if A does not make his planned trip, he will need groceries.

9. This is an oversimplification, since only positive questions are considered and only one of the two question-answering systems of American English is brought into the picture. Besides the *yes/no* system, in which a positive answer is accompanied by or represented by *yes* and a negative answer by *no,* there is also the *uh-huh/uh-uh* system (roughly equivalent to the *hai/iie* system of Japanese), in which *uh-huh* conveys agreement with the proposition that the question asks about and *uh-uh* conveys disagreement with it. The two systems diverge when the question asks about a negative proposition; for example, in response to the question *Did nobody challenge him on that point?,* a person who wishes to convey that nobody challenged him on that point could say either *No* or *Uh-huh.* What I said in the text is actually a more correct description of *Uh-huh* than of *Yes,* though the inaccuracy does not affect the points that I made in the text, which related to examples that are in the realm in which *Yes* and *Uh-huh* overlap. For a detailed cross-linguistic study of question-answering systems, see Pope 1973.

10. I am concerned here with the "neutral" pronunciation of 9.2.11a, in which *some* is not heavily stressed. If *some* is heavily stressed, the normalness of the answers is reversed. This is because *some* is then being contrasted with other items that could be used in its place, and 9.2.11b' is then an appropriate answer because *some* is not the "most correct" member of the set of contrasted items; however, in 9.2.11a with "neutral" pronunciation, the proposition that some men are mortal is being contrasted with its negation (the proposition that no men are mortal).

11. One further criticism of Grice by Cohen rests on a serious error, however. Grice takes it to be an important characteristic of conversational implicatures that they can be **cancelled** by putting the utterance in a context in which the possibility that the implicature is false is made explicit, as in 9.2.11b, where *as a matter of fact, all men are mortal* cancels the implicature that not all men are mortal, or in *Either Truman or*

Eisenhower was president in 1947, but I'm not going to tell you which, where the *but*-clause, since it suggests that the speaker is in a position to say which of the two was president, cancels the implicature that he does not know which of them was president. Cohen argues that not only implicatures but also parts of meaning can be cancelled, as in the expressions *a fake diamond* and *plastic flowers,* where *fake* and *plastic* cancel out (Cohen says) parts of the meanings of *diamond* and *flower.* However, Cohen is simply in error when he speaks of *fake,* etc., as cancelling parts of the meaning: a fake diamond isn't just something that you decline to call a diamond but rather something that masquerades as a diamond, and the color, shape, and surface texture of a piece of glass determine whether it is a fake diamond, a fake ruby, a fake emerald, or none of the above; *fake* doesn't cancel components of meaning any more than *not* does but merely embeds them in a frame. As far as I can tell, Grice's criterion of **cancellability** remains a valid test for conversational implicature. In this connection, though, see Sadock (1978).

12. See also Gruber 1967 for a statement of essentially the same principle and many instances of its application.

13. There is, however, a difference between the two cases that arises when they are used in yes-no questions:

    i.   Did only Southerners vote for Hubert?
         Yes, indeed only Lyndon did.
    ii. Did only Muriel vote for Hubert?
         ?Yes, indeed no one did.
         (?)No, indeed no one did.
    iii. Did only Muriel, Ed, and Lyndon vote for Hubert?
         ?Yes, indeed only Muriel and Ed did.

I am not yet clear as to what the significance of these facts is.

14. This is incorrect as it stands, in view of what Postal and Grinder (1971) call the **Missing antecedent phenomenon,** illustrated by such sentences as *Bill doesn't have a car, but Susan does, and it's parked in front of her house.* Note that the *it* refers to the understood *a car* of *Susan does (have a car).* The correct form of the generalization about existential NPs is probably that an existential quantifier creates a constant only if it occurs overtly or is anaphorically connected to something that occurs overtly. The zero V' of the second clause is an anaphoric device referring to the V' (*have a car*) of the first clause.

15. The discussion of 9.2.27 is based on Kamp's (1974) analysis of permission.

16. There is more than this to the difference between *lack* and *have not:* note that *John doesn't have ten dollars* implies that the amount of (available) money that John has is less than ten dollars, while *John lacks ten dollars* implies that the amount of money John has is ten dollars short of the amount he needs, although it could perfectly well be far more than ten dollars.

17. In saying this, I ignore the possibility that $f(x, p)$ might be neither true nor false; that possibility will be taken up in section 10.3, where a conception of truth values will

be developed that will allow $f(x, p)$ to lack a truth value in some cases in which p is true or false.

Chapter 10

1. I have used a "pseudo-cleft" construction rather than a "cleft" construction, since a cleft version of 10.2.10 would be very awkward by virtue of its having a clause in the middle of a clause (as noted in Ross 1967):

> ?*It's that he named Noriega attorney general that Bush regrets.

A pseudo-cleft example is equally relevant here, since cleft and pseudo-cleft constructions appear to have the same logical content, though there are different restrictions on their use.

2. Strictly speaking, what van Fraassen proposed was that the apparatus of supervaluations be supplemented by a relation **N** of "nonclassical necessitation" between propositions and that for any propositions A and B such that A **N** B, those supervaluations that make A T and B not T be excluded. In view of the fact that A **N** B makes it true that A $\vDash$ B (relative to the set of supervaluations that respect **N**), it does no harm to simply say that A $\vDash$ B **is** the meaning postulate. In this paragraph, I have tacitly excluded from consideration what van Fraassen calls "radical" presuppositional systems, which are taken up briefly later in this section. See van Fraassen 1969:76–77 and 1971:157–59 for a more precise description of his presuppositional systems.

3. We have # rather than T/# since the conditions under which $\supset(mA, A)$ might be T are not met here. Let v_x be a supervaluation for which $v_x(A) = v_x(mA) = \#$. For $v_x(\supset(mA, A))$ to be T, it must be the case that all classical valuations which make all of X T and make mA T also make A T. But there are classical valuations which make all of X T and make A F (that's what it means to say that $v_x(A) \neq$ T), and among those there must be classical valuations which make mA T, since in classical logic, A and mA are independent of each other. Thus, if $v_x(A) = v_x(mA) = \#$, then $v_x(\supset(mA, A)) = \#$.

4. According to 10.4.8, (i) should be $\sim$A $\gg$ C. However, since a proposition and its negation have the same presuppositions, it can be given in the form A $\gg$ C.

5. Example 10.4.15 should be distinguished from such sentences as

> Nixon regrets that he doesn't belong to the Elks, and, by the way, he dóesn't belong to the Elks.

which are quite normal but which do not affect the point being made here, since they involve afterthought. The function of the afterthought is, in effect, to replace the sentence that the speaker was originally going to utter (the first conjunct) by another sentence in which the material of the afterthought appears earlier.

6. This statement of the conditions under which a proposition A belongs to the "context" is somewhat misleading, in that what is at issue is not whether each partici-

pant in the discourse individually takes A for granted but whether the participants treat A as "common property" of the group that they form in conducting the conversation. In certain situations, propositions that none of the parties to the conversation believes may be "taken for granted" by them. For example, the proposition that there is a Santa Claus may belong to the context of a Christmastime conversation between a parent and his child, neither of whom believes that there is a Santa Claus or even believes that the other believes that there is a Santa Claus. The parties to the conversation may, of course, have conflicting conceptions of what their "common property" is; however, when such discrepancies become apparent, some sort of "repair" procedure is initiated (e.g., one might delete a proposition from the set that he had assumed to belong to the context or might challenge or query the other party so as to lead **him** to stop regarding a certain proposition as belonging to the context). See Smith (1982) for a variety of opinions about the notion "mutual knowledge."

7. We actually used the letters T and F at that point, but since we are now using capital letters for truth values based on a narrow conception of falsehood and small letters for truth values based on a broad conception of falsehood, it is small letters that are appropriate here.

8. Under the assumptions of standard logic, it makes no sense to speak of the logical structure of a V'; however, V's do have logical structures in the approach that is developed in section 8.3, in which every V' is associated with a formula of the form $(\lambda x)Fx$.

9. The full range of existential NPs may be found in the *if*-clause of conditional sentences that have a pronoun in the consequent clause that refers back to the quantified NP:

   i.   If Dave finds several copies of *Fanny Hill,* he'll give them all to the Wichita Public Library.
   ii.   If a lot of people come to Janet's party, they'll drink lots of beer.
   iii. If at least 10 people sign a petition to the chairman, they're entitled to present their grievance at a board meeting.
   iv.   If Sam buys two cars, he'll let me drive one of them.

These do not present an insuperable problem for the Quine analysis but do at least force its adherents to adopt an analysis in which a set variable is bound by a zero universal quantifier, for example (ii) would have to be analyzed as "For every set of a lot of people, if the members of that set come to Janet's party, they will drink lots of beer"; note that *a lot* cannot simply be taken itself to have wide scope—(ii) does not mean "There are a lot of people such that, if they come to Janet's party, they'll drink a lot of beer." A more serious problem that (ii) presents for Quine's analysis is that of getting *a lot* to pick out sets that are large by appropriate standards (e.g., *a lot* in [ii] might be around 30; but 30 fans attending a Vikings football game isn't a lot); for the Klima and Horn analysis, this is no problem: the antecedent of (ii) will be *A lot of people come to Janet's party,* and the standards relative to which *a lot* is interpreted will be the same as if the antecedent were an independent sentence.

10. Actually, it is available in a slightly more general slice of the discourse, namely,

those parts referring to states of affairs in which the antecedent is supposed true. In a sentence such as

> If a war breaks out in Uganda, it will spread to Tanzania, but I strongly doubt that it will spread to Mozambique.

the second *it* refers to the war mentioned in the antecedent. But the clause containing that second *it* is not part of the consequent of that conditional: the sentence cannot have the logical form "If *p*, then (*q* but *r*)," since your doubts, mentioned in the putative *r*, are real doubts that you have now, not something contingent on war breaking out in Uganda.

11. The context, CD, and salience relation are parts of what Lewis (1979) refers to as a **conversational score,** by analogy with information such as "two balls, one strike, Sandberg at bat in the bottom of the eighth, runners on first and third, Pirates leading the Cubs 3–1" that is given in reporting the progress of a sporting event. In both cases, the various parameter settings that make up the "score" determine what the participants are allowed to do and what particular events will count as (e.g., whether a use of *the dog* will count as a reference to Rover or to Fido, whether a foul ball will count as a strike or as nothing), and the actions of the participants bring about changes in the score (e.g., the conversational score is altered by adding things to the context and CD or by altering the salience relation among the members of the CD, and the baseball score is altered by adding 1 to the ball count or the strike count or by resetting those counts to 0 when the batter finishes his turn at bat). Conversational scorekeeping in Lewis's sense will play a major role in section 15.2.

12. Donnellan spoke of NPs such as *the man in the corner with the martini in his hand* as used **referentially**. A NP used referentially does not contribute its sense to the proposition that the sentence expresses but serves only to identify an entity that figures in that proposition; by contrast, a NP is used **attributively** if its sense is part of the proposition expressed by the sentence in which it occurs, as in the most obvious uses of (i)–(ii):

  i. The guy that's driving that car must be drunk.
  ii. The solution to equation 3 is greater than 10^{12}.

Definite NPs generally are neither inherently referential nor inherently attributive; for example *the man with the martini* can be used referentially in a sentence like 10.6.16, but it can also be used attributively, as it would be if the chairman of a temperance society learns that an unidentified intruder has come to one of its meetings with a martini in an innocuous-looking soft-drink cup and tells the master-at-arms *Find the man with the martini and make him leave*. It is often unclear how to apply the referential/attributive distinction in particular cases. Perhaps the most reliable way to determine whether a NP is used referentially is to determine whether a subsequent sentence can contain a pronoun having that NP as antecedent and having the "intended referent" of that NP as its referent irrespective of whether the NP correctly describes the referent, as when the interlocutor responds to 10.6.16 with *Yes, and I hear they're going to pay him a ridiculously high salary*. Among the highlights of the vast literature on the referential/attributive distinction are Recanati 1981 and Neale 1990.

13. Real world events may fail to conform to the relevant scripts. However, a hearer is entitled to take the events mentioned as conforming to the script if the speaker does not give him reason to believe that they may not conform to it.

14. In saying this, I assume that plural is the semantically unmarked number: in cases where it is indeterminate whether one entity or more than one is referred to, a plural is used, as in headings "Schools attended," "Previous positions," "Names of children" on forms that are to be filled out. *Any men who own donkeys beat them* clearly **does** imply that a man who owns one donkey beats it.

15. The treatment of donkey sentences sketched here has much in common with those of Kamp 1984 and Chierchia 1992, to which the interested reader is referred.

Chapter 11

1. Cf. Lycan's (1979:274) remark that "the identification of necessity with truth in all possible worlds . . . is almost universally credited to Leibniz, but I know of nowhere that it appears in Leibniz's standard texts—despite casual allusions to the doctrine, and even some (specious) page references, by a number of commentators."

2. To say that the R for epistemic possibility is reflexive is to say that *know* is a factive verb: that only what is true in a given state of affairs can be known in that state of affairs.

3. See Hughes and Cresswell (1968:58) for comments on the "somewhat tenuous" relationship of this formula to L. E. J. Brouwer and intuitionist mathematics.

4. As before, I include "axioms" under "rules of inference."

5. The systems S1, S2, and S3 of Lewis and Langford (1932) do not have this property (Hughes and Cresswell 1968:236).

6. The numbering of some of the additions to the Lewis hierarchy is confusing in that not all systems of the hierarchy are comparable. For example, S7, S8, and S9 are special cases of S3 but are not comparable with S4 or S5 (some theorems of S7 are not theorems of S4 and some theorems of S4 are not theorems of S7, etc.).

7. The introduction to Linsky 1971 provides a highly insightful survey of this entire controversy.

8. In a context where it makes sense to speak of events affecting properties of the individual in question, one can distinguish between essential and accidental properties by asking oneself whether the individual would continue to exist (and retain its identity) after some possible or imaginable change had taken place. We can imagine a wicked witch turning a handsome prince into a frog, an amoeba, or even an electron; in those cases, we regard the frog/amoeba/electron as continuing to be the prince only if it serves as a repository for the prince's mind or soul (e.g., if the prince continues to be conscious and his perceptions are now from the vantage point of the frog/amoeba/electron, of if the prince's consciousness is potentially recoverable from the frog/amoeba/electron through another magical event which will occur when, say, a princess kisses the frog or provides a positive ion for the electron-prince to combine with).

However, I am not up to the task of constructing a fairy tale in which a wicked witch turns a handsome prince into March the 21st or Planck's constant or the Tübingen dialect of German, or turns any of those three objects into a handsome prince. Thus, such properties as having a mind, being a period of time, being a number, and being a variety of language appear to be plausible candidates for being essential properties. One reasonable restriction on what properties can be "essential," attributed to G. H. von Wright, is that a property which is essential anywhere is essential everywhere; that is, if there is any element a such that fa is an essential property of a, then for any element b, if fb, then fb is an essential property of b, and if $\sim fb$, then $\sim fb$ is an essential property of b.

9. This should be interpreted with the qualification that such things as numbers can be treated as not strictly speaking **in** the various worlds and thus not participating in a cross-world counterpart relation.

10. Cross-world identification must take in not only persons and physical objects but also more abstract entities such as events. For example, when one says *That car could have run me over* after being narrowly missed by a recklessly driven car, one is not saying merely that there is an alternative world in which that car ran him over (say, a world in which the same near-miss occurred, whereupon the driver turned around and took a second shot at running the speaker over) but rather that there is an alternative world in which the same events that occurred in the real world (including the driver driving the way he did) had a different outcome.

11. I say "usually," since the terms "morning star" and "evening star" can refer to other planets. When Mercury is visible in the early evening and Venus is not, Mercury is referred to as the evening star; in Isaac Asimov's story "Heredity," which is set on the planet Mars, a character uses the expression *the morning star* to refer to the manifestation of Earth in the Martian sky. A necessary and sufficient condition for a visible planet to be a morning/evening star is that its orbit be inside that of the planet that one takes as vantage point.

12. A joke about a philosopher-astronaut who wants to pilot a spaceship to the morning star is just as funny as the one about the Polish astronaut who wants to pilot a spaceship to the sun, but philosophers usually fail to see the humor.

13. Hughes and Cresswell (1968) note that the symbol ⊰ first appeared in print in Lewis 1912, ◇ in Lewis and Langford 1932, and □ in Barcan 1946. Lewis of course wrote ⊰ between the items that it connected, for example, A ⊰ B. I will continue my policy of writing connectives at the left and write instead ⊰AB.

14. Since the various rules of inference perform set theoretic operations on the various index sets (as in 11.4.4) and since a supposition will behave in this regard as if it has a one-member index set, I will present suppositions as in fact having a one-member index set, as in the first line of 11.4.4, where I write $\{k\}$ rather than simply k.

15. Anderson and Belnap actually call this system FE→, reserving the name E→ for an equivalent system involving axioms that do the work of →-introduction. I will likewise write E⤳ below for the system that they actually call FE⤳.

16. Dunn (1986:152–53) gives a plausible rationale for why ∧-introduction should

require that the premises have the same index set. He adopts a condition that Prawitz (1965) had proposed imposing on systems of rules of inference: that the exploitation rule for any "logical" element not allow one to get more out of a formula than the corresponding introduction rule would put into the formula if one were to derive it by the introduction rule. Since ∧-exploitation has only one premise, and since index sets are simply sets, i.e., they have no internal structure, there is no alternative but to have the same index set for the conclusion as for the premise (as was tacitly assumed in line 4 of 11.4.7). Suppose that a given proof has a line ∧AB with index set N. Since A with index set N and B with index set N can both be inferred from that line (by ∧-exploitation), Prawitz's condition implies that if ∧AB were derived from A and B by ∧-introduction, it could not have any indices in its index set that were not indices of both A and B, since otherwise one could apply ∧-exploitation in such a way as to get more out of ∧AB than one had put into it, by deriving A and/or B with additional indices beyond the ones that they had to begin with. Thus, only 11.4.9 will avoid violations of Prawitz's condition.

17. While this rule is not one of the rules of inference for propositional logic given in chapter 3, it is available as a "derived" rule of inference: its effect can be simulated by a combination of other rules of inference. See now also Anderson et al. (1992: 498–506).

18. All that the distinguishability assumption tells us directly is that there is a proposition that is true in one of the two worlds and false in the other. However, if we had a proposition that was false in w_1 and true in w, we could take its negation as A_1. Thus the distinguishability assumption insures that for any worlds w' and w'', there will be a proposition true in w' and false in w''.

Chapter 12

1. The asterisks here relate only to nonreferential interpretations of the NPs in question; throughout this section, referential interpretations will be ignored.

2. The matter discussed here is considerably more complicated than this brief discussion suggests. For a more detailed treatment, see Reis 1974, where an account is developed that explains the puzzling fact that this phenomenon is largely restricted to first-person pronouns:

> *If you were Catherine Deneuve, you'd kiss you.

3. This amounts to saying that the interpretation of sentences involving world-creating predicates is subject to a principle of cooperativity: the speaker is taken as implying that the belief worlds, and so on, to which he refers agree with the real world in all relevant respects except those in which he has given the addressee reason to believe that they may differ from the real world. For example, the reason why (i) is so much more normal than (i′) is that the clause *Beethoven died at the age of forty* tells us that the dream world is one in which the events subsequent to Beethoven's fortieth year (such as his writing three more symphonies) did not occur, but provides us with no

information about Beethoven's tastes in food (for present purposes, I assumed that Beethoven in fact liked gebratene Leberkäse).

  i. Sam dreamed that Beethoven died at the age of forty and that Bernstein regretted that Beethoven had composed only six symphonies.
  i'. Sam dreamed that Beethoven died at the age of forty and that Bernstein regretted that Beethoven disliked gebratene Leberkäse.

The understanding of a sentence with a world-creating predicate is thus rather like the understanding of a counterfactual conditional. That is, (i) is acceptable for essentially the same reason that one would agree that if Beethoven had died at the age of forty he would have composed only six symphonies but would not agree that if he had died at the age of forty he would have disliked gebratene Leberkäse. The same point can be made about the relationship of (ii) to (ii'):

  ii. I dreamed that the Red Sox had won the 1977 American League pennant and that Billy Martin regretted that the Yankees had finished second.
  ii'. If the Red Sox had won the 1977 American League pennant, the Yankees would have finished second.

One will hold (ii') to be true if one believes that the Yankees and the Red Sox were bound to be the top two teams, and that proposition plus the counterfactual proposition that the Red Sox won the pennant implies that the Yankees finished second.

4. For perceptive remarks about the nature of pictorial representation, presented within a framework quite different from that of this chapter, see Jackendoff 1975 and Jackendoff 1983, chap. 11.

5. I am speaking of blanks being filled by individuals, real or fictitious, not by names of individuals. The individual need not be one to whom anyone has ever given a name, for example, the woman in Grant Wood's *American Gothic*.

6. Goffman 1974 provides much insightful discussion of the status of actions (including speech acts) carried out in theatrical performances, rehearsals, games, deceptions, and other "frames"; for applications of Goffman's ideas to issues in linguistics, see McCawley 1985b. See Fauconnier 1985 for extensive application of a scheme of "mental spaces" in which, as in the example of the theatrical performance and the events that are being enacted, a correspondence between the participants in two scenes allows participants in either scene to be referred to in terms of their counterparts in the other scene.

7. See Smith 1981, Prince 1982, and Eilfort 1985 for discussion of "futurate" uses of the present tense, which I will ignore in the remainder of this section. A futurate present differs from a future with *will* in that it implies that the world at present is constituted so as to make the future the way that the sentence indicates. For example, *The plane arrives at 4:37* says what the schedule currently is and is not a prediction about when the plane will actually arrive; *The White Sox will win tomorrow* is merely a prediction, while *The White Sox win tomorrow* suggests that the outcome of the game is already determined, i.e., the game is rigged.

8. Useful overviews of research in tense logic are given in Prior 1967, Rescher and Urquhart 1971, and Burgess 1984.

9. I will cite only English data in treating the various linguistic considerations that I take up. For valuable cross-linguistic treatments of linguistic categories related to time, see Comrie 1976, 1985, and Dahl 1985. I hope eventually to develop the approach to tense logic given in this section in such a way that it can be applied fruitfully to drawing the full range of semantic distinctions that these works survey.

In view of the fact that many languages, strictly speaking, do not have tense systems, I am not fully happy with the term "tense logic." It should be clear from what follows that much of the tense logic that I discuss in relation to English, though crucially involving temporal notions, has little to do with tense per se.

10. In much of the literature on tense logic, these operators are symbolised as F, G, P, and H, respectively. In view of the difficulty that I have always had in remembering which of these letters stands for which of the four notions, I have substituted symbols that are more transparent.

11. In determining what is a "normal" continuation of a world, the intentions of the relevant persons play at least as large a role as do physical laws. It is in virtue of Agnes being in the middle of executing a plan to write a letter in 12.2.10a that a future in which she completes the letter is "normal." Actually, it may be necessary to recast the discussion of progressives in terms not of "worlds" but of what Barwise and Perry (1983) speak of as "situations," i.e., possibly incomplete specifications of a world, since plans can conflict with each other and with the consequences of physical laws, as in such examples as *Smith was filling the pool and Brown was emptying the pool when they both were killed in the earthquake.* Here, each of the plans is doomed to be thwarted both by the other plan and by the unexpected geological event; neither a world in which Smith finishes filling the pool nor a world in which Brown finishes emptying the pool is a possible continuation of the world as it existed just prior to the earthquake. In using the progressive here, one is referring rather to ways things would have been had nothing stopped Smith from carrying out the one intention or had nothing stopped Brown from carrying out the other intention; these "ways things would have been" cannot be fully specified continuations of full specifications of the way things were at the given time, but they could be taken to be partially specified continuations of partial specifications of the way things were at that time.

12. See McCawley 1988b for arguments that adverbial NPs such as *yesterday* in 12.2.12b are P's with a zero P, e.g., here *yesterday* is the object of an understood preposition having the same meaning as the *on* of *on Tuesday* or the *in* of *in April*, and an element corresponding to that P is part of the logical form of sentences like 12.2.12b.

13. Reichenbach does give a few such formulas in his list of answers to exercises, but the formulas are makeshifts that I suspect he did not take very seriously.

14. In 12.2.19b, I use the makeshift of writing "$\exists_3$," to mean "there are three (values of the variable) such that . . .". This should be understood as an abbreviation of the sort of logical structure that I give in section 7.4 in which there is a bound set variable ("there is a set of three time intervals such that . . ."). As in the case of

12.2.11, the formulas in 12.2.19 are deficient by virtue of lacking any indication that the event (John's marrying Amy) is in the past.

15. While the relation between E and S never affects the choice of a tense and an auxiliary verb in the given clause (that is, in the clause expressing E), it may give rise to a conflict that renders a sentence unsayable. For example, if John arrived one week ago and will leave one week from now, the following sentences ought to be possible ways of expressing the relation between his arrival and his departure, but they sound quite odd because they violate a constraint requiring time adverbial clauses to agree in tense with the clauses that they modify:

> ??John will leave two weeks after he arrived.
> ??John arrived two weeks before he leaves.

This restriction has to do with tense and not with time reference, since corresponding sentences in which one of the tense markers is absent are acceptable:

> John will leave two weeks after his arrival.

16. English is unusual in using a present perfect in such sentences as 12.2.25. A simple present is much more common (e.g., German, French, Russian).

17. This is a good point at which to correct one oversight of Reichenbach's. The R in a present perfect is not always the speech act time, but can be any time that is expressed by the present tense. Thus, we find present perfects as in (i), where R is a future time that is expressed by a present tense in the antecedent of a conditional, as in (ii), where R is a variable time whose domain includes the speech act time, and as in (iii), where R is the time at which a narrative is set, which need not bear any determinate relationship to the time of the speech act:

> i.   If we ever find a linguist who <u>has done</u> field work on Burushaski, we'll offer him a job.
> ii. A country that <u>has been ruled</u> by a philosopher can't be all bad.
> iii. I've just read a novel in which someone who <u>has received</u> a Nobel prize gives up his career and enters a monastery.

Note that the most obvious interpretation of (i) has to do with the linguist doing field work on Burushaski prior to your finding him (which may be far in the future), not with his doing field work on it prior to the event in which the speaker utters (i). For further corrections to both Reichenbach's analysis and my 1971 reworking of it, see McCawley 1981b.

18. That the relevant state for 12.2.32c consists in the Dodgers being (based) in Los Angeles is confirmed by comparing it with (i):

> i.   ??The reason you can't say "The Boston Braves have won several pennants" is that the Braves have moved to Milwaukee and so the Boston Braves can't win any more pennants.

The difference here is that while the Dodgers have remained in Los Angeles since the move, the Braves moved to Atlanta after a few years and so are no longer in Milwaukee.

19. However, the stative present perfect excludes *already* and *by now*.

20. I allude here to the possibility of importing a superordinate line B into a subproof by conjoining it with any earlier line C of the subproof or of a superordinate proof, thus introducing ∧BC into the subproof by ∧-introduction, and then deriving B from ∧BC by ∧-exploitation.

Chapter 13

1. Note that Łukasiewicz's approach cannot keep **all** valid formulas of classical propositional logic valid; for example, ∨(A, ~A) will not be valid, since its value is I whenever A is I. Thus, Łukasiewicz appears to have been more attached to some formulas of classical propositional logic than to others. I find his preferences among the valid formulas quite reasonable; or at least, I could live more easily without ∨(A, ~A) than without ⊃AA. However, to get ⊃AA to be valid, one must accept a truth table that is at odds with the interpretation of I as "future contingent."

2. This truth table figures in an alternative version of many-valued logic proposed by Kurt Gödel (summarized in Rescher 1969:44–45). However, Gödel's system involved a different truth table for negation than Łukasiewicz's had: in Gödel's system, ~A is F except when A is F, that is, the negation of an I proposition is I for Łukasiewicz but F for Gödel.

3. It is not necessary to admit **all** numbers in the interval [0, 1] as truth values: the truth conditions given below require only that if a number a is admitted as a truth value, then so is $1 - a$, and thus one could take, for example, the five values that appear in 13.1.7 as the set of truth values. Important consequences of whether one admits infinitely or only finitely many truth values in a system of fuzzy logic such as is presented here are pointed out in Morgan and Pelletier 1977.

4. There are several distinct ways that one might replace Łukasiewicz's original truth table by formulas for the two classes of cases. For example: /⊃AB/ = 1 if /A/ ≤ /B/, /⊃AB/ = 1 − /A/ + /B/ if /A/ > /B/. These two parts could be combined into the single formula /⊃AB/ = min(1, 1 − /A/ + /B/), since "/A/ ≤ /B/" is equivalent to "1 − /A/ + /B/ ≥ 1."

5. Strictly speaking, we should say "least upper bound" rather than "maximum" and "greatest lower bound" rather than "minimum," since there need not be any element of the domain that makes /fx/ a maximum (or a minimum). For example, suppose that we took the truth value of "x is colossal" to be always less than 1 but allow it to get as close to 1 as one might like (say, if x ranges over numbers, /x is colossal/ might be taken to be $1 - 1/x$). In that case 1 is the "least upper bound" of the set of truth values that x can assume, but it is not the "maximum" value of /fx/, since /fx/ never takes the value 1. However, to simplify the exposition, I will say "minimum" where I should say "greatest lower bound," and "maximum" where I should say "least upper bound."

6. I ignore here the contribution of *person* to the content of 13.2.1.

7. This measure has the oddity that it comes out negative when $/ga/ > /fa/ > 0$. If one wishes, one can amend the proposal so as to make the degree of counterexamplehood be zero rather than negative in such cases.

8. The notion of a fuzzy alternativeness relation has some similarity to Lewis's notion of different worlds differing in how "close" they are to one another (see sec. 15.1) but has the important difference that for a fuzzy alternativeness relation, $/Rww'/$ may be 1 even if $w' \neq w$, whereas for Lewis any two distinct worlds are always "some distance apart."

9. To prove this properly, it would be necessary to refrain from assuming that $/fx/(/fx/ - /gx/)$ ever attains its least upper bound. The interested reader is invited to redo these proofs with that modification.

10. For a fuller treatment of the matters sketched in this section, see Zadeh 1965, 1971.

11. As 13.3.3 stands, it gives only the conditions under which $/A \subseteq B/ = 1$ and does not say under what conditions it might have a truth value greater than 0 and less than 1. If one wishes a sentence like *All fat persons are jolly* to have the same truth value as the proposition that the set of all fat persons is a subset of the set of all jolly persons, one will have to revise 13.3.3 to make it fit the conclusion about the truth value of universally quantified propositions that was arrived at in section 13.2. Note that if $/A \subseteq B/$ were simply taken to be 0 whenever the condition in 13.3.3 is not met, a weak counterexample to the proposition that $A \subseteq B$ (e.g., an entity that was to degree 0.1 a member of A and to degree 0.09 a member of B) would be enough to reduce its truth value to zero.

12. The effect of these arbitrary decisions remains attenuated in combinations put together with $\wedge$, $\vee$, and $\sim$, but can have a more profound effect on the truth values of conditional propositions, according to the truth conditions proposed in section 13.1.

13. For insightful discussion of expressions like *very, very tall* and *he ran and ran,* in which lexical items are repeated an arbitrary number of times, see Knowles 1979.

14. *Not quite* is not simply a negation of *quite,* in view of its different combinatoric properties:

> The watchman was not quite dead when the police arrived.

15. Combinations of *pretty well* with hedged adjectives make no sense, but that is because *pretty well* can only be combined with expressions referring to the end of a scale:

> *John is pretty well very tall.
> John is pretty well exhausted/*tired.

16. Lakoff (1972b, sec. 3) has stated that 13.5.4b "presupposes that Esther Williams is not literally a fish." However, *regular* in fact does not carry with it a presupposition that the predicate is literally inapplicable, since it is easy to imagine a situation in which both of the following would be correct things to say:

> Peoria is a regular disaster area.
> Technically, Peoria is a disaster area.

and thus the applicability of *a regular disaster area* does not require that the place under discussion fail to be literally a disaster area. Likewise, if Opus the penguin takes up hang gliding and becomes extremely good at it, it may be true that Opus is a regular bird, but it will also be true that technically, Opus is a bird.

17. Note that while a technical sense of *idiot* exists, it would not figure plausibly in the interpretation of 13.5.7.

18. The use of connotational properties is often highly conventionalized. For example, when we speak of Esther Williams as being "a regular fish" or "at home in the water," we refer only to the skill and effortlessness of her swimming: we know that she sleeps on a mattress and not under the water and that she eats off a plate and with a knife and fork rather than ingesting plankton and smaller fish (even smaller regular fish) while she swims.

19. Of course, if we broaden the notion of tautology to mean a formula that can assume only the values T and *t,* that is, if we take *t* as well as T to be a "designated" truth value, then exactly the same formulas will be tautologies here as in classical propositional logic.

Chapter 14

1. Strictly speaking, this is not correct, since according to this definition, two expressions could differ in intension without its being possible (relative to the given world) for their extensions to differ: their extensions might differ only at worlds that are not accessible from the given world. Since most work in intensional logic has ignored the possibility of a nontrivial accessibility relation, i.e., such authors as Montague have assumed a modal system in which every world is possible relative to every other world, this point is tangential to most of the literature in this area. There is of course nothing in principle to prevent one from doing intensional logic in terms of modal systems that have nontrivial accessibility relations.

2. It is not clear why *s* was chosen as the symbol for "worlds"; perhaps because it is the initial of Latin *saeculum*? Or of Chinese *shijie*?

3. A useful mnemonic for keeping straight what ˆ and ˇ stand for is that the one that points up raises the type (intension) and the one that points down lowers it (extension).

4. Montague's principal works in this area are conveniently collected in Montague 1974. For subsequent development of Montague's general approach, see Bach 1980, Cresswell 1973, Dowty 1979, Karttunen and Peters 1977, 1979, and Partee 1975, 1976. **Generalized phrase-structure grammar** (Gazdar et al. 1985) is a version of Montague grammar in which a very specific conception of syntactic rule takes the place of Montague's completely open-ended conception, and a particular componential approach to syntactic categories takes the place of Montague's ad hoc use of multiple slashes to distinguish syntactic categories that correspond to the same semantic type.

For comparison between Montague grammar and other syntactic approaches, especially transformational grammar, see McCawley 1977b, 1979b.

5. The second number in [S; 3, 0] indicates the value of i; the expression at the top of 14.2.1 is thus formed by substituting *every man* for he_0 in he_0 *loves some woman*.

6. I will follow Montague's informal practise of using primes to indicate the predicates of the system of intensional logic that correspond to English words that (in the given exposition) are not further analyzed, for example, love' (x, y) is the two-place predicate that figures in the translation of *love*. This practise is a direct analog to the capitalization (e.g., LOVE) employed by other linguists for the same purpose. Many steps in this translation are greatly oversimplified. The oversimplification will be corrected below.

7. The symbols x and P that appear here are used purely as illustrations. The actual choice of variables is made in such a way as to avoid incoherent combinations, as in 14.2.3a, where y rather than x appears as the variable bound by the universal quantifier.

While Montague grammarians have in fact commonly given their translations of quantified expressions in terms of unrestricted quantification, as in 14.1.2–3, nothing in the framework forces one to do so: one can do Montague grammar in terms of restricted quantifiers, as do Barwise and Cooper (1981) and other authors who have considered a broader range of quantifiers than the minuscule set that figures in early works in Montague grammar. Montague's treatment of the syntax of quantifiers was not exactly as in 14.2.1, in that he treated the quantifiers not as "basic expressions" but as inserted by syntactic rule: his rule actually formed *every man* from *man* rather than from *every* and *man*. This illustrates the point that in Montague grammar there is the same kind of nonuniqueness of analysis that there was in early transformational grammar, where elements such as *not* could be either present in "base structures" or inserted by transformations.

8. For Ajdukiewicz, any number of category symbols could appear after the slash; for example, $(s/n\ n)$ is the category of items that combine with two names to yield a sentence. Montague grammarians have generally confined their categories to those in which only one item appears after the slash, that is, to categories that yield "binary branching" analysis trees.

9. The general framework of Montague grammar does not force one to use an ad hoc device such as this for distinguishing categories whose denotations are of the same logical type. The multiple slashes amount to a numerical index combined with a "slash category": it would be only a minor change in typography to write $(t/e, 1)$ and $(t/e, 2)$ where Montague wrote t/e and $t//e$. If one adopts a "componential" conception of syntactic categories, in which a category of pristine categorial grammar is one of several components defining a category of Montague syntax, one could take as a second component not an arbitrary numerical index but the part of speech of the head of the expression, thus replacing Montague's t/e and $t//e$ by $(t/e, V)$ and $(t/e, N)$. This is in fact done in the version of Montague grammar whose syntax has been worked out in the greatest detail, namely Generalized Phrase Structure Grammar (GPSG; see Gazdar et al. 1985).

10. Kripke's definition of "rigid designator" (1972:269–70) is different from this in a small but important respect: Kripke only required that a rigid designator have the same denotation in all worlds in which it has a denotation and left it open whether it has a denotation in every world. However, this difference can be ignored here, since Montague did not require that the denotation of an individual constant in a given world be an object that exists in that world (i.e., the denotations of individual constants are possible entities, not necessarily actual entities), and thus he could take a constant as denoting the same entity in all worlds even if the entity that it denotes does not exist in all worlds. Kaplan (1989:569–71) gives a useful overview of the differences among the different conceptions of rigid designator.

11. Following Partee 1975, a double-shafted arrow is used to indicate "is translated into" and a single-shafted arrow for "is converted into" (by λ-conversion, meaning postulates, or other principles of equivalence). The end result in such "derivations" as 14.2.9 is, loosely speaking, a translation of the original expression into a formula of intensional logic, in that it is "equivalent to" a translation in the narrow sense.

12. The formula in 14.2.14 involves Montague's symbol ↔, standing for "if and only if."

13. This change will force us to introduce ˘ into the translations given earlier for *every* and *a:*

$$every\ man \Rightarrow (\lambda Q)(\forall x)\supset(man'(x), (\check{}Q)(x))$$
$$a\ man \Rightarrow (\lambda Q)(\exists x) \wedge(man'(x), (\check{}Q)(x))$$

14. Bach (1980) refers to this operation as "right-wrap"; it is one of a number of "elementary operations" that he proposes as part of a conception of syntactic rule that greatly narrows the essentially unlimited range of possible syntactic rules that Montague was willing to countenance.

15. While there is a consensus among Montague grammarians as to the general outlines of an analysis of passive clauses, there is no consensus as to the category to which passive V's should be assigned; I continue here the common practise of simply using an ad hoc name for whatever the appropriate category is.

16. The treatment described here covers only "reduced" passives, not full passives such as *Ted was given the money by Ann,* in which a translation is needed in which the semantic subject position is filled not by an existentially quantified NP but by something corresponding to the object of *by.* Giving an integrated treatment of full and reduced passives in Montague grammar is in fact a daunting task, and Montague grammarians have generally avoided it, simply giving a separate rule for full passives (and thus incorrectly treating *given the money by Ann* as if *given the money* is not a syntactic constituent of it). The way of treating full passives in Montague grammar that I find most attractive is one that adapts the conclusion of Langacker and Munro (1975) that (contrary to the nearly unanimous opinion of transformational grammarians) full passives are derived from reduced passives, with the *by*-phrase having the logical character of a *namely*-phrase (i.e., *John was bitten* is to *John was bitten by a dog* roughly as *Something bit John* is to *Something bit John, namely a dog*).

17. Strictly speaking, Dowty's rule has the false implication that *to Ted* in 14.2.47a′ is not a syntactic constituent: only if there were a rule forming such expressions as *to Ted* (which then might be combined by a separate rule into *give to Ted*) would the assumptions made by Montague grammarians allow *to Ted* to have any status as a syntactic unit. This illustrates the point (made in McCawley 1977b) that both Montague grammar and orthodox transformational grammar have adopted policies about constituent structure and category membership that make it impossible for a "transformationally inserted" element to belong to any syntactic category or to play any syntactic structural role. By contrast, in the approach of McCawley (1982b, 1988a), lexical units belong to a category inherently (e.g., *to* is a preposition, irrespective of whether it is present in deep structure or inserted in the course of the derivation), and deep structures have no direct relevance to the category membership of surface syntactic units.

18. Goldsmith (1980) argues that V's of the form [V NP NP] differ systematically in interpretation from those of the form [V NP P′], in that they imply (while the latter need not) that the person denoted by the first NP is supposed to have the thing denoted by the second NP. Thus, for Goldsmith, the reason that *I sent the package to Fred* has an alternative form *I sent Fred the package* but *I sent the package to New York* does not have the alternative form **I sent New York the package* is that the one event is supposed to result in Fred having the package but the other is not supposed to result in New York having the package (unless *New York* is used to mean, say, "our New York office," in which case the sentence is acceptable). Dowty's analysis could be revised to accomodate this observation by altering the semantic rule in 14.2.50, conjoining to the inner S another S that says roughly "$\mathcal{Q}$ is supposed to have $\mathcal{P}$ at the end of the event denoted by δ'" (or rather, a counterpart to that in which adjustments are made to get variables of the right types in the argument positions); alternatively, one could add a meaning postulate that allows a proposition of that form to be inferred from sentences whose predicate element is a $\delta'_{TV/T}$.

19. The term "generalized quantifiers," introduced in Mostowski 1957 and popularized by Barwise and Cooper 1981, refers to a semantic counterpart of quantified NPs. Since a "generalized quantifier" typically (though not necessarily) consists of a quantifier and an N′, i.e., it is something of which a quantifier is a proper part, I regard the (by now remarkably popular) term as misleading in much the same way that "generalized verbs" would be a misleading term for V's. I accordingly will avoid using the term here, though I have retained it (with scare quotes) in the title of this section for the benefit of readers who seek information about "generalized quantifiers" and the approach to quantification that is associated with that term.

20. I use $|X|$ here to mean "the number of members of X." In 14.3.3b I assume the treatment of *Two linguists were arrested* according to which it says that the number arrested was at least two and conversationally implicates but does not logically imply that only two were arrested. In treating *two* as a determiner here, I am of course being inconsistent with what I said in section 7.4 where I argued that in a NP such as *two linguists* there is a zero existential determiner combined with an N′ in which *two* is a modifier of *linguists*. The inconsistency can be removed if one broadens the notion of

"determiner" to include "derived determiners" consisting of a determiner in the narrow conception of section 7.4 plus one or more adjuncts to the N′ with which that determiner is combined. The conception of "determiner" that is prevalent in the generalized quantifier literature is sufficiently broad as to allow a huge range of such derived determiners; Keenan (1987), for example, explicitly includes the underlined expressions below in his class of determiners:

Neither every student's nor every teacher's car was stolen.
Exactly two of the ten students left early.
More of John's than of Mary's articles were accepted.

21. It is occasionally suggested that *many* is not constant, in view of the way in which contextual factors influence how many entities of a given class it takes to count as "many" members of it. However, in this case the interpretation depends not directly on the universe (e.g., adding chickens or Beatle records to the universe won't have any effect on the interpretation of *Many students did poorly on the German exam*) but only on the denotations of the constituents of the sentence and thus will reflect the universe only in that the universe places limits on the size of the denotations of various expressions.

22. Strictly speaking, being right monotone increasing or decreasing is a property of NPs rather than of determiners, in that it can be defined for arbitrary NPs irrespective of whether they are of the form Det N′: for any set X of sets of individuals (i.e., any object of the sort that is treated here as the denotation of a NP), X is (right) monotone increasing if whenever one set of individuals B is contained in another, B′, if XB is true, so is XB′; it is (right) monotone decreasing if whenever one set of individuals B contains another, B′, if XB is true, so is XB′. Among the NPs that are monotone increasing are proper names and conjunctions of monotone increasing NPs, e.g., *Senator Claghorn accepts huge bribes* entails *Senator Claghorn accepts bribes,* and *Some judges and many senators accept huge bribes* entails *Some judges and many senators accept bribes.*

Chapter 15

1. There actually is some doubt as to the validity of strengthening the protasis even for indicative conditionals; see the discussion of 15.2.5 below.

2. There is in fact some dispute as to whether inferences like 15.1.5 are valid in general; see 15.2.6 for discussion of a possible counterexample to its validity.

3. See McCawley 1976a for remarks suggesting that this condition may have to be dropped in order to avoid certain puzzles involving causation.

4. Throughout this section, I will assume that R is reflexive.

5. Kratzer (1989:628) has pointed out an undesirable consequence of simply taking $\lor pq$ always to be ranked above p. Suppose that p is something which one believes to be true and q is a blatant falsehood that is not logically impossible, e.g., p = "Nixon resigned in 1974" and q = "The Atlantic Ocean is drying up." If $\lor pq$ is ranked higher than p (which is not at all outlandish: no matter how improbable it is that the Atlantic

is drying up, there is an infinitesimally greater likelihood that either it is drying up or Nixon resigned in 1974 than that Nixon resigned in 1974), then the Rescher semantics will make counterfactuals such as the following true:

> If Nixon had not resigned in 1974, then the Atlantic Ocean would be drying up.

Since $\vee pq$ is consistent with $\sim p$, it will not be discarded in the construction of M', though p of course will be; consequently, $M' \cup \{\sim p\} \vdash q$.

To keep the Rescher semantics from having absurd consequences such as this, one must give up the idea that all propositions $\vee pq$ are ranked higher than a belief p. I wish to suggest that the fact that p is among a person's beliefs should not automatically require that $\vee pq$ count as one of his beliefs, even though the truth of p guarantees the truth of $\vee pq$. I tentatively propose that a disjunctive proposition should count as a belief only if a person believes it for some reason other than his belief in one of the conjuncts, as when, say, one believes that the plays generally attributed to Shakespeare were written by either Shakespeare or the Duke of Oxford, on the grounds that Shakespeare and the Duke of Oxford are the only plausible candidates for their authorship. On this understanding of "beliefs," a person who believes that the plays in question actually are by Shakespeare could have the belief that either Shakespeare or the Duke of Oxford wrote them without also having the belief that either Shakespeare or Mickey Spillane wrote them, even though both of these disjunctive propositions are logical consequences of the proposition that Shakespeare wrote the Shakespearean plays.

Note, by the way, that this policy on beliefs avoids one suspicious step in the construction of M' in the last paragraph: in constructing M', one discards p and retains $\vee pq$ even though one's sole grounds for having a "belief" that $\vee pq$ was his belief that p. This understanding of "belief" also allows one to avoid a technical problem that otherwise arises: if $\vee pq$ always counted as a belief when p did and was always ranked higher in confidence than p, one's beliefs could not be ranked in a sequence $p_1, p_2, p_3,$ . . . , since for any belief there would then always be infinitely many other beliefs ranked higher than it, and thus the procedure for constructing M' could not be carried out.

6. Within Rescher's approach, the most promising treatment of *might*-counterfactuals is to take them to be true when $M' \cup \{A\}$ is consistent with B.

7. A further difference between *unless* and *if . . . not* is that the clause introduced by *unless* has to be a "marked" possibility, while in *if not q*, neither q nor *not q* need be "marked." Thus, while (i) and (ii) would usually be perfectly normal things to say, (i') would be normal only in a situation in which the person is not expected to be able to pay by cash, and (ii') only in a situation in which it is a deviation from normality for a student to turn in his paper on time:

    i.   I'll take a check if you don't have cash.
    i'. I'll take a check unless you have cash.
    ii. I give students low grades if they don't turn in their papers on time.
    ii'. I give students low grades unless they turn in their papers on time.

References

Abbreviations

BLS	Berkeley Linguistics Society (Proceedings of Annual Meeting)
CLS	Chicago Linguistic Society (Papers from Annual Meeting)
ESCOL	Eastern States Conference on Linguistics (Papers from Annual Meeting)
FoL	*Foundations of Language*
HPhL	*Handbook of Philosophical Logic*
IULC	Indiana University Linguistics Club
JP	*Journal of Philosophy*
JPL	*Journal of Philosophical Logic*
LA	*Linguistic Analysis*
Lg	*Language*
LI	*Linguistic Inquiry*
L&P	*Linguistics and Philosophy*
NELS	North Eastern Linguistic Society (Papers from Annual Meeting)
PR	*Philosophical Review*
UCWPL	University of Chicago Working Papers in Linguistics

Abney, Stephen. 1987. The English noun phrase in its sentential aspect. Ph.D. diss., MIT.

Ajdukiewicz, Kazimierz. 1935. Über die syntaktische Konnexität. *Studia Philosophica* 1:1–27. English translation in Storrs McColl, ed., *Polish logic, 1920–1939*, pp. 207–31. Oxford: Clarendon.

Akmajian, Adrian, and Thomas Wasow. 1975. The constituent structure of VP and AUX and the position of the verb *be*. *LA* 1:205–45.

Anderson, Alan Ross. 1951. A note on subjunctive and counterfactual conditionals. *Analysis* 12:35–38.

Anderson, Alan Ross, and Nuel D. Belnap Jr. 1975. *Entailment*. Vol. 1. Princeton, N.J.: Princeton University Press.

Anderson, Alan Ross, Nuel D. Belnap Jr., and Michael Dunn. 1992. *Entailment*. Vol. 2. Princeton, N.J.: Princeton University Press.

Arnauld, Antoine. 1662. *The art of thinking*. Reprinted 1962. New York: Bobbs-Merrill.

Austin, J. L. 1957. A plea for excuses. *Proceedings of the Aristotelian Society* 57:1–30. Reprinted in Austin 1961:123–52.

————. 1961. *Philosophical papers*. Oxford: Oxford University Press.

————. 1962. *How to do things with words*. Oxford: Oxford University Press.

————. 1963. Performative-constative. In Caton 1963:22–54.

Bach, Emmon. 1970. Problominalization. *LI* 1:121–22.

————. 1980. In defense of passive. *L&P* 3:297–341.

Bakunin, Mikhail. 1871. *God and the state*. Translated 1916; reprinted 1970. New York: Dover.

Barcan [Marcus], Ruth. 1946. A functional calculus of first order based on strict implication. *Journal of Symbolic Logic* 11:1–16.

Barker, Chris, and Geoffrey K. Pullum. 1990. A theory of command relations. *L&P* 13:1–34.

Barwise, Jon. 1979. On branching quantifiers in English. *JPL* 8:47–80.

Barwise, Jon, and Robin Cooper. 1981. Generalized quantifiers and natural language. *L&P* 4:159–219.

Barwise, Jon, and John Perry. 1983. *Situations and attitudes*. Cambridge, MA: MIT Press.

Bastiat, Frederic. 1850. What is seen and what is not seen. In F. Bastiat, *Selected essays on political economy*. Princeton: Van Nostrand, 1962.

Belnap, Nuel D., Jr. 1977. A useful four-valued logic. In M. Dunn and G. Epstein, eds., *Modern uses of multiple-valued logic*, pp. 5–37. Dordrecht: Reidel.

Bencivenga, Ermanno. 1985. Free logics. *HPhL* 3:373–426.

Bennett, David. 1975. *Spatial and temporal uses of English prepositions*. London: Longmans.

Bouton, Lawrence R. 1970. Antecedent-contained pro-forms. *Papers from the sixth regional meeting, Chicago Linguistic Society*, pp. 154–67.

Braine, Martin D. S. 1978. On the relation between the natural logic of reasoning and standard logic. *Psychological Review* 85:1–30.

Bunt, Harry. 1976. The formal semantics of mass terms. In F. Karlsson, ed., *Papers from the third Scandinavian conference of linguistics*, pp. 81–94. Turku: Academy of Finland.

————. 1979. Ensembles and the formal properties of mass terms. In Pelletier 1979:249–77.

————. 1985. *Mass terms and model-theoretic semantics*. Cambridge: Cambridge Univ. Press.

Burgess, John. 1984. Basic tense logic. *HPhL* 2:89–133.

Cantrall, William. 1974. *Viewpoint, reflexives, and the nature of noun phrases*. The Hague: Mouton.

Carden, Guy. 1973. *English quantifiers: Logical structure and linguistic variation*. Tokyo: Taishukan; New York: Academic Press.

Carlson, Gregory. 1977. Reference to kinds in English. Ph.D. diss., University of Massachusetts at Amherst.

607   References

_____. 1981. Distribution of free choice *any*. *CLS* 17:8–23.

_____. 1982. General terms and generic sentences. *JPL* 11:145–81.

_____. 1989. On the semantic composition of English generic sentences. In Chierchia, Partee, and Turner 1989, vol. 2, pp. 167–92.

Carnap, Rudolf. 1943. *Formalization of logic*. Cambridge, MA: Harvard University Press.

_____. 1947. *Meaning and necessity*. Chicago: University of Chicago Press.

Caton, Charles E. 1963. *Philosophy and ordinary language*. Urbana and Chicago: University of Illinois Press.

Chierchia, Gennaro. 1992. Anaphora and dynamic binding. *L&P* 15.111–89.

Chierchia, Gennaro, Barbara H. Partee, and Raymond Turner, eds. 1989. *Properties, types, and meaning*. 2 vols. Dordrecht: Kluwer.

Chomsky, Noam A. 1957. *Syntactic structures*. The Hague: Mouton.

_____. 1965. *Aspects of the theory of syntax*. Cambridge, Mass.: MIT Press.

_____. 1966. *Topics in the theory of generative grammar*. The Hague: Mouton.

_____. 1970. Remarks on nominalization. In R. Jacobs and P. Rosenbaum, eds., *Readings in English transformational grammar*, pp. 184–221. Boston: Ginn.

_____. 1972. *Studies on semantics in generative grammar*. The Hague: Mouton.

_____. 1976. *Essays on form and interpretation*. Amsterdam: North Holland.

_____. 1981. *Lectures on government and binding*. Dordrecht: Foris.

_____. 1986. *Knowledge of language*. New York: Praeger.

Cohen, L. Jonathan. 1972. Remarks on Grice's analysis of logical particles in natural language. In Y. Bar-Hillel, ed., *Pragmatics of natural language*, pp. 50–68. Dordrecht: Reidel.

Cole, Peter. 1981. *Radical pragmatics*. New York: Academic Press.

Comrie, Bernard. 1976. *Aspect*. Cambridge University Press.

_____. 1985. *Tense*. Cambridge University Press.

Cresswell, M. J. 1973. *Logics and languages*. London: Methuen.

Croft, William. 1990. *Typology and Universals*. Cambridge University Press.

Dahl, Östen. 1975. On generics. In Edward Keenan, ed., *Formal semantics of natural languages*, pp. 99–111. Cambridge: Cambridge University Press.

_____. 1985. *Tense and aspect systems*. Oxford: Blackwell.

Davidson, Donald, and Gilbert Harman. 1972. *Semantics of natural language*. Dordrecht: Reidel.

Davis, Steven, and Marianne Mithun. 1979. *Linguistics, philosophy, and Montague grammar*. Austin: University of Texas Press.

Davison, Alice. 1973. Performative verbs, adverbs, and felicity conditions. Ph.D. diss., University of Chicago.

_____. 1980. Peculiar passives. *Lg* 56:42–66.

Dik, Simon. 1973. Crossing coreference again. *FoL* 9: 306–26.

Donnellan, Keith. 1966. Reference and definite descriptions. *PR* 75:281–304. Reprinted in Steinberg and Jakobovits 1971:100–114.

Doron, Edit. 1988. The semantics of predicate nominals. *Linguistics* 26:281–301.

Dowty, David. 1978. Governed transformations as lexical rules in a Montague grammar. *LI* 9:393–426.

————. 1979. *Word meaning and Montague grammar.* Dordrecht: Reidel.

Dummett, Michael. 1958. Truth. *Proceedings of the Aristotelian Society* 59:141–62. Reprinted in Strawson 1967:49–68.

————. 1977. *Elements of intuitionism.* Oxford: Oxford University Press.

Dunn, J. Michael. 1986. Relevance logic and entailment. *HPhL* 3:117–224.

Eilfort, William H. 1985. The English futurate: Just another tense. *UCWPL* 1:9–17.

Emonds, Joseph E. 1976. *A transformational approach to English syntax.* New York: Academic Press.

Fauconnier, Gilles. 1985. *Mental spaces.* Cambridge, MA: MIT Press.

Feldman, Fred. 1971. Counterparts. *JP* 68:406–9.

Feyerabend, Paul. 1987. *Farewell to reason.* London and New York: Verso.

Fiengo, Robert, and Howard Lasnik. 1973. The logical structure of reciprocal sentences in English. *FoL* 9:447–68.

Fillmore, Charles J. 1978. Pragmatics and the description of discourse. In Cole 1981:143–66.

Fillmore, Charles J., and Langendoen, D. T. 1971. *Studies in linguistic semantics.* New York: Holt, Rinehart and Winston.

Fitch, Frederic B. 1952. *Symbolic logic: An introduction.* New York: Ronald.

Fodor, Jerry A. 1975. *The language of thought.* New York: Crowell.

Fodor, Jerry A., and Jerrold J. Katz. 1964. *The structure of language.* Englewood Cliffs, NJ: Prentice-Hall.

Fraser, Bruce. 1974a. An examination of the performative analysis. *Papers in Linguistics* 7:1–40.

————. 1974b. An analysis of vernacular performative verbs. In R. W. Shuy and C.-J. Bailey, eds., *Towards tomorrow's linguistics,* pp. 139–58. Washington, D.C.: Georgetown University Press.

Frege, Gottlob. 1879. *Begriffsschrift.* English translation in J. van Heijenoort, ed., *From Frege to Gödel: A source book in mathematical logic, 1879–1931.* Cambridge, Mass.: Harvard University Press.

Gazdar, Gerald. 1979. *Pragmatics.* New York: Academic Press.

Gazdar, Gerald, Ewan Klein, Geoffrey K. Pullum, and Ivan Sag. 1985. *Generalized phrase structure grammar.* Oxford: Blackwell, and Cambridge, MA: Harvard University Press.

Geach, Peter T. 1962. *Reference and generality.* Ithaca: Cornell University Press. (Page references to 3rd edition, 1980.)

————. 1967. Intentional identity. *JP* 64:627–32. Reprinted in Geach 1972:146–53.

————. 1972. *Logic matters.* Oxford: Blackwell.

————. 1976. *Reason and argument* Oxford: Blackwell, and Berkeley and Los Angeles: University of California Press.

Geis, Michael. 1973. *If* and *unless.* In B. J. Kachru et al., eds., *Issues in linguistics:*

Papers in honor of Henry and Renee Kahane, pp. 231–53. Urbana and Chicago: University of Illinois Press.

Gentzen, Gerhard. 1969. *Collected papers of Gerhard Gentzen*. Amsterdam: North-Holland.

Gibbard, Alan. 1981. Two recent theories of conditionals. In Harper, Stalnaker, and Pearce 1981, pp. 211–47.

Gleitman, Lila. 1965. Coordinating conjunctions in English. *Lg* 41:260–93. Reprinted in Reibel and Schane 1969:80–112.

Goffman, Erving. 1974. *Frame analysis*. New York: Harper.

———. 1979. Footing. *Semiotica* 25:1–29. Reprinted in E. Goffman, *Forms of Talk*, pp. 78–123. Philadelphia: University of Pennsylvania Press, 1981.

Goldsmith, John. 1980. Meaning and mechanism in grammar. *Harvard Studies in Syntax* 3:423–49.

Goodman, Nelson. 1947. The problem of counterfactual conditionals. *JP* 44:113–28.

———. 1951. *The structure of appearance*. Cambridge, MA: Harvard University Press.

Goodman, Nelson, and Henry Leonard. 1940. The calculus of individuals and its uses. *Journal of Symbolic Logic* 5:45–55.

Grice, H. P. 1967. Logic and conversation. Lectures, Harvard University. Revised version appears in Grice 1989:1–143.

———. 1989. *Studies in the way of words*. Cambridge, MA: Harvard University Press.

Grinder, John. 1976. *On deletion phenomena in English*. The Hague: Mouton.

Gruber, Jeffrey. 1967. Functions of the lexicon in formal descriptive grammars. System Development Corporation report. Reprinted in Jeffrey Gruber, *Lexical structures in syntax and semantics*, pp. 213–367. Amsterdam: North Holland, 1976.

Gupta, Anil. 1980. *The logic of common nouns*. New Haven: Yale University Press.

Hankamer, Jorge, and Ivan Sag. 1976. Deep and surface anaphora. *LI* 7:391–428.

Harper, William L. 1981. A sketch of some recent developments in the theory of conditionals. Harper, Stalnaker, and Pearce 1981, 3–38.

Harper, William L., Robert Stalnaker, and Glenn T. Pearce. 1981. *Ifs*. Dordrecht: Reidel.

Hausser, Roland. 1978. How do pronouns denote? In F. Heny and H. Schnelle, eds., *Selections from the third Groningen Round Table*, pp. 93–139. Syntax and Semantics 10. New York: Academic Press.

Heim, Irene, Howard Lasnik, and Robert May. 1991. Reciprocity and plurality. *LI* 22:63–101.

Henkin, Leon. 1950. Completeness in the theory of types. *Journal of Symbolic Logic* 15:81–91.

———. 1961. Some remarks on infinitely long formulas. In *Infinitistic methods*, pp. 167–83. New York: Pergamon.

Herzberger, Hans. 1975a. Dimensions of truth. In D. Hockney et al., eds., *Contem-*

porary research in philosophical logic and linguistic semantics, pp. 71–92. Dordrecht: Reidel.

————. 1975b. Supervaluations in two dimensions. *Proceedings of the 1975 international symposium on multiple-valued logic,* pp. 429–35. Long Beach, Calif.: IIEE Computer Society.

Hintikka, Jaakko. 1969a. Semantics for propositional attitudes. In J. W. Davis et al., eds., *Philosophical logic,* pp. 21–45. Dordrecht: Reidel. Reprinted in Hintikka 1969b:87–111 and in Linsky 1971:145–67.

————. 1969b. *Models for modalities.* Dordrecht: Reidel.

————. 1973. *Logic, language-games, and information.* Oxford: Clarendon.

————. 1974. Quantifiers vs. quantification theory. *LI* 5: 153–77.

Hintikka, Jaakko, and Jack Kulas. 1985. *Anaphora and definite descriptions.* Dordrecht: Reidel.

Hintikka, Jaakko, and Veikko Rantala. 1976. A new approach to infinitary languages. *Annals of Mathematical Logic* 10:95–115.

Hintikka, Jaakko, and Esa Saarinen. 1975. Semantical games and the Bach-Peters paradox. *Theoretical Linguistics* 2:1–20.

Hintikka, Jaakko, and Gabriel Sandu. 1991. *The methodology of linguistics.* Oxford: Blackwell.

Hockney, Donald, et al. 1975. *Contemporary research in philosophical logic and linguistic semantics.* Dordrecht: Reidel.

Horn, Laurence R. 1969. A presuppositional analysis of *only* and *even. Papers from the fifth regional meeting, Chicago Linguistic Society,* pp. 318–27.

————. 1972. *On the semantic properties of logical operators in English.* Bloomington: IULC.

————. 1975. Neg-raising predicates: toward an explanation. *Papers from the eleventh regional meeting, Chicago Linguistic Society,* pp. 279–94.

————. 1978. Remarks on neg-raising. In P. Cole, ed., *Pragmatics,* pp. 129–220. Syntax and Semantics 9. New York: Academic Press.

————. 1984. In defense of privative ambiguity. *BLS*10: 141–56.

————. 1985. Metalinguistic negation and pragmatic ambiguity. *Lg* 61:121–74.

————. 1989. *A natural history of negation.* Chicago: University of Chicago Press.

Householder, Fred. 1971. *Linguistic speculations.* London and New York: Cambridge University Press.

Hudson, Richard A. 1976. *Arguments for a non-transformational grammar.* Chicago: University of Chicago Press.

Hughes, G., and M. J. Cresswell. 1968. *Introduction to modal logic.* London: Methuen.

Humberstone, Lloyd. 1975. Review of Davidson and Harman 1972. *York Papers in Linguistics* 5:195–224.

Jackendoff, Ray S. 1972. *Semantic interpretation in generative grammar.* Cambridge, MA: MIT Press.

————. 1975. Belief contexts. *LI* 6:53–93.

_____. 1977. *X̄ syntax: a study of phrase structure*. Cambridge, MA: MIT Press.

_____. 1983. *Semantics and Cognition*. Cambridge, MA: MIT Press.

Jackson, Frank. 1987. *Conditionals*. Oxford: Blackwell.

Jacobs, Roderick, and Peter S. Rosenbaum. 1967. *English transformational grammar*. Boston: Ginn.

Jacobson, Pauline, and Paul Neubauer. 1976. Rule cyclicity: Evidence from the intervention constraint. *LI* 7:429–61.

Jacobson, Pauline, and Geoffrey K. Pullum. 1982. *The nature of syntactic representation*. Dordrecht: Reidel.

Kamp, Hans. 1974. Free choice permission. *Proceedings of the Aristotelian Society* 74:57–74.

_____. 1984. A theory of truth and semantic representation. In Groenendijk, Jeroen, T. M. V. Janssen, and Martin Stokhof, eds., *Truth, interpretation and information*, pp. 1–41. *GRASS* 2. Dordrecht: Foris.

Kaplan, David. 1989. Afterthoughts. In Joseph Almog, John Perry, and Howard Wettstein, eds., *Themes from Kaplan*, pp. 565–614. Oxford: Oxford University Press.

Karttunen, Frances, and Lauri Karttunen. 1977. *Even* questions. *NELS* 7:115–34.

Karttunen, Lauri. 1971a. Definite descriptions with crossing coreference: A study of the Bach-Peters paradox. *FoL* 7:157–87.

_____. 1971b. Implicative verbs. *Language* 47:340–58.

_____. 1971c. *The logic of English predicate complement constructions*. Bloomington: IULC.

_____. 1973. Presuppositions of compound sentences. *LI* 4:169–93.

_____. 1974. Presupposition and linguistic context. *Theoretical Linguistics* 1:182–94. Also in Rogers, Wall, and Murphy 1977:149–60.

_____. 1976. Discourse referents. In McCawley 1976b:363–85.

Karttunen, Lauri, and P. S. Peters. Requiem for presupposition. *Proceedings of the third annual meeting, BLS*, pp. 360–71.

_____. 1979. Conventional implicature. In Oh and Dinneen 1979:1–56.

Kay, Paul. 1990. Even. *L&P* 13:59–111.

Keenan, Edward L. 1987. A semantic definition of "indefinite NP." In Eric J. Reuland and Alice ter Meulen, eds., *The representation of (in)definiteness*, pp. 286–317. Cambridge, MA: MIT Press.

_____. 1988. Complex anaphors and bind alpha. *CLS* 24(1):216–32.

Keenan, Edward L., and Jonathan Stavi. 1986. A semantic characterization of natural language determiners. *L&P* 9:253–326.

Kiparsky, Paul, and Carol Kiparsky. 1970. Fact. In M. Bierwisch and K. Heidolph, eds., *Progress in linguistics*, pp. 143–73. The Hague: Mouton. Reprinted in Steinberg and Jakobovits 1971:345–69.

Kiparsky, Paul, and Frits Staal. 1969. Syntactic and semantic relations in Panini. *FoL* 5:83–117.

Klima, E. S. 1964. Negation in English. In Fodor and Katz 1964:246–323.

Klooster, W. G. 1972. *The structure underlying measure phrase sentences*. Dordrecht: Reidel.

Knowles, John. 1979. Lexemic iteration. *Linguistics* 17:641–57.

Kratzer, Angelika. 1989. An investigation of the lumps of thought. *L&P* 12:607–53.

Kripke, Saul. 1959. A completeness theorem in modal logic. *Journal of Symbolic Logic* 24:1–14.

————. 1972. Naming and necessity. In Davidson and Harman 1972:253–355.

Kuno, Susumu. 1971. The position of locatives in existential sentences. *LI* 2:333–78.

Kuroda, S.-Y. 1971. Two remarks on pronominalization. *FoL* 7:183–98.

Lakoff, George. 1968. Pronouns and reference. IULC. Reprinted in McCawley 1976b:273–335.

————. 1971. Generative semantics. In Steinberg and Jakobovits 1971:232–96.

————. 1972a. Linguistics and natural logic. In Davidson and Harman 1972:545–665.

————. 1972b. Hedges: A study in meaning criteria and the logic of fuzzy concepts. *CLS* 8: 183–228. Corrected version in Hockney et al. 1975:221–71.

————. 1986. Frame semantic control of the coordinate structure constraint. *CLS* 22(2):152–67.

Lakoff, George, and P. S. Peters. 1969. Phrasal conjunction and symmetric predicates. In Reibel and Schane 1969:113–42.

Lakoff, Robin. 1971. If's, and's, and but's about conjunction. In Fillmore and Langendoen 1971:214–49.

Langacker, Ronald. 1969. Pronominalization and the chain of command. In Reibel and Schane 1969:160–86.

Langacker, Ronald W., and Pamela Munro. 1975. Passives and their meaning. *Lg* 51:789–830.

Langendoen, D. Terence. 1978. The logic of reciprocity. *LI* 9:177–97.

Langendoen, D. T., and Harris Savin. 1971. The projection problem for presuppositions. In Fillmore and Langendoen 1971:54–60.

Lasnik, Howard. 1976. Remarks on coreference. LA 2:1–22. Reprinted in Lasnik, *Essays on anaphora*, pp. 90–109. Dordrecht: Kluwer, 1989.

Laudan, Larry. 1976. *Progress and its problems*. Berkeley and Los Angeles: University of California Press.

Leech, Geoffrey. 1969. *Towards a semantic description of English*. London: Longmans.

LeGrand, Jean Ehrenkrantz. 1975. *Or* and *any:* The semantics and syntax of two logical operators. Ph.D. diss., University of Chicago.

Leśniewski, Stanislaw. 1916. *Podstawy Ogólnej Teoryi Mnogości,* vol. 1. Moscow: A. P. Poplawski.

Lewis, C. I. 1912. Implications and the algebra of logic. *Mind* n.s. 21:522–31.

————. 1918. *A survey of symbolic logic*. Berkeley: University of California Press.

Lewis, C. I., and C. H. Langford. 1932. *Symbolic logic*. New York: Dover.

Lewis, David. 1968. Counterpart theory and quantified modal logic. *Journal of Philosophy* 65:113–26.

_____. 1973. *Counterfactuals*. Cambridge, MA: Harvard University Press.

_____. 1979. Score-keeping in a language game. *JPL* 8:339–49. Reprinted in Lewis 1983:233–49.

_____. 1983. *Philosophical Papers*, vol. 1. Oxford: Oxford University Press.

Linebarger, Marcia. 1981. The grammar of negative polarity. MIT Ph.D. diss., distributed by IULC.

Link, Godehard. 1983. The logical analysis of plurals and mass terms: A lattice-theoretical approach. In R. Bäuerle, C. Schwartze, and A. von Stechow, eds., *Meaning, use, and interpretation of language*. Berlin: de Gruyter.

_____. 1984. Hydras: on the logic of relative constructions with multiple heads. In Fred Landman and Frank Veltman, eds., *Varieties of formal semantics*, pp. 245–57. Dordrecht: Foris.

Linsky, Leonard. 1971. *Reference and modality*. Oxford: Clarendon.

Lycan, William. 1979. The trouble with possible worlds. In Michael J. Loux, ed., *The possible and the actual*, pp. 274–316. Ithaca: Cornell University Press.

_____. 1984. A syntactically motivated semantics for conditionals. *Minnesota Studies in Philosophy* 9:437–55.

Lyons, John. 1977. *Semantics*. Cambridge: Cambridge University Press.

Massey, Gerald. 1970. *Understanding symbolic logic*. New York: Harper and Row.

May, Robert. 1985. *Logical form, its structure and derivation*. Cambridge MA: MIT Press.

McCawley, James D. 1968. Concerning the base component of a transformational grammar. *FoL* 4:243–69. Reprinted in McCawley 1973a:35–58.

_____. 1970. Semantic representation. In P. Garvin, ed., *Cognition: A multiple view*, pp. 227–47. New York: Spartan. Reprinted in McCawley 1973a: 240–56.

_____. 1971. Tense and time reference in English. In Fillmore and Langendoen 1971: 96–113. Reprinted in McCawley 1973a: 257–73.

_____. 1972. A program for logic. In Davidson and Harman 1972:157–212. Reprinted in McCawley 1973a:285–319.

_____. 1973a *Grammar and Meaning*. Tokyo: Taishukan; New York: Academic Press.

_____. 1973b. Where do noun phrases come from? [revised version]. In McCawley 1973a:133–54.

_____. 1974. On identifying the remains of deceased clauses. *Language Research* (Seoul, Korea) 9(2):73–85. Reprinted in McCawley 1979a:84–95.

_____. 1975a. Review of Chomsky 1972. *Studies in English Linguistics* 3:209–311. Reprinted in McCawley 1982a: 10–127.

_____. 1975b. Verbs of bitching. In Donald Hockney, William Harper, and Bruce Freed (eds.), *Contemporary research in philosophical logic and linguistic semantics*, pp. 313–32. Dordrecht: Reidel. Reprinted in McCawley 1979a: 135–50.

_____. 1976a. Remarks on what can cause what. In M. Shibatani, ed., *The grammar of causative constructions,* pp. 117–29. Syntax and Semantics 6. New York: Academic Press. Reprinted in McCawley 1979a: 101–12.

————. 1976b. *Notes from the linguistic underground.* Syntax and semantics 7. New York: Academic Press.

————. 1976c. Notes on Jackendoff's theory of anaphora. *LI* 7:319–41. Reprinted under the title "How to get an interpretive theory of anaphora to work" in McCawley 1982a: 128–58.

————. 1977a. Remarks on the lexicography of performative verbs. In Rogers, Wall, and Murphy 1977:13–25. Reprinted in McCawley 1979a: 151–64.

————. 1977b. Evolutionary parallels between Montague grammar and transformational grammar. *NELS* 7:219–32. Reprinted in McCawley 1979a: 122–32.

————. 1979a. *Adverbs, vowels, and other objects of wonder.* Chicago: University of Chicago Press.

————. 1979b. Helpful hints to the ordinary working Montague grammarian. Davis and Mithun 1979:103–25.

————. 1980. An un-syntax. In E. Moravcsik, ed., *Current approaches to syntax* (Syntax and Semantics 13), pp. 167–93. New York: Academic Press.

————. 1981a. The syntax and semantics of English relative clauses. *Lingua* 53:99–149.

————. 1981b. Notes on the English present perfect. *Australian Journal of Linguistics* 1:81–90.

————. 1982a. *Thirty million theories of grammar.* London: Croom Helm, and Chicago: University of Chicago Press.

————. 1982b. The nonexistence of syntactic categories. In McCawley 1982a: 176–203.

————. 1984. Anaphora and notions of command. *BLS* 10:220–32.

————. 1985a. What price the performative hypothesis? *UCWPL* 1:43–64.

————. 1985b. Speech acts and Goffman's participant roles. *ESCOL* 1:260–74.

————. 1986. Actions and events despite Bertrand Russell. In E. LePore and B. McLaughlin, eds., *Actions and Events,* pp. 177–92. Oxford: Blackwell.

————. 1988a. *The syntactic phenomena of English.* Chicago: University of Chicago Press.

————. 1988b. Adverbial NPs: Bare or clad in see-through garb? *Lg* 64:583–90.

————. 1991. Contrastive negation and metalinguistic negation. *CLS* 27:189–206.

————. 1992. The cyclic principle as a source of explanation in syntax. *CLS* 28.

Miller, George, and Philip Johnson-Laird. 1976. *Language and perception.* Cambridge, MA: Belknap Press.

Montague, Richard. 1970a. English as a formal language. In B. Visentini et al., eds., *Linguaggi nella Società e nella Tecnica,* pp. 189–224. Milan: Edizioni di Communità. Reprinted in Montague 1974: 188–221.

————. 1970b. Universal grammar. *Theoria* 36:373–98. Reprinted in Montague 1974:222–46.

————. 1973. The proper treatment of quantification in ordinary English. In J. Hintikka, J. Moravcsik, and P. Suppes, eds., *Approaches to natural language*. Dordrecht: Reidel. Reprinted in Montague 1974: 247–70.

————. 1974. *Formal philosophy*. New Haven: Yale University Press.

Morgan, Charles, and F. J. Pelletier. 1977. Some notes concerning fuzzy logics. *L&P* 1.79–97.

Morgan, J. L. 1973. Presupposition and the representation of meaning: Prolegomena. Ph.D. diss., University of Chicago.

Mostowski, Andrzej. 1957. On a generalization of quantifiers. *Fundamenta Mathematica* 44:12–36.

Neale, Stephen. 1990. *Descriptions*. Cambridge, MA: MIT Press.

Nute, Donald. 1975a. Counterfactuals. *Notre Dame Journal of Formal Logic* 16:476–82.

————. 1975b. Counterfactuals and the similarity of worlds. *JP* 72:773–78.

————. 1984. Conditional logic. *HPhL* 2:387–439.

Oh, Choon-Kyu, and Dinneen, David A. 1979. *Presupposition*. Syntax and Semantics 12. New York: Academic Press.

Ojeda, Almerindo. 1992. *Linguistic individuals*. Palo Alto, CA: Center for the Study of Language and Information.

Palmer, Frank. 1965. *The English verb*. London: Longmans.

Parsons, Terry. 1970. An analysis of mass terms and amount terms. *FoL* 6:362–88.

Partee, Barbara Hall. 1970. Negation, conjunction, and quantifiers: Syntax v. semantics. *Foundations of Language* 6:153–65.

————. 1974. Opacity and scope. In M. Munitz and P. Unger, eds., *Semantics and Philosophy*, 81–101. New York: NYU Press.

————. 1975. Montague grammar and transformational grammar. *LI* 6:203–300.

————. 1976. *Montague grammar*. New York: Academic Press.

————. 1989. Many quantifiers. *ESCOL* 6:383–402.

Partee, Barbara, Alice ter Meulen, and Robert Wall. 1990. *Mathematical methods in linguistics*. Dordrecht: Kluwer.

Pelletier, F. J. 1977. Or. *Theoretical Linguistics* 4:61–74.

————. 1979. *Mass terms*. Dordrecht: Reidel.

Perlmutter, David M. 1982. Syntactic representation, syntactic levels, and the notion of subject. In Jacobson and Pullum 1982:382–340.

Perlmutter, David M., and John Robert Ross. 1970. Relative clauses with split antecedents. *LI* 1:350.

Peterson, Philip. 1979. On the logic of *few, many*, and *most*. *Notre Dame Journal of Formal Logic* 20:155–79.

Pollard, Carl, and Ivan Sag. 1988. *Information-based syntax and semantics*. Chicago: University of Chicago Press.

Pope, Emily. 1973. Question-answering systems. *CLS* 9:482–92.

Popper, Karl. 1962. What is dialectic? In K. Popper, *Conjectures and refutations*, pp. 312–35. London: Routledge and Kegan Paul. Reprinted from *Mind* n.s. 49(1940): 403–26.

Postal, Paul M., and John T. Grinder. 1971. Missing antecedents. *LI* 2:269–312.

Prawitz, Dag. 1965. *Natural deduction: A proof-theoretical study.* Stockholm: Almqvist and Wiksell.

Prince, Ellen. 1982. The simple futurate: Not simply progressive futurate minus progressive. *CLS* 18:435–65.

Prior, A. N. 1960. The runabout inference-ticket. *Analysis* 21:38–39. Reprinted in Strawson 1967: 129–31.

―――. 1967. *Past, present, and future.* Oxford: Oxford University Press.

Quine, Willard van Orman. 1943. Notes on existence and necessity. *Journal of Philosophy* 40:113–27.

―――. 1953. Reference and modality. In Quine, *From a logical point of view,* pp. 139–57. Cambridge, Mass.: Harvard University Press. Reprinted in Linsky 1971: 17–34.

―――. 1956. Quantifiers and propositional attitudes. *JP* 53:177–87. Reprinted in Linsky 1971: 100–111.

―――. 1960. *Word and object.* Cambridge, MA: MIT Press.

―――. 1962. *Methods of logic.* 2d ed. London: Routledge and Kegan Paul.

―――. 1969. *Ontological relativity and other essays.* New York: Columbia University Press.

Recanati, François. 1981. On Kripke on Donnellan. In H. Parrett, M. Sbisa, and J. Verschueren, eds., *Possibilities and limitations of pragmatics,* pp. 595–630. Amsterdam: Benjamins.

Reibel, David, and Sanford Schane. 1969. *Modern studies in English.* Englewood Cliffs, NJ: Prentice Hall.

Reichenbach, Hans. 1947. *Elements of symbolic logic.* New York: Macmillan.

Reinhart, Tanya. 1976. The syntactic domain of anaphora. MIT Ph.D. thesis. [a more accessible reference is Reinhart 1983. *Anaphora and Semantic Interpretation.* Chicago: University of Chicago Press.]

Reis, Marga. 1974. Patching with counterparts. *FoL* 12:157–76.

Rescher, Nicholas. 1964. *Hypothetical reasoning.* Amsterdam: North Holland.

―――. 1969. *Many-valued logic.* New York: McGraw-Hill.

Rescher, Nicholas, and Urquhart, A. 1971. *Temporal logic.* New York: Springer.

Rice, Sally. 1987. Towards a transitive prototype: Evidence from some atypical English passives. *BLS* 13:422–34.

Rogers, Andy, Robert Wall and John Murphy eds. 1977. *Proceedings of the Texas Conference on performatives, presuppositions, and implicatures.* Arlington, VA: Center for Applied Linguistics.

Ross, John Robert. 1967. Constraints on variables in syntax. Ph.D. diss., MIT. Published in 1985 under the title *Infinite syntax!* Hillsdale, NJ: Erlbaum.

―――. 1969. The cyclic nature of English pronominalization. In Reibel and Schane 1969: 187–200.

―――. 1970. On declarative sentences. In Roderick Jacobs and P. S. Rosenbaum, *Readings in English transformational grammar,* pp. 222–72. Boston: Ginn.

―――. 1976. To have have and not to have have. In E. Polome et al., eds., *Linguistic and literary studies in honor of Archibald A. Hill.* Vol. 1, pp. 263–70. Lisse: de Ridder.

Russell, Bertrand. 1905. On denoting. *Mind* n.s. 14:479–93. Reprinted in I. Copi and J. Gould, *Contemporary readings in logical theory.* New York: Macmillan, 1967.

Russell, Bertrand, and A. N. Whitehead. 1910–13. *Principia mathematica.* London: Cambridge University Press.

Rutherford, William. 1970. Some observations concerning subordinate clauses in English. *Language* 46:97–115.

Saarinen, Esa, ed. 1976. Game-theoretical semantics. Dordrecht: Reidel.

Sadock, Jerrold. 1974. *Toward a linguistic theory of speech acts.* New York: Academic Press.

————. 1977. Truth and approximations. *BLS* 3:430–39.

————. 1978. On testing for conversational implicature. In P. Cole, ed., *Pragmatics* (Syntax and Semantics 9), pp. 281–97. New York: Academic Press.

————. 1981. Almost. In Cole 1981: 257–71.

Sag, Ivan. 1976. Deletion and logical form. Ph.D. diss., MIT.

Schank, Roger, and Robert Abelson. 1977. *Scripts, plans, goals, and understanding.* Hillsdale, NJ: Lawrence Erlbaum.

Schmerling, Susan F. 1975. Asymmetric conjunction and rules of conversation. In P. Cole, ed., *Speech acts*, pp. 211–31. Syntax and Semantics 3. New York: Academic Press.

————. 1982. How imperatives are special and how they aren't. *Nondeclaratives*, pp. 202–18. Chicago: Chicago Linguistic Society.

Schock, Rolf. 1968. *Logics without existence assumptions.* Stockholm: Almqvist and Wiksell.

Searle, John. 1969. *Speech acts.* Cambridge: Cambridge University Press.

Sharvy, Richard. 1979a. The indeterminacy of mass predication. In Pelletier 1979:47–54.

————. 1979b. Transitivity and conditionals. *Logique et analyse* 87:347–51.

————. 1980. A more general theory of definite descriptions. *PR* 89:607–24.

Smith, Carlota S. 1981. The futurate progressive: Not simply future + progressive. *CLS* 17:369–82.

Smith, N. V., ed. 1982. *Mutual knowledge.* New York: Academic Press.

Smullyan, A. F. 1948. Modality and description. *Journal of Symbolic Logic* 13:31–37. Reprinted in Linsky 1971:35–43.

Stalnaker, Robert. 1969. A theory of conditionals. In N. Rescher, ed., *Studies in logical theory,* pp. 98–112. Oxford: Blackwell.

————. 1975. Indicative conditionals. *Philosophia* 5:269–86. Reprinted in Harper, Stalnaker, and Pearce 1981: 193–210.

————. 1978. Assertion. In Peter Cole and J. L. Morgan, eds., *Pragmatics*, pp. 315–32. Syntax and Semantics 8. New York: Academic Press.

Steinberg, D., and L. Jakobovits. 1971. *Semantics: an interdisciplinary reader.* Cambridge: Cambridge University Press.

Strawson, P. F. 1950. On referring. *Mind* n.s. 59:320–44. Reprinted in Strawson 1971:1–27.

618   References

――――. 1964. Identifying reference and truth values. *Theoria* 30:96–118. Reprinted in Strawson 1971:75–95.

――――. 1967. *Philosophical logic*. Oxford: Clarendon.

――――. 1971. *Logico-linguistic papers*. London: Methuen.

Tarski, Alfred. 1944. The semantic conception of truth. *Philosophy and phenomenological research* 4:341–75.

Tateishi, Koichi. 1989. Subjects, SPEC, and DP in Japanese. *NELS* 19:405–18.

Thomason, Richmond. 1970. *Symbolic Logic*. New York: Macmillan.

van Fraassen, Bas. 1969. Presuppositions, supervaluations, and free logic. In K. Lambert, ed., *The logical way of doing things*, pp. 67–91. New Haven: Yale University Press.

――――. 1971. *Formal logic and semantics*. New York: Macmillan.

Vendler, Zeno. 1967a. *Linguistics in philosophy*. Ithaca: Cornell University Press.

――――. 1967b. Each and every, any and all. In Vendler 1967a: 70–96.

Wall, Robert. 1972. *Introduction to mathematical linguistics*. Englewood Cliffs, NJ: Prentice-Hall.

Wason, P. C., and Johnson-Laird, P. N. 1972. *Psychology of reasoning: Structure and content*. London: Batsford.

Wasow, Tom. 1973. More MIGs and pilots. *FoL* 9:297–305.

Westerståhl, Dag. 1985. Logical constants in quantifier languages. *L&P* 8:387–413.

Wierzbicka, Anna. 1972. "And" and plurality. In A. Wierzbicka, *Semantic primitives*, pp. 166–90. Frankfurt: Athenäum.

――――. 1980. *Lingua mentalis*. Orlando: Academic Press.

――――. 1985. *English speech act verbs: A semantic dictionary*. Orlando: Academic Press.

Williams, Edwin. 1977. Discourse and logical form. *LI* 8:101–39.

Wundt, Wilhelm. 1900. *Völkerpsychologie*. Vol. 1, part 2. Leipzig: Engelmann.

Zadeh, Lotfi A. 1965. Fuzzy sets. *Information and Control* 8:338–53.

――――. 1971. Similarity relations and fuzzy orderings. *Information Sciences* 3:177–200.

――――. 1972. A fuzzy-set-theoretic interpretation of linguistic hedges. *Journal of Cybernetics* 2:4–34.

Zwicky, Arnold M., and Jerrold M. Sadock. 1975. Ambiguity tests and how to fail them. In J. Kimball, ed., Syntax and Semantics 4. New York: Academic Press. 1–36.

List of Symbols

Notation Used in this Book	Other Current Notations	Informal Explanation
PROPOSITIONAL LOGIC		
$\wedge(p_1, p_2, \ldots, p_n)$ (p. 58)	none	$p_1, p_2, \ldots,$ and p_n
none	$p \wedge q$; $p \cdot q$; $p \ \& \ q$; Kpq	p and q
$\vee(p_1, p_2, \ldots, p_n)$ (p. 58)	none	$p_1, p_2, \ldots,$ or p_n
none	$p \vee q$; Apq	p or q
$\vee_e(p_1, p_2, \ldots, p_n)$	none	exclusive *or*
none	$p + q$	exclusive *or*
$\sim p$ (p. 57)	$\neg p$; $\bar{p}$; Np; $-p$	not p
$\supset pq$ (p. 62)	$p \supset q$; $p \rightarrow q$; Cpq	if p, then q
none	$p \equiv q$; $p \leftrightarrow q$; Epq (p. 601 n12)	p if and only if q
PREDICATE LOGIC		
$(\forall: Fx)_x Gx$ (p. 39)	$\underset{Fx}{\forall}\ Gx$	all F's are G
none	$(\forall x)Fx$; $(x)Fx$; $(\wedge x)Fx$ (p. 173)	everything is F
$(\exists: Fx)_x Gx$ (p. 42)	$\underset{Fx}{\exists}Gx$	some F's are G
none	$(\exists x)Fx$; $(\vee x)Fx$ (p. 173)	something is F
$(\imath: Fx)Gx$ (p.205)	$G(\imath x: Fx)$; $(\imath x: Fx)G(\imath x: Fx)$ (p. 575 n16)	the F is G
All M (p. 282)	none	all propositions in the set M are true
Some M (p. 283)	none	some propositions in the set M are true
$=xy$, $x=y$ (p. 168)		x is identical to y

619

SET THEORY

$\in a$A; $a \in$ A (pp. 136, 152)	$a \; \varepsilon \; A$	a is a member of A
$\subseteq$AB: A $\subseteq$ B (pp. 137, 152)		A is a subset of B
A $\cup$ B (p. 140)		union of A and B
A $\cap$ B (p. 140)		intersection of A and B
A $-$ B (p. 140)		the members of A not in B
none	$\bar{A}$; CA	complement of A
$\varnothing$ (p. 141)		empty set
$\{a_1, a_2, ..., a_n\}$ (p. 138)		set having $a_1, a_2, ...$ and a_n as its members
$\{fx \mid gx\}$; $\{fx: gx\}$ (pp. 139, 154)		set having as members all items fx for which x meets the condition gx
$\aleph_0$ (p. 144)		smallest infinite cardinal number
A $\times$ B (p. 149)		Cartesian product of A and B: set of all ordered pairs of a member of A and a member of B
A^B (p. 494)		set of all functions from B into A
$\lvert A \rvert$		number of members of A
R$\circ$S (p. 149)		composition of relations

METALINGUISTIC SYMBOLS

$\vdash$A (p. 116)		A is provable (by the given rules of inference)
$A_1, ..., A_n \vdash A$ (p. 53)		A is provable from the set of premises $\{A_1, ..., A_n\}$
A $\dashv\vdash$ B (p. 53)		A is deductively equivalent to B
$\vDash$ A (p. 124)	$\Vdash$A	A is valid, i.e., true in all states of affairs
$A_1, ..., A_n \vDash A$ (p. 125)	$A_1, ..., A_n \; \Vdash$A	$A_1, ..., A_n$ entail A, i.e., A is true in all states of affairs in which $A_1, ...,$ A_n are all true

A $\gg$ B (p. 327)

A/X (p. 350)

v_X (p. 334)

(a/x b/y ...) (p. 164)

A$^\alpha$ (p. 163)

A$^{\varrho,i}$ (p. 498)

/A/ (p. 463)

MODAL LOGIC

$\square$A (p. 374)   NA; LA

$\diamondsuit$A (p. 378)   MA

$\square$→AB (p. 531)   A $\square$→ B

$\diamondsuit$→AB (p. 542)   A $\diamondsuit$→ B

→AB (p. 401) Λ→B

Rw_1w_2 (p. 375)

$-\!3$AB (p. 399)   A $-\!3$ B

TENSE LOGIC

R$_i$(A) (p. 431)

Pt_1t_2 (p. 431)

TYPE THEORY, INTENSIONAL LOGIC

(λx)A (p. 255)

$\langle a,b \rangle$ (p. 254)

[a] (p. 254)

t, e, s (p. 496)

ˆX (p. 497)

A semantically
   presupposes B
A is acceptable relative to
   context X
supervaluation defined
   by the set of proposi-
   tions X
assignment of a as value
   of x, b as value of y, ...
denotation of A in
   interpretation α
denotation of A in world i
   of interpretation Q
truth value of A (in the
   given state of affairs)

necessarily, A
possibly, A
if A were the case, B
   would be the case
if A were the case, B
   might be the case
A implies B
w_2 is possible relative to
   w_1
necessarily, if A, then B

A is true at time t
t_1 is prior to t_2

A, treated as a function of
   x
logical type of functions
   from entities of type a
   to entities of type b
logical type of sets of
   entities of type a
types of truth values,
   entities, worlds
   (respectively)
intension of X

ˇX (p. 497)   extension of X

x^s, x^i, x^k (p. 266)   variables whose values
                                                   are (respectively)
                                                   stages, individuals, and
                                                   kinds

MONTAGUE GRAMMAR, CATEGORIAL GRAMMAR

A/B (p. 502)   syntactic category of
                                                   expressions that
                                                   combine with
                                                   expressions of category
                                                   B to yield expressions
                                                   of category A

A⇒α (p. 600 n11)   expression A translates
                                                   into logical formula α

α→β (p. 600 n11)   α is convertible into β by
                                                   λ-conversion and/or
                                                   meaning postulates

LINGUISTIC SYMBOLS

*, *?, ??, ? (p. 560 n12)   indicates that the example
                                                   to which the symbol is
                                                   prefixed is deviant in
                                                   some way, with *
                                                   marking strong
                                                   deviance and the other
                                                   "stigmata" marking
                                                   successively weaker
                                                   degree of deviance

X′ (p. 16)   phrasal unit whose head
                                                   belongs to the part-of-
                                                   speech X (e.g., V′
                                                   means "verb phrase")

S: NP V′ (p. 18)   a S may consist of a NP
                                                   followed by a V′

/NP_____ P′ (p. 29)   in the context:
                                                   immediately preceded
                                                   by a NP and
                                                   immediately followed
                                                   by a P′

Δ (p. 581 n5)   unspecified syntactic
                                                 constituent (e.g.,
                                                 underlying subject of
                                                 reduced passive)
<   derived from

Index

625